Criminal Law
and Procedure

Aspen College Series

Criminal Law and Procedure

An Introduction for Criminal Justice Professionals

NEAL R. BEVANS, J.D.

Wolters Kluwer
Law & Business

Published by Wolters Kluwer Law & Business in New York.

Wolters Kluwer Law & Business serves customers worldwide with CCH, Aspen Publishers, and Kluwer Law International products. (www.wolterskluwerlb.com)

To contact Customer Service, e-mail customer.service@wolterskluwer.com,
call 1-800-234-1660, fax 1-800-901-9075, or mail correspondence to:

Wolters Kluwer Law & Business
Attn: Order Department
PO Box 990
Frederick, MD 21705

Printed in the United States of America.

1 2 3 4 5 6 7 8 9 0

ISBN 978-1-4548-2477-0

Library of Congress Cataloging-in-Publication Data

Bevans, Neal R., 1961- author.
  Criminal law and procedure for criminal justice professionals / Neal R. Bevans, J.D.
     pages cm. — (Aspen college series)
  Includes bibliographical references and index.
  ISBN 978-1-4548-2477-0 (alk. paper) — ISBN 1-4548-2477-8 (alk. paper) 1. Criminal law —
United States. 2. Criminal procedure — United States. 3. Criminal justice personnel — United
States — Handbooks, manuals, etc. I. Title.
  KF9219.85.B49 2014
  345.73 — dc23
                              2014006910

About Wolters Kluwer Law & Business

Wolters Kluwer Law & Business is a leading global provider of intelligent information and digital solutions for legal and business professionals in key specialty areas, and respected educational resources for professors and law students. Wolters Kluwer Law & Business connects legal and business professionals as well as those in the education market with timely, specialized authoritative content and information-enabled solutions to support success through productivity, accuracy and mobility.

Serving customers worldwide, Wolters Kluwer Law & Business products include those under the Aspen Publishers, CCH, Kluwer Law International, Loislaw, ftwilliam.com and MediRegs family of products.

CCH products have been a trusted resource since 1913, and are highly regarded resources for legal, securities, antitrust and trade regulation, government contracting, banking, pension, payroll, employment and labor, and healthcare reimbursement and compliance professionals.

Aspen Publishers products provide essential information to attorneys, business professionals and law students. Written by preeminent authorities, the product line offers analytical and practical information in a range of specialty practice areas from securities law and intellectual property to mergers and acquisitions and pension/ benefits. Aspen's trusted legal education resources provide professors and students with high-quality, up-to-date and effective resources for successful instruction and study in all areas of the law.

Kluwer Law International products provide the global business community with reliable international legal information in English. Legal practitioners, corporate counsel and business executives around the world rely on Kluwer Law journals, looseleafs, books, and electronic products for comprehensive information in many areas of international legal practice.

Loislaw is a comprehensive online legal research product providing legal content to law firm practitioners of various specializations. Loislaw provides attorneys with the ability to quickly and efficiently find the necessary legal information they need, when and where they need it, by facilitating access to primary law as well as state-specific law, records, forms and treatises.

ftwilliam.com offers employee benefits professionals the highest quality plan documents (retirement, welfare and non-qualified) and government forms (5500/ PBGC, 1099 and IRS) software at highly competitive prices.

MediRegs products provide integrated health care compliance content and software solutions for professionals in healthcare, higher education and life sciences, including professionals in accounting, law and consulting.

Wolters Kluwer Law & Business, a division of Wolters Kluwer, is headquartered in New York. Wolters Kluwer is a market-leading global information services company focused on professionals.

For Nilsa Bevans with all of my love

Summary
of Contents

Contents

2 THE CRIMINAL JUSTICE SYSTEM

3   ATTEMPT TO COMMIT A CRIME; PRINCIPALS AND ACCESSORIES; CONSPIRACY

4 HOMICIDE

5 CRIMES AGAINST PERSONS

6 RAPE AND RELATED SEXUAL OFFENSES

7 OTHER SEX OFFENSES

8 BURGLARY AND ARSON

THEFT CRIMES

10 CRIMES AGAINST PUBLIC ORDER AND ADMINISTRATION

11   DRUG CRIMES

12 INTRODUCTION TO CRIMINAL PROCEDURE

13 THE LAW OF ARREST, INTERROGATION, AND *MIRANDA*

14 WARRANTS FOR ARREST, SEARCH, AND SEIZURE

15   POST ARREST, GRAND JURY, INDICTMENT

16 EVIDENCE

17 DEFENSES TO CRIMINAL ACCUSATIONS

18 ARRAIGNMENT AND DISCOVERY

19   THE DEFENDANT'S RIGHTS BEFORE AND DURING TRIAL

20 THE TRIAL

21   SENTENCING AND APPEAL

Criminal law and procedure is the core of all criminal justice programs. Unlike other texts on this topic, this book is written with the student, the instructor, and the criminal justice professional in mind. The author has extensive experience not only in teaching the topic, but also in living it. As an Assistant District Attorney in a major city, the author handled all types of cases from misdemeanors to murder trials. He brings his extensive knowledge of the topic to bear on each issue in this text. In Criminal Law and Procedure: An Introduction for Criminal Justice Professionals, the author offers in-depth and current research on criminal topics, as well as a personal view of the criminal justice system gleaned from years as both a prosecutor and a criminal defense attorney. The book provides a balance between theoretical discussions and practical, down-to to-earth examples of law in action at every phase of a criminal proceeding. The text emphasizes the practical aspects of criminal law and procedure and provides real-world examples, while still discussing the theoretical and academic bases of every aspect of a criminal case from the elements of offenses to procedural steps to the trial and subsequent appeal of a criminal case.

FEATURES OF THE TEXTBOOK

- Chapter objectives that are stated clearly and succinctly
- Terms and legal vocabulary set out in bold in the body of the text and defined immediately in the margin for the ease of student comprehension
- Figures and tables to illustrate crucial points, designed to capitalize on different learning styles among students
- Scenarios to help students develop their understanding of the material
- Excerpts from seminal or otherwise noteworthy appellate cases
- End-of-chapter questions, activities, and assignments to hone students' understanding
- Websites for further research and discussion

TEXTBOOK RESOURCES

The companion website for this text at http://www.aspenlegalcollege.com/books/ bevans_crimjust includes additional resources for students and instructors, including:

- Additional review materials to help students master the key concepts for this course.

- Instructor resources to accompany the text
- Links to helpful websites and updates.

Instructor resources to accompany this text include a comprehensive Instructor's Manual, Test Bank, and PowerPoint slides. All of these materials are available for download from our companion website.

ACKNOWLEDGMENTS

I would like to acknowledge the tremendous help, effort, and support that the following individuals provided in bringing this book to its final form: Sylvia Rebert, Jacqueline Landis, Betsy Kenny, and David Herzig. A sincere thank you to the following reviewers, whose suggestions, criticism, questions, and observations have helped me write a text that contains the essential material and is user-friendly, readable, and enjoyable:

Bruce A. Carroll, Texas Christian University
Patricia Erickson, Canisius College
John Feldmeier, Wright State Univesity
Eric A. Gentes, Rivier University
Reginia Judge, Montclair State University
Jeffrey Kleeger, Florida Gulf Coast University
James Lawrence McMonagle, Jr., Pennsylvania State University — Wilkes Barre
Johnnie Myers, Savannah State University
Carol M. Park, Fort Hays State University
Manswell T. Peterson, Darton State College
Howard Sokol, Athens Technical College
Roger E. Stone, Hilbert College
Michael Wright, Louisiana State University.

Criminal Law and Procedure

Introduction to Criminal Law

Chapter Objectives

- Define the basic differences between civil and criminal cases
- Explain the difference between a suspect and a defendant
- Describe the role of police officers in making a criminal case
- Describe the function of prosecutors and defense attorneys
- Define the importance of analyzing the elements of a criminal offense

I INTRODUCTION TO CRIMINAL LAW

This text is about the fascinating world of criminal law and procedure. As we go through future chapters, we will examine not only various types of crime, but also the procedural steps that must be followed by police, prosecutors, and judges once a defendant has been placed under arrest. We will begin the first part of the text with an examination of criminal law and then spend the second half of the text exploring criminal procedure. At every step of the process, during the collection of evidence, arresting the defendant, obtaining a statement from the defendant, arraigning, trying, and eventually sentencing guilty defendants, there are critical steps that must be followed and situations where the defendant is protected by rights guaranteed by the U.S. Constitution and individual state law.

However, before we can illustrate the various important points about both criminal law and criminal procedure, we must first take a broad view of law in general and discover where the field of criminal law lies in regard to many other types of law.

Broadly speaking, there are two branches of law: civil law and criminal law. We will examine these two categories to illustrate what makes them different from one another and also to show how criminal law is a world by itself, with its own rules, its own procedures, and its own personnel, and that it is as unique an area of practice as divorce law, wills, trusts, real estate, and personal injury and the many other categories of civil law.

THE BASIC DIFFERENCES BETWEEN CIVIL AND CRIMINAL CASES

At a basic level, we all have some understanding of criminal law. There are television shows, movies, books, and other forms of entertainment that often focus on the narrow issue of crime and its consequences. However, criminal law is not always accurately portrayed in the various media, and in this text we will get specific with the actual day-to-day workings of criminal law by examining not only the various features of the law, but also the people who work in the field.

We all know that people commit crimes and are arrested for those crimes. We also know that if these individuals are convicted or plead guilty to the crime with which they are charged, then they may go to prison. However, there are many other types of law that touch our lives every day that may not receive as much attention but are just as important for a working society.

In this chapter, we will address two basic fields of law: criminal law and civil law. One of the best ways to examine the important aspects of civil and criminal law is to look at the many differences between the two. The most obvious difference is that the state, not an individual, brings criminal actions. A victim may report a crime to the police, but it is the state, not the individual, who charges the defendant, prosecutes him or her, and, if necessary, brings the defendant to trial. In criminal law, the state takes action against an individual and imprisons that person for breaking the law. This is the most important distinction between criminal and civil law, but there are other key distinctions, such as:

- How the case originates
- The names and identities of the parties who bring and maintain the action

A. HOW THE CASE ORIGINATES

As we have already discussed, a victim can initially begin a criminal case by calling the police and reporting criminal behavior. Throughout this section, we will use the following scenario to help illustrate the differences between civil and criminal cases:

SCENARIO 1-1

THEO GETS PUNCHED

Theo is at a party and is having a good time. He sees a young lady that he finds very attractive and begins flirting with her. The young lady's boyfriend, Randall, sees Theo flirting with his girlfriend and takes offense. He confronts Theo and punches him in the nose.

How will this case be handled in a criminal as opposed to a civil case?

Assuming that Theo calls the police after being punched, the police will arrive on the scene and may arrest Randall for striking Theo. As we will see in future chapters, police officers and prosecutors have a great deal of latitude in deciding which cases they will prosecute and which ones they will not, but this case is very straightforward, so the police will almost certainly arrest Randall for punching Theo. The charge will probably be called "battery."

FIGURE 1-1

Amendment V

No person shall be held to answer for a capital, or otherwise infamous crime, unless on a presentment or indictment of a Grand Jury, except in cases arising in the land or naval forces, or in the Militia, when in actual service in time of War or public danger; nor shall any person be subject for the same offense to be twice put in jeopardy of life or limb; nor shall be compelled in any criminal case to be a witness against himself, nor be deprived of life, liberty, or property, without due process of law; nor shall private property be taken for public use, without just compensation.

Although Theo is the victim in the case, the moment that the police become involved, the case becomes the province of the state. Victims in criminal cases are often surprised to learn that they do not control how the case proceeds from that moment on. Suppose that Theo, after initially insisting on bringing charges against Randall, later changes his mind and decides that he wants to dismiss the case. Because this is a criminal matter, Theo does not have the power to make that decision. Criminal cases are brought by the government, not individuals. Police and prosecutors may take Theo's desires into account; then again, they may not. This brings us into the first bit of important terminology that anyone who intends to study criminal law must master: the difference between a suspect and a defendant.

SUSPECTS VS. DEFENDANTS

When the police have reason to believe that a person has committed a crime, but he or she has not yet been arrested, the person is referred to as a **suspect** (sometimes called the "perpetrator"). A suspect is not under arrest and is free to go about his or her business. If the police ask a suspect to come to police headquarters to answer questions, he or she is free to decline. When a suspect is being questioned by the police, he or she is free to leave at any time prior to being arrested. Once a suspect is arrested, his or her status changes: the person now becomes a **defendant**.

Why is the distinction between suspect and defendant so important? For one thing, several critical legal rights are triggered when a person becomes a defendant. A defendant has the right to a trial by jury, the right to be represented by counsel, the right to refuse to answer any questions, and not have that refusal used against him or her at a later time. One of the most important amendments of the U.S. Constitution comes into play when a person is placed under arrest. See Figure 1-1.

Sidebar

In a criminal case, the state controls how the case proceeds, not the victim.

Suspect
A person of interest to law enforcement and one whom they may believe has committed a criminal action, but is not under arrest.

Defendant
A person accused by the state of the commission of a crime

B. THE NAMES AND IDENTITIES OF THE PARTIES WHO BRING AND MAINTAIN THE ACTION

As we have already seen, another important difference between criminal and civil actions is the names of the parties who bring the actions. In a civil case, an individual, corporation, or company may bring a civil claim against another

Plaintiff
The name of the party who brings a civil suit.

individual, corporation, or company. The party who brings the suit is the **plaintiff**, and the person sued is the defendant. But the terminology goes much deeper than that. Consider our previous example of Theo being punched in the nose.

HOW WILL THEO PROCEED IN HIS CIVIL SUIT?

We have already discussed what will happen when Theo contacts the police about being punched by Randall. Once the government becomes involved, it is the government's case, and the prosecutor assigned to the case will make the ultimate decision about what to do. However, Theo decides that he wants to sue Randall. How will this case proceed?

Theo can hire a private attorney to bring a civil suit against Randall for punching him in the nose. This civil suit proceeds separately from the criminal case, and the two operate independently of one another. Theo can sue Randall before, during, or after the criminal case, although in most circumstances an attorney would advise Theo to wait until the criminal case has been completed for a very simple reason: If Randall goes to prison, there may not be very much that a civil case could get out of him that is worse than what he is already facing.

A criminal prosecution is brought by federal or state governments in the name of their citizens. A private individual brings a civil lawsuit. A crime is a violation of law, usually set out as a statute, and is viewed as an infraction against society as a whole. While there may be a specific victim, the prosecutor represents the government and brings charges in the name of the government. In the final analysis, a crime is a wrong committed against all of society. A civil action, on the other hand, is generally personal to the parties involved in the lawsuit. It is a private wrong and therefore a private lawsuit. These differences carry over into the pleadings or court documents filed in the different types of cases, which will be discussed in Chapter 2.

TERMINOLOGY USED IN CRIMINAL CASES

Criminal law has its own set of terms and phrases, and anyone who intends to study criminal law must be familiar with them. Later chapters will examine criminal law and procedure in great detail, but this chapter first examines the broader implications of criminal law. Perhaps the most important distinction to make is that between arrest and conviction.

To arrest a person is to take him or her into custody. An arrested person is not free to leave and will be taken to a local jail to be processed, assuming that the person does not immediately make bond. However, simply because a person has been arrested does not mean that he or she has lost any Constitutional rights. In fact, one could argue that the arrested person is protected by more Constitutional provisions than a person who is not under arrest. The important consideration about arrest is what it is not: An arrest is not a finding of guilt. An arrested person is not convicted of a crime, merely suspected of having committed one. A conviction is what comes at the end of the entire legal process. A person who has been convicted has been found guilty by a jury or has voluntarily pled guilty to a crime. Such a person loses important Constitutional protections. A convicted person can be sentenced to a term of confinement in a prison and may be compelled to pay a fine. An arrested person has not been guilty and even though the arrested person may await a hearing while being held in a detention facility, the arrested person has not been convicted.

A. THE "REAL WORLD"

Because this text has been written by an attorney who has worked as both a prosecutor and a defense attorney, there is great emphasis on the actual, day-to-day practices in criminal law and procedure. This text gives you the real world of criminal law, not the fictionalized account seen nightly on television shows and in movies. There is a great wealth of misinformation about criminal law and this text seeks to clear up some of those discrepancies.

B. FAMOUS CASES

To help separate fact from fiction, this text offers a feature that will appear throughout this book: Famous Cases. Each chapter introduces one of the many famous criminal cases that punctuate American criminal history. Each of these famous cases will tie in to the material in the chapter and will hopefully put a human face on the crimes being discussed. Criminals from Al Capone to Ted Bundy help to illustrate how, in the end, any textbook about criminal law is really about the people involved: the defendants, the victims, the law enforcement officers who build a case, and the prosecutors and defense attorneys who battle over the case in court. The participants are so important that they and their role in the criminal justice system are discussed next.

 **PARTICIPANTS IN THE CRIMINAL JUSTICE SYSTEM**

As you read the remaining chapters, you will encounter many different criminal justice professionals. Although this section introduces them, the parts that each play will be discussed throughout this book. The person who undoubtedly has the most authority, at least in the courtroom, is the judge.

Judges
A member of the judicial branch who is responsible for maintaining order in the courtroom, ruling on motions, making orders, and, in many circumstances, sentencing the defendant.

A. JUDGES

Judges are in charge of the courtroom, and during the trial they control all aspects of the case. They are responsible for keeping order in the courtroom and have the power of **contempt** to enforce it. If a judge orders someone to be held in contempt,

Contempt
A judge's power to enforce his or her orders, authority, or dignity by temporarily depriving the offending party of his or her liberty.

the person may be removed from the courtroom and taken to the local jail for a few hours to several days. The judge rules on evidentiary issues and objections during a trial, and in many states, it is the judge who passes sentence on a defendant who has been found guilty.

A judge is required to be neutral during all proceedings. Unlike other countries where judges can suggest important points to the jury for them to consider during their deliberations, American judges are not allowed to comment on the quality of the evidence or the credibility of witnesses. Judges enjoy a great deal of power in and out of the courtroom, and the position traditionally receives a great deal of respect from all other participants in the criminal justice system. The respect and the high salary make the position of judge very attractive for many attorneys. However, the temperament of a judge is critical. A judge who cannot remain neutral during proceedings, cannot control his or her temper, or makes consistently bad rulings will find the job challenging and may decide to resign from the position.

B. POLICE

Police
Law enforcement officers who are empowered to investigate criminal cases and to make arrests.

Police investigate crimes, make arrests, and generally keep the peace. They also gather evidence in criminal cases and must testify about their actions when a case goes to a preliminary hearing, a motion, or a trial. The conduct and requirements of police officers will be addressed throughout this text, but a quick word about police officers here is also warranted. Despite what is portrayed on television and in movies, being a police officer is not a glamorous job. Officers work long hours and do not make much money. In the recent economic recession, many police officers have been laid off as a cost-cutting measure. Those that remain on the job often work odd hours and have to supplement their income with part-time jobs. It is a difficult profession, with long periods of boredom punctuated by a few moments of heart-pounding action. Some officers may spend their entire careers and never become involved in a shoot out with a suspect, while others may be killed within a few months of joining the force. The job takes a toll on them, both physically and mentally.

C. PROSECUTORS

Prosecutor
An attorney who works for the state or federal government and is responsible for making decisions on cases and presenting cases to a judge and/or jury.

The **prosecutor** is the representative of the government in the courtroom. Prosecutors are, in most jurisdictions, members of the state bar, just like any other attorney. They are graduates of three years of intensive training in a law school, following four years in a bachelor's degree program. Like police officers, they are routinely portrayed incorrectly in television and movies. Prosecutors do not make high salaries. In fact, they enter the job knowing that they will never earn the same kind of money that their law school contemporaries will earn working for large firms or corporations. Why then do they take the job? Although the work is not quite what is portrayed on television, it can be exciting, and many prosecutors have high job satisfaction. Prosecutors often feel a strong sense of community, and the trial experience that they gain in even a few short years is more than most other attorneys will attain in a lifetime.

A quick review of the responsibilities of a prosecutor includes:

- representing the government in court
- charging defendants with crimes through indictments
- recommending sentences
- calling witnesses to testify
- introducing evidence to prove that a defendant committed the crime
- acting as legal advisors to the police

Most people are not aware that prosecutors advise police officers on legal issues. If a police officer has a legal question concerning an arrest or search warrant, the officer seeks legal advice from the prosecutor. However, prosecutors in most jurisdictions are barred from representing clients in civil matters or giving legal advice to anyone other than police officers, and then only when it involves a pending criminal case.

So far, we have used the term "prosecutor" to refer to the attorney who represents the government in a prosecution, but this position is known by many different names. They may be called district attorneys, state's attorneys, people's attorneys, solicitors, and other names. Whatever their title, this person works to seek justice in criminal cases and further the work completed by police and evidence technicians.

D. DEFENSE ATTORNEYS

A criminal **defense attorney** represents the person who is charged with a criminal violation. They are often seen as enemies of the prosecution and the police, but the reality is more nuanced. Many prosecutors become defense attorneys, and some defense attorneys become prosecutors. As a result, the depiction of prosecutors and defense attorneys as inimitable foes is often fiction. Most defense attorneys are ethical, honest, and trustworthy people. They view it as their job to make sure that the state does not skimp on the evidence or procedures and to ensure that the state proves that the defendant is guilty beyond a reasonable doubt. They fulfill a crucial role in our legal system: safeguarding the rights of the accused. Without them, there would be no one to monitor the actions of the prosecution and police who might be tempted to cut corners in certain cases to push a conviction. Some defense attorneys fall into the category of public defenders (see Figure 1-2), which will be covered later in this text.

E. DEFENDANTS

No discussion of the criminal justice system would be complete without reference to the people who are actually charged with crimes: **defendants**. Without a suspect, there would be no need for police, prosecutors, judges, or probation officers. See Figure 1-3 for a breakdown of felony defendants by charge. We will address the specific constitutional and statutory protections that are afforded all defendants in nearly every chapter of this text.

> **Sidebar**
>
> *Prosecutors usually draft the indictments relied upon by the grand jury in their deliberations and present the evidence at trial to prove a defendant is guilty.*

Defense attorney
An attorney who primarily or exclusively represents individuals who have been charged with criminal offenses.

Defendants
Individuals who have been charged with a crime.

FIGURE 1-2

Twenty-Two States Had Public Defender Programs in 2007

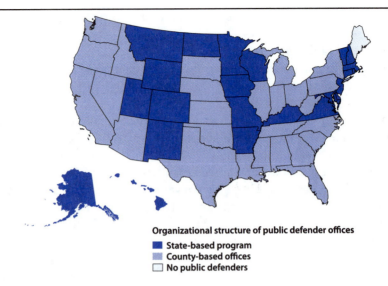

Organizational structure of public defender offices

- ■ State-based program
- ■ County-based offices
- □ No public defenders

FIGURE 1-3

Felony defendants, by most serious arrest charge, in 2006

Felony defendants in the 75 largest counties

Most Serious Arrest Charge	Number	Percent	95% Confidence Interval	
			Lower Bound	Upper Bound
All offenses	58,100	100.0%		
Violent offenses	13,295	22.9%	21.6%	24.2%
Murder	370	0.6	0.5	0.8
Rape	669	1.2	1.0	1.4
Robbery	3,451	5.9	5.2	6.8
Assault	6,386	11.0	10.1	12.0
Other violent	2,419	4.2	3.5	4.9
Property offenses	16,948	29.2%	27.7%	30.7%
Burglary	4,495	7.7	7.0	8.5
Larceny/theft	5,268	9.1	8.1	10.1
Motor vehicle theft	1,661	2.9	2.5	3.3
Forgery	1,416	2.4	2.1	2.9
Fraud	2,128	3.7	3.0	4.4
Other property	1,980	3.4	2.9	4.0
Drug offenses	21,232	36.5%	34.8%	38.3%
Trafficking	8,487	14.6	13.0	16.4
Other drug	12,745	21.9	19.9	24.1
Public-order offenses	6,624	11.4%	10.4%	12.5%
Weapons	1,958	3.4	2.9	3.9
Driving-related	1,837	3.2	2.5	3.9
Other public-order	2,830	4.9	4.3	5.6

Note: Data for the specific arrest charge were available for all cases. Detail may not add to total because of rounding.

F. CLERK OF COURT AND COURTHOUSE PERSONNEL

Clerks are government employees who work in the courthouse and are responsible for storing and maintaining all records of court proceedings. Clerk's offices are open to the public. Clerks and deputy clerks keep track of each case and store all documents relating to criminal and civil cases. They are the gatekeepers to the records of the criminal justice system. Without them there would be no way to track repeat offenders or to know who in the community is a convicted felon or sex offender. In order to do their jobs effectively, deputy clerks are often found in the courtroom during calendar calls and sentencing hearings so that they can keep track of the dispositions in each and every case.

G. PROBATION OFFICERS

As we will see in Chapter 21 on sentencing and appeals, one possible punishment for a defendant is to serve his sentence on probation. When the defendant is sentenced to probation (or parole), a **probation officer** is assigned to the defendant's case and is responsible for monitoring all activities of the defendant (see Figure 1-4). The probation officer ensures that the defendant obtains employment, stays away from other convicted felons, does not use illegal drugs, and pays his or her fine as ordered by the court. If a defendant is sentenced to community service, for instance, it is the probation officer who coordinates the defendant's service and keeps a record of his or her compliance. If a defendant violates any of the conditions of probation, then the probation officer will file a notice seeking to revoke the defendant's probation and request that the defendant be returned to prison. This

Probation officer
An individual employed by the government who monitors convicted defendants while they serve the balance of their sentences outside of prison or incarceration.

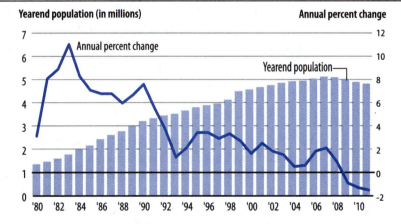

FIGURE 1-4

Adults on Probation at Year End, 1980–2011

Note: Annual change was based on the difference between the January 1 and December 31 populations within the reporting year. See *Methodology* for more details. The apparent decrease observed in the community supervision and probation rates between 2007 and 2008 was due to a change in scope for two jurisdictions and does not reflect actual declines in the populations. See *Probation and Parole in the United States, 2010,* BJS website, NJC236019, November 2011, for a description of changes in reporting methods.

Source: Bureau of Justice Statistics, Annual Surveys of Probation and Parole, 1980–2011.

notice will result in a probation revocation hearing where evidence will be presented. These hearings will be discussed in greater detail in Chapter 2.

H. OTHER PERSONNEL

The previous list is not exhaustive. Throughout this text, we will also encounter federal agents, prison counselors, federal and state correction agencies, federal and state law enforcement agencies, and many others, especially the victims of criminal activity and the important legislation that allows them to give a statement during the defendant's sentencing.

V ELEMENTS OF CRIMINAL OFFENSES

Elements
The factual points and statutory requirements of a criminal case that must be proven against the defendant beyond a reasonable doubt.

Throughout this text, we will often use the term **elements** when referring to crime. This word has a specific connotation in criminal law. The elements consist of the various points of the crime that the prosecutor must prove to the jury, beyond a reasonable doubt. Consider one of the worst crimes: murder in the first degree. As will be seen in Chapter 4 when homicide is discussed, the statute that makes murder a crime sets out the four elements of what constitutes this crime. For a person to be guilty of first degree murder, he or she must:

1 Intentionally
2 Kill a human being
3 With malice aforethought
4 Deliberately with premeditation

The elements come from the statute that criminalizes murder and when a prosecutor prepares a case for trial, he or she reviews each and every one of these elements to ensure that there is sufficient evidence to support every element. Consider Scenario 1-3, then ask yourself how the prosecutor will prove each element.

SCENARIO 1-3   MURDER IN THE FIRST DEGREE?

Andy knows a man named Carl. They haven't liked each other for a long time. One day while Andy is in his front yard, Carl drives by and yells an obscenity at Andy then drives off. Andy goes inside his home and thinks about what just happened. He doesn't like Carl, but now his dislike has become hatred. He knows enough about Carl to know that Carl sleeps during the day and works at night. Andy gets his shotgun, then spends an hour trying to find the shotgun shells. During that time, he gets a call from his girlfriend. Andy tells his girlfriend about what happened with Carl and she tells him to forget it. "Carl is always shooting his mouth off," the girlfriend says.

  "Maybe it's time somebody shot his mouth off," Andy says and hangs up. He doesn't answer when the phone rings again.

Andy places the loaded shotgun, extra shells, and some rope into his car. It takes 15 minutes to drive to Carl's house. During that time, Andy sees that his girlfriend has tried to contact him several more times. When Andy arrives at Carl's house, he finds that the front and back door are locked. He tries to pry open a basement window and, when that doesn't work, he goes back to his car to consider his options. He knows that Carl will get up around 5:00 p.m., which gives Andy three hours to wait. He thinks that he looks suspicious sitting in front of Carl's house, so he drives down the street to a playground and waits.

At 4:50 p.m., Andy drives back to Carl's house. When Carl comes out of his house, Andy gets out of his car and points the gun at Carl. He orders him back into the house, where Andy ties his hands and leads him to the basement. Once there, he shoots Carl in the face. On the way out, he wipes down surfaces he may have touched to remove any fingerprints. He then returns home, cleans the shotgun, and puts it away.

When police respond to the calls of Carl's neighbors, they find him dead in his basement. Several neighbors describe a man who had been lurking in the neighborhood earlier that day and one individual had written down the car's license plate number. Police run the tag and it comes back to Andy. They visit Andy who says he doesn't know anything about what happened. He denies owning a shotgun.

Later, five witnesses pick Andy out of a photographic lineup as the man they saw at Carl's house. Police recover the shotgun, and although they cannot run a ballistic test on a shotgun, the spent shells that were left at the scene are the same make and model as the ones that Andy owns. When they confront Andy with this evidence, Andy confesses to killing Carl, but says that it was an accident and that he never meant to hurt him.

We already know that the prosecutor assigned to Andy's case must prove that Andy:

1 Intentionally
2 Killed Carl
3 With malice aforethought
4 Deliberately with premeditation

The prosecutor must assemble evidence and witness testimony to substantiate each one of these elements. That is the important aspect of any discussion about the elements of a crime: Each one must be proven beyond a reasonable doubt. Prosecutors are not allowed to skip any of the elements or simply assume that everyone on the jury will agree that one element is established on the prosecutor's word alone. Instead, the prosecutor must present evidence on each and every one. If he or she fails to do so, the judge must enter a verdict in the defendant's favor. The case is dismissed.

The prosecutor assigned to Andy's case begins with the first element: that Andy acted intentionally. Proving this element is quite easy. The law assumes that each person acts intentionally unless there is some evidence that he or she was unconscious, drugged, or insane. The prosecution can show that Andy was apparently acting intentionally because he carried out a series of actions that showed he was neither unconscious or not in his right mind: He spoke on the phone with his girlfriend. He planned to kill Carl and took actions appropriate to carrying out that plan. He even took precautions by loading extra ammunition in his car and something to restrain Carl when he got to Carl's house. He drove for 15 minutes, then had to change his plans when he found that Carl's front and back doors were locked. All of these actions clearly show that he acted intentionally.

continued

For the second element of a first degree murder charge, the prosecutor must prove that the Andy killed Carl. First, the prosecutor will present the testimony of the Medical Examiner who will testify how Carl died. Then, the prosecutor will present testimony from the witnesses who saw Andy in the area. Finally, the prosecutor will present the shotgun and show how the shells that Andy owned matched those found in the freshly cleaned shotgun.

To prove the third element, the prosecution must show that Andy acted with malice. Although malice is discussed in greater detail in a later chapter, it is sufficient to show that Andy acted with ill will toward Carl. Loading the shotgun, telling his girlfriend that maybe someone should shoot Carl's mouth off, restraining Carl with rope and taking him downstairs, and shooting him in the face — all of these elements show malice and that Andy thought about them before he killed Carl.

The final element that the prosecution must prove is that Andy acted with deliberation or premeditation. As we will see in the chapter on homicide, premeditation refers to the ability and the time to consider one's actions before they are taken, to have time to reflect on what a person is about to do and then, despite knowing that the action was wrong, carrying out the crime anyway. The prosecutor can show considerable periods of time for Andy to reconsider his actions: He drove across town to commit the murder. He waited for Carl to wake up. He could have abandoned his crime at any time, but decided to go through with it. This shows premeditation. Finally, of course, there is Andy's confession that clearly shows that he knew what he was doing, that he thought through his actions, and that he committed murder anyway.

MENS REA

In almost every crime that can be prosecuted, the state must show two essential underlying elements: that the defendant knew what he or she was doing and that the defendant carried out some action. Without both of these elements, in almost all cases, a prosecution cannot proceed. Evaluate Scenario 1-4.

THEO HITS SOMEONE ELSE

Theo is staying with a bunch of friends at a cabin in the woods. After dinner, the friends bring out beer and wine and become intoxicated. Theo, realizing that he has had too much to drink, crawls into the top bed of a bunk. At 3:00 a.m., Don gets up from the bottom bunk to go to the bathroom. Theo, heavily asleep, rolls over smashing his hand into Don's face, immediately causing a bloody nose. Did Theo commit a crime?

Answer: No. To have a crime, the state must show that, at a minimum, the defendant acted with knowledge of his actions. An unconscious person cannot commit a crime.

Mens rea
Guilty intent, voluntary action, criminal intent.

Actus reus
A criminal action.

As you can see in Scenario 1-4, a person must act voluntarily before he or she can be charged with a crime, but in order to fully understand the basic building blocks of a criminal prosecution, one must go deeper and examine the terms **mens rea** and **actus reus**.

The basic equation for crime is simple: guilty intent (*mens rea*) + guilty act (*actus reus*) = crime. In almost all crimes, the defendant must have a mindset where he knows that he is acting voluntarily and that he has not been coerced or otherwise forced to carry out the action. This is *mens rea*, a Latin term.[1] The second element of a guilty act, known under the Latin term *actus reus*, is the wrongful deed, or the behavior that the defendant carried out. In the day-to-day practice of law, parties generally avoid the Latin terms and simply refer to *mens rea* as "intent." In most prosecutions, proving intent is straightforward. The state must simply prove the defendant had a general purpose or plan aimed at achieving a result. The state does not have to prove that the defendant had it in mind to commit a specific offense; the fact that the defendant intended to carry out an act is enough. That intent, coupled with a corresponding action, is the basis of crime. Consider Scenarios 1-5 and 1-6.

CRIME OR NO CRIME?

SCENARIO 1-5

Arty is at a bank, waiting for his wife to make a deposit. While he sits in his car, he comes up with what he believes is a foolproof plan to rob the bank. He even gets out of his car and checks the various sides of the bank to see if there are security cameras. He gets back into his car and draws out a diagram of the bank and writes down his idea for the bank robbery. He then waits for his wife to come out of the bank, and when she does, they go home. Has Arty committed attempted bank robbery?

Answer: No. Although the prosecution could clearly show that Arty had the intent to commit a robbery, there was no corresponding act to carry it out. Arty did not approach the bank with a gun or take any other illegal action. If arrested for attempted armed robbery, he can simply claim that he was working out a fictional plan for a book he was planning to write. The missing piece in this situation is *actus reus*.

CRIME OR NO CRIME, PART 2

SCENARIO 1-6

The following day, Arty goes back to the bank. This time he has a gun, a ski mask, a large sack, and several long plastic restraining ties. He gets out of his car, tucks the gun into his waistband, puts the bag with the other items under his arm and starts toward the bank. On his way he is stopped by a police officer who has been observing him. The officer charges him with attempted bank robbery. Has Arty committed this crime?

Answer: Yes. As we will see later in this text when we discuss attempted crimes, the closer a person gets to actually put the crime into action, the more likely that he will be considered to have committed it. In this case, Arty has both *mens rea* and *actus reus*. He has guilty intent from the plan he made the day before, coupled with the items that he brought with him (which certainly go beyond anything that someone would do to create a fictional bank robbery) and he committed an act, when he voluntarily got out of his car and began walking toward the bank.

---

[1] State v. Roberts, 948 S.W.2d 577, 587 (Mo. 1997).

CASE EXCERPT

In each chapter of this text, there is an example of a criminal case that has gone up on appeal. These cases are printed and made available in case reporters, as well as legal research sites and other online venues. The importance of reading appellate cases is that they explain the law and how it applies in particular cases. If a person is found guilty at the conclusion of a trial, he or she is permitted to appeal that conviction. When the appellate court reaches a decision in the case, it writes out the reasons for its decision. As we will see in the final chapter of this book, an appellate court has several possible alternatives in deciding an appeal. In many situations, the appellate court will write out the reasons for its decision and publish this in what is referred to as an opinion, or in common parlance, a "case." Reading these appellate opinions is helpful in understanding how all of the various aspects of criminal law and procedure come together in a specific trial.

In each of the cases in this book, the names are real and so are the crimes. These cases are not fiction. By reading them, you will gain a much better appreciation for how criminal law functions day to day. The cases have been edited for length. but none of the important details about the cases, or the real people involved, have been altered. In fact, after you read the cases in this text, you can find the same cases in other sources.

The first appellate case is a fairly straightforward appeal involving a charge of armed robbery and the accuracy of eyewitness identification. At the conclusion of the case, there are several questions to answer. In this first case, there are several specific areas of the case outlined to help understand how an appellate case is written and why specific portions are important.

PEOPLE v. MOHAMED

201 Cal. App. 4th 515, 525, 133 (Cal. Rptr. 3d 823, 830) (Cal. App. 4 Dist. 2011)

McCONNELL, P.J.

This is the style or caption of the case, where the parties are identified

The judge who wrote the opinion

INTRODUCTION

A jury convicted Abdi Mohamed of robbery (Pen.Code, § 211). The trial court sentenced him to five years in state prison. Mohamed appeals, contending there is insufficient evidence to support the jury's verdict.

This is a summary of what happened in the case

BACKGROUND

Prosecution Evidence

Around 12:45 a.m., Breanna Gomez was leaving a café when someone pushed her friend against her. Gomez fell against a wall. She heard someone refer to her and her friend as "b — s." She turned and saw three men wearing sheer, form-fitting masks. She felt an object she thought was a gun in her back and was pushed back against the wall. One man's mask ended up between his nose and lower lip. Gomez could see the man's jaw line and facial structure, including the shape of his chin, cheek, and nose. He was black, approximately six feet tall, and thin. He had a moderate beard defining his jaw line. He wore a black hooded sweatshirt, light colored pants, and a black beanie. He took her cell phone, car keys, and a $20 bill. One of the men also took her purse. Gomez then ran back into the café.

The owner of the café was standing with some customers outside when a man walked up. The man asked if the people outside were gang-banging, and when he learned they were not, he pulled a mask over his entire face and drew what appeared to be a gun. The man walked over to another group of people that included Gomez and her friend. Meanwhile, the owner went into the café and called 911. During the 911 call, the owner described the man he saw as a six-foot tall black man around 25-years-old. The man had a medium build and wore black pants, a black shirt, and a black and white striped jacket.

Another unidentified person told the 911 operator that one of the robbers was black and wore a black shirt, a black hooded sweatshirt, and gray sweats. The man also wore a black beanie as a mask. The unidentified person said that one of the other robbers was wearing a Spiderman backpack.

Froilan Medina was inside the café when the incident occurred. He saw a black man walk up to the restaurant and pull a black beanie mask down to his mouth area. The man was between five-feet-ten-inches and six feet tall. He had a thin patch of hair on his chin and was wearing dark pants and a red hooded sweater with designs.

Medina went out of the restaurant and saw the man run away with two other black men following him. One of the followers was around six feet tall and wore a mask, a black and gray hooded sweatshirt, and black baggie sweatpants. The other man wore a black hooded sweatshirt and gray sweatpants. He dropped what appeared to be a gun and went back to pick it up. Police officers found a magazine for a toy pistol in the same area. DNA testing of the magazine was inconclusive because there was not enough DNA for a comparison.

One of the police officers who responded to the incident drove around the neighborhood looking for suspects. Shortly after the robbery, the officer saw Mohamed walking along a street approximately four blocks from the café and holding an umbrella in a manner that partially blocked his face. Mohamed wore gray sweatpants, a black hooded sweatshirt, a beanie, and a neck scarf. The officer detained Mohamed, confirmed he fit the description of one of the robbers, and conducted curbside lineups with Gomez and two other witnesses.

Gomez told the officer who brought her to the lineup that she was 80-percent sure Mohamed was one of the men who robbed her because he was wearing the same clothing and had the same facial hair, facial features, and build. She could not be 100-percent sure because the men were wearing masks. Gomez later identified Mohamed as one of the robbers at both the preliminary hearing and the trial.

Medina also identified Mohamed as one of the robbers at the curbside lineup. At the time, he said he was "completely sure" about his identification because Mohamed was wearing the same clothes as one of the robbers. At trial, he said he had "a little bit" of doubt about his identification, but remained confident in it. The owner of the café said Mohamed was not the person he saw.

After Gomez and Medina identified Mohamed as one of the robbers, the officer arrested Mohamed and advised him of his rights under *Miranda v. Arizona*, 384 U.S.

In this section, the court presents a thorough overview of the facts of the case. Notice how detailed the court is in its presentation and how it emphasizes particular facts, especially eyewitness testimony.

436, 86 S.Ct. 1602, 16 L.Ed.2d 694 (1966). The officer searched Mohamed and found a nylon do-rag tucked between his body and his pants.

Mohamed told the officer he was coming from a friend's house where he had been playing video games since 5:00 p.m. The officer went to the friend's house, and the friend's mother told the officer she had not seen her son since about 1:00 p.m. and Mohamed had not been at her house after 5:00 p.m. playing video games. The following day the friend spoke with the officer and confirmed he had not seen Mohamed after 5:00 p.m. the prior evening. At trial, the friend testified he had been with Mohamed until dark, then they split up. He was not with Mohamed after then, and Mohamed was not at his house playing video games until 1:00 a.m.

Defense Evidence

Dr. Scott Fraser, an eyewitness identification expert, testified there are several variables affecting the accuracy of eyewitness identifications. These variables include lighting, distance, and duration of exposure. Generally, the better the lighting, the shorter the distance, and the longer the duration of exposure, the more likely an eyewitness identification is to be accurate. In addition, very small obstructions in a witness's view of the perpetrator, such as a partial face mask, can greatly reduce the accuracy of the witness's identification. Likewise, when there is more than one person involved in an incident, the rates of correctly recognizing any single person are significantly reduced. Stress can also affect the accuracy of eyewitness identifications. In very high stress situations, the accuracy of eyewitness identifications drops off rapidly.

> Although this evidence was presented for the defense, the court relies on it in other ways.

Conversely, the existence of distinctive cues, such as tattoos or scars, increases the accuracy of eyewitness identifications. If an eyewitness describes a perpetrator as having a scar in a particular place, the perpetrator will almost certainly have a mark or aberration in that place. If an eyewitness gives a description that omits a distinctive cue, such as the existence of facial hair on the chin, then the perpetrator's chin almost certainly did not have facial hair.

Errors in cross-racial identifications are two to two-and-a-half times higher than same-race identifications. Moreover, the errors in cross-racial identifications are almost exclusively false positives, such as saying a person is the perpetrator when the person is not the perpetrator.

Of the three recognition tests most commonly used by law enforcement officers — curbside lineups, photo lineups, and live lineups — curbside lineups have the highest error rate and are the least reliable. Like the errors in cross-racial identifications, the errors in curbside lineups are almost exclusively false positives. The error rates are especially high if the person displayed is the same race, size, and gender and is wearing clothing similar to what the perpetrator was seen wearing.

Moreover, once a witness makes an identification, whether through a curbside lineup or other method, the witness is predisposed to identify the same person again. Consequently, any subsequent identification of the same person, such as at a preliminary hearing or a trial, is not an independent assessment. Furthermore, if a witness does not specifically state the person is or is not the perpetrator, but instead makes feature-similarity declarations, such as the person has the same kind of clothes or jaw line as the perpetrator, the witness's remarks would more accurately be treated as a rejection than a selection.

DISCUSSION

Sufficiency of the Evidence Claim

Mohamed contends we must reverse his conviction because there was insufficient evidence to show he was one of the robbers. "In reviewing a claim for sufficiency of the evidence, we must determine whether, after viewing the evidence in the light most favorable to the prosecution, any rational trier of fact could have found the essential elements of the crime or special circumstance beyond a reasonable doubt. We review the entire record in the light most favorable to the judgment below to determine whether it discloses sufficient evidence — that is, evidence that is reasonable, credible, and of solid value — supporting the decision, and not whether the evidence proves guilt beyond a reasonable doubt. We neither reweigh the evidence nor reevaluate the credibility of witnesses. We presume in support of the judgment the existence of every fact the jury reasonably could deduce from the evidence. If the circumstances reasonably justify the findings made by the trier of fact, reversal of the judgment is not warranted simply because the circumstances might also reasonably be reconciled with a contrary finding. Apropos the question of identity, to entitle a reviewing court to set aside a jury's finding of guilt the evidence of identity must be so weak as to constitute practically no evidence at all."

> Here, the court sets out the law that is applicable to the charge and the facts of the case.

In this case, the evidence showed that a short time after the robbery, a police officer spotted Mohamed walking along the street four blocks from the crime scene. Mohamed fit the description of one of the robbers. During a curbside lineup, Gomez stated she was 80 percent sure Mohamed was one of the robbers because he was wearing the same clothing, had the same build, and had the same jaw line and chin hair. She also identified Mohamed as one of the robbers at the preliminary hearing and at trial. During a separate curbside lineup, Medina stated he was "completely sure" Mohamed was one of the robbers because Mohamed was wearing the same clothing. After Mohamed's arrest, a police officer found a thin, nylon do-rag on him, which Gomez testified matched the fabric the robbers used to mask their faces. In addition, Mohamed provided the officer with a false alibi, suggesting consciousness of guilt. We conclude this evidence amply supports the jury's verdict in this case.

Gomez's inability to be 100 percent certain of her curbside identification and Medina's expression of "a little bit" of doubt about his curbside identification at trial do not preclude the existence of sufficient support for the jury's verdict. "It is not essential that a witness be free from doubt as to one's identity. He may testify that in his belief, opinion, or judgment the accused is the person who perpetrated the crime, and the want of positiveness goes only to the weight of the testimony."

The fact that neither Gomez nor Medina saw the robbers' entire faces also does not preclude the existence of sufficient support for the jury's verdict. "It is not necessary that any of the witnesses called to identify the accused should have seen his face. Identification based on other peculiarities may be reasonably sure. Consequently, the identity of a defendant may be established by proof of any peculiarities of size, appearance, similarity of voice, features or clothing."

Similarly, the discrepancies between Gomez's and Medina's observations and their omission of certain information from their initial descriptions of the robber they identified as Mohamed, including his possession of an umbrella or the presence of a black stripe on the side of his pants, did not necessitate the jury's rejection of their identifications. "The strength or weakness of the identification, the incompatibility of and discrepancies in the testimony, if there were any, the uncertainty of recollection, and the qualification of identity and lack of positiveness in testimony are matters which go to the weight of the evidence and the credibility of the witnesses, and are for the observation and consideration, and directed solely to the attention of the jury in the first instance. . . ."

Moreover, although Dr. Fraser provided the jury with information explaining how certain discrepancies and omissions might indicate an eyewitness identification is inaccurate, the jury was not obliged to accept Dr. Fraser's opinions or find them applicable in this particular case. The jury is not bound to accept the opinion of any expert as conclusive, but should give to it the weight to which they shall find it to be entitled. The jury may, however, disregard any such opinion if it shall be found by them to be unreasonable. Furthermore, given the closeness of Gomez's and Medina's descriptions to Mohamed's physical appearance the night of the robbery, his proximity to the crime scene, his possession of a do-rag with similar characteristics to the masks worn by the robbers, and his false alibi, we are unable to conclude, as Mohamed asserts, that Gomez's and Medina's identifications of him were inherently improbable.

DISPOSITION

The judgment is affirmed.

WE CONCUR: HALLER and IRION, JJ.

> Here, the court quotes from another case. The citation to that case has been omitted because it was very lengthy

> The original finding of the trial court — that the defendant is guilty — is also the conclusion of the appellate court. The defendant has lost his appeal.

CASE QUESTIONS

1 In this case, the defendant Mr. Mohamed requests that his conviction for armed robbery be reversed. What reasons does he give for this request?
2 What standard does the appellate court use in determining the sufficiency of eyewitness testimony?
3 Were both witnesses 100% sure of their identifications?
4 Are the witnesses' doubts enough to overturn the conviction?
5 Does the fact that the witnesses never saw the defendant's entire face preclude a finding of guilt?

CHAPTER SUMMARY

At the conclusion of each chapter, there is a section called the Chapter Summary. This highlights many of the important concepts that have been explored in the chapter. The summary also serves as an excellent way to review the material from the chapter.

In this chapter, we have seen that criminal law is a specialized field with its own terminology, procedures, and rules. Most importantly, we have also seen that there are two broad categories of law: criminal law and civil law. Civil law deals with actions as diverse as child custody cases, contract suits, divorce, personal injury, and many others. In civil cases, one party sues another party and usually requests a monetary reward. In a criminal case, however, the government brings an action against an individual and charges that individual with violating a statute. The loser in a civil case may be forced to compensate the other side, but in a criminal case, if the accused is found guilty, he or she may face prison, fines, or both.

There is some important terminology that anyone who studies criminal law should know. For instance, there is a difference between a suspect and a defendant. A suspect is a person who is suspected of committing a crime, but has not been charged with an offense. A defendant is someone who has been charged with a crime.

There are many participants in the criminal justice field, including judges, prosecutors, police officers, defense attorneys, defendants, and others. Each of these participants plays a critical role in the process, and the defendant is protected by a wide variety of constitutional guarantees to ensure that the prosecution is fair.

For prosecutors and defense attorneys, the elements of an offense are extremely important. The elements refer to the basic allegations against the defendant and the evidence and testimony that the prosecutor must present in order to satisfy the jury, beyond a reasonable doubt, that the defendant is guilty. A defense attorney will often focus on attacking individual elements of an offense in order to show that the government's case is not strong and to introduce reasonable doubt.

There are two essential and underlying elements in almost all criminal offenses: *mens rea* and *actus reas*. To prove that a person is guilty of a crime, the government must prove that the defendant acted knowingly and voluntarily. That is the element of *mens rea*. The defendant must have intent. Involuntary actions or actions committed while the defendant is unconscious cannot be prosecuted because the government must prove that the defendant was aware and conscious of his or her actions. Coupled with the mental element, the government must also prove that the defendant took some action that was criminal in nature. This is the element of *actus reus* or, simply put, an illegal action. Illegal intent plus illegal action equals a crime.

KEY TERMS

Suspect	Police	Elements
Defendant	Prosecutor	*Mens rea*
Plaintiff	Defense attorney	*Actus reus*
Judge	Defendant	
Contempt	Probation Officer	

REVIEW QUESTIONS

1 Provide some general differences between civil law and criminal law.
2 Explain the differences between how a civil case originates versus a criminal case.
3 What is a prosecutor?
4 Explain case law and its significance.
5 What is the function of the judge?
6 What is the role of a defense attorney?
7 What is the difference between a suspect and a defendant?
8 What is a plaintiff?
9 Prosecutors and defense attorneys are both attorneys. What is the difference between them?
10 What are the "elements" of an offense?
11 Explain what a probation officer does.
12 What is the *mens rea* and why is it important?

WEB SURFING

NYC Public Defender Offices
http://www.nysacdl.org/legal-directories/new-york-city/public-defender-offices/

Los Angeles County District Attorney's Office
http://da.co.la.ca.us/

Miami Dade-County Police Department
http://www.miamidade.gov/police/

Illinois State Court System
http://www.state.il.us/court/

QUESTIONS FOR ANALYSIS

1 Why is the distinction between suspect and defendant so important?
2 Why would the law require the existence of *mens rea* in order to bring a prosecution?
3 How does a prosecutor use the elements of a crime to prove a case?

The Criminal Justice System

Chapter Objectives

- Define the differences between civil and criminal cases
- Describe the burden of proof in criminal cases
- Identify the various participants in the criminal justice system
- Explain the organization of the court system
- Distinguish between various sources of law

 I   INTRODUCTION TO THE CRIMINAL JUSTICE SYSTEM

As explained in the previous chapter, the world of criminal law is highly specialized and extremely interesting. Although there is a tendency to think about law as only involving an interpretation of statutes and appellate cases, criminal law is all about people. People commit crimes; other people investigate these crimes; and still others prosecute, represent, incarcerate, and monitor those accused of a crime. Criminal law is really about the interactions among and between human beings. This text will address not only the specific types of crimes that persons may commit against others, but also what happens after a suspect is arrested and processed through the criminal justice system. At every step of the process — during the collection of evidence, arresting the defendant, obtaining a statement from the defendant, arraigning, trying, and eventually sentencing guilty defendants — there are critical steps that must be followed and situations where the defendant is protected by rights guaranteed by the U.S. Constitution and individual state law.

As a broad distinction, there are two overall categories of law: criminal law and civil law. Chapter 1 showed how these were different from one another. In a criminal case, the government brings charges against a defendant. If a jury believes, beyond a reasonable doubt, that the defendant has committed the crime, then they may vote to find him or her guilty.

FIGURE 2-1

Examples of Civil Cases

- Slander
- Property boundary disputes
- Personal injury cases: when a person injured in a car wreck sues the other driver
- Medical malpractice

Examples of Criminal Cases

- Murder
- Rape
- Arson
- Armed robbery
- Forgery
- Battery
- Aggravated Assault
- Theft
- Criminal Damage to property

Guilty
The verdict in a criminal case where the jurors have determined that the defendant has committed a crime.

Liable
A finding in a civil case that a party has a duty or obligation to the other party to pay damages or to carry out some other action.

When a person is found **guilty** in a criminal case, that person faces imprisonment, fines, restitution, probation, or parole. That is not the situation in a civil case. At the conclusion of a civil case, a person may be found **liable**. A party who is found liable may be required to pay monetary damages to the opposing parties. However, no one who has lost a civil case will go to prison or face a term on probation or parole. See Figure 2-1 for examples of civil and criminal cases.

A. THE VERDICTS

Sidebar

The findings in a criminal case are guilty and not guilty; in a civil case it is liable or not liable.

Verdict
The jurors' determination of what they believe the facts of the case to be.

Not guilty
The jury's determination that the state has failed to prove, beyond a reasonable doubt, that the defendant committed the crime.

A **verdict** is the jurors' determination of what they believe the facts of the case to be. The verdict is the jury's final determination about who is telling the truth in the case and who is not. Looked at another way, the verdict refers to who wins and who loses. As already mentioned, the verdicts in civil and criminal cases are very different. At the conclusion of a civil trial, the losing party is found liable to the other party.

The verdicts in a criminal case are of a completely different order. At the conclusion of a criminal trial, a defendant may be found guilty, not guilty, guilty but mentally ill, or not guilty by reason of insanity. When a jury reaches a verdict of guilty in a criminal case, it means that the jurors believe that the defendant, to a level of proof beyond a reasonable doubt, committed the crime. This finding of guilt subjects the defendant to a possible prison sentence, probation, parole, or fines. The defendant may also be required to pay restitution to the victim during the course of his or her probation. A verdict of **not guilty** means one of two things: 1) that the jurors do not believe that the defendant committed the crime, or 2) that the state failed to prove that the defendant was guilty beyond a reasonable doubt.

The final two verdicts — guilty but mentally ill and not guilty by reason of insanity — are not available in all jurisdictions. When the jury finds the defendant

FIGURE 2-2

Amendment V

No person shall be held to answer for a capital, or otherwise infamous crime, unless on a presentment or indictment of a Grand Jury, except in cases arising in the land or naval forces, or in the Militia, when in actual service in time of War or public danger; nor shall any person be subject for the same offence to be twice put in jeopardy of life or limb; nor shall be compelled in any criminal case to be a witness against himself, nor be deprived of life, liberty, or property, without due process of law; nor shall private property be taken for public use, without just compensation.

is **guilty but mentally ill**, the court must sentence the defendant to a facility that includes some psychiatric counseling or monitoring. A finding of **not guilty by reason of insanity** is a verdict that will be explored in much greater depth in Chapter 17. At its simplest, the verdict means that the defendant lacks the mental capacity to know and understand the difference between right and wrong and therefore cannot be found guilty. Such defendants are often diverted to facilities that care for individuals suffering from severe mental disturbances.

When a defendant has been found not guilty, he or she will be set free (assuming that there are no other cases pending against the defendant). A not guilty verdict has specific legal and constitutional implications. For example, a defendant who has been found not guilty cannot be retried for the same offense. The Fifth Amendment to the U.S. Constitution specifically prohibits this practice under its double jeopardy clause. See Figure 2-2 for the entire text of the Fifth Amendment.

Guilty but mentally ill
A finding that the defendant is guilty of the crime charged, but has some mental problems or mental disease that mitigate his guilt to a small degree.

Not guilty by reason of insanity
A finding that the defendant did not understand the difference between right and wrong when he or she committed the offense and therefore lacks the mental capability to commit a crime.

VERDICTS IN CIVIL AND CRIMINAL CASES

In a civil trial, the jury can award monetary payments from one party to another. For instance, a jury can award compensatory **damages** — money payments from the defendant designed to compensate the plaintiffs for their losses. A civil jury can also award punitive damages and other types of damages against a defendant. **Punitive damages** are monetary assessments designed to punish the defendant and send a message to the community that behavior similar to that of the defendant will not be tolerated.

Damages are not available in criminal cases. Instead, the state may seek **restitution** for the victim's out-of-pocket expenses in repairing property destroyed by the defendant, but there are no provisions for punitive damages in criminal law. Instead, the punitive provisions come in the form of fines and prison time.

Unlike criminal cases, while the plaintiff who brings suit against a defendant will attempt to prove that the defendant is liable to the plaintiff, a defendant may also bring proof that the plaintiff is actually liable to him or her. In the end, a jury can as easily find the plaintiff liable to the defendant as it could the defendant liable to the plaintiff.

Damages
Money that a court orders paid to a person who has suffered damages by the person who caused the injury.

Punitive damages
Monetary assessments designed to punish the defendant and send a message to the community that behavior similar to that of the defendant will not be tolerated.

Restitution
Money that a court orders a criminal defendant to pay to the victim of a crime for damage or destruction of the victim's property.

B. THE BURDEN OF PROOF

Burden of proof
The amount of proof that a party must bring to sustain an action against another party. The burden of proof is different in civil and criminal cases.

Preponderance of the evidence
The standard of proof most closely associated with a civil case where a party proves that his or her version of the facts is more than likely to be true.

Beyond a reasonable doubt
The burden of proof in a criminal case; when one has a reasonable doubt, it is not mere conjecture but a doubt that would cause a prudent, rational person to hesitate before finding a defendant guilty of a crime.

The **burden of proof** in a legal action refers to the minimum level of evidence and facts that one party must establish as true against the other party. Standards of proof have been developed over centuries of legal hearings so that participants will understand what must be established as fact before another party can be liable in a civil case or guilty in a criminal case. Prosecutors in criminal cases have a much higher standard to meet in criminal cases than plaintiffs in civil cases.

The burden of proof is a phrase that refers to one side's obligation to prove the allegations against the other side. In most civil cases, that burden is **preponderance of the evidence**. This means that when a plaintiff brings a civil suit against a defendant, the plaintiff must prove his or her allegations are more likely true than not. Many commentators have compared this burden of proof to an old-fashioned scale, where putting more weight on one side makes the scale dip in one direction. When the plaintiff makes the scales tip in his or her direction, the plaintiff has met the civil standard of proof.

The standard that a prosecutor has to meet in order to convict someone is much higher than in civil cases. It is proof **beyond a reasonable doubt**. Although difficult to quantify, a reasonable doubt refers to the type of doubt that a person would have that might prevent him from making a major life decision. Proof beyond a reasonable doubt has been defined in various ways for centuries, but as most jurors learn at the conclusion of a criminal trial, this burden simply means that the state must prove each and every element of the offense against the defendant. If, at the end of the trial, a juror still believes that the state has failed to do that, and the juror has a specific, reasonable point of contention with the state's case, the juror is not only encouraged but required to find the defendant not guilty. This doubt has to be based on common sense and not mere fancy. Proving that someone has committed a crime beyond a reasonable doubt is quite a high standard. The individuals who founded our society based their legal model on the English system, which also required proof beyond a reasonable doubt to convict a person. The reason that the standard is so high is that it should not be an easy thing to deprive a person of his or her liberty or even the person's life. Conviction of a crime carries with it many legal and social consequences, and creating a low standard of proof would make it easy for prosecutors to prove that almost anyone is guilty of some offense. Judges often instruct jurors that even if they believe that the defendant committed the crime but the state has failed to prove it, then they must vote a "not guilty" verdict.

SCENARIO 2-1

THEO'S CASE GOES TO TRIAL

In the previous chapter, you were introduced to a factual scenario where Theo was at a party and was punched by Randall. Theo decides to press charges and Randall pleads not guilty to the charge of punching Theo in the nose. At the conclusion of the case, a juror is not sure if Theo is an American citizen or not. The fact was never brought up during the trial. Does this provide the juror with reasonable doubt about Randall's guilt?

Answer: No. Reasonable doubt must be based on the facts of the case and must be relevant. If the juror were unsure that Randall had punched Theo or thought that Theo may have started the fight, then that would qualify as reasonable doubt. However, Theo's citizenship status does not rise to the level of reasonable doubt.

There is an unfortunate use of legal terminology when it comes to discussing the parties to civil and criminal cases. The term used to refer to the person who is being sued in a civil case (in most jurisdictions) is the defendant. This is also the term that the state uses when it refers to a person charged with a crime. Because the terms are identical, it can sometimes lead to confusion when discussing a case. Often, it is necessary to ask if the defendant is a being sued or is a person charged with a crime. However, even though both of these parties are referred to as defendants, it is not proper to refer to the state as a "plaintiff" in a criminal action. States rarely sue individuals. It is far more likely that when the state brings an action against a person that the state is pursuing a criminal charge against the defendant.

A criminal prosecution is brought by federal or state governments in the name of their citizens. A private individual brings a civil lawsuit. A crime is a violation of law, usually set out as a statute, and is viewed as an infraction against society as a whole. While there may be a specific victim, the prosecutor represents the government and brings charges in the name of the government. In the final analysis, a crime is a wrong committed against all of society. A civil action, on the other hand, is generally personal to the parties involved in the lawsuit. It is a private wrong and therefore a private lawsuit. These differences carry over into the pleadings or court documents filed in the different types of cases.

> **Sidebar**
>
> *In criminal cases, the burden of proof is always on the state to prove that the defendant is guilty beyond a reasonable doubt. The defendant is never required to prove his or her innocence.*

C. THE PLEADINGS

A civil action is usually based on a private wrong suffered by an individual. The individual brings suit when he or she has suffered a financial, emotional, or physical loss. The right to bring a civil suit is not limited to natural persons only. Corporations and businesses may also sue in their own right. When cases from appellate courts are published, the first detail that is reported is the **style**, or caption, of the case. This is always given with the names of the parties involved. Civil cases are captioned *Plaintiff A v. Defendant B*. Because the government always brings criminal cases, the government is listed by name, not as a plaintiff. Criminal cases are captioned *Government (or State) v. Defendant*. The style of a case can tell you, usually within seconds, if the case is civil or criminal. There are times, however, when individuals also bring civil suits against the government, so it is important to examine additional details of the case, not just the style. See Figure 2-3 for an example of the style in a criminal case and how it compares to the style found in a criminal case.

Style (or caption)
The title or heading listing the parties to the case.

FIGURE 2-3

Style of Criminal and Civil Cases

Style of a Criminal Case

STATE OF XANADU
COUNTY OF BURKE
SUPERIOR COURT OF BURKE COUNTY

INDICTMENT NO: 13CR-12345

STATE OF XANADU   )
)
)
)
              v.   )
)
)
CHARLES FOSTER KANE,   )
)
Defendant.   )
)
_____   )

Style of a Civil Case

IN THE STATE OF PLACID
COUNTY OF BEVANS

IN THE GENERAL COURT OF JUSTICE
SUPERIOR COURT

Theo Baldwin,   *
                                   *
Plaintiff,   *
                                   *
              v.   *   COMPLAINT FOR DAMAGES
                                   *
                                   *   Civil Action File No.: 12CV-213
                                   *
Randall Nosepuncher,   *
                                   *
Defendant.   *
                                   *
_____   *

Pleadings refer to the legal documents that describe the nature of the claim against the parties. In a civil lawsuit, most states refer to the plaintiff's pleading as a **complaint** (also known as a petition). This document sets out the plaintiff's factual allegations against the defendant and requests the jury to award monetary damages to the plaintiff as a result of the defendant's actions. The defendant, on the other hand, responds with an **answer**, also known as a reply. In the answer, the defendant denies the plaintiff's factual allegations and also denies any responsibility for the plaintiff's injuries. In civil pleadings, the defendant may also request damages against the plaintiff.

In criminal cases, the state files charges against a defendant through various means. Although the defendant may have initially been arrested on a warrant or given a citation by a police officer, the prosecutor is allowed to alter the charges against the defendant, as long as they are supported by the evidence. In most states, prosecutors charge defendants with felonies through indictments. An **indictment** lists the known facts of the offense, including date, time, and location, as well as the name of the crime and the statute that the defendant is alleged to have violated. Should a prosecutor decide to charge the defendant with a lesser count, the prosecutor might use a different charging document (see Scenario 2-2).

Pleadings
1) In a civil case, the pleadings set out the wrong suffered by the parties against one another. 2) In a criminal case, the pleadings are often referred to as indictments (in felony cases) and accusations/informations (in misdemeanor cases), where the state sets out an infraction by the defendant that violates the law.

Complaint
The document filed by the plaintiff and served on the defendant that sets out the plaintiff's factual allegations that show the defendant is responsible for the plaintiff's injuries.

Answer
The defendant's written response to the complaint, usually containing denials of the defendant's responsibility for the plaintiff's injuries.

Indictment
An official charge against a defendant accusing him or her of a felony.

CIVIL OR CRIMINAL CASE?

SCENARIO 2-2

Marvin has a court date set for Monday morning at 9:00 a.m. He has just told you that it is "no big deal; just some civil thing." You look up Marvin's case online and see that the caption reads, "State v. Marvin." Is this is a civil or a criminal trial?

Answer: It is almost certainly a criminal case, despite what Marvin says. You might want to mention to Marvin the advantages of having an attorney represent him in his court proceeding.

D. CLASSES OF CRIMES: FELONIES VS. MISDEMEANORS

Crimes are broken down into two general classifications: felonies and misdemeanors. A **felony** is a crime punishable by more than one year in custody and often a substantial fine. These crimes include all of the major crimes against people, such as murder, manslaughter, sex crimes including rape, and theft crimes involving automobiles or items of a certain value. The definition also encompasses crimes as disparate as arson and habitual offender (recidivism). The maximum sentence under a felony is the death sentence, life in prison without the possibility of parole, or a term of years and parole, to name just a few options. By contrast, a misdemeanor is a less serious crime, punishable by less than a year in custody. In many states, misdemeanors also have a maximum limit of a $1,000 to $5,000 fine that may be imposed. Examples of misdemeanor offenses include driving while under the

Felony
A crime with a sentence of one year or more.

Misdemeanor
A criminal offense that is punished by a maximum possible sentence of one year or less in custody.

influence of alcohol, speeding, minor theft, and some forms of battery and assault, among many others.

FAMOUS CASES
AL CAPONE

Few cases illustrate the complexity of criminal law like that of Al Capone, otherwise known as America's most notorious gangster. He was the single greatest symbol of lawlessness during the Prohibition era of the 1920s.

Alphonse Gabriel Capone was born in a rough neighborhood in Brooklyn, New York in 1899 and quit school at the age of 14 after being expelled for getting into a fistfight with a teacher. His criminal career began early, when he joined two "kid gangs," the Brooklyn Rippers and the Forty Thieves Juniors, before graduating to the Five Points Gang in Manhattan. The Five Points Gang controlled brothels and gambling dens in lower Manhattan, turning the neighborhood into a crime-infested slum. The gang was known for its brutality, often killing rival gang members.

Capone's first arrest was for disorderly conduct during the time he worked as a bouncer at a bar. He is also reported to have murdered two men, but because of gangland's code of silence, he never came to trial for the killings.

When things got too hot for Capone in New York, he moved to Chicago in 1919, where he expanded his operations to include bootlegging, brothels, saloons, gambling houses, speakeasies, racetracks, and distilleries. From 1925 to 1930, his "businesses" were earning as much as $100 million per year. His cozy relationship with Chicago's corrupt mayor, William Hale Thompson, ensured that he was all but immune from arrest and prosecution.

Mayor Thompson, however, eventually saw Capone as a political liability and hired a new police chief to run him out of town. Capone physically moved to Palm Island, Florida in 1928 but continued his various criminal enterprises in Chicago, running them from afar.

Skillful at isolating and killing his enemies when they became too powerful, Capone's most notorious killing was the St. Valentine's Day Massacre in Chicago. On February 14, 1929, four of Capone's men (two disguised as police officers) cornered six members of rival bootlegger Bugs Moran's North Side gang in the garage of Moran's liquor headquarters. A seventh man, not a gang member, was just an unlucky friend in the wrong place at the wrong time. Using shotguns and machine guns, Capone's thugs fired more than 150 bullets into the victims. Moran himself was probably the real target, but he was out of the building at the time. Capone, of course, had an airtight alibi as he was in Florida.

The gangland code of honor ensured that Capone never faced trial for his most heinous crimes, even though he was arrested in 1926 for the murder of three people. Not surprisingly, he spent only a single night in jail because of a lack of evidence connecting him with the killings. He first saw the inside of a prison's walls in 1929 — serving eight months for carrying a concealed weapon. Demonstrating that his reach extended even into the prison system, an article in the *Philadelphia Public Ledger* described Capone's cell: "The whole room was suffused in the glow of a desk lamp which stood on a polished desk. . . . On the once-grim walls of the penal chamber hung tasteful paintings, and the strains of a waltz were being emitted by a powerful cabinet radio receiver of handsome design and fine finish."

What finally did Capone in was a common belief that the profits from illegal activities did not constitute taxable income. (A 1927 Supreme Court ruling, *United States v. Sullivan*, established that such income was indeed taxable.) Having failed in attempts to prosecute Capone for murder or racketeering, the government went after him for income tax evasion. He had never filed an income tax return, nor did he own anything in his own name. All of his business was conducted through front men.

Frank J. Wilson, from the IRS Special Intelligence Unit, was tasked with poring over a massive accumulation of documents related to Capone and his gang to try to isolate income linked directly to Capone's activities. This was no easy chore, however, because Capone took great pains to protect his anonymity. During his painstaking work, Wilson uncovered a cash receipts ledger confiscated years earlier during a raid. The ledger showed the operation's net profits for a gambling house, and it also contained something even more valuable: Capone's name. It was a record of his income.

In 1931, the U.S. government indicted Capone for income tax evasion. He was also charged with failing to file tax returns for the years 1928 and 1929. A third indictment was added, charging Capone with conspiracy to violate Prohibition laws. Confident in his belief that he would be able to plea bargain, Capone pleaded guilty to all three charges. However, Judge James Wilkerson would not agree to a deal, which prompted Capone to change his pleas to not guilty. He then changed tactics and tried to bribe the jury, but Judge Wilkerson switched jury panels at the last minute.

The jury found Capone guilty on five counts, and he was sentenced to a total of ten years in federal prison and one year in the county jail. On November 16, 1939, Al Capone was released from prison after serving seven years, six months, and 15 days.

While in prison, Capone experienced profound mental deterioration as a result of the syphilis he had contracted as a young man. He never again was mentally capable of regaining his gangland prominence and control. He remained in seclusion in his Florida home until his death on January 25, 1947 from cardiac arrest following a stroke and pneumonia.

That he never served prison time for his monstrous crimes can be viewed as a defeat for the criminal justice system, but the fact that he was brought to justice with persistence and more creative methods can surely be seen as a victory.

SOURCES OF LAW FOR THE CRIMINAL JUSTICE SYSTEM: STATUTORY LAW, CASE LAW, AND COMMON LAW

When discussing criminal law and criminal procedure, it is important to first address where law enforcement gets its authority to arrest individuals who have committed crimes, where prosecutors get the power to bring charges against defendants, where courts get the power to seat juries and hear cases, and finally, why the courts have the authority to sentence defendants who have been found guilty. What is the source of this authority? What are its limits? In criminal law, this question is answered in the following places:

1   U.S. Constitution
2   Statutory law
3   Judicial decisions
4   Court rules
5   Agency rules and regulations
6   Common law

A. THE U.S. CONSTITUTION

The Constitution of the United States provides that the government has the power to protect the welfare of its citizens and to pass laws that regulate behavior and punish those who break criminal statutes. This is the so-called "police power" of the Constitution, and it is the source of both federal and state criminal laws. However, as is often the case with the U.S. Constitution, there is no specific language empowering the Congress to enact criminal statutes and to authorize federal courts to impose sentences on criminal defendants. Similarly, the Constitution makes no reference to the states' power to do the same thing. This power has been inferred as a necessary and indisputable right of the government to set boundaries on the behavior of its citizens. Without such power, there would be little need for any kind of government. (The complete text of the U.S. Constitution is in the Appendix.)

The U.S. Constitution says that it is within the federal government's power to take action to protect the health, safety, and welfare of the citizens, and creating criminal statutes is a necessary offshoot of that power.

STATE CONSTITUTIONS

A state constitution functions for the state in virtually the same manner as the U.S. Constitution does for the federal government. However, unlike the U.S. Constitution which governs the entire nation, a state constitution governs only those actions occurring within the state's boundaries. The dual nature of the United States often causes some confusion for those not familiar with the process. There is a federal government and there are individual state governments. Most provisions of the U.S. Constitution apply to state residents, and the state constitution certainly applies to the state residents. Interestingly enough, state constitutions are permitted to give greater freedoms to their citizens under state constitutions than those that are given under the federal Constitution. A state constitution cannot, however, take away any of the rights granted to citizens under the U.S. Constitution. What happens when there is a conflict between the U.S. Constitution and the provisions of a particular state's constitution? In most situations, the U.S. Constitution will prevail. The framers of the U.S. Constitution anticipated such problems and included the Supremacy Clause in order to address this issue. The **Supremacy Clause** is found in Article VI of the Constitution (see Scenario 2-3 and Figure 2-4).

Supremacy Clause
The provision in Article VI of the U.S. Constitution which dictates that the U.S. Constitution, laws, and treaties take precedence over conflicting state constitutions or laws.

WHO IS SUPREME?

The State of Placid has just enacted a statute that provides in cases of alleged child molestation, a defendant does not have the right to a preliminary hearing or to bond and must remain in custody until the time of trial. However, the U.S. Constitution provides that all criminal defendants have the right to bond. Given the differences between the State of Placid and U.S. Constitution, will Placid's statute be ruled unconstitutional because of the Supremacy Clause?

Answer: Yes. The U.S. Supreme Court will undoubtedly rule that the Supremacy Clause controls in this case and that Placid's statute is unconstitutional and must be struck down.

There are times when a crime comes under both state and federal jurisdiction. This means that either the federal or state governments could prosecute. In such a situation, a conflict often arises as to which government takes priority. Fortunately, the Supremacy Clause also helps to clear up any problems of who gets priority in prosecuting the defendant. This constitutional provision dictates that when there is a conflict between federal and state law, federal law takes priority. When a person has committed an offense which could be seen as both a federal and a state law violation, the federal authorities have priority and may prosecute the defendant first.

B. STATUTORY LAW

Statutes consist of bills that are voted on by the legislative branch of government and enacted by the executive branch. Once a bill has been enacted, it is referred to as a statute. On the federal level, the U.S. Congress is the legislative branch, and it votes on bills before sending them to the president for signature. If the president signs the legislation, it becomes a binding law and thus a statute. On the state level, the legislature votes on bills and submits them to the governor for signature. In both instances, the laws that are created are referred to as statutes. It is tempting to think that statutes are the one and only source of laws that govern criminal activity, but that is not the case. Statutory law is only one part of the entire scheme of rules that govern criminal behavior.

Sidebar

The Supremacy Clause of the U.S. Constitution gives the federal authorities priority over state authorities in criminal actions.

Statute
A law that is voted on by the legislature branch of government and enacted by the executive branch.

FIGURE 2-4

Section 2: This Constitution, and the Laws of the United States which shall . . . be the supreme Law of the Land; and the Judges in every State shall be bound thereby, any Thing in the Constitution or Laws of any State to the Contrary notwithstanding.

Article VI

Code
A collection of laws.

Ordinance
A law passed by a local government, such as a town council or city government.

Case law
The written decisions by appellate courts explaining the outcome of a case on appeal.

Not all statutes involve criminal activity. There are many statutes created every year on both the federal and state levels that have nothing to do with criminal law. The statutes that deal with crime are usually grouped together in the federal and state codes for ease of reference. A **code** is a collection of laws, enacted by the legislative and executive process that has been published in bound volumes and is usually also available on the Internet. Most crimes are violations of state, not federal statutes. There are comparatively few federal crimes, but there are 50 states, and each state has its own set of criminal statutes. As a result, most crime in the United States is prosecuted on the state, not the federal level.

ORDINANCES

As we have seen, statutes are laws passed by a state or federal government. However, there is an entire class of laws passed by local governments, such as municipalities and towns which regulate behavior at a local level. These are not referred to as statutes. Instead, they are called **ordinances**. An ordinance has limited application. It has a strict geographic limit, such as the town limits or the county boundary. Ordinances cannot conflict with statutes. If they do, the ordinance is ruled unconstitutional and the statute takes precedence. Examples of ordinances include excessive noise, illegal parking, failure to leash a dog, and so on.

People who are charged with ordinance violations are usually given citations and told to report to a local court where they may face a small fine. Generally, there is no right to a jury trial for an ordinance violation.

C. JUDICIAL DECISIONS (CASE LAW)

In addition to statutory law, there is another, and equally important, source of law: **case law**. Case law is the huge body of published judicial decisions by appellate courts. People who are not familiar with the legal process often do not realize the significance of case law. Our first example of case law was in Chapter 1 which discussed the case against Abdi Mohamed for armed robbery. When an appellate court reaches a decision in a case on appeal, the reasons for the decision are encapsulated in a written opinion. This opinion discusses not only the facts of the case on appeal, but also how the statutes and facts interact with one another. In some ways, case law is like binding commentary on the statutes; it can amplify, refine, or restrict the application of a statute, based on its interpretation by the appellate courts. For attorneys and police officers, case law is just as important as statutory law and sometimes even more important. Case law generated by the U.S. Supreme Court has had a huge impact on criminal law and procedure and will continue to do so for the foreseeable future. In all later chapters, we will examine many of the important U.S. Supreme Court cases that have had a huge impact on criminal law.

CASE LAW AND THE UNITED STATES SUPREME COURT

The reason case law is so important is not simply that it interprets statutory law, but also that a case decision can invalidate an entire statute. If the U.S. Congress decides to create a statute that no longer requires police officers to read suspects their Miranda rights, this statute could (and probably would) be interpreted as a violation of the U.S. Constitution. In such a scenario, the U.S. Supreme Court can, and often has, invalidated a statute that has been voted on by the legislative branch and enacted by the executive branch. This is part of the checks and balances system found in the U.S. Constitution and is often lauded for maintaining the balance of power among the three branches of government.

   This is not to say that the only case law of importance is that created by the U.S. Supreme Court. Although the decisions of this court are binding on all U.S. courts, there are appellate courts on both the federal and state level that also interpret statutes every day and make rulings on specific cases. Unless a higher court overrules a court's interpretation of a statute, it remains binding.

> ## Sidebar
>
> *Case law consists of the written decisions of appellate courts that have interpreted statutes, and those decisions are made binding on everyone.*

D. COURT RULES

In addition to statutes and case law, courts also create their own internal rules that are extremely important to litigants in either civil or criminal cases. Court rules often focus on procedural steps, such as when and where a particular action can be filed and the types of motions that the parties to a case may file in a pending case. Motions practice will be examined in greater detail in Chapter 19.

E. AGENCY RULES AND REGULATIONS

Once a statute has been created, a governmental agency may create an administrative rule or regulation to put that statute into effect. For example, the 16th Amendment gave the federal government the power to levy and collect income taxes but provided no details on how the process should actually be carried out. The U.S. Department of the Treasury, an agency authorized under the federal government, has the power to create its own rules and regulations to enforce the 16th Amendment (see Figure 2-5). These rules and regulations carry the same force as a statute.

   A person who violates the U.S. Treasury's rules and regulations in regard to nonpayment of taxes (such as the Capone case) can face serious prison time and fines. They may also have their property confiscated by the government.

The Congress shall have power to lay and collect taxes on incomes, from whatever source derived, without apportionment among the several states, and without regard to any census or enumeration.

FIGURE 2-5

Amendment XVI

F. COMMON LAW

Common law
1) Either all case law or the case law that is made by judges in the absence of relevant statutes. 2) The legal system that originated in England and is composed of case law and statutes.

In addition to constitutional law, statutory law, ordinances, court rules, and agency regulations, there is one more source of law to examine: **common law**. The development of the common law in the United States has a very interesting history.

In 1776 when the newly formed colonies of the Americas rebelled from the monarchy in Great Britain and decided to form their own country, they were immediately faced with some pragmatic problems. Besides the issue of how a democracy would be organized, there was the more general question of what law would govern in the new United States of America. The founding fathers made up many of the rules for this new type of government as it was evolving, but they were not operating in a vacuum. They based many of their decisions on examples from ancient Greece and even former colonies in the Americas, but when it came to the law, they opted to take the easy route. Rather than reinvent the wheel, they chose to adopt the law with which they were most familiar: English common law.

WHAT IS THE COMMON LAW?

England has existed for centuries, and for most of that time many of its citizens were illiterate. Passing statutes and codifying them in books, although it was done, was not much use to a citizenry that could neither read nor interpret these laws. Instead, the citizens relied on judges to tell them what the law was and to dispense justice. In centuries past, English (and later American) judges, rode on horseback from town to town, dealing with both civil and criminal issues. Although they may have been accompanied by a few learned treatises, most of the rules of justice were in their heads. Many times, judges were faced with unique situations for which no written law had been created to address. In the absence of a written law, a judge would decide the case for himself. These decisions carried as much weight as a written law created by parliament. Judges from various jurisdictions would come together in meetings to discuss their decisions in their cases. Over time, as identical legal issues were presented, judges began to create a uniform system of rules which would help them and future judges to reach fair decisions. As there was no written law to interpret, the judges would come up with guidelines of their own. In order to show the legal system was fair, the judges agreed that each judge would be bound by decisions of other judges on specific issues. Many of these rules became known to the common people and thus were referred to as common law.

There is nothing particularly unusual or unique about common law. All of us have unwritten rules that we tend to follow. Many of these rules are understood to apply, even though they are not written down. When strangers meet for the first time, they often shake hands. There is no written rule requiring this behavior, but we all tend to do it and may take offense if someone refuses to offer his or her hand. English common law took this basic philosophy and elevated it to binding legal precedent. When the English colonies of the Americas became the United States of America, many of the states adopted this large body of rules, sayings, guidelines, and interpretations as American common law. We will examine only two out of hundreds of common law "rules" in order to illustrate how common law works.

"Possession is 9/10's of the Law." Possession is 9/10ths of the law is a maxim most people have heard, although probably not entirely understood. This is actually a common law rule. The origin of this law arises from a common problem in both rural England and rural America: wayward domestic animals.

Suppose that a judge is presented with a case in which a cow has wandered away from one farm and has been found by another farmer. In the Old West, for example, calves that had not yet been branded were referred to as "mavericks" and could be claimed by anyone who found them. If the cow had no identifying marks on it, how was the judge to decide who actually owned the animal? Farmer A might be correct in claiming that the cow is "Betsy" that he's owned for years, but Farmer B might just as easily claim that the cow is "Belle" and that he has also owned her for years. Rather than try to delve into the internal workings of the farms and who may or may not have seen the cow in one farmer's presence, judges fashioned a rule that stated that when ownership of an item of property — in this case a cow — cannot be confirmed to one person over another, then whoever has possession of it now is allowed to keep it. See Scenario 2-4 for another example.

TWIN MOTORCYCLES

SCENARIO 2-4

Evan and Mika both have identical motorcycles. They even purchased them on the same day. One day, Mika notices that his motorcycle is missing. He calls Evan and, while speaking with him, begins to suspect that the motorcycle currently in Evan's possession is actually Mika's. When Mika asks about a particular scratch on the front fender that closely resembles one that Mika had on his bike, Evan explains that he fell earlier that day and scratched the fender. Later, Mike learns from a mutual friend that Evan is bragging that he has two motorcycles, but keeps one hidden away. Is this a case of "possession is 9/10ths of the law"? Put another way, if it turns out that Evan actually does have Mika's motorcycle is he prohibited from challenging Evan's ownership?

Answer: No. This old common law rule only applies to objects that cannot be readily distinguished. Motorcycles, like automobiles, vehicle identification numbers (VIN) that are unique to each motorcycle. The common law rule would not apply. Mika can get his motorcycle back and can probably seek charges against Evan for stealing it.

These two examples are only a tiny fraction of the vast body of common law that arose over centuries of judicial decisions. It was this system that our country adopted shortly after its creation. One might be tempted to think that common law makes an interesting, if outdated, historical footnote, but that assumption would be incorrect. Common law is alive and well in the United States today.

THE IMPORTANCE OF COMMON LAW

Common law was adopted to create a body of law that the early colonial court systems could use as a ready-made legal framework. The common law found a valued place in situations where no other law was applicable. Common law was originally adopted by the thirteen colonies that later became the first thirteen states.

Many of those states took some or all common law principles, enacted them as legislation, then revoked the original English common law to avoid the confusing situation of having statutory law existing side–by–side with common law. However, several states never got around to the second part of that equation and never abolished common law. As a result, in those states, common law is as relevant as it ever was and does exist side by side with statutes, causing confusion for people not schooled in the meaning and importance of common law.

Some states, like Virginia and North Carolina, abolished only part of the common law and kept other parts. What this means is that for people in common-law states, it is possible to have two different kinds of criminal violations. For instance, in a common-law state, a defendant can be charged with two separate crimes for a single offense. A defendant could be charged with common-law burglary and statutory burglary, for example. However, when the case is resolved, the defendant can only be sentenced on one of the counts.

Proving someone guilty of a common law offense involves different evidence than would be required to prove someone guilty of a statutory offense. Under common law burglary, the state must prove the following elements beyond a reasonable doubt:

- Breaking and entering
- Of a house
- At night
- With the intent to commit a theft or felony

However, the elements of statutory burglary are different. Under statutory burglary, the state must prove that there was:

- Breaking and entering
- Of a dwelling
- With the intent to commit a theft or felony

As you can see, the elements of common-law burglary and statutory burglary are different. The most conspicuous difference is that common-law burglary can only be committed "at night." There is no such element in statutory burglary. Given the differences between the two crimes, one might ask why anyone would bother charging common law offenses when the statutory offenses appear to be broader in scope. The simple answer is that for some common law offenses, the sentence can be longer than the statutory offense. Common law offenses may also track the actual details of the crime better than the statutory offense. Finally, prosecutors may use both charges as a bargaining tool during plea negotiations, by offering to reduce the crime to the one with the lower possible punishment, whether the common-law crime or the statutory crime.

THE USES OF COMMON LAW

Although most states have abolished common law in favor of statutory law, a surprising number have either abolished only some aspects of common law while keeping others (such as abolishing all common-law crimes but keeping common-law marriage), while others have not abolished common law at all. In those states, there are powerful arguments for keeping common law, including sentencing and new legal issues.

When it comes to sentencing, a judge must follow the statutory guidelines for imposing the sentence. However, what happens when a legislature enacts a law but fails to provide a sentence? In that situation, a state that has abolished common law may find itself in a legal quandary that will require additional legislation. In common-law states, however, a judge is permitted to use common-law sentencing guidelines.

Common law dates back for centuries. Since that time nearly every type of legal question that has arisen has been addressed by a judge at one time or another. A judge who is presented with a seemingly new question could peruse the old common law to see if a similar argument has ever been raised. In such a situation, the judge could benefit from hundreds of years of cases and the accumulated wisdom of thousands of judges to help him or her decide the best course in a current case.

FEDERAL PROSECUTIONS VS. STATE PROSECUTIONS

As this chapter has shown, there are states that have a dual criminal justice system: common law and statutory law. However, there is another dual arrangement that sometimes causes confusion to individuals new to the criminal justice field. The United States itself exists as a dual arrangement, with state-based prosecution and federal-based prosecution existing side-by-side. A person may be prosecuted by the federal government or the state government or, in limited circumstances, by both. There are provisions that allow the federal government to charge a defendant with one crime and a state to charge a different crime for the same transaction. Examples abound everywhere, including the sniper attacks in the D.C. area several years ago where two men shot victims at random. In that case, the men were in violation of both state and federal laws. They were prosecuted by Maryland first, then prosecuted by the federal authorities, all based on the same actions. Why is this not a violation of the rule against double jeopardy?

The Fifth Amendment provides that a person cannot be tried twice for the same offense. If a defendant is found not guilty of a crime, the government that tried him is not permitted to try the defendant again. However, this rule applies to the specific **jurisdiction** that tried the defendant. The federal government and state governments are two different jurisdictions. Because of this, the federal authorities can prosecute a person who has committed a federal offense, then the state may also prosecute based on a state statute.

Jurisdiction
The persons about whom, and the subject matters about which, a court has the right and power to make decisions that are legally binding.

A. FEDERAL JURISDICTION

Jurisdiction refers to power or authority. If a court has jurisdiction, it can control the actions of the parties and make decisions that bind all parties in the prosecution.

If a judge has jurisdiction and rules that certain evidence produced by the prosecutor will not be admissible, then the evidence will not be allowed. Federal courts are courts of limited jurisdiction which essentially means that there are only a limited number of actions in which a federal court may become involved. Barring any statute expressly granting federal courts jurisdiction over a matter, the criminal action defaults to the states.

B. STATE JURISDICTION

State jurisdiction is based on the state's constitution and its own police power. However, simply because the U.S. Constitution imposes certain minimum standards on the states to allow for specific procedural steps, does not mean that the states are uniform in how they prosecute cases. In fact, states vary considerably in their procedural steps, hearings, and even the names that they apply to charging documents, law enforcement officials, and prosecutors. Because states have their own authority, they are free to develop any procedures that do not violate the U.S. Constitution or their own state constitution, even if this procedure is different from that used by another state.

States have the power to enact their own laws, not only to criminalize behavior, but also to include different procedural steps. Because most criminal prosecutions occur on the state level, this text discusses state-based procedural steps, but keep in mind that there is a great deal of variation among the states. Simply because an activity is illegal in one state does not necessarily mean that it is illegal in another state. California, for example, currently allows the cultivation of marijuana for medicinal purposes and allows the sale and possession of the drug for this purpose. Other states do not allow this activity. A person from California who suddenly moves to Alabama cannot use as a defense that his activity is perfectly legal in California. Alabama or any other state is free to criminalize any behavior, as long as it does not violate the U.S. Constitution.

Throughout this text, examples will address specific states and how they proceed with certain steps following the arrest of the suspect and continuing through to sentence and appeal. However, there is no way to address the differences among all of the states, so discussion will be limited to the most commonly found procedural steps and constitutional safeguards, while occasionally addressing the differences in particular states.

STATE LEVEL PROSECUTIONS

Most prosecutions occur on the state level. There are, after all, 50 states and only one federal government which explains why there are more state-level prosecutions than federal-level prosecutions. But the number of states is not the only reason why there are more state-based prosecutions. Federal courts have limited jurisdiction, but the states do not have that same limitation. States are free to criminalize any behavior they see fit, again, so long as it does not violate any of the rights guaranteed in the U.S. or state constitutions.

C. DIFFERENCES AMONG STATES

Individuals who are trained based on national standards are often surprised to learn just how regional some legal procedures are. States not only follow different sequences in prosecuting defendants; they even refer to their charging documents by different names and use different procedures. There is very little uniformity among the states and, as a result, an attorney who has been admitted to practice in one state might have difficulty adjusting to the differences in another state. In fact, many states limit the options that an attorney can use to transfer his or her license from one state to another. Referred to as reciprocity, some states allow an attorney who is a member in good standing to simply transfer his or her legal license to a new state, but a fair number require the attorney from one state to retake the bar exam for the new state. This fact tends to keep attorneys practicing in one or two states at most.

Most attorneys are members of one or maybe two bar associations at most. The reason is that procedures, rules, and hearings vary so much from state to state that it would be difficult to stay current on many different states' laws and variations.

 **FEDERAL VS. STATE COURT SYSTEMS**

When discussing the organization of the state and federal court systems, the material may, at first, appear daunting in its complexity. However, this is not the case. All court systems, whether on the state or federal level, are built on a simple premise: the actions of a lower court can be reviewed by a higher court. Seen this way, all court systems in the United States could be visualized as pyramids, with the lower courts forming the base and the higher courts forming the upper portions of the pyramid. The **U.S. Supreme Court** is the highest court in the federal system and so sits at the top of that pyramid.

U.S. Supreme Court
The name for the highest court of the United States federal and state court systems.

A. THE LEVELS OF THE FEDERAL COURT SYSTEM

We will now examine the pyramidal structure of the court system on the federal level by looking at the base then moving slowly up toward the top of the pyramid, the U.S. Supreme Court.

FEDERAL DISTRICT COURTS

The Federal Court system has courts that cover the entire United States and its territories. There are 94 U.S. District Courts with at least one for each state and some that share jurisdiction over American territories. Federal District Courts are the workhorses of the federal system. These are the courts where trials are held, where motions are heard, where defendants are sentenced, and where probationers may have their probation revoked, among many other procedures.

Federal District Courts are placed all over the United States, but the system is not based on geography, rather on population. In places where there are few people, there tends to be less crime. In more densely populated areas, crime tends to be

FIGURE 2-6

Map of Federal Circuits

Geographic Boundaries
of United States Courts of Appeals and United States District Courts

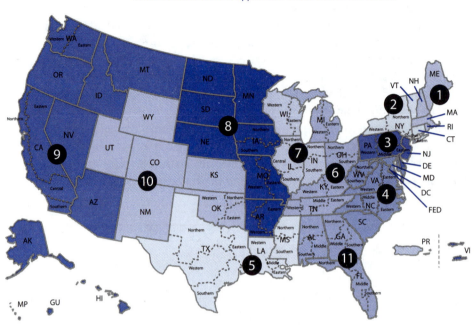

correspondingly larger. As a result, the east coast and the northeast in particular have higher numbers of federal district courts as opposed to portions of the western part of the United States, which have comparatively few. See Figure 2-6 for a map showing the location of the federal circuits. The courts are organized in 12 different circuits that encompass the entire United States and its territories. Any federal district court is identified by its affiliation with a particular circuit and a district within that circuit. A person who is charged with a federal offense in Raleigh, North Carolina, for example, would be tried in the North Carolina Eastern District Court for the 4th Circuit, while a man who is charged with a federal crime in Jacksonville, Florida would be charged in the Florida Middle District for the 11th Circuit.

APPELLATE COURTS: COURTS OF APPEAL

Each federal district court is established inside a particular circuit. The circuits of the federal judiciary encompass the entire United States and its territories. In criminal cases, when the defendant is found guilty, he or she will appeal the verdict to an appellate court. In the federal system, there are 12 separate circuits that are responsible for hearing appeals from the district courts located within their territory. (There is a thirteenth circuit, but it is reserved for special cases arising out of the DC Circuit.) When a case is heard on appeal from any district court, the case goes to the corresponding court of appeals for that circuit. The U.S. Courts of Appeal are the midlevel or intermediate courts between the trial courts (federal district court) and the U.S. Supreme Court. A judge who sits on any of the U.S. Circuit Courts of Appeals is nominated by the president and must be confirmed by the Senate before he or she can take the seat.

■ Chief Justice of the United States: JOHN G. ROBERTS, JR.
■ Associate Justices
  ☐ Antonin Scalia
  ☐ Anthony M. Kennedy
  ☐ Clarence Thomas
  ☐ Ruth Bader Ginsburg
  ☐ Stephen Breyer
  ☐ Samuel Alito, Jr.
  ☐ Sonia Sotomayor
  ☐ Elena Kagan

U.S. SUPREME COURT

The U.S. Supreme Court is the highest court in the federal system. It hears all appeals from the various federal Circuit Courts of Appeal located around the country. As we will see later in this text, the U.S. Supreme Court is not required to hear all appeals presented to it. The court may pick and choose, in most situations, which cases it will hear and which cases it will not hear.

Justices of the U.S. Supreme Court, once selected for the position, are allowed to serve as a Justice for the rest of their lives. They cannot be fired by the president or anyone else and may only be removed if they commit some crime and are impeached. When a position becomes vacant on the court, either through death or retirement, the president has the authority to nominate a replacement who must then be approved by the Senate. See Figure 2-7 for a list of the current members of the Supreme Court. The U.S. Supreme Court building is located in Washington, D.C., directly across from the Capitol. The Court begins its session on the first Monday in October and continues through the first Monday of the following May. The Court is in recess from June through October.

The U.S. Supreme Court is unlike any other court in the United States. For one thing, it is both the highest federal court and the highest state court, making it the final authority on all issues dealing with both the state and the federal Constitution (see Figure 2-8).

Sidebar

The average salary of a Federal Circuit Court of Appeals judge is $180,000 per year.

The judicial Power of the United States, shall be vested in one supreme Court, and in such inferior Courts as the Congress may from time to time ordain and establish.

B. THE LEVELS OF THE STATE COURT SYSTEM

The state court systems are often — but not always — similar to the federal system. There are trial courts where juries are empaneled and reach verdicts in criminal cases, and there are intermediate courts of appeal where a defendant may bring an appeal from that conviction. There is also a top state court that determines all issues of state law and is responsible for interpreting the state and the U.S. Constitution. One of the problems inherent in any examination of state court systems is the variation seen among the states. All states have trial courts, but they do not go by the same name or have the same powers as courts in other states.

TRIAL COURTS

In some states, there are State Courts that are empowered to hear misdemeanor cases, before juries of six people, while Superior Courts hear felony cases before juries of 12 individuals. In other states, there are no juries for misdemeanor cases and the defendant may appeal to the Superior Court for a new trial (and a jury) if he or she is convicted in State Court.

Because there is such variation among the states, we will simplify the process of examining state trial courts by using terms that are used by a majority of states and, for the moment, avoid the usage in the minority of states. For our purposes, we will assume that there is only one type of trial court on the state level, even though many states have two or more, each with different names. We will call our hypothetical trial court "Superior Court."

Superior Court is the court where criminal trials occur. Juries are empanelled in this courtroom, and defendants are brought to trial. These are the cases that you can see almost any night on television. In the fictionalized versions of Superior Court, witnesses often admit to committing the crime and attorneys give brilliant, and remarkably short, closing arguments. But the real world is considerably different, and we will be focusing on the real world of criminal law and procedure throughout this text.

If a defendant is found not guilty in Superior Court, he or she is released and there is no appeal. (The state is not allowed to appeal a not guilty verdict.) If a defendant is found guilty, then he or she will likely bring an appeal to the State Court of Appeals.

APPELLATE COURTS

Each state has its own version of an appellate court. Most states follow the federal model of a trial court, an intermediate court of appeals, and a state supreme court, but not all states use these names to refer to these courts. In most states, the intermediate appellate court is referred to as the State Court of Appeals. It may resemble the federal system closely. Defendants who are found guilty in Superior Court bring their appeal to this court. However, while there are 12 different Federal Circuit Courts of Appeal around the United States, there is only one State Appellate Court. If either the defendant or the prosecution loses the appeal at this level, either can bring an appeal to the State Supreme Court.

STATE SUPREME COURT

At the top of the state hierarchy is a court that hears all appeals from the State Court of Appeals. This court has the final say on all state law matters and is also empowered to interpret the U.S. Constitution. Although this court is not always called the State Supreme Court (New York, for example, calls this court State Superior Court), this text will use this term to refer to the states' highest court. In most cases, a criminal appeal will end at this level, but there are provisions that allow the U.S. Supreme Court to reach final and binding decisions on state law as well. These issues will be explored more thoroughly in Chapter 20.

STATE v. THOMAS
2012 WL 1995167 (N.C. App. 2012.)
June 5, 2012

Appeal by Defendant from judgment entered 3 September 2009 by Judge Ripley Rand, in Durham County Superior Court. Heard in the Court of Appeals 21 March 2012.

HUNTER, JR., ROBERT N., Judge.

I. FACTUAL & PROCEDURAL BACKGROUND

On 21 August 2006, Danny Lamont Thomas ("Defendant") was indicted for murder, first degree kidnapping, and robbery with a dangerous weapon. The matter came before Judge Ripley Rand at the 1 September 2009 session of the Superior Court for Durham County. The State's evidence at trial tended to show the following.

On July 2005, Charles Farrior and Ralph Joseph shared a house on Farthing Street in Durham. On the night of 15 July 2005, Valehia Williams, who was in a relationship with Farrior, testified that she went to Farrior and Joseph's house to take a shower. She testified that after taking a shower, she left the house and stopped to try and help a car with a flat tire. The four men in the car included two that she knew: Charles "Rock" Hightower and Defendant, who Williams referred to as "Cuban." Otis Crosby, Hightower's uncle, testified that Defendant and Hightower worked at a group home together and were friends.

Earlier that week, Hightower and Defendant had asked Williams about Farrior and stated that they had heard he had money and drugs. When Williams met the four men with the flat tire on 15 July 2005, they arranged to have her go back into Farrior and Joseph's house and leave the house quickly so they could get into the house before the door was locked in order to rob the house. According to Williams, she was not supposed to be in the house when the four men robbed the house.

Williams testified that she returned to the house to retrieve her earrings, which she had left there. While Williams was in the bathroom, she heard a commotion in the hallway, and when she came out of the bathroom, Hightower grabbed her and put her into a bedroom with Joseph, who was handcuffed behind his back and laying on his side. Hightower asked Joseph where the money was kept. Joseph stated that it was in a drawer, and Hightower retrieved the money from the drawer.

Hightower and Defendant beat Joseph while asking him where the money and drugs were. Both Hightower and Defendant shot Joseph multiple times, and Joseph died from the gunshot wounds. Williams testified she left the house and Defendant got into Williams' vehicle. Defendant had been wearing a mask, but removed his mask after getting in Williams' vehicle. Williams testified that Defendant directed her to drive down the street, at which point the other three men got into Williams' SUV and she drove them to their vehicle. Shortly thereafter, police stopped Williams' SUV and found a gun holster and a container of marijuana in the vehicle.

Around midnight on the night of the murder, Brandi Keith and Jason Sell visited the house which shared a driveway with Farrior and Joseph's house. While Sell went into the neighbor's house to pick up a friend's son, Keith stayed in the car. Keith observed a dark-colored SUV pull up in the driveway behind her car and then pull over behind Joseph's house. She saw a female get out of the driver's seat and heard car doors open a few more times before she saw the house door open. After about seven to ten minutes, Keith heard gunshots and then, about five minutes later, she saw the same female from earlier run out of the house with three men following her, one of whom was wearing a mask. All four jumped into the SUV and backed out of the driveway.

Keith got out of her car and went to ask Sell to go check on Joseph's house because she had heard gunshots. After Sell checked the house and discovered Joseph dead, 911 was called and the police arrived. Sell identified the SUV as belonging to Williams, who he knew to be Farrior's girlfriend.

A warrant was issued for Defendant's arrest on 25 July 2005. Willie Hayes, a coworker of Defendant, testified that on that day, a Monday morning, he met with Defendant at work and Defendant left to take grocery money to the group home where he worked. That same day, a SWAT team executed a search at the group home looking for Defendant but did not find him. Hayes did not see Defendant at work the rest of that day or again after that day.

Deputy Jason Hess of the El Paso County Sheriff's Office in Colorado testified that on 8 December 2005, at approximately 5:00 p.m., he was assisting United States Marshals in attempting to locate and apprehend Defendant. With the consent of the homeowner, who knew Defendant was in the residence, officers entered a residence in Colorado and announced their presence, requesting that Defendant show police his hands. Deputy Hess saw the barrel of a rifle pointing around a corner and, after moving back from that corner, saw the gun using a mirror. Defendant "began screaming at the officers to back up." After Deputy Hess tried to negotiate with Defendant, Defendant made threats, stating that "he was loaded with full metal jackets" and that if they attempted to arrest him "there was going to be a blood bath." After twenty or thirty minutes, the local police were brought in to handle the situation. Lieutenant James Patrick Rigdon of the Colorado Springs Police Department testified that he led the Colorado Springs Tactical Team into the residence at approximately 7:25 p.m. At approximately 9:45 p.m., Lieutenant Rigdon received a signed search warrant, and one of the officers deployed a tear gas canister. Lieutenant Rigdon heard two or three gunshots, then Defendant agreed to come out, at which point he was arrested.

In the residence, crime scene technicians found an SKS rifle, a .45 caliber semi-automatic handgun, and a backpack containing ammunition. Several of the bullets used in Joseph's murder were .45 caliber; however, testing at the North Carolina State Bureau of Investigation showed that the gun found in Colorado had not been used to shoot Joseph. A duffel bag containing a multi-colored mask and some bandanas was also found. After his arrest, Defendant told Detective Richard Gysin of the Colorado Springs Police Department that he knew the police were looking for him and that there was a warrant for his arrest. Defendant moved to dismiss all charges at the end of the State's evidence, and his motion was denied.

Hayes, Defendant's coworker, testified that on 15 July 2005, the day of Joseph's murder, Hayes and a group of friends, including Defendant, went to Kanki restaurant to celebrate Hayes' birthday. Hayes testified that Defendant had arrived by the time the group sat down at 9:30 p.m. and that Defendant was there until they finished having drinks and talked in the parking lot until just after midnight.

Gregory McBride, another coworker of Defendant, testified that he attended the party and that he either arrived at 10:30 p.m. and saw Defendant about twenty minutes later or arrived at 9:30 p.m. and saw Defendant at 10:30 p.m. FN1 McBride testified that he left at 11:35 p.m. and that Defendant and Hayes were still talking in the parking lot at the time. Sherwin Lacewell also testified that he attended the party at Kanki, arriving at about 11:00 p.m. or 11:30 p.m. and seeing Defendant there. Lacewell testified that when he left after midnight, Defendant was still talking to Hayes in the parking lot.

Defendant renewed his motion to dismiss at the close of all of the evidence, and it was again denied. During jury instructions, the trial court instructed the jury using the pattern jury instruction entitled "Flight — First Degree Murder Cases." N.C.P.I.-Crim. 104.36 (2011). On 3 September 2009, the jury found Defendant guilty on all counts. Defendant was sentenced to life imprisonment without parole. Defendant gave timely notice of appeal.

ANALYSIS

Defendant first argues that the admission of testimony about his arrest in Colorado was irrelevant and prejudicial and should not have been admitted under Rule 404(b) of our Rules of Evidence.

The determination of whether evidence was properly admitted under Rule 404(b) involves a three-step test. First, is the evidence relevant for some purpose other than to show that defendant has the propensity for the type of conduct for which he is being tried. Second, is that purpose relevant to an issue material to the pending case. Third, is the probative value of the evidence substantially outweighed by the danger of unfair prejudice pursuant to Rule 403.

State v. Foust, _____ N.C.App. _____, _____, 724 S.E.2d 154, _____ (2012). The first two steps involve questions of relevance as defined by Rule 401. This Court reviews questions of relevancy de novo but accords deference to the trial court's ruling. State v. Lane, 365 N.C. 7, 27, 707 S.E.2d 210, 222–23 (2011) ("A trial court's rulings on relevancy are technically not discretionary, though we accord them great deference on appeal."). The third step of the Rule 404(b) test — the Rule 403 balancing test — is reviewed for abuse of discretion. State v. Summers, 177

N.C.App. 691, 697, 629 S.E.2d 902, 907, appeal dismissed and disc. rev. denied, 360 N.C. 653, 637 S.E.2d 192 (2006).

Defendant asserts that the evidence introduced regarding his arrest in Colorado, including evidence of the .45 caliber gun that did not match the murder weapons, was irrelevant and was "overwhelmingly prejudicial." Defendant does not address, however, the State's argument at trial that the main purpose of the evidence was to show the circumstances of his flight from the crime in preparation for a jury instruction on flight. The trial court found the evidence of flight, including the evidence of the .45 caliber gun, relevant "to tell the entire story involved in the matter," and stated, "As long as it's made clear to the jury that the firearms seized there didn't have anything to do specifically with the events here in Durham . . . I think it is relevant to his capture in Colorado as part of the whole story being told."

"An accused's flight is universally conceded to be admissible as evidence of consciousness of guilt and thus of guilt itself." State v. Jones, 292 N.C. 513, 525, 234 S.E.2d 555, 562 (1977). Our Courts have long held that flight is competent on the question of guilt because "a guilty conscience influences conduct."

Defendant in the present case knew there was a warrant for his arrest. On the day the SWAT team executed a search of the group home where Defendant worked, Defendant disappeared in the middle of the work day and was not seen again by his coworker after that. Defendant was tracked to Colorado on 8 December 2005. As a part of his arrest in Colorado, Defendant engaged in a several hour standoff with police, threatening officers, which resulted in the use of tear gas to extract Defendant. The fact that Defendant was not found for several months does not negate the evidence of his flight. See State v. Tucker, 329 N.C. 709, 722, 407 S.E.2d 805, 813 (1991) (where the defendant was found in another state more than three years after the crime). It similarly does not matter that Defendant had not been arrested prior to his flight. See State v. Mash, 305 N.C. 285, 288, 287 S.E.2d 824, 826 (1982) ("The cases in which evidence of flight has been declared competent when the flight occurred before arrest or before the accused was in custody are legion.").

The evidence of the standoff in Colorado is relevant to show Defendant's consciousness of guilt, and the nature of the flight is important to the jury. Jones, 292 N.C. at 527, 234 S.E.2d at 562–63 ("For example, it is likely that a jury would attach a different significance where a defendant fled a short distance to a friend's house . . . - than where, as here, the defendant attempted to flee the state and in doing so assaulted a law enforcement officer."). "Flight is relative proof which must be viewed in its entire context to be of aid to the jury in the resolution of the case." The circumstances of Defendant's arrest in Colorado, including the weapons recovered at the residence, therefore, were relevant to Defendant's consciousness of guilt. The evidence was admissible, even if it disclosed the commission of separate crimes by Defendant.

Having found the evidence of Defendant's flight relevant, we turn to the Rule 403 balancing test to determine whether the danger of unfair prejudice outweighed the probative value of the evidence. Under the applicable abuse of discretion standard, we find no abuse of discretion by the trial court. "The term 'unfair prejudice' contemplates evidence having an undue tendency to suggest decision on an improper basis, commonly, though not necessarily, as an emotional one." State v. McDougald, 336 N.C. 451, 457, 444 S.E.2d 211, 214 (1994) (citation omitted).

"In light of our prior holdings regarding evidence of flight, the evidence of the defendant's flight could only be viewed as having a due tendency to suggest a decision on a proper basis ... We therefore find no abuse of discretion under Rule 403 and find no error in the trial court's admission of evidence regarding Defendant's arrest in Colorado.

CONCLUSION

For the foregoing reasons, we find No error.

CASE QUESTIONS

1 What crime was the defendant accused of committing in this case?
2 On what basis did the defendant move to dismiss the evidence procured in Colorado?
3 What counterargument did the State make in regard to the evidence obtained in Colorado?
4 How did the court rule on the defendant's motion?

CHAPTER SUMMARY

This chapter has shown that there are important differences between civil and criminal cases, including how the case originates, the names of the parties involved, the different levels in burdens of proof, and the ultimate decision and consequences for the parties involved in the cases. Criminal law is a specialized field, with its own terminology, procedures, and rules. There are various sources of authority for criminal law proceedings, including the U.S. Constitution, statutory law, case law, agency rules, and common law. Although common law is not found in all states, it remains an important part of legal history and is actively followed in a handful of states.

There are many participants in the criminal justice field, including judges, prosecutors, police officers, defense attorneys, defendants, and others. Each of these participants plays a critical role in the process, and the defendant is protected by a wide variety of constitutional guarantees to ensure that the prosecution is fair.

The court system is organized as a hierarchy, with trial courts at the bottom, appellate courts in the middle, and the Supreme Court at the top. On the state level, there is a court that examines appeals and makes final determinations of state law. The federal system is organized along the same lines, with federal district courts at the trial level, U.S. Courts of Appeals as the intermediate appellate courts, and the U.S. Supreme Court as the nation's highest court. The U.S. Supreme Court enjoys a unique position in that it is the court of last resort for both federal and state systems.

KEY TERMS

Guilty
Liable
Verdict
Not guilty
Guilty but mentally ill
Not guilty by reason of
insanity
Damages
Punitive damages
Restitution
Burden of proof
Prosecutor

Plaintiff
Beyond a reasonable
doubt
Preponderance of the
evidence
Defendant
Style
Pleadings
Complaint
Answer
Indictment
Felony

Misdemeanor
Supremacy Clause
Statute
Code
Ordinance
Case law
Common law
Contempt
Jurisdiction
U.S. Supreme Court

REVIEW QUESTIONS

1   What are the different burdens of proof between civil cases and criminal cases?
2   What are the possible verdicts in a criminal case?
3   What are damages in civil cases?
4   What is a prosecutor?
5   What are the names of the parties in a civil case?
6   Define "beyond a reasonable doubt."
7   What are pleadings?
8   What is an indictment?
9   Explain the difference between felonies and misdemeanors.
10 What is the Supremacy Clause?
11 Explain statutory law.
12 What are ordinances?
13 Explain case law and its significance.
14 Are federal and state agencies able to create their own rules and regulations? Explain.
15 What is the common law?
16 Provide two examples of common law rules.
17 What is the function of the judge?
18 What is the role of a defense attorney?
19 How do federal prosecutions differ from state prosecutions?
20 Explain "jurisdiction."
21 Provide a brief description of the organization of the federal court system.
22 What is the name of the highest court in the United States?
23 Describe the organization of most state court systems.

WEB SURFING

1   Locate the website for your state's court system. How is your court system organized? Is it similar or different from the description given in the text?
2   Go to the Federal Judiciary homepage and answer the following questions:
    a   How many justices serve on the United States Green court?
    b   How many federal district courts exist in the United States?
    c   Create a flowchart showing how a federal case proceeds from the trial court to the United States Supreme Court.

QUESTIONS FOR ANALYSIS

1   Should the court systems in the United States be simplified and streamlined? Do we have too many courts? Explain your answer.
2   In the states that still have common law, should it be abolished? Justify your answer.

HYPOTHETICALS

1   Placid state has recently amended its state constitution to provide a right of privacy for its citizens. Although this right is implied in the U.S. Constitution, it is not explicitly mentioned. Placid state legislators believe that in the light of expanding federal surveillance techniques that such an amendment is required. Can Placid pass such a statute?
2   In the case of State v. Z, individual jurors are convinced that Z actually murdered victim T, but they do not believe that the state has proven the case beyond a reasonable doubt. What are their options?
3   Placid has also enacted a recent law that allows the medicinal use of marijuana for those suffering from cancer and chronic pain. Federal law prohibits the sale of marijuana for any reason, but does make an exception for medicinal uses. Given the existence of the Supremacy Clause, what is the likely outcome of a dispute between federal and state authorities over whether medical marijuana is legal in Placid?

3

Attempt to Commit a Crime; Principals and Accessories; Conspiracy

Chapter Objectives

- Explain the legal standard used to determine when the crime of attempt has occurred
- Describe the elements of a conspiracy
- Define the differences between principals and accessories
- Explain the concepts of actual presence versus constructive presence
- Describe the crime of solicitation

I. INTRODUCTION TO THE CRIME OF ATTEMPT

When it comes to deciding whom to charge and what crime should be brought against a defendant, the responsibility falls to the prosecutor. Once the case is in the prosecutor's hands, the prosecutor may amend the original charges and also add new ones, as long as the facts support the new crime. One of the most important issues in this charging decision has to do with crimes that involve more than one defendant or ones where the crime was not completed. Multiple defendants will be discussed later in this chapter, but first we must address the issue of how a prosecutor proceeds when a defendant sets out to commit a crime but for some reason fails to complete it. When and under what circumstances can a person be charged for attempting to commit a crime?

Attempting to commit a crime is a crime by itself. However, this begs the question of how courts and statutes define what is and what is not attempt. The problem is that, unlike other crimes, an attempt, by its very nature, is a crime that is not completed. Should the defendant's attempt be considered a crime at all? Common law, statutes, and even common sense tell us that when a person sets out to a commit a crime and then is foiled at the last minute by something other than his own intent, this should be a crime. Making attempted crime into a crime by itself discourages people from committing a crime. However, charging a person with attempt to commit a crime raises some practical issues. For instance, just how far must a person go before he or she can be convicted of attempting to commit a crime? Is simply thinking about a crime considered to be an attempt? Obviously, that standard would be impossible to prove and even more damaging; many of us have thought about one crime or another but have never gone beyond that simple thought. Simply thinking about a crime is not enough to warrant a charge of attempt. However, if law enforcement were forced to wait until the defendant had actually committed a crime, then there would be no need for the crime of attempt at all. (Waiting for the crime to occur might also involve considerable danger to victims and innocent bystanders.) Police need guidance to know when they can charge a person with attempt to commit a crime, and prosecutors need the underlying facts to substantiate the charge and prove it beyond a reasonable doubt.

A. INCHOATE CRIMES

Inchoate
Incomplete, unfinished, an act begun but not finished.

Crimes of attempt are often referred to as **inchoate** crimes. An inchoate offense is a crime that has been set in motion but not completed. Rather than use this term, we will instead use "attempted crime" in its place. Inchoate is the word that is often used in common law jurisdictions, but this terminology has been abandoned in many locations. It is also a confusing term.

B. DEFINING ATTEMPT

Attempt
An act that goes beyond preparation but which is not completed.

When it comes to defining exactly what qualifies as **attempt**, the starting point should be the applicable statute. See Figure 3-1 for an example of a statute that provides some guidance about what constitutes the crime.

    Many jurisdictions follow the pattern set out in Figure 3-1. In these jurisdictions, the definition of an attempted crime is one where the defendant has taken a substantial step to complete it. However, this pattern is not followed in all jurisdictions. Under the common law, for example, attempt was defined as intent coupled with some act to further the crime.[1] Attempt can be, and often is, punishable as a separate crime.[2] Prosecutors often charge an attempt along with a completed crime. For instance, in a case where a man tries to kill one person and actually kills another, the prosecutor will charge attempted murder in the first instance and murder in the second.

---

[1] *Com. v. McClintock*, 433 Pa. Super. 83, 639 A.2d 1222 (1994).
[2] *Eakes v. State*, 665 So. 2d 852 (Miss. 1995)

FIGURE 3-1

Sec. 1. (a) A person attempts to commit a crime when, acting with the culpability required for commission of the crime, he engages in conduct that constitutes a substantial step toward commission of the crime. An attempt to commit a crime is a felony or misdemeanor of the same class as the crime attempted. However, an attempt to commit murder is a Class A felony.

(b) It is no defense that, because of a misapprehension of the circumstances, it would have been impossible for the accused person to commit the crime attempted.[3]

Attempt (Indiana)

THEO DRIVES TO A BANK

SCENARIO 3-1

Theo has decided to write a crime novel. The opening scene involves a bank robbery that ends with one of the characters being killed by a security guard. Theo has tried to write other books and one of his publishers advised him to get more "real world" experience before trying to write anything else. So, with this advice in mind, Theo drives to a local bank and takes some photos of the bank. He draws a diagram of the area and then works out a fictitious plan for how three of the characters in his book could rob an armored car.

SUBSTANTIAL STEP

A person crosses the line between merely thinking about an offense and actually committing one when she takes some action to further the crime. Different jurisdictions refer to this stage as "substantial step" or "overt act" or "direct act." We will refer to this stage as **substantial step**. A substantial step does not necessarily have to be some action that is just short of the crime itself. Instead, a substantial step is something that essentially sets the crime into motion. It places the person dangerously close to actually committing the crime.[4] Courts have consistently ruled that substantial step means coming very close to accomplishing the crime.[5] In Scenario 3-1, has Theo taken a substantial step toward the crime of armed robbery?

Substantial step
Intent and preparation to carry out a crime that is not completed because of some outside act.

Answer: No. Although Theo did drive to the bank and take photos and make a diagram of the bank, these actions are not enough by themselves to authorize a prosecution for attempted armed robbery. Looked at another way, have Theo's actions set the crime of armed robbery in motion? Has Theo taken a direct action that a jury could reasonably say made the crime of armed robbery likely? The answers are also no.

Under court rulings, a substantial step is more than preparing to commit a crime, but less than the act to complete the crime.[6] Given the fact that this definition is so hard to pin down, each case must be considered on its merits. Consider Scenario 3-2.

> **Sidebar**
>
> *A person is guilty of attempt to commit a crime when she takes some action that would have accomplished the crime had it not been for some intervening force.[7]*

---

[3] IC 35-41-5-1
[4] *People v. Johnson*, 186 A.D.2d 363, 588 N.Y.S.2d 162 (1992).
[5] *Com. v. Dixon*, 34 Mass. App. Ct. 653, 614 N.E.2d 1027 (1993)
[6] *State v. Walker*, 705 So. 2d 589 (Fla. Dist. Ct. App. 4th Dist. 1997)
[7] *People v. Carpenter*, 15 Cal. 4th 312, 63 Cal. Rptr. 2d 1, 935 P.2d 708 (1997), cert. denied, 118 S. Ct. 858, 139 L. Ed. 2d 757 (1998).

SCENARIO 3-2

THEO TAKES IT TO THE NEXT LEVEL

Theo has written up the first chapter of his novel, but he still feels that the actions he describes lack that sense of reality. He goes back to the bank and stays there for several hours. He notes the time that the employees arrive and when the armored car makes its delivery. He takes photos of who drives the armored car, how they unload the money, and what door they use to bring the bags of money into the bank.

Has Theo committed the crime of attempted armed robbery?

The answer is still no. Although some of Theo's actions are becoming questionable, he has yet to take a substantial step towards putting the crime of armed robbery into action.

C. PROSECUTING A CHARGE OF ATTEMPT

To prosecute someone for attempt, the government must show that the defendant acted with the intent to commit the crime and carried out some action that constituted a substantial step toward the commission of the crime.[8] The prosecution normally does this by showing the circumstances surrounding the defendant's actions. For instance, in a charge of attempted robbery, the prosecution might show that the defendant was short on money, that the defendant spent a considerable amount of time preparing to commit the crime, and that he also took some action toward carrying out the plan. This preparatory work would suggest that the idea of robbing a bank was no mere fancy, but a carefully laid-out plan (see Scenario 3-3).

SCENARIO 3-3

THEO BRINGS A GUN

Still feeling that his descriptions of an armed robbery lack the feeling of verisimilitude, Theo decides to take his fictitious armed robbery idea to the next level. He buys a ski mask and a gun. He drives to the bank shortly before the armored car is scheduled to make its delivery and he positions his car in such a way that if he were to rob the guards, he could make a quick getaway. He loads bullets into his gun and puts the ski mask on top of his head, but doesn't pull it over his face. He is sitting in his car, holding the gun, and reviewing the diagram and photos, when a police officer confronts him and demands that he drop the gun and get out of the car. He is arrested for attempted armed robbery. Has he committed the crime?

At this point, the answer is almost certainly yes. Why? In the previous scenarios, Theo did not have the requisite ingredients to bring the crime into existence. However, this time he is present, he has a gun, a ski mask, and his diagrams. The ski mask and the gun are the two most important factors because they show his intent. Although Theo could claim that he was simply trying to make his novel research more accurate, he has moved beyond

---

[8] *People v. Harris*, 892 P.2d 378 (1994); Moore v. State, 673 N.E.2d 776 (1996).

that claim by demonstrating his intent to actually carry through the crime. (Someone who had no intent to rob the bank would not have needed a real gun or a ski mask; they would also not have needed to position the car for a quick getaway.) Theo's "research" has moved into the realm of a criminal offense.

D. DEFENDING A CHARGE OF ATTEMPT

One of the defenses to attempt is **abandonment** — that the defendant voluntarily stopped the criminal enterprise before carrying it out. Abandonment, when proved, will relieve the defendant of all culpability in the case. However, proving abandonment is often not as easy as it sounds. A defendant can make out a defense of abandonment when he or she voluntarily renounces the crime, ceases efforts to carry it out, or finds a way to stop the crime from occurring.[9] Voluntariness is the key component here. The defense must present some evidence showing that he or she voluntarily decided not to carry out the crime. It is not a voluntary abandonment if the defendant changed her mind when she saw the police approaching.

> **Abandonment**
> When a defendant voluntarily stops the criminal enterprise before it is completed.

The question with abandonment is when a person is deemed to have abandoned the attempt. We can answer that question in the negative first: It is not abandonment when a person has already injured someone or where some act of danger has already happened. It is also not abandonment when the defendant fails to complete the crime because of some unanticipated problem.[10] Once the substantial step has been taken, abandonment is no longer a defense.[11] It is abandonment when a defendant voluntarily stops the criminal act and takes no part in its completion.

PRINCIPALS AND ACCESSORIES

When someone helps in the planning or carrying out of a crime, but is not physically present when the crime occurs, should that person be considered equally as guilty as the person who was physically present? What about a person who has no knowledge of the crime prior to it occurring, but who assists the defendant after it is over, with full knowledge she is helping someone avoid justice? As a natural extension, this text will address the crime of conspiracy to commit a crime when several defendants plan and execute a crime. It will also address the concept of solicitation of a crime, where one person persuades another person to commit a crime.

> **Principal**
> A person directly involved with committing a crime, as opposed to an accessory.

---

[9] *State v. Brown*, 999 A.2d 295 (N.H. 2010).
[10] *State v. Mahoney*, 264 Mont. 89, 870 P.2d 65 (1994).
[11] *State v. Devoid*, 2010 VT 86, 8 A.3d 1076 (Vt. 2010).

A. WHY IT IS IMPORTANT TO DETERMINE WHO IS A PRINCIPAL OR AN ACCESSORY

Accessory
A person who helps commit a crime without being present.

It is important to understand the difference between principals and **accessories** when assessing the culpability of the defendant. The principal is the person who actually commits the crime. An accessory is someone who helps in planning the crime or assists the principal in some way. The principal is someone who is actually present and who commits the crime. An accessory (or accomplice) is normally not physically present when the crime occurs, but may have given assistance to the principal either before the crime occurred or after. The reason that the distinction is important between principals and accessories is that they are punished differently. Principals, people who actually commit the crime, are normally punished more harshly than are accessories. In some states, for instance, a person classified as an accessory will receive only one half of the total sentence that a principal could receive. If the principal faces a maximum possible sentence of 20 years, then an accessory to the same crime will face a total maximum sentence of 10 years.

LEGAL DEFINITION OF "PRINCIPAL"

> ## Sidebar
>
> *Principals are present and participating when the crime occurs. Accessories are absent when the crime occurs; they aid and abet either before or after the crime, but do not participate in the actual crime.*

Constructive presence
A person who is deemed to be present when the crime occurs even if he or she was not actually in the immediate vicinity when the crime occurred.

In some states, there is a distinction made between principals in the first degree and principals in the second degree. However, because both are charged as principals and often receive identical sentences, we will not make these distinctions here. Instead, we will focus on issues surrounding actual presence versus constructive presence. The person who is actually present when the crime occurs and is taking an active role in the crime is actually present. However, there are times when a person can be considered a principal and not be physically present when the crime occurs. Suppose, for example, that during a bank robbery, two men are inside robbing the bank and a third is outside acting as a lookout and getaway driver. This person is usually considered to be *constructively* present at the scene of the crime. **Constructive presence** means that the person is actually helping the other principals commit the crime even though he or she may not be in the immediate vicinity of the actual crime. However, these persons are normally very close by. The farther away the person is from the scene of the crime, the more likely he or she will be considered an accessory or accomplice than a principal. Waiting just outside the bank behind the wheel of the getaway car is an example of someone who is close enough to the main action of the crime to be considered a principal. The law will constructively place the person at the scene. This person may not actually be inside the bank while the crime occurs, but because of the fact that he or she is close and playing an important role in helping the crime to occur, this person will be classified as a principal in the same way that the people inside the bank are considered to be principals. All will be charged with armed robbery. The only important feature of constructive presence arises during sentencing, when the constructive principal can legitimately say that he or she was not inside the bank when the crime occurred, and this might justify a somewhat lower sentence than the people who were inside. However, many judges will sentence defendants who were actually present and those who were constructively present in exactly the same way, reasoning that without all of them, the crime might never have occurred.

Present When the Crime Occurs. In order to be considered a principal, the person must be present when the crime occurs. A person who is not present, either constructively or actually, cannot be prosecuted as a principal. Someone who assists others to prepare for the crime, or assists after the crime, may be classified as an accessory, but if the person is not present, he or she cannot be considered to be a principal.

Actively Participating in the Crime. Another important point about principals is that they must be actively participating in the crime at the time that it occurred. It is not enough to simply be at the scene of a crime. The prosecution must show that the person had the intent to participate in the crime, that he or she was present, and that he or she actively participated in the crime, even if the participation was minimal.

LEGAL DEFINITION OF ACCESSORY

An accessory is someone who assists the principal but is not present when the crime occurs. An accessory often assists the principal in planning or preparing for the crime or assists the principal after the crime occurs but is not present and not participating when the crime actually occurs.

Accessory Before the Fact. There are two types of accessories. There are accessories before the fact, and there are accessories after the fact. An **accessory before the fact** is someone who helps the principal plan the crime, assists in acquiring items for the principal, aids or abets the principal to help with the crime, but is not present when the crime occurs. An accessory before the fact may be someone who provides resources to the principal, advice, or counseling.

Accessory before the fact
A person who, without being present, encourages, orders, or helps another to commit a crime.

An accessory before the fact is not physically or constructively present during the commission of the crime. If the person were present, he or she would be reclassified as a principal. An accessory before the fact helps organize the crime but is not actually present at the commission of the crime. When it comes to sentencing an accessory, the most common statutory scheme is that the accessory may receive up to half the maximum sentence as the principal. Consider Scenario 3-4.

ACCESSORY BEFORE THE FACT

SCENARIO 3-4

Ray is an accessory before the fact to the crime of first degree forgery robbery. The maximum sentence that the principal faces is ten years. What is the maximum possible sentence that Ray could face?

Answer: The maximum possible sentence for an accessory before the fact is half of the maximum sentence for the principal. Because the principal is facing a ten-year maximum sentence, the most that Ray could receive is five years.

Accessory After the Fact. The other type of accessory, **accessory after the fact**, is someone who helps the defendant avoid prosecution or arrest after the crime has been committed. An accessory after the fact was not involved in either the planning or organization of the crime. An accessory after the fact simply aids or abets the defendant in avoiding prosecution or arrest. If a person is involved in the planning

Accessory after the fact
A person who finds out that a crime has been committed and helps to conceal the crime or the criminal.

of a crime, that person becomes an accessory before the fact. The reason that this distinction is so important is that of the two, accessory before the fact and accessory after the fact, accessories before the fact are punished more harshly than accessories after the fact. A person can only be prosecuted as an accessory after the fact if he acted with knowledge that the person he assisted was in trouble with the law, and he gave that person help or assistance to flee the jurisdiction or otherwise avoid arrest.

An accessory after the fact usually does not face the same level of punishment as an accessory before the fact. In fact, many states place a maximum sentence on accessories after the fact of five years in prison, although the amount can vary considerably from state to state.

COMPLEXITIES IN THE LAW OF PRINCIPALS VS. ACCESSORIES

When it comes to the law concerning principals and accessories, there are some complexities that can creep into the analysis. As we have already seen, in order to be considered an accessory, a person must act with knowledge and intent. The person must know that the principal is about to commit a crime and must have the intent to assist the principal. Someone who simply furnishes goods or services to a person who later commits a crime cannot be considered an accessory. The same is true for accessories after the fact. The prosecution must prove, beyond a reasonable doubt, that the person provided aid and assistance to a principal, knowing that the principal had committed a crime. Consider Scenario 3-5.

| **SCENARIO 3-5** | ## HELPING AN ASSASSIN |

JWB has assassinated the president of the United States. As he flees the theater after shooting the president, he falls and breaks his leg. He manages to make it to a local doctor. The doctor, who does not know that JWB has just killed the president or that he is attempting to flee, sets JWB's leg. Later, the police discover that the doctor cared for JWB, and they charge him as an accessory after the fact. Is he?

Answer: No. The state cannot prove that the doctor was involved in the murder or that the doctor provided assistance, counseling, or protection to the principal, knowing that he was fleeing the authorities and a murder charge.

When the Principal Is Found Not Guilty. An interesting question arises when the principal is found not guilty at trial and then the accessory is brought to trial. Is it a proper defense for the accessory to state that the principal was acquitted? The answer is usually no. Most states that have addressed this question have held that the acquittal of the principal in a prosecution does not prohibit the conviction of an accessory before the fact.[12] The reason for this distinction is that each trial

---

[12] *State v. Massey*, 267 SC 432, 229 SE2d 332 (1976)

must stand on its own, and juries must make determinations based on the facts that are before them, not on the results or evidence that may have been presented in another case.

FAMOUS CASES
D.B. COOPER

The case of D.B. Cooper is the only skyjacking in the world that remains unsolved. On the day before Thanksgiving 1971, a rainy afternoon in Portland, Oregon, a man approached the ticket counter of Northwest Orient Airlines. He purchased a one-way ticket to Seattle under the name of Dan Cooper. Shortly after takeoff, Cooper gave a flight attendant a note, which read in part, "I have a bomb in my briefcase." To this day, no one has ever discovered if he worked alone or had accessories or co-conspirators. As ransom, he demanded $200,000, four parachutes, and a fuel truck to be waiting for the plane on arrival in Seattle.

The president of Northwest Orient approved the ransom demands, and for two hours, the plane circled the Seattle area while the money and parachutes were assembled. FBI agents gathered 10,000 unmarked $20 bills and photographed them so that there would be a record of the serial numbers. The plane landed in Seattle at 5:45 p.m., and the ransom money and parachutes were delivered. At that point, Cooper allowed the passengers and some of the flight attendants to leave the plane. After refueling, the plane took off with orders to fly to Mexico City. Also along for the ride were two fighter planes, close behind but out of Cooper's sight.

A few minutes after takeoff, Cooper ordered everyone into the flight cockpit, where they were to remain. The pilot soon saw a warning light, indicating that the rear stair mechanism had been activated. Shortly thereafter, the cockpit crew acknowledged a sudden change in air pressure, a sure sign that a door was open. Two hours later, the pilots landed the plane at the Reno, Nevada airport. A search confirmed that Cooper was gone. Somewhere over southwest Washington, Cooper had jumped from the plane.

For days, FBI agents scoured the forests in the area, looking for anything: a piece of parachute, a $20 bill, a body. They found nothing. Investigators recovered 66 unidentified fingerprints from the airplane, along with a clip-on tie, and tie clip Cooper had left behind. However, there was no evidence to link to a suspect. Neither of the pilots of the fighter planes had seen Cooper jump, but the weather had been poor that evening, so it's conceivable that they simply missed him.

Although the FBI mounted a massive investigation, they uncovered nothing to either confirm or deny that Cooper had successfully parachuted out of the plane with the ransom money. A reporter mistakenly repeated the wrong first name from a police source, and "D.B. Cooper" became etched into the collective minds of the public. However, D.B. Cooper did not exist, and even "Dan Cooper" was an alias. Oddly, many people were rooting for him because of the mythological quality of his story.

More than 1,000 suspects were investigated during the years following the skyjacking, but none was ever definitively identified as being the elusive D.B. Cooper. One investigator called him the "Bigfoot of the Pacific Northwest."

The FBI theorized that Cooper had to have died in the jump. The weather conditions were harsh, and the money probably blew away. However, in 1980 an eight-year-old boy camping with his family on the banks of the Columbia River uncovered a bag of bills, $5,800 in all. The bills had seriously deteriorated, but they were indeed part of Cooper's ransom money.

In 2011, 40 years after the crime, investigators uncovered new physical evidence: traces of pure titanium from Cooper's tie clip. The purity of the titanium led investigators to believe that Cooper was a metallurgist. The discovery did not produce a suspect, but it winnowed the field from millions to hundreds. But as time passes, the odds of solving the mystery continue to diminish greatly.

Abolishing the Definition of Accessory. In some states, the old common-law distinction between principals and accessories has been abolished by statute. In those states, a person may be charged as an accomplice to the crime committed by another person. Similar to an accessory, an accomplice must act in some way that aids, assists, or abets the crime.[13] In order to qualify as an accomplice, a person does not have to plan the crime. He or she could be someone who helps the main culprit commit the crime.[14]

Accomplice
A person who knowingly and voluntarily helps another person commit or conceal a crime.

Codefendants. Whether classified as principals in the first or second degree, or as accessories, codefendants are people charged with the same crime who are often tried together. At trial, they will all be lumped together under the single label "codefendant." The distinction between principals and accessories will only come after the trial during sentencing, if the parties are convicted.

CONSPIRACY

Conspiracy
A crime that may be committed when two or more people agree to do something unlawful.

The crime of **conspiracy** is as old as civilization itself. When a group agrees among its members to commit a crime, peer pressure alone is often sufficient to guarantee that they will actually carry it out. Because groups who commit crimes not only tend to follow through on their agreements, but often act in more violent and vicious ways, all states (and the federal government) have created a separate offense called conspiracy. This charge can be brought in addition to the charge for the underlying offense. Suppose, for instance, that a group has decided to carry out the kidnapping and beating of a specific individual. When the crime has been committed, each member of the group can be charged with three crimes: 1) kidnapping, 2) aggravated assault, 3) conspiracy to commit kidnapping. Conspiracy gives prosecutors additional leverage against gang or group members. Because of this societal view against the dangerousness of gangs and illegal group activities, the law takes a serious view of conspiracies and provides enhanced punishment for people involved in a conspiracy.

Groups who commit crimes generally bring more resources and resolve to the offense; they are also more likely to carry out the crime than an individual.

---

[13] *State v. Eyth*, 124 Kan 405, 260 P 976 (1927).
[14] *Smith v. State*, 229 Ind 546, 99 NE2d 417 (1951)

A. THE ELEMENTS OF A CONSPIRACY

A criminal conspiracy consists of the following elements:

1 An agreement between two or more persons
2 To work together to carry out an illegal act
3 One or more members commit an "overt act" in furtherance of the agreement

AGREEMENT

The most important element of a conspiracy is the agreement. The agreement has been called the essential ingredient of a conspiracy.[15] The prosecution must prove that there was an agreement between two or more persons to commit an unlawful act. However, the state is not required to prove that the members had worked out all of the actual details of the crime.[16] What makes conspiracy so interesting is that there is no requirement that the parties actually commit the crime. Just as with attempt, law enforcement is not required to wait for conspirators to actually complete the crime before bringing charges. If the state can show all three elements of the conspiracy, especially an agreement, then the parties can be prosecuted whether they were successful in committing the crime or not.[17]

In order to prove that there was an agreement, the state must show that the members of the conspiracy had knowledge of the agreement and the fact that the underlying action that they contemplated was illegal. The government must prove that each member of the group entered into an agreement to carry out the crime.[18]

However, there is no specific language that a defendant must utter before the agreement element of conspiracy is proven. There is certainly no formal declaration required, such as, "I hereby agree to the proposed conspiracy." Criminals often use vague language when communicating with others, especially when there is a chance that their communications can be monitored by law enforcement. Because of this, courts do not require that the defendant use specific words before the agreement element of conspiracy is proven. The government can prosecute several individuals under a conspiracy theory, even when the exact details of the agreement are not known, or have never been made clear.[19] Consider Scenario 3-6.

---

[15] *U.S. v. Broce*, 488 U.S. 563, 109 S. Ct. 757, 102 L. Ed. 2d 927 (1989).
[16] *U.S. v. Amiel*, 95 F.3d 135 (2d Cir. 1996).
[17] *U.S. v. Pinckney*, 85 F.3d 4 (2d Cir. 1996)
[18] *U.S. v. Jensen*, 41 F.3d 946 (5th Cir. 1994).
[19] *U. S. v. Varelli*, 407 F.2d 735 (7th Cir. 1969), affd, 452 F.2d 193 (7th Cir. 1971), cert. denied, 405 U.S. 1040, 92 S. Ct. 1311, 31 L. Ed. 2d 581 (1972).

| SCENARIO 3-6 | ## CONSPIRACY OVER THE PHONE |

Lou and Gina are speaking to one another on the telephone. Law enforcement, after obtaining a warrant, has intercepted previous communications between Gina, Lou, and Carl, where they have discussed purchasing a kilo of cocaine from a source known to Gina (but not known to the others). One day, police monitor the following exchange:

Gina: Hey, Lou. How's it going?
Lou: Great, Gina. What's up?
Gina: You know that thing we were talking about?
Lou: Yeah.
Gina: You good to go?
Lou: You bet.

    Later, police intercept another phone call.

Lou: Hey, it's me.
Carl: No names, okay? No names.
Lou: Sure, no names.
Carl: What have you got?
Lou: You know that thing with Gina?
Carl: Yeah.
Lou: She wants to know if you're ready to party.
Carl: Hell to the yeah. When does the party start?
Lou: Tomorrow. 2:00 p.m. We'll meet at the bridge. You know the one. Her guy will be there. We'll need your $5,000. I'll have mine with me.

Can the state prove that this is an agreement to commit a conspiracy?
    Answer: Yes. Although the words were vague and communicated over a period of time, prosecutors can show that each understood what the other was saying and that they agreed to broad outlines of the conspiracy.

Sidebar

In a conspiracy charge, as soon as the various members have reached an agreement to carry out an illegal act and at least one member has committed an overt act to set it in motion, the entire group can be charged with conspiracy.[23]

    As you can see in Scenario 3-6, there are no specific words that must be spoken to create a conspiracy. Members can speak in general terms, or even using "code" phrases, and this can still be considered a valid agreement.[20] The interesting point about conspiracy is that an agreement to commit an offense by several people can still be criminal even if one of the members could have performed the act legally. Price-fixing scams are an example. One individual is free to set the price for a particular item, but when he or she acts in concert with others to control the entire market, a legal action becomes an illegal conspiracy.[21] Courts have never required the state to prove that each member of a conspiracy carry out an individual criminal activity. A general understanding is enough to prosecute for conspiracy.[22]

---

[20] *People v. Edwards,* 74 Ill. App. 2d 225, 219 N.E.2d 382 (1966).
[21] *Gebardi v. U.S.,* 287 U.S. 112, 53 S. Ct. 35, 77 L. Ed. 206, 84 A.L.R. 370 (1932).
[22] *U.S. v. Knowles,* 66 F.3d 1146 (11th Cir. 1995), cert. denied, 116 S. Ct. 1449, 134 L. Ed. 2d 568 (U.S. 1996)
[23] *State v. Brewer,* 258 N.C. 533, 129 S.E.2d 262, 1 A.L.R.3d 1323 (1963), appeal dismissed, 375 U.S. 9, 84 S. Ct. 72, 11 L. Ed. 2d 40 (1963).

TO CARRY OUT AN ILLEGAL ACT

In many jurisdictions, the law requires that the object of the conspiracy be an illegal act. It is not a conspiracy for a group to agree to do something legal. However, some states provide that people can be prosecuted for a conspiracy even when they are carrying out a legal act, but doing it in an illegal manner. One of the best examples is price fixing. In some states, the conspiracy charge arises because the conspirators are attempting to complete a legal action, but use illegal means. In other states, the object of the conspiracy must be the commission of a crime.[24]

THE "OVERT ACT"

In some states, an overt act is not a requirement of a conspiracy charge. The agreement alone is sufficient. However, in most other jurisdictions, in order to prosecute for conspiracy, the state must point to some action that took place in furtherance of the conspiracy.[25] Overt acts are also a requirement of federal law.[26] The overt act does not have to be illegal; it can be any action that furthers the conspiracy or makes the goal of the conspiracy more likely to occur. This means that lawful actions, when used to further a conspiracy, can be the basis of an overt act and justify a prosecution.[27] This action can be taken by any member of the conspiracy and will be applied against the entire group.[28]

Overt act
An action that shows the intent to carry out a behavior; it does not have to be an illegal act, as long as it promotes or makes more likely an illegal activity, such as conspiracy.

An action by any member of the conspiracy is attributable to all of the other members. Simply put, if *one* member carries out an overt act in furtherance of the conspiracy, this act will be ascribed to *all* members.[29] The importance of the overt act in those jurisdictions where it is required is that this is a clear indication of the intent of the members to carry out a crime. The act does not have to be criminal in nature. Any act, even a legal one, that furthers the aim of the criminal conspiracy, is enough to satisfy this element. This overt act helps the government prove that something was actually being planned and that the people involved were serious in carrying out the crime. The requirement of an overt act also helps to show that the conspirators were prepared to put their plan in effect. Consider Scenario 3-7.

KILLING DARRYL

SCENARIO 3-7

Doug, Dan, and Dave have all decided that they want to kill Darryl. They discuss their plan in detail and agree that each will play a specific role in killing Darryl. Doug will lure Darryl to a remote cabin. Dan will be at the cabin waiting with a gun. Dave will be there, too, with a

continued

---

[24] *State v. Kaakimaka*, 84 Haw. 280, 933 P.2d 617 (1997), reconsideration denied, 84 Haw. 496, 936 P.2d 191 (Haw. 1997).

[25] *Williams v. State*, 665 So. 2d 955 (1994).

[26] 18 USCA § 371.

[27] *State v. Ellis*, 657 So. 2d 341 (La. Ct. App. 5th Cir. 1995); In Interest of P.A., 1997 ND 146, 566 N.W.2d 422 (1997).

[28] *People v. Morante*, 56 Cal. App. 4th 163, 65 Cal. Rptr. 2d 287 (1997)

[29] *Williams v. Aetna Fin. Co.*, 83 Ohio St. 3d 464, 700 N.E.2d 859 (1998).

knife. They have agreed to bury Darryl's body after they kill him. The next day, Doug goes to a local home store and buys a tarp and a shovel. Has he committed an overt act?

Answer: Yes. Although purchasing a tarp and a shovel are legal acts, they were obviously purchased with an eye toward carrying out the murder of Darryl. Because of this purchase, the state can prove that an overt act was carried out, and all three men can be charged with conspiracy to commit murder.

B. COMPARING/CONTRASTING PRINCIPALS/ ACCESSORIES TO CONSPIRATORS

The element distinguishing conspirators from accomplices or accessories is the agreement between the various people involved. An accomplice or an accessory can give aid without any agreement existing between the various participants. However, in order to have a conspiracy, there must be an agreement between two or more people. This is the core difference between persons who can be designated as accomplices or accessories and those who will be designated as coconspirators. The members of a conspiracy know that they are attempting to commit a crime and are working toward that ultimate goal. An accomplice or accessory may not be aware of the details and certainly have not agreed to coordinate his or her efforts toward the fulfillment of the plan. It is this concerted action and agreement that makes conspiracy a more serious crime.[30] In a prosecution for conspiracy, the focus is on the intent of the conspirators. In a prosecution against accomplices or accessories, the focus is on how this person (or persons) aided the principals. No agreement is required between principals and accomplices. It is the agreement to commit a crime and the concerted group action to achieve the goal that creates a conspiracy and justifies a harsher sentence.[31]

C. PROSECUTING CONSPIRACIES

Conspiracy prosecutions normally involve two different approaches: 1) the government focuses on the conspiracy to commit a particular crime, and 2) the crime itself. Just as we saw in the crime of attempt, there is no requirement that the conspirators actually commit the crime. If the state can show that the conspirators had an agreement, and they carried out an overt act, then that is enough. Of course, if the conspirators also completed the criminal act, then the prosecution can charge the conspirators with two crimes: conspiracy to commit a crime and carrying out the crime.

---

[30] *U.S. v. Peterson*, 524 F.2d 167 (4th Cir. 1975), cert. denied, 423 U.S. 1088, 96 S. Ct. 881, 47 L. Ed. 2d 99 (1976).
[31] *State v. Moretti*, 52 N.J. 182, 244 A.2d 499, 37 A.L.R.3d 364 (1968), cert. denied, 393 U.S. 952, 89 S. Ct. 376, 21 L. Ed. 2d 363 (1968).
[32] *U.S. v. Monroe*, 73 F.3d 129 (7th Cir. 1995), affd, 124 F.3d 206 (7th Cir. 1997).

LEGAL IMPEDIMENT: "WHARTON'S RULE"

Wharton's Rule regarding conspiracies is relatively simple: When it requires two people to actually commit a crime, such as gambling or prostitution, there can be no charge of conspiracy where only two people are involved. The reasoning behind this rule, which has been enacted in many states, is that conspiracies, by their very nature, bring together individuals with different resources and abilities. This group action is dangerous. However, where there are only two people involved in a crime that requires two people to commit it, there is no concerted group action. To prosecute gambling or prostitution as a conspiracy, most states require more than two people involved. The rule only applies to crimes that require two people to commit them, and one of the people cannot be a victim. For example, if one person attacks another person, one might argue that it requires two people to complete the crime, but Wharton's Rule contemplates that both people involved are committing a crime, not that one is an aggressor and the other an innocent victim.

Wharton's Rule
Known in some jurisdictions as the "concert of action rule"; a rule that states it is not a conspiracy for two persons to agree to commit a crime if the definition of the crime itself requires the participation of two or more persons.

 SOLICITATION

The crime of solicitation involves an offer or a request by one person made to another person to commit a crime. The person making the offer can be prosecuted for soliciting a crime.[33] The point of a solicitation prosecution is criminalizing a serious effort by the defendant to induce another person to commit a crime.[34] Because our society does not wish to condone criminal conduct, statutes have been created that make it a crime for one person to ask another person to commit a crime. The most common example of solicitation of a crime is when a prostitute solicits a client for paid sex. Solicitation cases are often seen in cases involving pedophiles who attempt to lure children to locations to engage in sex or when persons approach hired killers with the proposition that the killer murder his or her spouse or lover.

To distinguish solicitation from conspiracy, note that a conspiracy involves two or more persons, while solicitation only involves one person making a request of another. Solicitation does not require any agreement to further a criminal design, but a conspiracy does.

Solicitation
Asking for; enticing; strongly requesting; the crime of asking another person to commit a crime.

Sidebar

Like conspiracy, there is no requirement that the crime actually occur before a person can be prosecuted for soliciting it.[35]

STATE v. ALLAN
131 Conn.App. 433, 27 A.3d 19 (Conn.App.,2011)

CASE EXCERPT

ALVORD, J.

The defendant, Nemiah Allan, appeals from the judgment of conviction, rendered after a jury trial, of conspiracy to sell narcotics by a person who is not drug-

---

[33] *People v. Sanchez*, 60 Cal. App. 4th 1490, 71 Cal. Rptr. 2d 309 (1998).
[34] *U.S. v. Holveck*, 867 F. Supp. 969 (D. Kan. 1994).
[35] *People v. Hood*, 878 P.2d 89 (1994).

dependent in violation of General Statutes § § 53a–48 and 21a–278 (b). On appeal, the defendant claims that the trial court improperly denied his motion for a judgment of acquittal. Specifically, he argues that the evidence was insufficient to sustain his conviction, and, therefore, he was deprived of his federal due process rights. We affirm the judgment of the trial court.

The jury reasonably could have found the following facts. On the evening of April 15, 2009, the defendant was under surveillance by the Meriden police department, which was working in conjunction with agents of a Drug Enforcement Agency task force. The law enforcement officers, in unmarked cars, observed the defendant on Maple Street engaging in drug related activity. The officers also observed the defendant make a specific drug transaction with a man in a white van where money was provided to the defendant, who then entered the "stash house" on Maple Branch before returning to the van. The police followed the van and stopped its driver, Humberto Zarabozo, who told police that he had purchased crack cocaine from the defendant. The police recovered the crack cocaine from the van and subsequently arrested Zarabozo. The officers returned to their posts in the Maple Street area to observe the defendant further and again saw him engaged in activity consistent with drug dealing.

The law enforcement officers observed the defendant talking on a cell phone. Thereafter, they observed an Acura pull up outside 10 Maple Branch. The Acura flashed its lights, after which the defendant crossed the street and approached the passenger side of the vehicle. The defendant opened the door, causing the dome light to illuminate, so that he could lean into the vehicle through the open door to talk to the driver. After the defendant spoke to the Acura's driver for several minutes, the Acura departed Maple Branch. The officers followed the Acura and returned to the scene approximately one to two hours later to arrest the defendant.

When the police approached the defendant to arrest him, he resisted and attempted to flee the scene. The police subdued the defendant, arrested him, and read him his Miranda rights. The defendant subsequently told the police that the driver of the Acura went by the street name of "Fleet" and that Fleet had come to Maple Branch to "resupply" the defendant with crack cocaine, although he did not deliver the crack cocaine as promised. The police were familiar with the name Fleet, as he was a known drug supplier. The defendant also provided the police with Fleet's cell phone number, which was the last outgoing call on a cell phone in the defendant's possession. The defendant then led the police to a nearby gas station to identify Fleet's girlfriend, Brandy Clayton. Using information gleaned from the defendant and Clayton, the police apprehended Fleet, whose real name is Kareem Thomas. The defendant was transported to the police station where he asked the booking officer what had happened to the "big fat white guy." The booking officer testified that when he asked the defendant to whom he was referring, the defendant replied "the one that I sold drugs to," presumably meaning Zarabozo.

The state charged the defendant with illegal sale of narcotics by a person who is not drug-dependent, sale of narcotics within 1,500 feet of a school, possession of narcotics, conspiracy to sell narcotics by a person who is not drug-dependent, and interfering with an officer. The case was tried before a jury on December 2 and 3, 2009. Defense counsel made a motion to the trial court for a judgment of acquittal, which the court denied. The jury returned a verdict finding the defendant not guilty on the charges of sale of narcotics, sale of narcotics within 1,500 feet of a school, and possession of narcotics and found him guilty of conspiracy to sell narcotics and interfering with an officer. Following the jury's verdict, the court sentenced the defendant to a total effective term of twelve years incarceration. This appeal followed.

The defendant claims that the trial court should have granted his motion for a judgment of acquittal because there was insufficient evidence to allow the jury to find him guilty beyond a reasonable doubt of the crime of conspiracy to sell narcotics. First, he argues that there was insufficient evidence to prove that he and his coconspirator, Thomas, had an agreement to further distribute the narcotics. Second, he argues that the state failed to prove that he or his coconspirator committed an overt act in furtherance of the conspiracy. Both claims are without merit.

In reviewing sufficiency of the evidence claims, we apply a two part test. "First, we construe the evidence in the light most favorable to sustaining the verdict. Second, we determine whether upon the facts so construed and the inferences reasonably drawn therefrom the finder of fact reasonably could have concluded that the cumulative force of the evidence established guilt beyond a reasonable doubt. . . . - While . . . every element must be proven beyond a reasonable doubt in order to find the defendant guilty of the charged offense, each of the basic and inferred facts underlying those conclusions need not be proved beyond a reasonable doubt. . . . If it is reasonable and logical for the jury to conclude that a basic fact or an inferred fact is true, the jury is permitted to consider the fact proven and may consider it in combination with other proven facts in determining whether the cumulative effect of all the evidence proves the defendant guilty of all the elements of the crime charged beyond a reasonable doubt. On appeal, we do not ask whether there is a reasonable view of the evidence that would support a reasonable hypothesis of innocence. We ask, instead, whether there is a reasonable view of the evidence that supports the jury's verdict of guilty."

"To prove the crime of conspiracy, in violation of § 53a–48, the state must establish beyond a reasonable doubt that an agreement existed between two or more persons to engage in conduct constituting a crime and that subsequent to the agreement one of the conspirators performed an overt act in furtherance of the conspiracy. . . . The state is also obligated to prove that the accused intended that conduct constituting a crime be performed. . . . It is not necessary to establish that the defendant and his coconspirators signed papers, shook hands or uttered the words we have an agreement. . . . Indeed, because of the secret nature of conspiracies, a conviction is usually based on circumstantial evidence. . . . A conspiracy can be inferred from the conduct of the accused."

Section 53a–48 (a) sets forth the elements of the crime of conspiracy. The state bore the burden of proving beyond a reasonable doubt that the defendant (1) with intent that conduct constituting a crime be performed, (2) agreed with one or more persons to engage in or cause the performance of such conduct, and (3) any one of them committed an overt act in pursuance of such conspiracy.

The defendant first claims that the evidence is insufficient because the state failed to prove beyond a reasonable doubt that he had an agreement with Thomas in the past to distribute narcotics or to distribute narcotics in the future. In other words, he argues that the state did not prove that the agreement provided some additional benefit to Thomas in his selling the drugs to the defendant. The defendant misunderstands the elements of the crime of conspiracy. Here, the defendant admitted that he called Thomas on a cell phone and made arrangements for Thomas to resupply him with crack cocaine, which the defendant intended to resell. Thomas then drove to Maple Branch to meet the defendant and, once he arrived, flashed the lights of the Acura to signal the defendant to approach the vehicle. The defendant's statements show that he had intent to buy narcotics from Thomas and that the defendant made arrangements with Thomas to be resupplied with crack cocaine. That agreement, in concert with an overt act, which is the subject of the defendant's second claim, is sufficient under Connecticut law to constitute a conspiracy. There are no elements enumerated in § 53a–48 (a) requiring the state to prove any future or past criminal acts in order to prove the crime of conspiracy.

Despite the fact that the state did not have a burden to prove that the defendant engaged in a past conspiracy or a future conspiracy to sell narcotics with Thomas, the defendant argues that we should adopt the so-called federal "buyer-seller exception" in evaluating charges of conspiracy to sell narcotics. Under the federal exception, "the seller cannot be considered to have joined a conspiracy with the buyer to advance the buyer's resale unless the seller has somehow encouraged the venture or has a stake in it — an interest in bringing about its success." The government must prove that there exists a "shared intention between the transferor and the transferee that further transfers occur." The defendant has not provided a single Connecticut case endorsing the so-called "buyer-seller exception," and we decline to apply such an exception in evaluating the defendant's claim.

Second, the defendant claims that we should find the evidence insufficient because the state failed to prove beyond a reasonable doubt that there was an overt act committed in furtherance of the conspiracy. The defendant claims that because the meeting between the defendant and Thomas resulted in the breakdown of their agreement, Thomas' drive to Maple Branch and flashing of the Acura's lights, and the defendant's subsequent discussion with Thomas cannot qualify as overt acts in furtherance of the conspiracy. We disagree.

"In a conspiracy prosecution, the government is not limited to proof of only those overt acts charged in the indictment and in fact need not prove every overt act alleged." *State v. Forde,* supra, 52 Conn.App. at 169–70, 726 A.2d 132. "An overt act is an essential ingredient of the crime of conspiracy; it may be committed by either coconspirator." Further, an overt act need not be a criminal act in and of itself.

"The probative force of the evidence is not diminished because it consists, in whole or in part, of circumstantial evidence rather than direct evidence. . . . It has been repeatedly stated that there is no legal distinction between direct and circumstantial evidence so far as probative force is concerned. . . . It is not one fact, but the cumulative impact of a multitude of facts which establishes guilt in a case involving substantial circumstantial evidence. . . . Moreover, in considering the evidence introduced in a case, (triers of fact) are not required to leave common sense at the courtroom door . . . nor are they expected to lay aside matters of common knowledge or their own observations and experience of the affairs of life, but, on the contrary, to apply them to the facts at hand, to the end that their action may be intelligent and their conclusions correct."

In construing the evidence in the light most favorable to sustaining the verdict, the defendant's own statements show that there was an agreement with Thomas by which Thomas would "resupply" the defendant with crack cocaine. The defendant told the police that his meeting with Thomas that evening was for the specific purpose of being resupplied with crack cocaine and that Thomas was his drug supplier from Waterbury. The defendant admitted calling Thomas on his cell phone, and, thereafter, Thomas drove to Maple Branch in his Acura, flashing his lights to signal the defendant to approach the vehicle. The defendant approached the Acura, and the two men spoke, with the defendant leaning in the Acura through the open door of the car. According to the defendant, Thomas failed to resupply him with crack cocaine as planned. Upon the facts so construed and the inferences reasonably drawn therefrom, the finder of fact reasonably could have concluded that Thomas' drive to Maple Branch, his subsequent flashing of the Acura's lights, the defendant's walk to the Acura, and any discussion following between the defendant and Thomas were all overt acts in furtherance of the conspiracy. It is both reasonable and logical for the jury to have reached such conclusions.

The defendant's argument that he and Thomas had a breakdown in their agreement, which occurred when Thomas failed to resupply the defendant with crack cocaine as planned, is irrelevant. Under Connecticut law, a breakdown of an agreement does not end the conspiracy. Section 53a–48 (b) provides that, once the state has proved the elements of the crime, the only defense to a conspiracy charge is renunciation, that is, "the actor, after conspiring to commit a crime, thwarted the success of the conspiracy, under circumstances manifesting a complete and voluntary renunciation of his criminal purpose." The defendant made no argument that he attempted to thwart the conspiracy. Thus, even if a breakdown of the agreement did occur, such a breakdown would not disqualify the previously enumerated overt acts. Accordingly, the defendant's final argument has no merit.

The judgment is affirmed.
In this opinion the other judges concurred.

---

1 With what crime was the defendant charged?
2 According to the statute cited in the case, what elements must the state prove in order to meet its burden of proving a conspiracy?
3 What did the defendant claim that a conspiracy required, and why did the court rule against him?
4 What is the "buyer-seller" exception in conspiracy cases?
5 What was the defendant's second contention on appeal?

CASE QUESTIONS

CHAPTER SUMMARY

Even if a person does not commit a crime, he or she can be charged. In the crime of attempt, the state may prosecute someone for taking a substantial step toward committing a crime, although the person never actually completed it. The guilt between one or more people who commit or help others to commit a crime can also be apportioned. A principal is someone who actually commits the crime and is present when it occurs. An accessory is someone who assists the principal but is not present when the crime occurs. In many states, the category of accessory has been abolished in favor of a more general term: accomplice. When two or more people enter into an agreement to carry out an illegal act, they can be prosecuted for the crime of conspiracy. Most states require that before a conspiracy is complete, one or more members of the conspiracy must complete some overt act to make the crime more likely.

It is also a crime to ask someone else to commit a crime. This is referred to as solicitation, and the person who solicits the crime can be charged as well as the person who committed the crime at the first person's urging.

KEY TERMS

Inchoate	Accessory	Conspiracy
Attempt	Constructive presence	Overt act
Substantial step	Accessory before the fact	Wharton's rule
Abandonment	Accessory after the fact	Solicitation
Principal	Accomplice	

REVIEW QUESTIONS

1   What is an inchoate crime?
2   How is the crime of attempt defined?
3   Explain "substantial step."
4   What is one defense to the crime of attempt?
5   Explain the difference between a principal and an accessory.
6   What is the difference between an accessory before the fact and an accessory after the fact?
7   Is it significant in the prosecution of an accessory to a crime that the principal was found not guilty? Why or why not?
8   Explain how the definition of accomplice has modified the term "accessory."
9   What is the difference between a codefendant and an accessory?
10 Explain the elements of conspiracy.
11 What is the significance of an "overt act" to the definition of conspiracy?
12 What is "Wharton's Rule"?
13 Explain the crime of solicitation.
14 Explain the difference between solicitation and conspiracy.
15 Can a conspiracy be charged even if the crime is never committed? Explain.

QUESTIONS FOR ANALYSIS

1   Why would most jurisdictions require an overt act before a conspiracy can be charged?
2   Should the crime of solicitation be eliminated or expanded? Explain your answer.

HYPOTHETICALS

1   Just how far could Theo (from the beginning of the chapter) go in carrying out his research for his crime novel, short of bringing a gun and a ski mask to the bank, before he could still claim that he was researching instead of attempting to commit a crime?

2   Sheila works at a local restaurant and one afternoon she notices that the manager has put a great deal of cash into the office safe. She calls her boyfriend Robert and his friend Jesse and tells them about the case. She suggests that they come and rob the place. When they arrive, Jesse decides to deflect any suspicion from Sheila by striking her with the barrel of his gun. The men flee with the money. Sheila has been severely injured and when the police arrives she immediately tells them who committed the robbery. What crimes can you pin on Sheila, if any?

3   Two men meet at a local coffee house, and while they are surfing the web on their smart phones, they discuss what they believe would be the perfect crime: each would kill the other's wife. Each would make sure that he had a perfect alibi at the time of the killing. One of the men goes out the next day and kills the other man's wife. Is this a conspiracy? Is it solicitation? Is there a crime that can be charged against the man who did not commit the murder?

4

Homicide

Chapter Objectives

- Explain the difference between general intent and specific intent crimes
- Identify the elements of first-degree murder
- Describe the differences between first-degree, second-degree, and manslaughter murder
- Explain the concept of *corpus delicti*
- Explain how provocation or other defenses mitigate a charge of murder

I   INTRODUCTION TO HOMICIDE

Among the various crimes against persons discussed in this text, the most serious is homicide. Future chapters will examine crimes such as battery, assault, and kidnapping, but the focus of this chapter is exclusively on the taking of a human life. The term **homicide** is a broad term that simply means the killing of one human being by another. The term does not take into account the reasons for the killing or whether the killing was justified, such as in time of war, or whether the killing was excused, such as in self-defense. Because the term encompasses so many different types of human death, the term is almost useless when it comes to discussing the nuances of criminal law.

> **Homicide**
> The killing of a human being by another.

We recognize that not all killings are the same. Some are justified; some are not. Because of this, the law creates gradations or degrees of homicide, with the crime of **murder** being the most serious and negligent or accidental homicide the least.

As we saw in Chapter 1, there are provisions that allow the federal authorities to exert jurisdictional supremacy over the states in certain types of crimes. This is also true with the crime of homicide. See Figure 4-1, which shows the estimated number of homicides each year between 1950 and 2010. Although most homicides are prosecuted on the state level, the federal authorities can take precedence and prosecute an individual first if the murder victim falls into specific categories such as:

> **Murder**
> The unlawful killing of another human being that is done voluntarily, with premeditation or malice.

 President of the United States
 Vice-President of the United States

FIGURE 4-1

Estimated Number of
Homicides Between 1950
and 2010

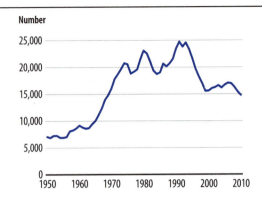

Note: Data are based on annual estimates of homicide from previously published versions of *Crime in the United States*. Data for 1989 to 2008 reflect updated homicide estimates from *Crime in the United States*, 2008. Data for 2009 and 2010 reflect updated homicide estimates from *Crime in the United States*, 2010.

Source: FBI, *Uniform Crime Reports*, 1950–2010.

- Members of Congress
- Candidates for federal office
- Foreign diplomats
- Members of the U.S. Supreme Court

However, before exploring the fascinating world of murder prosecutions, whether they are on the federal or state level, we must address a basic issue: How is a crime — any crime — evaluated? For that we consider two important terms: *mens rea* and *actus reus*.

GENERAL INTENT VS. SPECIFIC INTENT CRIMES

General intent
A showing that the defendant acted knowingly and voluntarily.

Specific intent
A requirement that the prosecution prove that the defendant acted with the intent to commit a specific crime.

As discussed in the first chapter, nearly all crimes have a very simple formula: There must be a guilty action coupled with guilty intent. Almost all crimes require *mens rea* (intent), as well as *actus reus* (action). But with the crime of murder — and a few other crimes — there is an additional classification to be considered. These two classes consist of **general intent** and **specific intent**. General intent refers to the simple intention on the part of the defendant to move his body or to take an action.[1] Specific action requires something more.

To prove that a defendant possessed general intent, a prosecutor need only show that the result the defendant put into motion was to be reasonably expected. Suppose, for example, that a defendant throws a rock into a crowd. Under general intent, it is a reasonable, and highly likely, result that the rock will hit someone.[2] As a result, proving general intent is relatively easy to do. One might inquire why such a question would be raised in the first place. General intent is obvious. However, there is a category of crime that requires the prosecution to prove more than simple

---

[1] *State v. Contreras*, 142 N.M. 518, 167 P.3d 966 (Ct. App. 2007).
[2] *State v. Domangue*, 649 So. 2d 1034 (La. Ct. App. 1st Cir. 1994).

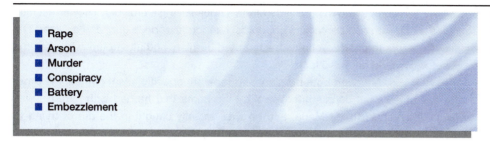

- Rape
- Arson
- Murder
- Conspiracy
- Battery
- Embezzlement

FIGURE 4-2

Examples of Specific Intent Crimes

intent. Instead, the government must prove what was in the defendant's mind at the time of his or her actions. That second category is referred to as specific intent.

A. SPECIFIC INTENT

Specific intent requires the prosecution to show that the defendant not only acted voluntarily, but also that he or she acted with an intended purpose. In other words, the prosecution must prove that the defendant intended to commit a specific crime. This is a higher standard than general intent. The reason that specific intent crimes carry this higher standard of proof is because they involve some of the more serious offenses and, in the past, many of these crimes were punishable by death. As a result, courts required a higher standard of proof before a defendant could be subjected to the death penalty. Although most of the specific intent crimes no longer carry the possibility of a death sentence, one of them — murder in the first degree — is still punishable by death in many states. See Figure 4-2 for a list of specific intent crimes.

To prove specific intent, the prosecution must not only show that the defendant acted voluntarily, but that the defendant had a particular crime in mind when he or she committed the act. In a murder prosecution, for example, the state must show that the defendant's intent was to murder another human being. How does a prosecutor prove what was in the defendant's mind? Obviously, prosecutors and police cannot read suspect's minds, but the law does not require this. Instead, the prosecutor can prove the defendant's state of mind based on his actions. This is a situation where actions speak louder than words. For instance, in a murder case, the state will often present evidence about the defendant's frame of mind, the statements that the defendant made both before and after the killing and any other evidence that will help give some idea of what was going on inside the defendant's mind. By contrast, a defendant who is charged with battery, which is not a specific intent crime, only requires that the prosecution prove that the defendant knew what he was doing and acted voluntarily. It is not a defense in a general intent crime for the defendant to claim that he did not intend the ultimate harm to the victim. However, such a defense is permitted in specific intent crimes. Consider Scenario 4-1.

Sidebar

General intent crimes are done voluntarily, not by accident or mistake.

SPECIFIC INTENT?

SCENARIO 4-1

Maria is home one night. Around midnight, she sees a man peeking in her window. The man is wearing a ski mask to disguise his features. Maria calls the police. When officers

continued

SCENARIO 4-1

(continued)

arrive they find John trying to break into Maria's house using a crowbar. They arrest him. John has a bag with him containing condoms, handcuffs, rope, a gun, and a Taser. The prosecutor wants to charge John with attempted burglary and attempted rape. Can the prosecutor succeed on these facts?

Answer: Yes. Although both burglary and rape are specific intent crimes, the prosecutor can show what John's intent was by the items that he had with him. He was obviously intending to rape Maria, and he was actually caught in the act of trying to pry open her back door.

Proving specific intent crimes is always more difficult than proving general intent crimes.

Transferred intent
A court doctrine that allows the state to apply the defendant's intent to harm one person to another person that the defendant may not have actually been trying to injure.

There are certain presumptions that can help the state to prove specific intent. For example, if the defendant uses a deadly weapon to commit an attack on the victim, and the victim dies from his or her injuries, the law allows the jury to assume that the defendant acted with specific intent to commit murder. There are other presumptions, such as the Felony-Murder Doctrine, discussed later in this chapter, that also provide specific intent when it might otherwise be difficult to prove.

The law also recognizes a concept called **transferred intent**. Under this doctrine, if the defendant was actually attempting to kill one person, but killed a different person, there is no defense that the defendant got it wrong. The defendant will be just as guilty for the murder, no matter who was killed. In this context, courts simply transfer the intent of the defendant to kill Victim A to Victim B, and a murder charge will stand. Under this rule, a defendant who attempts to kill someone known to him and instead kills a complete stranger is irrelevant. Intent is intent, and the fact that he committed the murder — and that his intent to kill can be transferred from the intended victim to the complete stranger — will mean that the defendant can be prosecuted under the same charge as if he had actually killed his original target.

B. WHEN *MENS REA* IS NOT REQUIRED

Strict liability offense
A crime where an illegal act occurs and the prosecution is not required to prove the defendant's intent.

After all of this discussion about the requirement of showing either general intent or specific intent as a subset of *mens rea*, it may be surprising to learn that there are some crimes that do not require *mens rea* at all. These crimes are often referred to as **"strict liability"** offenses, meaning that the mere fact that the crime occurred is enough to prosecute the defendant, regardless of his state of mind.

There are a limited number of crimes where the element of *mens rea* is eliminated. In these crimes, there is no responsibility on the part of the state to prove that the defendant acted with either general or specific intent. The only thing required of the state is to prove that the defendant acted voluntarily or, in some cases, that the defendant did not act when he or she should have. Because these strict liability offenses eliminate one of the most far-reaching elements found in almost all other criminal actions, the crimes that fall into this category are rare. However, because they do exist, it is important to know what they are and why legislatures have removed the *mens rea* element from these particular crimes. For instance, in the crime of statutory rape, most states have removed the *mens rea* requirement. In statutory rape, an adult has sex with a child under the age of 14 (the age varies in some states). The defendant's state of mind, or his intent (and many states are gender specific with this crime), is not an element that the state must prove in the

■ Statutory rape
■ Driving on a suspended driver's license
■ Driving after having been declared a habitual offender

FIGURE 4-3

Examples of Strict Liability Offenses

case. The fact that sexual intercourse occurred is enough, even if the other partner consented to the act.

In most cases, the crimes that fall into this category are considered minor offenses. No legislative initiative that attempted to eliminate *mens rea* from a murder prosecution would pass constitutional muster. In strict liability offenses the government is under no obligation to present evidence about the defendant's knowledge of the surrounding circumstances, that the defendant had any intent, that the defendant's actions were motivated by malice or that he or she had a deep-seated motive. All of those mental states are irrelevant in such crimes. See Figure 4-3 for examples of strict liability offenses.

PREMEDITATED MURDER

Because there are different types of homicide, ranging from the fully justified actions of a soldier in combat to the completely unjustified premeditated killing of another, this review of homicide must focus more narrowly on the issue of murder. Homicide is a general term referring to the death of a human being; murder

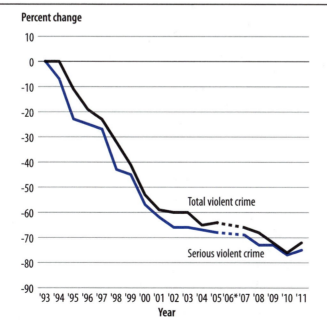

FIGURE 4-4

Percent Change in Rate of Violent Victimization Since 1993

*The 2006 percent change is not shown due to methodological changes in the 2006 NCVS. See *Criminal Victimization, 2007*, NCJ 224390, BJS website, December 2008, for more information.

Source: Bureau of Justice Statistics, National Crime Victimization Survey, 1993–2011.

is a specific term referring to the intentional killing of a human being by another. The most serious form of murder is premeditated killing, often referred to as first-degree murder. See Figure 4-4 for a description of violent crime trends, including premeditated murder.

There is no question that premeditated, or planned, murder is considered to be the most serious form of murder. The deliberate destruction of another human being has been outlawed in one form or another since human beings formed societies. For thousands of years, no distinction was made between a homicide involving premeditation (or planning) and the act of killing another person with simple malice. Generally, both actions were punishable by death. Most countries punished murder with execution and did not bother with nuances such as the fact that one murder was premeditated and the other was committed in the heat of passion or even through negligence. These countries also imposed the death penalty for crimes such as murder, rape, and even armed robbery in some instances.

The United States, which based its legal system on England's, similarly imposed the death penalty on a wide range of criminal activities, especially murder.

A. "DEGREES" OF MURDER

After the creation of the United States of America, some of the states began to question the system that made no clear distinction between one type of murder and another. This also coincided with a movement to restrict the death penalty to only the most serious crimes. These two movements were responsible for creating distinctions between various kinds of homicide. These distinctions, or "degrees," were based on the facts of the individual case. Classifying murder by various degrees reflected the different levels of guilt on the part of the defendant. To most people, it seemed fairly obvious that a man who had planned and committed a murder in cold blood was more culpable (and more dangerous to society) than someone who had killed in the heat of passion, perhaps even after being provoked. Should both of these types of killing face the same penalty?

Pennsylvania was the first state to enact legislation that divided various types of murder into degrees, with first degree being the most serious, second degree being less serious and so on. The determination of the degree of the murder would also dictate the punishment. Only first-degree murder could be punishable by death, while all other lesser forms of murder would face stiff sentences, but not the ultimate sanction. Those legal distinctions were eventually adopted, in one form or another, by all states.

FIRST-DEGREE MURDER

Under Pennsylvania's early statute, first-degree murder was defined as the unlawful killing of a human being with malice and premeditation. The statute gave additional guidance on what separates first-degree murder from all other forms of murder. For instance, as an example of premeditation, the statute listed killing someone by poison or by lying in wait for the victim. See Figure 4-5 for an example of California's First-Degree Murder Statute.

FIGURE 4-5

First-Degree Murder in California

§ 189. Murder; degrees

All murder which is perpetrated by means of a destructive device or explosive, a weapon of mass destruction, knowing use of ammunition designed primarily to penetrate metal or armor, poison, lying in wait, torture, or by any other kind of willful, deliberate, and premeditated killing, or which is committed in the perpetration of, or attempt to perpetrate, arson, rape, carjacking, robbery, burglary, mayhem, kidnapping, train wrecking, or any act punishable under Section 206, 286, 288, 288a, or 289, or any murder which is perpetrated by means of discharging a firearm from a motor vehicle, intentionally at another person outside of the vehicle with the intent to inflict death, is murder of the first degree. All other kinds of murders are of the second degree.[3]

Although the definition of first-degree murder varies from state to state, there are some common elements. They are:

- Unlawful killing
- Of a human being by another
- With malice aforethought
- With premeditation

Unlawful Killing. One might be tempted to ask: Is there ever a time when a killing is justified? The obvious answer might be a claim of self-defense. While self-defense is a justified killing, it is not a lawful killing. There are times when lawful killings are carried out. Police officers who engage in shoot-outs with suspects and kill them can have the killing ruled justified, but only after a lengthy investigation. Unlike television police officers, a real police officer who is involved in a fatality is immediately given administrative suspension while the killing is thoroughly examined. A solider who kills the enemy in a declared war has engaged in justified killing. But even in wartime, there are incidents where killing an enemy combatant is not justified. When the enemy surrenders, a solider no longer has the authority to kill the enemy soldier. Individuals who work as executioners for the state engage in justified killing.

With these examples in mind, we turn to the definition of unjustified killing. The prosecution always has the burden of proof in a criminal case and must prove this first element to that same burden as all of the others. However, actually showing that the killing was unjustified is straightforward. If the prosecution can show that the defendant was not legally justified in committing the homicide, the court will rule it to be an unjustified killing. Later, when we discuss defenses, we will see that defendants often claim self-defense to show that, although the person was killed, the

---

[3] West's Ann.Cal.Penal Code § 189.

killing was excused under the law because the defendant was trying to defend himself or someone else from a deadly threat.[4]

When Is a Murder Actually Committed? Although this would seem to be a rather obvious question, in day-to-day legal practice, the moment of death can be a complicating factor in a prosecution. Suppose that a person was attacked and severely injured in one jurisdiction, but then later died of his or her injuries in another jurisdiction. Where, exactly, did the murder occur? The reason that this question is important is that the site of the murder is the critical legal question for determining who will try the defendant. Fortunately, courts have been wrestling with these issues for hundreds of years, and case law (and the occasional statute) has made the question of where and when the murder occurs easier to determine.

There is a model act that helps to determine the moment of death. The Uniform Determination of Death Act defines the moment of death as: a) when the victim's breathing and circulatory system fails, or b) the moment when termination of all brain functions occurs.[5]

In most cases, the murder actually occurs at the time and place where the fatal blow or the wound that eventually killed the victim was delivered, regardless of where the victim ultimately died.[6] Consider Scenario 4-2.

SCENARIO 4-2

MURDER ACROSS COUNTY LINES

Murray lives in a home that is close to the county line. Officially, he lives in County A, but one evening, he is attacked in his home and fatally shot in the head. He staggers a few feet and dies in County B. Which county can prosecute the man who killed Murray?

Answer: County A. Even though Murray died in County B, his fatal wound was delivered in County A.

SCENARIO 4-3

MURDER ACROSS COUNTY LINES (2)

Sheila is standing in County A when Bryan, who is standing in County B, fires a gun and kills her. Which county will have the responsibility for prosecuting Bryan?

Answer: County A. Sheila was in County A when she was shot, and she also died there. County A clearly has jurisdiction for Bryan's prosecution.

Of a Human Being by Another. As we will see later in this chapter, when a person kills himself, it is not considered homicide, but suicide. In order to prove that a murder occurred, the prosecution must prove not only that the defendant killed the

---

[4] *Holloway v. McElroy*, 632 F.2d 605 (5th Cir. 1980), cert. denied, 451 U.S. 1028, 101 S. Ct. 3019, 69 L. Ed. 2d 398 (1981).
[5] Uniform Determination of Death Act § 1.
[6] *State v. Hare*, 190 Neb. 339, 208 N.W.2d 264 (1973).

victim, but also that the victim was a human being. Although this might also seem to be a self-evident item, there can be complications. For example, it is not considered murder when a person shoots a dead body.[7] Before states enacted statutes dealing with feticide, it was not a crime to kill an unborn child. The defendant could be charged with the injuries to the mother, but not the killing of the fetus. Many states have amended their statutes to change this old common law rule. Some states have attacked this particular problem in criminal law by enacting statutes that make it a crime to kill an unborn human being, no matter what stage of development the fetus may be.[8] Under these statutes, abortion would not qualify as murder, because the U.S. Supreme Court has determined that an abortion during the first trimester of the fetal development is not a crime. The Court has held that the mother has a privacy interest that outweighs the common law definition of viable fetus.[9]

It is not murder to kill someone who was already dead, and it is not murder to kill an animal. However, just as we saw with the first element of first-degree murder, proving the second element is also a straightforward proposition. The prosecution will call the coroner or medical examiner to the stand to detail the cause of the victim's death, including the time that the victim died, indirectly showing that the victim was alive before being injured. However, the prosecution will also call other witnesses to the stand to describe what the victim was like while he or she was alive. As this chapter's case excerpt will show, appellate courts prefer that the person who testifies and perhaps even identifies a photo of the victim while alive be someone other than a close family member. In many murder prosecutions, however, the victim's mother or father may still testify.

> **Sidebar**
>
> *The mother of an unborn child cannot be charged with murdering the fetus.[10]*

With Malice Aforethought. So far, our discussion of first-degree murder has set out two elements that are relatively easy for the prosecution to prove. However, the same cannot be said for the last two elements. The third element, malice, is a requirement found in both first- and second-degree murder charges. The state must prove that the defendant acted with malice at the time that he or she injured the victim. What is malice?

Malice is a state of mind that the defendant must have prior to killing the victim. Malice is the unlawful intent to kill; it is the intent to harm, to injure, or to carry out some evil intent. It can be formed in an instant and acted on in a few seconds. The state does not have to prove that the defendant developed malice over a period of time, only that at the time that defendant acted, he did so with the intent to kill. As you can see, malice sounds a great deal like specific intent. Both require proof of the defendant's state of mind. How does the state prove what was in the defendant's mind? The answer is to go back to the facts. If the defendant announces his intent to kill, that will satisfy malice. The state can also show from the actions

Malice
An intentional desire to inflict pain or death on someone that has no legal justification.

---

[7] *People v. Dlugash*, 41 N.Y.2d 725, 395 N.Y.S.2d 419, 363 N.E.2d 1155 (1977)

[8] *State v. Hampton*, 213 Ariz. 167, 140 P.3d 950 (2006), cert. denied, 127 S. Ct. 972, 166 L. Ed. 2d 738 (U.S. 2007).

[9] *People v. Davis*, 7 Cal. 4th 797, 30 Cal. Rptr. 2d 50, 872 P.2d 591 (1994).

[10] *State v. Geiser*, 2009 ND 36, 763 N.W.2d 469 (N.D. 2009).

that the defendant took, such as the savagery of the attack, or the fact that the defendant could have stopped his actions before the victim died and did not do so.

Proving malice is absolutely essential in a murder prosecution. It is an element of both first- and second-degree murder. Malice is the unlawful, deliberate intention to kill a human being without excuse, justification, or mitigation.[11] If the prosecution cannot show that the defendant acted in a vicious, angry, or deliberate way to kill the victim, the jury will not be authorized to return a verdict for either crime. Without the proof of malice, the crime must be manslaughter or some other lesser form of homicide.

Premeditation
Having sufficient time to think and consider one's actions and proceeding with the crime anyway.

With Premeditation. The final element in a first degree prosecution is **premeditation**. This element separates first-degree murder from all types of homicide and qualifies first-degree murder for a death sentence. No other form of homicide has this element. The reason is simple: As a society, we punish most severely those who had a chance to reconsider their actions, to stop themselves from killing, yet proceeded with the crime anyway. Persons who commit this crime may be beyond redemption, at least as far as the court system and society are concerned. They have also proven themselves to be capable of the worst thing that a human being can do to another.

What is premeditation? How long does it take to premeditate? Courts have been considering these issues for centuries and have come up with general guidelines. First of all, to premeditate is to think and consider what you are doing. When a person kills another with premeditation, he realizes that he is going to cause the death of another person, is conscious of the crime he is about to commit, and does it anyway. This moment to consider one's actions, to think about the repercussions, to think about the enormity of the crime considered is what separates first-degree murder from all other forms of murder. A person who had time to consider what he or she was going to do and then proceeds to do it anyway has shown that the person is extremely dangerous to society. In almost all states such a conviction of first-degree murder carries a life sentence; in other jurisdictions, this crime carries a sentence of life in prison without the possibility of parole. If the prosecution can show aggravating circumstances in the killing, such as rape, torture, or other action against the victim, the defendant may face the death penalty. The death penalty will be discussed in detail in Chapter 21.

Just as with malice, the prosecution must prove what was going on in the defendant's mind or at least show that the defendant had time to consider his actions, but decided to kill anyway. In a case of first-degree murder, the state must show that the defendant had time to consider what he was about to do, and then took the victim's life. How we define this amount of time varies from state to state, with most states simply providing that premeditation is an "appreciable period" of time, as little as a few seconds.

---

[11] *Mason v. Balkcom*, 487 F. Supp. 554 (M.D. Ga. 1980), rev'd on other grounds, 669 F.2d 222 (5th Cir. 1982), cert. denied, 460 U.S. 1016, 103 S. Ct. 1260, 75 L. Ed. 2d 487 (1983).

In the trial of a first-degree murder case, especially when the defendant has admitted to killing the victim, defense attorneys may focus their entire case on premeditation in an attempt to show that the defendant did not have time to form it or that surrounding circumstances so upset the defendant that he was incapable of thinking clearly. If the defense can establish a factual basis for this contention, juries will not be authorized to return a first-degree murder verdict. However, because we know that premeditation can be established in just a few seconds, it is not an easy defense to mount. If the jurors do believe that the defendant did not have time to premeditate, then the most they could find the defendant guilty of would be murder in the second degree or some form of manslaughter.

Although there are variations in many states on a wide variety of issues, most are remarkably consistent in defining premeditation. Almost all states define it as the defendant having time for forethought, that the defendant laid in wait for the victim (showing that he had time to consider his actions) or that the defendant poisoned the victim (which in most cases takes time, and often a considerable period of time and repeated doses before it is successful — again showing the time element). Premeditation can be formed in an instant. The important aspect of premeditation is that the defendant had the time to consider his actions and placed himself outside the law by deliberately committing a murder.

B. EXPANDING THE DEFINITION OF FIRST-DEGREE MURDER

Although some states have abandoned the death penalty, and some have restricted the definition of what counts as first-degree murder, some have expanded the definition. Some states, instead of opting for a definition of first-degree murder, simply refer to some types of murder as "capital murder," meaning that the person who commits it can be sentenced to death. For an example of an expanded definition of first-degree murder, see Figure 4-6.

C. MOTIVE

So far, in discussing the elements of first-degree murder, the topic of **motive** has not come up. The simple reason is that it is not required in murder cases. Motive is often the focus of television and film dramas, but the element is not included in the definition of first- or second-degree murder. Some might find that confusing. Surely we want to know why a person kills another? That is clearly true, but the important point about motive is that the prosecution is not required to present any evidence of what the defendant's motive was. Serial killers, for example, often have no clearly established motive beyond the simple pleasure they get from killing their victims. They often do not know their victims; there have been no arguments or disagreements between the serial killer and the victim. The killer kills because he wants to.

Motive
The reasons behind a person's actions.

FIGURE 4-6

Expanding Capital Murder in Texas

§ 19.03. Capital Murder

(a) A person commits an offense if the person commits murder as defined under Section 19.02(b)(1) and:

(1) the person murders a peace officer or fireman who is acting in the lawful discharge of an official duty and who the person knows is a peace officer or fireman;

(2) the person intentionally commits the murder in the course of committing or attempting to commit kidnapping, burglary, robbery, aggravated sexual assault, arson, obstruction or retaliation, or terroristic threat under Section 22.07(a)(1), (3), (4), (5), or (6);

(3) the person commits the murder for remuneration or the promise of remuneration or employs another to commit the murder for remuneration or the promise of remuneration;

(4) the person commits the murder while escaping or attempting to escape from a penal institution;

(5) the person, while incarcerated in a penal institution, murders another:

(A) who is employed in the operation of the penal institution; or

(B) with the intent to establish, maintain, or participate in a combination or in the profits of a combination;

(6) the person:

(A) while incarcerated for an offense under this section or Section 19.02, murders another; or

(B) while serving a sentence of life imprisonment or a term of 99 years for an offense under Section 20.04, 22.021, or 29.03, murders another;

(7) the person murders more than one person:

(A) during the same criminal transaction; or

(B) during different criminal transactions but the murders are committed pursuant to the same scheme or course of conduct;

(8) the person murders an individual under 10 years of age; or

(9) the person murders another person in retaliation for or on account of the service or status of the other person as a judge or justice of the supreme court, the court of criminal appeals, a court of appeals, a district court, a criminal district court, a constitutional county court, a statutory county court, a justice court, or a municipal court.

(b) An offense under this section is a capital felony.

(c) If the jury or, when authorized by law, the judge does not find beyond a reasonable doubt that the defendant is guilty of an offense under this section, he may be convicted of murder or of any other lesser included offense.[12]

---

[12] V.T.C.A., Penal Code § 19.03.

Even though motive is technically irrelevant to a murder prosecution, the state will often attempt to provide one for the jury. It is not a legal requirement, but jurors, just like everyone else, want to know why one person killed another. In most situations, the motive is clear: The defendant disliked the victim; the defendant was jealous of the victim; the defendant and the victim had problems in the past. However, consider the facts of Scenario 4-4, which is based on a real case.

WHAT IS THE MOTIVE?

A police officer is cruising through a high-crime area around 3:00 a.m. She stops her patrol car near an abandoned house that she knows from previous experience has been used for drug transactions. She looks around and is just about to leave when she hears something like a scream. The officer rushes into the house and shines her flashlight on two men. One is standing; one is lying on the ground. The one on the ground has blood gushing from his throat and quickly dies. The standing man has blood on his hands. Later, crime scene technicians recover a box cutter with the defendant's fingerprints on it where it could have easily been thrown when the defendant heard someone coming through the door. DNA tests confirm that the blood on the box cutter belongs to the victim. The defendant's fingerprints are on the box cutter. The victim is not identified. His fingerprints are not on file and no one in the neighborhood knows him. Media attention brings no identifications of the man.

The defendant is questioned but refuses to say anything. Later the case is assigned to a prosecutor who charges the defendant with first-degree murder. The prosecutor would like more evidence, but that is all that there is. The defendant has a prior record for armed robbery. No one ever establishes the identity of the victim. He is referred to as "John Doe."

The prosecutor presents the case to a jury and uses the physical evidence to establish the elements of murder. The defendant never testifies or offers a defense. At one point, the prosecutor wonders if the defendant has mental problems or is unable to speak or hear, but psychiatrists confirm that the man has no obvious problems. In fact, he is quite chatty with the nurses and seems to fully understand what he is charged with, but refuses to give a statement.

What is the motive for the murder?

Answer: Unknown. At the trial, the prosecutor argues a theory that the defendant went to the house armed with the box cutter determined to rob a drug dealer or a buyer or both, but instead found a homeless man and killed him. But that is just a theory. Fortunately, the prosecutor does not have to prove what the motive is because no one (aside from the defendant) knows.

Although there is no legal requirement to prove motive, prosecutors often present evidence of the defendant's motive anyway. The more evidence that the prosecutor can show establishing a motive, the easier it is for the jurors to understand what happened in the case. Of course, the same approach can be used by the defense team to show that the defendant had no motive or that the government's theory of motive is flawed. This argument is simply a sideshow in the trial and judges will often cut off lengthy testimony about motives, whether presented by the prosecution or the defense because motive is not an element in first-degree murder cases.

FAMOUS CASES
CHARLES MANSON

Homicide cases typically draw abundant public attention. However, the cases that truly grip the public's horrified fascination are those of serial killers and mass murderers. Ted Bundy was a serial killer: He confessed to 30 kidnappings, rapes, and murders during the mid-1970s. Seung-Hui Cho was a mass murderer: He killed 32 people and wounded 25 others during a rampage on the Virginia Tech campus in 2007. Then there is Charles Manson, who is harder to classify but continues to unnerve even the most jaded law enforcement professionals more than four decades after his crime.

Manson was neither a serial killer nor a mass murderer by the truest definition of the terms. He led a quasi-commune in California, which he called the Manson Family. Manson believed an apocalyptic race war was imminent, something he termed "Helter Skelter" after the Beatles' song of the same name. To help ignite the race war, he orchestrated two sets of grisly murders on successive nights. Because of the structure and timing of his murders, Manson can most accurately be described as a cult or spree killer.

Charles Milles Manson was born in 1934 in Cincinnati, Ohio. The son of an unwed alcoholic mother, he spent his childhood bouncing between various relatives and in reform schools. He began stealing by the age of nine and drifted in and out of prison during his young adulthood, mostly for auto theft, burglary, and pimping. During one six-year stint in the early 1960s, Manson learned to play the steel guitar and came to believe he had a future in music. Upon his release in 1967, he headed to San Francisco, where, with his guitar and a supply of drugs, he began to draw a following during the famous "Summer of Love" in the Haight-Ashbury district.

At the end of summer, Manson and his group of eight or nine followers piled into a van and started traveling, eventually setting up their commune on the Spahn Movie Ranch, near Topanga Canyon in Los Angeles. There the group began to grow, and Manson began his fixation with Helter Skelter. Manson was a skilled manipulator, taking bits and pieces of different religions to form his own philosophy. With that philosophy and a steady supply of drugs, he convinced his followers that they were an elite group who would escape the impending Armageddon. He was the godlike leader, and his followers were slavish in their worship.

To set off Helter Skelter, on August 9, 1969, Manson directed four of his followers to go a house in the Benedict Canyon area of Los Angeles and destroy everyone in it. In a gruesome scene, his disciples shot and killed a young man outside the house, and then broke into the house and slashed and stabbed to death the four occupants. One of the victims was actress Sharon Tate, wife of actor Roman Polanski and eight months pregnant at the time. Another of the victims was stabbed 51 times. As the assailants left, they scrawled "pig" on the front door in Tate's blood.

The next night, Manson accompanied six of his followers to the home of Leno and Rosemary LaBianca. The LaBiancas were both killed by multiple stabs with a bayonet. One of the assailants carved the word "war" in Mr. LaBianca's abdomen.

Following several months of painstaking investigation, the crimes were finally linked to Manson and his tribe. The 1970 trial was a circus. Manson's women followed a carefully scripted plan to absolve Manson of the crimes during their testimony, a ploy their defense attorney derailed by resting without presenting a defense. Manson shaved his head and trimmed his beard into a fork, claiming that he was the devil. When Manson took the stand to testify in his defense, he rambled for an hour, saying, among other things, that "The music is telling the youth to rise up against the establishment. Why blame it on me? I didn't write the music."

Although Manson technically did not commit any of the murders, he and the other defendants were nevertheless convicted on all 27 counts against them, including murder and conspiracy. All the defendants received the death penalty, which was converted to life in prison when California outlawed the death penalty in 1972.

Charles Manson's charisma gave him the power to control people. They did what he directed them to do and were essentially an extension of him. His unbreakable influence over them allowed him to commit multiple first-degree murders without ever wielding a weapon.

D. CORPUS DELICTI

In the past, it was necessary to produce the victim's body in order to prove that a murder had occurred. The phrase *corpus delicti* was used to explain this requirement. However, almost all states have done away with the old common law rule that there must be a body in order to prosecute a defendant for murder. Given the wide variety of ways that clever defendants have used to dispose of bodies, it may be possible to never find a victim's body. Under the modern usage, **corpus delicti** no longer refers to the victim's body, but the body of evidence against the defendant. When we talk about the *corpus delicti* in modern parlance, we are really talking about two separate phenomena: the fact that the victim is dead and that someone else caused the death.[13]

Corpus delicti
"The body of the crime," proof that the victim is dead and that the defendant caused the death.

E. FELONY-MURDER DOCTRINE

There are times when the necessary elements for a first-degree murder are absent, but courts have decided that such a prosecution can continue anyway. Many states have enacted so-called "felony-murder" statutes. Suppose, for example, that during an armed robbery, the defendant's gun goes off and kills a victim. Under the

Corpus delicti no longer refers to the victim's body in a murder case; it refers to the fact that the victim has been killed and that the defendant is responsible for the victim's death.

---

[13] *State v. Wilson*, 2011-NMSC-001, 248 P.3d 315 (N.M. 2010).

traditional analysis, premeditation would seem to be lacking. There is no clear delineation that the prosecution can point to and say that the defendant considered killing the store clerk, even for a few moments, and then went through with the murder. However, because the defendant is committing another felony at the time of the killing, courts and statutes have adopted a doctrine that supplies that missing element. Using the Felony-Murder Doctrine, a prosecutor can charge a defendant with first-degree murder when the defendant commits a different felony and a victim dies. The reasoning is very simple: If not for the defendant's actions, the victim would not have died. In this situation, who should bear the burden — the victim and the victim's family or the defendant? The answer seems very clear.

Felony-Murder Doctrine
A statute that exists in most states which allows the state to prosecute a defendant for first-degree murder when he or she causes the death of a person during the commission of a felony.

Under the **Felony-Murder Doctrine**, the law supplies the specific intent to murder, where it normally would not be present. There is also an important public-policy component to the Felony-Murder Doctrine. When a defendant knows that he or she could be charged with first-degree murder if someone dies during the commission of another felony, the defendant is less likely to bring deadly weapons with him or her to carry out the crime. The Felony-Murder Doctrine is often invoked in cases where a defendant kidnaps a victim, sexually assaults her and during the assault, the victim dies.

When the defendant uses a deadly weapon to inflict injury on the victim, the law will presume that malice is present. It is not a defense for the defendant to claim that, although he used a deadly weapon, he did not have specific intent to kill, or in a prosecution for manslaughter, that he lacked malice. Under this definition, what actually qualifies as a deadly weapon? The answer is that almost anything can fall into that classification. The most common forms of deadly weapons are:

- Guns
- Knives
- Axes
- Clubs
- Swords

Other articles, not normally thought of as "deadly weapons" also can be considered under that category when they are used in a deadly manner. Under this definition, a walking cane, a pocket knife, even a rock could be classified as a deadly weapon.[14] The jury must determine whether or not a particular item constitutes a deadly weapon.

IV SECOND-DEGREE MURDER OR "MALICE MURDER"

Second-degree murder has the same elements of first-degree murder except for the element of premeditation. As such, the elements of a second-degree murder are:

---

[14] *State v. Jennings*, 333 N.C. 579, 430 S.E.2d 188 (1993).

FIGURE 4-7

The Rate of Criminal Victimization

- The rate of violent victimization increased 17%, from 19.3 victimizations per 1,000 persons age 12 or older in 2010 to 22.5 in 2011.
- There was no statistically significant change in the rate of serious violent victimization from 2010 to 2011.
- A 22% increase in the number of assaults accounted for all of the increase in violent crime.
- No measurable change was detected in the rate of intimate partner violence from 2010 to 2011.
- Increases in the rates of violent victimizations for whites, Hispanics, younger persons, and males accounted for the majority of the increase in violent crime.
- Residents in urban areas continued to experience the highest rates of total and serious violence.
- The rate of property crime increased 11%, from 125.4 per 1,000 households in 2010 to 138.7 in 2011.
- From 2010 to 2011, household burglary increased 14% from 25.8 to 29.4 per 1,000 households.

- Unlawful killing
- Of a human being by another
- With malice

There are many instances where the prosecution sets out to prove a first-degree murder case against a defendant and fails to prove that the defendant acted with premeditation. In such a situation, the state can ask for a **lesser-included offense**, including second-degree murder and manslaughter (see Figure 4-7).

Lesser-included offenses are really crimes that have identical elements except for one or two. In murder, the distinction is easy to make. There is only one element that separates first-degree murder from second-degree: premeditation. If a jury cannot convict a person on first-degree murder because they do not believe, beyond a reasonable doubt, that the defendant premeditated the murder, then prosecutors are allowed to request that the jurors convict the defendant of the lesser-included offense of second-degree murder. The defendant's attorney may also ask the jury to convict the defendant of some lesser-included offense. However, instead of asking for second-degree murder, the defense attorney may ask the jury to convict the defendant of manslaughter instead.

Lesser-included offense
A crime that has many of the same elements as a more serious crime, but lacks one or two of the elements of that serious crime.

MANSLAUGHTER

When we have a situation where a murder has occurred, but the elements do not match either first- or second-degree murder, then the crime must be manslaughter. In this way, manslaughter is a kind of catch-all crime. What makes a death manslaughter instead of first- or second-degree murder? Manslaughter is the crime of taking a human life, without justification, without malice aforethought, and without premeditation. The most common example of manslaughter is when two people get

Manslaughter
The killing of another human being, done without premeditation or malice, often in response to an overwhelming passion or provocation.

into an argument and one kills the other. If the state cannot show that the defendant considered killing the victim prior to the argument, then there is no premeditation and therefore no first-degree murder. If the state cannot show malice, either because the defendant did not express ill will or hatred against the defendant and there is no deadly weapon brought to the confrontation, the state will be unable to prove malice and therefore a prosecution for second-degree murder will not prevail. However, if the state can show that the defendant satisfied the following elements, then a prosecution for manslaughter will be successful:

- Unlawful killing
- Of a human by another
- In a sudden passion or by some provocation

VOLUNTARY MANSLAUGHTER

Provocation
Words or actions by the victim or another that incite anger or passion that cloud the defendant's judgment and the ability to reason and therefore prevent him from being able to form the necessary intent.

Voluntary manslaughter is the intentional killing of a human being by another without justification or legal excuse, and committed under the influence of some overwhelming passion, often the result of **provocation**. Because the defendant did not have premeditation or even malice, the defendant cannot be prosecuted under first-degree murder or second-degree murder. However, the defendant has caused the death of another person. The defendant may have acted on some irresistible impulse or been caught up in some intense emotion. The point is that the defendant did not or could not form the specific intent necessary to charge him with murder in the first degree.

Provocation. In order for a prosecution to lower the charge from first-degree murder to manslaughter, it must be shown that the provocation was so great that a reasonable person would have responded in the same way that the defendant did. In order to establish the legal basis for provocation, the defendant must show that he or she was so overwhelmed with passion that the defendant essentially lost control of his or her emotions. This is the type of killing that is commonly referred to as "crime of passion." It has also been incorrectly referred to as "temporary insanity." Although insanity is a perfectly legitimate legal defense, temporary insanity has more to do with heat of passion and a sudden overwhelming emotion that essentially unhinges a defendant. The provocation must be something that a reasonable person would consider to be provoking. Consider the next two scenarios.

SCENARIO 4-5

PROVOCATION? (PART ONE)

Wallace and another man are at a party. Both men have been drinking. At one point, the man says to Wallace, "I hear that your girlfriend is hot." Wallace grabs a knife and stabs the man to death. When he is charged with second-degree murder, Wallace claims that at best the crime should be voluntary manslaughter because of sudden overwhelming passion. Is he correct?

Answer: No. Provocation falls under a reasonable person standard. The victim's statement might just as easily have been a compliment as opposed to a derogatory remark. The man's statement does not rise to the level of provocation that was so personal as to render him temporarily unable to think clearly.

PROVOCATION? (PART TWO)

Teresa's ten-year-old son, Ray, has been missing for two weeks. The police have been unable to find him. One day, John knocks on her front door. When she opens the door, John says, "I killed Ray and it was fun. I buried him in the woods." Teresa grabs a knife and stabs John to death. The state decides to charge Teresa with second-degree murder. Teresa claims that at best her crime was voluntary manslaughter. Is she correct?

Answer: Yes. Most people would agree that such a statement would be considered extreme provocation. It would not even matter if John's statement were true or not. Given the surrounding circumstances, this is a clear case of voluntary manslaughter.

As we have seen, provocation can reduce a second-degree murder charge to voluntary manslaughter, but there is an important limitation on provocation as a defense. The provoking act must be close in time to the defendant's actions. If the defendant has sufficient time to cool off, provocation is no longer available as a legal defense.

Provocation involves some action that renders the defendant so over-wrought with passion that he essentially loses control of his emotions. This is usually referred to as the "heat of passion." The theory is that the defendant has been so overcome with some emotion that he is unable to reason clearly and is therefore unable to form the specific intent necessary to commit pre-meditated murder. However, this heat of passion must be closely connected in time to the actual killing. There can be no "cooling-off period" — that is, some period of time in which the defendant could have calmed down. The jury usually decides the question of whether or not there was a sufficient cool-ing-off period.

Provocation and the Cooling-Off Period. It is the jury's duty to decide whether or not the defendant was provoked sufficiently to reduce a charge from second-degree murder to voluntary manslaughter. One of the considerations that the jury must take into account is whether or not the defendant had sufficient cooling-off time between the provoking events and the subsequent killing. The idea behind crime of passion is that, in the moment, the defendant becomes so overwhelmed that he or she is incapable of rational thought. However, this period of time is very brief. The longer the time period between the provoking act and the killing, the less likely that the defendant can claim provocation.

The question for the jury often is: "Did the defendant have enough time to cool off?" If the defendant had sufficient time to cool off and regain his or her compo-sure, then killed the victim, the crime may be second-degree or even first-degree murder. The question of the cooling-off period is judged not from what the defendant claims, but what a reasonable person would do. Courts have been reluctant to set a specific time period in which all persons should be capable of cooling off. Instead, the courts look at the situation on a case-by-case basis. In most states, any period of cooling off, no matter how brief, is enough. It is impossible to create a bright-line test for what always constitutes a cooling-off period. Each case must be taken on its own merits. It therefore becomes a jury question as to whether or not the facts support the defendant's contention that he was acting under a sudden, overwhelming passion or the state's contention that the defendant had sufficient time to cool off and is therefore guilty of premeditated murder.

VI INVOLUNTARY MANSLAUGHTER

When it comes to a discussion of involuntary manslaughter, the issue of intent, particularly special intent, disappears from the calculation. Essentially, involuntary manslaughter is the unintentional killing of another human being. It can be accomplished during the commission of some unlawful act (not a felony and not something that would normally endanger life — otherwise, that would fall under the felony-murder doctrine). It can also be caused by the actions on the part of the defendant that show a disregard for the health and safety of others, often referred to as the "wanton or reckless conduct" requirement. There is no malice requirement in the crime of involuntary manslaughter.[15] The element of "recklessness" or "wanton disregard" can be satisfied by showing that the defendant was aware of his or her actions but simply chose to disregard the risk that they posed to others. To prove involuntary manslaughter, prosecutors are not required to show that a person intended to kill; it is enough to show the defendant acted with wanton negligence.[16] Involuntary manslaughter convictions can also be had when the defendant suffers from some form of mental illness that prevents him from being able to form specific intent to kill.[17] Voluntary intoxication, however, does not qualify as a form of mental illness. Consider Scenario 4-7.

| SCENARIO 4-7 | NEGLIGENT HOMICIDE? |

Daniel is at home looking after his two-year-old son. The boy has a medical condition that requires an oxygen tube. Daniel changes out the boy's oxygen bottles twice a day. However, one day, he decides to get drunk and watch a football game. During the game, he passes out. As a result, he does not change out his son's oxygen bottle and the child dies. Can he be charged with involuntary manslaughter?

Answer: Yes. Because Daniel chose to become intoxicated to the point where he lost consciousness, he acted with reckless disregard for the safety of his child.[18]

---

[15] *State v. Fritsch*, 351 N.C. 373, 526 S.E.2d 451 (2000).
[16] *State v. Kaley*, 343 N.C. 107, 468 S.E.2d 44 (1996).
[17] *People v. Rogers*, 39 Cal. 4th 826, 48 Cal. Rptr. 3d 1, 141 P.3d 135 (2006), cert. denied 127 S. Ct. 2129 (2007).
[18] *People v. Ochoa*, 19 Cal. 4th 353, 79 Cal. Rpter. 2d 408, 966 P.2d 442 (1998).

When the facts do not suggest that there was any intent to do harm, let alone kill, the necessary elements to support premeditated murder or manslaughter are missing.

Just as with murder, manslaughter may be separated into various degrees. Not all states follow this pattern, but in the ones that do, voluntary manslaughter is considered manslaughter in the first degree, and involuntary manslaughter is considered manslaughter in the second degree. There are even some states that have the crime of manslaughter in the third degree, usually reserved for crimes involving homicides that occur as the result of traffic accidents. In the case of manslaughter in the third degree or vehicular homicide, which it is sometimes referred to in other states, the defendant would only be charged if he or she was violating some traffic law and caused the death of another. Obviously, if the defendant were committing some felony and caused the death of another, the Felony-Murder Doctrine would push the crime back up to murder in the first degree.

If a crime does not satisfy the elements of either voluntary manslaughter or involuntary manslaughter, then it is either a form of justifiable homicide or no crime at all. Justifiable homicide would encompass self-defense, which we will discuss in Chapter 17.

Some states label involuntary manslaughter as "negligent homicide."

VII SUICIDE AND ATTEMPTED SUICIDE

Suicide is the killing of oneself. Historically, suicide was frowned upon and those who had committed the act were not given burial within hallowed grounds or were buried under highways or highway markers. Suicide carried with it both a religious and ethical stigma. Many would argue that those who attempt to commit suicide still face social stigma. In the past, the property of the suicide victim was forfeited to the state. Some states still list suicide as a felony, while others list it as a misdemeanor, and still others do not make it a crime at all. New York, for example, does not consider suicide illegal.[19] However, in cases where a person attempts to commit suicide, the state can take action to intercede in the person's life and require him or her to obtain psychological counseling.

Even in situations where suicide is no longer considered a crime, attempted suicide can be. However, the most common course to take in the case of prosecuting someone for attempted suicide is to use that as a basis to have the person committed to some mental facility to receive care, rather than putting the person in the prison system.[20]

ASSISTED SUICIDE

Although it may not be a crime to kill oneself in many jurisdictions, it is not true for people who help other people commit suicide. **Assisted suicide** statutes have been

Assisted suicide
The crime of actively participating and abetting a person to kill himself or herself.

---

[19] *Stiles v. Clifton Springs Sanitarium Co.*, 74 F. Supp. 907 (W.D.N.Y 1947).
[20] *State ex rel. Swann v. Pack*, 527 S.W.2d 99 (1975).

enacted in most states and specifically draw out the actions that a person can take that will result in being charged with helping another person to die.

Regarding assisted suicide, the law makes a distinction between those who encourage another to commit suicide and those who actively participate in causing the death of another. In the first instance, a person who aids, assists, or even encourages a person to commit suicide, but does not actually perform any act that helps to cause the death, cannot be convicted for murder or assisted suicide, although this definition does vary from state to state.[21] On the other hand, a person who actively participates in helping another person to commit suicide can be found guilty. Perhaps the most famous proponent of actively participating in helping others to commit suicide was Dr. Jack Kevorkian. Kevorkian, who was stripped of his medical license, assisted numerous people to commit suicide. He was prosecuted on several occasions but was almost always found not guilty. However, in his final prosecution, he chose to represent himself after the law in the state of Michigan had been changed to redefine the crime of assisted suicide. Kevorkian was found guilty and sentenced to prison. He has since died.[22]

Many jurisdictions draw a distinction between assisting the person to commit suicide and withdrawing life-sustaining medical treatment. In fact, many states allow patients the option of selecting not to be revived should they slip into a coma or develop other medical problems that might facilitate their deaths. Medical personnel cannot be prosecuted for assisted suicide in such a scenario. Patients can also create living wills in which they specifically dictate that they do not wish to be kept alive in a persistent vegetative state following some accident or disease. In these instances, the executor or the person with power of attorney for the patient has a clear directive to allow the patient to die naturally. Some states have ruled that advocating suicide is not a crime and is actually protected under the First Amendment to the U.S. Constitution.[23]

If a person requests another to kill him, then the person who does the killing can be prosecuted for murder, not assisted suicide. The reason for this is that suicide is an action taken by the individual, while murder is carried out by another.[25] See Scenario 4-8.

Sidebar

It is not assisted suicide to put a defendant to death for capital murder when the defendant wishes to die.[24]

| SCENARIO 4-8 |

MURDER-SUICIDE PACT

John and his wife, Maria, entered into a suicide pact. Maria wanted to die first, so John put a rifle to her head and pulled the trigger, ending her life. However, when it was John's turn, he found that he could not commit the act. What crime will the state bring against John?

Answer: The most likely charge is second-degree murder. Maria did not kill herself; John killed her. Because John played an active role in the death, his actions satisfy the elements of second-degree murder. It would not qualify as assisted suicide, because although Maria apparently wanted to die, she took no action. The only actions were those of John. (It is

---

[21] *Grace v. State*, 44 Tex. Crim. 193, 69 S.W. 529 (1902).
[22] *People v. Kevorkian*, 447 Mich. 436, 527 N.W.2d 714 (1994).
[23] *Final Exit Network, Inc. v. State*, 290 Ga. 508, 722 S.E.2d 722 (2012).
[24] *Colwell v. State*, 273 Ga. 634, 544 S.E.2d 120 (2001).
[25] *State v. Goulding*, 2011 SD 25, 799 N.W.2d 412 (2011).

interesting to note, though, that some states might take a different view of these facts and charge John with assisted suicide, while others might also opt for first-degree murder. The various outcomes are dictated from the way that the statutes are worded.)

KLINECT v. STATE
269 Ga. 570, 501 S.E.2d 810 (1998)

CASE EXCERPT

HINES, Justice.

Christine Lynn Klinect appeals her conviction on one count of malice murder. For the reasons which follow, we affirm.

Evidence showed that the victim, Lewis Kalo, was Klinect's former husband and the father of Klinect's daughter. At the time of the murder, Kalo resided with Klinect, her common-law husband Mark Wilson, and Klinect's children, including the daughter by Kalo. On the evening of November 13, 1993, Kalo and a co-worker, Dennis Simpson, attended a party and returned to Klinect's house around midnight. Kalo remained asleep in the passenger seat of Simpson's vehicle while Simpson went behind the house where Klinect and Wilson had built a bonfire. Simpson told Klinect and Wilson that Kalo supplied the police with the information that had resulted in Klinect and Wilson being arrested on a marijuana charge a few days earlier. Simpson also told Klinect and Wilson that when he and Kalo were sharing a motel room and Klinect's daughter was present, he saw Kalo masturbate while lying next to the sleeping child.

Shortly thereafter, Klinect left the fire and went into the house, where she retrieved a pair of handcuffs. She then handcuffed the left wrist of the sleeping Kalo to the steering wheel of Simpson's car. Kalo awoke and began arguing with Klinect. Wilson and Simpson tried unsuccessfully to remove the handcuffs while Kalo and Klinect were yelling at one another.

According to Simpson's testimony, Klinect stated she would "shut Kalo up once and for all" and wrapped duct tape around Kalo's head and face, completely covering his mouth and nose; Kalo's body jerked for approximately a minute before he died. Simpson then cut the handcuff chain and he and Wilson took Kalo's body to a wooded area where Wilson removed Kalo's clothes and the tape around Kalo's head, and left the body. Simpson and Wilson returned to Klinect's home, where Wilson burned his own clothes, Kalo's clothes, and the tape. Klinect declared that they should all have a consistent story; that when Kalo and Simpson returned from the party they began to walk behind the house and a pickup truck turned into the driveway, Kalo went back to the truck, spoke with the driver, got into the truck stating he would be back shortly, and was not seen again. Simpson met with Klinect and Wilson a few days later, and she repeated the version of events she wanted them to report. Simpson left town shortly thereafter.

Three days after the murder, Klinect telephoned police and filed a report that Kalo was missing. She reported that Kalo had left the house with Simpson around 10:00 p.m. on November 13 to go to a party, and had not been seen since. After filing the report, Klinect repeatedly telephoned Kalo's pager and searched a mobile home where Kalo had resided, passing on information she found there to the police. When Kalo's body was discovered after approximately two months, Klinect told police that Simpson had returned from the party at about 2:00 a.m. and told her and Wilson that Kalo had left the party with someone in a black pickup truck.

Klinect and Wilson testified that Klinect handcuffed Kalo to the steering wheel as a joke and that Simpson then cut Kalo on the head and wrapped his head in tape. They testified that they did not inform the police that Simpson had killed Kalo because Simpson had threatened them and Klinect's children.

Klinect contends the evidence was insufficient to sustain the verdict because the only evidence showing her guilt is Simpson's testimony and a defendant cannot be convicted on the uncorroborated testimony of an accomplice. FN2 See OCGA § 24-4-8. The corroborating evidence connecting a defendant to a crime may consist entirely of circumstantial evidence, and evidence of the defendant's conduct before and after the crime was committed may give rise to an inference that the defendant participated in the crime. Whether the corroborating evidence is sufficient is a matter for the jury, and even slight evidence of corroboration connecting an accused to a crime is legally sufficient.

FN2. Simpson was also indicted for Kalo's murder. He was later tried and acquitted.

By her own testimony, Klinect actively deceived police, filing a false report that Kalo was missing and participating in efforts to locate him which she knew to be futile. This, coupled with her testimony that she handcuffed Kalo to the steering wheel, was sufficient corroboration. The jury was authorized to accept Simpson's testimony, and the evidence authorized the jury to find beyond a reasonable doubt that Klinect was guilty of malice murder.

At the time of his testimony in Klinect's trial, Simpson had not been tried for his alleged role in the crime. The State was under an obligation to reveal any agreement it had with Simpson concerning future prosecution, and failure to reveal such an agreement would constitute a due process violation.

At a pretrial hearing, and again before the jury, Simpson testified there was no agreement and he had received no promise of leniency or incentive to testify. After hearing testimony and reviewing evidence on the motion for new trial, the court ruled that no agreement had been formed. Although Klinect points to an affidavit of Simpson's attorney that arguably suggests the existence of an informal agreement, the attorney later clarified in a letter that no agreement existed, and testified at the hearing that no agreement existed. Additionally, the district attorney testified that no agreement was discussed before the completion of Klinect's trial, and that he made it clear to Simpson's counsel that no agreement would be discussed before that time. That Simpson or his counsel held a hope that testifying in Klinect's trial would benefit him later does not show an agreement. The trial court's finding was authorized, and there was no due process violation.

Klinect sought to question a police investigator about what Simpson's girlfriend told the investigator regarding an altercation between Simpson and a man named Triplett, and what the investigator learned about the altercation through other means. She urges that questioning of the investigator would tend to show that Simpson had a violent disposition, supporting her contention that he killed Kalo, although she made no proffer of the officer's expected testimony. Unlike the situation in *Butler v. State*, 254 Ga. 637, 332 S.E.2d 654 (1985), where it was error to refuse admission of evidence of a violent history between the person the defendant contended committed the murder and the victim, Klinect did not seek to introduce any evidence that Simpson had a violent history with Kalo, only that he had a generally violent disposition. Klinect was allowed to elicit testimony from the police investigator, Simpson, and Simpson's girlfriend about an altercation between Simpson and his girlfriend a month before the murder, for which Simpson was jailed.

Klinect contends that curtailing her cross-examination of the investigator nonetheless prevented her from showing that Simpson was the true murderer. Certainly a defendant is entitled to introduce relevant and admissible testimony tending to show that another person committed the crime for which the defendant is tried. However, the proffered evidence must raise a reasonable inference of the defendant's innocence, and must directly connect the other person with the corpus delicti, or show that the other person has recently committed a crime of the same or similar nature. Assuming that the desired cross-examination of the investigator would reveal that Simpson had an altercation with a man named Triplett, this testimony would reflect only on Simpson's character. It would not show any motive Simpson had to kill Kalo. Nor would it connect Simpson to the corpus delicti or show that he had committed a similar crime by similar methods.

The court's ruling did not violate Klinect's Sixth Amendment right to confrontation or her statutory right to cross-examine witnesses. The defense is entitled to a thorough cross-examination, but the scope of cross-examination is within the sound discretion of the trial court, and under the facts of this case, there was no abuse of discretion.

The court admitted into evidence photographs of Kalo's body in the condition in which it was found; it was partially decomposed and the skull was essentially skeletonized. Photographs showing the condition and location of the victim's body are admissible where alterations to the body are due to the combined forces of the murderer and the elements.

Nor was it error to admit a photograph of Kalo while he was alive. Although the better practice is to have the photograph identified by one not a close family member, Ledford v. State, 264 Ga. 60, 66(14), 439 S.E.2d 917 (1994), Klinect did not object that the identification of the photograph was made by Kalo's father rather than by a nonrelated witness. Under these circumstances, there was no error.

On cross-examination, the State questioned Klinect about whether she ever called the police to report the crime, and during closing argument commented on her failure to do so. Klinect contends this violated her right to pre-arrest silence. However, she did not object or move for a mistrial and cannot raise the issue for the first time on appeal. Further, the State's cross-examination of Klinect, and its comments concerning her filing a false missing persons report and her failure to tell police investigators that Simpson had killed Kalo, occurred after Klinect had testified on direct examination that she had taken those actions, and why she had done so.

It was not error to allow the admission of testimony to the effect that Klinect and Wilson were arrested on a marijuana charge a few days before the murder. This evidence was relevant because the State contended that Klinect's motive for the murder was her belief that Kalo had informed police about her drug activities, resulting in her arrest, and that the pending charges raised the possibility that Kalo would gain custody of Klinect's daughter, who Klinect feared Kalo might molest. This evidence of motive was admissible even though it incidentally put Klinect's character in issue.

Nor was it error to admit Simpson's testimony that he had overheard Kalo tell another person at the party that, because of Klinect's arrest, Kalo might gain custody of his daughter. Testimony is considered hearsay only if the declarant's out-of-court statement is admitted to prove the truth of the statement. Simpson testified that after he told Klinect of Kalo's statement, and told her of the prior incident concerning her daughter, Klinect murdered Kalo, stating that Kalo "won't snitch or child molest nobody else." Kalo's former statement was admitted to show the motive for the murder, not to prove that Klinect actually had been arrested, or that Kalo actually would gain custody.

It was not error to charge the jury on the law of parties to a crime pursuant to OCGA § 16–2–20. Klinect's own testimony was that she handcuffed Kalo to the steering wheel, Simpson killed Kalo, and she then participated in efforts to conceal the crime. This authorized a charge on parties to a crime.

Lastly, the court did not err in failing to charge the jury on the law of accessory after the fact. Klinect was not indicted for the separate crime of obstruction of justice. See OCGA § 16–10–24; Jones v. State, 250 Ga. 11, 13, 295 S.E.2d 71 (1982). She did not submit a written request to charge on accessory after the fact or obstruction of justice, but contends such a charge should nonetheless have been given, citing Tarvestad v. State, 261 Ga. 605, 409 S.E.2d 513 (1991). Tarvestad held that a defendant's sole defense must be charged even when no written request is made. In addition to the court's charge on parties to a crime, the court instructed that the defendant's mere presence at the scene of the crime, without participation in the crime, would not authorize a conviction, and that mere association with one who committed the crime, without participation in the crime, would not authorize a conviction. The court also charged that to convict, the jury would have to find that the State proved beyond a reasonable doubt that Klinect knew the crime of murder was being committed and knowingly assisted in some way, and that if the jury did not so find, its duty was to acquit. The charge as a whole fairly presented the issues, including Klinect's theory that she was only an accessory after the fact.

Judgment affirmed.

CASE QUESTIONS

1 What was the charge brought against the defendant in this case?
2 How did the state contend that the defendant committed the crime?
3 Did Simpson enter into any agreement with the state before he testified?
4 What was the court's finding concerning the defendant's contention about Simpson's interaction with a man named Triplett and the *corpus delicti* in the case?
5 Was it error for the prosecutor to comment on the fact that the defendant and her boyfriend had been arrested a week before on a drug charge?

CHAPTER SUMMARY

In this chapter, we have seen that the primary elements of a criminal action involve criminal intent and a corresponding criminal action. These two terms are known by their Latin names as *mens rea* and *actus reus*. Without these two elements, in almost all cases, the state is not permitted to prosecute a defendant. However, there are a few crimes in which the *mens rea* requirement has been removed. In these prosecutions, the state need only prove that the defendant committed an action without regard to the defendant's criminal intent. The requirement of proving criminal intent is further broken down into two subcategories. General intent refers to the fact that the defendant acted knowingly and voluntarily. The vast majority of crimes simply require a proof that the defendant had general intent at the time that he committed the offense. In a small but significant group of criminal infractions, the state is required not only to prove that the defendant acted knowingly and voluntarily, but that the defendant acted with the intent to commit a specific type of crime. Specific intent crimes include murder, rape, and others. In these prosecutions, the prosecutor must meet a higher standard as these crimes were traditionally punishable by death and are still considered to be the most serious crimes committed.

The crime of murder is divided into subcategories based on the severity of the crime. The most severely punished form of homicide is first-degree murder. That crime requires that the prosecution prove the defendant unlawfully caused the death of another human being with malice and premeditation. First-degree murder can be punishable by death. Other forms of murder include second-degree murder, which lacks the element of premeditation, and voluntary manslaughter, which often lacks the element of malice. Some states have also enacted crimes such as involuntary manslaughter or negligent homicide that punish a defendant for causing the death of another person but without the specific intent to kill.

Finally, although most states no longer criminalize suicide, most states have statutes that do make it illegal to assist someone else in committing suicide.

KEY TERMS

Homicide	Strict liability offense	Felony-Murder Doctrine
Murder	Malice	Lesser-included offense
General intent	Premeditation	Manslaughter
Specific intent	Motive	Provocation
Transferred intent	*Corpus delicti*	Assisted suicide

REVIEW QUESTIONS

1 What is *mens rea* and how does it differ from *actus reus*?
2 What is the definition of homicide?
3 How did the terms homicide and murder differ from one another?
4 Provide three examples of crimes where the federal authorities would take precedence in a murder investigation.
5 What is the difference between general intent and specific intent?
6 Are there crimes in which mens rea is not required? If so, what are they?
7 Why do some crimes require specific intent while the vast majority do not?
8 What is the doctrine of transferred intent?
9 What is a strict liability offense?
10 Provide some examples of strict liability offenses.
11 What is premeditation?
12 Explain the system that came up with "degrees" of murder.
13 What are the elements of first-degree murder?
14 How do courts determine exactly where a defendant should be prosecuted for murder?
15 Is it murder to kill a fetus?
16 What is malice?
17 Some states have expanded the definition of first-degree murder. Provide some examples.
18 What role does motive play in a murder prosecution?
19 Why is Charles Manson infamous?
20 What is corpus delicti?
21 Explain the Felony-Murder Doctrine.
22 Define the elements of second-degree murder.
23 Explain the difference between voluntary manslaughter and involuntary manslaughter.
24 What is provocation, and why is it important in a manslaughter prosecution?
25 What is the crime of assisted suicide?

WEB SURFING

1 Find your state's statutes online and look up the definition for first- and second-degree murder. How do your statutory definitions compare with those in the text?
2 Does your state recognize voluntary and involuntary manslaughter, or does it have some other scheme to refer to these crimes?
3 Is assisted suicide illegal in your state? Find your online statutes and see if you can discover the answer.

QUESTIONS FOR ANALYSIS

1 Should suicide be made legal in all states? Explain your answer.
2 If a person wishes to commit suicide and there is someone who is prepared to assist, why should that person be prosecuted for assisted suicide?
3 Should strict-liability crime be expanded into other areas?
4 Some states, like Texas, have expanded the definition of first-degree murder. Should other states follow suit? Explain.
5 Should a defendant be allowed to claim "temporary insanity" in the face of sudden provocation to relieve them of all guilt in a killing? Why or why not?

HYPOTHETICALS

1 Terry, a police officer, is home one evening cleaning his service pistol as he sits in the kitchen. He does this activity every week at the same time and in the same location. The gun goes off and the bullet strikes Terry's wife, Megan, in the head killing her instantly. When other officers arrive, Terry claims that it was an accident. What crime, if any, do you believe Terry should be charged with?

2 Using the same facts as above, consider the following additional information: Two days after Megan's death, a woman comes forward and claims that she has been having an affair with Terry for over two years. She says that Terry wanted his wife to die. She tells the authorities that Terry discussed his plans with her to kill his wife and pretend that it was an accident. In addition to her testimony, the woman reveals that Terry enhanced the life insurance payout on his wife from $100,000 to $500,000 two months before her death. She also has emails from Terry where he discusses how much better their life would be if Terry's wife, "weren't around." You are the prosecutor assigned to this case. Besides what you know from the first hypothetical, there is no additional forensic evidence. The coroner can only state that the gun went off and that the bullet killed Megan. No expert can give you an opinion about the circumstances surrounding the gun's discharge. No other witness has claimed that Terry and his wife were having any problems. The woman who makes these claims appears to be completely reliable, but she will not "wear a wire" to confront Terry. She has passed a lie detector test. What charge do you bring against Terry, if any?

3 Using the same facts from hypothetical number 1 above, you, as the prosecutor, learn that Megan was dying of pancreatic cancer. It is a very painful form of cancer and the chances of her surviving the disease are less than 4 percent. Several days after her death, Terry admits to other police officers that his wife wanted to kill herself, but lacked the courage. He tells the officers that Megan pleaded with him to kill her. He states, "I helped her to end the suffering." What crime, if any, do you bring against Terry?

Crimes Against
Persons

5

Chapter Objectives

- Compare and contrast assault and battery
- Describe the elements of aggravated assault
- Explain what constitutes a deadly weapon
- Define the basic elements of kidnapping
- Demonstrate understanding of cyberstalking and bullying

I. ASSAULT AND RELATED OFFENSES

This chapter focuses on crimes against persons short of murder. It will first address the concepts of assault and battery and show how a certain amount of confusion has crept into the use of these terms.

A. ASSAULT

An **assault** occurs when a defendant causes a victim:

 Fear or apprehension
 Of a harmful or offensive contact

Under the strict definition of assault, there is no contact between the defendant and the victim. Touching is an element of the crime of **battery**, not assault.

Although the terms are often used interchangeably, assault and battery are actually two different legal concepts. In its strictest definition, assault does not involve touching, merely the fear or apprehension of harmful or offensive contact. Battery, on the other hand, involves actual harmful or offensive touching. The reason that the two are so closely linked is that a person who is charged with battery is often charged with assault because the defendant may swing and miss the victim

Assault
The apprehension or fear of harmful or offensive touching.

Battery
Harmful or offensive touching without consent.

Apprehension
Dread of an upcoming and an unwanted event.

on one occasion and then swing and make contact on the second occasion.[1] At its simplest, assault demonstrates the defendant's intent to inflict injury or harmful or offensive contact on the victim. The assault must be immediate. The victim must feel apprehension or fear at the moment. There is no such thing as future assault.[2]

FEAR OR APPREHENSION

In an assault, actual fear is not a requirement. The victim must simply have **apprehension** of the contact. Since awareness is a requirement, a victim cannot be assaulted if he or she is unconscious. Unconscious people cannot be fearful or apprehensive, so a simple assault cannot be committed against them. As you can see, this runs counter to the way that the term assault is used in everyday parlance. Here the term is used in its correct, legal sense, not the way that it is misused in the media.

In many ways, assault is an attempted battery. Attempt and related offenses were discussed earlier in this text. If the crime of assault is viewed as an attempted battery, how is attempted assault classified? In some jurisdictions — Connecticut, Indiana, and Kansas to name a few — there is no such crime.[3]

Assault by Words Alone? Can a person commit the crime of assault simply through words? The answer in most jurisdictions is no. That may come as a surprise to individuals who believe that when someone issues a threat to another person, that is a criminal action. However, the words by themselves will not be enough to initiate a prosecution.[4] The simple answer is that people often say things that they regret later, and prosecuting people based simply on what they say would bring about a great many more prosecutions. In general, a threat is not a crime. However, that can change by adding additional facts. For instance, a threat followed by an action that appears to put the threat into play will qualify as an assault. In most situations, words must be followed by some type of action before they qualify as a crime. There are many exceptions to this general rule. As we will see in later chapters, when a person uses an electronic device to forward a threat, it may be criminal violation. It is also true that certain individuals receive greater protection under the law. Sending a threatening letter to the president of the United States may be considered a federal offense.

HARMFUL OR OFFENSIVE CONTACT

Assault involves the fear or apprehension of contact. However, the intended contact must be harmful or offensive. There is no requirement that the intended victim would be seriously injured had the contact occurred. Because people have different

---

[1] *Saucier ex rel. Mallory v. McDonald's Restaurants of Mont., Inc.*, 2008 MT 63, 342 Mont. 29, 179 P.3d 481 (2008).

[2] *City of Seattle v. Allen*, 80 Wash. App. 824, 911 P.2d 1354 (Div. 1 1996).

[3] *State v. Scheck*, 106 Conn. App. 81, 940 A.2d 871 (2008), certification denied, 286 Conn. 918, 945 A.2d 979 (2008); *Ott v. State*, 648 N.E.2d 671 (Ind. Ct. App. 1995); *Spencer v. State*, 264 Kan. 4, 954 P.2d 1088 (1998)

[4] *State v. Deprow*, 937 S.W.2d 748 (Mo. Ct. App. S.D. 1997); *State v. Sanders*, 92 S.C. 427, 75 S.E. 702 (1912).

standards about what constitutes "offensive" contact, we do not judge the word by the subjective view of the victim. Instead, the law uses the reasonable person standard to determine if an intended contact was offensive. Under this definition, if a hypothetical reasonable person would believe that the contact was offensive, then the state has met its burden, despite the fact that the specific victim believes that any contact is offensive.

Conditional Assault. Instead of a simple situation where the defendant places the victim in fear of an immediate harmful or offensive contact, in **conditional assault** the defendant instead places a condition on the violence. A common formulation is, "Give me all of your money, or I will hit you in the head with this weapon." Under these terms, the normal definition of assault might not be sufficient to bring a prosecution against the defendant. However, in states that recognize conditional assault, inserting the condition that the defendant will harm the victim if the victim fails to take a certain action is enough to prosecute for assault. Many, but not all, jurisdictions recognize the crime of conditional assault.

Conditional assault
A form of assault in which the defendant places a condition on the violence.

Apparent Ability to Carry Out the Threat. Inherent in the definition of assault is that the defendant has the **apparent ability** to carry out whatever threat he or she makes. If the defendant lacks that apparent or present ability, then there may be no crime. Both assaults and batteries must be coupled with the immediate and apparent ability to carry through on the threatened action.[5] Consider Scenario 5-1.

Apparent ability
The defendant's obvious capability of carrying through on a threat.

THEO'S AFTER-SCHOOL THREAT

SCENARIO 5-1

Theo is attending a class on criminal law and procedure. When the class ends, Danny stops Theo in the hallway and says, "I'm going to beat you up at 3:00 p.m." It is now 10:00 a.m. Has Danny committed the crime of assault?

Answer: No. Setting aside for the moment whether or not Danny's words are enough to constitute the crime of assault, there is an essential element missing: the immediate threat of action. Although Theo may be uncomfortable while waiting for three o'clock, he cannot accuse Danny of assault.

THEO'S THREE O'CLOCK DEADLINE

SCENARIO 5-2

Theo walks out to the parking lot to get to his car, and Danny is standing next to it. Danny balls his fists and says, "Remember what I said to you this morning? Now you're going to pay." Danny takes a swing at Theo and misses. Has Danny committed the crime of assault?

Answer: Yes. Danny has placed Theo in fear of an immediate harmful or offensive contact. All of the elements of simple assault have been established. If Danny subsequently lands a punch, then Danny will also be guilty of battery.

---

[5] *McVay v. Delchamps, Inc.*, 707 So. 2d 90 (La. Ct. App. 5th Cir. 1998).

SCENARIO 5-3

THE HOLDING CELL THREAT

Keisha is an Assistant District Attorney. While on a short recess, she walks into the holding cell area behind the courtroom to get a drink of water. There are several inmates inside the cell. One of them says, "I'm going to punch you in the nose, Ms. Prosecutor." Can Keisha seek a warrant against the inmate for assault?

Answer: No. The inmate lacks the apparent ability to carry out the threat. Because the inmate is behind bars and is unable to reach Keisha, there is no way that he can put his threat into action. Unless Keisha is protected by a statute that makes threatening her a separate crime, no prosecution will result.[6]

B. SIMPLE BATTERY

When the law classifies a crime as "simple," such as "simple battery," it usually means the lowest and least threatening form of the crime. **Simple assault** is the crime of putting a person in fear or apprehension of a harmful or offensive touching. **Simple battery** is the lowest form of battery and consists of the intentional touching of another that is either harmful or offensive. Earlier, assault was listed as an attempted battery. From that vantage point, battery is an assault that involves touching.

UNLAWFUL VS. LAWFUL TOUCHING

Not every touch is a battery, because not all touches are harmful or offensive. Just as with assault, battery refers to the act of touching as seen from the reasonable person standard. There may be individuals who think that any type of touch is objectionable. For such a person, being bumped into while standing in a crowd would constitute a battery. Fortunately, the law does not recognize such actions as the crime of battery. Instead, the law focuses on the nature of the touch. A person who jostles against you in the crowd has not committed battery for two reasons: 1) the touching was accidental, therefore without *mens rea*, and 2) the touch was neither harmful nor offensive. However, change the facts slightly, and the outcome is completely different. The person in the crowd deliberately sets out to touch you by jabbing a finger in your eye. Here, we have both *mens rea* and a harmful touching. The man has committed battery. In another situation, the person in the crowd intentionally touches another person in an inappropriate place. A battery has also occurred.

There are also individuals who receive protection under the law from being prosecuted for battery even when the touching is harmful or offensive. Police officers, for example, often must subdue suspects. Obviously, allowing the suspect to bring a charge of battery against a police officer for doing his or her duty would not make sense. (A police officer could be charged with battery if he or she used

---

Sidebar

Assault can be defined as the offer of violence, coupled with the contemporaneous apparent ability to carry through on the threat.[7]

Simple assault
The crime of putting a person in fear or apprehension of a harmful or offensive touching.

Simple battery
The intentional touching of another that is either harmful or offensive.

---

[6] *Nkop v. U.S.*, 945 A.2d 617 (D.C. 2008).
[7] *In re T.Y.B.*, 288 Ga. App. 610, 654 S.E.2d 688 (2007).

excessive force in the arrest, but that issue will be addressed in Chapter 13.) Doctors who must care for seriously injured or ill individuals often must touch their patients in areas that most would consider private or inappropriate. They are also immune from being charged with battery for carrying out normal medical procedures.

Finally, a touching that might ordinarily qualify as harmful or offensive could be ruled lawful when the victim consents to the touching. Consent is discussed in the next section.

HARMFUL OR OFFENSIVE TOUCHING

In construing what makes touching a battery, the courts usually require that the touching be done in anger or done in a rude or resentful manner. Battery does not require injury. As long as the contact is harmful or offensive, the elements of battery are satisfied, assuming that the defendant acted with intent.[8]

Using Objects to Touch. While a battery can be committed by a defendant who reaches out and offensively touches a victim with his hands, it is also possible to use objects to touch. A person can commit the offense of battery by using some device, other than his or her own hands, to effect harmful or offensive touching. Objects that are held by a defendant or thrown by him are considered to be extensions of the defendant's body and thus justify a charge of battery. As long as the state can prove that the defendant was the source of the touching, a prosecution for battery can be successful.[9] Consider Scenario 5-4.

THE POKING STICK

SCENARIO 5-4

John sees a man lying asleep on the beach. He takes a long stick and puts it in the man's ear, causing the man to cry out in pain. Has John committed a battery?

Answer: Yes. The fact that John did not touch the man with John's own hands is irrelevant. John used the stick to inflict harmful contact and therefore is just as guilty of the crime of battery as if he had used his own hands.

THE ROCK

SCENARIO 5-5

John is in his backyard one day and sees his neighbor planting some roses in the next yard. He grabs a rock and throws it at the neighbor, striking the neighbor on the back of the head. Has John committed a battery?

Answer: Yes. Under the same theory as we saw in the previous scenario, it was John who put the events into motion that resulted in harmful contact to the victim. Because of this, John is guilty of battery.

---

[8] *Tower Ins. Co. of New York v. Old Northern Blvd. Restaurant Corp.*, 245 A.D.2d 241, 666 N.Y.S.2d 636 (1st Dep't 1997)
[9] *Friedrich v. Adesman*, 146 Or. App. 624, 934 P.2d 587 (1997).

In many jurisdictions, the "touching" element of battery can be satisfied by any type of physical contact, no matter how minimal. However, even a slight touching must be harmful or offensive. Consider Scenario 5-6.

SCENARIO 5-6	## THE ALZHEIMER'S PATIENT

Maria is caring for an elderly gentleman who is suffering from Alzheimer's disease. Today, when Maria greeted her patient, he mistook her for his wife. He touched her in an inappropriate place but barely made contact. Has the patient committed a battery?

Answer: Assuming that the patient's Alzheimer's disease is not progressed to the point where he is incapable of forming intent, then the answer is yes.

Some jurisdictions actually require proof of bodily injury or physical harm before the crime of battery is established. However, all states include the provision of offensive touching that does not require proof of bodily injury. In such cases, the victim's testimony will be sufficient to establish the element.[10]

Common law was discussed in the Chapter 2 which also explained how common law has had an impact on many different crimes. It should come as no surprise that there are common law crimes of assault and battery. Under the old common law definition of battery, no injury was required. Instead, the focus of the prosecution was on the invasion of the plaintiff's person, essentially proving that the contact was offensive.[11] Common law also provided that in addition to the crimes of assault and battery, there are also civil actions with the same names. This can occasionally cause some confusion in common law states.

Wanton or reckless acts
Activities carried out by a defendant who shows a complete indifference to the safety of others.

Reckless Conduct. A person may also be charged with assault and battery for committing **wanton or reckless acts**. In such a situation, the defendant may not have targeted a specific individual, but may have acted with reckless disregard for the safety of others and caused injury. Suppose, for example, that a defendant shoots a gun into a passing train. One of his bullets strikes one of the passengers. The defendant will be charged with aggravated battery or aggravated assault with a deadly weapon.[12]

Horseplay or Practical Jokes. Suppose that a person is not acting with reckless indifference to the safety of others, rather is actually attempting to carry out a practical joke in which someone is injured. Does the law allow a "horseplay" or "practical joke" defense? It does not. Even when the defendant acts in fun, but still causes harmful or offensive contact, the crime is battery.[13]

Consent
Voluntary and knowing agreement to a proposed action.

Consent. Of course, one of the most basic elements for both assault and battery is that the defendant's actions were taken without the **consent** of the victim. If the

---

[10] *State v. Cabana*, 315 N.J. Super. 84, 716 A.2d 576 (Law Div. 1997), aff'd, 318 N.J. Super. 259, 723 A.2d 635 (App. Div. 1999).
[11] *Lounsbury v. Capel*, 836 P.2d 188 (Utah Ct. App. 1992).
[12] *Bentley v. Com.*, 354 S.W.2d 495 (Ky. 1962).
[13] *State v. Mowery*, 115 W. Va. 445, 176 S.E. 851 (1934).

defendant acts with consent, there is no assault and there is no battery.[14] However, simply because the victim has given consent to a form of battery does not mean that the victim has given consent to all possible forms of battery. The law is quite clear on consent. If the victim consents to one type of touching, but the defendant exceeds the scope of that consent, then the defendant can still be prosecuted for battery. Suppose, for example, two men are playing a game where each slaps the palm of the other. Each man is attempting to see how long the other man can last without showing signs of pain. However, at one point during the game, one of the participants produces a hammer and uses that to strike the other man's palm. In such a case, the defendant would not be able to use the defense of consent because the consent was limited to the particulars of the game, in this case, slapping one palm with the other man's hand.[15]

In a similar vein, if the defendant obtains consent through fraud or duress, then there is no valid consent at all. Consider Scenario 5-7.

THEO'S MOCK FIGHT

Theo and his friend are playing around. Theo's friend suggests that Theo learn how to take a fake punch. The friend instructs Theo how he should turn his head suddenly as the friend's fist goes by his face. They work it out several times and then decide to demonstrate their mock-fighting technique to others. However, when the friend throws the punch, he hits Theo squarely on the jaw, knocking him out. Will the friend have the defense that Theo consented to the battery and that therefore there is no crime?

Answer: No. Theo's consent was based on fraud. Theo had every reason to believe that they were going to engage in a mock fight, not a real one. As a result, Theo's consent was no consent at all.

Parents. Criminal law makes special provisions for parents when they are dealing with their children. It is not battery for a parent to inflict reasonable corporal punishment on his or her child. Obviously, this legal protection does not allow a parent to inflict any type of injury on the child that he or she wishes. However, it is not battery to spank a recalcitrant child.[16]

Teachers. When it comes to corporal punishment of students, teachers are held to the same standard as parents. Their punishments must be "reasonable." The definition of what constitutes reasonableness varies from case to case, and when a teacher is charged with battery, it will be the jury's responsibility to determine what is reasonable under the circumstances in the case.[17]

Sexual Battery. We will discuss sexual battery in the chapter on sexual offenses.

---

[14] *Com. v. Feijoo*, 419 Mass. 486, 646 N.E.2d 118 (1995).
[15] *Gnadt v. Com.*, 27 Va. App. 148, 497 S.E.2d 887 (1998).
[16] West's F.S.A. § § 741.28(2), 741.30(1)(a). *G.C. v. R.S.*, 71 So. 3d 164 (Fla. Dist. Ct. App. 1st Dist. 2011).
[17] *People v. Ball*, 58 Ill. 2d 36, 317 N.E.2d 54 (1974).

AGGRAVATED ASSAULT OR AGGRAVATED BATTERY

A battery or an assault can be classified as aggravated when a weapon is used, when the victim is severely injured, or under other circumstances. When an assault or battery is classified as "aggravated," it means that the possible sentence the defendant could receive is more severe. Simple battery or simple assault is normally a misdemeanor. **Aggravated assault** and **aggravated battery** are felonies, with a maximum sentence in many states of twenty years in prison.

Figure 5-1 shows the age at arrest of felony defendants.

Just as with murder, many states divide the crimes of assault and battery into various degrees. While some states simply refer to simple assault or simple battery versus aggravated assault and aggravated battery, some states divide into as many as

Aggravated assault
A felony in most states, the victim is either seriously injured or the defendant uses a deadly weapon in the attack.

Aggravated battery
Used interchangeably with the term "aggravated assault."

FIGURE 5-1	Age at arrest of felony defendants

			Percent of felony defendants who were—							
Most Serious Arrest Charge	**Number of Defendants**	**Total**	**Under 18**	**18-20**	**21-24**	**25-29**	**30-34**	**35-39**	**40 or older**	**Average Age at Arrest (Years)**
All offenses	57,948	100%	3	14	17	16	13	12	26	32
Violent offenses	13,246	100%	6	16	17	16	12	10	23	31
Murder	370	100%	7	19	18	24	13	7	11	28
Rape	665	100%	4	15	15	16	16	15	18	30
Robbery	3,451	100%	13	27	17	12	8	8	15	27
Assault	6,376	100%	3	13	17	17	14	11	25	32
Other violent	2,385	100%	2	11	15	15	14	12	31	34
Property offenses	16,882	100%	2	15	15	17	13	13	25	32
Burglary	4,486	100%	3	19	16	15	11	13	23	31
Larceny/theft	5,259	100%	2	14	13	16	12	14	29	33
Motor vehicle theft	1,653	100%	4	23	17	16	14	11	16	29
Forgery	1,416	100%	1	9	18	19	14	11	28	32
Fraud	2,091	100%	1	8	12	19	16	16	29	34
Other property	1,977	100%	2	16	20	18	14	10	20	30
Drug offenses	21,223	100%	2	13	17	15	13	12	28	32
Trafficking	8,482	100%	3	17	22	17	11	10	21	30
Other drug	12,741	100%	2	10	14	14	13	13	33	34
Public-order offenses	6,597	100%	2	12	17	16	14	11	28	32
Weapons	1,958	100%	3	25	27	20	10	4	12	27
Driving-related	1,836	100%	0	3	12	18	16	12	39	36
Other public-order	2,805	100%	2	9	13	13	16	16	31	34

Note: Data on age of defendants were available for 99.7% of all cases. Detail may not sum to total because of rounding.

four degrees of assault. This is the pattern used in Washington State, for example.[18] Aggravated assault generally refers to someone who intentionally (or recklessly) causes great bodily harm to the victim.[19]

Any of the following can qualify as aggravated assault:

- Inflicting serious pain on the victim
- Causing serious physical injuries to the victim
- Bodily injury that is likely to cause death
- The victim suffers disfigurement[20]

There are some states that include language in their aggravated assault and aggravated battery statutes that require the state to establish that the defendant acted with "depraved indifference" to the victim's life. The prosecution can prove this element by showing that the defendant acted with great cruelty, recklessness concerning the consequences to the victim or that the defendant ignored his or her social duty not to injure others.[21] Consider Scenario 5-8.

SERIOUS ENOUGH TO WARRANT AGGRAVATED ASSAULT CHARGE?

SCENARIO 5-8

Manny is out walking his dog and becomes involved in an argument with a neighbor. During the argument, the neighbor punches Manny in the face and Manny falls to the ground. He goes to the hospital where doctors discover that he has a slight tear on his lip. They use small staples to close the wound. Manny never loses consciousness and the wound will not leave a scar. Manny goes to the local magistrate and demands a warrant against his neighbor for aggravated assault. What charge, if any, is the magistrate likely to issue?

Answer: Simple battery. Because Manny's injuries were not life-threatening, he was not permanently scarred, he never lost consciousness, and did not suffer extreme pain, there is no basis for a charge for aggravated assault.[22]

THEO VISITS A BANK AT THE WRONG TIME

SCENARIO 5-9

Yesterday, Theo went to the bank to cash a check. When he walked in, he immediately saw that everyone in the bank was holding their hands above their heads and one man, wearing a ski mask, was pointing a gun at them. The man with the gun told everyone, including Theo, to lie down. The defendant said, "Your safety depends on your

continued

---

[18] West's RCWA 9A.36.041(1). *State v. Hahn*, 271 P.3d 892 (Wash. 2012).
[19] *Com. v. Patrick*, 2007 PA Super 289, 933 A.2d 1043 (2007), appeal denied, 940 A.2d 364 (Pa. 2007).
[20] *State v. Cunningham*, 1998 ME 167, 715 A.2d 156 (Me. 1998); *State v. Cepeda*, 588 N.W.2d 747 (Minn. Ct. App. 1999).
[21] *Com. v. McClendon*, 2004 PA Super 164, 874 A.2d 1223 (2005).
[22] *Jackson v. U.S.*, 970 A.2d 277 (D.C. 2009).

cooperation." The man grabbed a bag of money and ran. There's no question that the man will be charged with bank robbery, but has Theo been the victim of an assault?

Answer: Yes. Theo was placed in imminent fear or apprehension of a harmful or offensive contact. The fact that the man's statement wasn't more specific does not affect the analysis.[23]

A. CONFUSION OF TERMS: AGGRAVATED ASSAULT AND AGGRAVATED BATTERY

It is important to note that a certain amount of confusion has crept into the definition of the crime using a weapon or inflicting serious injury on a person. Technically speaking, a battery is a harmful or offensive touching. Aggravated battery would then be the term used to describe serious bodily injury or when a weapon is used to inflict the injuries. However, this crime is usually referred to as "aggravated assault." Because an assault involved no actual touching, how can the crime of *aggravated* assault even exist? One could argue that the use of a weapon to cause a person fear or apprehension of a harmful or offensive contact would qualify for this crime, but this is not how the term is used in the everyday practice of law. Instead, aggravated assault is often used to describe a situation where a person has been seriously injured or where a weapon has been used. Technically, this crime should only be called "aggravated battery." There are some states that use this — or some other close formulation of words — to describe the crime, but most have retained the use of aggravated assault.

B. ENHANCEMENT STATUTES

Aggravated assault and aggravated battery statutes often contain provisions that may enhance the sentence that the defendant receives when he or she injures a specific type of person or commits the offense in a particular place. For example, many states have statutes that will add additional years to a sentence for aggravated assault if the attack occurs on public property, especially public schools.[24]

SERIOUS ENOUGH TO WARRANT AGGRAVATED ASSAULT CHARGE (2)?

Paul is out for an evening run. He sees a neighbor and becomes involved in an argument. The neighbor knocks Paul to the ground, kicks him repeatedly in the ribs, bangs Paul's head against the road surface, then briefly chokes him. Fortunately, Paul is a retired veteran who served in both Iraq and Afghanistan and manages to fend the neighbor off. Paul calls the police. What charges are the police likely to bring against the neighbor?

---

[23] *People v. Schwartz*, 2 Cal. App. 4th 1319, 3 Cal. Rptr. 2d 816 (4th Dist. 1992).
[24] *People v. Ojeda*, 921 N.E.2d 490 (Ill. App. Ct. 2d Dist. 2009), appeal pending, (Mar. 1, 2010).

Answer: Aggravated assault. Unlike the previous scenario, Paul was kicked, obviously causing serious pain. He was also choked and had his head struck against the road surface. The fact that Paul was able to use some of his own training to avoid even more serious injuries is not relevant to the defendant's actions.[25]

What separates simple battery from aggravated battery? The answer is that for a crime to be considered aggravated battery, the defendant must have caused serious bodily injury to the victim, disfigured the victim, or used a deadly weapon.[26]

C. DEADLY WEAPONS

A battery or assault can be reclassified as aggravated, and thus more severely punished, when a **deadly weapon** is used. The use of a deadly weapon in a simple assault is sufficient to increase the charge to aggravated assault, even if the victim is uninjured. Even apparently innocuous objects can be classified as deadly weapons under the right circumstances. The court focuses on the object's ability to inflict serious harm and the victim's awareness that the object could cause serious bodily injuries or death. Consider Scenario 5-11.

Deadly weapon
Any item or device that is likely to cause serious bodily harm to a victim, especially items designed to inflict wounds or death, such as guns or knives.

BUT I ONLY MEANT TO SCARE HER

SCENARIO 5-11

Donny and Clara are going through a contentious divorce. Donny appears at Clara's house one day, brandishing a knife, and chases Clara into the kitchen where he corners her. Fortunately, a neighbor saw Donny get out of his car with the knife. When the police arrive, they rush into the house and hear Donny shout out, "I never meant to hurt her. I could've killed her or cut her, but I didn't." Clara is, in fact, unharmed, but has been seriously frightened by the experience. Although he could have injured his estranged wife, he did not. At Donny's trial for aggravated assault with a deadly weapon, will that be a valid defense resulting in the case being dismissed? In fact, he claims that because he didn't hurt her, he obviously had no intention of doing so.

Answer: No. The fact that he used a knife to threaten her is enough. Donny's actions in this context speak louder than his words to the officers and to the jury.

What is a deadly weapon? Figure 5-2 shows some real-life examples. Obviously, there are some items that can be classified as deadly weapons without great thought. Knives, guns, and other items that are designed to kill people are deadly weapons. In some circumstances, courts have ruled that a person's feet or hands could be deadly weapons, especially if the defendant has received specialized martial arts training.[27]

---

[25] *People v. Audi*, 88 A.D.3d 1070, 931 N.Y.S.2d 418 (3d Dep't 2011).
[26] *State v. Smith*, 39 Kan. App. 2d 64, 176 P.3d 997 (2008), review denied, (July 3, 2008).
[27] *McCallum v. State*, 311 S.W.3d 9 (Tex. App. San Antonio 2010).

Victimizations Involving Any Theft and Firearm Theft

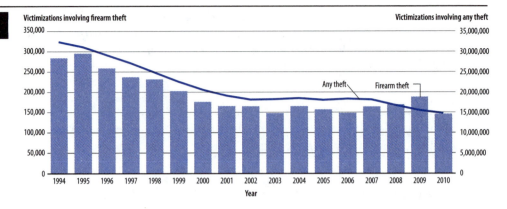

Note: Data based on two-year rolling averages.

Source: Bureau of Justice Statistics, National Crime Victimization Survey, 1993–2010.

To make the definition clearer, courts have developed several tests to help juries determine when an item qualifies as a deadly weapon. These tests include:

- Is it designed as a weapon, and is it capable of killing or seriously injuring a human being?
- Did the defendant have the apparent ability to use the item to inflict death or serious injury to the victim?[28]

IS A TELEVISION SET A DEADLY WEAPON?

Stan and Cato are roommates. They get into an argument one evening about which show to watch on television. At one point, Stan unplugs and picks up the television, which is very large and heavy, and rushes toward Cato. At the last second, Cato jumps out of the way and the television crashes down inches from Cato's head. Can Stan be charged with aggravated assault with a deadly weapon?

Answer: Yes. Although we generally do not think of television sets as deadly weapons, many innocuous objects can be classified as deadly weapons if they are capable of causing serious injury or death and the victim is aware of that fact.

D. "SPECIAL" VICTIMS

A battery or assault may also be classified as aggravated when the victim falls into a special category. For instance, many states classify any battery on a police officer as aggravated battery, justifying a more severe sentence. In many states, if the victim is

---

[28] *Com. v. Sexton*, 425 Mass. 146, 680 N.E.2d 23 (1997).

over 65 years of age, a battery may be reclassified as aggravated, even though it would be considered simple battery if the victim were younger. These statutes were enacted as a means to protect certain classes of individuals and to discourage people from committing batteries on them. In addition to creating special victims' categories through legislation, states have also identified specific instances that may require mandatory minimum sentences of a year or more. Some of these subcategories of assault and battery include:

- Assault or battery of a law enforcement officer
- Assault or battery on a correctional officer
- Domestic violence
- Assault on special victims, such as the elderly or the mentally challenged

A defendant convicted of assault or battery under these circumstances can receive a mandatory minimum sentence of five years or more.

E. LESSER-INCLUDED OFFENSES

Aggravated assault can contain lesser-included offenses. In fact, an aggravated battery contains all of the elements of simple battery. The jury is permitted to reach a decision on either verdict, depending on the facts of the case and the jury charge.

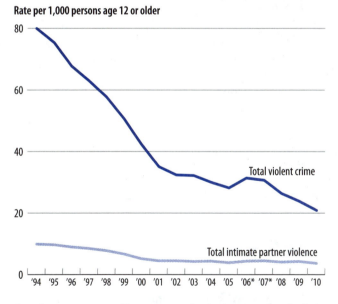

FIGURE 5-3

Total Violent Crimes and Intimate Partner Violence, 1993–2010

Note: Estimates based on two-year rolling averages beginning in 1993. Includes rape or sexual assault, robbery, aggravated assault, and simple assault committed by current or former spouses, boyfriends, or girlfriends.

*Due to methodological changes, use caution when comparing 2006 NCVS criminal victimization estimates to other years. See *Criminal Victimization, 2007*, NCJ 224390, BJS website, December 2008, for more information.

Source: Bureau of Justice Statistics, National Crime Victimization Survey, 1993–2010.

DOMESTIC VIOLENCE

Unfortunately, domestic violence remains a common occurrence in the United States. As Figure 5-3 shows, although the rate of domestic violence has decreased over time, it still remains high.

Domestic violence is defined as physical and verbal abuse, generally carried out by a man against a woman in a romantic relationship. This is not to say that domestic violence cannot occur in other relationships, but the most common form is an abusive boyfriend or husband. There is a common cycle in these relationships: tension builds in the relationship until some event, often trivial, triggers an overreaction by the man in the form of physical and verbal abuse. After the incident, the man is normally remorseful and promises never to do such a thing again. The relationship proceeds in a loving manner for some period of time until tension begins mounting again and the inevitable explosion happens. The problem with domestic violence is not only that there is the constant threat of violence hanging in the air between the couple, but also that the violence tends to escalate over time.

Individuals who have not observed or been involved in such relationships find it difficult to understand the complex interdependence between the partners. The man may actually love the woman that he abuses, and the woman often loves the man who abuses her. Both may have grown up in households where domestic violence was prevalent, and although each may have resolved to never replicate that same situation, they ultimately find themselves in an almost identical relationship.

Why would an abused woman continue to remain in such a relationship? The answer, like the relationship itself, is complex. The woman may be financially dependent on the man. They may also have children. Abusers often threaten to kill themselves or the woman, and even the children, if the woman should leave. In some instances, the woman suffers from low self-esteem and does not believe that any other relationship would be different. The woman may also believe that she can help the man overcome his violence. Unfortunately, the statistics are clearly against them. Men who tend toward violence in intimate relationships rarely abandon the practice, and most tend to increase, not decrease, the level of violence.

Although our discussion has focused on the man as the abuser and the woman as the abused, it is true that there are relationships where this is not the pattern. However, given the fact that the majority of domestic violence involves a man abusing a woman, we have limited our discussion to these roles.

FAMOUS CASES
O.J. SIMPSON

O.J. Simpson's infamous murder trial is a familiar tale. In June 1994, Simpson, in a fit of rage, allegedly slashed the necks of his ex-wife, Nicole Brown Simpson, and her friend Ronald Goldman outside her condominium in Los Angeles. Despite an abundance of evidence incriminating Simpson, the jury acquitted him after a nine-month trial, largely because defense attorney Johnnie Cochran convinced the jury that lab technicians had mishandled DNA evidence. Additionally, Cochran alleged misconduct on the part of the L.A. Police Department, planting a seed of doubt in the jury members' minds that the defense was not able to overcome.

Public opinion ran high that Simpson was guilty and that the prosecution team had done a shoddy job. To bolster that opinion, the families of Brown Simpson and Goldman sued for wrongful death in a civil trial. That jury unanimously agreed by a preponderance of evidence that Simpson was liable for wrongful death and damages of $38 million to the Goldman family and $24 million to the Brown family.

Nevertheless, many people still believed that Simpson had literally gotten away with murder. His life following both trials was that of an outcast. He lived in self-imposed exile in Miami, but legal troubles continued to haunt him. The State of California imposed on him a $1.44 million tax lien; he was arrested in Miami for battery and burglary following a traffic incident; he was sued in federal court for stealing satellite signals; he was arrested for speeding in his boat through a manatee-protected area in Florida. But the crime that finally sent him to prison was robbery.

On a mid-September night in 2007, Simpson and five other men burst into a room at the Palace Station Hotel-Casino in Las Vegas. Brandishing a gun, they accosted two men who had been led to believe the group was meeting them to purchase sports memorabilia. Simpson and his cohorts relieved the two men of their sports memorabilia and fled the hotel.

When police questioned Simpson about the crime, he admitted taking the items, saying that he was only trying to retrieve what had been stolen from him. In a *Los Angeles Times* article, Simpson was quoted as saying, "I'm not walking around feeling sad or anything. I've done nothing wrong." Besides, he quipped, "I thought what happens in Las Vegas stays in Las Vegas."

Nevertheless, three days later, Simpson was arrested and held without bail. He was charged with 13 counts, including armed robbery, kidnapping, assault with a deadly weapon, and felony coercion. During jury selection for the trial, defense attorneys grilled prospective jurors about their knowledge and views of Simpson's earlier acquittal. The defense was justifiably concerned that lingering hostility about his acquittal would taint the current proceedings.

Whether or not the jury members held a grudge that influenced them is unknowable. Nonetheless, on October 3, 2008 they convicted Simpson of all thirteen charges against him. Coincidentally, it was 13 years to the day that he had been acquitted of murder. The judge sentenced him to a maximum term of 33 years, with parole a possibility after 9 years, in 2017.

Although Simpson was never convicted of the ultimate crime against a person, his conviction and incarceration for a lesser crime brought some measure of satisfaction to those who believe he was unjustly acquitted in the murder case.

 CHILD ABUSE

Physical, emotional, and sexual abuse of children is outlawed in all jurisdictions in the United States. Child abuse is defined as any act that puts a child in danger of serious physical or mental harm. Here, the word "act" is also defined as neglect or abandonment.

Prosecutions for child abuse can be based on a single incident or a continuing series of incidents. Like domestic violence, a child is far more likely to be abused by a member of his or her household than by a stranger. Individuals who abuse children, like those who commit domestic violence, have often been victims of abuse themselves. This does not condone or mitigate their actions, but does show a disturbing trend from generation to generation.

 ## ELDER ABUSE

There are studies showing that over 2 million elderly Americans are abused every year. Just like domestic violence or child abuse, elder abuse can take many different forms. It can be both physical and mental and, like child abuse, can also involve neglect or abandonment. The surprising detail about elder abuse is that more of it occurs within the family home than in nursing homes or other facilities. The abuse is often the outcome of stress within the family unit that taking care of an elderly parent or relative can generate. This crime is often under-reported. In many ways, an elderly person makes the perfect victim for a disturbed individual. The elderly person may be physically weak and easy to intimidate, or may suffer from some form of mental disability that would make it difficult if not impossible for the person to report the crime. Finally, from a prosecutor's viewpoint, taking these cases to trial is problematic. The elderly abuse victim may not be able to testify due to health or mental issues and may even die before the case comes to trial.

 ## KIDNAPPING AND FALSE IMPRISONMENT

There is a wide variation among states and federal statutes in the terms used to define kidnapping. However, the basic idea is the same in any jurisdiction: The victim is restrained from moving about freely and is taken some distance away. Kidnapping, like many criminal offenses, arose under English common law and was defined as the forcible abduction of a man, woman, or child. Usually, the goal of kidnapping was the sale of the person to a slave market or to some form of indentured servitude.[29] In the early 20th century, kidnapping was seen as a means of gaining money. Wealthy individuals would be kidnapped, held for ransom and, in most cases, returned. There is a similar pattern in many underdeveloped countries in the modern era. In the United States, cases involving kidnapping for ransom have become rare. It is far more likely for an individual to be kidnapped as part of some other criminal enterprise, such as a prelude to rape or murder.

Most jurisdictions define the crime of kidnapping by the:

- Unlawful taking and confinement
- Asportation of the victim
- Against his or her will, or through the use of force, threat, or deception

---

[29] *Doss v. State*, 220 Ala. 30, 123 So. 231, 68 A.L.R. 712 (1929).

A. UNLAWFUL TAKING AND CONFINEMENT

The first element of kidnapping is that the victim be taken and confined. This does not mean that the victim must be carried away some significant distance and held by force. As we will see later in this discussion, taking simply means that the victim was removed from his or her surroundings and that the victim's liberty was circumscribed. Confinement can be accomplished by threats, fraud, or deceit. When a defendant tricks a person into accompanying him, he has restrained his victim as much as if he had seized the victim. Consider Scenario 5-13.

THEO IS ARRESTED

Theo is at the mall, and a man approaches him. The man produces a badge and tells Theo that he is under arrest for suspicion of shoplifting. Theo protests that he has not taken anything without paying for it. The man insists that Theo accompany him to the parking lot where the man puts Theo in the back of the man's car. At this point, Theo realizes that the car is not a police car. Has the first element of kidnapping — taking and confinement– been established?

    Answer: Yes. There is no requirement that anyone use force against a victim to take and confine him. In this case, the man used trickery to get Theo to accompany him.

LAWFUL VS. UNLAWFUL RESTRAINT

Police officers do not commit kidnapping when they arrest suspects. Of course this is only true when police officers are acting in their official capacity. On duty, police officers cannot be charged with kidnapping for lawfully taking a suspect into custody. However, when police officers exceed their authority, or engage in unlawful acts, the law no longer shields them. Consider Scenario 5-14.

THEO IS ARRESTED . . . ?

After Theo realizes that he is not sitting in a police car, he asks the man if he is a real police officer. The man replies, "That's none of your business."

    Theo opens the door and gets out. The man rushes after him and points a gun at Theo, saying, "Yes, I am a police officer, but I work in another state. Now, get back into the car."

    Assuming that the man is a police officer from another state, can he be charged with kidnapping Theo?

    Answer: Yes. A police officer outside of his or her jurisdiction has no greater right to make arrests than any other citizen. The statutory protection for police officers that prevent them from being prosecuted for valid arrests does not apply in this situation. This is not a valid arrest, and the man can be prosecuted for kidnapping.

THEO IS PLACED UNDER CITIZEN'S ARREST . . . ?

We have all heard about the term "citizen's arrest." When the man who brought Theo to his car is faced with prosecution, the man realizes that his defense of being a police officer will not work. Instead, he claims the right to make a citizen's arrest. Is this a valid citizen's arrest?

Answer: Arrest and citizen's arrest will be discussed in later chapters, but this is not a citizen's arrest. Citizens can detain individuals whom they have seen commit a crime, but only to detain them for the police. They are not authorized to take anyone into custody and certainly cannot remove them from the scene of the supposed crime.

B. ASPORTATION OF THE VICTIM

Asportation
The movement of the victim, usually against the victim's will or without the victim's consent or, in the case of theft, of the victim's property.

The term **asportation** refers to movement. In a kidnapping charge, the defendant must move the victim some distance. The element of asportation is what separates a kidnapping from a lesser charge of false imprisonment. Behind the theory of asportation is that, when the defendant moves the victim away from safety and security, the defendant is decreasing the victim's chances of finding someone who may rescue the victim or allow the victim to contact someone who could assist.

The concept of asportation is simple: The defendant moves the victim without the victim's consent. However, states vary widely when it comes to defining exactly how far the defendant must move the victim before the element is considered satisfied. For example, some states interpret asportation to mean a substantial distance, such as several yards, while other states define asportation as any slight, almost undetectable, distance. For instance, some states have said that when the defendant moves the victim, by force, only a foot, that is enough to satisfy this element. In some states, the movement must be more than a few feet. Why would a jurisdiction have the requirement of asportation at all? Because kidnapping is a major felony, which can be punished by life imprisonment, the crime requires that the defendant take an active role in moving the victim. Where the statute does not specify what distance is required to satisfy asportation, the courts must determine it from the facts in a particular case.

Sidebar

In order to have a kidnapping, the defendant must move the victim, either by force, threat or deceit, some distance from where the victim was originally. This element is called asportation.

C. BY USE OF FORCE, THREAT, FRAUD, OR DECEPTION

Kidnapping can be accomplished by force, but also by taking and detaining a person through intimidation, fraud, or trickery, as in the previous scenario involving Theo. There is no requirement that the defendant actually touch the victim to satisfy the elements of kidnapping. In the scenario involving Theo, there was never any point where the man touched Theo; nonetheless, Theo was kidnapped. Tricking a victim into going with the kidnapper is just as sufficient from a legal perspective as holding a gun to the victim's back and demanding that the victim leave with the defendant. The important point about force, threat, fraud, or deception is that in each case, the victim's free will was overcome.

FIGURE 5-4

Kidnapping (Georgia)

§ 16-5-40. Kidnapping

(a) A person commits the offense of kidnapping when he abducts or steals away any person without lawful authority or warrant and holds such person against his will.

(b) A person convicted of the offense of kidnapping shall be punished by:

(1) Imprisonment for not less than ten nor more than 20 years if the kidnapping involved a victim who was 14 years of age or older;

(2) Imprisonment for life or by a split sentence that is a term of imprisonment for not less than 25 years and not exceeding life imprisonment, followed by probation for life, if the kidnapping involved a victim who is less than 14 years of age;

(3) Life imprisonment or death if the kidnapping was for ransom; or

(4) Life imprisonment or death if the person kidnapped received bodily injury.[30]

As we have seen with other crimes against persons, if the victim voluntarily goes with the defendant, or consents, then there is no unlawful taking and there is no case for kidnapping. Of course, it is not consent for a defendant to trick someone into going with him or her. Trickery overcomes free will just as brute force does. There are times when a person initially gives consent and then revokes it. What happens in such a case?

If the victim goes with the defendant willingly, at least at first, then there is a valid consent. However, if the victim should revoke consent, then the taking is unlawful and a kidnapping charge can be sustained against the defendant. The moment that the victim was restrained against her will, even if this should come several minutes or even hours into the trip on which she had initially consented, the "unlawful" element of the detention is triggered.

D. AGGRAVATING CIRCUMSTANCES IN KIDNAPPING

Under the old common law, kidnapping was usually classified as a misdemeanor, but in most states, it is a felony. In fact, in some states, kidnapping that involves bodily injury of the victim can result in a life sentence for the defendant.

Many states follow the pattern set out in the statute in Figure 5-4.

FALSE IMPRISONMENT

False imprisonment has many of the same elements of kidnapping. It is the:

- Unlawful restraint of the victim
- Through force or threats

---

[30] O.C.G.A. § 16-5-40.

False imprisonment
The crime of restraining another's movement through force, threat, or intimidation.

False imprisonment occurs when someone unlawfully detains another through force, threat, or intimidation, and the person is not free to leave.

Unlike kidnapping, there is no asportation requirement in **false imprisonment**. Like kidnapping, the victim's restraint can be obtained through force, threat, fraud, or deception. The most common type of false imprisonment claim does not arise from prisons or even police custody, but with retailers. When a merchant detains someone he or she believes has committed shoplifting, the retailer must be sure that the victim actually is a shoplifter. If it turns out that the person detained is innocent, then the restraint was unlawful and the merchant can be prosecuted for false imprisonment. If, on the other hand, the merchant detained a person who really had committed shoplifting, then the first element would not apply. A merchant is within his or her rights to detain a person who steals. This would again be a form of citizens' arrest, which will be examined in greater detail in Chapter 13.

STALKING

Stalking
Following, contacting, harassing, or annoying another for the purpose of causing emotional distress.

Men and women have followed, harassed, and annoyed one another for thousands of years, but it was only in the 1990s that legislatures in the United States began criminalizing the behavior. It was not that law enforcement did not think that **stalking** was serious; it was just that it was often prosecuted under different statutes or as a part of an overall scheme of criminal behavior. However, there was a strong push to make the act itself illegal, and all states have now enacted some form of statute that clearly makes stalking a criminal offense. The elements of stalking are, in general:

- A course of conduct
- Designed to harass or intimidate a person
- The conduct serves no legitimate purpose
- Carried out over a period of time
- That causes the victim to have a credible fear of injury or death

A. THE ELEMENTS OF STALKING

Most states follow the elements set out above, although there is considerable variation in how stalking is defined among the various states. Stalking as a crime is often considered a little vague, and over time statutes have attempted to specify precisely what is and what is not considered stalking. Consider Scenario 5-16.

SCENARIO 5-16

KEISHA AND THE STALKER

Keisha, as we have already seen, is an assistant district attorney. Last week, she was given seven related cases concerning a group of skinheads who kidnapped and tortured an Asian American teenager. As she was leaving work yesterday, she noticed a man with numerous tattoos and a shaved head standing near her car. The man walked several feet away as she approached, then turned and made a show of writing down the license number of her car. Can Keisha seek charges against the man for stalking?

FIGURE 5-5

Stalking in Florida

(1) As used in this section, the term:

(a) "Harass" means to engage in a course of conduct directed at a specific person that causes substantial emotional distress in such person and serves no legitimate purpose.

(b) "Course of conduct" means a pattern of conduct composed of a series of acts over a period of time, however short, evidencing a continuity of purpose. Constitutionally protected activity is not included within the meaning of "course of conduct." Such constitutionally protected activity includes picketing or other organized protests.

(c) "Credible threat" means a threat made with the intent to cause the person who is the target of the threat to reasonably fear for his or her safety. The threat must be against the life of, or a threat to cause bodily injury to, a person.

(d) "Cyberstalk" means to engage in a course of conduct to communicate, or to cause to be communicated, words, images, or language by or through the use of electronic mail or electronic communication, directed at a specific person, causing substantial emotional distress to that person and serving no legitimate purpose.

(2) Any person who willfully, maliciously, and repeatedly follows, harasses, or cyberstalks another person commits the offense of stalking, a misdemeanor of the first degree.

(3) Any person who willfully, maliciously, and repeatedly follows, harasses, or cyberstalks another person, and makes a credible threat with the intent to place that person in reasonable fear of death or bodily injury of the person, or the person's child, sibling, spouse, parent, or dependent, commits the offense of aggravated stalking, a felony of the third degree.

(4) Any person who, after an injunction for protection against repeat violence, sexual violence, or dating violence pursuant to s. 784.046, or an injunction for protection against domestic violence pursuant to s. 741.30, or after any other court-imposed prohibition of conduct toward the subject person or that person's property, knowingly, willfully, maliciously, and repeatedly follows, harasses, or cyberstalks another person commits the offense of aggravated stalking, a felony of the third degree.

(5) Any person who willfully, maliciously, and repeatedly follows, harasses, or cyberstalks a minor under 16 years of age commits the offense of aggravated stalking, a felony of the third degree, punishable as provided in s. 775.082, s. 775.083, or s. 775.084.[31]

Answer: Probably not. Stalking usually requires a course of conduct, and a one-time event will usually not satisfy the statute. Even though she is an Assistant District Attorney, this by itself, coupled with the man's behavior, does not rise to the level of a crime, but Keisha should obviously start taking precautions.

Most statutes that define stalking also add a provision referred to as a "reasonable person" standard. The stalking activity must be something that would cause a reasonable person to suffer substantial emotional distress (see Figure 5-5).

---

[31] West's F.S.A. § 784.048.

CYBERSTALKING

Cyberstalking
The crime of using electronic means, including the Internet and social media, to cause the victim emotional distress.

Many states have expanded the definition of stalking to include some form of **cyberstalking**. With sites like Facebook and other social media becoming commonplace, the damage that a technically savvy person could do to a person's reputation could be enormous should that person decide to harass or intimidate someone over the Internet.

As Figure 5-6 shows, Florida's definition of cyber-stalking encompasses "a course of conduct to communicate, or to cause to be communicated, words, images, or language by or through the use of electronic mail or electronic communication, directed at a specific person, causing substantial emotional distress to that person and serving no legitimate purpose."

B. BULLYING

Although there is nothing new about bullying, high profile cases in recent years have caused many state legislatures to enact anti-bullying laws. Almost every state has proposed legislation that seeks to criminalize some or all of the following behaviors:

- Harassment
- Intimidation
- Violence
- Threats
- False accusation
- All occurring on or near a public or private school setting

In most situations, these activities are classified as misdemeanors, and because they involve individuals who are not yet legal adults, they are prosecuted in juvenile court. The problem that some of these statutes face is a certain vagueness when it

---

FIGURE 5-6

Cyberstalking Techniques

Among the techniques used by people who engage in cyberstalking are some or all of the following:

- Listing the person's name, address, and home telephone number at dating sites and other personal sites where individuals seek out others for romantic or sexual encounters.
- Using the victim's email to send out resignation letters from their current employment or to repeatedly harass others pretending to be the victim.
- Denial of service attacks that flood the victim's email with so many emails that the victim essentially cannot use the service.
- Releasing the victim's credit card and other sensitive information to others.
- Portraying the victim as sexually promiscuous or posting photos of the victim that claim to show a pattern of sexually promiscuous conduct.

comes to balancing the rights of students to live free of bullying and the rights of others to freedom of expression. Admittedly, First Amendment rights are already curtailed for those who have not yet reached adulthood, but some statutes certainly come close to crossing the line between safety and freedom of speech.

COM. v. SEXTON
425 Mass. 146, 680 N.E.2d 23 (1997)

FRIED, Justice.

The defendant, Everett Sexton, was convicted on a joint venture theory of assault and battery by means of a dangerous weapon and willful and malicious destruction of property. On appeal, the Appeals Court affirmed his conviction of willful and malicious destruction of property, but reversed his conviction of assault and battery by means of a dangerous weapon on the ground that concrete pavement, the instrumentality at issue, is not a dangerous weapon. Commonwealth v. Sexton, 41 Mass.App.Ct. 676, 678–680, 672 N.E.2d 991 (1996). We granted the Commonwealth's application for further appellate review and affirm the conviction by the Superior Court.

I

On the evening of August 28, 1992, Jeffrey Czyzewski and a female companion went to a bar in Holyoke. At the bar, Czyzewski played a game of pool with the wife of Donald Sexton. Czyzewski briefly left the pool table. On his return, he accused Sexton's wife of cheating by moving the pool balls during his absence. Ending the game, Czyzewski left the pool table and was thereafter approached three separate times by an agitated Donald Sexton, who demanded an apology. Czyzewski testified that after the second request, the defendant, Everett Sexton, the brother of Donald Sexton, approached Czyzewski and said that he would stand by his brother if anything happened. On the third occasion, Donald Sexton smashed a beer bottle on the bar, but was restrained before he could threaten Czyzewski further. Following this incident, the defendant, his brother, and his brother's wife left the bar.

Shortly thereafter, Czyzewski and his companion went out to the parking lot and got into their car. Immediately a van pulled up alongside them and the defendant, his brother, and a third man got out. The defendant and his brother kicked in the window on the passenger side where Czyzewski was sitting. The defendant reached through the shattered window to grab Czyzewski, attempting to pull him through the window. At that moment, Czyzewski's companion was able to start the car and drove out of the parking lot. As they pulled out, the Sextons said, "Let's go get him," and returned to the van to follow Czyzewski. Because their car was about to run out of gas, Czyzewski and his companion were forced to return to the parking lot, with the van following behind. Czyzewski left the vehicle and Donald Sexton, the defendant, and their companion left their van. The defendant and his brother immediately approached Czyzewski; they began to push and shove him. The defendant restrained Czyzewski by lifting Czyzewski's jacket over his head and the brothers threw Czyzewski to the ground. On the ground, Donald Sexton banged Czyzewski's head against the pavement a number of times while the defendant repeatedly kicked him. The beating was interrupted by the bar owner and another man. The Sexton brothers left before the police arrived.

II

The Appeals Court held that the defendant possessed the requisite intent and knowledge to be guilty of assault and battery by means of a dangerous weapon on a joint venture theory, but reversed this conviction on the ground that "concrete pavement" is not a dangerous weapon under G.L. c. 265, § 15A. Commonwealth v. Sexton, supra at 678–679, 672 N.E.2d 991. At trial, the judge had instructed the jury that "concrete pavement" could be considered a dangerous weapon if the jury found that it was "used in such a way that it was capable of causing death or serious bodily injury to a person." While the Appeals Court agreed that "ordinarily the determination whether an object that is not dangerous per se is a dangerous weapon under § 15A is a question of fact for the jury," the Appeals Court reached this holding by reading *Commonwealth v. Shea*, supra, to conclude that a dangerous weapon "is an object or instrumentality that the batterer is able to wield to inflict serious injury or death upon another." *Commonwealth v. Sexton*, supra. Because the pavement was not an item with which the defendant "could arm himself," but was instead "simply part of the surroundings in which the defendant found himself while perpetrating an assault," id., the Appeals Court rejected the Commonwealth's argument that, in the circumstances, the pavement met the statutory requirements because it was "used . . . in a manner that was capable of producing serious bodily harm."

The Appeals Court also supported its decision by noting that "it is a well settled principle of statutory construction that criminal statutes are to be strictly construed." In construing G.L. c. 265, § 15A, we note that the phrase "dangerous weapon" is not defined. Instead, we have consistently looked to our precedent in applying this label. We find nothing in our case law which precludes our holding today, nor do we think it contravenes the intent of the Legislature, which chose to invoke greater penalties for assaults which threatened serious injury because an actor chose to employ a dangerous weapon.

This case presents an issue of first impression, in that we have not previously addressed whether stationary objects can be considered dangerous weapons in Massachusetts. The statute, G.L. c. 265, § 15A, does not define the term "dangerous weapon," but we have stated previously that there are things which are dangerous per se and those which are dangerous as used. *Commonwealth v. Appleby*, 380 Mass. 296, 303, 402 N.E.2d 1051 (1980). We have defined the former class as "instrumentalities designed and constructed to produce death or great bodily harm." Id. In the latter class are things which become dangerous weapons because they are "used in a dangerous fashion." Id. at 304, 402 N.E.2d 1051. In such cases it is generally "a question for the fact finder whether the instrument was so used in a particular case." In evaluating different situations, the determination has invariably turned on "use," and our courts have repeatedly held that ordinarily innocuous items can be considered dangerous weapons when used in an improper and dangerous manner. See Commonwealth v. Scott, 408 Mass. 811, 822–823, 564 N.E.2d 370 (1990) (gag); Commonwealth v. Barrett, 386 Mass. 649, 655–656, 436 N.E.2d 1219 (1982) (aerosol spray can); Commonwealth v. Appleby, supra at 304–305, 402 N.E.2d 1051 (riding crop); Commonwealth v. Tarrant, 367 Mass. 411, 418, 326 N.E.2d 710 (1975) (German shepherd dog); Commonwealth v. Farrell, supra at 615, 78 N.E.2d 697 (lighted cigarettes); Commonwealth v. Mercado, 24 Mass.App.Ct. 391, 395, 509 N.E.2d 300 (1987) (baseball bat); Commonwealth v. LeBlanc, 3 Mass.App.Ct. 780, 780, 334 N.E.2d 647 (1975) (automobile door swung knocking police officer down). Our courts have also noted, with approval, decisions in other jurisdictions which have found otherwise innocent items to fit this classification when used in a way which endangers another's safety.

We do not agree with the Appeals Court that, to be a dangerous weapon, the defendant must be able to wield the item at issue, nor do we think it relevant that the pavement was present as part of the environment in which the defendant chose to participate in this assault. Prior to the Appeals Court's decision in *Commonwealth v. Shea*, supra, the only explicit restriction on our use-based categorization of dangerous weapons held that human teeth and other parts of the human body were not dangerous weapons because they are not "instrumentalities apart from the defendant's person." *Commonwealth v. Davis*, supra at 193, 406 N.E.2d 417. In Shea, a case in which the defendant pushed two women from his boat and sped off, leaving them five miles off shore, the Appeals Court found that, while "the ocean can be and often is dangerous, it cannot be regarded in its natural state as a weapon within the meaning of § 15A," because "in its natural state it cannot be possessed or controlled." *Commonwealth v. Shea*, supra at 15–16, 644 N.E.2d 244. We believe that this is too narrow a reading of the instrumentality and use language we have employed when we have defined dangerous weapons as "an instrument or instrumentality which, because of the manner in which it is used, or attempted to be used, endangers the life or inflicts great bodily harm." *Commonwealth v. Farrell*, supra at 615, 78 N.E.2d 697. While one might not be able to possess the ocean or exercise authority over it in a traditional sense, *Commonwealth v. Shea*, supra at 16, 644 N.E.2d 244, one could certainly use it to inflict great harm, such as by holding another's head underwater.[1]

Likewise, it is obvious that one could employ concrete pavement, as the defendant and his brother did here, to cause serious bodily harm to another by banging the victim's head against the hard surface. As the Commonwealth points out, there would be no problem in convicting a defendant of assault and battery by means of a dangerous weapon if he used a broken slab of concrete to bludgeon his victim. We see no reason to hold that such a conviction cannot

---

[1] While we take issue with some of the reasoning in Shea, we do not necessarily disagree with the result the court reached in that case. In Shea, the danger posed by the ocean was not a result of the defendant bringing his victims into contact with that body of water, but rather the circumstances which followed when he deserted them, five miles from shore. We contrast this to a situation in which a defendant might drop his victim into a vat of acid, in which the mere contact with the substance would directly pose the risk of serious bodily harm.

stand merely because the instrumentality in question is a fixed thing at the time of its dangerous use.

A number of other jurisdictions which have considered this question have also held that an object's stationary character does not prevent its use as a dangerous weapon. *United States v. Murphy*, 35 F.3d 143, 147 (4th Cir.1994), cert. denied, 513 U.S. 1135, 115 S.Ct. 954, 130 L.Ed.2d 897 (1995) (steel cell bars); *State v. Brinson*, 337 N.C. 764, 766, 448 S.E.2d 822 (1994) (cell bars and floor); *People v. O'Hagan*, 176 A.D.2d 179, 179, 574 N.Y.S.2d 198 (1991) (cell bars); *People v. Coe*, 165 A.D.2d 721, 722, 564 N.Y.S.2d 255 (1990) (plate glass window); *State v. Reed*, 101 Or.App. 277, 279–280, 790 P.2d 551 (1990) (sidewalk).FN2 As North Carolina recognized, an item's dangerous propensities "often depend entirely on its use," and not its mobility, for "whether the pitcher hits the stone or the stone hits the pitcher, it will be bad for the pitcher." *State v. Reed*, supra at 280, 790 P.2d 551, quoting Cervantes, Don Quixote, Part II, ch. 43 (1615). We hold that one who intentionally uses concrete pavement as a means of inflicting serious harm can be found guilty of assault and battery by means of a dangerous weapon.

FN2. While other jurisdictions have taken a contrary position, we do not find them sufficiently apposite. In *Edwards v. United States*, 583 A.2d 661, 663–664 (D.C.1990), in determining whether bathroom fixtures could be considered dangerous weapons, the court was applying a statute which addressed crimes committed by a person "armed with or having readily available any pistol or other firearm . . . or other dangerous or deadly weapon," which went on to enumerate the types of specific instrumentalities the statute contemplated, carrying with its violation a possible life sentence. Although the Supreme Court of Louisiana rejected concrete as a dangerous weapon, it did so in the context of a defendant striking his victim and "causing him to fall upon the concrete and sustain injuries," *State v. Legendre*, 362 So.2d 570, 571 (La.1978), a scenario quite different from the purposeful and deliberate use of the pavement as a means of beating another which we must examine. Likewise, a Missouri appellate court found it "untenable to suggest that the dangerous instrument or deadly weapon components" of its statute were implicated in a case where the defendant beat a woman against a door casing and plumbing fixtures, but only considered whether the defendant's fists met this definition, never addressing the defendant's use of stationary objects he employed. Only *State v. Houck*, 652 So.2d 359, 360 (Fla.1995) (pavement and other passive objects not considered weapons as matter of law), directly contradicts our holding.

The conviction of assault and battery by means of a dangerous weapon is affirmed.

So ordered.

CASE QUESTIONS

1 How did the fight between the defendant and the victim initially start?
2 What was the "dangerous weapon" used in this case?
3 Is a "dangerous weapon" defined under the statute?
4 What is the "issue of first impression" before the court?
5 How does the court rule that the concrete pavement qualifies as a dangerous weapon?

CHAPTER SUMMARY

Assault is the apprehension or fear of a harmful or offensive contact. Battery occurs when the victim receives a harmful or offensive contact. Assault and battery are often prosecuted together because of their close relationship. In order to prosecute someone for either crime, the defendant must have the apparent ability to carry out the threatened action. There is no requirement that the victim must receive a severe injury in a simple battery case, only that the injury is either harmful or offensive. However, in felony cases of aggravated assault and battery, the defendant must have used a deadly weapon to hurt the victim or have caused serious bodily injury to the victim. Domestic violence is another form of crimes against persons. In a domestic violence case we often see men who use violence against their partners. Domestic violence cases often spiral downward into increasingly more serious injuries to the victim.

Kidnapping is the taking and asportation of a victim without the person's consent. Asportation refers to moving the victim against the victim's consent and is made an element of the crime because in moving the victim, the defendant takes the victim away from potential help. False imprisonment is a lesser-included crime of kidnapping and has similar elements except that there is only a restraint of the victim and no asportation.

Finally, crimes such as stalking, cyberstalking, and bullying, have all received greater attention in recent years because of the serious injuries and even deaths that these actions have brought about.

KEY TERMS

Assault	Simple battery	Asportation
Battery	Wanton or reckless acts	False imprisonment
Apprehension	Consent	Stalking
Conditional assault	Aggravated assault	Cyberstalking
Apparent ability	Aggravated battery	
Simple assault	Deadly weapon	

REVIEW QUESTIONS

1 What is the definition of assault?
2 How does the definition of assault differ from the definition of the crime of battery?
3 What is conditional assault?
4 What is the definition of a "deadly weapon?"
5 What are the elements of stalking?

6   Explain lesser-included offenses.

7   What are the elements of false imprisonment?

8   How does the term asportation apply to kidnapping?

9   What is the crime of aggravated assault?

10   Explain the basic aspects of domestic violence.

11   Provide at least three examples of "special victims" as the term applies to aggravated assault cases.

12   Is it necessary that the victim of a simple battery receive serious bodily injury?

13   Why is it important that the defendant have the apparent ability to carry through on a threat?

14   Is there such a crime as attempted simple assault? Explain.

15   Is it possible to commit assault using only words? Explain your answer.

16   Are there examples of lawful touchings vs. unlawful touchings?

17   Give an example of a way that a defendant can commit battery without actually touching any part of his or her body with that of the victim.

18   Is there such a thing as common law assault and battery?

19   How does reckless conduct interact with the law of battery?

20   Is it a defense to a battery for the defendant to say, "I was just carrying out a practical joke"? Explain.

21   What effect does valid consent have on the crime of battery or aggravated assault?

22   Is consent obtained through deceit still a valid defense to battery? Why or why not?

23   Can parents be prosecuted for battery for spanking their children? Why or why not?

24   Explain the role of enhancement statutes in aggravated assault cases.

25   According to the case excerpt, can background objects be considered deadly weapons? Explain.

QUESTIONS FOR ANALYSIS

1   Provide some reasons why kidnapping for ransom is rare in the United States, while it is increasing in some underdeveloped countries.

2   Will legislation stop bullying? Why or why not?

3   Should stalking statutes be expanded to protect celebrities from intrusive reporters and photographers? Justify your answer.

HYPOTHETICALS

1   Toure' is out with some friends at a bar and he gets into an argument with Rich. At one point, Rich tells Toure', "Why don't we step outside and settle this?"

     Has an assault occurred? Why or why not?

2   Danny and Neal are at work and it is a quiet Friday afternoon. Most of the other employees have left for the day. The men decide to take a small football and playing a game of catch in the long hallway near their offices. They toss it back and forth for several minutes and as they do, they increase the distance between them and begin throwing the ball harder, trying to make it more difficult for the other man to catch the ball. Kacey steps out of her office and is hit in the side of her head. What crime, if any, has occurred?

3   Ben and Katie are in the front yard of their house. They are brother and sister and both are over the age of 18. Ben decides to demonstrate some of his "trick riding" techniques on his motorcycle for his sister. He rides the bike up and down the street, sometimes standing on the seat and sometimes doing other tricks. He suggests that Katie try to hit him with some of the rocks in the front garden. He claims that no matter what she does, he will be able to avoid the rocks because of his prowess on his motorcycle. On her first throw, Katie hits Ben in the face and he falls off the motorcycle, breaking his nose and his leg. He calls the police and wants to have his sister charged with aggravated battery.

　　　Is such a charge warranted in this case? Why or why not?

Rape and Related Sexual Offenses

Chapter Objectives

- Define the elements of rape
- Differentiate between common law rape and modern, statutory rape
- Explain the relationship between lack of consent and force
- Compare and contrast the crimes of rape and statutory rape
- Explain date rape

I. INTRODUCTION

In the last chapter, we examined various crimes against the person, including assault and battery. Rape is both an assault and a battery, but carries with it much more psychological (and physical) impact.[1] This chapter examines rape and sexual battery. These crimes demand their own chapter because of the many issues that surround them which are not normally seen with other types of crimes against persons. For instance, a person who has been beaten may have a bad reaction and might even suffer from post-traumatic stress disorder, but the chances that a rape victim will have negative physical, emotional, and psychological issues are much higher. Rape is a crime of violence coupled with intense humiliation. It raises numerous issues with survivors.

It is not only the impact on the victim that makes these crimes so different from other crimes against persons; it is also the motivation of the defendant. Where a defendant might be motivated by anger in an aggravated assault case, a rape case is motivated, in many cases, by the defendant's need to sexually dominate another person. This chapter will explore the differences between sexual assault and other forms of assault and battery, including the tremendous technological innovations that have developed in recent decades which have made prosecution of rape cases considerably easier for prosecutors, even if they are not any easier for victims.

---

[1] *Girden v. Sandals Intern.*, 262 F.3d 195, 51 Fed. R. Serv. 3d 112 (2d Cir. 2001).

RAPE

Before we delve into the complex world of rape, we must address some concerns about terminology. Throughout this chapter, we will refer to the defendant as "he" and the victim as "she." This terminology is based on most state statutes that limit the definition of rape to an act committed by a man against a woman. However, with the recognition that sexual assault can involve male victims or female attackers, numerous states have removed the gender-specific aspects of prior legislation. For instance, under the old statutes, it would **not** be rape when:

- A woman sexually assaults a man
- A woman sexually assaults another woman
- A man sexually assaults another man

These actions might still have been prosecuted, but they were prosecuted under a different statute than rape. In all of the previous examples, the prosecution would fall under the category of sodomy. However, with legislative changes on the federal level and a recognition by the U.S. Attorney General that the definition of rape should be expanded to encompass all forced sex, no matter the gender of the victim or the assailant, many states have reworded their statutes to define rape as: the penetration of a man's or woman's anus or the female's vagina by another person by any means without the person's consent, or penetration of the mouth of another person by the sexual organ of the actor without the person's consent. See Figure 6-1.

However, for the sake of clarity, and because most rape cases involve female victims and male attackers, this text will use the masculine pronoun for the defendant and the feminine pronoun for the victim, unless the situation calls for a different configuration. This text will also stick with the traditional definition of rape, except in cases where it is illustrative to examine recent changes in legislation or proposed legislation.

Why do men rape women? That question has existed for centuries, and even today there is no clear answer. There are experts that see rape as a crime more about control and domination than about sexual urges. Regardless of the reason, forcing a woman (or a man) to have sex is a crime in all jurisdictions. Societal attitudes have changed a great deal about the topic of rape. In the past, the victim was often ostracized and even accused of having provoked the crime. Fortunately, these attitudes are slowly disappearing, but they have not completely gone away. In the past, rape victims were seen as tainted or stigmatized and sometimes driven from society. We are extremely fortunate that those attitudes, at least in the United States, have changed dramatically. Because rape carries with it so many complex emotions and reactions, we will examine the modern law of rape to show how much the perception, the prosecution, and even the sentencing of defendants has changed over many decades. We will also explore how **rape** was handled under the common law and how it still casts a shadow over modern rape prosecutions and some societal attitudes. See Figure 6-2 for an overview of rape in the context of other serious crimes.

Rape
When a person forces sex on another without the victim's consent.

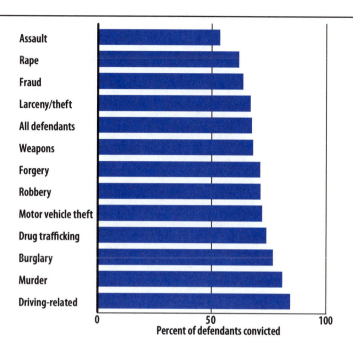

FIGURE 6-1

Probability of Conviction for Felony Defendants

Assault
Rape
Fraud
Larceny/theft
All defendants
Weapons
Forgery
Robbery
Motor vehicle theft
Drug trafficking
Burglary
Murder
Driving-related

0   50   100

Percent of defendants convicted

A. THE ELEMENTS OF RAPE

The simplest definition of rape is when a man has sexual intercourse with a woman against her will through the use of force, threat, or intimidation.[2] However, this simple definition belies a great deal of complexity. In the first instance, what criminal law means by the term "intercourse" and how does the state prove that the defendant committed this action? Also, what are the issues surrounding "force, threat, or intimidation" and what are the types of defenses commonly used in rape cases?

The general elements of the crime of rape are:

- Vaginal sexual intercourse with any degree of penetration
- Without the consent of the victim[3]

> **Sidebar**
>
> *Rape is a crime of violence. When a woman is raped, her will and her consent are overcome by the defendant. It is in many ways the worst form of assault and battery.*

VAGINAL SEXUAL INTERCOURSE WITH ANY DEGREE OF PENETRATION

In the strictest sense, rape involves the penetration of the woman's vagina by the man's penis. Other forms of sexual assault, including forced oral sex and others,

---

[2] *Com. v. Sherman*, 68 Mass. App. Ct. 797, 864 N.E.2d 1241 (2007), aff'd, 451 Mass. 332, 885 N.E.2d 122 (2008).
[3] *People v. Hovarter*, 44 Cal. 4th 983, 81 Cal. Rptr. 3d 299, 189 P.3d 300 (2008).

FIGURE 6-2	Number of Violent Victimizations and Percent Change					
	Number of victimizations			**Percent change, 2002-2011**[a]	**Percent change, 2010-2011**[a]	**Average annual change, 2002-2010**[a]
Type of violent crime	**2002**	**2010**	**2011**			
Violent crime[b]	7,424,550	4,935,980	5,805,430	−22%[†]	18%[†]	−5%
Rape/sexual assault	349,810	268,570	243,800	−30	−9	−3
Robbery	624,390	568,510	556,760	−11	−2	−1
Assault	6,450,350	4,098,900	5,004,860	−22[†]	22[†]	−5
Aggravated assault	1,332,520	857,750	1,052,080	−21[†]	23[‡]	−5
Simple assault	5,117,840	3,241,150	3,952,780	−23[†]	22[†]	−5
Domestic violence[c]	1,308,320	1,129,560	1,353,340	3	20[‡]	−2
Intimate partner violence[d]	929,760	773,430	851,340	−8	10	−2
Violent crime involving injury	1,889,880	1,289,830	1,449,300	−23[†]	12	−4
Serious violent crime[e]	2,306,710	1,694,840	1,852,650	−20%[†]	9%	−3%
Serious domestic violence[c]	449,990	380,030	368,820	−18	−3	−2
Serious intimate partner violence[d]	300,530	268,780	262,830	−13	−2	−1
Serious violent crime involving weapons	1,603,440	1,067,530	1,192,970	−26[†]	12	−5
Serious violent crime involving injury	762,220	668,160	689,510	−10	3	−1

Note: Detail may not sum to total due to rounding. Total population age 12 or older was 231,589,260 in 2002; 255,961,940 in 2010; and 257,542,240 in 2011.

† Significant at 95%.
‡ Significant at 90%.
[a] Calculated based on unrounded estimates.
[b] Excludes homicide. The NCVS is based on interviews with victims and therefore cannot measure murder.
[c] Includes victimization committed by intimate partners (current of former spouses, boyfriends, or girlfriends) and family members.
[d] Includes victimization committed by current or former spouses, boyfriends, or girlfriends.
[e] Includes rape or sexual assault, robbery, and aggravated assault.

Source: Bureau of justice Statistics, National Crime Victimization Survey, 2002, 2010, and 2011.

have fallen under the broad definition of "sodomy" and were often punished just as severely as rape. Actual penetration is a requirement of rape and is synonymous with sexual intercourse. The defendant does not have to ejaculate to complete the offense of rape. Although some penetration must be shown in order to convict the defendant, it does not have to be full penetration. In many states, slight penetration is sufficient. Under rape statutes, any penetration of the woman's vagina by the man's penis is sufficient to establish the first element of rape.[4]

---

[4] *Wightman v. State*, 289 Ga. App. 225, 656 S.E.2d 563 (2008).

To prove penetration, there are several avenues open to the prosecution showing that the first element of rape was completed, such as:

- The victim's testimony
- Witness testimony
- Medical testimony

The Victim's Testimony. In the first instance, it is often difficult for a rape victim to testify as to the specifics of the attack. No person wants to admit to being a victim, and this is especially true for rape victims. Add to that the fact that the victim must testify about extremely intimate and embarrassing details in front of a group of strangers including the judge, the prosecutor, the jury, the court bailiff, and anyone seated in the courtroom observing the trial and there is a strong potential that the victim will freeze up, have difficulty in remembering, or have suffered enough trauma during the event itself that she will have difficulty recalling what happened.

Witness Testimony. In order to have a witness testify that the man's penis entered the woman's vagina, the witness would have had to be present when the crime occurred. This is extremely unusual and if the witness were present, he or she might actually be a co-defendant, so the state would be unable to call this person to testify unless the state had worked out some agreement with the witness.

Medical Testimony. The first two methods of proving penetration are insufficient to prove this critical element. Victims are often traumatized to the point where they cannot remember specifics of the attack, and having a witness on hand to provide details of the sexual attack is extremely rare. Instead of using either of these methods, the state relies on medical testimony. In some states, medical testimony is required — a holdover from the old days of the common law — but even when it is not required, having a medical professional testify about the victim's condition is the best way to prove penetration.

How does a medical professional, usually a medical doctor or a Sexual Assault Nurse Examiner (SANE), establish that there was penetration? This person examines the victim and obtains evidence. Although there is no requirement that the state prove that the defendant ejaculated or that sperm was present following the assault, the presence does indicate that the penetration occurred.[5] This is **circumstantial evidence**. It suggests, rather than proves, a contention. However, simply because the law labels evidence circumstantial does not make it inadmissible. Circumstantial evidence is used in courtrooms across the country every day in trials. The reason that we call the evidence of sperm, or the defendant's pubic hairs, circumstantial evidence is not because it is somehow less reliable; it is because the medical professional cannot state conclusively the circumstances of how it got there. A doctor who testifies about the rape victim's condition cannot draw a conclusion that the victim was raped. That decision is left to the jury. Instead, the

Circumstantial evidence
Proof or facts that suggest a conclusion.

---

[5] *Woolridge v. State*, 97 Okla. Crim. 326, 263 P.2d 196 (1953).

doctor or SANE can simply testify that this evidence was present. The medical professional can also testify about any tearing, bruising, or discoloration in and around the vagina that would be consistent with nonconsensual sex. The medical testimony is presented with the testimony from the victim and any other corroborating evidence to prove to the jury that the defendant penetrated the victim's vagina.

In nonconsensual or forced sex it is common for the vagina to undergo a great deal of trauma. A medical professional can offer a medical opinion about how these injuries occurred and whether they are consistent with forced sex. However, the value of the testimony lies in the length of time between the assault and the medical examination. The longer the victim waits to report the crime, the more likely that valuable evidence will disappear. If the victim cleans herself after the attack, valuable DNA and other evidence will be eliminated, making it difficult to prove that a rape occurred.

Medical testimony is often required in rape cases to establish some of the basic elements of the offense.

WITHOUT THE CONSENT OF THE VICTIM

The second element that the prosecution must prove is that the defendant committed the sex act without the victim's **consent**. Because consent is often the central issue in a rape case, with the defendant claiming that all sexual contact was consensual and therefore not illegal (at least with adult victims) and the victim claiming that the sex act was nonconsensual, the government must show that the victim did not give consent. One method of doing so is by showing that she actively resisted the defendant.

Consent
Knowing and voluntary agreement to an act.

In addition to opposing the defendant's advances, the law makes certain presumptions about a woman's consent. For instance, when a woman is unconscious, and therefore unable to give consent, the law presumes no consent. The sexual assault of an unconscious woman qualifies as rape. Lack of consent is presumed when the defendant has sexual relations with a woman who is either unconscious, in a coma, or suffering from some other medical condition that makes it impossible for her to give consent.[6] The same situation would apply to a woman who is incapable of giving consent for other reasons, such as mental incapacity. Females below a certain age are presumed not to be able to give consent to any sexual contact. In most states, the age of consent is 16, but it can be as low as 14. See Figure 6-3 for one state's rape statute.

When we examine issues such as consent or whether or not force was used, the law does not address the circumstances from the defendant's viewpoint. When courts consider the issue of consent, they focus on whether or not the victim knew and understood the nature and consequences of defendant's proposed action. If the victim does not or cannot understand, then there is no valid consent.[8] A defendant would, of course, state that he believed that the victim had consented to his advances. Instead, the jury is required to view the situation from the victim's

The law imposes no requirement of force when the defendant has sex with an unconscious woman.[7]

---

[6] *Com. v. Widmer*, 560 Pa. 308, 744 A.2d 745 (2000).
[7] *People v. Hernandez*, 200 Cal. App. 4th 1000, 2011 WL 4963866 (2d Dist. 2011), review filed (Nov. 29, 2011).
[8] *State v. Ice*, 27 Kan. App. 2d 1, 997 P.2d 737 (2000).

FIGURE 6-3

Ohio's Statute on Rape

Rape.

(A)(1) No person shall engage in sexual conduct with another who is not the spouse of the offender or who is the spouse of the offender but is living separate and apart from the offender, when any of the following applies:

(a) For the purpose of preventing resistance, the offender substantially impairs the other person's judgment or control by administering any drug, intoxicant, or controlled substance to the other person surreptitiously or by force, threat of force, or deception.

(b) The other person is less than thirteen years of age, whether or not the offender knows the age of the other person.

(c) The other person's ability to resist or consent is substantially impaired because of a mental or physical condition or because of advanced age, and the offender knows or has reasonable cause to believe that the other person's ability to resist or consent is substantially impaired because of a mental or physical condition or because of advanced age.

(2) No person shall engage in sexual conduct with another when the offender purposely compels the other person to submit by force or threat of force.[9]

perspective. The jury is allowed to take into account numerous factors about the victim, including the victim's:

- Age
- Mental status
- Physical size in relation to the defendant
- Relationship, if any, with the defendant[10]

Age. As we saw earlier in this chapter, there is a point where the law presumes that individuals below a certain age cannot legally consent to sexual activity. Although this "age of consent" varies from state to state, there is no question that having sex with a child aged 12 or under is illegal in the United States and qualifies as child molestation, a topic examined in detail in the next chapter (see Figure 6-4).

FAMOUS CASES
ROMAN POLANSKI

Oscar-winning film director Roman Polanski, acclaimed for his work on *Rosemary's Baby, Chinatown,* and *The Pianist,* became embroiled in a rape scandal

---

[9] Ohio Rev. Code Ann § 2907.0.2.
[10] *Maslin v. State,* 718 N.E.2d 1230 (Ind. Ct. App. 1999) (overruled on other grounds by, *Ludy v. State,* 784 N.E.2d 459 (Ind. 2003)).

FIGURE 6-4

Florida's Sexual Battery
Statute

> **(2) (a)   A person 18 years of age or older who commits sexual battery upon, or in an attempt to commit sexual battery injures the sexual organs of, a person less than 12 years of age commits a capital felony, punishable as provided in ss. 775.082 and 921.141.**
>
> **(b)   A person less than 18 years of age who commits sexual battery upon, or in an attempt to commit sexual battery injures the sexual organs of, a person less than 12 years of age commits a life felony.[11]**

in 1977. An acquaintance, a model and actress, granted Polanski permission to do a photo shoot of her 13-year-old daughter, Samantha Gailey, for the French edition of *Vogue* magazine. The photo shoot took place at the Los Angeles home of actor Jack Nicholson, who was away on a skiing trip. Behind a closed bedroom door, Polanski took photos of a topless Samantha drinking champagne, and he allegedly gave her part of a Quaalude, a sedative-hypnotic drug. After he finished shooting in the bedroom, they moved to a Jacuzzi where he took photos of her nude before removing his own clothing and joining her. Samantha became uncomfortable and returned to the bedroom. Polanski followed and then performed a variety of sex acts on her, including oral, vaginal, and anal sex.

The truth is murky about whether Samantha was a willing participant or forced to have sex with Polanski. But murky or not, the act constituted statutory rape. Polanski was arrested the next day and charged with rape by use of drugs, sodomy, lewd and lascivious act upon a child under the age of 14, perversion, and furnishing a controlled substance to a minor.

Wanting to avoid the ordeal of a trial for Samantha, her attorney arranged for a plea bargain in which Polanski would plead guilty to a single charge of unlawful sexual intercourse with a minor. Under the terms of the plea bargain, Polanski spent 90 days in a state prison for psychiatric evaluation. He was released after 42 days, and the expectation was that his sentence would be probation. However, Polanski learned through one of his attorneys that even though the examining psychiatrist, the probation officer, and the victim herself recommended no prison time, Judge Laurence J. Rittenband had other ideas. The judge, it seemed, believed it to be a miscarriage of justice to allow a man who had "drugged and raped a 13-year-old child" to go free.

Polanski fled to his native France, where he could avoid extradition because of his citizenship. The United States kept tabs on him, however, for if he visited another country from which he could be extradited, he could be returned to face sentencing. Over the years, Polanski and his lawyers tried numerous maneuvers to have his case dismissed on the grounds of prosecutorial and judicial misconduct. He claimed that, among other things, Judge Rittenband violated the plea bargain by communicating details of the case to a deputy district attorney who was not involved.

In consideration of this motion, Judge Peter Espinoza (Rittenband had since died) admitted in February 2009 that there were problems with the case, but he

---

[11] Fla.Stat.ch.794.011.

declined to throw the charges out. He did state, however, that he would issue a ruling if Polanski would return to Los Angeles and appear in court. Fearing he would be taken into custody, Polanski refused.

Then on September 26, 2009, more than 30 years after the original crime, U.S. officials learned that Polanski would be traveling to Switzerland to accept an award at the Zurich Film Festival. In cooperation with the United States, the Swiss police detained him at the airport, and a lengthy extradition process commenced. Polanski remained in custody in Zurich for two months then was placed under house arrest at his home in Gstaad while the extradition fight played out. On July 12, 2010, the Swiss court rejected extradition because of flaws in the United States' request. The court immediately released Polanski from house arrest and declared him a free man.

Roman Polanski remains a wanted man in the United States. Should he travel to another country that has an extradition treaty with the United States, it is likely that the scenario will repeat itself. In an odd coincidence, Polanski's arrest in Zurich came just two days after the death of Susan Atkins, the Charles Manson Family member who stabbed to death Polanski's wife, Sharon Tate, in 1969.

Mental Status. If age can be taken into account when determining whether or not valid consent was given, so too can the victim's mental status. If the victim is incapable of giving consent, either because she is not conscious or suffers from some mental impediment, then it is legally impossible for her to give consent. Persons who suffer from mental disease to the point where they cannot make rational decisions or understand the nature and consequences of their actions, are incapable of giving valid consent, and a defendant cannot claim as a defense that such a person actually did consent, when the defendant knew that she suffered from mental problems.[12] It should be noted that when this question arises in a rape prosecution, the victim's mental status is obvious for anyone to see, including the defendant. This provision of the law is not invoked for mental problems that might have a slight impact on the victim; it is used when the victim suffers from a severe form of mental disease. Consider Scenario 6-1.

VICTIM WITH A LOW IQ AND A MENTAL AGE OF 6

SCENARIO 6-1

Dan is accused of having sex with Mary, who is in an institution. Mary has an IQ of 45 and a mental age of 6 years old, although she is physically 30 years old. She responds to everything in her world as if she is a 6-year-old and will always be that way. Dan asked if her she wanted to have sex and she said yes. After he had sex with her, he was charged with rape. Is this a valid charge?

Answer: Yes. The victim had a mental age of 6 years old and was unable to understand the consequences or the nature of giving consent to sexual contact. In fact, she was institutionalized for this condition.[13]

---

[12] *People v. Giardino*, 82 Cal. App. 4th 454, 98 Cal. Rptr. 2d 315 (4th Dist. 2000).
[13] *State v. Ortega-Martinez*, 124 Wash. 2d 702, 881 P.2d 231 (1994).

Physical Size in Relation to Defendant. Intimidation can also satisfy the elements of rape. There is no requirement that the victim actually suffer bodily injury before submitting to a rape. Sexual contact that is obtained through intimidation is no more consensual than brute force. There is no requirement that the victim cry out or resist, at least in most states. Intimidation can substitute for force, and this is true even if the victim's fear of the attacker is not reasonable or rational and the attacker takes advantage of that unreasonable fear to intimidate the victim into having sex with him.[14]

Relationship, if Any, with the Defendant. A woman may revoke her consent at any time, even after the sexual act has begun. If the man continues, after he is aware that consent has been withdrawn, then the crime is rape.[15] This is true even if the victim and the defendant had once had a consensual relationship. If the relationship is no longer consensual, and the man forces sex on the woman, then the elements of rape are satisfied.[16]

Consent and Force. Proving that the victim did not consent is only part of the proof required to establish the second element of the offense. As we have seen, there is no requirement to prove that the victim was forced into a sex act when she was unconscious, below a certain age or suffered from some form of mental disease. However, suppose the victim in a rape case has no such impediment? In that case, the prosecution must still establish that the attack was not consensual, but it must also address the issue of how the attack was carried out. See Figure 6-5.

This is not simply a matter of asking the victim if she consented. The prosecutor will definitely ask that question, but in order to bolster the case, the prosecution will also show surrounding circumstances that establish that the victim did not consent. One of those surrounding circumstances is the use of force.

Force. If the state can prove that the defendant used force to overcome the victim, then there is no consent. Forcing a person to carry out an act does not make it something that she did of her own free will. The element of force can be satisfied in any of a number of ways, including physically restraining the victim, tying the victim up, or beating her to the point of unconsciousness.[18]

What is "force"? At first glance, this would seem to be an obvious question. Force is force. But how is force defined? Obviously it is force when a defendant seizes a victim and drags her away, but not all rapes occur in that manner. Is it force to point a gun at the victim? The answer is yes. Force, threats of

---

Sidebar

Most states have laws that make it a crime for a police officer or corrections officer to have sex with a detainee. In these situations, consent is irrelevant. The fact that the officer had sexual relations with the detainee is enough to meet the elements of the crime.[17]

---

[14] *People v. Bermudez*, 157 Cal. App. 3d 619, 203 Cal. Rptr. 728 (5th Dist. 1984).

[15] *People v. Ireland*, 188 Cal. App. 4th 328, 114 Cal. Rptr. 3d 915 (5th Dist. 2010), review filed (Oct. 20, 2010).

[16] *Scott v. State*, 281 Ga. App. 106, 635 S.E.2d 582 (2006).

[17] *State v. Torres*, 151 Wash. App. 378, 212 P.3d 573 (Div. 1 2009), review denied, 167 Wash. 2d 1019, 224 P.3d 773 (2010).

[18] *U.S. v. Simmons*, 470 F.3d 1115, 71 Fed. R. Evid. Serv. 1019 (5th Cir. 2006).

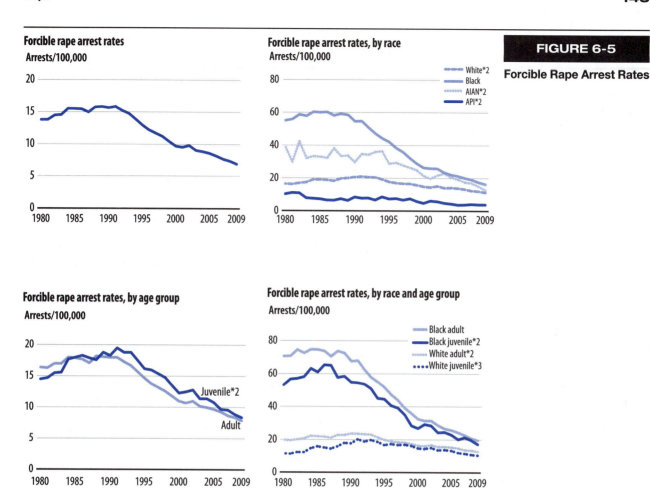

FIGURE 6-5

Forcible Rape Arrest Rates

force, or any fear of serious bodily injury is enough to satisfy the element of force.[19] With victims who are under the age of consent, intimidation can substitute for force.[20]

The terms "forcibly" and "against her will" are actually two separate elements in rape cases. "Against her will" means without consent. "Forcibly" means any physical violence, a show of force, or threats of death or physical bodily harm. It can also mean mental coercion, such as intimidation. In most situations, this term will be satisfied by a threat of physical force or violence coupled with the defendant's apparent ability to carry out the threat. There is also no requirement that the defendant actually utter a threat before the force element can be satisfied. The act of rape can be

---

[19] *State v. Tucker*, 154 N.C. App. 653, 573 S.E.2d 197 (2002), writ denied, review denied, 356 N.C. 691, 578 S.E.2d 597 (2003).
[20] *Wightman v. State*, 289 Ga. App. 225, 656 S.E.2d 563 (2008).

carried out without the defendant ever saying a word. The fact that he has a weapon is sufficient.[21]

SCENARIO 6-2	## BLACKMAIL

David, who has been divorced from Brenda for over a year, recently learned that Brenda is having an affair with a married co-worker. He approaches Brenda and demands sex or he will reveal the affair. Brenda submits to his demands. Later, she wishes to file a rape charge. Have the elements of rape been met?

Answer: No. In this case, blackmailing a woman into having sex is not the same thing as using force, threat, or intimidation to overcome the victim's will. Even if the defendant had revealed his ex-wife's affair, she would not have faced any criminal charges or economic loss, there was no other force used and even though the threat of blackmail made Brenda uncomfortable, it did not rise to the level of forcing her to submit to sex.[22] However, the crime of blackmail would certainly apply.

When a deadly weapon is used, for instance, the force requirement is satisfied. Generally, courts have held that the element of force is satisfied when the defendant uses words or acts that would place a reasonable person in apprehension or fear of the consequences to her or others. The force element can also be established if the prosecution can show that the defendant put the victim in fear, that he coerced her, or that he put her under duress.[23] Consider Scenario 6-3.

SCENARIO 6-3	## THE CHILD

Very early one morning, Sheila is awakened by a noise in her bedroom. A man is standing there holding a knife. He also has Sheila's 3-year-old son, Kaya, with him. The man says, "You know what will happen to him if I don't get what I want."

The man puts Kaya on the other side of the door and then rapes Sheila. At trial, the man insists that the sex was consensual because he never actually forced Sheila and never even explicitly mentioned any threat against the son. Can the state show that Sheila was forced to submit to sex under this situation?

Answer: Yes. Threatening to kill a child, even by implication, is enough to establish force and overcome the victim's consent. In fact, most mothers would readily agree that they would do almost anything to protect the lives of their children.

---

[21] *State v. Brooks*, 263 P.3d 161 (Kan. 2011).
[22] *State v. Brooks*, 263 P.3d 161 (Kan. 2011).
[23] *State v. Baptista*, 894 A.2d 911 (R.I. 2006).

BURNING DOWN THE HOUSE

Alisha wakes up in her bed to find a strange man standing in her bedroom. He has a gas can in one hand and a cigarette lighter in the other. He tells Alisha that unless she has sex with him, he will burn down her house. Is this sufficient "force" to charge the man with rape when he has sex with Alisha?

Answer: Yes. If the victim has a reasonable belief that threat to burn down her house is real, that is enough to establish force.[24]

Consent Through Fraud? Jurisdictions are split on the question of whether obtaining consent by fraud qualifies as rape. Suppose that the defendant slips into bed with a woman and pretends to be her husband. In some states, this fraud would rise to the level of overcoming consent, while in others it does not.[25]

Technological Advances in Rape Cases. Once a report of rape has reached law enforcement, the first task is to secure the victim and catch the perpetrator. The victim will be taken to a local hospital or some other medical facility for a medical examination. The sooner this examination occurs, the better the chance of recovering valuable evidence. These days, many states have facilities with specially trained personnel on hand who know how to go about obtaining the evidence and preserving it for later testing. In some states, there are specially Registered Nurses who are called Sexual Assault Nurse Examiners (SANE). A SANE is trained not only in gathering evidence, but also in how to present this evidence to a jury. A SANE will often work in conjunction with counselors or a victim's advocate so that the victim will have some help through the ordeal of reporting the crime and being examined for evidence.

DNA Databases. Collecting evidence is more important now than ever before. If the state can obtain a specimen of the defendant's DNA, either from his sperm, saliva, or other substances, then the chances of catching the suspect are much higher. However, DNA will not take the place of a proper investigation. The best that DNA can do is to tell the jury, with almost absolute certainty, that *this* defendant was the source of this bodily fluid. However, DNA will not explain motives, human emotions, or why a person would commit such a crime. DNA will not even tell a jury if the sex was consensual; it only provides the answer as to whether or not a particular defendant had sex with the victim.

As most of us know, DNA databases have been set up in all states and on the national level. There are still some issues about sharing information among and between these various databases, but these local rivalries are giving way to a greater concern for catching criminals. Some have raised civil-liberties objections to obtaining DNA specimens from convicted criminals, but challenges to the constitutionality of such databases has passed scrutiny from the courts. In recent years, the U.S.

---

[24] *State v. Brooks*, 263 P.3d 161 (Kan. 2011).
[25] *State v. Navarro*, 90 Ariz. 185, 367 P.2d 227, 91 A.L.R.2d 586 (1961).

Supreme Court has even ruled that obtaining DNA from people who have been arrested is acceptable in certain circumstances. Even with these advances in DNA technology, there still remain regional variations in rape victimization across the United States as shown in Figure 6-6.

RAPE AND THE COMMON LAW

DNA databases have been a huge boon to law enforcement, helping them to identify rapists who have previously provided DNA material to the DNA database.

Rape under the common law was a substantially different crime. The differences lay not so much in the actions of the defendant, but in the focus on the victim. The basic elements of rape were the same under common law as they are under most statutory definitions of the crime. The biggest difference came in relation to the victim. The issue of consent was a complex and troublesome feature of common law. First of all, to prove the sex was not consensual, the victim had to show that she resisted the attack. That element is still present in modern rape prosecutions, but the definition of resistance has changed dramatically from the days of common law rape. In some jurisdictions, the victim had to show that she fought her attacker to the point of death; otherwise, it would be assumed that she consented. In other jurisdictions, the victim had to show that she had used "maximum and reasonable resistance" in

| FIGURE 6-6 | Rate and Percent Change of Violent Victimization, by Household Region |

	Violent crime					Serious violence crime[a]				
	Rates[b]			Percent change[c]		Rates[b]			Percent change[c]	
Household location	2002	2010	2011	2002-2011	2010-2011	2002	2010	2011	2002-2011	2010-2011
Total	32.1	19.3	22.5	−30%[†]	17%[†]	10.0	6.6	7.2	−28%[†]	9%
Region										
Northeast	28.5	17.2	20.3	−29%[†]	18%	7.1	6.8	6.4	−9%	−6%
Midwest	38.8	22.0	26.3	−32[†]	19[‡]	11.5	7.6	7.8	−32[†]	3
South	27.4	16.6	18.3	−33[†]	10	10.8	5.4	6.5	−40[†]	20
West	35.6	22.4	27.1	−24[†]	21[‡]	9.5	7.5	8.4	−12	12
Location of residence										
Urban	41.0	24.2	27.4	−33%[†]	13%	15.2	9.5	9.7	−36%[†]	3%
Suburban	28.3	16.8	20.2	−29[†]	20[†]	7.8	5.5	5.7	−27%[†]	4
Rural	28.6	17.7	20.1	−30[†]	14	7.9	4.7	6.7	−15	42

† Significant at 95%.
‡ Significant at 90%.
[a] Includes rape or sexual assault, robbery, and aggravated assault.
[b] Per 1,000 persons age 12 or older.
[c] Calculated based on unrounded estimates.

Source: Bureau of Justice Statistics, National Crime Victimization Survey, 2002, 2010, and 2011.

fighting off her attacker. States interpreted this phrase in different ways. While some states interpreted it to mean any resistance to the assault, many states required the victim to put up a heroic effort before they would consider the victim to have properly resisted. Essentially, this placed the burden on the victim. If she did not resist enough, then she must have consented to the sex act and therefore it was not rape.

Fortunately, this view began to change in the mid-20th century. Many courts began questioning why the victim would have to show such dramatic resistance to a sexual assault, when victims of other types of batteries were not required to show similar resistance. The idea that the victim had to show that she resisted "with all her power and strength" or that she must have consented slowly gave way to a more commonsense view that a rape was an act of violence, not simply a romantic act taken too far.[26] Along with this change in viewpoint, studies showed that less than 2 percent of all rapes were false claims. There was a strong push to put the burden on the state to prove that the defendant overcame the victim's will, rather than placing the burden on the victim to prove that if she had not resisted to the point of death, then her submission must have been consensual. In the few jurisdictions where resistance still remains an element, it is not enough for the victim simply to resist by words. She must use some type of physical resistance. Although common law used to require that a woman resisted to the point of death, it is no longer the case in United States.[27] Even in these jurisdictions, a woman is only required to resist the attack, not to continue the resistance after the sexual act is completed.[28] In most other jurisdictions, the focus of the prosecution is not on whether or not the victim physically resisted, but on whether the defendant knew that the victim had not consented and acted anyway.[29]

In many ways, when it comes to proving the first element of rape, states continue to follow the common law definition. Under that definition, penetrating the victim's vagina with a finger or some other object does not strictly meet the standard of penetration. However, that does mean that it is not a crime. It may simply be referred to as sexual battery or forced sodomy.[30]

A. SPOUSAL IMMUNITY UNDER COMMON LAW

Common law presented some other interesting issues in rape prosecutions. The common law prevented a husband from being charged and convicted with raping his wife. The theory actually developed along two lines, the first of which was eventually abandoned. Under the original construction of the marital relationship, wives were considered property of their husbands. A husband need not obtain consent from his own property before engaging in any activity, so there could be

Under the common law, it was typical to require that the victim show active resistance to the rapist. Many jurisdictions have done away with that requirement.[31]

---

[26] *Curtis v. State*, 236 Ga. 362, 362, 223 S.E.2d 721 (1976).

[27] *State v. Lopez-McCurdy*, 266 S.W.3d 874 (Mo. Ct. App. S.D. 2008).

[28] *People v. Nazworth*, 152 Cal. App. 2d 790, 313 P.2d 113 (4th Dist. 1957).

[29] *Jimmy v. State*, 206 P.3d 750 (Alaska Ct. App. 2009).

[30] *Com. v. Sherman*, 451 Mass. 332, 885 N.E.2d 122 (2008).

[31] *Com. v. Andrulewicz*, 2006 PA Super 309, 911 A.2d 162 (2006).

no rape prosecution. However, this extremely antiquated view was eventually modified, especially in the face of the expansion of women's rights and their eventual grant of the right to vote, to a view that because the wife had married the husband, she had given prior consent to sexual activity and could not revoke that consent within the marital relationship. That view persisted in the law until the 1970s and 1980s when movements began to recognize that women had the right to invoke their own human rights and refuse to give consent, especially in situations where the wife and husband were estranged and living apart. Eventually, all states adopted legislation and changed the common law rule that a husband could not be prosecuted for raping his wife. The so-called **spousal immunity** in rape cases was eliminated, and now a husband who forces his wife to submit to sex can be prosecuted for rape, although these cases often involve difficult questions of proof, especially where the couple has had a complicated and violent history.

Spousal immunity
The legal doctrine that prevents a husband from being charged with the rape of his wife.

B. CORROBORATION REQUIRED UNDER THE COMMON LAW

Common law continues to cast a long shadow in rape cases. Originally, common law required that any victim's report of rape must be corroborated. That meant that some other person would have to bolster the victim's statement with sworn testimony. In many cases, this was impossible as the only people present during the attack were the victim and the attacker. Most states have eliminated this requirement, and the few that kept it have modified it so that medical testimony from an examination of the victim will satisfy the **corroboration** element.[32]

Corroboration
Presentation of evidence that supports or adds details to a claim.

RAPE SHIELD STATUTES

Although we have all seen rape cases portrayed on television and in movies, they are almost universally incorrect in their depictions of the reality of a rape trial. One of the most gut-wrenching parts of a rape trial occurs when the defense attorney cross-examines the rape victim and points out that she has had sex with other men, that she may, in fact, be a "loose woman" who routinely engages in sex with a wide variety of men, drawing the clear indication that the victim should not be believed in this case, because she has sex with strange men on a regular basis. Not only does this line of questioning do a disservice to the criminal justice system; there are undoubtedly rape victims who see these depictions, believe them, and fail to report assaults because they do not wish to be subjected to such an attack while they are on the witness stand.

However, all states have statutes that specifically prevent exactly this type of questioning. A victim of a sexual assault cannot be questioned about her prior sexual history, unless the defense can show that it has some bearing on the facts

---

[32] *Baker v. State*, 245 Ga. 657, 266 S.E.2d 477 (1980).

California's Rape Shield Statute

§ 782. Sexual offenses; evidence of sexual conduct of complaining witness; procedure for admissibility; treatment of resealed affidavits

(a) In any of the circumstances described in subdivision (c), if evidence of sexual conduct of the complaining witness is offered to attack the credibility of the complaining witness under Section 780, the following procedure shall be followed:

(1) A written motion shall be made by the defendant to the court and prosecutor stating that the defense has an offer of proof of the relevancy of evidence of the sexual conduct of the complaining witness proposed to be presented and its relevancy in attacking the credibility of the complaining witness.

(2) The written motion shall be accompanied by an affidavit in which the offer of proof shall be stated. The affidavit shall be filed under seal and only unsealed by the court to determine if the offer of proof is sufficient to order a hearing pursuant to paragraph (3). After that determination, the affidavit shall be resealed by the court.

(3) If the court finds that the offer of proof is sufficient, the court shall order a hearing out of the presence of the jury, if any, and at the hearing allow the questioning of the complaining witness regarding the offer of proof made by the defendant.

(4) At the conclusion of the hearing, if the court finds that evidence proposed to be offered by the defendant regarding the sexual conduct of the complaining witness is relevant pursuant to Section 780, and is not inadmissible pursuant to Section 352, the court may make an order stating what evidence may be introduced by the defendant, and the nature of the questions to be permitted. The defendant may then offer evidence pursuant to the order of the court.

(b) As used in this section, "complaining witness" means:

(1) The alleged victim of the crime charged, the prosecution of which is subject to this section, pursuant to paragraph (1) of subdivision (c).[33]

of the current case. Defense attorneys are not permitted to ask broad questions about a victim's sexual history. The statutes that were passed to protect the privacy of rape victims are commonly referred to as **"Rape Shield Statutes."** See Figure 6-7 for an example.

Consider this scenario:

Rape Shield Statute
A statute that prevents a rape victim from being cross-examined about her sexual history, unless that history involves the defendant; these statutes also protect the name of the rape victim from being released to the media.

THE MAN IN HER ROOM

During the trial of Ron X for rape, the victim testifies. On cross-examination, the victim tells the defense attorney that she woke up around 2:00 a.m. and found a man standing in her

continued

---

[33] West's Ann.Cal.Evid.Code § 782.

SCENARIO 6-5

(continued)

bedroom. The defense attorney asks, "Surely you've had strange men standing in your bedroom before?"

The prosecutor objects, citing the rape shield statute. How does the judge rule?

Answer: The judge is likely to rule that this question falls within the spirit, if not the letter of the rape shield statute and will likely instruct the victim not to answer the question and the attorney to move on to another question.

A. CROSS-EXAMINING RAPE VICTIMS

During the course of a trial, the rape victim will testify on direct examination where she will be questioned by the prosecutor about the facts and circumstances surrounding the attack. Once direct examination is complete, the defendant's attorney has the right to question the witness on cross-examination. Unlike what is often dramatized on television, most defense attorneys are not sleazy, immoral people who are willing to try any tactic to get their client found not guilty. Cross-examination of rape victims is one area that has been especially embellished and fictionalized on television and in movies. The truth is that in most rape cases, the defense attorney does not scream and yell at the rape victim. This is not necessarily because the defense attorney is a nice person, rather the reason is more pragmatic. In a fictionalized rape trial when the victim is brought to tears by a sneering, sarcastic, and brutal cross-examination, we feel sorry for the victim and, by extension, feel great animosity toward the defense attorney and his or her client. Defense attorneys know this. They do not want the jury to feel sorry for the victim or to hate the defendant. That is one way to ensure a conviction.

Instead, defense attorneys use entirely different tactics than what are commonly portrayed in the media. They do not scream and accuse the victim of being a sexually promiscuous person. Depending on the nature of the defense, they will use one of several approaches. If the defense is that the victim has identified the wrong person, the defense attorney will often be very solicitous of the victim and attempt to show that there is at least a possibility that the victim has identified the wrong person. In cases where the defense is consent, the defense attorney will focus on the particulars of the relationship between the victim and the defendant, if there is one, or that the victim exercised poor judgment by meeting a stranger and then later regretted the action and found a claim of rape was the only way to rectify personal difficulties, such as having to admit to an extramarital affair.

V AGGRAVATED SEXUAL ASSAULT

An assault may be classified as aggravated sexual assault when any of the following occurs:

- When a deadly weapon is used
- When the victim is seriously injured
- When the victim was kidnapped

What is the significance of calling one crime rape and another aggravated sexual assault? The practical consequence is that the defendant's sentence can be enhanced. Instead of a 10-year sentence for rape, a defendant may be sentenced to 20 years for aggravated rape or aggravated sexual assault. In many cases it is either the use of a weapon or the degree of force that will dictate whether the crime is classified as rape or aggravated sexual assault (sometimes called aggravated sexual battery).[34] Depending on the severity of the injuries to the victim, a defendant can even face a mandatory life sentence for aggravated sexual assault.

 ## VI DATE RAPE

It is an unfortunate fact that most victims know their rapists. The statistics are depressingly clear: A woman is far more likely to be raped by someone she knows, perhaps even trusts. Her rapist may be a friend, a co-worker, an ex-boyfriend, or a date. Date rape has received increased publicity in recent years, as more victims have come forward to reveal that they have been assaulted on first or second dates. The fact that the rape occurs during a romantic date does not make the rape any less serious or the rapist any less culpable.

A. DATE RAPE DRUGS

So-called "date rape drugs" have become widely available in recent years. These drugs, marketed under a wide variety of names, are generally clear, odorless and tasteless liquids that would-be rapists put into victims' drinks. Once imbibed, the drug renders the victim unconscious. She is then raped. Following the rape, the attacker will attempt to arrange things so that it will appear that the victim simply passed out from drinking too much alcohol. Often the victim has no clear idea of what happened. See this chapter's case excerpt for an example of a case involving the rape of a woman who was not aware that it had even happened. Consider Scenario 6-6.

PRIOR CONSENT?

SCENARIO 6-6

Rob and Victoria have recently met through an online dating service. They have never actually spoken, but they have exchanged emails. In the emails, their exchanges have increasingly taken on sexual overtones. Rob is convinced that Victoria wants to have sex with him, even though they have never actually met. When they finally go out on a date, Victoria has too much to drink and passes out in Rob's car when they leave the restaurant. Rob has sex with Victoria. Has he committed rape?

continued

---

[34] *State v. Dixon*, 900 So. 2d 929 (La. Ct. App. 5th Cir. 2005).

SCENARIO 6-6

(continued)

Answer: Yes. Rob did not have consent from Victoria and, although their previous emails may have led him to believe that she was interested in him sexually, he cannot infer her consent or attempt to show that Victoria had given prior consent to a sex act in his car.

VII   STATUTORY RAPE

Statutory rape is one of the few *strict liability* crimes. A strict liability crime is one that does not require the two elements of any criminal offense: *mens rea* (intent) and *actus reus* (action). As discussed in Chapter 2, most crimes require both intent on the part of the defendant as well as a corresponding behavior to put that intent into action. This is not the case with strict liability crimes. In a strict liability crime, the act alone is sufficient to charge the defendant. To be guilty of statutory rape the only requirement is that the defendant had sexual intercourse with an underage victim. The fact that the defendant may have believed that the victim was of proper age is not a defense to **statutory rape**. The fact that the victim consented to the action — which normally would eliminate any criminal charge — is also irrelevant.

Statutory rape
The crime of an adult having sex with an underage boy or girl.

States have different rules when it comes to what does and does not qualify as statutory rape. Traditionally, the statutes were phrased so that they only applied to men having sex with underage girls. But in recent years, many high profile cases involving adult women having sex with underage boys have resulted in a change in the statutes so that they now apply to both men and women and to boys and girls. In addition to states having considerable variation as to what age a child must be when the crime is considered statutory rape (15 years of age is one example, but some states go as low as 12), there are also provisions in some state laws that impose an age difference between the parties. For instance, in North Carolina, there must be a greater than six-year difference in age before the adult can be prosecuted for having sex with an underage person (see Figure 6-8).

FIGURE 6-8

Statutory Rape in North Carolina

> Statutory rape or sexual offense of person who is 13, 14, or 15 years old.
>
> (a) A defendant is guilty of a Class B1 felony if the defendant engages in vaginal intercourse or a sexual act with another person who is 13, 14, or 15 years old and the defendant is at least six years older than the person, except when the defendant is lawfully married to the person.
>
> (b) A defendant is guilty of a Class C felony if the defendant engages in vaginal intercourse or a sexual act with another person who is 13, 14, or 15 years old and the defendant is more than four but less than six years older than the person, except when the defendant is lawfully married to the person.[35]

---

[35] N.C.G.S. § 14–27.7A.

PEOPLE v. HERNANDEZ
200 Cal.App.4th 1000, 1007, 133 Cal.Rptr.3d 229, 235)
(Cal.App. 2 Dist.,2011)

YEGAN, J.

Ramon Ruiz Hernandez appeals his conviction, by jury, of rape of an unconscious person. (Pen.Code, § 261, subd. (a)(4).) He was sentenced by the trial court to a term of three years in state prison. Appellant contends there was insufficient evidence that the victim was unconscious or that he was aware of this fact. He further contends the trial court erred when it failed to instruct the jury on simple battery (§ 242) as a lesser included offense. We affirm.

FACTS

A.B. spent the night of July 4, 2009 at the Glendale apartment of her godmother, Alejandra Garcia. It was Garcia's birthday and she was having a party with some family members and friends, including her cousin, appellant. By around midnight, most of the guests were gone, but A.B., Alejandra, and appellant were still playing video games and drinking beer. During the evening, A.B. told Alejandra that she did not want to be left alone with appellant. Alejandra told A.B. and appellant that they should both stay the night because they had been drinking. A.B. changed into pajama bottoms and a t-shirt and went into the bedroom to sleep. Appellant stayed in the living room, on the couch. Alejandra got into bed with A.B.

A.B. woke up at about 4:00 a.m. and went to the bathroom. She noticed that her vagina was wet, she was not wearing her underwear and her pajama bottoms were on inside out. She felt scared and wanted to call someone but could not find her phone in the bedroom, where she had left it the night before. Appellant was sleeping on the living room couch. A.B. woke him up and asked if he had done anything to her. Appellant denied doing anything. Then he got down on his knees, used his fists to strike himself in the head and repeated in Spanish, "I didn't do anything, I swear." A.B. found her phone in the kitchen and called her brother, Ivan, to pick her up. She didn't want to stay in the apartment, so she went outside and started walking. She met Ivan and he drove her home.

Once at home, A.B. called her best friend, appellant's sister, Linda. She told Linda that she thought appellant raped her. Later that morning, A.B. went to the hospital with her mother, Ivan, and Linda where she was given a sexual assault examination. The forensic nurse examiner testified that A.B. had lacerations on the entrance of her vagina that were consistent with blunt penetrating trauma and were more severe than she would expect to see with consensual sex. DNA tests confirmed that saliva found on A.B.'s neck and sperm found on her external and internal genitalia were appellant's.

When questioned by police, appellant initially denied having sex with A.B. Then, appellant said that A.B. and Alejandra told him they were gay and wanted him to leave so they could "do their thing." He told them he would leave if they each kissed him. They did and then went into the bedroom. He stayed in the living room and eventually went to sleep. When he got up in the night to use the bathroom, he walked past A.B.'s bed.[2] The two started kissing and eventually had sex. Appellant first told the police that A.B. was awake and that she moved her hips and legs so that he could remove her pajama bottoms. After some additional questioning, he stated that A.B. was asleep when he first started kissing her and when he removed her pants, but that she lifted her legs behind his head once he started having sex with her. Appellant later said that A.B. was "knocked out" or "out cold" the entire time and that she did not give him permission to have sex with her.

At trial, appellant testified that the sex was consensual. He told the jury that he had been confused by the police officer's questions because he does not speak English very well. He testified that, before anyone went to bed, he was massaging A.B.'s feet and she seemed to like it. Alejandra told him, "No leave her alone. She's mine tonight." They asked him to leave because they said, "'We are gay and we could not do our thing,'" with him there. Both women kissed him, so that he would leave. He stayed anyway. The women went into the bedroom together. Later, he walked past A.B.'s bed as he left the bathroom. The two started kissing. She was awake and responsive. They had consensual sex.

Appellant's sister, Linda, testified that A.B. called her at about 5:30 a.m. on July 5 to say she thought she'd had sex with Linda's brother and that she'd been very drunk. A.B. did not say she had been raped. They went to the hospital because A.B. wanted to get a "morning after" pill, to avoid pregnancy. Two days later, A.B. called Linda and told her that she remembered having consensual sex with appellant. She wanted to tell the police but was afraid she'd get in trouble. Linda did not tell the police or appellant's trial counsel about this conversation before she testified.

DISCUSSION

Appellant contends there was no substantial evidence A.B. was unconscious or that he knew she was unconscious while they were having sex. He further contends the trial court erred in failing to give an instruction on battery as a lesser included offense of the charged crime, rape of an unconscious person. Neither contention has merit.

SUBSTANTIAL EVIDENCE

In determining whether appellant's conviction is supported by substantial evidence, we apply a familiar standard. We review the entire record in the light most favorable to the judgment, to determine whether it contains evidence sufficient to permit any rational trier of fact to find the essential elements of the crime beyond a reasonable doubt. We presume in support of the judgment the existence of every fact the trier could reasonably deduce from the evidence, but we do not re-weigh the evidence or re-evaluate the credibility of the witnesses.

Rape, as defined by section 261, subdivision (a)(4), includes an act of sexual intercourse accomplished, "Where a person is at the time unconscious of the nature of the act, and this is known to the accused. As used in this paragraph, 'unconscious

---

[2] Alejandra's apartment has one bedroom and one bathroom, which is reached through the bedroom.

of the nature of the act' means incapable of resisting because the victim meets one of the following conditions: (A) Was unconscious or asleep." (§ 261, subd. (a)(4)(A).) The trial court instructed the jury that it could find appellant guilty only if the prosecution proved beyond a reasonable doubt that, when A.B. had sexual intercourse with appellant, she was unable to resist because she was unconscious of the nature of the act and that appellant knew A.B. was unable to resist because she was unconscious of the nature of the act.

Appellant concedes there is ample evidence that A.B. was very drunk when she went to bed that night, and she could not remember the next morning what had happened. He contends that her memory lapse establishes drunkenness, not unconsciousness. This contention essentially invites us to re-weigh the evidence and infer that A.B. was drunk rather than unconscious when he had sex with her. We decline the invitation because the record contains substantial evidence supporting the inferences drawn by the jury: that A.B. was unconscious and that appellant knew it. In his tape-recorded interview with Glendale Police Department Detective Ernest Gaxiola, appellant admitted that A.B. was unconscious when he had sex with her. According to appellant, A.B. never told him she wanted to have sex; in fact, she said nothing during the entire encounter. She did not "wake up" and barely even moved while they were having sex. In fact, appellant agreed that she was "knocked out," or "out cold" while they were having sex. Appellant also admitted that A.B. never gave him permission to have sex with her and that he knew she "didn't want to have sex with him." A rational trier of fact could find from these statements alone that A.B. was unconscious during the assault and that appellant knew it. When considered in light of A.B.'s testimony that she was intoxicated, had no memory of the assault and never consented to have sex with appellant, appellant's statements provide substantial evidence of both A.B.'s unconsciousness and his knowledge of it.

INSTRUCTION ON LESSER INCLUDED OFFENSE

Appellant contends the trial court erred when it denied his request for an instruction on simple battery as a lesser included offense because the jury might have concluded that appellant kissed A.B. without her consent but that the subsequent sexual intercourse was consensual. We are not persuaded.

As our Supreme Court has explained, the trial court must instruct the jury on "any uncharged offense that is lesser than, and included in, a greater charged offense, but only if there is substantial evidence supporting a jury determination that the defendant was in fact guilty only of the lesser offense." In this context, substantial evidence is "evidence that a reasonable jury would find persuasive" that the lesser offense was committed, but not the greater. "An uncharged offense is included in a greater charged offense if either (1) the greater offense, as defined by statute, cannot be committed without also committing the lesser (the elements test) or (2) the language of the accusatory pleading encompasses all the elements of the lesser offense (the accusatory pleading test).

Simple battery is not a lesser included offense of the charged crime, rape of an unconscious person. Battery includes "any willful and unlawful use of force or violence upon the person of another." (§ 242.) Even a slight touching may constitute a battery, "if it is done in a rude or angry way." The force at issue here need not be violent or severe, and it need not cause bodily harm or pain; rather it includes "'any wrongful act committed by means of physical force against the person of another. . . . '"

Rape of an unconscious person, by contrast, requires proof that: (1) the defendant had sexual intercourse with the victim; (2) the defendant was not married to the victim at the time; (3) the victim was unable to resist because she was unconscious of the nature of the act; and (4) the defendant knew the victim was unable to resist because she was unconscious of the nature of the act. (§ 261, subd. (a)(4); CALCRIM No. 1003.) There is no requirement that the defendant use force or violence to accomplish the act of sexual intercourse . . . regarding rape of an intoxicated woman, neither force upon the part of the man, nor resistance upon the part of the woman, forms an element of the crime. The act of sexual intercourse with an unconscious person is itself illegal, regardless of "the victim's 'advance consent' or the perpetrator's belief that the victim has consented in advance to the prohibited act." (*People v. Dancy*, 102 Cal.App.4th 21, 37, 124 Cal.Rptr.2d 898 (2002). Thus, an unconscious person could be raped within the meaning of section 261, subdivision (a)(4) without having been subjected to force or violence, or even to a harmful or offensive touching. As a result, battery is not a lesser included offense of rape of an unconscious person.

Even if battery was a lesser included offense, the trial court did not err in refusing the requested instruction because there was no substantial evidence to support it. Appellant's defense was that A.B. was conscious and the sex was consensual. There was no evidence that he kissed A.B. in a rude, angry, or violent way, but immediately thereafter had consensual sex with her. His testimony was that she was not harmed or offended by the kissing and that they had consensual sex. Thus, the kissing he described did not amount of a battery. There was no evidentiary basis for an instruction on battery as a lesser included offense.

CONCLUSION

The judgment is affirmed.
We concur: GILBERT, P.J., and PERREN, J.

CASE QUESTIONS

1. What was the victim's first intimation that she may have been raped?
2. What did the forensic nurse examiner find on her examination?
3. What claim did the defendant make regarding whether or not the victim was unconscious?
4. How did the court deal with this assertion?
5. Is it rape to have sex with an unconscious person?

CHAPTER SUMMARY

This chapter has shown that the crime of rape involves the elements of non-consensual sex often accomplished by force, threat, or intimidation. In order to prove that a rape has occurred, the prosecution must present testimony from the victim and frequently from medical professionals that the victim was the subject of force and trauma. The use of DNA databases has revolutionized the way that rape cases are prosecuted. In many cases, a defendant's DNA can match him to the specimens collected from the victim with absolute certainty. We have also seen in this chapter that modern statutes concerning rape are considerably different from the old common law rules. For one thing, under the common law, a husband could not be prosecuted for raping his wife. In many jurisdictions, the victim would have also had to show active resistance to the attacker, sometimes even to the point of death. The common law rules about rape have been replaced or modified in all jurisdictions. Besides changing the common law, all states have enacted some version of a rape shield statute that not only protects the identity of the victim during the trial, but prevents defense counsel from asking questions about the victim's prior sexual history, unless it specifically involved the defendant. In addition to rape and date rape, this chapter examined the crime of statutory rape. A person can be prosecuted under statutory rape charges even when the victim consents to the act because the victim is under the age of consent. That age varies from state to state, and there are even some states that will not prosecute a statutory rape charge unless there is a significant age difference between the defendant and the victim.

KEY TERMS

Rape	Spousal immunity	Statutory rape
Circumstantial evidence	Corroboration	
Consent	Rape Shield Statute	

REVIEW QUESTIONS

1   Why is rape considered to be a crime of violence?
2   What are the basic elements of the crime of rape?
3   How does the state prove penetration in a rape case?
4   Why is the victim's testimony problematic in establishing penetration?
5   Explain the use of medical testimony in a rape trial.
6   What is a SANE?
7   What is circumstantial evidence?

8   How can age factor into a consideration of whether or not the victim gave consent?

9   What is the relationship between consent and the force used by the defendant?

10 Is it considered force for the defendant to threaten to hurt someone other than the rape victim?

11 How have DNA databases changed the way that rape cases are investigated?

12 Explain the requirement of the victim's resistance under the old common law crime of rape.

13 Under the common law, could a husband be prosecuted for raping his wife?

14 What is corroboration, and why was it required under common law?

15 What are rape shield statutes?

16 How does the cross-examination of a rape victim in a real trial differ from that shown on television and in movies?

17 What qualifies as aggravated rape?

18 What is date rape?

19 What are date rape drugs?

20 What are the elements of statutory rape?

21 Why is statutory rape considered to be a strict liability offense?

QUESTIONS FOR ANALYSIS

1   Is it still necessary to protect the identity of the rape victim? Haven't we, as a society, progressed to the point where this is no longer necessary? Explain your answer.

2   Under the strict legal definition of assault, can an unconscious person be assaulted? Can an unconscious person be battered?

HYPOTHETICALS

1   John has had a crush on Megan for several months. One night, at a party, Megan has too much to drink and John offers to drive her home. As they drive to her home, Megan makes some suggestive comments to John that lead him to think that she may be interested in a sexual relationship with him. However, when he parks the car in an out of the way area, Megan asks him what he is doing. As he tries to kiss her, she passes out. John has sex with her. Afterward, he puts her clothes back on, revives her, and takes her to her house. He bids her goodnight. Has John committed rape? Why or why not?

2   Chuck has been charged with rape and the victim in the case is on the witness stand. She testifies that she woke up early in the morning and found Chuck in

her bedroom. She testifies that she knew Chuck from her work, but that he had never been inside her home and she was shocked to see a man standing in her room. The defense attorney, on cross-examination, asks the victim how many other men have been in her bedroom. The prosecutor objects. How is the judge likely to rule? Will the defense attorney be allowed to get an answer to his question? Why or why not?

3   Why is it so common to have cases where men are charged with raping women and not women raping men or women raping other women?

Other Sex Offenses

7

Chapter Objectives

- Explain the difference between the crimes of public indecency and voyeurism
- Describe the importance of the "Miller" test in defining obscenity
- Define child molestation
- Explain the modern definitions of sodomy and aggravated sodomy
- Describe what child pornography is and what makes it illegal

I. INTRODUCTION

This chapter examines other sexual offenses that do not necessarily fall under the definition of rape. The first three sex offenses discussed in this text — fornication, adultery and cohabitation — are rarely, if ever, prosecuted. However, when the topic turns to sodomy, there is a dramatic change. Aggravated or forced sodomy cases are frequently prosecuted, while consensual acts between adults in the privacy of their own homes are protected by a U.S. Supreme Court decision. This chapter will also examine the law surrounding child molestation and conclude with a discussion of obscenity law.

A. FORNICATION

Fornication is the crime of unmarried men and women having consensual sex. Many Americans are unaware that this is a crime, and even though it is rarely prosecuted, it remains on the books as a listed crime and could be prosecuted. However, given society's attitudes about sexuality, such charges are rarely brought.

B. ADULTERY

Many people are surprised to learn that when a spouse has sex with someone outside the marriage, it is actually a crime. Like fornication, this crime is almost never prosecuted. With the demands on police departments and prosecutors to pursue more serious crimes, this crime is not a priority.

C. COHABITATION

It is also a crime, usually a misdemeanor, for an unmarried couple to live together and engage in sexual relations. Crimes like fornication, adultery, and cohabitation are holdovers from previous decades (and centuries) when the government took a more intrusive role in people's day-to-day lives. Although this crime remains illegal in most states, such crimes are rarely prosecuted for the simple fact that a large majority of people in our country have, at one time or another, lived together in a romantic relationship without being married. Some spend their entire lives with a partner and never marry. Some states have actually repealed these statutes, although most have not. It is difficult for a politician to run on a platform of making fornication, adultery, and cohabitation legal.

D. SEX ACTS THAT ARE PROSECUTED

Other sex-related offenses are prosecuted every day across the country. Because these crimes involve public acts, force, threat, or nonconsensual behavior, law enforcement gives these crimes higher priority and assigns more resources to these offenses than the first three discussed in this chapter.

Essentially, states prohibit specific acts, especially when they are carried out in public. In the past, these crimes were classified as **lewd** acts. Lewdness is a broad term that encompasses almost any act by a person that involves sexual lust.[1] The problem with using such an all-encompassing term is that its very imprecision gives rise to numerous questions about what is and what is not criminal behavior. As a result, many states have specified exactly what they mean by lewd behavior. Rather than simply lumping crimes together under the sweeping category of lewdness, this text will examine specific crimes such as:

Lewd
An act that shows an unlawful indulgence of lust; gross indecency in matters pertaining to sexual relations.

- Public indecency and indecent exposure
- Voyeurism
- Sodomy

---

[1] *State v. Stamper*, 615 So. 2d 1359 (La. Ct. App. 2d Cir. 1993).

PUBLIC INDECENCY AND INDECENT EXPOSURE

A person commits the offense of indecent exposure when he exposes his or her sexual organs in public. In most such prosecutions, the defendant is a man who is exposing himself to others as a means of sexual gratification.

The elements of indecent exposure are that the defendant:

- Willfully exposed
- His or her sex organs
- In a public place for a sexual purpose
- (In the presence of a member of the opposite sex)[2]

The last element is placed in parentheses because not all jurisdictions list this as an element of **public indecency**. All jurisdictions require that the nudity occur in either a public place or a place open to public view. There are many jurisdictions that not only require that the defendant exposed his or her sex organs in a public place, but also that the state prove that the defendant's motive was sexually based. California, for example, imposes this requirement.[3] However, not all jurisdictions follow the requirement that there must be a sexual element to the exposure. To clarify these varying approaches, most law enforcement agencies adopt a policy that they will charge individuals with this offense when they expose themselves to others for the purposes of the defendant's own gratification. States follow an objective test in order to prosecute this offense. Did the defendant act in a way that was designed to offend, alarm, harass, or annoy another person? If the answer is yes, then the defendant can be prosecuted for public indecency.[4] It is normally punished as a misdemeanor.

Public indecency
Exposure of a person's sex organs in public.

PUBLIC INDECENCY?

SCENARIO 7-1

Tom, who is 44-years-old and married, last week asked three girls to go with him to a popular swimming area near the river. When they got there, he asked them to strip. The girls ranged from 13 to 19 years of age. The swimming area is commonly used by members of the public. While they all swam naked, Tom took photographs of the girls. Has he committed the crime of public indecency?

Answer: Yes. Tom knew that he was encouraging the girls to remove their clothes, thus satisfying the elements of public indecency and obviously had additional plans of making use of their nudity with the photos he'd taken.[5] He may also face additional charges given that one of the girls was 13 years of age.

---

[2] *Schmitt v. State*, 590 So. 2d 404 (Fla. 1991).
[3] *Nunez v. Holder*, 594 F.3d 1124 (9th Cir. 2010).
[4] *State v. Moss*, 2008 SD 64, 754 N.W.2d 626 (S.D. 2008).
[5] *Com. v. Tiffany*, 2007 PA Super 162, 926 A.2d 503 (2007).

SCENARIO 7-2

NUDITY AT THE CONCERT

Sam is attending an outdoor concert and wanders off. He decides that his clothing is too restrictive and, after looking around, does not see anyone close. He takes off all of his clothes and feels much better. A police officer sees Sam naked and arrests him. Has Sam committed the offense of public indecency?

Answer: Yes. Even though there weren't any people in Sam's immediate area, the fact that Sam disrobed in a public area where it was quite conceivable that some of the other concert-goers could see him is enough to establish the elements of the crime.[6]

FAMOUS CASES
BILL CLINTON AND PAULA JONES

Although this particular case does not involve a criminal prosecution, it was part of a pattern that involved the impeachment of President Clinton. Paula Jones was a young Arkansas state employee who claimed that then-Governor Bill Clinton propositioned her and exposed himself to her in a Little Rock hotel room in 1991. Three years later, just a few days before the statute of limitations expired, she filed a sexual harassment lawsuit against Clinton, who by that time was president of the United States. Little did Jones know that her lawsuit would permanently tarnish, and nearly bring down, a sitting president.

Jones anchored her suit in the assumption that, because she was a state employee, Clinton was her boss, and he therefore had sexually harassed her. Although no one witnessed the incident, she had spoken of it to a friend. Subsequently, several other women came forward saying that they had experienced similar behavior by Clinton.

Clinton fought back, stating that the event in question never happened, and Jones was an opportunist who was trying only to make money and harm him politically. His reaction was partially borne out by the fact that Jones was seeking more than half a million dollars in damages, and her cause was immediately taken up by conservative backers with a rabid desire to besmirch the president.

Clinton also tried another tactic: challenging her right to bring a lawsuit for something that allegedly happened before he became president. He argued that the trial should be delayed until after he left office. This defense wound its way through the courts, until the U.S. Supreme Court ruled in 1997 that the suit could proceed.

The case concluded before it came to trial with Judge Susan Webber Wright's summary judgment that Jones could not show that she had suffered any damages. If, in fact, the incident actually took place, she had not demonstrated any emotional damage, nor had she been punished in the workplace for refusing his advances. Jones appealed, and Clinton ultimately offered an $850,000 settlement with no apology or admission of guilt.

The entire case might have been no more than a footnote in history had it not been for the revelation of Clinton's affair with Monica Lewinsky. While the case was

---

[6] *Parnigoni v. District of Columbia*, 933 A.2d 823 (D.C. 2007).

unfolding, Judge Wright ruled that Jones was entitled to any information regarding Clinton's actual or attempted sexual relations with any employees, either on the state or the federal level. Jones's lawyers were trying to show a pattern of behavior that would support her claim.

During depositions, Monica Lewinsky denied having a relationship with Clinton, and Clinton flatly denied having sexual relations with her. However, Pentagon employee Linda Tripp, a confidant of Monica Lewinsky's, had recorded telephone conversations with Lewinsky during which she shared details of her affair with Clinton. Tripp turned the recordings over to Independent Counsel Kenneth Starr, which was enough to investigate Clinton for perjury. On the basis of Tripp's information and Clinton's denial, he was impeached on two charges: one for perjury and another for obstruction of justice.

Clinton, of course, escaped removal from office because he was acquitted by the Senate. Needing a two-thirds majority to convict, the Senate could muster only 45 senators who voted guilty on the perjury charge and 50 on the obstruction of justice charge. The vote split largely along party lines.

A lurid moment in an obscure hotel room, whether real or imagined, resulted in only the second impeachment of a president in the history of the United States.

VOYEURISM

A **voyeur**, commonly known as a "peeping tom," is someone who spies on other people, often for sexual satisfaction. This person might simply peek through the windows of other people's homes at night, or the intrusion can take on a more high-tech flavor with video and audio surveillance. This invasion of privacy is illegal in all states. In the past, the crime was not considered to be very serious, but then law enforcement began seeing patterns: A man who starts out looking through women's windows often graduates to more serious offenses, such as rape and forced sodomy. Figure 7-1 gives an example of one state's statute on voyeurism.

Voyeur
One who views another, either through a door or window, or by electronic means, in order to achieve sexual gratification.

FIGURE 7-1

Voyeurism (Ohio)

(A) No person, for the purpose of sexually arousing or gratifying the person's self, shall commit trespass or otherwise surreptitiously invade the privacy of another, to spy or eavesdrop upon another.

(B) No person, for the purpose of sexually arousing or gratifying the person's self, shall commit trespass or otherwise surreptitiously invade the privacy of another to videotape, film, photograph, or otherwise record the other person in a state of nudity.

. . .

(E)(1) Whoever violates this section is guilty of voyeurism.

(2) A violation of division (A) of this section is a misdemeanor of the third degree.

(3) A violation of division (B) of this section is a misdemeanor of the second degree.[7]

---

[7] Ohio Rev.Code Ann § 2907.08.

SODOMY

Sodomy
A generic term for any "crime against nature" or sexual act that has been branded as degenerate; it includes oral sex, anal sex, homosexual acts, or sex with animals.

Bestiality
Sexual acts with animals.

Necrophilia
Sexual acts with human corpses.

Over time, **sodomy** has been referred to under various names, including "crimes against nature" and "lewd and lascivious acts."[8] Sodomy has been defined differently in many states and covers such a broad spectrum of behavior that the term has virtually lost any coherent legal meaning. Depending on the state, sodomy can be limited to anal intercourse or can include acts as disparate as **bestiality**, **necrophilia**, and virtually any sexual interaction beyond what is considered "normal."[9] In almost all states, homosexual acts are considered to be sodomy. Consenting, heterosexual couples may also be guilty of sodomy if they carry out their activities in public. Some states even went so far as to outlaw these practices among married couples. However, many of these statutes have been held to be unconstitutional. A distinction should be drawn here between consensual acts of sodomy and those involving force. Consensual acts, unless they are carried out in public, are generally not illegal, while forced acts of sodomy are often brought in cases where rape has also been charged.

The theory underlying the criminalization of these various acts goes beyond moral repugnance of the early founders of our country and the common law of the England. There was actually a biological argument against these acts: They did not contribute to procreation. That view has been abandoned by modern statutes and legal scholars.[10]

Lawrence v. Texas. The U.S. Supreme Court ruled in 2003 that a statute which prohibited adults from consensual homosexual acts in the privacy of their own homes was unconstitutional, reversing a decision that it had made in the case of *Bowers v. Hardwick*, 478 U.S. 186 (1986).[11] This ruling does not apply to acts of nonconsensual sodomy, where the acts are committed with minors, or in cases charging prostitution.[12] Although in the past, cases of adult, consensual sodomy were prosecuted, in light of the *Lawrence* decision, law enforcement has shifted focus to aggravated sodomy.

Aggravated sodomy
Nonconsensual "crimes against nature" that are carried out with force, threat, or cause serious bodily injury to the victim.

Aggravated Sodomy. In **aggravated** or forced **sodomy,** the defendant's actions with the victim are not consensual and are often encompassed within a rape prosecution. However rape prosecutions, especially in states where the rape statutes were drawn narrowly to refer only to the actions of a man raping a woman, often did not allow the state to prosecute a man for raping another man. Although some states have begun to expand the definition of rape to include actions that were formerly considered aggravated sodomy, many states still refer to any nonconsensual action involving anything other than penetration of the woman's vagina by the man's penis as sodomy. Under those state laws, the only option available to prosecutors for homosexual rape was a charge of *aggravated sodomy*.

---

[8] *State v. Cook*, 146 Idaho 261, 192 P.3d 1085 (Ct. App. 2008).
[9] *Phillips v. State*, 248 Ind. 150, 222 N.E.2d 821 (1967).
[10] *Lawrence v. Texas*, 539 U.S. 558, 123 S. Ct. 2472, 156 L. Ed. 2d 508 (2003).
[11] *Lawrence v. Texas*, 539 U.S. 558, 123 S. Ct. 2472, 156 L. Ed. 2d 508 (2003).
[12] Ibid

Sodomy is classified as aggravated when the victim does not consent to the contact and the victim receives serious bodily injury, or when a deadly weapon is used.[13] Other factors that can lead to a charge of aggravated sodomy include the fact that the victim was under the age of consent, although in many cases, where the victim is very young, the charge will revert to child molestation.[14]

INCEST

If certain family members cannot legally marry, then they cannot legally engage in sexual activities. The closer the relation, the more likely that sexual contact will be considered **incest**. This crime is based on ancient religious and societal taboos forbidding close family members from engaging in sexual relations with one another. The following would qualify as incest if the parties engage in sexual intercourse with one another:

Incest
Sexual intercourse between members of a family who, according to state law, are too closely related by blood or adoption to legally marry.

- Father-daughter
- Mother-son
- Brother-sister
- (First cousins)

The last category is not universally recognized. Although most states bar first cousins from marrying one another, and thus if they have sex, it would by definition qualify as incest, there are some states where the rules are vague on the subject of cousins. In many states, this law has also been extended to adopted children.

By its very nature, a parent who has sex with a minor child is committing two offenses: child molestation and incest. Although most people know that there are societal taboos against incest, few are aware that there are also criminal statutes that prohibit this behavior among adults. The fact is, however, that incest prosecutions do not carry as heavy a possible sentence as child molestation statutes, and so, when the act involves a child, prosecutors will invariably seek to bring a charge for child molestation. Suppose that the two persons involved in a sexual act are both consenting adults, but the act still qualifies as incest. Prosecuting adults for incest is technically possible, but few such prosecutions are ever brought. Police and prosecutors are zealous in protecting the rights of children, but when it comes to consenting adults, they often take a more hands-off approach.

CHILD MOLESTATION

In criminal law, just as in other areas of law, children receive special protections. Because they have not fully developed mentally and physically, the law must sometimes protect them from themselves. This is especially true when the subject is sexual contact.

---

[13] *Oeth v. State*, 775 N.E.2d 696 (Ind. Ct. App. 2002).
[14] *Brewer v. State*, 271 Ga. 605, 523 S.E.2d 18 (1999).

Child Molestation;
Aggravated Child
Molestation (Georgia)

(a) A person commits the offense of child molestation when such person:

(1) Does any immoral or indecent act to or in the presence of or with any child under the age of 16 years with the intent to arouse or satisfy the sexual desires of either the child or the person; or

(2) By means of an electronic device, transmits images of a person engaging in, inducing, or otherwise participating in any immoral or indecent act to a child under the age of 16 years with the intent to arouse or satisfy the sexual desires of either the child or the person.

(b)(1) Except as provided in paragraph (2) of this subsection, a person convicted of a first offense of child molestation shall be punished by imprisonment for not less than five nor more than 20 years and shall be subject to the sentencing and punishment provisions of Code Sections 17-10-6. 2 and 17-10-7. Upon a defendant being incarcerated on a conviction for a first offense, the Department of Corrections shall provide counseling to such defendant. Except as provided in paragraph (2) of this subsection, upon a second or subsequent conviction of an offense of child molestation, the defendant shall be punished by imprisonment for not less than ten years nor more than 30 years or by imprisonment for life and shall be subject to the sentencing and punishment provisions of Code Sections 17-10-6.2 and 17-10-7; provided, however, that prior to trial, a defendant shall be given notice, in writing, that the state intends to seek a punishment of life imprisonment.

. . .

(c) A person commits the offense of aggravated child molestation when such person commits an offense of child molestation which act physically injures the child or involves an act of sodomy.

(d)(1) Except as provided in paragraph (2) of this subsection, a person convicted of the offense of aggravated child molestation shall be punished by imprisonment for life or by a split sentence that is a term of imprisonment for not less than 25 years and not exceeding life imprisonment, followed by probation for life . . . [15]

Child molestation
Any sexual act with a child.

The laws prohibiting **child molestation** state that any sexual activity with a child is a felony. In most states, the age at which a person is considered to be a "child" for purposes of child molestation statutes is 12, although the age varies from state to state. Child molestation is a serious offense that can often lead to psychological trauma which will last the victim's entire life. Because society abhors the use of children as sexual objects, a person charged with child molestation can face a lengthy prison sentence. See Figure 7-2 for an example of a child molestation statute.

What is child molestation? The simple answer is that it is any sexual act involving a child, from fondling to rape. Some states spell out the actions that are prohibited in very specific terms. For instance: It is unlawful to touch or penetrate the sexual organ of a child with the mouth, anus, or sexual organ of another person or to contact or penetrate of the mouth, anus, or sexual organ of a child with the anus or sexual organ of another person. Figure 7-3 shows the rate of federal prosecutions of child sex exploitation offenders.

---

[15] O.C.G.A.§ 16-6-4.

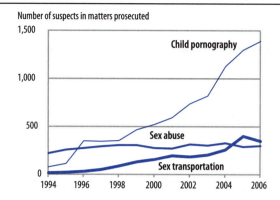

Number of suspects in matters prosecuted

Child pornography

Sex abuse

Sex transportation

FIGURE 7-3

Federal Prosecutions of Child Sex Exploitation Offenders

Note: Includes matters with a child sex exploitation offense as lead charge.

Source: Executive Office for U.S. Attorneys, National LIONS database, fiscal year 2006.

Consent Is Not an Issue in Child Molestation. The previous chapter on rape discussed that the issue of consent is frequently brought up as a defense. If the

FIGURE 7-4

Fondling Child; Punishment (Mississippi)

(1) Any person above the age of eighteen (18) years, who, for the purpose of gratifying his or her lust, or indulging his or her depraved licentious sexual desires, shall handle, touch or rub with hands or any part of his or her body or any member thereof, any child under the age of sixteen (16) years, with or without the child's consent, or a mentally defective, mentally incapacitated or physically helpless person as defined in Section 97-3-97, shall be guilty of a felony and, upon conviction thereof, shall be fined in a sum not less than One Thousand Dollars ($1,000.00) nor more than Five Thousand Dollars ($5,000.00), or be committed to the custody of the State Department of Corrections not less than two (2) years nor more than fifteen (15) years, or be punished by both such fine and imprisonment, at the discretion of the court.

(2) Any person above the age of eighteen (18) years, who, for the purpose of gratifying his or her lust, or indulging his or her depraved licentious sexual desires, shall handle, touch or rub with hands or any part of his or her body or any member thereof, any child younger than himself or herself and under the age of eighteen (18) years who is not such person's spouse, with or without the child's consent, when the person occupies a position of trust or authority over the child shall be guilty of a felony and, upon conviction thereof, shall be fined in a sum not less than One Thousand Dollars ($1,000.00) nor more than Five Thousand Dollars ($5,000.00), or be committed to the custody of the State Department of Corrections not less than two (2) years nor more than fifteen (15) years, or be punished by both such fine and imprisonment, at the discretion of the court. A person in a position of trust or authority over a child includes without limitation a child's teacher, counselor, physician, psychiatrist, psychologist, minister, priest, physical therapist, chiropractor, legal guardian, parent, stepparent, aunt, uncle, scout leader or coach.[16]

---

[16] Miss. Code Ann. § 97-5-23.

victim consents to the sexual act, then there is no rape. However, children cannot legally consent to sex, no matter what the context, so there is no defense of consent available to child molesters. The reason again is society's extra protection of its most vulnerable and the recognition that children lack the degree of emotional and physical development to understand the nature of the sexual act.

Enticing a Minor for Immoral Purposes. A variation on the charge of child molestation is the offense of **enticement** of a child for sexual purposes. When a person entices a child, he or she offers to take the child to someplace where the child will have fun or toys or candy, but the real intent is to take the child away from safety and then abuse the child. In recent years, several news programs have placed ads in various media and then responded to potential child predators as though they were children. The programs have then aired various men coming to locations to engage in sex with someone they believe is an underage girl or boy.

Enticement
Attempting to persuade a child to come to some secluded place with the intent to commit an unlawful sexual act.

INTERNET ENTICEMENT

Pedophile
An adult who has a strong or even overpowering sexual attraction to children.

Pedophiles have become computer-savvy and spend a great deal of time online, attempting to contact potential victims. They often pose as children themselves, and because of the anonymity granted by the Internet, they can be quite successful in disguising their actual age. A child predator may have several potential victims developing at any one time. The pedophile may push the chat room conversation to sexual matters and even offer to send a photo of "himself" when it is actually of a previous victim. In this way, he gains the trust of the victim and then arranges to meet. It is only when the victim is confronted with someone very different from what he or she expected that they realize the truth. For a profile of sex offenders, see Figure 7-5.

OBSCENITY

Obscene
Sexually oriented lewd and offensive depictions that are in violation of accepted standards of decency.

Sale, distribution, shipment, or distributing by electronic means of **obscene** material is a violation of both state and federal law. However, that simple statement belies a world of U.S. Supreme Court cases and challenges to obscenity laws on every front. To understand the crime of obscenity, we must discuss the impact on the First Amendment in cases involving freedom of expression (see Figure 7-6). The First Amendment to the U. S. Constitution guarantees the right to freedom of speech for all citizens. The difficulty in evaluating a case of obscenity is attempting to fix a definition that will allow the state to prove the case beyond a reasonable doubt while simultaneously upholding the principles set out in the First Amendment. In the past, the U.S. Supreme Court was called on time and again to rule exactly what obscenity is.

The problem with defining obscenity is that it is extremely hard to do. What is obscene to one person is art to another. The frustration of trying to come up with a workable definition of obscenity led one Supreme Court justice to quip: "I know it when I see it." That single statement puts in relief the difficulty of establishing what obscenity is. The U.S. Supreme Court finally settled many, but by no means all, questions about obscenity in its decision in *Miller v. California*.

Defendant characteristics	Total	Sex abuse	Child pornography	Sex transportation
Number of defendants	1.863	249	1.275	339
Gender				
Male	97.0%	96.4%	98.7%	91.2%
Female	3.0	3.6	1.3	8.8
Race				
White*	75.8%	15.9%	88.9%	70.2%
Black/African American*	4.9	2.9	3.2	12.5
Hispanic	8.1	8.9	6.6	13.1
American Indian/ Alaska Native*	9.9	70.7	0.3	1.5
Asian/Native Hawaiian/other Pacific Islanders*	1.3	1.6	1.0	2.7
Age				
Under 21	5.0%	21.7%	2.8%	1.5%
21-30	23.2	29.3	20.2	30.1
31-40	24.1	23.3	23.1	28.6
41-50	23.6	14.9	25.5	23.0
51-60	16.8	6.4	19.9	12.4
Over 60	7.3	4.4	8.5	4.4
Median age	39yrs	29yrs	42yrs	36yrs
Education level				
Less than high school graduate	14.0%	48.1%	7.9%	13.7%
High school graduate	34.1	31.6	34.0	36.5
Some college	29.6	15.6	33.0	26.0
College graduate	22.3	4.7	25.1	23.9
Citizenship				
U.S. citizen	95.8%	96.3%	97.7%	88.5%
Non-U.S. citizen	4.2	3.7	2.3	11.5
Criminal record				
No prior felony conviction	78.6%	78.6%	79.9%	74.0%
Prior felony conviction	21.4	21.4	20.1	26.0

Note: Percents based on non-missing data.

* Excludes persons of Hispanic or Latino origin.

Source: Administrative Office of the U.S. Courts. Pretrial Services data file, fiscal year 2006.

FIGURE 7-5

Characteristics of Federal Sex Exploitation Defendants

FIGURE 7-6

First Amendment to the
U.S. Constitution

"Congress shall make no law respecting an establishment of religion, or prohibiting the free exercise thereof; or abridging the freedom of speech, or of the press; or the right of the people peaceably to assemble, and to petition the Government for a redress of grievances."

A. THE MILLER TEST

By 1973, the U.S. Supreme Court had realized that its previous attempts to create a test that could be used in all situations to evaluate whether or not material was obscene had all failed. Courts, including the Supreme Court, were barraged with criminal prosecutions from across the nation and defendants who were claiming First Amendment guarantees of expression in a wide range of activities. As outlined in the book, *The Brethren*, the justices actually watched some of the movies under contention. Faced with the daunting task of creating a nationwide standard for obscenity, the justices fashioned a test and used the case of *Miller v. California* as the vehicle to establish this test. Under the new "Miller" test, obscene material must pass all three steps in order to be considered obscene and thus prosecutable. If any of the steps were not met, then the Court would rule that the material was not obscene and the convictions obtained were unconstitutional. The Miller test sets out the following:

> (1) whether "the average person, applying contemporary community standards" would find that the work, taken as a whole, appeals to the prurient interest; (2) whether the work depicts or describes, in a patently offensive way, sexual conduct specifically defined by the applicable state law; and (3) whether the work, taken as a whole, lacks serious literary, artistic, political, or scientific value. *Miller v. California*, 413 U.S. 15, 93 S. Ct. 2607, 37 L. Ed. 2d 419 (1973).

This text will examine two out of three of these steps, the first and the third. The second step is the easiest part of the Miller test to prove and simply requires that the material conform to the definition of obscenity under applicable state law. The first and third elements, however, present real difficulties to prosecutors.

"PRURIENT INTEREST"

Obscenity law is limited to sexual material, but just because some material depicts sexual activity does not automatically make it obscene. Art, video, paintings, or any other medium that presents sexual content is only considered obscene when it satisfies all three elements of the Miller test. The first element,

Sidebar

Under the Miller test, if the material under consideration does not meet all three requirements, then the prosecution may not proceed and a jury is not authorized to return a guilty verdict on the charge of obscenity.[17]

---

[17] *State v. Harrold*, 256 Neb. 829, 593 N.W.2d 299 (1999).

that the material taken as a whole appeals to the **prurient interest** means that the work arouses a person to the point that he or she has an obsessive or unusual sexual desire. As many commentators have pointed out, a depiction of a sexual event that might cause intense sexual desire might just as easily cause disgust in another. The first problem in using the Miller test in a day-to-day setting is proving that the material is prurient. Because obscenity cases in the United States only involve sexual acts, this hurdle is difficult, but not impossible, for prosecutors to meet.

Prurient interest
A work that, taken as a whole, is designed for the purpose of arousing intense, obsessive, or overwhelming sexual intensity.

EQUUS

SCENARIO 7-3

The local community college drama department has decided to present the play, "Equus." In the play, a scene shows the lead actor naked while blinding several horses with a spike. Local groups have lodged protests and have asked law enforcement to shut down the production. Can the police charge the production with obscenity and therefore keep the play from being shown?

Answer: No. The Miller test prevents action. Although one of the actors is nude, there is nothing to indicate that the material is presented for erotic or prurient interests. It is also not obscene to present a fictional act of animal cruelty, although there are many who would argue that it should be.

TAKEN AS A WHOLE LACKS SERIOUS LITERARY, ARTISTIC, POLITICAL, OR SCIENTIFIC VALUE

The third criterion of the Miller test requires not only that the work must appeal to the prurient interest, but also that it lacks serious literary, artistic, political, or scientific value. That last hurdle is difficult to meet for the simple reason that one person's art is another person's trash. Who is to say that erotica does not provide an important artistic expression?

What does "taken as a whole" mean? The Court requires that a viewer cannot cherry-pick a particular scene as obscene. Instead, the entire work must be viewed to see if the whole production appeals to the prurient interest and lacks serious artistic, political, scientific, or literary value. This standard is difficult to meet, simply because almost all works are considered to have some value.[18] On the other hand, a depiction that satisfies all of the elements of the Miller test cannot be saved by inserting a minor bit of legitimate or artistic material. Consider Scenario 7-4.

SHAKESPEARE AND THE PORN MOVIE

SCENARIO 7-4

A movie has just been released that shows only sex acts and apparently passes each of the three elements of the Miller test, but the producers, apparently fearing that this

continued

---

[18] *U.S. v. Tupler*, 564 F.2d 1294 (9th Cir. 1977).

SCENARIO 7-4

(continued)

might be the case, put in a two-minute clip of an actor reading Macbeth's soliloquy from act 5, scene 5, that contains the famous lines beginning, "Tomorrow and tomorrow and tomorrow creeps in this petty pace from day to day . . ." Will this insertion be enough to prevent the movie producers from being prosecuted for obscenity?

Answer: No. Because the work, taken as a whole, passes the Miller test, one scene containing a Shakespearean quote will not be enough to tilt the work back to non-obscene.

Another aspect of obscenity law, at least in the United States, is that obscenity only refers to sexual matters. It is not obscene to show a real person being killed, but it may very well be obscene to show two adult human beings engaging in consensual sexual behavior.[19]

SCENARIO 7-5

SPRINGFIELD'S NEW STATUTE

Springfield town council has passed a new ordinance. It is aimed at protecting the youth of Springfield who seem to be spending a great deal of time playing violent video games. The Springfield statute provides that it is illegal to sell, possess, distribute, or play any video game that presents violence in a stylized, fictitious and unrealistic manner or that lessens the consequences of violence on the players. Such video games will be deemed obscene and will be prosecuted as a misdemeanor. Last week, Jeff, the owner of DEF video games was arrested and charged under the statute after putting on sale "Grand Death Auto," which gives points to players when they run over pedestrians in a cross-county race. Will Springfield's ordinance survive a constitutional challenge?

Answer: Almost certainly no. The statute does not incorporate the Miller test, and the video game does not meet all of the elements of the Miller test. As such, it is not legally obscene and therefore is protected under the First Amendment.[20]

Is indecency the same thing as obscenity? Many courts say no. There are elements found in obscenity that are not found in indecency. Public indecency involves displaying one's sex organs in public. But the elements of obscenity, especially as they are described in Miller, involve several other factors.[21]

B. PORNOGRAPHY AND OBSCENITY

Pornographic
Any material that depicts sexual behavior and nudity designed to cause sexual excitement.

It is important to draw a distinction between items that are **pornographic** and those that are obscene. Pornography is a general term that refers to any sexual material. The problem, like so many things in the interpretation of the law of obscenity, is that the term is far too broad to be useful. As we have all heard at one time or another, one person's pornography is another person's art. What prosecutors and police really need in order to prosecute cases is a way of defining obscenity so

---

[19] *Video Software Dealers Ass'n v. Webster*, 968 F.2d 684 (8th Cir. 1992).
[20] *American Amusement Machine Ass'n v. Kendrick*, 244 F.3d 572 (7th Cir. 2001).
[21] *F.C.C. v. Pacifica Foundation*, 438 U.S. 726, 98 S. Ct. 3026, 57 L. Ed. 2d 1073 (1978).

everyone can know when they are crossing the line from something that is merely pornographic to something that is obscene.

C. POSSESSION OF OBSCENE MATERIAL

Even in situations where material satisfies all of the elements of the Miller test, it is not a crime to possess it. Curiously, it is a crime to distribute obscene material, to sell it, to ship it, or to send by electronic means. However, this does not apply to child pornography. It is never legal to possess child porn.[22] The twist to obscenity law, that is not unlawful to possess it, raises the question of how the person who lawfully possesses it in his home got it in the first place.[23] However, the state cannot prosecute simply because the only way that a person could be in possession of obscene material is by receiving it through an illegal source. The government must prove that the defendant had it shipped to him or that he got it through some other illegal means. Simply having it will not prove that crime beyond a reasonable doubt.

OBSCENE?

SCENARIO 7-6

ABC Theaters presented a midnight showing of the movie *Brokeback Mountain*, which depicts some homosexual activity between two actors. The town of Springfield has recently enacted a statute that prohibits the public display of any motion picture that is obscene, indecent, or immoral. Is this statute a violation of the U.S. Supreme Court's standards as set out in *Miller v. California*?

Answer: Yes. The statute is overbroad. Unless the movie satisfies all three elements of the Miller test, the city is prevented from making the movie illegal and cannot prosecute the theater owner for violating the statute.[24]

D. OBSCENITY AND NUDE DANCING

Many cities have attempted to close down or at least limit the types of places where patrons can go to see women strip. The clubs have countered that stripping and dancing naked is a form of expression that is protected under the First Amendment. When cities ban such establishments, they violate the U.S. Constitution. However, when they simply limit the area where such businesses may be established, they remain on the safe side of the Constitution.[25] Obviously, nude dancing is not considered a protected form of speech when the dancers do more than dance. If they also perform sex acts for money on the patrons, the activity has moved beyond freedom of expression into the sphere of prostitution.[26]

---

[22] *U.S. v. Thomas*, 726 F.2d 1191 (7th Cir. 1984).
[23] *U.S. v. 12 200-Foot Reels of Super 8mm. Film*, 413 U.S. 123, 93 S. Ct. 2665, 37 L. Ed. 2d 500 (1973).
[24] *ABC Interstate Theatres, Inc. v. State*, 325 So. 2d 123 (Miss. 1976).
[25] *Young v. City of Simi Valley*, 216 F.3d 807 (9th Cir. 2000).
[26] *2025 Emery Highway, L.L.C. v. Bibb County, Georgia*, 377 F. Supp. 2d 1310 (M.D. Ga. 2005).

E. CAN WORDS BE OBSCENE?

In general, four-letter words are not classified as obscene, even if they are considered to be taboo in polite society. Such language can be regulated on television, but not in daily life.[27] Some states do make it a crime to use "four-letter words" in front of children. In that case, as in the case of child pornography, the state can show a compelling interest in protecting children that may outweigh the individual's First Amendment rights. In constitutional law, no right is absolute and must always be weighed against another. The First Amendment does not always trump protection of children and vice versa.

F. CHILD PORNOGRAPHY

Child pornography
Any depiction of a child intended to be viewed as a sexual object or for sexual pleasure.

So far, our discussion about obscenity has focused on the difficulties in prosecuting these cases because the definitions and standards created in *Miller v. California* make it difficult to label many activities as obscene. However, the Miller test does not apply to **child pornography**. The U.S. Supreme Court has recognized that states have a compelling interest in the protection of children. Child porn is illegal, and anyone possessing it, selling it, transporting it, or handling it in any other way can be prosecuted for those actions. In this case, the prosecution is not based on whether the material is obscene, but is instead based on the protection of children from being used as sexual objects. States are given greater latitude when dealing with child pornography as opposed to pornography involving consenting adults. However, what exactly is child pornography? Is any photo or video of a naked infant considered to be child pornography? Certainly not. Instead, statutes clearly indicate that material is considered child pornography when a child is depicted in a sexual manner and for the sexual gratification or stimulation of the person viewing the material.[28]

Any material that displays a child's genitals in a lewd or sexual manner is child pornography.[29]

In prosecuting a case of child pornography, the government does not have to show that the material involving children appeals to the prurient interest. All that the state must show is that the material is a lewd display of the child's sexual organs and that the defendant knew that the material contained such exhibitions. All states have enacted statutes outlawing child pornography.

What makes child pornography different is that the government always has a compelling interest to protect those who are least able to protect themselves. As we will see throughout this text, there are many examples where children receive special treatment and special protection from adults. As a result, states have much greater authority to regulate activities involving children than they do in regulating adult behavior.[30]

---

[27] 18 U.S.C.A. § 1468.
[28] *Com. v. Tiffany*, 2007 PA Super 162, 926 A.2d 503 (2007).
[29] *People v. Hebel*, 174 Ill. App. 3d 1, 123 Ill. Dec. 592, 527 N.E.2d 1367 (5th Dist. 1988).
[30] *Ginsberg v. State of N.Y.*, 390 U.S. 629, 88 S. Ct. 1274, 20 L. Ed. 2d 195 (1968).

Unlike obscene materials, individuals cannot possess child pornography without fear of prosecution. Child pornography is considered **contraband**, illegal wherever it is found and can be seized by law enforcement whenever it is discovered.

It is no defense that the work may have some literary merit. Any images that are the result of the abuse of a child for sexual purposes will justify a prosecution for possession of child pornography.[32]

Child pornography statutes apply to all of the following:

- Movies
- Photos
- Cartoons
- Drawings
- Sculpture
- Or any other visual media[33] (although there have been rulings by the U.S. Supreme Court that images that have been digitally altered may not fall into the category of child pornography)

Contraband
An object that is illegal to possess, including child pornography, certain types of weapons, and illegal narcotics, among others.

The Miller test does not apply to child porn.[31]

---

(1) "Child" means any person under the age of 16 years.

(2) "Electronic device" means any device used for the purpose of communicating with a child for sexual purposes or any device used to visually depict a child engaged in sexually explicit conduct, store any image or audio of a child engaged in sexually explicit conduct, or transmit any audio or visual image of a child for sexual purposes. Such term may include, but shall not be limited to, a computer, cellular phone, thumb drive, video game system, or any other electronic device that can be used in furtherance of exploiting a child for sexual purposes;

. . .

(8) "Visual depiction" means any image and includes undeveloped film and video tape and data stored on computer disk or by electronic means which is capable of conversion into a visual image or which has been created, adapted, or modified to show an identifiable child engaged in sexually explicit conduct.

. . .

(2) Any person convicted of violating paragraph (1) of this subsection shall be punished by a fine of not more than $10,000.00 and by imprisonment for not less than one nor more than 20 years.

(d)(1) It shall be unlawful for any person intentionally or willfully to utilize a computer on-line service or Internet service, including but not limited to a local bulletin board service, Internet chat room, e-mail, on-line messaging service, or other electronic device, to seduce, solicit, lure, or entice, or attempt to seduce, solicit, lure, or entice a

continued

FIGURE 7-7

Computer or Electronic Pornography and Child Exploitation Prevention Act of 2007[34]

---

[31] *Ashcroft v. Free Speech Coalition*, 535 U.S. 234, 122 S. Ct. 1389, 152 L. Ed. 2d 403 (2002).
[32] *Ashcroft v. Free Speech Coalition*, 535 U.S. 234, 122 S. Ct. 1389, 152 L. Ed. 2d 403 (2002).
[33] 18 U.S.C.A. § 1466A(a).
[34] O.C.G.A. § 16-6-4.

child or another person believed by such person to be a child to commit any illegal act described in Code Section 16-6-2, relating to the offense of sodomy or aggravated sodomy; Code Section 16-6-4, relating to the offense of child molestation or aggravated child molestation; Code Section 16-6-5, relating to the offense of enticing a child for indecent purposes; or Code Section 16-6-8, relating to the offense of public indecency or to engage in any conduct that by its nature is an unlawful sexual offense against a child.

(2) Any person who violates paragraph (1) of this subsection shall be guilty of a felony and, upon conviction thereof, shall be punished by imprisonment for not less than one nor more than 20 years and by a fine of not more than $25,000.00; provided, however, that, if at the time of the offense the victim was 14 or 15 years of age and the defendant was no more than three years older than the victim, then the defendant shall be guilty of a misdemeanor of a high and aggravated nature.

SELLING CHILDREN FOR CHILD PORNOGRAPHY

In addition to outlawing child pornography, federal statutes also make it a crime to sell children, or even offer a child for sale, when the child will be used in child pornography.[35] Unfortunately, there is an international black market in children who are used for child pornography, including some countries where pedophiles can go to have prearranged meetings with children for the express purpose of having sex with them.

CASE EXCERPT

GARCIA v. STATE
936 N.E.2d 361 (2010)

OPINION
BAKER, Chief Judge.

Appellant-defendant Lucio Garcia appeals the denial of his petition for post-conviction relief. Garcia contends that the post-conviction court erroneously determined that he did not receive the ineffective assistance of trial and appellate counsel. Finding no error, we affirm.

FACTS

The facts underlying Garcia's convictions, as described in Garcia's direct appeal, are as follows:

Between December 31, 2004, and January 29, 2005, Garcia engaged 12-year-old A.S. in sexual intercourse on three occasions. At the time, Garcia was 32 years old

---

[35] 18 U.S.C.A. § 2251A.

and had led A.S. to believe that they were "boyfriend-girlfriend." On February 2, after receiving a report that A.S. may have been raped, Detective Steve Buchanan of the Indianapolis Police Department interviewed A.S. and learned of her relationship with Garcia.

On February 14, the State charged Garcia with three counts of child molesting, each as a Class A felony. The State subsequently amended the charging information to include three counts of attempted sexual misconduct with a minor, each as a Class B felony. . . .

Garcia's trial occurred on August 8, 2006, in which the State called A.S. and Detective Buchanan as witnesses. A.S. testified that on each of the three dates in question, Garcia engaged her in sexual intercourse. . . .

The jury found Garcia guilty as charged, and the trial court merged the attempted sexual misconduct with a minor convictions into his child molestation convictions. Following a sentencing hearing, the trial court sentenced Garcia to twenty-year terms on each of the child molesting convictions, with two of the terms to run consecutively, for an aggregate forty-year term. Garcia appealed, and this court affirmed.

On October 4, 2007, Garcia filed a pro se petition for post-conviction relief, later filing an amended petition after retaining counsel. Garcia contended that his appellate counsel was ineffective for failing to contend that the child molesting convictions should have been overturned because, by convicting Garcia of attempted sexual misconduct with a minor, the jury found beyond a reasonable doubt that Garcia believed that A.S. was fourteen years of age. Garcia also claimed that appellate counsel should have challenged the consecutive twenty-year terms imposed by the trial court. Finally, Garcia argued that trial counsel was ineffective for failing to bring caselaw to the trial court's attention that tends to suggest that consecutive sentences would be disfavored under these circumstances. Following a hearing, the post-conviction court denied Garcia's petition on April 8, 2010. Garcia now appeals.

DISCUSSION AND DECISION

Assistance of Counsel

A. Defendant's Burden

When making a claim of ineffective assistance of counsel, the defendant must first show that counsel's performance was deficient. *Strickland v. Washington*, 466 U.S. 668, 687, 104 S.Ct. 2052, 80 L.Ed.2d 674 (1984). This requires a showing that counsel's representation fell below an objective standard of reasonableness and that the errors were so serious that they resulted in a denial of the right to counsel guaranteed to the defendant by the Sixth and Fourteenth Amendments. Second, the defendant must show that the deficient performance resulted in prejudice — in other words, that there is a reasonable probability that but for counsel's unprofessional errors, the result of the proceeding would have been different. If a claim of ineffective assistance can be disposed of by analyzing the prejudice prong alone, we will do so.

Claims of ineffective assistance of appellate counsel are reviewed using the same standard applicable to claims of trial counsel ineffectiveness. *Bieghler v. State*, 690

N.E.2d 188, 193 (Ind.1997). Ineffectiveness is rarely found when the issue is the failure to raise a claim on direct appeal.

B. Appellate Counsel

1. Inconsistent Verdicts

Garcia first argues that his appellate counsel was ineffective for failing to challenge his child molesting convictions. It is a defense to child molesting that the defendant believed the victim to be fourteen years of age or older.

Here, Garcia was also convicted of three counts of attempted sexual misconduct with a minor. The jury was instructed on this offense as follows:

Before you may convict the Defendant of Attempted Sexual Misconduct With a Minor, as charged in Count IV, the State must have proved each of the following elements beyond a reasonable doubt.

1. The Defendant, Lucio Garcia
2. acting with the culpability required to commit the crime of Sexual Misconduct With a Minor
    a. intentionally
    b. performed or submitted to sexual intercourse
    c. with (A.S.)
    d. the defendant, Lucio Garcia, was at least twenty-one (21) years of age and
    e. believed (A.S.) to be fourteen (14) years of age
3. did place his penis in the vagina of (A.S.)
4. which was conduct constituting a substantial step toward the commission of the crime of Sexual Misconduct With a Minor.

Therefore, by convicting Garcia of this crime, the jury necessarily found beyond a reasonable doubt that he believed that A.S. was fourteen years old, which is a defense to the child molesting conviction.

Although Garcia attempts to frame his argument in other ways, what he argues, in essence, is that his appellate counsel should have challenged these verdicts as inconsistent. Very recently, our Supreme Court held that "jury verdicts in criminal cases are not subject to appellate review on grounds that they are inconsistent, contradictory, or irreconcilable." *Beattie v. State*, 924 N.E.2d 643, 649 (Ind.2010). Although Beattie had not been handed down at the time of Garcia's direct appeal, we now know that even if Garcia's appellate counsel had raised this issue, our Supreme Court would have declined to address this claim of inconsistent verdicts. Consequently, Garcia cannot establish prejudice as a result of counsel's failure to raise the claim on appeal, and we decline to reverse on this basis.

2. Sentencing

Garcia also argues that appellate counsel was ineffective for failing to make an argument regarding the two consecutive sentences imposed by the trial court. He directs our attention to a number of cases in which our Supreme Court ordered consecutive sentences in child molesting cases to run concurrently. Estes v. State, 827

N.E.2d 27, 29 (Ind.2005) (revising 267–year term to 120 years); Serino v. State, 798 N.E.2d 852, 856 (Ind.2003) (revising 385–year term to three consecutive standard terms, or 90 years total); Ortiz v. State, 766 N.E.2d 370, 377 (Ind.2002) (revising consecutive thirty-year terms to run concurrently); Walker v. State, 747 N.E.2d 536, 538 (Ind.2001) (consecutive forty-year sentences for two counts of child molestation ordered to be served concurrently).

Garcia was sentenced on three convictions for class A felony child molesting. At that time, the "presumptive" term for a class A felony was thirty years, with a maximum of fifty and a minimum of twenty years. I.C. § 35–50–2–4 (Burns 2004). Had the trial court imposed three fully executed consecutive terms, therefore, Garcia faced a maximum of 150 years imprisonment. Instead, the trial court elected to impose twenty-year sentences, which is the minimum term. Furthermore, it chose to run only two, rather than all three, of the terms consecutively. Consequently, Garcia received an aggregate term of 40 years, which is still ten years less than the maximum possible term he faced for one conviction alone, and far less than the possible maximum term of 150 years.

To impose consecutive sentences, the trial court must identify at least one aggravating circumstance. The record herein reveals that one of the instances of sex between Garcia and his twelve-year-old victim took place in the presence of Garcia's one-year-old nephew. That fact constitutes a proper statutory aggravator; consequently, that requirement was met. Ind.Code § 35–38–1–7.1(a)(4)(B).

Additionally, Garcia made his young victim wait alone in his car before joining him in their hotel room, persisted when she initially declined to have sex, and dropped her off away from her home when they were finished. Thus, the nature and circumstances of the offenses were an additional aggravator that supported the imposition of consecutive sentences.

Finally, Garcia's criminal history included a conviction for driving under the influence in Georgia, charges of battery with family violence, battery, and operating a vehicle while intoxicated that were ultimately dismissed, and a charge of failure to stop after an accident that was pending at the time Garcia was sentenced herein. It is well established that past wrongs may be considered as part of sentencing even if they did not result in convictions. Although his criminal history, alone, may not have justified consecutive sentences, it provides additional support for the trial court's decision to do so.

We acknowledge that the above authority cited by Garcia could have led this court to revise his sentence. It is equally likely, however, that we would have affirmed the sentence given the above-discussed aggravators, his criminal history, and the fact that the trial court imposed less than the presumptive term for the individual sentences. To establish ineffective assistance of counsel for failing to raise an issue on appeal, Garcia is required to show that the unraised issue is "clearly stronger" than the issues that were presented. We conclude that Garcia has not met that burden. Garcia must also establish that the evidence as a whole unerringly and unmistakably leads to a conclusion opposite that reached by the post-conviction court, and we conclude that he has not met that burden either. Consequently, we decline to reverse on this basis.

C. Trial Counsel

Finally, Garcia contends that his trial counsel was ineffective for failing to bring the Walker/Ortiz line of cases to the trial court's attention at sentencing, arguing that if counsel had done so, he would not have received consecutive sentences. As noted above, it is possible that the trial court would have imposed different sentences had counsel brought these cases to its attention. It is equally possible, however, that the result would have been the same, for all of the reasons discussed above.

In other words, we cannot find that there is a reasonable probability that the result would have been different. Therefore, Garcia has failed to establish prejudice and has also failed to show that the evidence unerringly and unmistakably leads to a conclusion opposite that reached by the post-conviction court. Consequently, we decline to reverse the post-conviction court on this issue.

The judgment of the post-conviction court is affirmed.

NAJAM, J., and MATHIAS, J., concur.

CASE QUESTIONS

1. What are the underlying facts of this case?
2. What was Garcia's sentence?
3. What is the defendant's burden when attempting to show ineffective assistance of counsel?
4. Is it a proper appellate argument to state that the verdicts were inconsistent with another?
5. Garcia challenged his total sentence. According to the court, what was the maximum sentence that Garcia could have been given?

CHAPTER SUMMARY

This chapter showed that there are some sex-related crimes that are rarely prosecuted, including fornication, adultery, and cohabitation. We have also seen that crimes involving more serious situations, such as voyeurism and public indecency continue to receive strong attention from the law enforcement community. Sodomy is defined as any "unnatural" sexual act and encompasses a wide range of activities. After the U.S. Supreme Court's decision in *Lawrence v. Texas*, consensual sodomy between adults was made virtually impossible to prosecute. However, aggravated sodomy cases, where the victim did not consent or where the victim received serious bodily injury, are actively prosecuted every day in the United States.

When a person touches a child in a sexual way, it is child molestation. Sexual acts with children are illegal across the nation, including child pornography, which consists of graphic video or other media depictions of children in sexual activity.

Obscenity is an area of law that has undergone a great deal of change in the past few decades. Nowadays, the U.S. Supreme Court uses the so-called Miller test to define what is and what is not obscene. In *Miller v. California*, the Supreme Court created a three-step process to define when something is considered to be obscene and can be prosecuted. If an item fails to meet each of the steps outlined in the Miller test, it cannot be prosecuted as obscenity. The Miller test does not apply to child pornography.

KEY TERMS

Lewd	Sodomy	Obscene
Public indecency	Aggravated sodomy	Pornographic
Voyeur	Incest	Prurient interest
Bestiality	Child molestation	Child pornography
Necrophilia	Enticement	Contraband

REVIEW QUESTIONS

1 What are the elements of indecent exposure?
2 How does the law classify the word "lewd"?
3 What allegations were made against President Clinton by Paula Jones?
4 What is voyeurism?
5 Why does the text refer to the term "sodomy" as a general, not a specific crime?
6 What is the significance of the *Lawrence v. Texas* decision?
7 What makes a crime qualify as aggravated sodomy?
8 Define the term "incest."
9 Under the definition of incest provided in the text, is it legal for second or third cousins to have consensual, adult sexual relations with another?
10 What is child molestation?
11 Is consent of the victim an issue in child molestation cases? Why or why not?
12 Explain "enticement" of a child.
13 What is a pedophile?
14 What is the Miller test, and how does it apply to obscenity prosecutions?
15 What is the relationship between pornography and obscenity? Are they the same thing? Explain.
16 List and explain the three prongs of the Miller test.
17 What is prurient interest?
18 Why is it difficult to prosecute most obscenity cases these days?
19 Explain the relationship between findings of obscenity and nude dancing.
20 If it is legal to possess obscene materials, why is it illegal to possess child pornography?
21 What is the relationship of the Miller test and child pornography?

22   According to the text, what are the ranges of punishment for exploiting a child or using an electronic device to create child pornography?

QUESTIONS FOR ANALYSIS

1   These days, children know a great deal more about the world than they did 50 years ago. Should the law acknowledge this greater knowledge by lowering the age of consent for sexual activity? Explain your response.

2   If the crimes of fornication, adultery and cohabitation are rarely, if ever, prosecuted, why do they remain crimes in most states?

HYPOTHETICALS

1   Matt is a fireman who is required to live at the firehouse for four days a week. His living quarters consist of a bunk and a private area where he can read or answer emails. During an inspection of the living quarters by the fire chief, the chief discovered that Matt had pornographic magazines in his possession. The magazines clearly satisfy all of the elements of the Miller test. Can the state prosecute Matt and if so, does he have a defense that will negate the charges?

2   Steve has been charged with child molestation for fondling a four-year-old girl. In his defense, Steve states that he is a member of a religious order that believes that children should be touched in all parts of their bodies and also taught that sexuality is a key component of human existence and children must be instructed in sexual activity as early as possible. Does Steve's religious convictions outweigh the state's right to prosecute him for child molestation? What do you think?

3   What is a justification for a ruling that states that adult, consensual homosexual acts should be legal? What is an argument against such a position?

Burglary and Arson

I INTRODUCTION

This chapter will explore crimes against property, sometimes called crimes against habitation. Specifically, we will examine burglary and arson. Burglary is the intentional breaking and entering of a structure with the intent to commit a theft or a felony. Arson, on the other hand, is the intentional burning of a structure. We begin with burglary.

II BURGLARY

Burglary is a relatively straightforward crime that often evokes strong feelings in victims. The laws criminalizing burglary are based on the obvious premise that having an intruder in a person's home is a potentially life-threatening situation. The burglar may harm or kill the occupants; the occupants may do the same to the burglar. At a minimum, the burglar may steal the occupants' personal belongings and disrupt their sense of security. The basic elements of burglary are:

Burglary
The intentional breaking and entering of a structure with the intent to commit a theft or a felony.

 Breaking
 Entering
 Of a dwelling house of another
 With the intent to commit a theft or a felony

This text will examine each of these elements in turn, beginning with a legal analysis of what "breaking" means in the context of a burglary charge.

A. BREAKING

Breaking
Any force, even slight force, used to gain admittance to a dwelling.

The elements of **breaking** and entering are best explored by separating them into disparate units. Despite how it sounds, "breaking," as set out in burglary statutes, does not actually require anything to be broken. There is no requirement, for instance, that a window must be broken or a door forced to satisfy this element.[1] Breaking can be established by the simple act of the defendant turning a door knob to get inside a dwelling.[2] Instead, it means the application of force to create a way inside the structure. This force must be without the consent of the occupant. If the occupant consents, then there is no illegal breaking and therefore no burglary. Under the definition of breaking, even slight force is enough to establish the element of breaking. Opening a window, twisting an unlocked door, and even pushing open a window would all qualify as "breaking" under burglary statutes.[3] Some states have gone so far as to define breaking as simply moving an item out of the way that blocks entrance to the structure.[4] In some states, however, walking through an open door might not be considered "breaking" and would thus make prosecution difficult.[5]

| SCENARIO 8-1 | BREAKING? |

BREAKING?

Maria hears her front doorbell ring and opens the door only a few inches to look out. When she sees a man she doesn't recognize, she starts to close the door, but the man pushes the door open with his foot and enters. Do his actions qualify as "breaking" under burglary statutes?

   Answer: Yes. Even though the victim initially opened the door, she did not consent to his entry, and the use of his foot to push open the door satisfies the element of breaking.[6]

Under the law of burglary, there are two types of breaking: actual breaking and constructive breaking. Actual breaking is the use of any force, even slight force, to gain entry, but constructive breaking is a different animal.

CONSTRUCTIVE BREAKING

Constructive breaking
Using fraud, trickery, or deceit to gain access to a dwelling that a person has no right or consent to enter.

Under the **constructive breaking** doctrine, the state can prove that the defendant satisfied the element of breaking when he or she used fraud, deceit, or trickery to gain entrance to the dwelling.[7] Consider Scenario 8-2.

---

[1] *Sample v. State*, 629 S.W.2d 86 (Tex. App. Dallas 1981).
[2] *Templeton v. State*, 725 So. 2d 764 (Miss. 1998).
[3] *State v. Simpson*, 611 A.2d 1390 (R.I. 1992).
[4] *Finney v. Com.*, 277 Va. 83, 671 S.E.2d 169 (2009).
[5] *State v. Styles*, 93 N.C. App. 596, 379 S.E.2d 255 (1989).
[6] *State v. McDowell*, 246 Neb. 692, 522 N.W.2d 738 (1994).
[7] *Finney v. Com.*, 277 Va. 83, 671 S.E.2d 169 (2009).

PIZZA DELIVERY

Dennis is home one evening when he hears a knock on his door. He looks through the peephole in his front door and sees a man dressed as a pizza delivery man and carrying a large pizza. Dennis did not order a pizza, so he is confused. He opens the door and the pizza delivery man says, "Here's your pizza." Dennis tells the man that he didn't order a pizza. The man looks confused and then asks Dennis if he can step inside and call the restaurant to see what is wrong. Once inside, the man attacks Dennis, restrains him and then steals several items from his home. At trial, the man claims that he entered the home with Dennis's consent. Is this consent or constructive breaking?

Answer: Constructive breaking. The defendant used deceit to gain entrance to the victim's home.[8]

If a person has the right to enter the dwelling, then a burglary charge cannot be sustained against him or her. Spouses have the right to enter the marital home. Managers have the right to enter stores before or after store hours. However, the situation changes when the spouse has been subjected to a temporary restraining order. In that case, the spouse no longer has the privilege of entering the marital residence and can be charged with burglary.[9] A store manager who has had his or her privileges revoked faces the same dilemma. It is also true that an employee may have the right to enter some parts of the commercial setting, but not others. When he or she enters the forbidden area, with the intent to commit a theft or felony, the employee can be guilty of burglary.

CONSENT

Another method to prove that the defendant committed breaking and entering is to establish that he or she did not have permission or consent to be on the premises.[10] Like many criminal offenses, consent is a valid defense. If the victim gives knowing and voluntary consent to the defendant's presence, then his actions of opening a door and stepping inside do not satisfy the elements of breaking and entering, and the first two elements of a burglary charge are not met.[11]

B. ENTERING

In addition to breaking, the state must also show that the defendant **entered** the dwelling. Usually, this is quite easy to prove, either because there are witnesses that the defendant was inside or because the defendant left fingerprints while committing the theft or felony. But the law is specific; the state must show entry, and that

Entering
Proof that any part of the defendant's body entered the victim's dwelling after the defendant satisfied the element of "breaking."

---

[8] *State v. Abdullah*, 967 A.2d 469 (R.I. 2009).
[9] *In re Richard M.*, 205 Cal. App. 3d 7, 252 Cal. Rptr. 36 (2d Dist. 1988).
[10] *Nickell v. State*, 722 So. 2d 924 (Fla. Dist. Ct. App. 2d Dist. 1998).
[11] *Smith v. State*, 362 P.2d 1071, 93 A.L.R.2d 525 (Alaska 1961).

Sidebar

Under burglary statutes, a defendant is guilty if he or she enters a building with the intent to commit a theft or a felony. It is not burglary if the person is permitted to enter the premises.

Sidebar

There are some jurisdictions that also include breaking and entering of automobiles under the category of burglary, but many do not.[13] Instead, they include this crime under criminal damage to property or as part grand theft automobile, which will be discussed later in this text.

Dwelling
An occupied structure, one that is designed for human beings.

Sidebar

A structure still qualifies as a dwelling even if it is temporarily unable to be occupied, such as a house that is being refurbished or a cabin that is being repaired.[15]

means that the state must present specific evidence to establish this element. If the state can prove that any part of the defendant's body entered the premises, then the element has been established. That means that if the defendant remained outside the dwelling, but pushed open a window and reached inside to take an item, the state can proceed with a burglary charge.[12]

C. OF A DWELLING HOUSE OF ANOTHER

The crime of burglary requires an unlawful entry into a building or other structure. In some states, the burglary statute specifically requires a **dwelling**. Dwellings are places that are normally used by people for sleeping and general living. Apartments, mobile homes, and holiday cabins are all examples of dwellings. To avoid confusion this text will refer to all structures that can be the subject of a burglary as a "dwelling." Dwellings are considered to be occupied structures or structures that are designed to house human beings. In most states, it is not important whether the owners of the premises were home. The breaking and entering are sufficient to prove burglary.[14]

What qualifies as a dwelling? Simply put, a dwelling for purposes of a burglary statute is any structure designed to house human beings (see Figure 8-1). These include:

- Homes
- Apartments
- Mobile homes
- Stores
- Garages
- Porches (as curtilage, see below)
- Storage areas
- Dormitory rooms
- Vacant cabins
- Unoccupied apartments, to name just a few

In establishing what is and what is not a dwelling, courts look to issues such as how the structure is used, whether or not it is typically occupied, whether the owner maintains it, and what period of time it has been vacant.[16] The temporary absence of the occupant does not affect the status of a building as a dwelling for purposes of a burglary prosecution, but what happens when the occupant leaves the premises and demonstrates an intention of never returning? In such a situation, the structure may

---

[12] *State v. Spikes*, 111 Conn. App. 543, 961 A.2d 426 (2008), certification denied, 291 Conn. 901, 967 A.2d 114 (2009).
[13] *State v. Lindsay*, 77 Wyo. 410, 317 P.2d 506 (1957).
[14] *State v. Smith*, 677 So. 2d 589 (La. Ct. App. 2d Cir. 1996), writ denied, 703 So. 2d 1287 (La. 1997).
[15] *Michael v. State*, 51 So. 3d 574 (Fla. Dist. Ct. App. 5th Dist. 2010).
[16] *State v. Scarberry*, 187 W. Va. 251, 418 S.E.2d 361 (1992).

FIGURE 8-1

§ 19-1. Burglary. (Illinois)

(a) A person commits burglary when without authority he knowingly enters or without authority remains within a building, housetrailer, watercraft, aircraft, motor vehicle as defined in the Illinois Vehicle Code, railroad car, or any part thereof, with intent to commit therein a felony or theft. This offense shall not include the offenses set out in Section 4-102 of the Illinois Vehicle Code.

(b) Sentence.

Burglary is a Class 2 felony. A burglary committed in a school, day care center, day care home, group day care home, or part day child care facility, or place of worship is a Class 1 felony, except that this provision does not apply to a day care center, day care home, group day care home, or part day child care facility operated in a private residence used as a dwelling.[19]

no longer qualify as dwelling, and the defendant might not be guilty of burglary for entering it.[17] However, this does not mean that the defendant has not committed a crime. Instead of burglary, the state may bring a trespass and theft charge against the defendant.

It is never necessary for the person who lives in the dwelling to be home before a burglary charge can be brought against someone who breaks into the dwelling.[20]

> ## Sidebar
>
> *When a structure becomes uninhabitable, it no longer qualifies as a dwelling for purposes of a burglary charge.*[18]

THEY BOUGHT A ZOO

One evening, after closing time, Tim jumps the fence at a local zoo and pries open a vending machine just outside the zoo's main office. When he is caught, he is charged with burglary. Tim raises the claim that a zoo is not a dwelling and therefore he can't be charged with burglary, only damage to property and theft, both of which are misdemeanors. Is he right?

Answer: Yes. A zoo is not designed for the housing of people, and the structure does not qualify as a dwelling.[21]

Does a hotel room qualify as a dwelling for purposes of a burglary? Jurisdictions are split on this issue, with some saying that it is and some saying that it is not.[22] In some cases, a single structure can contain several dwellings. An apartment house,

---

[17] *Rash v. Com.*, 9 Va. App. 22, 383 S.E.2d 749 (1989).

[18] *State v. Albert*, 426 A.2d 1370, 20 A.L.R.4th 342 (Me. 1981).

[19] 720 ILCS 5/19-1.

[20] *State v. Calderwood*, 194 Ohio App. 3d 438, 2011-Ohio-2913, 956 N.E.2d 892 (8th Dist. Cuyahoga County 2011).

[21] *In Interest of E. S.*, 93 Ill. App. 3d 171, 48 Ill. Dec. 711, 416 N.E.2d 1233 (2d Dist. 1981).

[22] *People v. Fleetwood*, 171 Cal. App. 3d 982, 217 Cal. Rptr. 612 (4th Dist. 1985).

for example, might contain several distinct units. A person who enters any of the apartments without permission could be guilty of burglary for each unit.

Who is permitted to enter the premises? In some cases, a spouse can be convicted of burglary if he or she enters the marital home after the custody and control of the house has been transferred to the other spouse and the defendant no longer has a property interest in the home or permission to be there.[23]

CURTILAGE OF A DWELLING

Curtilage
An area associated with the immediate area of the house, but not necessarily inside the dwelling.

As you saw in the first description of the places that could be considered dwellings, houses and apartments were listed, but there were also entries for garages, storage buildings, and carports. How do these areas qualify as dwellings? Courts include these in the immediate area of the dwelling. The term for this area is **curtilage**. This area is used for normal family functions and includes lawns, gardens, and so on. The reason that curtilage is so important is that a person can be convicted of burglary when he or she enters the curtilage of the house. This means that a person can be guilty of burglary even if she does not actually enter the house.

D. WITH INTENT TO COMMIT A THEFT OR FELONY

The last element of a burglary is that the defendant broke and entered with the intent to commit a theft or a felony. If the state is unable to show the defendant's intent, or that the defendant merely walked into an area with no particular intent in mind, the state's charge of burglary cannot be sustained. Proving theft is relatively easy to do: If the defendant takes something that does not belong to him, then he has committed theft. When the defendant has entered the home to commit a theft, there is no minimum monetary value that the defendant must take before the crime becomes burglary. The actual value of the stolen items is not important: Any theft is enough to justify a prosecution for burglary. But what about entering for the purposes of committing a felony? We have already seen that a felony is any crime that is punishable by more than one year in custody. Examples of felonies are murder, rape, and robbery. How does the state prove that the defendant intended to commit a felony? Again, the answer comes from the surrounding circumstances. If the defendant breaks and enters and is carrying handcuffs, duct tape, and condoms, it is fairly certain that the defendant was entering with the intent to commit rape. Similarly, if the defendant enters with a handgun and is actively seeking out the occupant, the jury is allowed to infer that the defendant intended to commit murder.

The most common way to prove the defendant's intent is by the items in his or her possession at the time of the break in. For a summary of burglary victimizations, see Figure 8-2.

Sidebar

In a burglary prosecution, if the defendant is in possession of burglary tools, this will often be enough to establish that the defendant entered with the intent to commit a theft.[24]

---

[23] *State v. O'Neal,* 87 Ohio St. 3d 402, 2000-Ohio-449, 721 N.E.2d 73 (2000).
[24] *People v. Glazier,* 186 Cal. App. 4th 1151, 113 Cal. Rptr. 3d 108 (2d Dist. 2010).

FIGURE 8-2	Number of Property Victimizations					
	Number of victimizations					
Type of property crime	2002	2010	2011	Percent change, 2002-2011*	Percent change, 2010-2011*	Average annual change, 2002-2010*
Total	18,554,320	15,411,610	17,066,780	−8%[†]	11%[†]	−2%
Household burglary	3,251,810	3,176,180	3,613,190	11%[‡]	14%[†]	—
Motor vehicle theft	1,018,690	606,990	628,070	−38[†]	3	−6%
Theft	14,283,820	11,628,440	12,825,510	−10[†]	10[†]	−2

Note: Detail may not sum to total due to rounding. Total number of households was 110,323,840 in 2002; 122,885,570 in 2011.

† Significant at 95%.
‡ Significant at 90%.
— Less than 0.5%.
* Calculated based on unrounded estimates.

Source: Bureau of Justice Statistics, National Crime Victimization Survey, 2002, 2010, and 2011.

SPECIFIC INTENT AND BURGLARY

Burglary is a specific intent crime. Just as we saw with homicide, the state must prove not only that the defendant acted voluntarily, but also that he or she acted with the specific goal of committing a burglary.[25] However, proving specific intent is not as difficult as one might imagine. The fact that the defendant entered the premises by force, took objects inside the dwelling, and was caught with them once he left is enough to establish specific intent to commit burglary.[26]

E. DEGREES OF BURGLARY

In some jurisdictions, burglary is divided into different degrees, while in others, there are separate offenses: residential burglary and burglary. As you might imagine, the offense of residential burglary involves the breaking and entering of a residence with the intent to commit a theft or felony, while "burglary" requires the same elements, except that the structure is something other than a residence.[27] In states that organize burglary into various degrees, there are usually three categories: first-, second-, and third-degree burglary.

First-degree burglary, in these states, occurs when a person breaks and enters with the intent to commit a theft or felony and causes serious injury to the victim.[28] In some jurisdictions, first-degree burglary is committed when the defendant breaks and enters, with the intent to commit a theft or felony and the occupants are at

---

[25] *In re D.A.*, 40 Kan. App. 2d 878, 197 P.3d 849 (2008).
[26] *Grissam v. State*, 2009 WL 673084 (Tex. App. Fort Worth 2009).
[27] *People v. Willard*, 303 Ill. App. 3d 231, 236 Ill. Dec. 679, 707 N.E.2d 1249 (2d Dist. 1999).
[28] *State v. Parker*, 350 N.C. 411, 516 S.E.2d 106 (1999).

FIGURE 8-3

Burglary Arrest Rates

Burglary arrest rates

Arrests/100,000

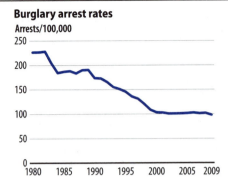

Burglary arrest rates, by sex

Arrests/100,000

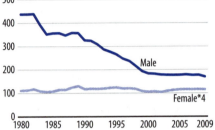

Burglary arrest rates, by age group

Arrests/100,000

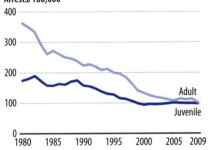

Burglary arrest rates, by race

Arrests/100,000

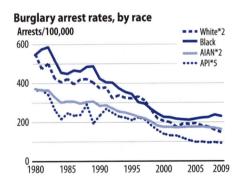

home.[29] Second-degree burglary has the same elements as first degree, with the important exception that the residents were not at home when the burglary occurred. In states that have third-degree burglary, the elements are that the defendant knowingly entered a dwelling with the intent to commit a crime.[30] See Figure 8-3 for burglary arrest rates.

COMMON-LAW BURGLARY

In the few remaining states where common-law offenses are still followed, the crime of burglary takes an unusual turn. In those states, the elements of burglary are:

- Breaking
- Entering
- Of a dwelling house of another
- At night
- With the intent to commit a theft or felony once entry has been gained

One of the obvious problems with common-law burglary is proving that the burglary occurred at night. If it occurred during the day, it was not burglary, but trespass with a possible theft charge. Because common-law burglary requires that the burglary occur at night, when the government fails to prove that the crime did occur at night, the charges against the defendant must be dismissed.

These days, in states that do not follow the common law, the time of day that the burglary occurs is not relevant, except that it may be an aggravating factor if the burglar broke into a dwelling during the night when people were asleep inside. This could justify a more severe sentence.[31]

 ARSON

Arson is generally defined as:

- The malicious
- Burning of a
- Dwelling house or structure

Arson
Intentional (and malicious) burning of a structure.

The elements of arson have changed over time. In previous centuries, arson was considered one of the most serious crimes to be perpetrated on an individual and by extension, the community. Before the advent of fire departments and other technology, there was a real chance that any fire set to burn down a house might spread

---

[29] *State v. Rich*, 130 N.C. App. 113, 502 S.E.2d 49 (1998).
[30] *Green v. State*, 424 So. 2d 704 (Ala. Crim. App. 1982).
[31] *Goodroad v. Solem*, 406 N.W.2d 141 (S.D. 1987).

FIGURE 8-4

Arson (Michigan)

Sec. 72. Burning dwelling house — Any person who willfully or maliciously burns any dwelling house, either occupied or unoccupied, or the contents thereof, whether owned by himself or another, or any building within the curtilage of such dwelling house, or the contents thereof, shall be guilty of a felony, punishable by imprisonment in the state prison not more than 20 years.[32]

to the entire community. Cities such as San Francisco, Chicago, and London have all been decimated by fires.

A. MALICE ELEMENT OF ARSON

In order to prosecute someone for the crime of arson, it is first necessary to show that the fire was started out of malice, not negligence. This means that the person who started the fire must have done so deliberately. Without this deliberate intent, the first element of arson is not met, and the case against the defendant will fail. A person may be charged with some lesser crime for negligence in burning down a structure, but not with first-degree arson. Figure 8-4 provides an example of an arson statute.

PROVING INTENT IN ARSON CASES

In some states, a defendant must not only set fire to a structure, but he or she must have done so "willfully and maliciously." This is a holdover from the old common-law offense of arson. Although almost all states have eliminated common-law crimes in favor of statutorily defined crimes, the old common-law element often remains in the newer version of the law. Under the common law, if the prosecution could not prove that the fire was set willfully and with malice, then, at best, the crime would be a form of trespass. No doubt the additional elements for common-law arson had a direct relationship with the enhanced punishment that an arsonist would receive under the common law, including the death penalty.[33]

How does the prosecution prove intent in a case of arson? Put another way, a defendant's intention is clear when he or she splashes gasoline around a house and then sets fire to it, but what about situations where the defendant might claim that the fire was an accident? How can the government prove the defendant's intent? As is true in so many other situations, we look to the surrounding circumstances. If a defendant sets a fire and it is almost certain to burn, then he has the intent to commit arson.[34] The state must often rely on circumstantial evidence to prove the defendant's intent in an arson case. This would consist of the defendant's prior

---

[32] M.C.L.A. 750.72.
[33] *People v. Fanshawe*, 137 N.Y. 68, 32 N.E. 1102 (1893).
[34] *State v. Smith*, 170 Wis. 2d 701, 490 N.W.2d 40 (Ct. App. 1992).

threatening statements, the items that the defendant took with him to the scene, his or her reactions after the fire was set (such as failing to call for help) and his relationship with the owner or occupant of the property, among other things.

B. DEFINING "BURNING"

At first glance, defining what is and what is not a **"burning"** would seem to be a matter of common sense. However, because prosecutors must prove each and every element of the crime beyond a reasonable doubt, this means that the prosecutor must also focus on defining exactly what constitutes burning. Under arson statutes, the defendant must have burned real or personal property, for which there are legal differences. The basic definitions are simple. Real property consists of land and anything permanently attached to land. The land that a house is built upon qualifies as real property, as does the house. Personal property refers to items, anything from automobiles to zoom lenses. Essentially, personal property is anything that does not qualify as real property. Obviously, setting fire to real property, especially a person's home, poses a greater danger to society than burning an item of personal property. As a result, setting fire to a home or other structure carries a higher penalty than burning an automobile. If a person dies as a result of the fire, the defendant can be charged with murder under the felony-murder doctrine. In many states, the strict definition of arson is the burning of a building or other structure. Burning personal property is often classified as criminal damage to property or falls under some other category.

Burning
Setting a flame to real or personal property.

BURNING THE LICENSE

Edward has discovered that his bride, Ella, has been cheating on him. He takes their marriage license out to the front yard of their house and burns it in front of her, then tells her that he is going to seek a divorce. Bella calls the police and says that the Edward has committed arson? Has he?

Answer: No. In the strictest sense, arson is the intentional burning of a building or other structure. Because Edward has burned a piece of paper (which qualifies as personal property), he cannot be charged with arson.

SCENARIO 8-4

C. DWELLING HOUSE OR STRUCTURE

Under the original formulation of the law, arson applied only to dwelling houses. However, arson law has been expanded from a simple focus on dwelling houses to all structures. These days, when a person sets fire to almost any type of structure it can be classified as arson.

Sidebar

The common-law definition of arson has been expanded in all states to include all structures that qualify as real property, encompassing private and public structures.[35]

---

[35] *Com. v. Cross*, 769 S.W.2d 63 (Ky. Ct. App. 1988).

D. ARSON UNDER COMMON LAW

Under the common law, arson was defined as the:

- Malicious, voluntary
- Burning
- Of another's dwelling[36]

Under the common law, arson was punished severely, with lengthy prison terms and even death sentences. The reason for this is simple: Arson presented a great threat to communities that had no established fire departments, pressurized water, and other modern methods to put out fire.[37] Most jurisdictions have abandoned the old common-law definition of arson and instead have switched to statutory definitions. These statutes have actually expanded the definition and elements of arson.[38]

Under the common-law definition of arson, a person was guilty when he or she burned "another's" dwelling. Under common law, it was not arson to burn down your own house. However, even under the common law, if the defendant shared ownership with another person, such as a husband with a wife, then the defendant could still be charged with arson.[39] Not all states recognized this division. In many of the original common-law states, the husband and wife were regarded as a single unit, and therefore the act of one spouse burning down the marital residence was not a crime against the other.[40] In order to clear up this question, all states have expanded the definition of arson to include burning a person's own home, as well as including provisions for prosecuting a defendant for arson with the intent to defraud an insurance company.

E. NEW STATUTORY APPROACHES TO ARSON

Modern statutes have expanded the common-law definition. There were some obvious problems with it, not the least of which was that under common-law definition a person could not be prosecuted for burning down her own home. Another obvious problem is that it applies only to "dwelling houses." Under this definition, businesses and other commercial enterprises, when burned, would not constitute arson. Modern statutes have addressed these problems, labeling it arson to burn either a home or a building, whether owned by the perpetrator or not.

The newer statutory approaches to arson expand the definition to include a fire set within the curtilage of a building. As we have already seen in the discussion on

---

[36] *State v. Britt*, 132 N.C. App. 173, 510 S.E.2d 683 (1999).
[37] *State v. Campbell*, 332 N.C. 116, 418 S.E.2d 476 (1992).
[38] *State v. Cuthrell*, 235 N.C. 173, 69 S.E.2d 233 (1952).
[39] *Ex parte Davis*, 548 So. 2d 1041 (Ala. 1989).
[40] *Daniels v. Com.*, 172 Va. 583, 1 S.E.2d 333 (1939).

burglary, curtilage refers to the space immediately outside the structure. Setting a fire there also qualifies as arson.[41]

ARSON IN THE FIRST DEGREE

Like burglary (and homicide), arson is often divided into various degrees with first degree considered the most serious and punished the most severely. First-degree arson, for example, would include burning when there is a risk to human life. By dividing the crime of arson into varying degrees, states can punish certain forms of arson more severely. Consider Scenario 8-5.

BURNING THE APARTMENT

SCENARIO 8-5

Todd is angry with girlfriend. She has asked him to move out. On the day that he comes to the apartment building to collect his things, he decides to set fire to her apartment. He lights the bed on fire and leaves. Has he committed arson? Would this qualify as arson in the first degree, assuming that he has committed the crime of arson?

   Answer: Yes, Todd has committed arson. His actions have satisfied all of the elements of arson, and the fact that he set the fire in an apartment building qualifies as arson in the first degree. However, depending on the state, Todd might be charged with one count of arson or with several.[42]

F. USING ARSON TO DEFRAUD INSURANCE COMPANIES

In modern times, the use of arson as a means to defraud insurance companies has increased dramatically. As a consequence, many states have expanded the definition of arson to include not only residences but also businesses, warehouses, and other structures. Business owners facing financial loss might try to recoup their investments by burning the structure simply to collect the insurance proceeds.

 **FAMOUS CASES**
JOHN ORR

In a small hardware store in South Pasadena, California, a swift-moving fire broke out on October 10, 1984. The fire destroyed the store. Four people, including two employees, a grandmother, and her two-year-old grandson, died in the flames. Arson investigators initially concluded that the cause of the fire was electrical, but veteran arson investigator John Orr, disagreed. Orr insisted that the fire was arson. Further investigation revealed that Orr was correct: The fire had started in an area of the store that contained highly flammable products, including glue and

---

[41] *U.S. v. Potts*, 297 F.2d 68 (6th Cir. 1961).
[42] *People v. Anderson*, 38 A.D.3d 1061, 831 N.Y.S.2d 582 (3d Dep't 2007).

varnish, which gave it a quick and volatile start. Despite the fact that the fire was deemed arson, no suspect was identified.

Three years later, arson investigators from all over California attended a conference in Fresno. During the conference and in the days immediately following, several arson fires flared up in and around Fresno as well as 100 miles south, in Bakersfield. Each of the fires was set during the middle of the day in a business, and each was ignited by a time-delay incendiary device. No one was killed in these fires, but they resulted in millions of dollars in damage.

During his investigation, Captain Marvin G. Casey of the Bakersfield Fire Department began to suspect that the arsonist was a firefighter, probably from the Los Angeles area. Among the clues he uncovered was a time-delay device containing a piece of notebook paper. On the paper was a single fingerprint. The fingerprint had no match to anyone in the criminal database, however, and again no suspect could be identified.

In 1989, arson investigators attended yet another conference, this time in Pacific Grove, California, a small community adjacent to the coastal city of Monterey. Yet again, more arson fires were set along the California coast during the time of the conference. Acting on his suspicions, Captain Casey compared the list of attendees from the Pacific Grove conference to those who attended the Fresno conference. From those names, he came up with 10 possible suspects, including an arson investigator from Glendale, California: John Orr.

During 1990 and 1991, several arson fires broke out around the Los Angeles area, and the *modus operandi* in each was again a specific time-delay device. Searching for leads, the Los Angeles Arson Task Force learned of Captain Casey's fingerprint and his suspicions that the arsonist was a firefighter from the Los Angeles area. Members of the task force met with Casey and obtained the fingerprint. It was a match — to John Orr.

At that point Orr came under intense scrutiny and surveillance. As the investigation proceeded, Orr began to realize that he was a suspect, a suspicion borne out when he discovered and removed a tracking device attached beneath the bumper of his vehicle. However, Orr was not aware that a separate device had been installed behind his dashboard. The second device proved that Orr was at the scene of yet another suspicious fire before dispatchers were even aware of it, and he was arrested on December 4, 1991.

During the 1992 trial, two key pieces of evidence helped sway the jury in federal court to convict Orr of three counts of arson. First was a set of videotapes that Orr had taken of suspicious fires, including several he was accused of setting. Second, and possibly more damning, was a manuscript for a novel he had written about a serial arsonist who was a firefighter. Many of the details in the novel, titled *Points of Origin*, were identical to those of the fires attributed to him. Furthermore, although not included as evidence, the incidence of brush fires in the Los Angeles hills decreased by more than 90 percent after Orr's arrest.

On June 25, 1998, a California state court convicted Orr of four counts of first-degree murder stemming from the South Pasadena hardware-store fire. He was sentenced to life plus 25 years, with no parole.

John Leonard Orr is considered the worst serial arsonist of the 20th century. The Bureau of Alcohol, Tobacco, and Firearms believes that he set more than

2,000 fires between 1984 and 1991. Author Joseph Wambaugh chronicled Orr's saga in *Fire Lover*, a true-life account of a man who led a double life. Orr's story was also re-created in an HBO special titled *Point of Origin*, starring Ray Liotta.

G. TECHNOLOGICAL ADVANCES IN ARSON INVESTIGATIONS

Arson prosecutions have shown a dramatic downturn in recent decades. This is due, in some measure, to the advances in technology that authorities bring to bear on arson investigations. Armed with computer modeling, burn patterns, and even dogs trained to sniff out accelerants (such as gasoline), it is a great deal harder to successfully elude an arson investigation.

STATE v. COOK

2010 ME 85, 2 A.3d 333 (Me. 2010)

CASE EXCERPT

GORMAN, J.

Daniel O. Cook appeals from a judgment of conviction entered in the Superior Court (Hancock County, Cuddy, J.) for twenty-five total counts: four counts of burglary (Class B), 17-A M.R.S. § 401(1)(A), (B)(4) (2009); four counts of burglary (Class C), 17-A M.R.S. § 401(1)(A) (2009); one count of theft by unauthorized taking or transfer (Class C), 17-A M.R.S. § 353(1)(A), (B)(4) (2009); one count of theft by unauthorized taking or transfer (Class D), 17-A M.R.S. § 353(1)(A), (B)(5) (2009); eleven counts of theft by unauthorized taking or transfer (Class E), 17-A M.R.S. § 353(1)(A) (2009); three counts of criminal mischief (Class D), 17-A M.R.S. § 806(1)(A) (2009); and one count of unlawful possession of a firearm (Class C), 15 M.R.S. § 393(1)(A-1)(1) (2009), following a jury trial. Cook challenges the sufficiency of the evidence for each count of the conviction. We affirm in part and vacate in part.

I. BACKGROUND

"Viewed in the light most favorable to the State, the following evidence was admitted at trial." *State v. Cook*, 2010 ME 81. In November and December of 2006, Cook and his father, David Cook,FN2 along with his nephew Christopher Cook, and Christopher Lapointe, a friend of Cook's nephew, engaged in a series of burglaries and thefts of seasonal camps in Dedham. During this period, all four lived together in David Cook's home in Dedham, and Lapointe had outstanding warrants in Bangor. The purpose of the spree was to locate and steal copper pipe in order to sell it for scrap metal. The men damaged several doors and windows in the course of the break-ins, stole copper and personal property from the victimized residences, and brought all the stolen property back to the Cook residence. After law enforcement officers came to the Cook residence seeking a suspicious person and inquiring about Lapointe on December 9, 2006, Cook and David Cook dumped the stolen property into a culvert in Ellsworth.

> FN2. Recently we also decided the appeal of David O. Cook, Cook's father and co-defendant, State v. Cook, 2010 ME 81, 2 A.2d 313.

Lapointe was arrested on his outstanding warrants on December 14, 2006, and became a cooperating witness for the State. The Hancock County Sheriffs Department executed a search warrant at the Cook residence on February 13, 2007. The deputies found a locked gun cabinet along with the key in Cook's bedroom. The guns inside the cabinet were in working order, and Cook had been seen handling the guns.

A grand jury returned an indictment on June 5, 2007, charging Cook with thirty-two total counts against fifteen separate victims: nine counts of burglary (Class B), 17-A M.R.S. § 401(1)(A), (B)(4); five counts of burglary (Class C), 17-A M.R.S. § 401(1)(A); two counts of theft by unauthorized taking or transfer (Class C), 17-A M.R.S. § 353(1)(A), (B)(4); one count of theft by unauthorized taking or transfer (Class D), 17-A M.R.S. § 353(1)(A), (B)(5); eleven counts of theft by unauthorized taking or transfer (Class E), 17-A M.R.S. § 353(1)(A); three counts of criminal mischief (Class D), 17-A M.R.S. § 806(1)(A); and one count of unlawful possession of a firearm (Class C), 15 M.R.S. § 393(1)(A-1)(1). Pursuant to M.R.Crim. P. 8(b), the State filed a notice of joinder for Cook and David Cook on the same day.

Lapointe pleaded guilty to charges arising from the camp break-ins, and testified at trial in December 2007. At trial, Cook stipulated that he "was convicted on June 22, 2001 in Penobscot Superior Court in Bangor, Maine, in Docket No. CR-00-685 of unlawful trafficking in scheduled drugs, a crime under the laws of Maine punishable by imprisonment . . . for one year or more." At the close of the State's case, Cook moved for a judgment of acquittal based on insufficient evidence, which the court denied. The court instructed the jury on both principal and accomplice liability, and the jury returned a guilty verdict on all counts of the indictment except for five Class B burglaries, one Class C burglary, and one Class C theft by unauthorized taking or transfer.

The court entered a judgment on the verdict and sentenced Cook to three years in prison, suspended all but two years, and imposed two years of probation on Cook's eight burglary convictions and one Class C theft by unauthorized taking conviction. The court sentenced Cook to one year in jail on the count of unlawful possession of a firearm and ninety days in jail for the remaining fifteen Class D and Class E convictions. All sentences were to be served concurrently. The court also ordered restitution in the amount of $20,027.50, jointly and severally with David Cook, to be paid through probation. Cook's appeal is timely pursuant to 15 M.R.S. § 2115 (2009) and M.R.App. P. 2.

II. DISCUSSION

Cook's sole challenge on appeal is the sufficiency of the evidence supporting each of his convictions. "Upon a claim of insufficient evidence, we view the evidence in the light most favorable to the State to determine whether the fact-finder could rationally find every element of the offense beyond a reasonable doubt." *State v.*

Milliken, 2010 ME 1, 19, 985 A.2d 1152, 1158. As the fact-finder, the jury's "determinations of the weight and credibility to be afforded the evidence are within its exclusive province," and it "is permitted to draw all reasonable inferences from the evidence." Evidence is sufficient to support a conviction when the facts presented are proved beyond a reasonable doubt; to prove facts beyond a reasonable doubt, the jury must be convinced of the defendant's guilt by having a conscientious belief that the charged offense is almost certainly true.

The jury convicted Cook on twenty-five counts of four crimes in varying degrees of severity: burglary (Class B and C), theft by unauthorized taking or transfer (Class C, D, and E), criminal mischief (Class D), and unlawful possession of a firearm (Class C). Cook's arguments regarding the sufficiency of the evidence on Counts 1, 2, 6, 8, 12, 14 through 16, 18, 21 through 23, 26 through 29, 31, and 32 are unpersuasive and merit no further discussion. Viewed in the light most favorable to the State, a rational fact-finder could have found each element of those eighteen offenses beyond a reasonable doubt based on the evidence presented and the reasonable inferences that may be drawn from that evidence. We affirm those eighteen convictions. The remaining convictions warrant further analysis. We begin with a discussion of the elements that the State was required to prove for each crime and then examine the sufficiency of the evidence for Counts 5, 10, 13, 19, 24, 25, and 30.

A. State's Burden of Proof

Burglary to a structure is a Class C offense. 17-A M.R.S. § 401(1)(A). To prove burglary to a structure, the State must show that the defendant entered or surreptitiously remained in a structure knowing that he was "not licensed or privileged to do so, with the intent to commit a crime therein." A structure is "a building or other place designed to provide protection for persons or property against weather or intrusion." 17-A M.R.S. § 2(24) (2009).

To prove theft by unauthorized taking or transfer, the State must prove the defendant "(1) obtained or exercised unauthorized control (2) over the property of another (3) with the intent to deprive the owner of that property." The basic offense of theft by unauthorized taking or transfer is a Class E offense. 17-A M.R.S. § 353(1)(A). When the State proves that the value of the property taken is "more than $500 but not more than $1,000" at the time of the offense, theft by unauthorized taking is a Class D crime. 17-A M.R.S. § 353(1)(B)(5).

Criminal mischief is a Class D offense. 17-A M.R.S. § 806(2) (2009). To support a conviction for criminal mischief, the State must prove that the defendant "intentionally, knowingly, or recklessly . . . damaged or destroyed the property of another, having no reasonable grounds to believe that the (defendant had) a right to do so."

B. Sufficiency of the Evidence

1. Counts 5 and 30-Burglary (Class C)

Cook's convictions for Counts 5 and 30 are for the burglaries at the Zimmerman and Delucia camps. The evidence is sufficient to support the jury's finding, beyond a reasonable doubt, that Lapointe and Christopher Cook, without authorization, crawled under both camps with the intent to steal the copper pipe underneath each location. Cook assisted Lapointe and Christopher Cook in the commission of these crimes by picking them up in a vehicle after each break-in. Although Cook contends that he was merely present at each scene, the jury could reasonably infer that Cook knowingly aided Christopher Cook and Lapointe. Further, the intent of all three men may be inferred from the evidence. The evidence is sufficient to support Cook's convictions for burglary on a theory of accomplice liability only if the area underneath the camp is in fact part of the "structure" of the camp.

When we have previously examined whether an area is a structure for purposes of the burglary statute, we have only dealt with areas designed to accommodate a standing adult in either a building or storage area. See, e.g., *State v. Miller*, 626 A.2d 343, 344 (Me.1993) (concluding that an office with a locked door within a building qualifies as a structure under the statute); *State v. Hillman*, 565 A.2d 1012, 1013 (Me.1989); *State v. Wing*, 426 A.2d 1375, 1376-77 (Me.1981) (affirming the defendant's conviction for burglary of a storage shed adjacent to a restaurant as part of the restaurant's structure). The offense of burglary, however, "is one primarily against the security of habitation," and encompasses entries into a structure that is purposefully designed to keep "persons out whose entrance is not desired." *State v. Cookson*, 293 A.2d 780, 784-85 (Me.1972). The statutory definition of a structure reinforces this principle. A structure is "a building or other place designed to provide protection for persons or property against weather or intrusion." 17-A M.R.S. § 2(24). The statute thus protects not only a traditional building; the statute also protects any "place designed to provide protection for persons or property against weather or intrusion."

At trial, Deputy Jeffrey McFarland of the Hancock County Sheriff's Department testified that the space underneath both camps had been closed or secured against the weather by skirting or lattice and that the latticework on the Zimmerman camp had been cut in order to gain access to the copper pipe. Because the testimony established that the space under each camp was designed to protect the area from weather, we conclude that the area underneath the camp is part of the structure.

Cook's convictions for burglary and theft at the Brookings camp are based on allegations that Cook entered the camp without authorization and stole copper pipe from underneath the residence. At trial, Brookings testified that no one had permission to go under the camp and steal the copper pipe located there. The only other direct evidence that the State presented regarding these crimes was the testimony of Lapointe. FN6 Lapointe testified that he committed these crimes with Christopher Cook, and that David Cook picked them up after the break-in.

> FN6. Several witnesses testified to the fact of the burglary, but Lapointe was the only witness that could connect either Cook or his co-defendant to the crimes.

The State contends that because Cook orchestrated, participated in, and profited from the string of burglaries, the evidence is sufficient to support these convictions. The State, however, presented no evidence that Cook was present at Brooking's camp during the commission of these crimes, or any evidence that Cook assisted in these particular acts. "Although we view the evidence in the light most favorable to the State," without any evidence of Cook's involvement in these particular crimes, a fact-finder could not rationally find beyond a reasonable doubt that Cook either committed or assisted in the burglary and theft of the Brookings camp, We therefore vacate Cook's convictions for Counts 24 and 25.

III. CONCLUSION

In sum, we vacate five of Cook's twenty-five convictions. We also vacate the order of restitution, which was ordered jointly and severally with David Cook. The sentencing court may only order restitution for the amount of the victim's actual economic loss resulting from the specific crime for which a defendant has been convicted. Of the $20,027.50 Cook was ordered to pay in restitution, $4527.50 was payable to the owner of the Cross camp for the loss she sustained from the burglary of both her house and garage. As Cook has only been convicted of the burglary of her home, the court should reexamine the loss attributable to each crime and apportion the restitution accordingly between the co-defendants as necessary.

CASE QUESTIONS

1 What were the crimes involved in this case?

2 What was Cook's only challenge on appeal?

3 According to the court, what must the state prove about structures in a burglary?

4 How did the court address the issue of whether or not the Zimmerman and Delucia camps were "structures" as defined in the burglary statute?

CHAPTER SUMMARY

Burglary is the crime of breaking and entering a structure with the intent to commit a theft or felony. As we have seen in this chapter, originally, burglary was limited to "dwelling houses" but has been expanded to include nearly all types of structures. A person can commit "constructive breaking" by using fraud or deceit to gain entrance to the building. Once inside, the prosecution must prove that the defendant entered with the intent to commit a theft or a felony. Proof of that is usually accomplished by examining the surrounding circumstances and facts of the particular case. Burglaries can also occur within the curtilage of a building, which is the area outside, but closely associated with the building and can include areas such as carports, porches, and other commonly used areas. In many states there are degrees of burglary, from first degree to third degree.

Arson is the crime of maliciously burning a building. Originally, just as with burglary, arson was limited to dwelling houses and under the common law, limited even further to the dwelling house "of another." Under the common-law crime of arson, it was not a crime to burn your own home. However, all states have changed the common-law definition and greatly expanded the definition of dwelling to include all structures and, in some states, even automobiles and other items of personal property. It is also a crime to burn a structure to defraud insurance companies. These days, arson cases are not as common as in the past because the techniques used to investigate them have become very sophisticated and fire investigators can often tell when a person has deliberately set a fire.

KEY TERMS

Burglary	Entering	Arson
Breaking	Dwelling	Burning
Constructive breaking	Curtilage	

REVIEW QUESTIONS

1 What are the basic elements of burglary?
2 Why is it necessary to prove that the defendant in a burglary case had no permission to enter the dwelling?
3 What qualifies as a "dwelling" for purposes of burglary?
4 How does the state prove the defendant's intent to commit a theft or a felony in a burglary prosecution?
5 What are some of the important differences between common-law burglary and statutory burglary?
6 Why is the defendant in the case excerpt guilty of burglary when he never actually entered the cabin?
7 Explain the various degrees of burglary, including first, second, and third.
8 What is "constructive breaking"?
9 What does it mean when we say that burglary is a specific intent crime?
10 How does the state prove the defendant's intent on breaking and entering a dwelling?
11 What is curtilage?
12 When a dwelling becomes uninhabitable, can a person be charged for burglary when he or she breaks into it?
13 Give an example of how someone would use deceit to gain entry to a dwelling.
14 The text mentions that there are not as many arson prosecutions as there have been in previous decades. Why is that?
15 Historically, why has arson been considered such a serious crime?
16 Under the old common law, why was it not illegal to burn your own home but was illegal to burn some other person's?
17 How do arsonists attempt to defraud insurance companies?

18 Explain the difference between the original definition of a "dwelling house" for purposes of an arson prosecution and the common definition of the structures that can be the subject of an arson charge.
19 Are there degrees of arson? If so, what are they?
20 What is the legal definition of "burning"?

QUESTIONS FOR ANALYSIS

1 Some commentators have gone so far as to say that although not all burglars become rapists, nearly every rapist has been a burglar. What do you suppose explains this phenomenon?
2 There are some people who feel compelled to set fires. Should these people receive the same kind of sentence as a person who sets a fire in retaliation of a failed love affair or to defraud an insurance company? Why or why not?

HYPOTHETICALS

1 Tanner is a computer and electronic expert and creates a remote-controlled robot that has gripper arms and other functions. She uses this robot to open the door of a neighbor's home, while Tanner remains inside her own residence, and guides the robot to take specific items belonging to her neighbor. Can she be successfully prosecuted for burglary? Explain your answer.
2 Rick joined a new movement called "Tiny Houses." These are self-contained units that have living space, a bathroom, and a kitchen, but have a floor plan no larger than an average-sized walk-in closet. They are also mobile. Rick has set up a Tiny House on his mountain land. While he is gone, someone breaks into his home and steals his wallet. Is this a case of burglary or trespassing and theft? Support your conclusion with the specific elements of burglary.
3 You own an out building in your backyard. The building is small and was once used to store your lawnmower, but has become unsafe. You decide that the best way to remove this eyesore is to burn it down. You apply for a burn permit but do not specify that you intend to burn an outbuilding. (Typically, 'burn permits' are issued for people who intend to burn some leaves.) Should you be allowed to burn your outbuilding and avoid being charged with arson? Why or why not?

Theft Crimes

Chapter Objectives

- Explain the basic elements of larceny
- Describe asportation as it applies to theft cases
- Define fair market value and why it is important in theft cases
- Describe the elements of various theft offenses from theft by shoplifting to embezzlement
- Explain the difference between larceny and robbery

I   THEFT

Stealing — has always been considered wrong, and all societies have created rules that ban it. This chapter will examine many different theft-related crimes and explain not only the elements of each, but also how the prosecution and defense teams prepare their cases to either prove (or disprove) these elements.

The problem with a word like "theft" is that its meaning has been extended to include so many different types of crime that the word practically loses all meaning. Under the Model Penal Code and various state statutes, "theft" can refer to:

- Theft of services
- Theft by taking
- Theft by receiving stolen property
- Theft involving fraud
- Theft involving unauthorized use of property
- Theft by deception, among others[1]

---

[1] Model Penal Code § § 223.2 to 223.9.

A. LARCENY

Larceny is a general term used to refer to any form of theft. We face a similar problem with the term that we faced with theft. Larceny has often been used to refer to the original common law crime of theft, but has also been expanded over time to include crimes as diverse as writing bad checks and embezzlement.

Because of this confusion of terms, this text will use the term "larceny" to refer to all general types of crimes where a person takes property of another. The term *theft* will be reserved for those specific crimes where a statute incorporates it into the name of the offense. Larceny is essentially a trespass on the rights of a person's property. As long as that trespass occurs without permission and with the taker's intent to permanently deprive the owner access to the property, the actual means involved are almost irrelevant. Because people constantly come up with new and ingenious ways to commit theft, the means of carrying out the crime are only relevant when they involve force, threat, or some other aggravating circumstance. These aggravating circumstances will only enhance the defendant's sentence, not take away from the basic crime.[2]

The general elements of larceny are:

- A person takes the property of another
- Without permission
- Moves the property (asportation)
- With the intent to permanently deprive the owner of the property[3]

PERSON TAKES THE PROPERTY OF ANOTHER

Taking consists of gaining custody, dominion, and control of property that belongs to someone else.[5] Usually, proving that a taking has occurred is relatively straightforward: the item was in one place, often in the victim's possession, then is later recovered in the defendant's possession. However, there are some unique issues that arise when examining what the defendant actually took. For instance, there is the original view of larceny as not applicable to land.

Under the common law, larceny was not applicable to **real property** (land), only personal property. The term **personal property** refers to movable things such as automobiles, household goods, and almost anything else that does not qualify as real property. In larceny, there is no requirement that violence accompany the taking. In fact, if violence is used, the crime is robbery, and the perpetrator is likely sentenced to a much harsher sentence. See Figure 9-1 for larceny and theft rates in the United States.

It does not affect the analysis of the crime that the defendant took an item that he or she could not possibly earn any money on. The state is only responsible for

---

[2] *Stewart v. State*, 44 S.W.3d 582 (Tex. Crim. App. 2001).
[3] *State v. Calonico*, 256 Conn. 135, 770 A.2d 454 (2001).
[4] *Britt v. Com.*, 276 Va. 569, 667 S.E.2d 763 (2008).
[5] *State v. Donaldson*, 663 N.W.2d 882 (Iowa 2003).

FIGURE 9-1 Arrest in the United States by Sex, Race, and Age Group

		Sex		Age group		Race			
		Male	Female	Juvenile under age 18	Adult	White	Black	AIAN[a]	API[b]
Total	13,122,110	9,792,190	3,329,920	1,642,650	11,479,470	9,122,010	3,655,620	186,120	158,370
Property									
Burglary	289,770	245,770	44,000	65,200	224,570	195,780	88,740	2,500	2,750
Larceny-theft	1,271,410	717,770	553,640	281,060	990,350	875,620	359,080	18,130	18,570
Motor vehicle theft	71,490	58,980	12,500	15,760	55,730	45,340	24,200	890	1,060
Arson	11,300	9,350	1,950	4,560	6,740	8,520	2,520	130	130
Forgery and counterfeiting	78,100	48,780	29,320	1,690	76,410	51,860	24,890	440	900
Fraud	187,890	109,740	78,150	5,770	182,120	123,420	61,190	1,560	1,730
Embezzlement	16,620	8,230	8,390	440	16,170	11,020	5,160	110	330
Stolen property offenses	94,800	76,230	18,570	14,640	80,160	61,860	31,250	760	940
Vandalism	252,750	204,860	47,890	77,070	175,690	186,570	59,180	4,210	2,790

proving that the defendant took the item, that it had value, and that the defendant intended to permanently deprive the victim of the property. Consider Scenario 9-1.

MINOR VALUE

SCENARIO 9-1

Ted recently visited the home of his nephew and, while there, decided to take all of the condiments inside the refrigerator. He removed the mayonnaise, relish, and mustard and took them home with him while his nephew was at work. When confronted, Ted claims that the items had no value and that he couldn't possibly earn anything by trying to sell these items to someone else, so no theft has occurred. Is Ted right?

Answer: No. The items do have some value, and simply because the defendant can't sell them for a profit to someone else does not affect the analysis of the elements of the crime. It is, however, unlikely that Ted will receive a severe punishment for this particular taking.[6]

In order to satisfy the legal requirement of "taking," the defendant must exercise control or "dominion" over the property and convert the property to his use. In this context, **conversion** refers to the defendant reducing the item to his or her custody and removing it from the possession of the rightful owner. Without possession, the defendant cannot exercise dominion over the property. However, this dominion or

Conversion
An act that transfers the possession of an item from the rightful owner to a person who does not have the owner's consent to possess.

[6] *Ehrhardt v. State*, 334 S.W.3d 849 (Tex. App. Texarkana 2011).

control over the property does not have to be for a long period of time. In most jurisdictions, it is only necessary for the state to prove that the defendant exercised this control for a few seconds.

Constructive taking
When the defendant removes an item from the victim's possession and places it in a place where the victim cannot access it.

Constructive Taking. **Constructive taking** occurs when the defendant takes the items and places them in some place that is inaccessible to the owner but available to the defendant. Because the state can show that the defendant placed the items in a location where the original owner could not regain custody and control of the property, the law refers to this as a "constructive taking."[7]

WITHOUT PERMISSION

To tackle some of the easiest elements of larceny, the state must obviously prove that the taking occurred without the victim's consent. If the defendant did have consent to take the item, then there is no theft. If the defendant originally had consent, but then kept the item beyond the agreed-upon period, the crime becomes embezzlement, which is addressed later in this chapter. Obviously, the defendant cannot be charged with taking an item that belongs to him, even in situations where the defendant shares ownership with someone else. The defendant may not use fraud, trickery, or deceit to gain consent. In fact, consent gained through these means is no consent at all.

ASPORTATION

Asportation (theft)
Movement of an item some distance from its original location.

To prove larceny, the state must also prove that the taking involves the carrying away, or **asportation**, of the property. This term was already referenced in the discussions of kidnapping in Chapter 2. Essentially it means the same thing here. In both instances, the term refers to movement. To satisfy the elements of theft, property must be moved from its original location. Asportation can be proven by any slight movement of the property, although what constitutes "slight" movement varies from state to state.[8] In most states, moving the property even a few inches would satisfy the element of asportation.

Sidebar

In order to prove theft, the state must show not only that the defendant took the item, but also that following the unlawful taking, the defendant committed asportation of the item. Simply put, the state must show that the defendant carried away the item.

WITH INTENT TO PERMANENTLY DEPRIVE THE OWNER

The final element in a larceny case is proof that the defendant took the item with the intent to permanently deprive the owner of it. Obviously, the state must prove that the defendant had no rights to the property itself and had no ownership interest in it. How does the government prove that the defendant intended to permanently deprive the owner of the property? The answer is simple. If the defendant takes the item and does any act that shows his intention to keep the property or dispose of it in a way that is unknown to the victim, then the state can establish this element.

---

[7] *People v. Lardner*, 300 Ill. 264, 133 N.E. 375, 19 A.L.R. 721 (1921).
[8] *Barnett v. State Farm General Ins. Co.*, 200 Cal. App. 4th 536, 132 Cal. Rptr. 3d 742 (4th Dist. 2011).

There is no requirement that the thief know the identity of the owner of the property. The only thing that is required is that the defendant is aware that the property does not belong to him.

Many states have modified the original language of common-law larceny so it now reads "with intent to steal" as opposed to with "intent to permanently deprive the victim of the property." Intent to steal has proven to be far easier to prove at trial than intent to permanently deprive.

Establishing the Value of the Stolen Property. In addition to the four main elements that the prosecution must prove in a larceny case, the state has an additional burden. For instance, in many jurisdictions theft of an article worth more than $500 is a felony, while theft of an item valued less than $500 is considered a misdemeanor. As you can imagine, the valuation of an item makes a great deal of difference to the defendant, given that a felony carries a potential sentence of several years in custody versus 12 months or less for a misdemeanor. Because the valuation of the property can have such a significant impact on the case, it is important to discuss exactly how the state proves the value of the property taken.

The most common method for the state to establish value for a stolen item is by use of fair market value. In a theft prosecution, the state must present evidence, usually from an expert, what the fair market value of the item is and whether or not it is valued higher than $500 or is some lower amount.

> Sidebar
>
> *The only difference between simple theft (sometimes called "petty" (petit) or misdemeanor theft) and grand larceny involves the value of the items taken.[9]*

Fair Market Value. **Fair market value** does not mean that the particular item has a legal market for sale. In many instances, the test used to determine the value of an item boils down to a simple equation: How much would a willing buyer spend to acquire the item from a willing seller at the time of the theft?[10] This means that someone, a person with extensive knowledge of buying and selling or valuation of the particular stolen property, takes the stand and testifies as to what the value of this particular item is. In most situations, it is not enough for the state simply to present the price tag on the particular item. A used bicycle, for example, will have a lower value than a brand-new one. The value of the used bicycle has to be established by the state. Fair market value is not derived from the object's sentimental value to the owner, but what an expert would testify as to the item's objective value.[11] It is also not based solely on the original purchase price or the replacement value of the item — it is often a combination of both factors.[12]

Fair market value
An estimate of what a willing, knowledgeable buyer, acting without coercion or pressure, would pay for an item.

Where an item has no obvious cash value, the court may look to replacement costs as one way to value the item.[13] Consider Scenario 9-2.

---

[9] *State v. Fluker*, 139 N.C. App. 768, 535 S.E.2d 68 (2000).
[10] *U.S. v. Perry*, 638 F.2d 862 (5th Cir. 1981).
[11] *People v. Dyer*, 157 Mich. App. 606, 403 N.W.2d 84 (1986).
[12] *State v. Stephens*, 263 Kan. 658, 953 P.2d 1373 (1998).
[13] *State v. Campbell*, 721 S.W.2d 813 (Tenn. Crim. App. 1986).

STEVE'S SHOES

Steve is a former soldier who was seriously injured during the conflicts in Iraq. Because his feet have been damaged, he requires special shoes to allow him to walk without a limp. These shoes are unique in the world and no one else would be able to wear them. Lenny steals these shoes and is caught. How can the court set a value on these shoes?

Answer: Because trying to set a fair market value on these shoes would be difficult, given that they only fit one person on the planet, the court would probably look to the replacement cost in order to set the value. In this case, the shoes cost more than $1,000 to replace, and once the state has proven that at trial, the court allows the felony charge against the defendant to remain in place when it is challenged by Lenny's defense attorney.

In felony prosecutions, the state must establish the value of the item stolen.[14]

In cases where it may be impossible to determine an object's value, the state may still proceed on misdemeanor theft charges because there is no requirement to prove the value of an item taken in a misdemeanor case, only that the item belonged to someone else and that the defendant unlawfully took it and moved it, all with the intent to permanently deprive the owner of the object.[15]

When retail property is stolen, the price tag for the item is often the best (and easiest) way to establish fair market value.[16] In such cases, the prosecution will present testimony from a store employee who will testify as to the retail item price posted on the price tag.

B. SPECIFIC THEFT OFFENSES

Now that we have discussed the general elements of larceny, we will turn our attention to specific types of theft charges, including:

- Theft by shoplifting
- Theft by receiving stolen property
- Theft of services
- Embezzlement
- Grand larceny and grand theft

THEFT BY SHOPLIFTING

Theft by shoplifting occurs when a person steals items from a store or retail establishment. The victim in this case is not an individual, but a business. However, this does not make the crime any less serious. Shoplifting is a common occurrence in businesses and drives up the price for other consumers, not only because merchants

---

[14] *State v. Burns*, 2011 ME 92, 26 A.3d 817 (Me. 2011).
[15] *People v. Smith*, 121 P.3d 243 (Colo. Ct. App. 2005).
[16] *Maisel v. People*, 166 Colo. 161, 442 P.2d 399 (1968).

must make up for lost inventory, but also because of the need to install security cameras and other equipment to monitor potential theft. The crime of shoplifting is not a victimless crime.

Shoplifting can occur in a variety of ways, including:

- Concealing an item on the defendant's person
- Switching price tags from a less expensive item to a costlier one
- Hiding an item inside another item and then paying for the larger item

To add insult to injury, some thieves will take an item from a store and then seek to return it for money or store credit, even though they obviously do not have a receipt to prove that they paid for the merchandise. Shoplifting cases are often complicated by store regulations that prevent store employees from detaining suspected shoplifters after a great many high-profile cases where suspected shoplifters brought civil suits against stores for false imprisonment.

Shoplifting is also handled differently depending on the state. In most states, proof that an item is valued higher than $500 will result in a felony conviction. However, in many states that amount is lowered to $100 in the case of shoplifting. Doubtless these changes were brought about as a way to stop the surge in shoplifting cases over the last few decades.

THEFT BY RECEIVING STOLEN PROPERTY

When a person receives stolen property from another person, it is a crime. In prosecuting, theft by receiving stolen property, the state is not required to prove that the person in possession actually committed the theft. Instead, the state must simply show that the defendant "knew or should have known" that the property was stolen. These statutes were created to punish people like **"fences"** who deal in stolen merchandise.

Fence
A common term for a person who makes a living receiving stolen property from another and then selling it to others.

THEFT OF SERVICES

Theft of services occurs when someone obtains a service, such as cable or telephone service, then refuses to pay for it. This crime is not based on a person's failure to pay for a service he or she legitimately ordered. Instead, the person accused has obtained the service illegally, either by plugging a device into the cable service or hooking into the electrical grid without permission. In many states, this is a misdemeanor crime. However, the accrued monetary amount of services obtained might be enough to satisfy the threshold amount for felony prosecution.

EMBEZZLEMENT

Embezzlement occurs when someone who has been entrusted with property decides to violate that trust and keep the property for his own use.[17] This crime

Embezzlement
The wrongful retention of property, with the intent to permanently deprive the owner of it, after the person has been given temporary consent to possess the property.

---

[17] *People v. Talbot*, 220 Cal. 3, 28 P.2d 1057(1934).

is often carried out by employees who routinely have access to cash or other items of value and exceed their authority by converting the property to their own use. The important point here is that the person who committed the theft actually had legal custody of the item, but then exceeded that authority by retaining the property after he or she should have. Consider Scenario 9-3.

SCENARIO 9-3	## DON'S SCHEME

Don works for a fast-food restaurant as a manager. When working the evening shift, Dan makes a regular habit of dismissing the drive-through cashier after 9:00 p.m. Then Dan works the cash register himself. This is unusual behavior. The method of ordering food at the restaurant is simple: A customer calls out his order through the microphone by the drive-through menu, and the cashier calls out the order over a microphone to the people in the kitchen who prepare the meal.

Lisa, an employee in the kitchen, is confused about why Don works the register. One evening while taking out the trash, she notices a large amount of "No Sale" receipts stuffed into a bag. She realizes what Don is doing: He is receiving orders from customers, calling them out on the loudspeaker, then ringing up no sale and making change for the customers. Then, when the shift is over, he takes the cash register drawer back to the office and pockets the money he has made on several hours' worth of orders. What crime has Don committed?

Answer: Embezzlement. Why wouldn't his actions qualify as simple theft? His activity satisfies most of the elements of regular theft, but, as a manager, he is allowed to handle the cash register drawers, so his crime more closely fits the elements of embezzlement. Prosecutors also prefer to bring this charge because, in this situation, the possible punishment that Don faces is more severe than a simple theft case.

GRAND LARCENY AND GRAND THEFT

Grand larceny or grand theft statutes refer to theft of items above a certain value, or theft of certain items. In many states, theft of an item worth more than $500 ($400 in some states) constitutes felony theft or grand larceny. In many states the theft of an automobile, no matter what the car is actually worth, is considered to be grand larceny. The significance of these statutes is that the value of the items taken makes the crime a felony instead of a misdemeanor. The added significance is that the possible sentence for grand theft is much greater than misdemeanor theft. In all states, theft of an automobile is classified, not because of the value of the auto, but for the more practical reason that stealing a person's mode of transportation can have a devastating effect on that person's life. (In the Old West, stealing a horse — a person's mode of transportation — could be punished by death.)

What happens when a defendant is charged with grand larceny, but the state forgets to present any evidence of value? As this chapter has already shown, value is an important element in a felony theft case. In such a situation, the most that the

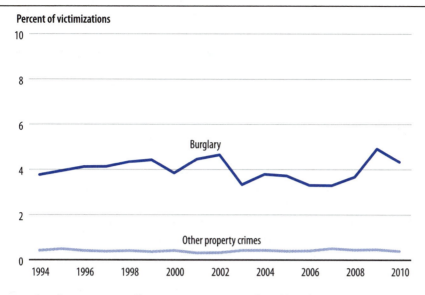

FIGURE 9-2

Completed Burglaries and Other Property Crimes Involving the Theft of at Least One Firearm

Note: Data based on two-year rolling averages. See appendix table 3 for standard errors.

Source: Bureau of Justice Statistics, National Crime Victimization Survey, 1993–2010.

defendant could be convicted for is misdemeanor larceny — there is no requirement to prove value in misdemeanor cases.[18]

In addition to classifying the taking of automobiles as felonies, some jurisdictions also qualify other items as felonies when they are taken, including the theft of a:

- Will or testamentary document
- Firearm (see Figure 9-2)
- Explosives
- Livestock, to name a few[19]

 # ROBBERY

Robbery is actually an aggravated form of larceny. Robbery requires the use of violence, fear, or threat of an immediate harm to obtain property of another.[20] In robbery there is also the additional requirement that the property be taken from the person or the immediate presence of the victim. Because the core elements of robbery are the same as theft, this text will only address the elements of robbery that are different from other forms of theft. In some jurisdictions, where an item is

Robbery
The unlawful taking of property belonging to another, through the use of force, threat, or intimidation.

---

[18] *Miller v. State*, 338 So. 2d 1145 (Fla. Dist. Ct. App. 2d Dist. 1976).
[19] *State v. Grappin*, 427 So. 2d 760 (Fla. Dist. Ct. App. 2d Dist. 1983); *State v. Callaghan*, 33 Or. App. 49, 576 P.2d 14 (1978).
[20] *State v. Owens*, 20 S.W.3d 634 (Tenn. 2000).

taken from the victim's person, often by sudden taking, such as purse snatching, the crime may be classified as a form of larceny from the person, instead of robbery. Because of that, the defendant often faces a lower possible sentence.[21] In most jurisdictions, armed robbery or robbery by sudden snatching is not only a felony, but one that is punished severely, often with long prison sentences.

Sidebar

Robbery is larceny plus violence.

A. FROM THE PERSON OF THE VICTIM

Just as with larceny, robbery requires that the defendant take property from the victim. However, robbery is different because the taking is accomplished from the "person" of the victim. This is not a requirement in larceny or other forms of theft. In fact, it is this element of proximity, and the possibility of injury or death to the victim, that elevates robbery into a higher-order crime and also explains the more severe punishment doled out to people who commit robberies instead of thefts.

Because robbery also involves the threat of violence or actual violence itself, as well as the fact that the property was taken from the immediate presence or person of the victim, robbery is one of the more dangerous felonies. As such, robbery is often punished by terms in prison of 20 years or more. In fact, as we will see below, armed robbery is often punished severely.

B. WITHOUT THE VICTIM'S CONSENT

Like theft, the taking must have occurred without the victim's consent. This element is easily satisfied by putting the victim on the stand in a robbery trial and asking him or her if the defendant had permission to remove the property from the person of the victim. When the victim testifies that the defendant did not have consent, this element is met. Putting the victim on the witness stand also helps the prosecution in other ways. The victim can testify to what happened, can identify the defendant as the person who committed the crime, but can also make an abstract crime into something more real and personal.

C. ASPORTATION

Like larceny, robbery also requires that the defendant move the property. This element of asportation is the same as discussed earlier in this chapter. The reason that asportation is important is that by moving the item of property, the defendant is showing his intent to deprive the owner of possession and satisfies the requirement of the defendant's control over the property.

---

[21] *People v. Haynes*, 91 N.Y.2d 966, 672 N.Y.S.2d 845, 695 N.E.2d 714 (1998).

D. THROUGH FORCE, THREAT, OR INTIMIDATION

So far, the discussion of robbery sounds like any other analysis of a theft crime. However, the final element, the use of force, threat, or intimidation, sets robbery apart from other theft crimes by introducing physical danger into the mix. Violence, or the threat of it, is an essential element to proving the crime of robbery.[22] Robbery is essentially theft with force or the threat of force. Because this force or threat of force is almost always brought about by the use of a weapon, armed robbery is the most severely punished of all of the theft statutes. The existence of violence also helps explain why robbery, especially armed robbery, carries a higher sentence than a simple theft case.

FAMOUS CASES
THE GREAT BRINK'S ROBBERY

On a cold January evening in 1950, 11 men pulled off what is widely known as the crime of the century. Shortly before 7:30 p.m. on January 17, a group of men emerged from the Brink's Incorporated building in Boston. Brink's was and continues to be the largest provider of security-related transport services for banks, retailers, and governmental entities. The men carried with them canvas bags filled with more than $1.2 million in cash and $1.5 million in checks, money orders, and other securities.

Five employees were present in the building during the robbery, and they reported to investigators that between five and seven men carried out the actual crime. All of the men wore Navy-style pea coats, gloves, and chauffeur's hats. Additionally, each concealed his face behind a Halloween mask. The robbers spoke little and moved with precision, suggesting that they had carefully rehearsed the crime and knew exactly what they were doing.

They forced all five employees to lie face down on the floor, with hands tied behind their backs and adhesive tape covering their mouths. Then they filled the canvas bags with all the money and noncash securities that Brink's had collected from its customers that day. All totaled, the bags weighed approximately half a ton. The only thing they missed was the box containing money for the General Electric Company's payroll — they couldn't get the box open.

The robbers fled and left precious few clues — only the rope and adhesive they had used to bind the employees, and a single chauffeur's cap. The FBI came down heavily on known underworld figures in the Boston area, hoping to get a lead, any lead. They also compiled detailed descriptions from Brink's customers of packaging materials and any identifying marks on the stolen currency. The figured that the cash would soon start to surface and with luck would lead to the perpetrators. What the FBI did not know was that the robbers had agreed to stay out of trouble and sit on their loot for six years, at which time the statute of limitations would expire. They very nearly made it.

---

[22] *Spencer v. Com.*, 42 Va. App. 443, 592 S.E.2d 400 (2004).

For six years, the FBI was relentless in its investigation, and Brink's itself offered a $100,000 reward for information leading to the arrest of the robbers. The FBI tried creative tactics, including monitoring racetracks to see if anyone was wagering large sums of money or if any of the cash might be in circulation. This so disturbed the regular gamblers that they laid low and expressed a strong desire that the case be solved.

As the investigation continued, thousands of leads proved to be nothing but dead ends. Nevertheless, FBI investigators had their suspicions, and the list of suspects began to narrow. The break they needed finally came from Joseph "Specs" O'Keefe. O'Keefe was indeed one of the robbers, but he had to leave his share of the loot with one of his cohorts because he had a prison sentence to serve on an unrelated crime. Investigators interviewed O'Keefe while he was in prison, but he denied any knowledge of the crime.

However, once he was released, he faced trial for another burglary. He needed money, so he kidnapped another member of the Brink's gang and demanded his share of the money as the ransom. He was paid a small portion, but Anthony "Fat" Pino, one of the original masterminds, began to worry that O'Keefe would talk, so Pino ordered a hit on him. The hit man seriously wounded O'Keefe, and while he was recovering in the hospital, he decided it was time to talk. On January 12, 1956, just five days before the statute of limitations was set to expire, the FBI arrested six of the robbers, including Pino and the other masterminds, Joseph "Big Joe" McGinnis and Stanley "Gus" Gusciora. Two others were apprehended later that year. Of the two remaining robbers, one was already dead and another died before trial.

All of the men were charged with conspiracy to commit theft of government property, robbery of government property, and bank robbery by force and violence and by intimidation. Additional charges were committing an assault on Brink's employees and conspiracy to receive and conceal money. O'Keefe pleaded guilty on January 18, 1956 and testified against the others during trial. His sentence was four years. The eight remaining men were sentenced to life in prison. One died in prison, and the others were paroled in 1971.

Only $58,000 of the more than $2.7 million that was stolen was ever recovered. The Great Brink's Robbery still maintains its reputation as the great robbery of the 20th century.

E. ARMED ROBBERY

Armed robbery is robbery carried out with a weapon. A person charged with armed robbery may receive an enhanced sentence when he or she uses a weapon to threaten or injure the victim in order to steal. A robbery may also be classified as "aggravated" when certain conditions are met. For example, a defendant may receive a harsher sentence if he commits any of the following during a robbery:

- Serious injury to the victim
- Use of a deadly weapon
- Victimizes a "special victim," such as a person over the age of 65, or a person under the age of 18 or a disabled person

FRAUD AND FALSE PRETENSES

The crime of theft by false pretenses does not involve any change to the basic definition of larceny: A person takes the property of another with the intent to permanently deprive the owner of it. However, the crime of false pretenses focuses on the means that the defendant used to obtain possession of the property. In a simple theft, the defendant takes the property of another. In false pretenses, the defendant uses trickery, deceit, or fraud to obtain possession. See Scenario 9-4.

FAKE REPOSSESSION

SCENARIO 9-4

Tony has fallen behind on his car payments. It comes as no real surprise to him when he hears a knock on his door one evening and a man is standing there claiming to be from the finance company with orders to repossess the car. The only thing Tony finds disconcerting is that it is midnight, but Tony has seen plenty of television shows about men and women who repossess cars for a living and realizes that contesting this repossession would be a waste of time. Given the time of day, he also can't call the finance company to work out some arrangement. The man asks for the key to the car and Tony gives it to him. The next day, Tony discovers that the finance company did not order a repossession and that Tony was tricked into giving his keys to an unknown man who has stolen Tony's car. When the man is caught, he claims that Tony willingly gave him the keys to the car, so no theft has occurred. Is the man correct?

Answer: No. Because the man used trickery to obtain possession of Tony's car, he can be charged with theft of an automobile by means of false pretenses.

The crime of false pretenses involves a misrepresentation of a **material fact**. This is a fact that is critical to the parties' understanding of the transaction and, if made plain, would change their actions. For instance, a defendant commits false pretenses when he or she claims ownership in an item when in fact there is no such ownership. Selling something that you do not own is false pretenses, and the material fact is misrepresenting who actually has title to the property. Many statutes phrase misrepresentation in terms of a "material past or present fact." This simply refers to the kind of misrepresentation made. It is not false pretenses to claim that a used car is the "best car in the world." Salesmanship, "puffing," and other exaggerations are common among salespersons and are usually not actionable as false pretenses.

Material fact
A fact that is central to the negotiations; a fact that is so important to the transaction that, if changed, would alter the outcome.

FIGURE 9-3	Statements That Would and Would Not Qualify as False Pretenses

Would not qualify as false pretenses	Would qualify as false pretenses
Opinions: "I think this workmanship is the finest I've ever seen."	Statements of fact: "I own this car" when the person does not.
"This painting could be an early work by Picasso."	"This painting is an early work by Picasso."

However, when the salesperson deliberately lies about a material fact, then the crime of false pretenses can be proven. See Figure 9-3 for examples of statements that would and would not qualify as false pretenses.

FORGERY

Forgery is a different type of theft crime. In forgery, a person does not steal an item, but presents an item as real when it is not. The most common type of forgery is when a person signs someone's name to a check or other negotiable instrument when he or she does not have permission to do so, then presents the check as genuine in order to cash it. But forgery can occur in a wide variety of other ways. Under common law, forgery consisted of writing someone else's signature on a document and passing it off as authentic. Forgery is a specific intent crime and, as we have seen in previous chapters, that means the prosecution must prove that the defendant specifically intended to commit the crime of forgery. Forgery can be committed by any of the following:

- Writing a person's name on a document without permission and passing it off as genuine
- Copying (sometimes through the use of computer programs) a person's legitimate signature and transferring it to a new document
- Creating an "original" (such as a signed photo by a celebrity) when no such original ever existed

A. DEGREES OF FORGERY

In many states, forgery is divided into different degrees, with first-degree forgery being punished more severely than second-degree. This is a similar pattern with murder, arson, and even battery. See Figure 9-4 for an example of a forgery statute.

DISCUSSING THE ELEMENTS OF FORGERY

As you can see in Figure 9-4, the elements of first degree forgery are:

- He or she forges a writing
- With the intent to defraud or harm another
- Utters the document

Forges a Writing. What does it mean to "forge" a writing? At its simplest, forging means to sign some other person's name as though it is authentic. Usually, this involves copying a person's handwriting and placing it on a document that the victim has no knowledge of. But there is another question that arises from

FIGURE 9-4

Forgery (Texas)

FORGERY

(a) For purposes of this section:

(1) "Forge" means:

(A) to alter, make, complete, execute, or authenticate any writing so that it purports:

(i) to be the act of another who did not authorize that act;

(ii) to have been executed at a time or place or in a numbered sequence other than was in fact the case; or

(iii) to be a copy of an original when no such original existed;

(B) to issue, transfer, register the transfer of, pass, publish, or otherwise utter a writing that is forged within the meaning of Paragraph (A); or

(C) to possess a writing that is forged within the meaning of Paragraph (A) with intent to utter it in a manner specified in Paragraph (B).

(2) "Writing" includes:

(A) printing or any other method of recording information;

(B) money, coins, tokens, stamps, seals, credit cards, badges, and trademarks; and

(C) symbols of value, right, privilege, or identification.

(b) A person commits an offense if he forges a writing with intent to defraud or harm another.

(c) Except as provided in Subsections (d) and (e) an offense under this section is a Class A misdemeanor.

(d) An offense under this section is a state jail felony if the writing is or purports to be a will, codicil, deed, deed of trust, mortgage, security instrument, security agreement, credit card, check or similar sight order for payment of money, contract, release, or other commercial instrument.

(e) An offense under this section is a felony of the third degree if the writing is or purports to be:

(1) part of an issue of money, securities, postage or revenue stamps[23]

this element: What qualifies as a writing, at least for purposes of forgery prosecutions?

DEFINING A "WRITING" FOR PURPOSES OF FORGERY

As you can see in the statute provided in Figure 9-4, writings are defined broadly to encompass "printing or any other method of recording information, money, coins, tokens, stamps, seals, credit cards, badges, trademarks, symbols of value, right,

---

[23] V.T.C.A., Penal Code § 32.21.

privilege, or identification."[24] This means that almost any type of representation can be the subject of a forgery.

INTENT TO DEFRAUD

Although writing another person's signature on a document would seem to qualify as forgery, the most important element of forgery is not making a signature, but doing so with the intent to defraud. Consider Scenario 9-5.

SCENARIO 9-5

NILSA'S SIGNATURE

Nilsa has received a check in the mail that is addressed to her husband. He is currently away on a trip, and Nilsa needs to deposit this check as soon as possible. She calls her husband and tells him about the check, and he insists that she sign his name on the back and deposit it into their bank account. Nilsa signs his name and makes a deposit. Has she committed forgery?

Answer: No. There are two reasons why this cannot be a forgery case. In the first instance, Nilsa obtained permission to sign the other person's name. In the second instance, it is not forgery because Nilsa has no intent to defraud the bank. The check is legitimate and can be deposited into their account.

UTTERS A DOCUMENT

Utter
To offer as genuine.

The element that distinguishes first-degree forgery from other lesser offenses of forgery is "uttering." To **utter** a forged document means to present it to another person as a genuine document. If a person merely possesses a forged document, this is classified as second-degree forgery. But presenting the document as legitimate (uttering it) is more serious than simple possession. In the first example, the defendant simply has possession of a document, but in the second example he or she is actively attempting to defraud someone by pretending that a document is real when it is not. Most states that make a distinction between first- and second-degree forgery place the dividing line at uttering and simply possessing a forged document.

CREDIT CARD THEFT AND FRAUD

The use of credit and debit cards to make purchases has become so widespread in all industrialized societies that a person can charge almost any type of purchase. Crimes involving credit cards have skyrocketed in the past few decades. The federal government recognized the growing problem of credit card fraud when it passed Title 18, Section 514 of the U.S. Code. This statute was specifically designed to

---

[24] V.T.C.A., Penal Code § 32.21.

address the increasing amount of fraud through the use of credit cards and other fraudulent finance instruments. The Secret Service was given jurisdiction to investigate and prosecute credit card cases.

Theft of a card is an offense by itself. Subsequent use of the card qualifies as credit card fraud. In a case where a person steals a card and uses it to make purchases, the individual can be charged with a single count of credit card theft (which can be punished by a sentence of up to five years in some states) and then a charge for every credit card purchase made with the stolen card (each transaction can face a potential sentence of three to five years in prison).

A. SKIMMING

The crime of credit card theft and fraud are not the only crimes associated with credit cards. Individuals can also obtain credit card information and use that to charge for services and items without ever actually possessing the physical card. Criminals obtain credit card information from a wide variety of sources. One method of getting credit card information is called **skimming.** This procedure involves the use of a small, handheld device through which the card is swiped. The machine can read all relevant information and stores it for later retrieval. This information can be sold to other individuals who develop new cards based on the encrypted information.

Skimming
Use of an electronic device to surreptitiously acquire credit card information.

 ## VI COUNTERFEITING

The U.S. Secret Service is responsible for investigating and prosecuting cases involving counterfeit U.S. currency. In recent years, the Secret Service has noted an alarming trend: criminals printing U.S. currency on home-based color printers. Using a sophisticated scanner, a counterfeiter could scan a 20-dollar bill, and then recreate as many copies of it as he wished. Before the advent of this technology, it was far more common for counterfeiters to be members of a large, organized group, one with the resources necessary to process the color plates and buy the other equipment necessary to reproduce fake currency. It was partly out of the concern that small-time crooks could reproduce their own currency that all major denominations of U.S. bills were redesigned, adding features that a typical scanner and home color printer would find difficult if not impossible to reproduce.

 ## VII WHITE-COLLAR CRIME

White-collar crime refers to any crime in which technology, nonviolent, or indirect methods are used. Examples of white-collar crime include embezzlement, computer hacking, and fraud. The term was first coined in the 1930s to describe crime carried out by the rich and powerful. However, there is nothing especially noble or anything

White-collar crimes
A type of theft that is carried out without the direct use of violence and often involves scams, fraud, or the use of technology to defraud victims.

that makes this type of theft better than any others. Consider, for example, the case of Bernie Madoff, who took millions of dollars from people's pension funds. You could easily argue that this was a far worse tragedy than stealing someone's wallet or purse.

A. IDENTITY THEFT

Identity theft
Unlawful and nonconsensual use of another person's identifying information, such as Social Security number, address, and name, to create new credit accounts with no intention of repaying the debts incurred.

The crime of **identity theft** is a relatively recent development in the criminal world. The term itself is so new that credit card companies, lending institutions, and law enforcement cannot agree on what exactly constitutes identity theft. The most commonly accepted definition of identity theft occurs when someone uses personal information belonging to another to pass himself or herself off as that person to obtain financial gain. A criminal can gain access to a surprisingly small amount of personal information belonging to someone else (full name, date of birth, Social Security number) and use this information to obtain credit cards, personal loans, car financing, and even buy a home using the victim's credit history and personal information. Later, all of these assets will be liquidated, leaving the original person liable for all of the debts. The victim may find it very hard to convince the credit card companies and others that someone

FIGURE 9-5	2005		2010	
Income, Location, and Size of Households That Experienced Identity Theft				
Household characteristic	**Number**	**Percent in each category**	**Number**	**Percent in each category**
Total	6,424,900	5.5%	8,571,900	7.0%
Household income				
Less than $7,500	240,400	4.7%	238,600	5.3%
$7,500-14,999	315,300	3.7	334,500	4.8
$15,000-24,999	455,900	3.9	470,500	4.6
$25,000-34,999	547,500	4.9	616,900	6.0
$35,000-49,999	773,300	5.5	884,700	6.6
$50,000-74,999	1,059,500	6.8	1,152,100	7.9
$75,000 or more	2,050,300	9.5	2,835,300	12.3
Unknown	982,600	3.3	2,039,400	5.1
Location				
Urban	2,037,300	5.8%	3,083,100	7.6%
Suburban	3,526,100	5.9	4,718,500	7.6
Rural	861,400	3.9	770,300	3.9
Number of persons age 12 or older in household				
1	1,519,000	4.2%	2,130,000	5.5%
2-3	4,148,000	5.9	5,468,300	7.5
4-5	677,400	6.8	898,800	8.5
6 or more	80,400	10.8	74,800	8.3

FIGURE 9-6

Percent of Households That Experienced Identity Theft

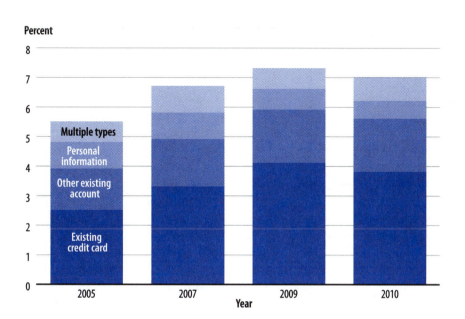

Percent

- Multiple types
- Personal information
- Other existing account
- Existing credit card

Year

*Annual estimates not available for 2008 because six months of identity theft data were collected.

else racked up all of these charges. The effects on the victim's credit history can be devastating. It frequently takes years and a large financial investment for victims to clear their names. See Figure 9-5 for statistics about identity theft.

With a victim's full name, date of birth, and Social Security number, a wide variety of lending institutions will extend credit, issue credit cards, and allow a criminal almost limitless access to financial opportunities. Both federal and state initiatives have attempted to make access to Social Security number information more difficult to obtain, but even these days acquiring some else's Social Security number is much easier than it should be. Here are some of the common methods that criminals use to obtain this information:

- Social engineering — asking the victim for the information while posing as a legitimate business.
- Trash — people often dispose of items containing important reference information, including their Social Security numbers, bank account statements, credit card numbers, and a wide variety of other information that criminals can put to ready use.
- Purchase — criminals may pose as legitimate companies requesting background information or credit histories on individuals.
- Theft — criminals may simply steal the information from legitimate companies.

CASE EXCERPT

STEWART V. STATE,
44 S.W.3d 582 (2001)

OPINION

MEYERS, J., delivered the opinion of the Court, joined by KELLER, P.J., PRICE, HOLLAND, JOHNSON, KEASLER, HERVEY and HOLCOMB, JJ.

Appellant was convicted of theft in a bench trial and sentenced to two years in a state jail facility. The trial court suspended the sentence, placed appellant on community supervision for five years, confined him to the county jail for ten days, assessed a $1,000 fine, and ordered him to perform 400 hours of community service. The Ninth Court of Appeals reversed appellant's conviction and entered a judgment of acquittal. *Stewart v. State*, 8 S.W.3d 832 (Tex.App. — Beaumont 2000). We granted the State's petition for discretionary review to determine whether the appellate court erred in holding that the State failed to establish venue in Montgomery County.

I

Appellant, the complainant's ex-husband, placed a phone call from his home in Harris County to the complainant's home in Montgomery County. During the call, appellant threatened to distribute nude pictures of the complainant to organizations in her community if she did not send him $5,000 within 48 hours. The complainant reported the incident to the Conroe Police Department. Detective Gene De Forrest told the complainant that, at the time, there was no evidence of a crime and nothing he could do to help.

Prior to the deadline threatened by appellant, the complainant received a letter at her home in Montgomery County from appellant. The letter was accompanied by a flier for the complainant's business, depicting a nude photograph of the complainant. In the letter, appellant threatened to mail the fliers out to "the Conroe business and church community" if the complainant failed to pay appellant within seven days. The complainant took the flier and the letter to Detective De Forrest.

De Forrest collaborated with U. S. Postal Service Inspector Bruce Beckham, who had been contacted by the complainant's husband, in an attempt to orchestrate "a little 'sting' operation" and catch appellant committing theft. De Forrest and Beckham obtained $1,600 in cash from the complainant at her home in Montgomery County, had her fill out a mailing address label, and took all items to Beckham's office in Harris County. The money was placed in an express mail envelope and delivered to appellant at his home in Harris County by a different postal employee. After De Forrest and Beckham witnessed the delivery, they waited 20 minutes, then stopped appellant as he backed out of his driveway holding the money in his hand. Appellant was arrested, taken to Beckham's office where he signed a written statement, and transported to Montgomery County jail. Appellant was then charged by indictment with having committed theft "by acquiring and exercising control of corporeal personal property, to-wit: U. S. Currency."

During trial, appellant argued that the State's failure to show appellant committed an offense in Montgomery County precluded venue in that county under Texas Code of Criminal Procedure Article 13.18, the general venue statute. The State countered that venue was proper in Montgomery County under the theft-specific venue statute, Texas Code of Criminal Procedure Article 13.08, because appellant exercised control over the money in that county. The trial judge did not make a specific finding as to which venue statute was applicable in appellant's case, however, it appears from his stated ruling that he found the general venue statute, Article 13.18, to be proper. The trial judge then found that the theft was complete at the time the complainant transferred the money to the authorities because of appellant's threats. The judge stated that the "gravity [sic] of the crime is the deprivation" and that physical delivery of the money was not necessary to complete the crime of theft.

On appeal, appellant argued again that the general venue statute, Article 13.18, was applicable to his case and not the theft-specific venue statute, Article 13.08. Appellant then argued that the State failed to establish venue in Montgomery County under Texas Code of Criminal Procedure Article 13.18 because there was no evidence that Stewart "appropriated" the money in that county, therefore no "offense was committed" in Montgomery County. The Court of Appeals held that Article 13.08 was the proper venue statute because "the Court of Criminal Appeals has concluded article 13.08 applies to all of the offenders who are prosecuted under the consolidated theft statute." Stewart at 833 (quoting Jones v. State, 979 S.W.2d 652 at 657 (Tex.Crim.App.1998)). The Court of Appeals went on to hold that the State failed to show that appellant appropriated the money in Montgomery County under Article 13.08. Utilizing the Penal Code's definition of theft, the appellate court found no evidence that appellant "acquired or otherwise exercised control over the currency in Montgomery County." FN4 The Court of Appeals held that "the only action taken by appellant in Montgomery County was the inducement of the transfer of the currency. In Montgomery County, appellant did not conduct or direct the transfer of the money, or any instrument representing the money, and did not re-direct any packages containing the money." Stewart, 8 S.W.3d at 837. The Court of Appeals reversed and rendered a judgment of acquittal.

FN4. Texas Penal Code § 31.03, Theft, provides in part:

(a) A person commits an offense if he unlawfully appropriates property with intent to deprive the owner of property.

Texas Penal Code § 31.01, Definitions, provides in part:

(4) "Appropriate" means:

(B) to acquire or otherwise exercise control over property other than real property.

II

We granted the State's petition for discretionary review to determine whether the Court of Appeals erred in holding that venue was not proper in Montgomery County, under Article 13.08, because appellant did not acquire or otherwise exercise control over the money in that county.

The State first asserts that it does not contest the Court of Appeal's finding that Article 13.08 is the applicable venue statute in this case. Relying on the Penal Code definitions of "theft" and "appropriate," the State argues appellant exercised control over the property "when his extortive threats succeeded in compelling the victim to part with her property." The State maintains that one can exercise control over property without having actual possession of the property, and that, because complainant parted with her money in Montgomery County as a result of appellant's actions, venue lies within that county.

Appellant initially claims that the proper venue statute in this case is Article 13.18, the general venue statute, as he argued before the Court of Appeals. Appellant also claims that regardless of whether the general statute, Article 13.18, or the theft-specific venue statute, Article 13.08, is applicable here, venue is not proper in Montgomery County because no theft was committed in that county. Appellant says there is no evidence that he acquired, possessed or exercised control over the property in Montgomery County.

III

We begin by addressing the issue of which venue statute is proper here, Article 13.08 or Article 13.18. The determination of whether one venue statute or another applies to a particular case is a mixed question of law and fact. The trial court must examine the facts of the case and apply the statutory requirements to those facts to determine whether the general venue statute or the theft-specific venue statute is appropriate. We review mixed questions of law and fact under an abuse of discretion standard when the resolution of the question turns on an evaluation of credibility and demeanor because, in such a situation, the trial judge is in an appreciably better position than the reviewing court to make such an evaluation. *Guzman v. State*, 955 S.W.2d 85 at 87–89 (Tex.Crim.App.1997). However, if the mixed question of law and fact does not involve an evaluation of credibility and demeanor, we review the decision de novo. Id. Determining which venue statute is applicable does not involve an evaluation of credibility or demeanor. It involves an examination of the facts as they appear on the record, and a determination of which venue statute is proper in light of those facts. The trial court does not have any particular advantage over the reviewing court in making such a determination. Therefore, we will review the holding by the Court of Appeals that the theft-specific venue statute is applicable de novo.

Article 13.08 is a specific venue statute, applicable when "property is stolen in one county and removed by the offender to another county." Therefore, the theft-specific venue statute can only be proper if the property was transported by the offender from one county to another. We have said that Article 13.08 attaches venue "at the point where the accused takes control of the property." *Jones*, 979 S.W.2d at 657. It is not necessary that the offender physically remove the money from one county to another. Once appellant took control of the property and directed its removal from one county to another, he was responsible for that removal and Article 13.08 is applicable. Therefore, for the theft-specific venue statute to apply to appellant's case, appellant must have had control of the money when the complainant was dispossessed of it and he must be responsible for its removal to Harris County. If appellant did not have control of the money until it reached him in Harris County, and he was not responsible for its removal from one county to another, then we look to the general venue statute to resolve where venue properly lies.

For the reasons given in our analysis below, we conclude that appellant did have control of the complainant's money and was responsible for its removal to Harris County from Montgomery County and Article 13.08 is the proper venue statute.

IV

Article 13.08 provides: "where property is stolen in one county and removed by the offender to another county, the offender may be prosecuted either in the county where he took the property or in any other county through or into which he may have removed the same."

Whether venue properly lies in Montgomery County depends initially upon whether the $1600 was, in fact, "stolen" in that county. The term "stolen" is not defined in Article 13.08 or anywhere else in the Code of Criminal Procedure. It is logical to interpret the theft-specific venue provision in light of the terms of the consolidated theft statute to which it applies. Accordingly, we look to Texas Penal Code § 31.03, which defines and addresses the crime of theft. FN7 The word "steal" is defined in § 31.01(7) as "to acquire property or service by theft". "Stolen" is the past participle of "steal". Webster's New Collegiate Dictionary 1137 (1980). Therefore, property is "stolen" for the purposes of Article 13.08 at the moment it is "acquired . . . by theft."

> FN7. The term "stolen" is used in Texas Penal Code § 31.03(b), which provides in part:
> (b) Appropriation of property is unlawful if:
> (2) the property is stolen and the actor appropriates the property knowing it was stolen by another; or
> (3) property in the custody of any law enforcement agency was explicitly represented by any law enforcement agent to the actor as being stolen and the actor appropriates the property believing it was stolen by another.

When is property "acquired . . . by theft?" According to § 31.03(a), theft occurs when an individual "unlawfully appropriates property with intent to deprive the owner of the property." Furthermore, "appropriate" is defined as "to acquire or otherwise exercise control over property." FN8 Tex.Pen.Code § 31.01(4)(B). In short, the complainant's property was "stolen" in the county in which appellant "acquired or otherwise exercised control" over it with the intent to deprive the complainant of the property.

> FN8. "Appropriate" is also defined as, "to bring about a transfer or purported transfer of title to or other nonpossessory interest in property, whether to the actor or another." Tex.Pen.Code § 31.01(4)(A).

The question is whether the complainant's $1,600 was "stolen" by appellant in Montgomery County. All parties concede that appellant did not "acquire" the money until it was delivered to him in Harris County. Therefore, the only issue is whether appellant "otherwise exercised control" over the money in Montgomery County.

The Court of Appeals held that appellant could not have exercised control over the money without having "actual or 'possessory'" possession of it. *Stewart*, 8 S.W.3d at 835. Because appellant did not have possession of the money until it was delivered to him in Harris County, the appellate court held that venue was improper in Montgomery County.

We have previously said that Article 13.08 "applies to offenders at the moment they take control over property, either to unlawfully appropriate it or to move it." *Jones*, 979 S.W.2d at 657. We have also held that "the 'manner of acquisition' is inconsequential to the evil of a theft: the gravamen of theft is in depriving the true owner of the use, benefit, enjoyment or value of his property, without his consent." *McClain v. State*, 687 S.W.2d 350, 353 (Tex.Crim.App.1985).

In a separate line of cases, we have said that, upon a defendant's motion, an indictment alleging theft by unlawful appropriation of property must specify whether the defendant is alleged to have appropriated the property by transfer of title or by acquiring or otherwise exercising control over it. *Gorman v. State*, 634 S.W.2d 681 (Tex. Crim.App.1982). We reasoned that the statutory definition of "appropriate" encompasses more than one method of appropriation, and that each of those methods comprise more than one way of meeting the definition. We stated that, although "'exercising control' was primarily directed at 'those thefts that involve only possession,' it also 'encompasses conduct that does not involve possession.'" Id. at 683 (quoting Practice Commentary following § 31.03).

Although Gorman did not elaborate on the type of conduct which would qualify as "exercising control" without involving possession, the commentary referred to in that case goes on to state that "a shipping clerk who reroutes a package to a friend by substituting a new address label might not have possession, but his conduct constitutes an exercise of control. Anyone who is in a position to take some action that deprives the owner of property is in a position to exercise control." Branch's 3d Edition, Texas Annotated Penal Statutes § 31.03 at 401 (Bancroft Whitney Company 1974).

We hold that the crucial element of theft is the deprivation of property from the rightful owner, without the owner's consent, regardless of whether the defendant at that moment has taken possession of the property. Appellant "exercised control" over the property and committed theft when, by his threats, he caused the complainant to release the money to the police in Montgomery County.FN10 Further, because appellant directed the removal of the money from Montgomery County to Harris County, he is responsible for that removal. Article 13.08, the theft-specific venue statute, is appropriate here and venue is proper in Montgomery County. The Court of Appeals erred in holding that venue was not proper in Montgomery County because appellant did not "exercise control" over the money in that county.

> FN10. The complainant testified on direct examination that giving up the money was a hardship for her and that she did not consent to appellant taking the $1,600.

We vacate the judgment of the Court of Appeals and remand to that court to address appellant's remaining points of error.

WOMACK, J., filed a concurring opinion.

CASE QUESTIONS

1 What was the crime that the defendant was accused of committing?
2 What claim did the defendant raise concerning venue during the trial?
3 What ruling did the Court of Appeals make?
4 How did the Texas Supreme Court rule?
5 How does the Court define the actual moment of theft?

CHAPTER SUMMARY

This chapter addressed the issues surrounding larceny in general and theft in particular. The basic elements of larceny are the unlawful taking of property of another, movement of the property, and the intent to permanently deprive the owner of the use of the property. Taking can be as simple as reducing an object to the person's custody, dominion, and control or it can be constructive. In constructive taking, the defendant places the victim's item out of reach of the victim, but also outside the immediate possession of the defendant. Just as we have seen in other crimes, theft also requires asportation of the item taken, which can be as little as a few inches. In felony case, the prosecution must prove that the value of the item stolen is greater than a stated amount, usually $500. The prosecution must prove this value by presenting expert testimony to establish the fair market value of the item stolen.

There are many different types of theft crimes, ranging from theft by shoplifting to embezzlement. Each has its specific elements, but most share the basic elements of larceny. Robbery is theft coupled with violence or the threat of violence. When robbery occurs through the use of a deadly weapon, it is referred to as armed robbery and is punished severely. Fraud or false pretenses occurs when a person uses deception to gain possession of an item. False pretenses must involve a material fact — one that is so important to the transaction that had it not been concealed would have changed the entire agreement. One of the most frequently abused material facts in false pretenses prosecutions is the claim that the defendant owns merchandise that he sells another when in fact he does not. Forgery consists of making or altering a writing as though it were the product of someone else, such as signing another person's name to a check without permission. In order to prosecute for forgery, the state must show that the defendant not only altered a writing, but did so in order to defraud another. When a person presents an altered or faked writing as real, this is called uttering and marks the difference between first-degree forgery and second-degree forgery.

KEY TERMS

Larceny

Real property

Personal property

Conversion

Constructive taking

Asportation (theft)

Fair market value

Fence

Embezzlement

Robbery

Material fact

Utter

Skimming

White-collar crimes

Identity theft

REVIEW QUESTIONS

1 What is larceny?

2 What is the difference between real and personal property?

3 Explain the legal requirement of "taking" in the context of theft.

4 What is conversion and how does it compare to constructive taking?

5 Explain asportation.

6 How does the prosecution prove that the defendant intended to permanently deprive the victim in a case of theft?

7 What is "fair market value" as it applies to proof of value in a theft case?

8 Who is responsible for establishing value in a theft case? Why?

9 Distinguish between theft by shoplifting and theft of services.

10 What are the elements of embezzlement?

11 Explain the element in theft by receiving stolen property where a defendant knew or "should have known" that the item was stolen. How can the state prove that a defendant should have known?

12 Explain the different between simple theft and "grand" larceny.

13 List and explain the elements of robbery.

14 What is a 'material fact' as that phrase applies to fraud case?

15 What are examples of statements that can constitute false pretenses?

16 Explain the difference between first and second degree forgery.

17 What is "uttering" as that term applies to first degree forgery?

18 Who is responsible for investigating federal crimes of credit card theft and why?

19 What is white collar crime?

20 Explain some of the ways that white collar criminals and hackers obtain information from their victims.

QUESTIONS FOR ANALYSIS

1   One of the examples given in this chapter concerns a spouse signing a check for another spouse. Is there a situation where this action could become a case of forgery? Provide an example.

2   Besides creating new accounts under a person's name, what are some other dangers of identity theft? Explain.

HYPOTHETICALS

1   Carl hacks Steve's blog and reroutes the small amounts of money that Steve makes when people pay for his content. What type of theft has he committed? Why?

2   Frank approaches Keisha and tells her that unless she pays him $500 he will post unflatteringly comments about her on her Facebook page. Is this a crime? If so, what?

3   Theo creates a false identity with a fake Social Security card and date of birth, then uses it to obtain a credit card. He uses the card to buy items and then does not pay for them. Has he committed a crime?

Crimes Against Public Order and Administration

 **I   INTRODUCTION TO CRIMES AGAINST PUBLIC MORALITY AND HEALTH**

Crimes against public morality, health, and administration of justice cover a wide variety of behaviors. We will begin with a discussion of various crimes against morality and health and then move swiftly to crimes involving administration of justice. In that area, we will encounter crimes as diverse as bribery and riot.

 **II   CRIMES AGAINST PUBLIC MORALITY**

There are several crimes against public morality, but two of the most important are gambling and prostitution. This chapter will examine both.

A. GAMBLING

Gambling is a generic term used for any type of game of chance where there is a monetary or other gain.[1] Because the term is so broad, the word has been applied to

Gambling
Paying money for the chance of winning more money or something else of value.

---

[1] *In re Initiative Petition No. 363*, State Question No. 672, 1996 OK 122, 927 P.2d 558 (Okla. 1996).

"gaming," video poker, and a wide range of other activities, including Internet-based gambling.[2] Under the old common law, gambling itself was usually not illegal. However, gambling was often seen as part of a symptom of greater moral decline. Gambling statutes were enacted because of breaches of the peace and other crimes that often went hand in hand with gambling. In the Old West, boomtowns would spring up to help relieve rich gold miners of their profits through gambling and prostitution. These days, gambling is not a top priority for law enforcement, but there are enough cases made to warrant a discussion of the crime.

The elements of gambling are:

▧ Payment of money (or something else of value)
▧ For the chance
▧ To win a prize or an item of value[3]

To meet the second element, courts have defined "chance" to mean that the person placing the wager has no control over the outcome.[4] The third element can be satisfied not only by the payment of money, but also by receiving additional free games.[5]

In some jurisdictions, it is a crime to be present at an illegal gambling event. In many states, gambling at a private house where the general public is not allowed is exempted under the statute. This means that a local Friday night poker party is probably not subject to prosecution, at least in certain states.

What is the difference between gambling and playing the lottery? For one thing, in a lottery, the winner is chosen from many players and is randomly selected. The problem with this definition is that it is not sufficiently different from gambling to make a case that there really is any moral difference between gambling and playing the state lottery. The word "lottery" has no set legal definition, making the distinction between the two acts even more difficult to distinguish. Having said that, "gambling" is illegal and playing the lottery is not.[6]

B. PROSTITUTION

Prostitution
The crime of offering a person's body to another for sexual purposes in exchange for money.

Prostitution is often referred to as the "world's oldest profession." There is no doubt that individuals have been offering sex to others for money or something else of value for thousands of years. Prostitution is mentioned and denounced in the Bible. The selling of sex services has been considered a moral and legal violation in many societies, but the crime has never been eradicated. Although prostitution was originally defined as offering sexual intercourse by a woman to a man, many states

---

[2] *People v. Tillman*, 13 Misc. 3d 736, 820 N.Y.S.2d 511 (City Crim. Ct. 2006).
[3] *Barber v. Jefferson County Racing Ass'n, Inc.*, 960 So. 2d 599 (Ala. 2006), cert. denied, 551 U.S. 1131, 127 S. Ct. 2975, 168 L. Ed. 2d 703 (2007).
[4] *Barber v. Jefferson County Racing Ass'n, Inc.*, 960 So. 2d 599 (Ala. 2006), cert. denied, 551 U.S. 1131, 127 S. Ct. 2975, 168 L. Ed. 2d 703 (2007).
[5] *Trinkle v. Stroh*, 60 Cal. App. 4th 771, 70 Cal. Rptr. 2d 661 (3d Dist. 1997).
[6] *Harris v. Missouri Gaming Com'n*, 869 S.W.2d 58 (Mo. 1994).

have expanded on the definition to include not only same-sex partners, but also the scope of activities that fall under "sexual practices."[7] Jurisdictions are split on whether soliciting sex for money and engaging in sex for money qualify as the single crime of prostitution or two separate offenses: solicitation of prostitution and prostitution.[8] There is no requirement that the party charged with prostitution actually set a fee for the service. Merely offering sex for some payment is enough.[9]

Is prostitution a "victimless" crime? Many people who advocate against it point to the fact that it is often associated with drug use; exploitation of women; the spread of sexually transmitted diseases, such as syphilis and AIDS; or giving incentives to organized crime to use women as a source of income and even corrupting law enforcement agencies.[12]

In cases where prostitution statutes have been challenged as unconstitutional, for instance, as a violation of the right to privacy or that they are overbroad, courts have routinely upheld the statutes.[13]

Prostitution involves engaging in a sexual act for money.[10]

Both men and women can be charged with prostitution.[11]

"STATUS" OFFENSE

This is the first point in this text where that deals with a "status" offense. The law does not penalize someone for being a specific thing, only doing a specific thing. Therefore, it is not illegal to be a drug or alcohol addict. It is also not illegal to be a prostitute. It is illegal to possess illegal drugs, and it is illegal to engage in prostitution, but a person cannot be prosecuted even if he or she self-identifies as a criminal. The person must still engage in some activity.[14]

PROSECUTING "JOHNS"

Recently, many states have enacted legislation specifically targeted at prostitutes' clients (sometimes called "johns"). In these states, it is a crime, usually a misdemeanor, to solicit sex from a prostitute.[15] These new crimes have resulted in cleaning up certain areas that had traditionally been known as "red light districts." Despite these legislative changes, prostitution is generally a low priority for law enforcement.

FEDERAL LEGISLATION

On the federal level, the Mann Act has been in effect since 1910 and prohibits the transportation of women across state lines for "immoral" purposes. Although the enforcement of the Mann Act has had a checkered history, it has been limited in

---

[7] *State v. B Bar Enterprises, Inc.*, 133 Ariz. 99, 649 P.2d 978 (1982).
[8] *State v. Kittilstad*, 231 Wis. 2d 245, 603 N.W.2d 732 (1999).
[9] *People v. Emig*, 188 Mich. App. 687, 470 N.W.2d 504 (1991).
[10] *Com. v. Johnson*, 448 Pa. Super. 42, 670 A.2d 666 (1996).
[11] *Plas v. State*, 598 P.2d 966 (Alaska 1979).
[12] *Com. v. DeStefanis*, 442 Pa. Super. 54, 658 A.2d 416 (1995).
[13] *People v. Hill*, 333 Ill. App. 3d 783, 267 Ill. Dec. 456, 776 N.E.2d 828 (2d Dist. 2002).
[14] *Ford v. U.S.*, 533 A.2d 617 (D.C. 1987).
[15] *State v. Ellis*, 853 S.W.2d 440 (Mo. Ct. App. E.D. 1993).

the modern era to the practice of trafficking in prostitutes across state lines.[16] The Mann Act is also known as the "White Slavery Act."[17]

CRIMES AGAINST ADMINISTRATION OF JUSTICE

Crimes against the administration of justice are acts that go to the very heart of what is supposed to be a fair, unbiased criminal justice system. Corruption in general and bribery in particular can have a devastating effect on a community. When people begin to believe that justice and even regular governmental services are only available to the highest bidder, society begins to break down. We have a right to expect that public servants will do their jobs and will not be bought and sold like commodities.

A. BRIBERY

Bribery
Offering money (or something of value) to a public official to influence his or her decisions.

Bribery is the illegal offer of money to a public servant to receive an action helpful to the person making the offer. Public servants can be police officers, municipal employees, or building inspectors, among others. Courts look at bribery as a form of fraud that is perpetrated against all the members of the public.[18]

States have set up their own bribery definitions in their various statutes. Although there are important differences between and among the states, some general rules can be culled out. It is always considered bribery to offer a public official money (or something of value) to either do a thing that he or she did not have to do, or refrain from doing a thing that he or she had a right to do.[19]

ITEM OF "VALUE"

What is an item of value? Obviously cash has inherent value, but bribery requires only that the person receive cash or "something of value." Although courts generally follow an objective viewpoint in most areas of criminal law, this is one area where the subjective viewpoint is used. Prosecutors are not required to prove that the thing of value was something that *all* persons would value, but only that the *defendant* valued it. Consider Scenarios 10-1 and 10-2.

SCENARIO 10-1

COMPLETING THE COLLECTION

Police officer Danny has been collecting miniature pewter sculptures of Civil War scenes for years. He has only one figurine left to complete the collection and, curiously enough, it is not the most valuable. It is simply a small figurine of a wounded soldier. The piece is difficult to find.

---

[16] 18 U.S.C. § 2421.
[17] 18 U.S.C. § 2421.
[18] *Alvarez v. State*, 800 So. 2d 237 (Fla. Dist. Ct. App. 3d Dist. 2001).
[19] *Stanton v. State*, 2006 WY 31, 130 P.3d 486 (Wyo. 2006).

Carl, who is facing arrest on drug charges, asks Danny to destroy the evidence that will be used against him. To give Danny some incentive, he offers Danny the very figurine that Danny has been searching for. The actual monetary value of the figurine is less than $200, but to Danny, its value is almost priceless. Danny accepts the figurine and destroys the evidence. Has Danny accepted a bribe?

Answer: Yes. In bribery prosecutions, it is not necessary for the prosecution to prove that the item given to the officer was something that all people would value, only that it was something that Danny would value.[20]

PAULA, THE PROSECUTOR

Paula has received the case against Carl and intends to bring charges of bribery and conspiracy against Danny. In order to do this, Paula offers Carl the following: In exchange for his testimony in the bribery trial against Danny, she will lower the charge that Carl is facing to a misdemeanor. Danny hears about this deal and insists that Paula be charged with attempting to bribe a witness. Has Paula bribed Carl?

Answer: No. Lowering charges or offering a lower sentence has never been construed to be a "thing of value" for purposes of a bribery prosecution. In fact, this arrangement is used all over the country to induce defendants to plead guilty and forego trials and also to encourage codefendants to testify against one another. There is also the additional point that Carl is not a public official.[21]

● FAMOUS CASES
ROBERT HANSSEN

By all appearances, Robert Philip Hanssen was a devoted family man who, along with his wife and six children, attended Mass every Sunday. A typical suburban dad, he worked hard to pay his mortgage and put his kids through Catholic schools and colleges. But Robert Philip Hanssen was also responsible for what might be the worst intelligence disaster in U.S. history.

Hanssen joined the FBI as a special agent in 1976 and later began working in counterintelligence. His task as a counterintelligence agent was to compile a database of Soviet intelligence. But for 15 years, from 1985 until his arrest in 2001, Robert Hanssen spied for the Soviet Union and later for Russia.

As a spy, Hanssen led a true double life. The Soviet Union and then Russia were sworn enemies of his FBI counterintelligence team and also of his beloved church. Nevertheless, in October 1985 he contacted KGB agents in Washington, D.C., and offered to provide information in exchange for cash, diamonds, and goodwill. His

---

[20] *U.S. v. Crozier*, 987 F.2d 893 (2d Cir. 1993).
[21] *U.S. v. Moore*, 525 F.3d 1033 (11th Cir. 2008).

vision of goodwill was an escape plan, which would allow him to retire to Moscow, teach college courses, and train future spies.

His initial deal was to sell the names of three KGB agents working secretly for the FBI. Moscow recalled the three agents, executed two of them, and sentenced the third to prison.

Hanssen's espionage activities continued in subsequent years. Among the information he passed along to the Soviets was a complete list of all American double agents. Additionally, he compromised the investigation of Felix Bloch, another suspected spy. Hanssen alerted the KGB that Bloch was under suspicion, which eventually caused the FBI's investigation to crumble. In 1989, he passed along information about America's plans to electronically collect intelligence, including radar, underwater hydrophones, spy satellites, and signal intercepts.

Hanssen first came under suspicion when he hacked into a fellow agent's computer in 1993. He gave a cover story that he was testing security, but his real motive was to determine whether or not he himself was under investigation. When he found nothing, he requested a transfer in 1994 to the new National Counterintelligence Center. When he learned that he would have to take a lie detector test in order to make the transfer, he withdrew himself from consideration.

Suspicion about Hanssen grew, and in 1997 computer specialists impounded his computer. He had reported a computer failure, and while the specialists were examining it, they found a password-cracking program that Hanssen had installed. Even more incriminating, Hanssen got careless about monitoring his own status. He frequently used FBI computers to search for his own name in connection with any investigation. Progress was slow, however, and it wasn't until several years of forensic investigation and tips from other agents that the FBI became certain that Hanssen was indeed a spy. But they needed hard evidence, ideally to catch him in the act.

To monitor him more closely, the FBI promoted him to the job of supervising computer security. The assistant assigned to him was actually tasked with monitoring Hanssen's activities. The assistant determined that Hanssen was using a handheld PDA to store information, and when he had an opportunity to get his hands on it briefly, he had other agents download the incriminating evidence.

Unaware that he was under round-the-clock surveillance, Hanssen arranged another drop for the Russians. FBI agents followed him to Foxstone Park, a small county park in Vienna, Virginia, and observed him placing a garbage bag full of classified material beneath a footbridge. It was the last drop he would make. Ten agents surrounded him and ordered him to freeze. His only response was "What took you so long?"

Hanssen was accused of sending 27 letters and 22 packages to the KGB and its successor agency, the SVR. In exchange, he collected more than $600,000 in cash, some $50,000 in diamonds, and the promise of another $800,000 in a Russian bank account. His sole motivation was money.

Hanssen negotiated a plea bargain that allowed him to escape the death penalty in exchange for life in prison without parole. He pleaded guilty to 15 counts of espionage. The director of the FBI at the time, Louis Freeh, noted that the damage Hanssen had caused was grave. He compromised the safety of untold numbers of intelligence agents, as well as that of numerous sensitive FBI programs and operations.

B. PERJURY

The elements of **perjury** are:

Perjury
Giving false testimony under
oath about a material fact.

- Taking an oath before a court or other official
- Giving a false statement of a material fact
- Knowing that the fact was false when it was given[22]

Perjury is something more than simply lying on the stand. In order to meet the elements of a perjury charge, the prosecution must first prove that the witness took an oath. What is an oath? A person takes an oath when he or she takes the witness stand in a court of law and is administered an oath by a qualified person. The statutes on perjury (see Figure 10-1) do not limit perjury to courtrooms, but to any "tribunal." The key is that the person who gives the testimony realizes that he or she is under oath, and this procedure normally takes place by the witness raising his or her hand and promising to tell the truth, the whole truth, and nothing but the truth. See Scenario 10-3.

PERJURY?

Harry has been called to testify at a civil court proceeding involving a child custody matter. Harry does not like the child's mother and is a close friend to the child's father. After being sworn in, the attorney representing the father asks Harry if he has ever seen the child's mother act in an overly aggressive manner toward the child. Harry answers, "Yes. There was one time that I saw her really get angry and go way over the top."

When asked to explain, Harry says that he was raised in a home where any type of violence was frowned upon and he again insists that the child's mother acted in an "inappropriate way." Pressed for details, Harry says, "I'm telling you, it wasn't right."

Has Harry committed perjury?

Answer: Probably not. In examining the elements of perjury, Harry is under oath and is in a court of law. However, his statement sounds more like an opinion than a factual statement. Furthermore, he has not given any details that are clearly untrue. His opinion, by itself, does not rise to the level of an untruthful statement.

Because the prosecution must prove that a valid oath was administered, if the evidence shows that the defendant was a notary who signed a misleading document or that the defendant was a witness before a local board hearing, neither situation would satisfy the element of taking an oath, because neither involves someone taking an oath or having one administered by a qualified official.[23]

In addition to proving that the defendant was under oath, the prosecution must also prove that the defendant made a false statement and that he or she knew it was

---

[22] *People v. Garcia*, 39 Cal. 4th 1070, 48 Cal. Rptr. 3d 75, 141 P.3d 197 (2006).
[23] *Stiley v. Block*, 130 Wash. 2d 486, 925 P.2d 194 (1996).

FIGURE 10-1

Sample Perjury Statute

(1) A person is guilty of perjury, a Class III felony, if in any official proceeding he or she makes a false statement under oath or equivalent affirmation, or swears or affirms the truth of a statement previously made, when the statement is material and he or she does not believe it to be true.

. . .

(3) A falsification shall be material, regardless of the admissibility of the statement under rules of evidence, if it could have affected the course or outcome of the proceeding. It shall not be a defense that the declarant mistakenly believed the falsification to be immaterial. Whether a falsification is material in a given factual situation shall be a question of law.

. . .

(7) No person shall be convicted of an offense under this section when proof of falsity rests solely upon contradiction by testimony of a single person other than the defendant.[24]

Material fact
A fact that is central to winning or deciding a case.

false at the time. Many jurisdictions also add one more element: that the statement must involve a **material fact**. A material fact is one that is crucial to a case, and if changed might well alter the outcome of the case. A material fact is one that focuses on the important questions of a case: who, what, when, or where. False testimony about these matters could result in a perjury prosecution. Prosecutions for perjury are relatively rare for the simple reason that most people shade their meaning when they testify as opposed to outright lying. It is not perjury for a witness to offer an opinion or a belief.[25] If a person offers an opinion, based on facts, it is still not perjury if that opinion is wrong. It is also true that the witness must know that the statement is false at the time that it is made. If the witness believes that the statement is true, then it is not perjury.[26] Opinions, feelings, and other speculations, even if false, are usually not actionable.

C. OBSTRUCTION OF JUSTICE

All states have laws that make it a crime to hinder prosecution or police action, or that prevent law enforcement from locating, bringing charges, or punishing a person charged with committing a crime.[27] Examples of obstruction of justice include:

- Giving false information to police
- Tampering with evidence
- Obstructing or resisting arrest

---

[24] Neb.Rev.St. § 28-915.
[25] *State v. Hawkins*, 620 N.W.2d 256 (Iowa 2000).
[26] *U.S. v. Stotts*, 113 F.3d 493 (4th Cir. 1997).
[27] *State v. McCullough*, 347 Or. 350, 220 P.3d 1182 (2009).

GIVING FALSE INFORMATION TO POLICE

In addition to a charge of obstruction of justice for hindering prosecution, it is also a crime to give false information to the police or other investigators. Examples of giving false information to police include:

- Providing a false name to investigators
- Giving false or misleading information to law enforcement
- Obstructing a criminal investigation (see this chapter's Case Excerpt)[28]

TAMPERING WITH EVIDENCE

It is a crime to destroy, hide, or create false evidence in a criminal prosecution. Many states include this crime in a larger statute that makes it a crime to tamper with evidence.[29] (This crime is also discussed in this chapter's Case Excerpt.)

OBSTRUCTING OR RESISTING ARREST

In addition to tampering with evidence, it is a crime to obstruct a police officer in his or her duties. The problem with this crime is defining exactly what is and what is not considered to be "obstruction." It is obvious that when a person violently opposes being taken into custody, she may be charged with resisting arrest. This charge would be in addition to whatever crime she was originally charged with. However, what about situations where violence is not clear? How does one define "obstructing" an arrest? Courts have wrestled with this definition for decades. In order to define it clearly, the courts have come up with some basic guidelines to help determine when obstruction has occurred. These include:

- The obstruction does not have to be successful, simply attempting it is sufficient.[30]
- The obstruction does not have to actually delay an investigation, only present the possibility of such a delay.
- The obstruction can consist of attempting violence on the person of a police officer.[31]
- The obstruction can consist of the use of "fighting words."[32]

Based on these guidelines, states have come up with a basic set of essential elements that define obstructing an arrest. They are that:

- The defendant intentionally resisted, obstructed, or delayed a police officer,
- The officer was engaged in official duties, and

---

[28] *State v. Coddington*, 135 Ariz. 480, 662 P.2d 155 (Ct. App. Div. 2 1983).
[29] *Timberlake v. U.S.*, 758 A.2d 978 (D.C. 2000).
[30] *State v. Silva*, 285 Conn. 447, 939 A.2d 581 (2008).
[31] *Mattis v. U.S.*, 995 A.2d 223 (D.C. 2010).
[32] *State v. Bower*, 725 N.W.2d 435 (Iowa 2006).

◾ The defendant knew or should have known that the police officer was acting in his or her official capacity.[33]

Generally speaking, resisting arrest involves some physical resistance. Mere statements, insults, or even mild threats, generally do not constitute resisting arrest (see Scenario 10-4). Only when an officer has a reasonable belief that the person may carry out the threat will the suspect's actions be considered resisting arrest. It is also obstruction of justice to shield others from arrest or actively interfere in the arrest of others. As we have already seen, obstruction of justice can take many forms. If a person refuses to identify himself or herself to police after being requested to do so, this can qualify as obstruction of justice.[34]

SCENARIO 10-4

A CASE OF OBSTRUCTION?

Paula is a police officer in uniform who has arrived at a location to serve an arrest warrant. When she knocks on the door, a man answers. She asks, "Are you John Smith?"

"Who wants to know?" the man answers.

"I need you to answer my question," Paula continues.

"I'm called lots of things by lots of people," the man says.

Paula asks again, "Are you or are you not John Smith?"

The man replies, "You got a warrant or are you just wasting my time?"

"I have an arrest warrant for John Smith," Paula continues. "You match the description given. Are you John Smith?"

"Like I said, officer," the man says, "They call me all kinds of things. Besides, what's in a name? I bet some people call you 'officer' and some other people call you 'pig' and other people call you . . ."

"That's enough. I am arresting you for obstruction of justice." After he is arrested, the man admits that he is John Smith.

Is this a case of obstruction of justice?

Answer: Probably. But this is a close call. The question concerning obstruction of justice has to do with deliberately delaying an officer or actively preventing the officer from carrying out his or her duties. The man's actions are certainly annoying, but whether this rises to the level of obstruction is a question that a jury may have to decide.

> **Sidebar**
>
> *It is not obstruction of justice for a person to advise another of his or her constitutional rights, including the right to an attorney.*

Flight
When a suspect attempts to elude the police or runs away when confronted by police.

Flight. Fleeing the police may be prosecuted as obstruction of justice. Fleeing, or **flight**, has an interesting history in criminal law. In the context of constitutional law, flight may be a factor in giving police reasonable belief to conduct a *Terry* stop (discussed in Chapter 13). In some cases, flight may rise to the level of probable cause when it is coupled with other factors. In addition to providing probable cause

---

[33] *Yount v. City of Sacramento*, 43 Cal. 4th 885, 76 Cal. Rptr. 3d 787, 183 P.3d 471 (2008).

[34] *State ex rel. Bailey v. City of West Monroe*, 418 So. 2d 570 (La. 1982).

> **2C:29-2. Resisting Arrest; Eluding Officer. a. (1)** Except as provided in paragraph (3), a person is guilty of a disorderly persons offense if he purposely prevents or attempts to prevent a law enforcement officer from effecting an arrest. **(2)** Except as provided in paragraph (3), a person is guilty of a crime of the fourth degree if he, by flight, purposely prevents or attempts to prevent a law enforcement officer from effecting an arrest. **(3)** An offense under paragraph (1) or (2) of subsection a. is a crime of the third degree if the person:
>
> **(a)** Uses or threatens to use physical force or violence against the law enforcement officer or another; or
> **(b)** Uses any other means to create a substantial risk of causing physical injury to the public servant or another.
>
> It is not a defense to a prosecution under this subsection that the law enforcement officer was acting unlawfully in making the arrest, provided he was acting under color of his official authority and provided the law enforcement officer announces his intention to arrest prior to the resistance.

FIGURE 10-2

New Jersey 2C:29-2. Resisting Arrest, Eluding Officer

to detain the individual, if a person flees from the police, after being told to remain still, he or she can be charged with obstruction of justice.[35]

Resisting Arrest. **Resisting arrest** is considered to be a form of obstructing justice (see Figure 10-2). In most cases, resisting arrest can take the form of physical resistance. When a person uses fighting words or other nonphysical behavior, the crime may be considered obstruction of justice and not resisting arrest. In either event, both charges are usually classified as misdemeanors.

Resisting arrest
Actively preventing a police officer from arresting a person.

D. WIRETAPPING AND EAVESDROPPING

Law enforcement officials are authorized to listen in on telephone conversations — **wiretap** — or private conversations only after they have obtained a warrant to do so. Private individuals are barred from listening in on telephone conversations to which they are not a party. It is also illegal to listen in on other people's private conversations (see Scenario 10-5). In some states it is a felony to place recording instruments on private individuals' telephones in order to listen in on their conversations. With the advent of the Internet, whole new areas of invasion of privacy concerns have arisen. For instance, is email a private communication? Most of us would agree that it is, but courts have not ruled that way. No doubt there will be additional cases that come out refining the constitutional status of email is. There are some strong indications that, although email is not currently classified the same way or given the same protection as a person's papers or telephone calls, email may

Wiretap
Using electronic devices to listen in on a person's telephone calls, whether they are land-based lines or cell calls.

---

[35] *State v. Williams,* 192 N.J. 1, 926 A.2d 340 (2007).

one day receive similar constitutional protections. Before government officials can listen in on telephone calls, either cellphone or old-fashioned landlines, they must obtain a warrant to do so. This also holds true for intercepting text messages.

EAVESDROPPING

Marvin is a police officer who works at the local jail. Teddy has recently been arrested for armed robbery and is awaiting his preliminary hearing. A man appears at the jail and identifies himself as Teddy's lawyer. Marvin escorts the man back to an interview room and waits there while another officer brings Teddy to the same location. When Teddy arrives Marvin prepares to leave, but the other officer takes him aside and whispers to him that he overhead Teddy telling the other men in his holding cell that the man who has identified himself as Teddy's attorney is not in fact an attorney at all and is simply one of Teddy's friends who is there to supply him with illegal narcotics. The other officer departs, but before Marvin leaves the room, he plants a small microphone in the room and listens in from another location. He does not hear anything that would make him think that the man is not an attorney. Has he committed illegal eavesdropping?

Answer: Yes. A criminal defendant has the right to meet with his or her attorney and to engage in confidential (and unmonitored) communications. If Marvin had suspicions that the man was not an attorney, he could have used different methods to satisfy his doubts other than listening in on the conversation. He could simply have asked the man for some identification to prove who he was.

E. JURY TAMPERING

Jury tampering
Influencing or attempting to influence a juror's vote in a civil or criminal case.

Embracery
Another term for jury tampering.

Jury tampering (or **embracery**) is a crime in all jurisdictions. A person commits jury tampering when he or she influences or tries to influence a juror's decision in a civil or criminal case. Jury tampering can take the form of physical threats, coercion or bribery.

F. WITNESS TAMPERING

Witness tampering
Attempting to influence a witness's testimony during a civil or criminal trial; encouraging a witness to commit perjury.

It is also a crime to attempt to influence a witness's testimony or to encourage the witness to commit perjury. **Witness tampering** can take the same form as jury tampering. If a person threatens, coerces, bribes, or uses some other means to induce a witness to commit perjury, he or she is guilty of witness tampering. Like jury tampering, most states classify witness tampering as a felony.

CRIMES AGAINST PUBLIC ORDER

Statutes creating crimes against public order are based on the belief that when large groups of people act in concert, they can do far more damage than an individual acting alone. Throughout our history and that of other nations, we have seen that when groups decide to go on a rampage, they can do incredible destruction and can cause great loss of life. As a result, law enforcement takes such actions seriously.

A. RIOT

A **riot** is defined as a public disturbance involving a group of three or more people who engage in destruction of personal property or who injure people. The problem with prosecuting is determining when police officers are permitted to make an arrest for inciting a riot. There is an inherent tension between protecting the public from property destruction and danger to human beings and the First Amendment's guarantee of freedom of expression and the right to lawfully assemble. To determine when an action crosses the line from constitutional protected speech into riot, the court used the case of *Brandenburg v. Ohio*, 89 S.Ct. 1827 (1969) to create the "imminent lawless action test." Under this test, police may arrest individuals for incitement to riot when they can show that:

Riot
A public disturbance involving three or more persons who create the danger of imminent lawless action.

1 the defendants are actively advocating behavior which is likely to produce imminent lawless action, and
2 the defendants' actions are likely to incite or produce imminent lawless action.

Under this test, for the prosecution to be successful in a charge of incitement to riot, it must show not only that the defendants advocated unlawful behavior but also that their advocacy was closely tied to circumstances where violence was likely. Without both elements, an incitement to riot charge will fail.

B. TERRORISM

In recent years, the dangers of both domestic and international terrorism have become painfully aware. The federal government has responded to incidents such as the Oklahoma City bombing and 9/11 by making acts of terrorism where U.S. citizens are killed punishable by death (see Figure 10-3).

(a) Homicide. - Whoever kills a national of the United States, while such national is outside the United States, shall -

(1) if the killing is murder (as defined in section 1111(a)), be fined under this title, punished by death or imprisonment for any term of years or for life, or both

FIGURE 10-3

18 USC § 2332. Criminal Penalties for Terrorism

Terrorism can be prosecuted on both the state and federal level. Many states have enacted their own statutes on terrorism, and these can be prosecuted independently of federal actions, although the Supremacy Clause of the U.S. Constitution gives the federal authorities the right to bring criminal charges before any state can proceed.

C. CARRYING CONCEALED WEAPONS

All states have laws restricting the possession of weapons, especially handguns. Even states that allow citizens to obtain permits to carry concealed weapons do not allow the person to carry the weapon into all facilities. With or without a permit, a person is often barred from bringing a handgun to a school, courthouse, or other government facility. For many decades, the exact application of the Second Amendment's right to bear arms was an open question. However, the U.S. Supreme Court finally weighed in on this question by establishing that citizens have the right to possess and carry weapons.[36] However, the Supreme Court's ruling does not prevent the states from enacting statutes that proscribe certain individuals from possessing handguns, including convicted felons and those who have been found to be mentally incompetent, among others. Consider Scenario 10-6.

A person commits the offense of carrying a concealed weapon by:

- Knowingly carrying on his or her person (unless in an open manner, not fully exposed to view outside his or her home) any of the following:
  - brass knuckles
  - firearm
  - knife designed for offense or defense
  - martial arts weapons

SCENARIO 10-6

CARRYING A CONCEALED WEAPON

Christopher is driving his car one afternoon and does not realize that his back taillight is broken. Donna, a police officer, notices the tail light and pulls Christopher over. While she is talking with him, she notices the butt of a handgun sticking out under the driver's seat and places him under arrest for carrying a concealed weapon. Christopher states that he has a Second Amendment right to possess a handgun. Do the facts rise to the level of carrying a concealed weapon?

Answer: Yes. The handgun was concealed and although the Second Amendment allows individuals to have firearms, it does not override the carrying concealed weapon statutes.

Generally, a conviction for this offense is a misdemeanor. However, when the person carrying the concealed weapon is a convicted felon or has been convicted of this offense before, many jurisdictions make it a felony.

---

[36] *District of Columbia v. Heller*, 128 S. Ct. 2783, 171 L. Ed. 2d 637 (2008).

Possessing a weapon during other crimes can also enhance the sentence. For instance, when a gun or knife is used to commit robbery, the offense becomes armed robbery and is punished more severely.

HANDGUN PERMITS

In all jurisdictions a person is allowed to apply for a handgun permit or license. This permit allows a person to conceal the pistol in a holster or purse and provides a statutory exception to the rule that a person must always display a weapon in his or her possession. However, simply because a person can apply for a handgun permit doesn't necessarily mean that a person will get one. The U.S. Supreme Court has given states wide discretion in denying handgun permit applications.

"STAND YOUR GROUND" LAWS

In recent years, some states have enacted so-called "Stand Your Ground" laws. These statutes modify a much older concept sometimes referred to as the "castle" doctrine or "duty to retreat" doctrine. Under the common law and even under statutory law in many states, an individual who was threatened with violence in a public setting had a duty to retreat or to seek safety if such action was reasonable. However, most states also had a separate doctrine that did not require retreat of any kind when the person was being attacked inside his or her home. The castle doctrine derives from the old saying "your home is your castle." A person was then faced with two different rules: In public, if he could reasonably retreat, then he must do so, but if the same person was presented with a threat of violence in his home, then there was no such duty. Several states expanded on the castle doctrine by creating "Stand Your Ground" statutes. These laws changed the duty-to-retreat provision by no longer requiring a person confronted with violence in public to retreat. In fact, some of these statutes provide that if a person is in legal possession of a handgun and is presented with a lethal threat, that person could respond with deadly force, even in public. These laws also provide for both criminal and civil immunity if the person's actions are governed by the statute. That means that if the person can successfully plead a Stand Your Ground law, he or she cannot be prosecuted for use of violence, including causing the death of another person. See Figure 10-4 for an example of a Stand Your Ground law.

FIGURE 10-4

Stand Your Ground Law (Florida)

776.012 Use of force in defense of person. — A person is justified in using force, except deadly force, against another when and to the extent that the person reasonably believes that such conduct is necessary to defend himself or herself or another against the other's imminent use of unlawful force. However, a person is justified in the use of deadly force and does not have a duty to retreat if:

continued

FIGURE 10-4

Stand Your Ground Law (Florida) *(continued)*

(1) He or she reasonably believes that such force is necessary to prevent imminent death or great bodily harm to himself or herself or another or to prevent the imminent commission of a forcible felony; or

(2) Under those circumstances permitted pursuant to s. 776.013.

776.013   Home protection; use of deadly force; presumption of fear of death or great bodily harm. —

(1) A person is presumed to have held a reasonable fear of imminent peril of death or great bodily harm to himself or herself or another when using defensive force that is intended or likely to cause death or great bodily harm to another if:

(a) The person against whom the defensive force was used was in the process of unlawfully and forcefully entering, or had unlawfully and forcibly entered, a dwelling, residence, or occupied vehicle, or if that person had removed or was attempting to remove another against that person's will from the dwelling, residence, or occupied vehicle; and

(b) The person who uses defensive force knew or had reason to believe that an unlawful and forcible entry or unlawful and forcible act was occurring or had occurred.

(2) The presumption set forth in subsection (1) does not apply if:

(a) The person against whom the defensive force is used has the right to be in or is a lawful resident of the dwelling, residence, or vehicle, such as an owner, lessee, or titleholder, and there is not an injunction for protection from domestic violence or a written pretrial supervision order of no contact against that person; or

(b) The person or persons sought to be removed is a child or grandchild, or is otherwise in the lawful custody or under the lawful guardianship of, the person against whom the defensive force is used; or

(c) The person who uses defensive force is engaged in an unlawful activity or is using the dwelling, residence, or occupied vehicle to further an unlawful activity; or

(d) The person against whom the defensive force is used is a law enforcement officer, as defined in s. 943.10(14), who enters or attempts to enter a dwelling, residence, or vehicle in the performance of his or her official duties and the officer identified himself or herself in accordance with any applicable law or the person using force knew or reasonably should have known that the person entering or attempting to enter was a law enforcement officer.

(3) A person who is not engaged in an unlawful activity and who is attacked in any other place where he or she has a right to be has no duty to retreat and has the right to stand his or her ground and meet force with force, including deadly force if he or she reasonably believes it is necessary to do so to prevent death or great bodily harm to himself or herself or another or to prevent the commission of a forcible felony.

(4) A person who unlawfully and by force enters or attempts to enter a person's dwelling, residence, or occupied vehicle is presumed to be doing so with the intent to commit an unlawful act involving force or violence.

D. DISTURBING THE PEACE

All states have enacted some version of a crime that can be referred to as "disturbing the peace," but there is considerable variation about what each state considers to be the bedrock elements of this offense. At its simplest, this crime has been defined as words or acts that tend to disturb the peace, or actions that endanger the morals, safety, or health of the community. The closely related offense of "disorderly conduct" is often defined in similar terms. By their very nature both disorderly conduct and disturbing the peace are difficult to define. Because the actions of individuals can vary considerably, police have wide latitude in determining when someone has disturbed the peace or committed disorderly conduct. It is that vagueness of definition that often gets these statutes into trouble with the constitutional interpretation by the Supreme Court. For instance, a statute that defined disorderly conduct as acts that "annoy, disturb, interfere with or obstruct, or are offensive to others" was declared unconstitutional by the United States Supreme Court, specifically because it was too broad in its terms and definitions of what constituted disorderly conduct.

E. PUBLIC FIGHTING

In addition to disturbing the peace or engaging in disorderly conduct, it is a crime to engage in public fighting. This crime is also referred to as "affray." An affray is an old common law offense, based on the understandable need to prevent people from fighting in the streets. In order to have an affray, the state must prove three elements:

1 two or more defendants
2 were fighting
3 in a public place

If a person is acting in self-defense, his or her actions may be excused and no charge of public fighting may be brought. However, self-defense is often in the eye of the beholder, and what one person claims to be self-defense might easily qualify as an aggressive action against another. That is why self-defense must be substantiated by the defendant before it will be excused. Self-defense is discussed in greater detail in Chapter 19.

F. HARASSMENT

The crime of harassment encompasses a wide range of activities. There are statutes that make it a crime to deliberately annoy, threaten, or intimidate a person over a telephone or even through email. Harassment may also lead to the crime of stalking, which was discussed in depth in Chapter 3.

G. THREATS

Although most would readily agree that threatening violence against another person sounds like a crime, it turns out that to charge someone with issuing threats — sometimes called "terroristic threats," although the term has nothing to do with international terrorism — the state must prove several elements that may be difficult to establish. First of all, a threat must usually be coupled with some action. Most people have said regrettable things in the past, and the simple statement "I'm going to kill you" would get many people into trouble with the law if it were taken out of context. If the person who makes a threat couples that with some action, like possessing a weapon, then it may qualify as assault. If the person threatens a specific type of person, such as the president of the United States, then it may be a violation of a federal law. In most instances, a person who is charged with issuing a threat must not only direct the threat to a specific person, but also issue the threat with some commensurate action, such as moving toward the victim in a threatening way. The defendant must also have the apparent ability to carry out the threat. As seen in discussions about assault in Chapter 5, a person who has no ability to carry through on his or her words cannot be prosecuted for assault. Similarly, a prosecution for issuing threats will fail without this element.

Prosecutors benefit if a person uses an electronic device, such as a telephone, to issue a threat, and the threat is heard by someone other than the victim, then the defendant can be charged with making a threat. The theory is that the defendant is more serious in his threat if he or she goes to the trouble of using a device to issue it and is aware that the threat could be overheard by a third party.

H. PUBLIC DRUNKENNESS

In the United States, public drunkenness is outlawed in all 50 states. Police may bring charges against a person who is obviously intoxicated, and these types of arrests are made every day across the nation.

I. CRUELTY TO ANIMALS

All states have legislation criminalizing cruel treatment of pets and also make it illegal to neglect them. Many states specifically prohibit people from torturing animals for pleasure. However, even with these laws, it is not always an easy proposition to prosecute owners for cruelty or abandonment of their animals. The Michael Vick case brought animal cruelty to national attention several years ago, but often these prosecutions do not take lower priority in prosecutors' offices, where there are few enough resources to prosecute individuals who have committed crimes against other human beings, let alone acts of cruelty to animals.

J. TAX CRIMES

According to Benjamin Franklin, there are only two certainties in life: "death and taxes." Failure to pay state or federal income taxes that are due is a crime. On the federal level, the U. S. Treasury Department and the Internal Revenue Service have many tools available to them to punish those people who engage in **tax evasion** — paying less tax than is owed or paying no taxes — and **tax fraud**, deliberately falsifying records to make it appear that a person owes less taxes or no taxes at all. Taxes are a continuing requirement of citizenship, and despite recent movements to dramatically reduce or eliminate them, no doubt they will be with us all for some time to come.

Tax evasion
When a person pays less tax than is legally required.

Tax fraud
Creating false documentation or tax schemes that illegally hide income and reduce some or all of the taxes an individual owes to federal or state governments.

CASE EXCERPT

STATE v. LYLES–GRAY
328 S.C. 458, 492 S.E.2d 802 (1997)

GOOLSBY, Judge:

Henrietta Lyles–Gray was convicted of two counts of common-law obstruction of justice and two counts of official misconduct in office as an officer in the Camden Police Department. Lyles–Gray appeals. We affirm.

FACTS

On the evening of December 2, 1994, Betty Kennedy was working as a security manager at the Belk's store in Camden when she saw two suspicious women, later identified as Renee Lyles and Valerie Drakeford. Drakeford carried an unzipped purse around the store while Lyles carried a shopping bag. The women carried clothing into the fitting rooms without looking at the price tag or size. Kennedy, therefore, suspected the women were shoplifting because of their strange behavior.

While observing Drakeford and Lyles, Kennedy pretended to shop with her daughter Linda. Lyles tossed a sweater into the air, allowing it to drop to the floor; then Lyles placed the sweater into the shopping bag. Lyles and Drakeford were chatting with Niki Hinson, a sales clerk, when Lyles said she needed a checkbook and left to go outside. Kennedy then asked Linda to follow Lyles outside. Linda saw Lyles unlock a blue Ford Escort parked near the store entrance. Lyles placed the bag on the floorboard, locked the car, and returned to the store.

While Lyles was outside, Kennedy asked someone to call the police and asked Stephanie Griffin, a sales manager, for help. Kennedy also asked Hinson to identify the shoplifter. Hinson then identified the woman carrying the shopping bag as Renee Lyles and Valerie Drakeford as her companion.

Linda reported the theft to Sergeant George Waters. When Sergeant Waters arrived at the scene, he shined his flashlight in the Escort and saw the shopping bag on the floorboard. Sergeant Waters waited in his patrol car for the owner of the Escort to leave.

As Drakeford and Lyles left the store, Kennedy followed them outside, identified herself, and asked to look in the car. Sergeant Waters drove his patrol car behind the Escort and blocked it from leaving. Lyles offered to allow Sergeant Waters to search a Hyundai that either Lyles or Drakeford was driving. Lyles denied any knowledge of the Escort. During this conversation, Lyles repeatedly stated, "Let's go. Let's go." Lyles and Drakeford eventually left in the Hyundai.

Sergeant Waters ran a license check on the Escort and learned that Lyles–Gray owned the Escort. Lyles–Gray is Renee Lyles's mother and was at that time a Camden city police officer. Sergeant Waters had the police dispatcher call Lyles–Gray. When Lyles–Gray was on the telephone, Waters asked if a locksmith could open the Escort. Lyles–Gray told Sergeant Waters to "leave it alone." Following this conversation, Sergeant Waters called Chief Jack Cobb at home. After Sergeant Waters explained to Chief Cobb that the evidence was in Lyles–Gray's car, Chief Cobb instructed Sergeant Waters to tell Kennedy that the vehicle belonged to a police officer and that the police officer would take care of it as soon as she got there.

When Sergeant Waters left, Kennedy, Adele Holbrook, and Stephanie Griffin waited for the owner of the Escort. After Griffin and Holbrook went inside, Kennedy saw a light-colored car park beside the Escort. Lyles–Gray got out of that car and unlocked the Escort.

Kennedy testified that when she walked to Lyles–Gray's Escort and tapped on the window, Lyles–Gray ignored her. When Kennedy knocked again, Lyles–Gray asked, "Do you know who I am?" Kennedy identified herself and told Lyles–Gray she believed there was stolen merchandise in the Escort. Lyles–Gray responded, "I'm Henrietta Gray with the Camden City Police Department, and I think not." When Kennedy asked Lyles–Gray for the merchandise, she said, "I think not, lady," and drove away.

Chief Cobb later met with Kennedy and other store personnel at the station. After Kennedy described the incident, Chief Cobb spoke to Lyles–Gray, who told Chief Cobb, "It's my car, I'll drive it anywhere I want to" and "Them [sic] people are crazy, and I'll go up and tell them." Chief Cobb ordered Lyles–Gray to go home and prepare a warrant when she returned to work. Chief Cobb also stated he wanted the merchandise brought to the station. On the following Monday, Lyles–Gray showed Chief Cobb an arrest warrant for Nechelle Drakeford, and he considered the matter closed.

When Kennedy went to the magistrate's office on December 5th to sign several arrest warrants, she saw Drakeford's arrest warrant. The warrant stated what Kennedy observed on that night, including that she observed Drakeford putting the sweater into the shopping bag and later placing it into the Escort. Kennedy, however, testified Lyles–Gray never interviewed her about the case. Kennedy refused to sign the warrant. Kennedy denied seeing Drakeford place the sweater into the Escort as the warrant stated. Moreover, Kennedy identified the shoplifter as Renee Lyles when she reported the crime and denied seeing Nechelle Drakeford in the store.

Kennedy reported the defective arrest warrant to store manager Will Kuhne, who later met with Chief Cobb. Chief Cobb met with Lyles–Gray and Sergeant Herbie Frazier and turned the investigation over to Sergeant Frazier. Chief Cobb also ordered Lyles–Gray to give the evidence to Sergeant Frazier. Sergeant Frazier asked Lyles–Gray for any evidence in her possession, but she never gave the evidence to Sergeant Frazier.

On December 8, 1994, after interviewing the Kennedys and Niki Hinson, Sergeant Frazier charged Renee Lyles with shoplifting. When the case was called to trial in March 1995, however, the assistant solicitor discovered the police did not have the sweater. The solicitor learned that Renee Lyles's attorney, Doug Robinson, had the sweater. Lyles had retained Robinson to represent her in January. Robinson testified that, at the time he agreed to represent Lyles, he learned that Lyles–Gray still had the sweater in her car. Chief Cobb testified that when he asked Lyles–Gray about the sweater, she confirmed she gave it to Attorney Robinson. At Chief Cobb's request, Robinson brought the sweater to the station. Chief Cobb testified he kept the sweater in his desk rather than in the evidence locker because the chain of custody was already broken.

At Chief Cobb's request, SLED [State Law Enforcement Department] agent Alice Shealy investigated Lyles–Gray in her conduct of the shoplifting investigation. Following this investigation, the Kershaw County grand jury indicted Lyles–Gray for obstruction of justice and misconduct in office.

At trial, Nechelle Drakeford stated she stole the sweater from Belk's while shopping with Lyles and Valerie Drakeford. Nechelle Drakeford also stated that she admitted the shoplifting when Lyles–Gray questioned her.

DISCUSSION

I

Under common-law obstruction of justice, "it is an offense to do any act which prevents, obstructs, impedes, or hinders the administration of justice." *State v. Cogdell,* 273 S.C. 563, 567, 257 S.E.2d 748, 750 (1979). Section 16–9–340, codified under article 4 of the criminal code concerning interference with judicial process, provides in pertinent part as follows:

16–9–340. Intimidation of court officials, jurors or witnesses.

(A) It is unlawful for a person by threat or force to:

(1) intimidate or impede a judge, magistrate, juror, witness, or potential juror or witness, arbiter, commissioner, or member of any commission of this State or any other official of any court, in the discharge of his duty as such; or

(2) destroy, impede, or attempt to obstruct or impede the administration of justice in any court.

The two indictments for obstruction of justice do not allege that Lyles–Gray obstructed justice by "threats or force." Moreover, section 16–9–340 principally applies to those acts that use threat or force against court officials and members of administrative agencies. Although the statute codifies "various common law crimes," it does not purport to codify or supersede all of them. Indeed, a person can commit obstruction of justice by use of force or threats; however, such conduct is neither an essential element of, nor the only means of committing, the crime of common-law obstruction of justice.

We, therefore, conclude section 16–9–380 does not prohibit the State's prosecution of Lyles–Gray for conduct amounting to common-law obstruction of justice.

II

Lyles–Gray also argues the trial court erred in denying her motion for a directed verdict. We disagree.

The trial court should grant a directed verdict in a criminal case if evidence fails to raise more than a mere suspicion that the accused is guilty. In reviewing a trial court's refusal to grant a directed verdict, this court must view the evidence in the light most favorable to the state to determine whether there is any direct or any substantial circumstantial evidence that reasonably tends to prove the guilt of the accused or from which guilt may fairly and logically be deduced.

As mentioned above, common-law obstruction of justice is conduct that "prevents, obstructs, impedes or hinders the administration of justice." *Cogdell*, 273 S.C. at 567, 257 S.E.2d at 750. Misconduct in office occurs when persons in public office fail to properly and faithfully discharge a duty imposed by law.

The indictments allege Lyles–Gray obstructed justice and committed misconduct in office because she (1) failed to interview witnesses after Renee Lyles was identified as a suspect, (2) obtained a false arrest warrant for Nechelle Drakeford's arrest, and (3) refused to turn over the sweater to Belk's personnel or the investigating officer.

Lyles–Gray argues she was unaware Renee Lyles was the shoplifting suspect; she attempted to contact Belk's employees after the incident; she did not knowingly refuse to return the evidence to Belk's; and her investigation pointed toward Nechelle Drakeford, rather than her daughter, as the shoplifter.

Renee Lyles testified she drove Lyles–Gray's Escort. Brenda Johnson, George Waters, Sergeant Waters, and Kennedy all testified they informed Lyles–Gray the shoplifter placed stolen goods in her car. Kennedy stated that Lyles–Gray never attempted to contact her before obtaining the warrant for Drakeford's arrest and that Lyles–Gray refused to discuss the stolen goods after the witness identified herself. Chief Cobb testified Lyles–Gray should have interviewed the security personnel when she retrieved her car. Chief Cobb also testified Lyles–Gray should have removed the stolen merchandise from the car when she met with the Belk's employees. Although Chief Cobb ordered Lyles–Gray to give the sweater to Sergeant Frazier, when Sergeant Frazier asked for the sweater, Lyles–Gray "just sort of avoided him and didn't bring it back to him."

These facts should have given Lyles–Gray notice that her daughter was a possible suspect. Finally, Lyles–Gray's conduct at the crime scene and her mishandling of the evidence is circumstantial evidence of her knowledge that her daughter was a suspect.

Although Nechelle Drakeford testified she was the shoplifter, this admission is not dispositive because the trial court is concerned with the existence of evidence and not its weight when deciding a directed verdict motion. Apart from that, the *467 evidence shows Lyles–Gray failed to follow proper investigatory procedures when she refused to cooperate with Kennedy or Frazier after learning that her car contained stolen merchandise from a shoplifting.

We find the State presented sufficient evidence from which a jury can logically conclude Lyles–Gray committed the crimes of obstruction of justice and official misconduct.

AFFIRMED.

CURETON and CONNOR, JJ., concur.

CASE QUESTIONS

1   What activity initially drew the security manager's attention to the women?
2   Why was Lyles–Gray indicted for obstruction of justice and misconduct in office?
3   What is the common law definition of obstruction of justice?
4   What are the incidents of obstruction of justice and misconduct in office that Lyles-Gray was charged with?
5   Did the fact that Drakeford confessed to the shoplifting help Lyles–Gray on her appeal?

CHAPTER SUMMARY

This chapter has shown that there are a wide variety of crimes against public morality and justice. Gambling is paying money for a chance to win something of value. Prostitution is the offer of sex in exchange for money. In the category of crimes against the administration of justice, bribery is offering a public official money, or something else of value, to influence the official's actions. Courts view bribery as a fraud against society in general. When a person tells a deliberate lie while under oath, that is the crime of perjury. This crime usually involves deceit about a material fact, some feature about the case that is so important that changing it would have dire consequences for the parties.

There are various ways for a person to be guilty of obstructing justice. A person who gives false information to the police can be prosecuted for doing so. Similarly, anyone who tampers with evidence in a criminal case can be charged with an offense. One of the most common obstruction of justice offenses is resisting arrest. When a person resists arrest, he or she uses physical force to try to prevent the officer from carrying out a lawful arrest. When a person attempts to influence the outcome of a trial, either by intimidating witnesses or attempting to influence jurors, the person can be charged with witness and jury tampering — felonies in most states.

Riot is another form of crime against the administration of justice. A riot is an act by three or more people that threatens property or persons. The U.S. Supreme Court, in its famous Brandenburg decision, set out a test to determine when a person has crossed the line from speech that is protected by the First Amendment into the realm of incitement to riot. If the speech promotes the destruction of property and is about to cause the destruction of property or danger to people, it is called imminent lawless action and the police may arrest. In recent years, carrying-concealed-weapon cases have come up in a variety of ways, including the Stand Your Ground laws that do not require persons to retreat in a public setting. Finally, failure to pay taxes, or creating false documentation to disguise income, are both federal and state law violations and can result in severe penalties and even prison time.

KEY TERMS

Gambling	Flight	Witness tampering
Prostitution	Resisting arrest	Riot
Bribery	Wiretap	Tax evasion
Perjury	Jury tampering	Tax fraud
Material fact	Embracery	

REVIEW QUESTIONS

1   What are the elements of bribery?
2   Explain the crime of gambling.
3   How does gambling compare to the lottery? Are they the same or different? Explain.
4   What is the Mann Act?
5   What is a "status" offense?
6   What is perjury?
7   Explain the relationship between perjury and material facts.
8   Why is it a crime to give false information to the police?
9   What are some ways that an individual can be charged with obstruction of justice?
10 Explain how flight can be a form of obstruction of justice.
11 Why is there a physical element required in resisting arrest?
12 What is wiretapping?
13 Explain the elements of jury tampering.
14 What are some of the constitutional concerns in prosecuting a person for incitement to riot?
15 What is the *Brandenburg* case and why is it important?
16 Explain "Stand Your Ground" statutes.
17 What is the Castle doctrine?
18 Explain why a defendant must have the apparent ability to carry out an action before he can be charged with making a threat.
19 What is the difference between tax evasion and tax fraud?
20 What is the significance of the Michael Vick case to cases involving animal cruelty?

QUESTIONS FOR ANALYSIS

1   Why shouldn't every misstatement or lie that a witness makes on the stand be subject to a perjury prosecution? Explain your answer.
2   Is there a moral difference between gambling and playing a state lottery? Why or why not?

HYPOTHETICALS

1   A federal agency listens in on citizens' phone calls without a warrant. Under the strict definition of the crime of eavesdropping, can they be prosecuted? Why or why not?

2   Suppose that Z follows T one night. Z is armed. T is not. Z confronts T and they get into a fight. Z shoots T. The state where this occurs has adopted the Stand Your Ground law. Z claims that he was in fear for his life when he shot T. How would this case come out under Stand Your Ground laws? How would it come out in a state that maintained the traditional approach to self-defense (or the "Retreat Doctrine")?

3   M is being questioned by federal agents concerning insider trading by her broker. She knowingly gives false and misleading answers to their questions. Is there a crime or a number of crimes with which she can be charged?

Drug Crimes

11

Chapter Objectives

■ Define what makes a particular drug a "controlled substance"
■ Differentiate between actual possession and constructive possession
■ Explain the elements of possession with intent to distribute controlled substances
■ Describe the impact that alcohol and other drugs have had on society in general
■ Explain how a person can be proven guilty of operating an automobile while under the influence of alcohol or some other drug

I   REGULATING ILLICIT DRUGS

This chapter will examine various crimes associated with drugs. Obviously, not all drug use is illegal, so this text will focus on the situation where controlled substances are used in violation of the law or situations where legal drugs, such as alcohol, are used in such a way that violates the law.

Both the federal and state constitutions give the government power to regulate the use, sale, and possession of narcotics in general and controlled substances in particular.[1] These crimes fall under the jurisdiction of protection of public health, as well as the obligation of the government to provide for the safety and welfare of its citizens.[2] It is important to point out some distinctions in terms before we go any further into a discussion about illegal drugs. Although the term **"narcotic"** is often used to describe an illegal drug, this term covers a broad category of drugs. Rather than use this term, this text will refer to controlled substances. A **controlled substance** is any drug whose use is restricted or forbidden according to state or federal law. Later this chapter will discuss how particular drugs are listed as controlled substances.

Narcotic
A drug that induces sleep, affects the senses, or induces hallucinations.

Controlled substance
Any drug, including narcotics, which is regulated by the government or classified under state or federal Controlled Substances Acts.

---

[1] *Buford v. Com.*, 942 S.W.2d 909 (Ky. Ct. App. 1997).
[2] *Rutherford v. U.S.*, 429 F. Supp. 506 (W.D. Okla. 1977).

Before discussing the particulars of controlled substance offenses, it is important to note that the enforcement of these laws may sometimes come up against constitutional rights. The right of the government to regulate controlled substances can supersede other constitutional protections, such as the First Amendment's guarantee of freedom of religion. Suppose, for example, that a religious group insists that the use of a specific narcotic is part of its religious practices. In such a case, the right of the government to protect the health, safety, and welfare of society will outweigh the rights of the religious group. Consider Scenario 11-1.

SCENARIO 11-1

RELIGIOUS FREEDOM VS. DRUG USE

A local religious group uses the drug cocaine as part of its ceremonies. Will the religious group be allowed to use it by claiming that it falls under the protections of the First Amendment to the U.S. Constitution?

Answer: No. The government has a compelling interest in regulating the use of narcotics, and in this case, the government's interest outweighs the group's freedom of religion claim. However, these results vary, and the government's interest in controlling all drugs does not always outweigh a religious group's practices. In some cases, individual exceptions will be allowed for certain drugs, and the court always balances the government's interest against the rights of the individual group.

DRUG CRIMES

There are many types of drugs in the world, and many of them carry no legal consequences whatsoever. The use of drugs as diverse as aspirin to allergy medication is not regulated under **controlled substances acts**. Instead, those statutes focus on what we might consider the more serious drugs. See Figure 11-1 for a list of the various schedules listed under state and federal controlled substances acts.

Controlled substances acts
State and federal laws that regulate, restrict, or forbid the use of certain types of drugs, usually in the form of schedules that list the drug and the associated penalty.

A. CONTROLLED SUBSTANCES

A controlled substance is what most people would consider an illegal drug. Examples of controlled substances include cocaine, hashish, marijuana, and many others. These are drugs that normally affect a person's mental equilibrium or mood. Some of these drugs cause hallucinations. To regulate (and prosecute) use of these drugs, they have been organized into **schedules**, as mentioned in Figure 11-1. Sentences vary with the type of schedule. As noted, there are five schedules in all. Generally,

Schedules
A list of assorted items, organized under some guiding principle.

---

[3] *Gonzales v. O Centro Espirita Beneficente Uniao Do Vegetal*, 126 S. Ct. 1211, 163 L. Ed. 2d 1017 (U.S. 2006).

FIGURE 11-1

Schedules (DEA listing)[4]

Schedule I Controlled Substances

Substances in this schedule have a high potential for abuse, have no currently accepted medical use in treatment in the United States, and there is a lack of accepted safety for use of the drug or other substance under medical supervision.

Some examples of substances listed in schedule I are: heroin, lysergic acid diethylamide (LSD), marijuana (cannabis), peyote, methaqualone, and 3,4-methylenedioxymethamphetamine ("ecstasy").

Schedule II Controlled Substances

Substances in this schedule have a high potential for abuse which may lead to severe psychological or physical dependence.

Examples of single-entity schedule II narcotics include morphine and opium. Other schedule II narcotic substances and their common name brand products include hydromorphone (Dilaudid), methadone (Dolophine), meperidine (Demerol), oxycodone (OxyContin), and fentanyl (Sublimaze or Duragesic).

Examples of schedule II stimulants include amphetamine (Dexedrine, Adderall), methamphetamine (Desoxyn), and methylphenidate (Ritalin). Other schedule II substances include cocaine, amobarbital, glutethimide, and pentobarbital.

Schedule III Controlled Substances

Substances in this schedule have a potential for abuse less than substances in schedules I or II, and abuse may lead to moderate or low physical dependence or high psychological dependence.

Examples of schedule III narcotics include combination products containing less than 15 milligrams of hydrocodone per dosage unit (Vicodin) and products containing not more than 90 milligrams of codeine per dosage unit (Tylenol with codeine). Also included are buprenorphine products (Suboxone and Subutex) used to treat opioid addiction.

Examples of schedule III non-narcotics include benzphetamine (Didrex), phendimetrazine, ketamine, and anabolic steroids such as oxandrolone (Oxandrin).

Schedule IV Controlled Substances

Substances in this schedule have a low potential for abuse relative to substances in schedule III.
An example of a schedule IV narcotic is propoxyphene (Darvon and Darvocet-N 100).

Other schedule IV substances include alprazolam (Xanax), clonazepam (Klonopin), clorazepate (Tranxene), diazepam (Valium), lorazepam (Ativan), midazolam (Versed), temazepam (Restoril), and triazolam (Halcion).

continued

---

[4] http://www.deadiversion.usdoj.gov/schedules/index.html#list

FIGURE 11-1

Schedules (DEA listing)
(continued)

Schedule V Controlled Substances

Substances in this schedule have a low potential for abuse relative to substances listed in schedule IV and consist primarily of preparations containing limited quantities of certain narcotics. These are generally used for antitussive, antidiarrheal, and analgesic purposes.

Examples include cough preparations containing not more than 200 milligrams of codeine per 100 milliliters or per 100 grams (Robitussin AC and Phenergan with Codeine).

the first and second schedules contain the "hard" drugs, while later schedules contain lesser-known, and less-powerful drugs.

The schedules list the drugs not by their similar chemical makeup, but for their real or imagined potential damage to society and to the individuals who abuse them. As a result, as you can see in Figure 11-1, Schedule I includes LSD, heroin, and marijuana. Although most people would be surprised to find that marijuana is lumped together with LSD and the street drug "ecstasy," the organization has more to do with perceived threat than underlying chemistry.

The government is authorized to regulate such drugs under the police powers granted to it under the federal and state constitutions.[5]

Not all drugs that affect a person's mood are considered to be controlled substances. The effects of tobacco, caffeine, and alcohol on human beings has been seen, but these drugs are not listed in the schedules at all.

PROVING THE DRUG IS A CONTROLLED SUBSTANCE

The government is required to prove that the item recovered from the defendant's possession is a controlled substance. To do this, the suspected drug must be tested. A state crime lab or other agency normally conducts these tests. Experts in drug identification perform several different chemical tests on the suspected drug and can confirm its chemical structure. At trial, this same expert will testify about the tests that were performed and give an opinion that the drug is in fact a controlled substance.

FAMOUS CASES
"FREEWAY" RICKY ROSS

Ricky Donnell Ross didn't intend to become the leader of a drug empire; his early dreams were far more conventional. At Dorsey High School in South Central Los Angeles, he played tennis, hoping to earn a scholarship. The talent was there, but his coach soon realized that Ricky was functionally illiterate and

---

[5] *Employment Div., Dep't of Human Resources v. Smith*, 485 US 660, 108 S Ct 1444. 99 L Ed 2d 753 (1988).

dashed his hopes for college. Nevertheless, a new road opened for him when a teacher at a local job center introduced him to cocaine, and Ricky soon began selling for him. He was good at it, and when he saw how much money he could make, he started his own business.

Ricky invested $125 in his first three grams of cocaine. From there he established himself as one of the largest cocaine dealers in Los Angeles, earning upwards of $2 million a week from the mid-1980s to the mid-1990s. As Ricky's success grew, his clientele expanded beyond the poor people of South Central L.A. to include wealthy, respected members of the community and celebrities from upscale neighborhoods like Beverly Hills. In time the reach of his empire extended throughout the country. Ricky himself invested much of his profits in real estate, including some properties adjacent to an L.A. freeway, thus earning him the nickname "Freeway."

The key to Ricky's phenomenal success in the cocaine industry came from his decision to buy directly from Nicaraguan connections instead of from middlemen. By cutting out the middleman, he could sell his drugs far cheaper than his competition. Furthermore, he offered his customers "smoke ready" crack cocaine that had already been cooked and rendered into rocks. However, after a decade of selling drugs, during which he earned an estimated $600 million, Ricky began to assess the damage that crack was doing to his neighborhood. He knew the dangers of cocaine, and he was adamant that his family and girlfriend not use it. But he was keenly aware that he was selling it to other people's families and loved ones, and the hypocrisy began to wear on him.

He was still selling, though, and both local and federal authorities were determined to take down the so-called King of Crack. Crack cocaine was a plague that ravaged cities across the country, and Ricky was the source of much of it. His arrest came in 1996 for attempting to purchase 100 kilograms of cocaine from an informant. Ricky was convicted of conspiracy, and his initial sentence was life without parole. But a federal appeals court threw that decision out. Ultimately he was sentenced to 20 years, which was further reduced by good behavior. Ricky was released from prison in 2009 after serving 13 years.

What set "Freeway" Ricky Ross apart from other kingpin dealers was the fact that he had a conscience. Most major drug traffickers, such as Manuel Noriega and the Arellano Felix cartel, were obsessed with amassing money and power through their drug empires and gave scant thought to the destruction they wrought. Not Ricky. While in prison he learned to read, and following his release was determined to mitigate some of the damage he had inflicted on the black community.

Today he visits drug rehab programs, where he sometimes sees old customers. He also visits and talks with schoolchildren about the dangers of drugs. Every day he selects a couple of teens from his Los Angeles neighborhood to spend the day working with him at his trucking company. He uses their time together wisely, talking to them about drugs. He hopes that he is planting some healthy seeds that will take root. Unlike most career criminals, Ricky has been both the hero and the villain, and these days he seems far more comfortable in his role as the hero.

POSSESSION OF CONTROLLED SUBSTANCES

Possession (controlled substances)
When a person has unlawful dominion, custody, or control of a controlled substance.

Possessing a controlled substance is a violation of law, whether or not it is being used or intended to be sold to another. A person can also be charged with **possession** of controlled substances by having the component parts of a drug, such as unrefined cocaine, or cocaine "base," or other substances that can be combined into a controlled substance.[6]

Whenever the state brings a charge for illegal possession of a controlled substance, there are two essential elements that the prosecution must prove:

1   That the item recovered was a controlled substance, and
2   That the defendant possessed the controlled substance.[7]

When the drug is in a person's hand, there are no real issues about whether or not she possessed it. Simple possession (or possession solely for the use of the defendant) is a lesser-included offense of possession with intent to distribute. A defendant will often request that the jury be given a jury instruction informing the jurors that they can find the defendant guilty of the lesser crime based on the amount that was in the defendant's possession, especially if the defendant had a small amount and it was not apparently repackaged for sale to others. Obviously, this finding will be based on the facts of the case. The defendant's request for such a jury instruction could have a huge impact on his case. For example, simple possession of a Schedule I drug could result in a maximum 10-year sentence, while possession with intent to resell the same drug could result in a 20-year sentence or even a life sentence.

How do the narcotics statutes define possession? There are a variety of ways. For instance, a person can be in possession of a controlled substance when he:

■ Exercises control and dominion over the controlled substance
■ Has knowledge that the controlled substance is present on or near his person
■ Knows that the drug is a controlled substance
■ Possesses the controlled substance with the intent to sell it to others[8]

Clearly, possession of a drug is easy to prove when it is found in the suspect's hand and the state can prove that the defendant knew that it was a controlled substance. However, the question becomes more complicated when the drug is found in her purse, luggage, or car. As far as the law is concerned, there are two kinds of possession: actual and constructive.

Actual possession
When a person has a controlled substance in or on his person, with full knowledge of what the substance is.

Actual possession refers to the simple act of having a drug in your immediate possession. Holding a drug in your hand or your shirt pocket would constitute actual possession. It is also possession to have the narcotic in your inner or outer clothing or in a container, such as a book bag, purse, etc. When the possession is more removed, the law of constructive possession is triggered.

---

[6] *U.S. v. Clay*, 355 F.3d 1281 (C.A.11Ga., 2004).
[7] *State v. Staley*, 123 Wash. 2d 794, 872 P.2d 502 (1994).
[8] *State v. Salinas*, 181 Ariz. 104, 887 P.2d 985 (1994).

Constructive possession refers to the defendant's custody and control over an item where drugs are found. If the accused happens to be standing by a trash can at the local mall where drugs are recovered, it could hardly be said that she had exclusive custody and control over the trash can. After all, any member of the public could have put an item in that trash can without the suspect knowing it. In order for the government to charge a person with possession of items not found on the person of the accused, the government must show that the item was in the exclusive custody and control of the accused. Consider Scenario 11-2.

> **Constructive possession**
> When a person has a controlled substance inside or contained in some other object over which the defendant has dominion, custody, or control.

WHO IS CHARGED?

SCENARIO 11-2

Police have received information that a man in a hotel room has several kilos of marijuana in his possession and is planning on selling it to others. They execute a search warrant on the room and find three individuals inside. The man to whom the room is registered is taken aside and readily admits that he is in possession of the drug and tells the officers where to find it. The marijuana is cleverly concealed in the bottom of a footlocker belonging to the man who rented the room. Police also arrest the other two individuals and charge them with possession with intent to distribute. Both men deny any knowledge of the other man's possession and say that they were not involved in any conspiracy to sell marijuana. Does the government have enough evidence to charge the other two men with constructive possession?

Answer: No. Because there was no evidence presented that linked the men to the marijuana or any paraphernalia found in the room and nothing that indicated that they knew that the drug was present or even that they were anywhere near the trunk at the time of the arrest, there is nothing under the constructive possession doctrine that will permit them to be convicted.[9]

Proving Constructive Possession. In order to prove the accused guilty of constructive possession of drugs, the government must prove 1) that the accused had knowledge of the presence of the drugs, and 2) the accused exercised custody, control, or dominion over the item. Proving the second item can be as simple as showing that the defendant had exclusive contact with the item or that she owned the item and no one else was permitted to use it. Defendants have been prosecuted for drugs found in luggage, cars, and other items, all under the theory of constructive possession.

CONSTRUCTIVE POSSESSION AND CARS

A driver is pulled over on a routine traffic stop, and the police ask for permission to search the car for drugs. The driver gives permission and narcotics are found. Is this an open and shut case? Not really. The mere fact that the accused was driving a car in which narcotics were found is usually not enough to justify a conviction. The government must prove that the accused had exclusive access to the car or that the

---

[9] *State v. Slaughter*, 718 S.E.2d 362 (N.C. 2011).

car was her property. Showing that the car belonged to the accused raises a presumption that the accused owned the drugs, but not in all jurisdictions. In order to deal with this situation, or where several people are in the car when it is pulled over, courts have developed various tests to justify the driver's conviction for possession. The court will often ask: Were the narcotics in "plain view"? Were the drugs found in the defendant's personal effects? Were the drugs found in close proximity to the defendant? Is the accused the owner of the car? Did the defendant act in a suspicious manner? If the answer to all of these questions is yes, then the defendant can be convicted of possession. In many states, statutes provide a presumption that the persons in a car where a controlled substance is found are all in possession of it. Some states have a **"car owner's presumption"** that states that the owner of the vehicle is presumed to be in possession of anything found in the car, with certain exceptions, although there are also states that do not make this presumption. Instead, these states may presume that everyone in the car is in possession of the controlled substance.

In many states, the owner and operator of an automobile is presumed to be in possession of any contraband drugs found in it.[10] The idea is that the owner or operator is in the best position to know what is being transported in the car. However, not all states impose this presumption.[11] Those states must show that the owner or operator has some connection with the controlled substances, such as the drugs being in plain view, in the personal effects of the operator, or recovered from an area of the car that only the operator could access, like a locked glove compartment.[12]

POSSESSION OF DRUG PARAPHERNALIA

Both state and federal law make it illegal to sell **drug paraphernalia**. Defining drug paraphernalia has been an ongoing challenge. Originally, the term was limited to items such as pipes and bongs that could be used to smoke marijuana or needles that could be used to inject narcotics. However, the creativity of drug users and those who wish to sell to them is almost endless and the term has gradually expanded to include a wide variety of items, including:

- Metal, wooden, acrylic, glass, stone, plastic, or ceramic pipes with or without screens, permanent screens, hashish heads, or punctured metal bowls;
- Water pipes;
- Carburetion tubes and devices;
- Smoking and carburetion masks;
- Roach clips: meaning objects used to hold burning material, such as a marijuana cigarette, that has become too small or too short to be held in the hand;
- Miniature spoons with level capacities of one-tenth cubic centimeter or less;

Car owner's presumption
A legal presumption that the owner or operator of an automobile has knowledge and is in possession of any items that are recovered from the automobile at the time he or she was driving it.

> **Sidebar**
>
> *To establish constructive possession, the state must prove that there is some connection between the controlled substance and the defendant. Without that proof, the defendant cannot be convicted of possession of a controlled substance.*[13]

Drug paraphernalia
Any item that can be used to inhale, consume, inject, or imbibe a controlled substance.

[10] *Pittman v. State*, 208 Ga. App. 211, 430 S.E.2d 141 (1993).
[11] *State v. Harris*, 807 S.W.2d 528 (Mo. Ct. App. W.D. 1991).
[12] *State v. Abbott*, 277 Kan. 161, 83 P.3d 794 (2004).
[13] *O'Neill v. State*, 285 Ga. 125, 674 S.E.2d 302 (2009).

- Chamber pipes;
- Carburetor pipes;
- Electric pipes;
- Air-driven pipes;
- Chillums;
- Bongs;
- Ice pipes or chillers;
- Wired cigarette papers; or
- Cocaine freebase kits[14]

SALE OF CONTROLLED SUBSTANCES

Sale of a controlled substance is illegal. States have set up a sliding scale of punishments that can be imposed on a defendant, all of them depending on the amount of drug that he or she sells to another (see Figure 11-2). In these prosecutions, the state must prove, beyond a reasonable doubt, the exact weight of the substance. To do this, the state will call an expert — usually the person at the crime lab who actually carried out the weighing procedure. The prosecutor will ask the technician how he or she went through the process of weighing the drug in question and how the exact weight was determined. The general rule is that the greater the amount, the more severe the sentence.

Suppose that a person merely acts as a go-between, arranging a willing buyer and a willing drug seller? Can that person be charged with sale of controlled substances? The answer is yes.[15]

In some jurisdictions, a person is guilty of differing degrees of a sale of a controlled substance based on the weight of the mixture sold during a specified time period, and in such circumstances, the weight of the mixture is an essential element of the offense and must be proven by the state beyond a reasonable doubt.

The word "sell" often becomes an issue in drug cases. It is obvious that a sale has occurred when a defendant exchanges money for the drug, but what about situations where the defendant trades the drug for something else of value? To address this issue, all states have inserted language in their sale-of-controlled-substances legislation which makes it a crime to do any of the following with controlled substances:

- Sell
- Give away
- Exchange for something else of value
- Barter[16]
- Exchange for sexual favors[17]

> **Sale (controlled substance)**
> To exchange a controlled substance for cash or something else of value.

---

[14] 21 USC § 863.

[15] *Haywood v. State*, 562 So. 2d 297 (Ala. Crim. App. 1990); *Pidkameny v. State*, 569 So. 2d 908 (Fla. Dist. Ct. App. 5th Dist. 1990).

[16] *State v. Robinson*, 517 N.W.2d 336 (Minn. 1994).

[17] *State v. Varner*, 643 N.W.2d 298 (Minn. 2002).

FIGURE 11-2

Sample Statute — Trafficking in Cocaine, Illegal Drugs, Marijuana, or Methamphetamine: Penalties

(a)(1) Any person who knowingly sells, manufactures, delivers, or brings into this state or who is knowingly in possession of 28 grams or more of cocaine or of any mixture with a purity of 10 percent or more of cocaine, as described in Schedule II, in violation of this article commits the felony offense of trafficking in cocaine and, upon conviction thereof, shall be punished as follows:

(A) If the quantity of the cocaine or the mixture involved is 28 grams or more, but less than 200 grams, the person shall be sentenced to a mandatory minimum term of imprisonment of ten years and shall pay a fine of $200,000.00;

(B) If the quantity of the cocaine or the mixture involved is 200 grams or more, but less than 400 grams, the person shall be sentenced to a mandatory minimum term of imprisonment of 15 years and shall pay a fine of $300,000.00; and

(C) If the quantity of the cocaine or the mixture involved is 400 grams or more, the person shall be sentenced to a mandatory minimum term of imprisonment of 25 years and shall pay a fine of $1 million.

(2) Any person who knowingly sells, manufactures, delivers, or brings into this state or who is knowingly in possession of any mixture with a purity of less than 10 percent of cocaine, as described in Schedule II, in violation of this article commits the felony offense of trafficking in cocaine if the total weight of the mixture multiplied by the percentage of cocaine contained in the mixture exceeds any of the quantities of cocaine specified in paragraph (1) of this subsection. Upon conviction thereof, such person shall be punished as provided in paragraph (1) of this subsection depending upon the quantity of cocaine such person is charged with knowingly selling, manufacturing, delivering, or bringing into this state or knowingly possessing.[18]

Sale on or Near School Grounds. In addition to making the sale of a controlled substance illegal, both state and federal jurisdictions have made it illegal to sell controlled substances in certain areas, for example in or near a school ground. Many states follow the model set out in Figure 11-3, which enhances the punishment for sale of a controlled substance when it occurs on school grounds. Some states go so far as to make it an additional crime to sell a controlled substance within 1,000 feet of a school ground or school zone.

POSSESSION WITH INTENT TO SELL

Most jurisdictions provide enhanced sentences for individuals who possess items with the clear intent of reselling them. Possession with intent to sell can be shown by the amount of the drug in the defendant's possession. For instance, if the defendant has numerous small packages in her possession, it may indicate that the accused is in the business of selling drugs. Other indicators include might be that the defendant had a large amount of small bills on her person, or that the amount

---

[18] O.C.G.A.§ 16-13-31.

FIGURE 11-3

Criminal Sale of a
Controlled Substance in
or near School Grounds

A person is guilty of criminal sale of a controlled substance in or near school grounds when he knowingly and unlawfully sells:

1. a controlled substance in violation of any one of subdivisions one through six-a of section 220.34 of this article, when such sale takes place upon school grounds; or

2. a controlled substance in violation of any one of subdivisions one through eight of section 220.39 of this article, when such sale takes place upon school grounds; or

3. a controlled substance in violation of any one of subdivisions one through six of section 220.34 of this article, when such sale takes place upon the grounds of a child day care or educational facility under circumstances evincing knowledge by the defendant that such sale is taking place upon such grounds; or

4. a controlled substance in violation of any one of subdivisions one through eight of section 220.39 of this article, when such sale takes place upon the grounds of a child day care or educational facility under circumstances evincing knowledge by the defendant that such sale is taking place upon such grounds.[19]

of drugs in her possession was more than a person would have for personal use.[20]

A person can also be guilty of possession with intent to distribute even if he or she does not actually sell the drug, but offers it to friends.[22] The important factor in a prosecution for possession with intent to distribute is the amount in the defendant's possession and the way that it is packaged. Consider Scenario 11-3.

Sidebar

It is illegal for a person to manufacture, distribute, or sell a controlled substance.[21]

DISTRIBUTION?

SCENARIO 11-3

Mel, a local drug dealer, meets Shelly and offers her one of his "packages." This package consists of a small amount of cocaine. Shelly accepts the package and both are immediately arrested. Has Mel "distributed" a controlled substance under the definition of the statute?

Answer: Yes. Sharing a controlled substance is the same as selling it or offering it for trade, and Mel can be convicted under the statute.[23]

In an era when methamphetamine has become the drug of choice for some, individuals will set up "meth labs" inside their homes or other areas. Because creating methamphetamine requires several chemical combinations, there are

---

[19] NY St. Ann § 220.44.
[20] *U.S. v. Andrade*, 94 F.3d 9 (1st Cir. 1996).
[21] 21 U.S.C.A. § 841(b).
[22] *U.S. v. Wallace*, 532 F.3d 126 (2d Cir. 2008).
[23] *U.S. v. Wallace*, 532 F.3d 126 (2d Cir. 2008).

statutes that allow the state to bring charges against an individual for bringing together the various ingredients to create the drug, such as anhydrous ammonia — a critical component in manufacturing methamphetamine.[24]

DRIVING UNDER THE INFLUENCE

Operating a motor vehicle while under the influence of alcohol is a crime in all states. In previous decades, this crime was often considered harmless, but since the late 1980s, both public perception and judicial temperament have changed dramatically. Among the changes are mandatory jail terms for repeat offenders, community service requirements for all offenders, a lowering of the "legal limit" from .12 to .10 or .08 percent, and even provisions for publishing the pictures of convicted drunk drivers in local newspapers. **Driving under the influence** (DUI) is now treated as a serious offense, and this attitude has begun to permeate throughout society, with individuals realizing, even when they are inebriated, that the dangers of drunk driving, and the chances of arrest, are simply not worth the risk.

Driving under the influence
A charge that can be brought against a driver for operating a motor vehicle with greater than a certain percent of blood-alcohol or operating a vehicle under the influence to the extent that the driver is a threat to others; often abbreviated DUI or DWI (driving while intoxicated).

A. BRINGING A DUI CASE

Persons can be charged with DUI or DWI if they are found to be operating a motor vehicle with more than a certain percent of blood alcohol in their systems. This is true whether they are driving erratically or are driving as safely as a non-intoxicated person. Simply having this blood-alcohol level is enough to be guilty of the crime. However, there is a second way that a person can be charged with DUI: They can be a less safe driver.

LESS SAFE DRIVER

A person may be charged for operating a motor vehicle with greater than a certain baseline blood-alcohol level (which can be as low as .04 grams/percent for commercial truck drivers). Drivers can also be charged for being a less safe driver, no matter how much alcohol they have in their systems. Being a less safe driver can be charged as an alternative to operating with a certain blood-alcohol level or can be charged in addition to the first charge. In many cases, a defendant is often surprised to find that he or she has been charged with two different types of DUI or DWI. However, when the case is resolved, a defendant can only be sentenced under one offense. Consider Scenario 11-4.

---

[24] *Nash v. Com.*, 2008 WL 465198 (Ky. Ct. App. 2008).

GUILTY OF A SLOW METABOLISM?

Carl was out drinking last night with friends and doesn't think that he had too much to drink, but actually suffers from a metabolic condition that prevents his body from metabolizing alcohol at a normal rate. In fact, he metabolizes alcohol much more slowly than most people. This means that any alcohol that he consumes remains in his system longer than it does for most people. He is not committing a traffic offense when he is driving, but an officer following behind notices that his license tag is expired. When the officer pulls Carl over, he smells alcohol on Carl's breath. Although it is 9:00 a.m., the officer suspects that Carl is operating under the influence. He has Carl take a breath test and the results are .11 grams/percent. Carl is then arrested for Driving Under the Influence. Does he have a valid defense because his body does not metabolize alcohol and that he wasn't doing anything dangerous at the time that he was stopped?

Answer: No. Because he voluntarily consumed alcohol the night before, even though his metabolism is different, and even though he was not driving in a less safe manner, he is still guilty of the crime.

Why would the state charge a defendant as a less safe driver when it can simply charge a person with DUI or DWI based on blood-alcohol levels? The answer is simple: If the breath or blood test given to the defendant turns out to be defective in some manner, the prosecution can still proceed on the second charge — assuming that the defendant exhibited some form of unsafe driving before he or she was arrested.

B. PROVING DUI OR DWI

One of the problems that police have when pulling an individual over for suspected drunken driving is establishing that the person is, in fact, intoxicated. Erratic driving could be the product of alcohol, but it could also be the product of fatigue or other problems. **Roadside sobriety tests** help the officer establish whether or not the person is operating under the influence of alcohol or some other drug.

Roadside sobriety tests
A series of physical evaluations to test a person's responses, balance, and verbal abilities in order to determine if the person is under the influence of alcohol or some other drug.

ROADSIDE SOBRIETY TESTS

When a police officer suspects that a person is operating under the influence of alcohol or some other drug, the officer can request the driver to submit to roadside field sobriety tests. These evaluations are well known and are often portrayed on television and in movies. They include the famous "walk a straight line" and "touch finger to nose" as well as repeating the alphabet for the officer. Though not definitive proof, these tests are designed to give the officer a better indication that the person is operating a vehicle while intoxicated. No single test is determinative of alcohol or other drug use, but taken together they can form a fairly accurate picture that the driver is under the influence, as opposed to simply being tired or having some other difficulty.

IMPLIED CONSENT

Implied consent
A legal doctrine that provides that when a driver is issued a driver's license under state law, he or she has given consent in advance to any officer who requests a blood or breath test.

All states have passed **implied consent** statutes. These statutes declare that a driver has already given consent for a blood or breath test simply by receiving a license. When a driver is pulled over and the officer suspects that the driver may be operating under the influence, she can request that the driver submit to a test. If the driver refuses, his driver's license can be revoked under the provisions of the implied consent law.

BLOOD AND BREATH TESTS

A police officer can request either a blood or a breath test. In most cases, when an officer suspects that the driver has been drinking, a breath test will be requested. A breath test machine — there are numerous brands available to law enforcement — takes a breath sample from the defendant and compares it to a known sample stored inside the machine. The comparison results in a fairly accurate representation of the defendant's current blood-alcohol level. However, if the defendant is operating under the influence of some other drug, a breath test will not be effective. There are no current breath test machines that can test for drugs such as cocaine or marijuana. In those cases, the defendant's blood must be drawn. When the officer suspects that the defendant is operating under the influence of some drug other than alcohol, the suspect is transported to a local hospital or some facility authorized to draw blood, and a sample is taken that will later be submitted to the crime lab for analysis.

CASE EXCERPT

O'NEILL v. STATE
285 Ga. 125, 674 S.E.2d 302 (2009)

HUNSTEIN, Presiding Justice.

We granted Brian O'Neill's petition for writ of certiorari to review whether the Court of Appeals erred by finding the evidence was sufficient to uphold O'Neill's conviction for possession of methamphetamine. Because the Court of Appeals improperly relied on a statement by O'Neill's co-conspirator that was not admissible against O'Neill pursuant to OCGA § 24-3-52 and the admissible evidence in the record failed to exclude every other reasonable hypothesis except the guilt of the accused, OCGA § 24-4-6, we reverse.

The law is well-established that "to warrant a conviction based on circumstantial evidence, the State must prove not only that the evidence is consistent with the hypothesis of guilt, but that every other reasonable hypothesis of nonguilt is excluded." *Carr v. State*, 251 Ga.App. 117, 118(1), 553 S.E.2d 674 (2001).

"When the circumstantial evidence supports more than one theory, one consistent with guilt and another with innocence, it does not exclude every other reasonable hypothesis except guilt and is not sufficient to prove the defendant's guilt beyond a reasonable doubt. Circumstantial evidence is worth nothing in a criminal case, if the circumstances are reasonably consistent with the hypothesis of innocence, as well as the hypothesis of guilt. *Johnson v. State*, 159 Ga.App. 497, 499, 283 S.E.2d 711 (1981).

The evidence in this case established that law enforcement officers, acting on information obtained after a drug arrest, knocked on a motel room in Stapleton. Three men were in the room: Bryant, who answered the door; Horton, who had rented the room and was awake on the bed; and O'Neill, who was passed out on the bed. Bryant admitted the officers into the room. Because the first officer saw several knives, including one within a few feet of O'Neill's hand, the officers asked Horton and O'Neill to get off the bed. When Horton complied, officers saw on the bed an ashtray containing two glass pipes of a type used for smoking methamphetamine. In response to seeing the pipes, the officers placed all three men in handcuffs and searched them. O'Neill was difficult to rouse and so "out of it" that he had to be "sat up" while the officers searched him. Nothing incriminating was found on O'Neill. However, after a packet with suspected methamphetamine in it was found in Horton's front pocket, the officers searched other containers in the room. Boxes claimed by Bryant and Horton were found to contain methamphetamine and other illegal drugs. Additionally, a ring-sized jewelry box containing 2.8 grams of methamphetamine was found "close to O'Neill . . . between where O'Neill and Horton were laying [sic] on the bed."

In regard to the charge against O'Neill, the Court of Appeals upheld his conviction for possession of methamphetamine relying on three evidentiary items: O'Neill's unconscious condition on the bed in the motel room; his proximity to the jewelry box and glass pipes on the bed; and a statement Bryant or Horton made to a law enforcement officer "attributing O'Neill's unconscious state to the fact that he was having marital problems and had been drinking or smoking the entire night." *Bryant v. State*, supra, 288 Ga.App. at 868(2), 655 S.E.2d 707. However, for the reasons that follow, we find that the last item was inadmissible as evidence against O'Neill and the remaining items failed to exclude the reasonable hypothesis that O'Neill had no knowledge of and did not possess the methamphetamine in the jewelry box, inasmuch as his physical condition was due to excessive alcohol consumption or other legal means and the methamphetamine in the jewelry box and the pipes was possessed and smoked by Bryant and/or Horton.

Turning first to the "drinking or smoking" statement, OCGA § 24-3-52 expressly provides that "the confession of one joint offender or conspirator made after the enterprise is ended shall be admissible only against himself. A conspirator's post-arrest statement to police incriminating a co-conspirator terminates the conspiracy, rendering the statement admissible only against the declarant." *Fetty v. State*, 268 Ga. 365, 371(7), 489 S.E.2d 813 (1997). The evidence establishes that the officers took Horton and Bryant into custody upon spotting the glass pipes on the bed, at a time when the officers did not know whether O'Neill was actually sleeping or just "playing possum." The "drinking or smoking" statement to the officers came as the officers struggled to search and handcuff the unresponsive O'Neill, i.e., after the defendants had been taken into custody. Thus, whether the incriminating statement was made by Horton or Bryant, it was made after the conspiracy was terminated and, pursuant to OCGA § 24-3-52, was admissible only against the declarant. The Court of Appeals erred by considering this statement as evidence against O'Neill in assessing the sufficiency of the evidence to support his conviction.

Moreover, even if consideration of this statement were not precluded by OCGA § 24-3-52, the statement positively supports a reasonable hypothesis other than O'Neill's guilt. The officer's testimony is that Bryant or Horton claimed that O'Neill "had been either drinking or smoking the entire night." The use of the disjunctive "or" provides a reasonable alternative to explain O'Neill's condition so as to indicate that he may have passed out as a result of "drinking . . . the entire night."

The Court of Appeals also relied upon evidence of O'Neill's condition even though no evidence was introduced that his unconscious state was the result of smoking methamphetamine. The State introduced no evidence of any laboratory test results that may have been conducted to prove the presence of methamphetamine in O'Neill's body. No expert testimony was introduced regarding the effects of methamphetamine and none of the law enforcement officers testified that O'Neill's condition appeared consistent with that of a person under the influence of methamphetamine. Nor was any evidence introduced that excluded the possibility that O'Neill was passed out on the bed for a reason unrelated to methamphetamine, such as from an excessive consumption of alcohol. Not one of the three officers and two co-defendants who testified was asked about the presence or absence of any alcohol containers in the room or the presence or absence of any smell of alcohol on O'Neill. Under these circumstances, the fact that O'Neill was "passed out" on the bed could not establish that he had smoked methamphetamine as this fact did not exclude the reasonable possibility that O'Neill's condition resulted from alcohol intoxication, exhaustion or the ingestion of some legal substance, rather than methamphetamine.

O'Neill's conviction cannot be sustained by his proximity to the jewelry box containing methamphetamine and the glass pipes used for smoking the drug found on the bed between where he and Horton were lying. As to the jewelry box, the record reflects the complete absence of evidence that O'Neill made any claim to or exerted any dominion or control over the box. See *Lockwood v. State*, 257 Ga. 796, 797, 364 S.E.2d 574 (1988) (constructive possession shown where person has "both the power and the intention at a given time to exercise dominion or control over a thing"). It is well established that a finding of constructive possession must be based upon some connection between the defendant and the contraband other than mere spatial proximity. *Mitchell v. State*, 268 Ga. 592, 492 S.E.2d 204 (1997). The three officers who testified were never questioned whether they had asked Horton and Bryant about their possible ownership of the jewelry box. Although both Horton and Bryant testified and variously claimed ownership of other containers in the room, neither defense counsel on direct nor the prosecutor during his cross-examination asked either of them about the jewelry box. In the absence of any denial of ownership, the evidence did not exclude the reasonable hypothesis that the jewelry box belonged to either Bryant or Horton, who had equal access to it and who, unlike O'Neill, were found with methamphetamine either on their person or in their belongings.

As to the two glass pipes, the State introduced no evidence of any laboratory test results that may have been conducted to prove O'Neill used either of the pipes or, as noted earlier, to prove the presence of methamphetamine in his body. Nor was there any evidence regarding where Bryant had been located in the motel room in relation to the glass pipes before he went to answer the door to the officers' knock so as to indicate he lacked equal access to the pipes. Given that there were three men in the room and only two glass pipes, the evidence adduced failed to exclude the reasonable possibility that only Bryant and Horton smoked the pipes.

Davis v. State, 270 Ga.App. 777(1), 607 S.E.2d 924 (2004), cited by the Court of Appeals, does not support its affirmance of O'Neill's conviction based on his "joint possession" of the methamphetamine with Horton and Bryant because, in that case, the persons convicted were all conscious when police officers found them in possession of contraband. There may exist factual situations where possession of contraband can be established notwithstanding the defendant's unconscious or asleep condition at the time the contraband was found by police, e.g., *Combs v. State*, 271 Ga.App. 276, 609 S.E.2d 198 (2005) (conviction for possession of methamphetamine upheld where defendant found unconscious in driver's seat of parked vehicle with drug paraphernalia in lap); *United States v. Tyler*, 2006 WL 334212, 2006 U.S. Dist. LEXIS 5348 (M.D.Fla., February 13, 2006) (although defendant was unconscious when police found him in car with cocaine and firearm, fact that defendant's car was running, transmission was in drive and doors locked supported conclusion that defendant had recently and consciously transported firearm and cocaine so as to sustain convictions). In the instant case, however, where there is only O'Neill's spatial proximity to the contraband, with nothing more to show his participation in any illegal act, and where there are two co-defendants who had equal access to the contraband and equal opportunity to possess it, the proved facts failed to exclude every other reasonable hypothesis save that of O'Neill's guilt. OCGA § 24-4-6.

Accordingly, we reverse the Court of Appeals' affirmance of O'Neill's conviction for possession of methamphetamine.

Judgment reversed.

---

1 What is the rule about basing a conviction on circumstantial evidence as set out by the court in this case?
2 What condition was O'Neill in when the officers entered the motel room?
3 What evidence did the court of appeals rely on to uphold O'Neill's conviction?
4 Why couldn't the court rely on the constructive possession doctrine to find that O'Neill was guilty?
5 What would have been better proof of the defendant's constructive possession, according to the court?

CASE QUESTIONS

CHAPTER SUMMARY

In this chapter, we have seen that certain drugs are considered to be controlled substances, and their use is tightly restricted and even forbidden, depending on the type of drug. A controlled substance is any drug that is considered to be dangerous and addictive. Some controlled substances can be legally purchased through a pharmacist, while others, like cocaine and heroin, cannot be legally purchased anywhere in the United States. When it comes to prosecuting controlled substance cases, prosecutors often look to the surrounding circumstances to determine whether a person possessed a drug or was engaged in selling it. The difference is that a person will receive a higher sentence for selling a controlled substance than simply possessing it. A person can have actual possession of a controlled substance by having it in his or her dominion, custody, or control. A person can also be guilty of possessing a controlled substance when he or she has constructive possession. Under the doctrine of constructive possession, a person can be guilty of possession when he or she has control over an item that contains a controlled substance, even though the drug is not on the suspect's person. Constructive possession cases are often a feature when a person is pulled over in an automobile and a subsequent search reveals that there are controlled substances inside the vehicle. Some, but not all states, impose a duty on the driver that presumes he or she is in possession of the items recovered in the car.

In addition to possession of controlled of substances, it also illegal to possess drug paraphernalia or items that enable a user to engage in drug use. A person can be charged with possession with intent to distribute controlled substances. In this scenario, a suspect has several drugs, packaged for resale. The significance of this charge is that it carries the heaviest penalty because it is aimed at drug dealers.

Besides charges involving controlled substances, drug crimes also include driving under the influence of alcohol or other drug. If a person operates an automobile with greater than a specific amount of blood-alcohol level or while under the influence of some other drug, the person can be charged with driving under the influence, also known as driving while intoxicated. When a driver is suspected of operating a vehicle under the influence of alcohol or some other drug, a police officer is authorized to request a breath or blood test. Implied consent laws in all states provide that as a condition of receiving a driver's license, all drivers have consented to giving a breath or blood test when requested by law enforcement.

KEY TERMS

Narcotic	Possession	Sale
Controlled substance	Actual possession	Driving Under the
Controlled Substances	Constructive possession	Influence
Acts	Car owner's presumption	Roadside sobriety tests
Schedules	Drug paraphernalia	Implied consent

REVIEW QUESTIONS

1 What is a controlled substance?
2 What is the difference between a controlled substance and a narcotic?

3   How do constitutional rights, such as the First Amendment, impact the enforcement of controlled substances crimes?

4   In what schedule would you find cocaine?

5   What are schedules, and why are they important?

6   How does the prosecution prove that a drug is a controlled substance?

7   When and how is expert testimony used in drug prosecutions?

8   How do the statutes define possession of controlled substances?

9   What is possession with intent to distribute under controlled substances laws?

10 What is the difference between actual possession and constructive possession?

11 What is the rule about constructive possession and automobiles?

12 What is the "car owner's presumption"?

13 What is drug paraphernalia?

14 What are some other methods that drugs can be "sold" other than simply exchanging a controlled substance for cash?

15 What is the difference between "possession" of a controlled substance and "possession with intent to distribute"?

16 What are the two ways that a driver can be charged with DUI or DWI?

17 What are roadside sobriety tests?

18 What is implied consent?

QUESTIONS FOR ANALYSIS

1   Many people have called for the legalization of so-called "hard drugs" like cocaine and heroin. Is there a valid argument for this approach? Create one and justify the position.

2   Have stiffer penalties in DUI and DWI cases actually resulted in a change of behavior of people who are intoxicated and have the ability to drive their cars to another location? Why or why not?

HYPOTHETICALS

1   Sal acts as a go-between for Mary and John. Mary wishes to sell 50 kilos of cocaine to John. Sal will receive 10 percent of the sale price for putting the parties together. He never actually handles either the cocaine or the money that John carries. Can he be charged with sale of a controlled substance? Should he be? Why or why not?

2   Mary approaches Theo and offers to sell him one ounce of marijuana in exchange for his motorcycle. When she is charged with sale of a controlled substance, she claims that Theo was simply giving her the motorcycle as a gift and that she was giving Theo the marijuana as a gift. Can she be prosecuted for sale of a controlled substance?

3   Sal is arrested for driving under the influence of alcohol. The officer pulled Sal over because his license plate light was not working, and when she began speaking with Sal, she smelled alcohol on his breath. Sal performed some of the roadside tests well, but did not complete the recitation of the alphabet and was unable to touch his index finger to his nose. When Sal is given a breath test, the result is .08. At trial, Sal argues that he was not a less safe driver because there was no indication that he was dangerous to anyone. He asks the jury to acquit him. You are a juror in this case. How do you vote and why?

Introduction to Criminal Procedure

Chapter Objectives

■ Define when a person is considered to be under arrest
■ Explain the concept of probable cause
■ Describe the purpose of initial appearance and probable cause hearings
■ Explain the purpose of the grand jury
■ Describe the importance of sentencing and appeals

I. INTRODUCTION TO CRIMINAL PROCEDURE

This chapter will examine the basic steps involved in bringing a prosecution, from arrest, search, and seizure, through the charging decision and the grand jury presentation. It will also provide a sketch of the trial process and what occurs during sentencing and appeal. All of these topics will be examined in detail in succeeding chapters, but it is important to provide a framework here that sets the stage for the material that comes in the second half of this text.

II. ARREST

In almost all situations, a criminal case begins with an **arrest**. To arrest someone is to detain a person suspected of committing a crime. Only law enforcement officers are empowered to make arrests. But what is the legal definition of arrest?

To arrest a person is to place him in custody and prevent him from leaving the area. When a person is under arrest, he or she is often physically restrained and the person's liberty is taken away. The suspect is also handcuffed or restrained in some other way.

Arrest
Detention and restraint of a suspect by a law enforcement official; a person who is under arrest is not free to leave.

Later chapters will examine all of the aspects of when and under what circumstances a person is under arrest, but determining the precise point when a person is considered to be under arrest has important constitutional law consequences. A person who is under arrest has the right to an attorney, the right to petition for bond, the right to be told about the charges against him, and the right to remain silent, among many others. When a suspect is under arrest, any statement that he or she makes can be used against him. Consider Scenario 12-1.

SCENARIO 12-1

ARREST?

Mike calls the local police after he finds that his roommate, who is currently away, has a substantial amount of cash and what appears to be marijuana hidden under the kitchen sink. The officer who takes the call tells Mike that based on what he has told him, his roommate should be placed under arrest and should surrender himself at the police station. The officer tells Mike to relay this information to his friend. Is the roommate under arrest?

Answer: No. A police officer must personally interact with a suspect to arrest him or her. There is no such thing as a telephonically relayed arrest.

A. ARREST AND PROBABLE CAUSE

Probable cause
The constitutional requirement that law enforcement officers have reasonable belief that a person has committed a crime.

In order for an arrest to be legally valid, it must be supported by **probable cause**. The Fourth Amendment requires that when a suspect is placed under arrest, the officer making that arrest must have probable cause to believe that the person committed a crime (see Figure 12-1).

If we were called upon to come up with the simplest definition of probable cause, we might rely on how courts have defined it. According to numerous court decisions, probable cause refers to the reasonable belief that the suspect has committed a crime. An officer must have probable cause before arresting a suspect and cannot wait to develop facts later that justify the initial arrest. The existence of probable cause to arrest is based on objective standards and is determined from the viewpoint of what a prudent person would believe when presented with the same facts and circumstances as the officer. If a hypothetical, reasonable person would believe, based on the facts presented, that the suspect had committed a crime, then a police officer would also have probable cause and can make an arrest. The Fourth Amendment was written in such a way as to make sure that officers could not arrest anyone on a whim or on a "gut feeling." Consider Scenario 12-2.

Sidebar

Probable cause, in its simplest form, refers to the objective evidence that a crime has been or is about to be committed.

FIGURE 12-1

Fourth Amendment to the U.S. Constitution

The right of the people to be secure in their persons, houses, papers, and effects, against unreasonable searches and seizures, shall not be violated, and no Warrants shall issue, but upon probable cause, supported by Oath or affirmation, and particularly describing the place to be searched, and the persons or things to be seized

HUNCHES

Officer John Doe is on patrol one evening and sees a car being driven by an African American male. Officer Doe is familiar with this area of town and knows that very few African Americans live in this area. He pulls the man over and arrests him. Does he have probable cause?

Answer: No. It is not a crime to be an African American in a car driving through a predominately white neighborhood, and without additional evidence, there is no probable cause for the arrest.

FAMOUS CASES
PATTY HEARST

Patricia Campbell Hearst grew up in an affluent environment, daughter of media magnate Randolph A. Hearst and heiress to his fortune. Patty Hearst was also the victim of a violent kidnapping who subsequently participated in a bank robbery.

In 1974 Hearst was 19 years old and living with her fiancé, Steven Weed, in a Berkeley, California, townhouse. On the night of February 4, members of a left-wing guerilla group called the Symbionese Liberation Army (SLA) broke into the townhouse, brutally beat Weed, and dragged a screaming Hearst from the house at gunpoint, shoving her into the trunk of a car and taking her to a hideout in South San Francisco.

The SLA tried to swap Hearst for jailed members of the group, but authorities refused. When that failed, the SLA then demanded that the Hearst family distribute millions of dollars of food to needy Californians. Randolph Hearst immediately arranged to distribute more than $6 million of food to poor people in the Bay Area. Nevertheless, the SLA deemed the food to be of poor quality and refused to release their captive.

Meanwhile, Hearst was being held in a locked closet, subjected to the group's philosophical rants, physical abuse, and rape. The leader of the SLA, Donald "Cinque" De Freeze, recognized that he had a valuable asset in Hearst because of her family's high visibility and wealth; he could use her to showcase his cause. DeFreeze undertook a calculated program of brainwashing, keeping her isolated, and telling her that no one would come to her rescue. He and the other SLA members told her she might die at any moment, and they fed her tales of how the "establishment" oppressed them. They even forced her to record messages that were critical of her family. Their tactics worked. On April 3, 1974, the SLA released an audiotape of Patty Hearst saying that she had joined the SLA and adopted the name "Tania."

On April 15 of that same year, the SLA robbed a branch of the Hibernia Bank in San Francisco. Hearst, brandishing an M1 carbine, was recognized as one of the robbers, and the attorney general formed the opinion that her participation was voluntary. In the days that followed, more audiotapes surfaced in which Hearst claimed to be committed to the goals of the SLA. Accordingly, an arrest warrant was issued.

A month after the bank robbery, Hearst was involved in a shootout at a Los Angeles sporting goods store, where two other SLA members, Bill and Emily Harris, had been apprehended for shoplifting. As Hearst emptied her M1 carbine, the Harrises escaped. They ditched the van they had been driving and successfully got away, but a parking ticket led police to where the group was hiding. The next day, May 17, 1974, Police engaged in a gun battle with the SLA in their East Los Angeles hideout. The building went up in flames, and six SLA members, including DeFreeze, died. Police expected to find Hearst's body in the burned-out wreckage, but she and the Harrises had not returned to the hideout. Instead, they watched the shootout and fire on television from a motel room near Disneyland. With the majority of the SLA members dead, Hearst and the Harrises went on the run.

Eighteen months after her kidnapping, the FBI finally caught up with Hearst in a San Francisco apartment, where she was arrested with other SLA members. Hearst was charged with armed bank robbery and use of a firearm in the commission of a felony. Her family hired famed attorney F. Lee Bailey to defend her in court. The trial began February 4, 1976, two years to the day of Hearst's kidnapping. The defense brought in numerous medical and psychiatric experts to describe the extreme physical and mental stress she had experienced and how she had been thoroughly brainwashed. One psychologist who had examined Hearst testified that her IQ had fallen dramatically since the time of her kidnapping. The prosecution countered with its own experts who testified that Hearst was simply a spoiled rich girl, a rebel looking for a cause.

Unfortunately for Hearst, it was not F. Lee Bailey's finest hour. During his closing argument, his hands were shaking, his face was flushed, and he appeared to be inebriated. He rambled and at times seemed incoherent. Worse, he knocked a glass of water from the podium, and it spilled on his crotch. For the remainder of his closing argument, it appeared that he had wet his pants. Many legal experts believe that it was Bailey's poor performance that decided Hearst's fate.

The jury returned with a verdict of guilty on both charges, and the judge sentenced her to 35 years. That sentence was later reduced to 7 years. President Jimmy Carter commuted her sentence in 1979, and Patty Hearst left prison after serving 22 months. President Bill Clinton granted her a full pardon in 2001.

Following her release from prison, Hearst married her bodyguard, Bernard Shaw. She essentially returned to the life she had led before her kidnapping, settling in Connecticut and having two daughters. She wrote an autobiography in 1982 and acted in a few movies. Hearst has never wavered from her claim that she was a victim of brainwashing. With a less bumpy defense, she might have convinced the jury.

INTERROGATION

Interrogation
The questioning by law enforcement of a suspect concerning the commission of a crime.

It may be thought that everyone who is arrested is immediately interrogated by the police, but this is not the case. There are numerous instances where a defendant will not be interrogated. Before an **interrogation** can be carried out, police must determine that the defendant is not under the influence of drugs or alcohol, which would affect the accuracy, quality, and veracity of his or her statements. Consider Scenario 12-3.

UNDER THE INFLUENCE

Sally has been arrested for driving under the influence of alcohol. She is very intoxicated as a breath test has confirmed. Can or should the police interrogate Sally?

Answer: No. First of all, police will not need to question Sally. Why should they? She has been arrested for operating a motor vehicle under the influence. What additional questions do they need to ask? Even if they did, Sally is demonstrably acting under the influence of alcohol. If the police wished to question her, then they would have to wait until she sobered up.

When police wish to interrogate someone who has been arrested, there are strict rules that they must follow. The most obvious — and most famous — is administering the *Miranda* warnings.

A. *MIRANDA* WARNINGS

Once defendants have been placed under arrest they have several constitutional rights that immediately protect them. Among them are the right to remain silent and the right to have an attorney present when they are being interrogated. Anyone who watches television shows or movies about police work has come into contact with the ***Miranda* warnings**. Under the *Miranda v. Arizona*[1] decision, the U.S. Supreme Court requires police officers to read a suspect a summary of his or her rights before law enforcement can interrogate that suspect. One version of the *Miranda* rights is provided in Figure 12-2.

One of the biggest myths about arrest and *Miranda* warnings is that an arrest is somehow invalid if the police do not read the *Miranda* rights to the suspect. This is not true. As we have already seen, there are many times when the police have no intention of questioning a suspect after arrest. Only if the police intend to question the suspect are they required to read the *Miranda* rights. The issues surrounding interrogation and *Miranda* will be discussed in greater detail in Chapter 13.

Miranda **warning**
Rights that must be read to persons who have been placed under arrest and who the police intend to interrogate; required by the U.S. Supreme Court in the case of *Miranda v. Arizona*.

FIGURE 12-2

You have the right to remain silent. If you give up this right to remain silent, anything you say can and will be used against you at trial. You have the right to an attorney during any questioning. If you cannot afford an attorney, one will be appointed to represent you. Do you understand these rights?

The *Miranda* Rights Warning

---

[1] 384 U.S. 436, 86 S.Ct. 1602, 16 L.Ed.2d 694 (1966).

EVIDENCE

Evidence
Any type of information, including testimony, documents, and physical objects that are presented during a trial to prove or disprove a point in contention.

Direct evidence
Evidence that proves a fact without the need to resort to any other fact. Direct evidence that the defendant held the murder weapon would be his fingerprints on the object.

Circumstantial evidence
Facts that suggest a conclusion or indirectly prove a main fact in question.

In deciding what charges to bring against a suspect, police and prosecutors must review the available evidence. Although chapter 16 will explore the issues of evidence, this introductory chapter will examine the basic concepts of the use of evidence in criminal trials. **Evidence** refers to anything that tends to prove or disprove any fact in a case. Both prosecutors and defense attorneys rely on evidence to establish facts in a case (or to question the veracity of the other side's evidence).

The first way to approach evidence is to categorize it into direct and circumstantial. **Direct evidence** refers to any object or testimony that has an immediate connection with the facts in the case. The defendant's fingerprints found on the murder weapon are an example of direct evidence. The fingerprints directly link the defendant to the murder weapon and form part of the proof that the defendant committed the crime, beyond a reasonable doubt. **Circumstantial evidence**, on the other hand, suggests conclusions and inferences but has no direct connection with the facts of the case. An example of circumstantial evidence that has been used in law schools for years is the famous "trout in milk" scenario. Suppose that you wake up one morning and find a trout sticking out of a glass of milk in your kitchen. What conclusions can you reach? Obviously, your first conclusion is that someone must have put the fish in your glass of milk. You may not be able to immediately discern who put the trout there, but there is no doubt that someone did. Consider Scenario 12-4.

SCENARIO 12-4

BLOODY HANDS

Maria walks into an all-night grocery store and finds the clerk slumped behind the cash register. He has been severely beaten and the cash register drawer is open and empty. Maria takes out her cellphone and calls the police. Just as she does, she sees a man outside the store. He has blood on his hands and on the front of his shirt. He looks guilty. At this point, without any additional testing, would you classify the man's appearance as direct or circumstantial evidence?

Answer: Circumstantial evidence. Without more evidence, such as a test showing that the blood on the man matches the clerk's blood, this evidence is merely suggestive of guilt.

Although circumstantial evidence is often considered to be weaker than direct evidence, any trial will have a combination of both types of evidence. The problem with circumstantial evidence is that under criminal law, circumstantial evidence must not only suggest a conclusion, but also exclude every other reasonable possibility. It is possible to convict a person on circumstantial evidence alone, but the evidence must prove that the defendant committed the crime beyond a reasonable doubt and that the evidence excludes every other reasonable possibility other than the defendant's guilt.

Direct evidence can be broken down into subcategories, such as:

- Physical evidence
- Documentary evidence

- Testimonial evidence
- Demonstrative evidence

A. PHYSICAL EVIDENCE

Physical evidence refers to objects and things. In a criminal case, the prosecution may enter into evidence a wide range of objects to prove that the defendant committed a crime. Although we tend to think of physical evidence as the murder weapon, there are many other types of physical evidence, ranging from DNA, carpet fibers, fingerprints, and almost any other object that can be retrieved from a crime scene and that ties the defendant to the area or the crime.

Physical evidence
Any object that tends to prove that a defendant committed (or did not commit) a crime; physical evidence can consist of murder weapons or other types of physical evidence like DNA.

B. DOCUMENTARY EVIDENCE

Documentary evidence obviously refers to documents. Why would documents have their own separate classification from physical evidence? The answer is that documents can be altered. Because a document can be forged, altered, or redacted, it is important to have a different set of rules regulating how and when documents can be used to prove that a defendant committed a crime.

Documentary evidence
A writing that contains facts or data that tend to prove or disprove that a defendant committed a crime.

C. TESTIMONIAL EVIDENCE

When a witness testifies on the stand, this is classified as **testimonial evidence**. Because witnesses are human beings, they are obviously treated differently than physical objects or documents. A person can testify about direct evidence, such as observing the defendant commit a crime, or provide circumstantial evidence. When a witness is called to the stand, he or she first testifies on direct examination and then is cross-examined by the opposing attorney. The attorneys will either attempt to show how the witness is telling the truth or how the witness is biased, prejudiced, or lying, depending on whom they represent in the criminal case.

Testimonial evidence
Evidence given by a witness under oath.

D. DEMONSTRATIVE EVIDENCE

The final category of evidence for this chapter involves the use of **demonstrative evidence**. This is evidence that is actually prepared by the attorneys or parties to assist in the trial. Because it has been prepared by the parties, it has an inherent bias and judges will often instruct jurors to approach demonstrative evidence carefully. Demonstrative evidence usually comes in the form of charts, diagrams, and even PowerPoint presentations prepared by the attorneys to help illustrate specific points in the case and to assist in giving an opening statement or a closing argument. Unlike other types of evidence, jurors are usually not allowed to take demonstrative evidence into the jury room with them during deliberations.

Demonstrative evidence
Pictorial displays, charts, scale models, and other displays designed to persuade the jury.

INITIAL APPEARANCE

Initial appearance
A hearing that takes place within days of the suspect's arrest, where the suspect is advised of his or her constitutional rights and given the opportunity to request a court-appointed attorney, and where the court can confirm the defendant's identity.

The primary purpose of the initial appearance is to ensure that the defendant is aware of his or her constitutional rights.

In some jurisdictions, the **initial appearance** is also called the preliminary examination. No matter what the term, the purpose of the hearing is the same. Shortly after the defendant is arrested, the defendant is brought before a judge — often a magistrate judge — and again reminded of his or her rights and also asked if it will be necessary to appoint an attorney to represent the defendant.

During the initial appearance, the magistrate will often advise the defendant of the charges currently pending against him or her. These are usually preliminary charges, and the defendant may have additional charges added once the prosecution team has had an opportunity to review the defendant's case.

The final purpose of the initial appearance is to ensure that the defendant has been correctly identified. The judge will confirm that the person whom the state believes that it has in custody is in fact the person being held. To that end, the judge may order fingerprint comparisons or some other procedure to properly identify the defendant.

PRELIMINARY HEARING

Preliminary hearing
A court hearing that determines if there is probable cause to believe that the defendant committed the crime with which he or she is charged.

Within a few days of the initial appearance (the actual time period varies by state), the defendant will be brought before another magistrate or court officer. However, this hearing is not an initial hearing. Instead, the court will hold a hearing to determine if there is sufficient probable cause to believe that the defendant committed the crime. The **preliminary hearing** (also known as a probable cause hearing) is held within days of the defendant's arrest. It is a hearing where the defendant will appear, represented by an attorney, and the case will be presented by a prosecutor. Preliminary hearings are usually reserved only for felony cases. Misdemeanor cases, in most states, do not have preliminary hearings.

During this hearing, the prosecutor will call witnesses to the stand, swear them in and then ask them some basic questions about the case. The purpose of the preliminary hearing is not to determine the defendant's guilt. Instead, it is to establish that the police had probable cause to arrest him. This is a relatively low threshold to meet, and winning a preliminary hearing is not a difficult thing for the prosecution.

GRAND JURY

Grand jury
A group of citizens who consider felony charges against defendants and make a determination that there is sufficient evidence to warrant further prosecution.

If a defendant is charged with a felony, the next step in the criminal process is to convene a **grand jury** to consider the charges against him or her. Grand juries are required under the U.S. Constitution, and most states, but not all, follow this example. The grand jury is not the same as the jury that hears a criminal charge. Instead, the grand jury is composed of 16–23 persons, and they consider the basic facts of the prosecution's case. The purpose of the grand jury is to act as a buffer between the state and the defendant. The grand jury considers witness testimony and then makes a ruling as to whether or not the case should continue. If the grand jurors determine that there is a **prima facie** case of guilt, then they will authorize continued prosecution.

Prima facie
Facts that are considered true as presented until they are disproven by some contrary evidence.

A. TRUE BILL VS. NO BILL

When the grand jurors reach a decision that the prosecution against a particular defendant should continue, they record their vote as a **true bill**. A true bill authorizes the prosecution to bring formal charges against the defendant and to summon him or her to trial. On the other hand, if the grand jurors do not believe that a case should continue, then they vote **no bill**. A vote of no bill effectively stops the prosecution in its tracks. At this point, the prosecution can either wait until a new grand jury is empaneled, which could be as long as a year or more, or seek to charge the defendant with a misdemeanor.

If the grand jury returns a true bill against a defendant, the next step in the prosecution is the arraignment.

True bill
A grand jury's determination that there is sufficient probable cause to continue the prosecution against the accused.

No bill
A grand jury's determination that there is insufficient probable cause to continue the prosecution against the accused.

 **ARRAIGNMENT**

Once a grand jury has returned a true bill, the defendant will be summoned to court for an **arraignment**. The arraignment is normally scheduled several weeks or even months after the grand jury meets. In some jurisdictions, a defendant can be arraigned on the day of the trial, but most follow a pattern that sets the arraignment several weeks before the next scheduled trial date. At the arraignment, the defendant is told exactly what the charges are against him or her and is given an opportunity to enter an official plea. The defendant may plead guilty or not guilty. If the defendant pleads guilty, he or she may be sentenced immediately. However, if the defendant enters a not guilty plea, the case will be scheduled for trial.

Arraignment
A court hearing where the defendant is informed of the charge against him or her and given the opportunity to enter a plea of guilty or not guilty.

 TRIAL

If a defendant pleads not guilty, his or her case will be scheduled for trial. We will examine the trial of a criminal case in depth in Chapter 20, but a few words here about a criminal trial are also important.

A defendant enters a trial with several presumptions in his or her favor. For instance, a defendant is presumed innocent unless and until the prosecution can prove, beyond a reasonable doubt, that the defendant committed the crime. If the state fails to meet this burden, the jurors are instructed that they must vote a not guilty verdict.

A. BASIC OVERVIEW OF A CRIMINAL TRIAL

Trials proceed in a similar pattern all across the United States. When the defendant's case is called for trial, the judge will summon local citizens who will act as jurors in the case. Jury selection will occur prior to trial.

Once a jury is empaneled, the parties will give their opening statements. The usual pattern is for the prosecutor to go first, outlining the evidence that it has against the defendant and the witnesses who will testify in the case. Once the prosecutor has finished his or her opening statement, the defense will have its opportunity. A defense attorney will often use the opening statement as a way to introduce the defense in the case or to simply challenge the state's version of events.

Following the opening statements, the case actually begins. The prosecutor calls witnesses to the stand, questions them about the case and establishes the basic facts against the defendant. After each witness has answered questions posed by the prosecutor, the defense attorney is allowed to question the witnesses to dispute their version, question their veracity or to show that they have some bias against the defendant. The case proceeds in this fashion, with the state calling a witness, the witness testifying and the prosecutor using the witness as a means to present direct or circumstantial evidence. Each witness can be questioned by the defense. When the state has presented all of its witnesses and evidence, it rests its case.

At this point, the defense has two options. The defense attorney can present witnesses and evidence to support the defendant's version of the case or to establish a legally recognized defense, or the defense can simply rest without presenting anything. Jurors are instructed that simply because the defense presented no evidence, they are not permitted to infer that the defendant admits his guilt. In fact, the jurors are told the opposite. The burden of proving that the defendant is guilty is always on the state, and it never shifts to the defendant to prove that he or she is not guilty.

When the case concludes, the prosecutor and defense attorney will address the jury in one last presentation, referred to as a closing argument. During the closing argument, the prosecutor will argue how the evidence proves the defendant guilty beyond a reasonable doubt. When it is the defense attorney's time, he or she will undoubtedly argue that the state's version is incorrect and that the prosecution has failed to meet the burden of proving the defendant guilty beyond a reasonable doubt.

Following closing arguments, the judge instructs the jurors about what law applies to the crime with which the defendant is charged. Then the judge sends the jurors out to deliberate in the jury room. No one else is allowed to be present while they discuss the case. In most states, the jury's verdict must be unanimous — agreed to by all. If even one juror does not vote for the defendant's guilt, and the other jurors cannot change this juror's mind, the judge will have no choice but to suspend the proceedings. The prosecution can then decide whether or not to schedule a new trial against the defendant.

If the jurors reach a unanimous verdict of guilty, then the court moves on to the next stage in the criminal process: sentencing.

SENTENCING

At the conclusion of a criminal trial, if a defendant is found guilty, the judge usually **sentences** him or her. Although there are provisions that allow juries to recommend sentences in some states, the most common method is for the judge to impose a sentence based on the applicable statutes. In most jurisdictions, the judge has specific restrictions on the ultimate sentence that he or she can impose on the defendant. The legislature imposes maximum sentences on all types of crimes, and a judge may not exceed the statutory limit. As part of the sentence, a judge may impose a prison term, parole, or probation as well as fines that the defendant must pay over the course of his probationary sentence.

Sentence
The punishment, which can consist of some combination of prison time and probation, that is imposed on a defendant who has been found guilty at trial or who has pled guilty.

A. PRISON VS. PROBATION

When a judge sentences a defendant to a term in prison, he or she may order that the sentence be served consecutively to other prison terms or concurrently with other terms. When a defendant is released from prison, he will often continue to serve the balance of his sentence on **probation** or parole. This chapter will consider probation and parole to be the same thing. However, as Chapter 21 will show that, although these terms are similar, they are handled differently. Probation officers ensure that the defendant follows the conditions of his sentence. For instance, if the defendant has been ordered to pay fines or restitution, the probation officer is the person who monitors these payments. In addition, the probation officer also makes sure that the probationer obtains employment and refrains from drug use, among other conditions.

A judge may sentence a defendant to a strictly probationary sentence, without any prison time. If a defendant violates the terms or conditions of his probation, the judge may revoke the defendant's probation and have him serve the balance of his sentence in prison.

Probation
Allowing a person convicted of a criminal offense to avoid serving a jail sentence imposed on the person, so long as he or she abides by certain conditions (usually including being supervised by a probation officer).

STATE v. JENKINS
143 Idaho 918, 155 P.3d 1157 (2007)

TROUT, Justice.

I. FACTUAL AND PROCEDURAL BACKGROUND

Boise police officers responded to an alleged battery at a Boise residence, in which the victim indicated that William H. Jenkins (Jenkins) had battered her and attempted to drive over her in his car. The victim gave the police a physical description of Jenkins as well as a description of his vehicle and his license plate number, all of which were forwarded to dispatch. Using the license plate number, the police located Jenkins's home address and drove to his home. Finding no one at the Jenkins residence, the responding officer parked in front of a neighbor's house and waited for

Jenkins to return home. Approximately fifteen to twenty minutes later, a car matching the description of Jenkins' car drove up to the house. Because it was dark, the officers could not see the license plate number or determine whether the driver matched the physical description of Jenkins. As the car pulled into the driveway, the officer turned on his overhead lights and pulled in behind the car. After waiting for the garage door to open, the suspect car proceeded into the garage. The driver began to get out of the car, but the officer instructed him to stay seated. At that point, the officer confirmed the identity of the driver as Jenkins. The officer questioned Jenkins about the battery and, because Jenkins smelled of alcohol, conducted field sobriety tests.

The State charged Jenkins with misdemeanor battery and driving under the influence (DUI). The Court of Appeals first concluded there was no probable cause to arrest under the facts of this case. The Court of Appeals then applied this Court's decision in State v. Maland, 140 Idaho 817, 103 P.3d 430 (2004) and reversed, holding that the officer was not entitled to follow Jenkins when he retreated into the garage. This Court granted review.

II. DISCUSSION

The Fourth Amendment to the U.S. Constitution and Article I, § 17 of the Idaho Constitution protect people against unreasonable searches and seizures. U.S. Const. amend. IV; Idaho Const. art. I, § 17. The guarantees under the U.S. Constitution and the Idaho Constitution are substantially the same. *State v. Fees*, 140 Idaho 81, 88, 90 P.3d 306, 313 (2004). When seizure occurs without a warrant, the government bears the burden of proving facts necessary to establish an exception to the warrant requirement. Evidence obtained in violation of these constitutional protections must be suppressed in a criminal prosecution of the person whose rights were violated.

A. Reasonable Expectation of Privacy

Before addressing whether the State complied with Fourth Amendment requirements in this case, it is necessary to determine whether Fourth Amendment protections apply. The Fourth Amendment prohibits police from making a warrantless, nonconsensual entry into a suspect's home in order to make a routine, non-exigent arrest. However, the warrantless arrest of an individual in a public place upon probable cause does not violate the Fourth Amendment. In *United States v. Santana*, 427 U.S. 38, 96 S.Ct. 2406, 49 L.Ed.2d 300 (1976), the Supreme Court found that a person standing on the threshold of her home in her doorway was in a public place not subject to Fourth Amendment protection. The Court relied on the proposition that "what a person knowingly exposes to the public, even in his own house or office, is not a subject of Fourth Amendment protection." Because Santana "was not in an area where she had any expectation of privacy," the Court reasoned that she was in a public place subject to arrest upon probable cause, with no warrant required. *Santana*, 427 U.S. at 42, 96 S.Ct. at 2409, 49 L.Ed.2d at 305.

Probable Cause to Arrest

The magistrate judge analyzed this encounter as an investigatory stop and thus did not address whether the officer had probable cause to arrest Jenkins at the moment of seizure. We conclude that the facts found by the magistrate judge support a determination that the officer had probable cause to arrest Jenkins at the time of the stop.

A police officer may, without a warrant, arrest a suspect "when a felony has in fact been committed and he has reasonable cause for believing the person arrested to have committed it." I.C. § 19–603. To have probable cause for a felony arrest, an officer must have information that would lead a person of ordinary care to believe or entertain an honest and strong presumption that such person is guilty. *State v. Julian*, 129 Idaho 133, 136, 922 P.2d 1059, 1062 (1996). Probable cause is not measured by the same level of proof required for conviction. As the Court explained in State v. Alger, 100 Idaho 675, 603 P.2d 1009, "in dealing with probable cause . . . , as the very name implies, we deal with probabilities." Id. at 677, 603 P.2d at 1011, quoting *Brinegar v. United States*, 338 U.S. 160, 175, 69 S.Ct. 1302, 1310, 93 L.Ed. 1879, 1890 (1967). Judicial determination of probable cause focuses on the information and facts the officers possessed at the time.

Jenkins challenges the State's assertion of probable cause for a felony arrest not on the basis that the alleged crime was not a felony, but rather on the basis that the officer was unable to identify the driver as Jenkins. Clearly, the officers had probable cause to believe a felony had been committed based on the victim's statements. Further, we conclude the arresting officer had probable cause to believe that the driver of the vehicle he stopped committed that crime. The question is not whether the police had probable cause to believe that Jenkins was the driver of the car; rather, the question is whether the victim provided an adequate description of her assailant to allow the officers to corroborate that the driver of the stopped car was the person who attempted to injure her. In this case, the victim's identification of the suspect's license plate number led the officers to Jenkins' home; Jenkins was not at home when the police knocked; there was close proximity in time between the victim's call to the police and the time the suspect vehicle pulled up to Jenkins' house; the vehicle pulling into Jenkins' home matched the victim's description of the car the suspect used in attempting to run over her; and the driver activated the garage door opener from the vehicle. The magistrate judge's findings of fact sufficiently demonstrate that the officer had probable cause to believe the driver of the vehicle had committed the crime alleged. When the officers turned on their overhead lights in Jenkins' driveway, they acted on probable cause to arrest in a public place, regardless of whether they articulated this exact purpose.

Under Santana, "a suspect may not defeat an arrest which has been set in motion in a public place . . . by the expedient of escaping to a private place." 427 U.S. at 43, 96 S.Ct. at 2410, 49 L.Ed.2d at 306. Like the suspect in Santana who could not thwart an arrest initiated on her threshold by fleeing inside her home, Jenkins could not thwart the arrest, validly initiated upon probable cause in his driveway, by fleeing inside. As in Santana, "the fact that the pursuit here ended almost as soon as it began did not render it any the less a 'hot pursuit' sufficient to justify the warrantless entry into the suspect's house." Id. The police had probable cause to arrest Jenkins and the rightful authority to follow him into his garage in order to complete the arrest. Because we find that the officer had probable cause to arrest Jenkins, we need not discuss the validity of the encounter as a Terry stop.

IV. CONCLUSION

The magistrate judge's order denying Jenkins' motion to suppress evidence is affirmed.

Chief Justice SCHROEDER and Justices EISMANN, BURDICK and JONES concur.

CASE QUESTIONS

1 Why did officers arrest Jenkins in the first place?
2 How do the constitutional guarantees of the U.S. Constitution and the Idaho Constitution compare?
3 When may an officer arrest a suspect without a warrant?
4 Is the standard of probable cause different from that required to convict a person? Explain your answer based on the case.
5 Jenkins countered that the officers had no probable cause, because they did not know that he was the driver of the car. How did the court address this issue?

CHAPTER SUMMARY

This introductory chapter on criminal procedure has shown that an arrest triggers several significant procedural steps. To arrest a person is to detain him or her and render the suspect not free to leave. Once a person is under arrest, he or she may be interrogated by the police. If the suspect is interrogated, then the police must advise the suspect of his or her *Miranda* rights. These rights are mandated by the U.S. Supreme Court and require that the police tell a suspect that he or she has the right to remain silent and the right to an attorney, among other rights. All arrests must be supported by probable cause, which is a reasonable belief that the suspect was committing a crime.

Following the arrest, the defendant is brought before a court for an initial appearance hearing where he or she is again advised of any applicable constitutional rights and given the opportunity to request an attorney if the suspect cannot afford to hire one. In order to support a charge and a subsequent conviction, police must gather evidence to prove that the defendant committed the crime beyond a reasonable doubt. Evidence can be divided into two broad categories: direct and circumstantial. Direct evidence establishes a fact while circumstantial evidence suggests a conclusion. Direct evidence can be broken down into other subcategories including physical, documentary, testimonial and demonstrative.

As an additional safeguard, most states require preliminary hearings in felony cases. The purpose of a preliminary hearing is to establish, to a judge's satisfaction, that there was sufficient probable cause to arrest the defendant. This hearing is adversarial, with the defendant, defense attorney, and prosecutor all present. The prosecutor presents witness testimony to establish probable cause, and if the judge agrees, the case is transferred to another court. Following the preliminary hearing, many states require that the case be considered by a grand jury. This body of citizens is responsible for reviewing cases to determine if there is a *prima facie* showing of guilt against the defendant. If they agree, then they return a vote of true bill. If they do not believe that sufficient evidence has been presented, they will return a vote of no bill, which essentially dismisses the case. After the return of a true bill, the defendant will be brought to court for his or her arraignment and given the opportunity to hear the official charges and a chance to enter a plea to those charges. If a defendant pleads not guilty at arraignment, then the case will be scheduled for trial. Defendants who are found guilty have the right to appeal their cases to higher courts. These appellate courts review the record and evidence and make a determination whether the case involved no error (affirm), had error that was damaging to the defendant (reverse) or that the court requires additional information and sends it back to the trial court for a hearing (remand).

KEY TERMS

Arrest	Physical evidence	No bill
Probable cause	Documentary evidence	Arraignment
Interrogation	Initial appearance	Sentence
Miranda warnings	Preliminary hearing	Appeal
Evidence	Grand jury	Affirm
Direct evidence	*Prima facie*	Reverse
Circumstantial evidence	True bill	Remand

REVIEW QUESTIONS

1 What is the definition of arrest?
2 Define probable cause.
3 What constitutional amendment governs probable cause?
4 What is an initial appearance hearing?
5 What is the purpose of a preliminary hearing?
6 What is the standard of proof at a preliminary hearing?
7 Explain the *Miranda* warnings.
8 What is the difference between direct and circumstantial evidence?
9 Provide some examples of direct evidence.
10 How many people normally serve on a grand jury?
11 What is the difference between a true bill and a no bill?
12 What is the purpose of an arraignment?
13 What is plea bargaining?
14 What are the possible verdicts in a criminal case?

15   What factors does a judge consider in sentencing a defendant who has been found guilty?

16   What is the difference between a prison sentence and a probationary sentence?

17   What actions are appellate courts authorized to take?

18   What is an appeal?

19   What is the difference between an order affirming an appeal and one that remands an appeal?

QUESTIONS FOR ANALYSIS

1   Are all of these procedural steps, including initial appearance, preliminary hearings, and grand jury proceedings really necessary? Has the U.S. court system gone too far in trying to protect the rights of people accused of crimes? Explain your answer.

2   There have been cases where innocent people have been convicted of crimes that they did not commit. Is there an inherent weakness in our system that would allow something like this to happen? Explain.

HYPOTHETICALS

1   Tony is asked to accompany a police officer to police headquarters for questioning. Tony is told that he is free to leave at any time and that he is not under arrest. However, the officer locks the door to the interrogation room and tells Tony that he's not going anywhere until he "clears things up." Does this meet the definition of arrest? Why or why not?

2   In some countries, a defendant can be tried even if he never actually appears in the courtroom. In fact, the defendant may never have been arrested. However, his or her trial proceeds and if the defendant is found guilty, he or she will be sentenced. If the defendant is caught, then he or she is put into prison. Why doesn't our system allow such a procedure? Would it make things easier for prosecutors and police?

3   Arnise is arrested and placed in a holding cell. She is never read her *Miranda* rights and is never questioned. Shortly before her trial begins, her attorney challenges her arrest by saying that it is unconstitutional and uses the example of the failure to be read the *Miranda* rights as the primary example. Will the attorney be successful?

13

The Law of Arrest, Interrogation, and *Miranda*

I   THE LAW OF ARREST

As explained in Chapter 12, arrest is detaining a suspect who police believe has committed a crime. The U.S. Constitution places strict limits on the arrest powers of police officers. The Fourth Amendment requires that when police arrest someone either with or without a warrant, they must have probable cause. The previous chapter's definition makes it clear that probable cause is a reasonable belief that the suspect has committed a crime. In some cases, probable cause is described differently. These courts describe probable cause as a factor of the "totality of the circumstance," including the location, time of day, and suspect's demeanor, all viewed through the eyes of a reasonable, prudent police officer.[1] However, this chapter will go beyond these generalities and explore the law of arrest in much greater depth.

An arrest can occur under a wide variety of situations. There is no requirement that the police must use the word "arrest" before a detention is considered to be an arrest. The problem with defining arrest is that there are so many interactions between police and suspects in so many varied locations — and under such a

---

[1] *Bost v. State*, 406 Md. 341, 958 A.2d 356 (2008).

wide variety of circumstances — that simply defining arrest as taking someone into custody is not sufficient. The real issue with defining arrest has to do with constitutional rights. There are vital constitutional issues that figure into the arrest of a suspect. Before a person is legally considered under arrest, he or she does not have the right to a trial by jury, the right to have an attorney present during questioning, or many other rights.

There is a natural tension between suspects and police when it comes to defining the precise moment when an arrest occurred. Suspects would, quite naturally, want that moment to occur as early in the interaction with police as possible. Police, on the other hand, would like to delay the official moment of arrest as long as possible, in order to sidestep some of the limitations that are placed on them when that moment occurs. Because of this, courts do not look to the subjective belief or intent of either the suspect or the police officer in determining when the exact moment of arrest occurred. Instead, courts will look to the surrounding circumstances. A person is under arrest when a third party, viewing the facts and circumstances, would believe that the suspect was not free to leave.[2] This classification of not being free to leave is the linchpin of the definition of arrest, and it this definition that defines precisely when a suspect's numerous post-arrest rights are triggered (see Figure 13-1).

A. WHO CAN ARREST

In the United States, hundreds of individuals are arrested on a daily basis. Law enforcement officers make arrests under all types of situations. Some are inherently dangerous, such as serving an arrest warrant on a person who is armed and dangerous. Arrests may occur without warrants, such as when officers have reason to believe that a person has committed a crime.

In the typical situation, an arrest is made under the authority of an arrest warrant, which is discussed in Chapter 14. But police officers are also allowed to make arrests without warrants and do so every day in this country.

ARRESTS BY POLICE OFFICERS AND OTHERS

In most situations, a certified law enforcement officer is the only person who can make an arrest. These officers are specifically empowered by the local, state, or federal government to conduct arrests and have been through extensive training before being given that power. When a person becomes a police officer, he or she is authorized to make arrests either on duty or off duty, either in uniform or in civilian clothes. No matter the circumstance, the arrest must be supported by probable cause.

When a person desires to become a police officer, he or she usually attends a police academy that is governed and supervised by state agencies. Their trainers

---

[2] *U.S. v. Hastamorir*, 881 F.2d 1551, 1556 (11th Cir.1989); *United States v. Hammock*, 860 F.2d 390, 393 (11th Cir.1988).

FIGURE 13-1

"The right of the people to be secure in their persons, houses, papers, and effects, against unreasonable searches and seizures, shall not be violated, and no Warrants shall issue, but upon probable cause, supported by Oath or affirmation, and particularly describing the place to be searched, and the persons or things to be seized."

Amendment IV: Search and Seizure

are older, more experienced police officers and attorneys. Police officers train the recruits in the methods of carrying out the physical actions involved in arrests, hostage situations and gun battles, while attorneys train officers in the complexities of constitutional law and how to make sure that they abide by the law in their professional lives.

After graduating from a police academy or other training program, new officers are usually placed on a probationary period. They ride with other, more seasoned officers who go out on patrol. They watch and observe other officers in the normal course of their day-to-day activities. While the new officer learns, he or she is also being closely monitored and observed for reactions in stress situations and other police activities. Not everyone is cut out to be a police officer. Some cannot handle the stress. Some cannot handle the power of their positions.

Once officers are fully authorized to carry out arrests, they are normally limited to a specific geographic region where they are allowed to make arrests. This term is frequently — and somewhat incorrectly — referred to as an officer's "jurisdiction." The term jurisdiction is a legal term that refers to a person's or a court's power to take some action. In most cases, the geographic limitations of that power are referred to as **venue**, a term that designates the limits of where a court or a police officer can carry out his or her duties. However, because jurisdiction is the most commonly used term, this text will use it from this point forward. Just as a judge cannot make a ruling that binds a judge in some other county, a police officer is usually barred from making arrests in another county (assuming that the venue is limited to county, not state, boundaries, which is the most common limitation).

Venue
The particular geographic area where a court or an official can exercise power; an example of venue would be the county's borders.

FAMOUS CASES
BERNIE MADOFF

By all appearances, Bernard Lawrence "Bernie" Madoff had the magic touch. Madoff founded and ran an investment securities firm that provided consistent double-digit annual returns to its investors, a rate of return unmatched in the industry. Dating back to the 1970s, his firm cultivated exclusive clientele, including celebrities such as Steven Spielberg and Kevin Bacon, and they reaped the benefits of his purported investment genius — until Madoff's arrest for securities fraud. Madoff, it seems, had been perpetrating a massive Ponzi scheme.

Charles Ponzi, an Italian immigrant, began advertising in 1920 that he could give investors a 50 percent return on their money. Ponzi took money from people all over New England and New Jersey. He, of course, was making millions as people scraped together whatever they could beg, borrow, or steal to invest with him. When the scheme collapsed, Ponzi was indicted on 86 counts of fraud, and tens of millions of dollars invested with him had simply vanished.

Bernie Madoff was born April 29, 1938, and began his investment firm with $5,000 he earned as a lifeguard and a sprinkler installer. The company began as a penny stock trader in 1960 and then made the transition into investment securities. By the 1980s, Madoff's firm handled as much as 5 percent of the trading on the New York Stock Exchange. Like Ponzi, Madoff lived lavishly, supposedly on the profits from his business.

The secret to his success, as Madoff claimed, was a closely guarded computer system that helped him make trades. The system supposedly alerted him when to buy and when to sell. He attracted many high-profile investors; the owners of the New York Mets had some $300 million invested with him. His firm was also attractive to nonprofit organizations, such as religious groups, hospitals, and foundations.

Madoff kept his firm small, with his two sons as his primary employees. Toward the end of 2008, Madoff confided in one of his sons that he was having trouble fulfilling $7 billion in redemption requests. But a few days later, he told his son Mark that he planned to pay out $173 million in bonuses. Mark and his brother, Andrew, confronted Madoff, demanding to know how he could pay out bonuses when he was having trouble paying their customers. Realizing that the firm's collapse was imminent, Madoff confessed that the operation was a Ponzi scheme. All along he had used the money from new investors to pay older investors, an unsustainable structure.

Mark and Andrew went to federal authorities and reported what their father had told them. The next day, December 11, 2008, Madoff was arrested and charged with securities fraud. He confessed that he had lost more than $50 billion of investors' money (which later proved to be closer to $65 billion). On March 12, 2009, he pleaded guilty to 11 felony counts, including securities fraud, investment adviser fraud, mail fraud, wire fraud, three counts of money laundering, false statements, perjury, false filings with the U.S. Securities and Exchange Commission, and theft from an employee benefit plan.

Until his guilty plea, Madoff had been out on $10 million bail and confined to house arrest in his posh New York Upper East Side penthouse. After his plea, he was held in jail until sentencing because the judge feared his age, wealth, and the prospect of life in prison made him a flight risk. On June 29, 2009, Madoff was sentenced to 150 years in prison, the maximum allowable sentence for the 71-year-old man.

The big question is how Madoff managed to get away with his scheme for so many years. The answer seems to be that no one really wanted to know the truth about his operation. Fraud investigator Harry Markopolos tried in vain to convince the Securities and Exchange Commission in 2000 that Madoff was a fraud, but no one would listen. Markopolos believed it was mathematically impossible to produce the kinds of returns that Madoff was generating. He looked at Madoff's numbers and tried for hours to replicate them, with no success. He took his findings to both the Boston SEC and the New York SEC and was ignored.

Additionally, despite the size of Madoff's operation, none of the major derivatives firms would trade with him because they doubted the validity of his numbers.

Likewise, none of the major Wall Street firms would invest with him because of suspicions that he was not legitimate. Nevertheless, Madoff was allowed to continue until the Ponzi scheme's inevitable collapse.

Although Mark and Andrew, Madoff's sons, saw themselves as honest whistle-blowers who tried to do the right thing, the press and many of those involved in the Madoff case portrayed them as bungling money managers who profited greatly while doing nothing to protect investors. On December 11, 2010, on the second anniversary of Bernie Madoff's arrest, Mark Madoff hanged himself in his Manhattan apartment. Andrew Madoff became a pariah in New York City, unable to find anyone who would even rent him an apartment.

Arrests Outside of the Officer's Jurisdiction. Although the general rule is that police officers cannot arrest a person outside their territorial jurisdiction, there are exceptions. One such exception is the **fresh pursuit doctrine.** Under this ruling, if a police officer is pursuing a suspect who has committed a felony, then the officer can chase that person across county or state lines and arrest him, even though the officer has no lawful authority to arrest in that jurisdiction. Of course, the fresh pursuit doctrine has its own limitations, including rulings on just how "fresh" the pursuit must be. It is obviously not fresh pursuit if the officer arrests the suspect hours or even days after the pursuit has ended. In court rulings, fresh pursuit means just what it suggests, an ongoing, immediate pursuit that happens to cross some boundary. Without that showing of immediacy, officers would have no greater authority to arrest someone outside their jurisdiction than would a citizen.

Fresh pursuit doctrine
A court-created doctrine that allows police officers to arrest suspects without warrants and to cross territorial boundaries while they are still pursuing the suspect.

Citizen's Arrest. In some situations, individuals who are not police officers can detain a suspect. This is often referred to as **citizen's arrest**, but the term is misleading. Citizens, or anyone else, can detain a person who has committed a crime and then hand that person over to the police, but citizens do not make arrests. An arrest has a very specific meaning and involves constitutional rights, none of which apply when one or more citizens detain a criminal for the police. However, this term has been in popular use for decades, so this text will continue to use it. Many states allow citizens to make arrests when a crime has been committed in the citizen's presence or within his immediate knowledge. Some states even go so far as to say that private citizens have as much power to arrest a felon — in an emergency situation — as does a police officer. Private citizens can make a citizen's arrest — in most states — for a felony occurring in their presence. They may also have the right to arrest someone to prevent a felony from occurring. Generally, there is no right of citizen's arrest to prevent a misdemeanor. Usually the citizen can only arrest a person if the citizen actually saw the person commit the crime. Many states have dramatically curtailed the right of citizen's arrest, preferring to leave it in the hands of the people who have been specifically trained to carry it out, namely, police officers.

Citizen's arrest
A legal doctrine that holds harmless a citizen who detains a person observed to have committed a crime. When a person makes a citizen's arrest, he or she is immune from civil suit for battery or false imprisonment of the person detained, provided the person detained actually committed a crime.

Under the citizen's arrest doctrine, persons have the right to physically restrain a person who has committed a crime in their presence and hold this person for the police. A citizen's arrest is used most commonly in cases of shoplifting — a store manager or employee detains a person suspected of shoplifting until the police arrive. This doctrine has more importance in the area of civil law, where it protects

Sidebar

Citizen's arrest is not actually an arrest at all. Citizens are not empowered to arrest anyone. The phrase should, more correctly, be called citizen's detention.

the citizen from being sued for battery in restraining the individual and holding him or her until the police arrive to make a real arrest.[3]

MAKING AN ARREST

Although in some countries a police officer must actually touch the person before he or she is considered to be under arrest that is not true in the United States. Here police officers can make a legal arrest simply by giving a verbal command to a suspect. In most cases, of course, the officer does touch the person, usually by restraining him or her. Often, the officer will place the suspect in handcuffs and transport the suspect to police headquarters, so there is no question that the person has been restrained and is not free to leave, the two most important factors in determining when an arrest has been made.

There is no requirement that a police use force to make an arrest. Conversely, if a police officer must use force, that force must be reasonable and only that force necessary to effect an arrest and nothing more. A person can always voluntarily submit to an arrest. When this happens, the person is considered legally arrested.

DETERMINING WHEN THE SUSPECT IS UNDER ARREST

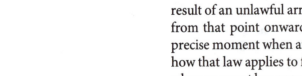

The test to determine when a person is under arrest is when a reasonable person, reviewing the facts, would believe that the suspect is not free to leave.

If a person is arrested without probable cause, then the arrest is unconstitutional. There is often no direct penalty against the officer for making an unconstitutional arrest, so why is the issue of arrest so important? If an arrest is not supported by probable cause, or if some other irregularity occurs during the arrest, then the primary punishment faced by law enforcement is not a civil suit, but the exclusionary rule. This rule, developed by the U.S. Supreme Court in *Weeks v. U.S.,*[4] holds that any evidence obtained after an unlawful arrest (or in violation of the suspect's rights) is not admissible. We will explore the application of the exclusionary rule in Chapter 16.

Court Tests to Determine the Moment of Arrest. The question of *when* a person is under arrest is critically important for the entire criminal process. Because the result of an unlawful arrest is so drastic — the suppression of any evidence obtained from that point onwards — police and prosecutors are very keen to pinpoint the precise moment when an arrest occurred and to make sure that police officers know how that law applies to factual scenarios. In order to determine the precise moment when an arrest has occurred, the U.S. Supreme Court has created a test that does not rely on the subjective impressions of either the suspect or the officer to make the determination. As discussed in the previous chapter, both of these individuals have vested interests in stating that the moment of arrest occurred at different times. The defendant will attempt to say that an arrest occurred as early as possible in the

---

[3] *State v. Garcia*, 146 Wash. App. 821, 193 P.3d 181 (Div. 3 2008).
[4] 232 U.S. 383 (1914).

interaction between the suspect and the officer so that any evidence obtained after this point may be challenged. An officer, on the other hand, has a vested interest to delay the moment of arrest as long as possible, because officers have more latitude in what they are permitted to do before the suspect is considered to be under arrest.

Courts have created an objective test to determine when an arrest has occurred. The elements of the test are whether under the circumstances at the time, a reasonable person would believe that he or she was under arrest and not free to leave. The subjective beliefs of the police officer and the suspect are irrelevant under this test. As an example, a police officer testifying during a pretrial motion might state unequivocally that the suspect was not under arrest and that he or she was free to leave, but the objective facts might give a completely different interpretation. Consider Scenario 13-1.

FREE TO LEAVE?

SCENARIO 13-1

Andrew has been asked to come to the police department to answer some questions about burglaries in his neighborhood. He voluntarily comes to the police department, and during questioning a detective accuses him of being the person who has committed the burglaries. As he is being questioned, a uniformed officer stands in front of the door to the interrogation room with a gun drawn and pointed at the floor. Andrew asks if he is under arrest and the detective says, "Absolutely not. You can walk out any time you want." Is Andrew under arrest as that term is defined by the courts?

Answer: Yes. Despite what the detective says, the physical actions of the police speak louder than their words. The fact that there is a uniformed officer standing in front of the door with a gun drawn would suggest to a reasonable person that Andrew is under arrest.

III PROBABLE CAUSE AND ARREST

Probable cause has been discussed in this chapter and the previous one, but what constitutes probable cause?

A. WHAT IS PROBABLE CAUSE?

At its simplest, probable cause refers to the reasonable suspicion that a particular set of facts is true. In this particular case, the set of facts is that a police officer believes that a suspect has committed a crime. Although an officer does not need to prove that the defendant committed an offense beyond a reasonable doubt, the officer cannot base probable cause on mere suspicion, gut feelings, or hunches.[5] Instead an

---

[5] *U.S. v. Lopez*, 482 F.3d 1067 (9th Cir. 2007).

officer must have reasonable suspicion that a crime has occurred.[6] The existence of probable cause to arrest is based on objective standards and is determined from the viewpoint of what a prudent person would believe when presented with the same facts and circumstances as the officer.

Probable cause exists if, at the time of the arrest, the officers had knowledge and reasonably trustworthy information about facts and circumstances sufficient to warrant a prudent man in believing that the defendant had committed the offense. If the officer can demonstrate that she had such objective facts at the time that she made the arrest, then the courts are likely to rule that probable cause existed and the arrest was constitutionally valid.

Determining probable cause is often not a simple matter. "In dealing with probable cause . . . as the very name implies, we deal with probabilities. These probabilities are technical; they are the essentially factual and practical considerations of everyday life on which reasonable and prudent men, not legal technicians, act."[7] Probable cause at the time of arrest means that at the moment the arrest was made, the officers had reasonable belief that a crime had been (or was about to be) committed.

What is the process for making the determination of probable cause? First, it must exist at the moment of arrest. An officer may be called on to testify about specific, articulable facts that led him or her to believe that a crime had occurred (or was occurring). The standard to prove probable cause is that the facts and circumstances, at the moment of the arrest, "warrant a man of reasonable caution in the belief that an offense had been committed."[8] Probable cause must be based on something more substantial than mere rumor or speculation.[9] This means that police officers must often independently verify facts related to them before they will have sufficient probable cause to make an arrest. Probable cause is a middle ground between proof beyond a reasonable doubt and mere suspicion that a criminal act occurred. Police officers must be able to articulate the precise elements that made them believe that a crime was occurring.

B. CONTINUUM OF CONTACTS AND THEIR CONSTITUTIONAL REQUIREMENTS

There is a continuum of contacts between individuals and police officers. Each of these interactions carries its own dangers and its own constitutional standards. We will break these interactions down into three disparate settings:

- Voluntary interactions between police and individuals
- *Terry* stops
- Arrests

---

[6] *Denson v. State*, 159 Ga. App. 713, 285 S.E.2d 69 (1981).
[7] *Brinegar v. United States*, 338 U.S. 160, 69 S.Ct. 1302, 93 LE 1879 (1948).
[8] *Carroll v. United States*, 267 U.S. 132, 45 S.Ct.280, 69 LE 543 (1925).
[9] *Clark v. State*, 189 Ga. App 124, 375 SE2d 230 (1988).

VOLUNTARY INTERACTIONS BETWEEN POLICE AND INDIVIDUALS

There are times when a person might choose to interact with a police officer on a purely voluntary basis. A person might simply ask a police officer a question. The officer might also ask an individual a question. In either of these scenarios, there is no legal requirement that the police must show before they can engage in voluntary interactions. The Fourth Amendment does not prohibit voluntary interaction between citizens and the police.[10] Consider Scenario 13-2.

VOLUNTARY INTERACTION

Officer Mike is walking down the street, and he meets a man going in the opposite direction. Officer Mike asks the man, "Where you headed?"

The man answers, "I'm heading home."

Later, the man seeks to challenge Officer Mike's actions as unconstitutional. Are they?

Answer: No. A police officer is free to ask questions such as this without having to show any legal basis. Similarly, the person being asked is under no compulsion to answer the question.

There would be nothing gained, and a great deal lost, if the police were required to have a legal basis for asking a simple question such as "What's your name?" However, if the officer wishes to detain the person briefly, there is a legal requirement: reasonable suspicion. These brief detentions are referred to as "*Terry* stops."

TERRY STOPS

A police officer may briefly detain a person to ask questions and conduct a short investigation. This detention is not an arrest, and therefore probable cause is not required. This type of stop is a middle ground between a voluntary encounter and a full-blown arrest. They are called ***Terry*** **stops** because of the case in which the concept was developed: *Terry v. Ohio.*[11] Under the *Terry* ruling, an officer who does not have probable cause may briefly detain a suspicious individual in order to determine his identity or to gather more information. In fact, the U.S. Supreme Court's own wording explains it best: "Not all personal interactions between policemen and citizens involve seizures of persons. Only when the officer, by means of physical force or show of authority, has in some way restrained the liberty of a citizen have the Courts concluded that a seizure has occurred."[12] Under this ruling, police do not have to establish probable cause in order to briefly detain a suspect.

Terry **stops**
A brief detention of a suspect to follow up on specific investigative issues.

---

[10] *Coolidge v. New Hampshire*, 403 U.S. 443, 91 S.Ct.2022, 29 L.Ed2d 564 (1971).
[11] 392 U.S. 1, 88 S.Ct.1868, 20 L.Ed2d 889 (1968).
[12] *Terry v. Ohio*, 392 U.S. 1, 88 S.Ct.1868, 20 L.Ed2d 889 (1968).

When Does a "Brief Detention" Become an Arrest? In a *Terry* stop there is often a question about a very simple issue: How "brief" is brief? When does a brief detention cross the line into an arrest? In a real-life situation, activities are fluid, and what began as reasonable suspicion for a stop and frisk can move to probable cause to arrest in just a few seconds.[13] The U.S. Supreme Court has refused to put a specific time period on how long a *Terry* stop should be. Instead, they have opted for a more case-specific approach that takes into account all of the surrounding circumstances. Generally, the facts of the case and the kind of investigation required will determine how reasonable the officer was. In some cases, it will only take a few minutes to verify information. Holding the person longer than that time period would be considered an arrest — and a ruling that the arrest was unconstitutional. However, in other cases, it may take an hour or longer to verify certain information. Whatever the situation, under *Terry* a detention is no longer "brief" when a police officer requests that the suspect accompany him to the police station. The test for an arrest does not change: A *Terry* stop becomes an arrest when a reasonable person, presented with the facts, would conclude that the defendant was under arrest, not simply being detained.[14]

Stop and Frisk. In some situations, a police officer is authorized to actually pat down the outer clothing of an individual he or she has briefly detained. Patting down, or a **stop and frisk**, is permitted under various U.S. Supreme Court decisions, especially *Terry v. Ohio*. However, *Terry* only authorizes such a frisk when it is supported by a reasonable belief that the suspect is armed and dangerous.[15] During a *Terry* stop, an officer can engage in behavior that would normally be considered a seizure of the suspect's person, specifically by patting the suspect down and removing potentially dangerous items from his or her person.[16]

During a *Terry* stop, an officer is permitted to pat down and then "intrude beneath the surface only if he confirms his reasonable belief or suspicion by coming upon something which feels like a weapon."[17] The idea behind pat down and frisk is that when a police officer briefly detains a suspect, there is a greater chance that violence might ensue. The only way to minimize the potential for violence is to allow police officers to pat down the suspect and remove any weapons that they find. "A *Terry* investigation . . . involves a police investigation at close range, when the officer remains particularly vulnerable in part because a full custodial arrest has not been effected, and the officer must make a quick decision as to how to protect himself and others from possible danger."[18]

Stop and frisk
The right of a law enforcement officer to pat down a person's outer clothing for weapons, whether the person is under arrest or not.

---

[13] *People v. Flow*, 37 A.D.3d 303, 831 N.Y.S.2d 129 (1st Dep't 2007).
[14] *United States v. Hill*, 626 F2d 429 (5th Cir 1980).
[15] *Adams v. Williams*, 407 U.S. 143 (1972); *Terry v. Ohio*, 392 U.S. 1, 88 S.Ct.1868, 20 L.Ed2d 889 (1968).
[16] *Adams v. Williams*, 407 U.S. 143, 92 S.Ct.1921, 32 L.Ed2d 612 (1972).
[17] *Hayes v. State*, 202 Ga. App 204, 414 SE2d 321 (1991).
[18] *Michigan v. Long*, 463 U.S. 1032, 103 S.Ct.3469, 77 L.Ed2d 1201 (1983).

THE GUN

During a stop and frisk, a police officer discovers that a suspect has a concealed weapon for which he has no permit. Does this give the officer probable cause to arrest?

Answer: Yes. Because the defendant did not indicate that he had the weapon, an officer in a *Terry* stop can establish probable cause to arrest when the officer recovers a concealed weapon.[19]

When the suspect and the officer are dealing with one another face-to-face, it only makes sense that the officer can take some precautions for his or her safety. Pat downs and frisks are not considered to be searches, and police may not use the pretext of a pat down under *Terry* as carte blanche to search anyone that they please.[20]

Arrest. The final type of interaction between individuals and police is an arrest, which must be supported by probable cause. A person who is under arrest is not free to leave and, at the moment that he or she is arrested, a host of constitutional protections are triggered. These protections will be discussed in Chapter 14.

DEGREE OF PROOF NEEDED TO ESTABLISH PROBABLE CAUSE

Police officers are not required to establish that a suspect is guilty of a crime beyond a reasonable doubt. That standard must be met by the prosecutor during the trial, not by the police officer at the scene of the arrest. The officer must have probable cause that is based on something more substantial than mere rumor or speculation.[21] This means that police officers must often independently verify facts related to them before they will have sufficient probable cause to make an arrest. Probable cause is a middle ground between proof beyond a reasonable doubt and mere suspicion that an action may be a criminal act.

SPECIFIC ACTS THAT ESTABLISH PROBABLE CAUSE

This section will examine specific factual scenarios to determine whether they do or do not establish probable cause, including the following:

- Description over the radio
- Suspicious or unusual behavior
- Information provided by confidential informants
- Anonymous phone calls
- Stops at sobriety or roadside check points

---

[19] *U.S. v. Pontoo*, 666 F.3d 20 (1st Cir. 2011).
[20] *United States v. Berry*, 670 F2d 583 (5th Cir 1982).
[21] *Clark v. State*, 189 Ga. App 124, 375 SE2d 230 (1988).

■ Pretextual Stops
■ Flight
■ Presence at crime scene
■ "Gut feelings" or hunches

Description over the Radio. The Court has stated that an arresting officer does not need personal or direct knowledge of the facts that support probable cause. For instance, an officer may arrest a person simply because he matches a description relayed to him over the police radio.[22]

SCENARIO 13-4	## PROBABLE CAUSE?

Officers Smith and Jones are on patrol when they receive a description of an alleged armed robber's clothing and the car he was driving when he committed the robbery. Smith and Jones stop a car that matches the description and a person who matches the description of the armed robber. They conduct a *Terry* stop and find a bag in the car that has the same name as the gas station where the robbery occurred. They arrest the man. Do they have probable cause?

Answer: Yes. A prudent officer would have believed that the defendant had committed the crime of armed robbery and had reasonable suspicion that a crime had occurred.[23]

Suspicious or Unusual Behavior. Officers who observe individuals acting in strange or bizarre ways may conduct a *Terry* stop. Suspicious behavior, coupled with additional information about a crime having occurred, will provide probable cause.[24]

Information Provided by Confidential Informants. In *Illinois v. Gates*,[25] the U.S. Supreme Court determined that probable cause may be based on an informant's tip. However, probable cause will only exist if "under the totality of the circumstances, including the veracity and basis of knowledge of the informant, there is a fair probability that contraband or evidence of a crime will be found in a particular place."[26] Corroboration of the informant's tip can come from the officer's previous knowledge of the defendant's criminal activities and other investigations.[27] The rules change, though, when the informant is another police officer. In that situation, the reliability of the information is presumed as a matter of law.[28]

---

[22] *Whiteley v. Warden*, 401 U.S. 560, 91 S.Ct.1031, 28 L.Ed2d 306 (1971).
[23] *Chambers v. Maroney*, 399 U.S. 42, 90 S.Ct.1975, 26 L.Ed2d 419 (1970).
[24] *Brinegar v. United States*, 338 U.S. 160, 69 S.Ct.1302, 93 LE 1879 (1949).
[25] 462 U.S. 273, 103 S.Ct.2317, 76 L.Ed2d 527 (1983).
[26] 462 U.S. 273, 103 S.Ct.2317, 76 L.Ed2d 527 (1983).
[27] *Brinegar v. United States*, 338 U.S. 160, 69 S.Ct.1302, 93 LE 1879 (1948).
[28] *Quinn v. State*, 132 Ga. App 395, 208 SE2d 263 (1974).

Anonymous Phone Calls. When police receive an anonymous phone call stating that a specific individual has committed a crime, that fact coupled with the officers' independent investigation or corroboration can provide sufficient probable cause. However, anonymous phone calls by themselves cannot establish probable cause.[29] Courts give them a much higher degree of scrutiny. In a U.S. Supreme Court case, the court ruled that an arrest was unconstitutional when police officers responded to a location after receiving an anonymous phone call and immediately arrested the suspect. Because they did not corroborate the details of the anonymous independently, they lacked probable cause.[30]

Even when the anonymous phone caller gives detailed descriptions, probable cause may not be established. Additional investigation is still required. Courts will look to questions such as, "Can the anonymous caller state with specificity what the defendant's actions would be?" What the courts are looking for with confidential informants is some indication the caller had inside information on the defendant.[31]

Stops at Sobriety or Roadside Check Points. It is very common for police to set up roadblocks to check drivers to see if they have their drivers' licenses and to incidentally determine if anyone is operating under the influence of alcohol or some other drug. Such roadblocks have been ruled constitutional, as long as the officers follow specific procedures. For instance, police must determine how they will stop cars before they set up the roadblock and then follow that procedure during the roadblock. If they have determined that they will stop every car, then they must follow that procedure. Law enforcement is not permitted to single out specific cars for special treatment or to set up a roadblock as subterfuge to catch a particular defendant. Consider Scenario 13-5.

FAKE ROADBLOCK

SCENARIO 13-5

Several police officers have strong suspicions that Calvin is transporting narcotics. They decide that they will set up a roadblock checkpoint near Calvin's home and then not bother to stop any drivers until Calvin comes along. The roadblock will just be a ruse to find an excuse to talk with Calvin and perhaps see what he has in his car. Is this roadblock constitutional?

Answer: No. Officers cannot use a roadblock as a way to secretly check on one motorist. Once the checkpoint is established, they must stop every car or follow the procedure that they instituted at the beginning.[32]

Pretextual Stops. A police officer's decision to stop a suspect for the commission of a traffic violation is not unlawful merely because the officer had reason to believe

---

[29] *Florida v. J.L.,* 529 U.S. 266 (2000).
[30] *Florida v. J.L.,* 529 U.S. 266 (2000).
[31] *Alabama v. White,* 496 U.S. 325, 110 S.Ct.2412, 110 L.Ed2d 301 (1990).
[32] *Michigan Dept. of State Police v. Sitz,* 496 U.S. 444, 110 S.Ct.2481, 110 L.Ed2d 412 (1990).

that the suspect was implicated in committing other crimes. The officer must have valid reason to pull over a suspect, independent of the officer's suspicion regarding the other crimes. Police officers are authorized to stop motor vehicles, even if the reason that they are doing so is something other than a traffic violation. These are referred to as **pretextual stops** and are constitutional, as long as the stop is based on a real violation.[33] (See this chapter's Case Excerpt.)

Pretextual stops
The detention or arrest of a person for a minor offense when the officer really suspects that the defendant has committed a more serious crime.

Flight. One question that often comes up is what happens when the police encounter a person on the street, and after they begin to question him or her, the person flees? Courts have ruled that flight gives the officers probable cause to arrest.[34]

SCENARIO 13-6

FLIGHT

Officer Jo has been alerted that a white male, approximately 50 years of age with black hair, has been reported to have committed a murder in a specific neighborhood. Officer Jo spots a man who roughly matches the description. The man is walking into a store. Officer Jo gets out of her car and confronts the man, asking him to show his hands. Instead, the man runs into the store. Officer Jo tackles the man and arrests him. However, he is not the murder suspect Does she have probable cause anyway?

Answer: Yes.[35] Because the man ran away from Officer Jo, he displayed flight, which satisfies probable cause.

SCENARIO 13-7

FLIGHT?

Officer Dan is on patrol when he receives a call that a man has been seen in a neighborhood, threatening residents with a gun. The officer cruises the neighborhood and sees a man who roughly resembles the 911 description. He stops the man and arrests him, recovering a weapon. It turns out that the man is not the suspect who had threatened others. Does Officer Dan have probable cause to arrest?

Answer: No. Unlike the previous example, the man did not flee when confronted by the officer, so there was no independent action by the suspect that would give the officer probable cause. Officer Dan could have done a *Terry* stop, but he did not have sufficient facts to establish probable cause.[36]

Presence at a Crime Scene. Simply because a person is present at the scene of a crime does not give police the probable cause to arrest. Consider Scenario 13-8.

---

[33] *U.S. v. Randolph*, 628 F.3d 1022 (8th Cir. 2011).
[34] *U.S. v. Laville*, 480 F.3d 187 (3d Cir. 2007).
[35] *Jewett v. Anders*, 521 F.3d 818 (7th Cir. 2008).
[36] *U.S. v. Wali*, 811 F. Supp. 2d 1276 (N.D. Tex. 2011).

WRONG PLACE, WRONG TIME

Jimmy is at a party and someone has called the police. When the police arrive, they pat down the man standing next to Jimmy and recover drugs from him. The police then arrest everyone in the immediate area including Jimmy. Do police have probable cause under these facts?

Answer: No. Mere presence when drugs are recovered from another individual does not give the police probable cause to arrest other people.[37]

"Gut Feelings" or Hunches. Although we often see portrayals of fictional police officers following "hunches" or "gut feelings," the real world is more complex. An officer may well have a feeling that a particular person has committed an offense, but until he or she can present some proof to substantiate it, that feeling cannot form the basis for probable cause, and any arrest based on a hunch will be ruled unconstitutional.

ACTIONS FOLLOWING ARREST

Although you might think that police interrogate everyone after arrest, this is not true. There are many suspects that the police have no need to interrogate. A person who has been arrested for driving under the influence, for instance, will usually not be interrogated. There is very little that the defendant could tell the police that would be helpful to the prosecution. Why the defendant chose to drink that night or where he got drunk is not going to be an issue in the case.

However, there are numerous other circumstances where the police will want to question a suspect after he or she has been arrested. In that event, police must follow a specific procedure or risk violating the Constitution.

The first step in a valid interrogation of a suspect is that he or she must be read the *Miranda* rights. Television and movies often portray these rights being read to suspects, and most people can actually quote the warning from memory. The reason that the *Miranda* warnings are required is that police must inform the defendant that he or she has the right to remain silent, and if the suspect gives up that right, anything the defendant says can and will be used against him or her during the trial.

A. INTERROGATION

Police usually interrogate a suspect in a room or some other secure location, often private. This setting allows the police officers to concentrate on what the defendant is saying and to design questions that will hopefully keep the defendant talking. There are some common misconceptions about **interrogations.** For one thing, police officers are not allowed to use violence against a suspect. Police cannot

Interrogation
Questioning of a suspect to determine if he or she has committed a crime.

---

[37] *U.S. v. Castro-Gaxiola*, 479 F.3d 579 (8th Cir. 2007).

deprive a person of sleep or food or bathroom privileges as a means to "break" the suspect. Although police can use loud tones of voice, they are not allowed to use any physical violence. Another common misconception concerns who is present at the interrogation. If the defendant requests that an attorney be present while he or she is being questioned, then the attorney must be present. Police are not allowed to delay or trick the attorney into going to another location and then to question the defendant "while the attorney is on the way." If a defendant invokes his or her right to remain silent, then questioning must cease. If the defendant states that he or she does not wish to answer any more questions, then questioning must cease.

In addition to these misconceptions, there is at least one other that should be addressed. Prosecutors are generally not present during an interrogation. They do not participate in questioning a suspect, and they rarely observe the questioning while it is going on. The reasons for this are very simple: Unlike police officers, prosecutors are not trained to interrogate anyone. Prosecutors have a different skill set. In addition, should the prosecutor actually decide to be present when an interrogation is being conducted and the defendant says something that will be used in evidence against him or her, then the prosecutor may well become a witness. Because an attorney cannot be both a witness and an attorney in a case, most prosecutors opt not to be present when the interrogation occurs.

ORAL AND WRITTEN STATEMENTS

When the police question a suspect, they do so verbally. They often use recording devices, such as audio or video recorders, but even with this technology, officers usually write down the defendant's statement after he or she has made it. Officers have the defendant review the written statement to make sure that it is actually what the defendant said, then ask for the defendant to sign it.

MIRANDA

Once a defendant has been placed under arrest, a number of important constitutional rights are triggered, including the right to have an attorney, the right to a trial by jury, the right to be presumed innocent, the right not to incriminate oneself and the right to remain silent, among others. These are collectively referred to as *Miranda* **warnings** based on the case through which they were developed.

Miranda **warnings**
The rights that must be read to a person who has been arrested and then questioned by the police.

Before the decision in *Miranda v. Arizona*, there was an open question about these rights. Police officers acknowledged that suspects had these rights and courts were in agreement that suspects should be made aware of them, but the question was who would advise the defendant? Police officers argued that they were in the worst position to advise the suspect of his or her rights. They are not lawyers and have no pretense to understanding the nuances of constitutional interpretation. In briefs submitted during the appeal in *Miranda v. Arizona*, police agencies urged that the court require that defense attorneys be responsible for advising suspects. However, the court determined that although many defendants might have access to defense counsel, many would not. Nevertheless, the court could be sure that there would be at least two people present in every interrogation: the police officer and the suspect. Because of this certainty, the U.S. Supreme Court ruled that police officers were responsible for advising suspects of their *Miranda* rights before they began any post-arrest questioning.

Miranda v. Arizona[38] was a highly controversial case when it was first decided, but it did put an end to speculation about when a suspect should be advised of his or her constitutional rights and who should do the advising. As anyone who watches television or movie legal dramas knows, police officers are responsible for advising suspects, and they must be advised before they are interrogated.

Background of the Miranda *Decision.* Ernesto Miranda was arrested for the kidnapping and rape of a young woman. After his arrest, he was interrogated by police officers for several hours and eventually confessed to the crime. The *Miranda* decision came about when Miranda's attorney appealed his conviction on the basis that his confession should not have been used in his trial because he had never been informed of his rights under the law. The U.S. Supreme Court consolidated Miranda's case with several others in which the same issue was raised and then reached its famous decision. Because Miranda's name was first on the Court's opinion, the ruling became known as the *Miranda decision*, and the requirements imposed by the Court on police became known as *Miranda warnings*.

Under the ruling, the prosecution may not use any statement that was made by the defendant until the state has proven that the defendant knew all of his or her constitutional rights, had the ability to invoke them, then waived them and gave a statement to police. Among these rights, police must specifically tell a suspect that the Fifth Amendment provides the right to remain silent and not incriminate oneself, and if a person waives that right, any statement that he or she makes may be used against that person during the trial to prove that he or she committed the crime. Before the prosecution can introduce the defendant's confession at trial, the prosecutor must call police witnesses to testify that they read the defendant his rights, that he appeared to understand them, that he was not coerced or promised anything to waive his rights, and that he gave his statement after waiving his constitutional rights.

The *Miranda* decision gives little latitude to police officers. The rights must be read, even if the suspect is an attorney, a police officer, or a judge. It does not matter how many times the suspect has been arrested before; he or she must be read the rights again before being questioned in the present case. The only variation that the Court allows is that, as long as the substance of the rights is conveyed to the suspect, it does not matter in what order they are read to him or her.[39]

When Miranda *Does Not Apply.* *Miranda* rights must be read to a suspect who is taken into custody or arrested, *if he is going to be questioned.* An arrest is not unconstitutional if the police fail to read a suspect his or her *Miranda* rights. A suspect must be read the rights before being questioned, but there are circumstances, as noted previously, in which the police have no intention of questioning

---

[38] 384 U.S. 436, 86 S.Ct. 1602, 16 L.Ed.2d 694 (1966).
[39] *Florida v. Powell*, 559. U.S. 722 (2010)

a defendant and therefore do not read the suspect *Miranda* warnings. There is also no requirement that the police must read a person the *Miranda* warnings before being arrested. *Miranda* applies only to post-arrest questioning and interrogation. One might be tempted to think that the police would wish to question everyone that they arrest, but there are numerous circumstances when such questioning never occurs.

There are also other circumstances in which the *Miranda* rights warnings are not required:

- Background or routine police questioning
- Exigent circumstances
- Voluntary statements
- Traffic stops

Background or Routine Police Questioning. When police arrive at the scene of a crime, they will likely ask some typical questions: What happened? Who did it? Where is the person who did the crime? What is the relationship of the people to one another, the victim and the defendant? In these situations, the police are not required to preface their questions with the *Miranda* warnings. When they focus their attention on a specific suspect and begin to ask questions that could incriminate him, they have moved beyond background or routine questioning, and *Miranda* rights apply. However, until that time, officers may question people at the scene without any need to Mirandize everyone they meet.

Exigent circumstance
An emergency situation that poses a threat to persons or to evidence.

Exigent Circumstances. The U.S. Supreme Court has ruled that *Miranda* warnings are not required in **exigent circumstances.** An exigent circumstance is a situation that is inherently dangerous to people or evidence. In an emergency situation, officers are permitted to ask questions that will help them prevent harm to others or prevent evidence from being destroyed. There is no requirement to read the *Miranda* warnings in this situation. Of course, once the situation has been resolved and there is no longer an emergency, the *Miranda* warning requirement resurfaces.

Voluntary Statements. If a suspect voluntarily agrees to speak with police, then *Miranda* does not apply. By volunteering, the suspect is waiving his or her constitutional rights—the very rights spelled out in the *Miranda* warnings. A suspect always has the right to waive the application of those rights to his or her case and freely discuss it with the police. However, law enforcement officers are not permitted to use subterfuge to trick the defendant into giving a "voluntary" statement. For instance, police cannot address one another within earshot of the suspect and say that the suspect is hiding behind his rights or that a "real man would own up to what he had done." Unfortunately, this rule is routinely and almost universally abused by television detectives.

When It Is Lawful to Use Trickery. We have just established that law enforcement cannot use trickery or deceit to make a suspect give up his or her constitutional rights. However, that prohibition does not extend to other areas. Police may lie to a defendant, so long as the lie is not designed to overcome any constitutional protections. Law enforcement might lie to a suspect and tell him or her that a witness saw the suspect or that they have evidence tying him to the scene when they actually do not. Trickery and deception are not commonplace during most interrogations because of the difficulties involved in maintaining the deception. Lies often lead to other lies. If the defendant knows that he wore gloves during the crime and the detectives claim that they recovered his fingerprints from the scene, the defendant will realize that they are lying and may question just how much evidence they actually have that incriminates him. In cases where police use trickery, courts always examine the officers' actions closely, and that is yet another reason to avoid wandering into this legal minefield.

Traffic Stops. When police officers pull over automobile drivers for routine infractions, such as speeding or improper passing, this stop is not considered to be an arrest, and therefore *Miranda* warnings are not required.[40] However, *Miranda* warnings would apply if the police officer were to remove the driver from his or her automobile and place the driver under arrest or transport the driver back to police headquarters for questioning.[41]

B. INVOKING THE RIGHT TO REMAIN SILENT

A criminal suspect has an absolute right to remain silent. When a defendant states that he has nothing to say, police are not permitted to force him to make incriminating statements. A statement obtained in a coercive way is not admissible at trial. When the suspect states that he does not wish to say anything until he speaks with his attorney, questioning must also stop at that point. Police officers are not allowed to try to talk the suspect out of his need for an attorney or to continue questioning him until his attorney arrives. A recent Supreme Court case has held, however, that a defendant must tell the police that he or she intends to remain silent. The suspect cannot simply refuse to answer and have the police infer that he or she intends to remain silent.[42]

C. REQUESTING AN ATTORNEY

During questioning, the suspect has the right to request an attorney. Police officers are not allowed to try to talk the defendant out of his right to an attorney or to state that only someone who was guilty would want an attorney. However, if the suspect's request for an attorney is vague, police may continue to question him or her until he either refuses to answer any more questions or makes an unequivocal request for an attorney. Consider Scenarios 13-9 and 13-10.

---

[40] *Pennsylvania v. Bruder*, 488 U.S. 292 (1990).
[41] *Berkemer v. McCarty*, 103 S.Ct. 3138 (1984).
[42] *Berghuis v. Thompkins*, 130 S.Ct. 1499 (2010).

SCENARIO 13-9   UNEQUIVOCAL REQUEST FOR AN ATTORNEY (1)

Tad is being questioned by the police in connection with a series of burglaries. During the questioning, Tad says, "I wonder if I should to talk to my lawyer."

The officer responds that he certainly has that right, but they would like to get some more information from him to clear up the charges. Is any continued questioning by the police constitutional?

Answer: Yes. Because the defendant did not give an unequivocal request for an attorney, questioning can continue.

SCENARIO 13-10   UNEQUIVOCAL REQUEST FOR AN ATTORNEY (2)

It's about an hour later, and Tad is still being questioned.

The police officer asks Tad, "Why did you commit these burglaries? Did you need the money?"

Tad responds, "I want my lawyer."

Can police continue questioning Tad?

Answer: No. Tad's request is now definitely unequivocal, and all questioning must cease until Tad's attorney arrives.

In most situations, when an attorney arrives at the interrogation, he or she usually advises the suspect to stop answering any questions and to end the interview.

D. REINITIATING INTERROGATION

A question often arises during the course of repeated interrogations of a suspect: How long are the *Miranda* rights "good" for? Put another way, is it sufficient to read the suspect his or her *Miranda* rights once and then never read them again? Do the rights eventually expire? When police officers initially question a suspect and read that suspect the *Miranda* warnings, must they be read every time that they question the suspect after that?

Police officers are not required to re-Mirandize a suspect each and every time that they question him. However, once the suspect has invoked his right to remain silent, the situation changes. In one case, *Edwards v. Arizona*,[43] a suspect (Edwards) was arrested on burglary and murder charges. During questioning, Edwards said that he wanted to consult with an attorney before making any further statements. The police officers stopped the interview and returned Edwards to his cell. At this point, the officers had acted in accordance with *Miranda*. However, the following day, two other police officers appeared at the jail and asked to see Edwards. He refused to speak with the officers but was told by a guard that he must. He was read

---

[43] 451 U.S. 477 (1981).

his *Miranda* rights again, and during this interrogation made incriminating statements that were later used against him at trial. The U.S. Supreme Court held that the use of his statement violated his right to have an attorney present during his questioning. Edwards, according to the Court, had made an unequivocal request for an attorney. His questioning the next day did not waive that right.

A suspect must knowingly and intelligently relinquish his rights. The U.S. Supreme Court has placed the burden for showing compliance with its decisions squarely on the shoulders of the state. Therefore, the state must show that the defendant voluntarily waived his rights before the statement can be read to the jury. When police reinitiate questioning of a suspect, they may rely on the fact that they Mirandized the suspect the first time; however, if any appreciable period of time has passed between the first questioning and the second, police must read the suspect his or her *Miranda* rights again. Courts have been vague on just how long this appreciable period is. The safest course for a police officer to follow when there is any doubt about whether the first reading of *Miranda* rights was sufficient is to Mirandize the suspect again.

E. PROCEDURE AFTER ARREST

Once a person is placed under arrest, he or she is then transported to the local detention facility where the typical book-in procedures take place. The person will be fingerprinted, have all belongings taken away and stored for safekeeping, issued a jail uniform with sandals and then assigned to a cell. However, there are numerous instances in which this procedure is not followed. For instance, suppose that a suspect has been arrested on a misdemeanor count. Many jail facilities post bond amounts for specific types of offenses. For example, a first-offense theft by shoplifting might carry a bond of $500. If the defendant can pay the bond, then he or she will be released on the bond after being fingerprinted. If the defendant cannot make bond, then he or she will be held at the local detention facility until the initial appearance.

STATE v. BARROW
408 N.J.Super. 509, 975 A.2d 539 (N.J.Super.A.D.,2009)

On appeal, defendant raises the following contentions:

POINT I

BECAUSE THE PROVISIONS OF N.J.S.A. 39:3–74 DO NOT APPLY TO A PAIR OF MINIATURE BOXING GLOVES THAT ARE HANGING FROM THE REARVIEW MIRROR, THERE WAS NO OBJECTIVELY REASONABLE LEGAL BASIS FOR THE POLICE TO STOP MR. ROSATO'S VEHICLE ON OCTOBER 25, 2005, AND THE EVIDENCE OBTAINED FROM THAT UNLAWFUL STOP MUST BE SUPPRESSED.

A. The otherwise lawful operation of a vehicle with small items hanging from a rearview mirror does not violate the provisions of N.J.S.A. 39:3–74 that prohibit the operation of a motor vehicle with items upon the front windshield or side windows, and a resulting traffic stop based on this premise is unlawful.

B. There is no reasonable articulable basis to believe that the operation of a motor vehicle with small items hanging from a rearview mirror unduly interferes with the driver's vision, in violation of the third paragraph of N.J.S.A. 39:3–74, and a resulting traffic stop based on this premise is unlawful.

We reject these contentions and affirm.

The following facts are summarized from the record. On October 21, 2005 at 12:26 a.m., Officer Ted Wittke of the Hazlet Township Police Department was on routine patrol in uniform and in a marked patrol car. While stopped at a red traffic light on Holmdel Road, at its intersection with Route 35, the officer saw a small Acura sports car also stopped at the light facing him in the opposite direction. At some point, Wittke also saw two rounded objects hanging from the Acura's rearview mirror.

Wittke testified that he will stop a vehicle on a case-by-case basis for items hanging from a rearview mirror based on the size of the items, how far they hang down from the rearview mirror, and whether he believed they obstructed the driver's view. In this case, he decided to stop the Acura because the items hanging from the rearview mirror were larger than a Christmas tree air freshener, and were swaying and hanging approximately seven inches from the rearview mirror at the driver's eye level. The officer said that he "observed the Acura had items hanging from the rearview mirror, which he believed obstructed the view of the driver." It was later discovered that the hanging items were boxing gloves measuring 3-1/2 inches high and 3-1/2 inches wide.

Wittke continued that when the light turned green, both vehicles turned onto Route 35 north, with the Acura in front of his patrol car. He activated his overhead lights, but the Acura did not immediately stop. Instead, it coasted to the shoulder, traveled approximately two hundred feet, and entered a parking lot. Wittke became uncomfortable with the time it took the driver to stop. He illuminated the inside of the Acura with a spotlight and saw the passenger, later identified as defendant, leaning forward with his shoulders moving. At this point, the officer suspected that defendant may be either reaching for a weapon or destroying narcotics. He was afraid for his safety, so he radioed for back-up.

After the Acura stopped, Wittke exited his patrol car and cautiously approached the driver's side. When he looked inside the vehicle, he saw defendant sit straight back and stop moving. He then advised the driver that he stopped him because of the items hanging from the rearview mirror. While the driver was taking the items down, the officer saw that defendant moved around and placed his left hand in his left pant pocket. Wittke immediately instructed defendant to remove his hand from the pocket and place his hands where the officer could see them. Defendant complied and told the officer not to worry about him.

Wittke also testified that as a result of defendant's actions, he became increasingly apprehensive and anxious and radioed for additional backup. Officer Michael Duncan and Canine Officer Kevin Geoghan arrived at the scene. Wittke then had defendant exit the vehicle, at which time the officer observed that defendant was "very, very nervous . . . his hands were shaking . . . and his speech wasn't very clear." Based on Wittke's experience in prior narcotics arrests, he believed that defendant was concealing narcotics. Thus, he asked Officer Geoghan to conduct a canine "sniff of the vehicle." The dog indicated the presence of narcotics on the passenger side door; however, a search of the passenger area revealed no narcotics.

Wittke then advised defendant "that the dog did alert positively for the smell of narcotics on defendant's side of the vehicle." Defendant responded, "I don't understand, I don't do drugs. You go ahead and search me." Defendant then began pulling items from his pocket, including a pack of cigarettes. Wittke's search of the cigarette pack revealed a glassine plastic bag containing a white substance, which based on his training and experience, he believed was cocaine. Wittke advised defendant of his *Miranda* rights and placed him under arrest. A further search of defendant's person revealed another glycine bag containing "six yellowish pills," which defendant admitted were ecstasy (methamphetamine).

Wittke also issued the driver a summons for violating N.J.S.A. 39:3–74, based on the items hanging from the rearview mirror. The driver pled guilty and paid a fine.

Defendant filed a motion to suppress, contending that the stop was unlawful because N.J.S.A. 39:3–74 does not prohibit items hanging from a rearview mirror, and because the boxing gloves did not unduly interfere with the driver's vision. Finding Wittke's testimony credible, the motion judge denied the motion, concluding that the officer had a reasonable and articulable suspicion that the driver had committed a motor vehicle violation. The judge reasoned that:

> I think that it arguably falls within the definition of this statute. I think that the purpose that windshields be unobstructed that if there is something that is swinging back and forth, it could obstruct or interfere with a driver's vision.

> Did it unduly, I mean, that would be a question for the Court trying that traffic offense. But it was enough to bring it to the officer's attention and I find that it was a reasonable decision on his part and it falls within the broad parameters of Paragraph 3 of N.J.S.A. 39:3–74.

> It's true that there is no case in New Jersey that says that this is acceptable and that it — it's also true it doesn't outright specify that items can't hang from the rearview mirror. But as I indicated, it can be construed as unduly interfering in the larger, the obstruction that would go toward whether the motorist would be convicted of the offense, whether it would unduly interfere. And as I said, that's not before me. It's whether the officer acted reasonably in stopping the car for that infraction.

Law enforcement officers "may stop motor vehicles where they have a reasonable or articulable suspicion that a motor vehicle violation has occurred." *State v. Murphy*, 238 N.J.Super. 546, 553, 570 A.2d 451 (App.Div.1990). "Reasonable suspicion" means that "the police officer must be able to point to specific and articulable facts which, taken together with rational inferences from those facts, reasonably warrant that intrusion." *Terry v. Ohio*, 392 U.S. 1, 21, 88 S.Ct. 1868, 1880, 20 L.Ed.2d 889, 906 (1968). "Reasonable suspicion" is "less than proof . . . by a preponderance of evidence," and "less demanding than that for probable cause," but must be something greater "than an 'inchoate or unparticularized suspicion or' 'hunch.'" *United States v. Sokolow*, 490 U.S. 1, 7, 109 S.Ct. 1581, 1585, 104 L.Ed.2d 1, 10 (1989).

The fact that the officer does not have the state of mind hypothesized by the reasons which provide the legal justification for the search and seizure or investigatory stop does not invalidate the action taken, so long as the circumstances, viewed objectively, support the police conduct." A Fourth Amendment violation is assessed based upon an objective viewing of the officer's actions considering the circumstances confronting him at that time, not his actual state of mind.

Ultimately, courts will not inquire into the motivation of a police officer whose stop of an automobile is based upon a traffic violation committed in his presence. The fact that the justification for the stop was pretextual . . . is irrelevant," The State need not prove that the suspected motor vehicle violation has in fact occurred, only that the officer had a reasonable, articulable, and objective basis for justifying the stop. Investigatory stops are valid in situations where the objective basis for the stop was a minor traffic infraction.

Here, in denying the motion to suppress, the judge found Wittke's testimony credible, and concluded the officer had a reasonable suspicion that defendant committed a motor vehicle violation justifying the stop. We agree.

N.J.S.A. 39:3–74 provides as follows:

Every motor vehicle having a windshield shall be equipped with at least one device in good working order for cleaning rain, snow or other moisture from the windshield so as to provide clear vision for the driver, and all such devices shall be so constructed and installed as to be operated or controlled by the driver.

No person shall drive any motor vehicle with any sign, poster, sticker or other non-transparent material upon the front windshield, wings, deflectors, side shields, corner lights adjoining windshield or front side windows of such vehicle other than a certificate or other article required to be so displayed by **546 statute or by regulations of the commissioner.

No person shall drive any vehicle so constructed, equipped or loaded as to unduly interfere with the driver's vision to the front and to the sides.

The State concedes that the first two paragraphs of the statute do not apply to items hanging from a rearview mirror. Accordingly, we need not address defendant's contentions regarding those paragraphs and the cases he cites interpreting paragraph two. However, the State posits that Wittke had a reasonable basis for the stop because the third paragraph of N.J.S.A. 39:3–74 applies to the boxing gloves.

Defendant responds that the third paragraph only applies to a vehicle that is "constructed, equipped or loaded" with an offending item. Thus, because the boxing gloves are not part of the vehicle's construction, and do not represent the vehicle's equipment or load, defendant concludes that Wittke lacked a reasonable articulable basis to believe that they violated the statute.

Defendant's argument lacks merit. The third paragraph of N.J.S.A. 39:3–74 applies to vehicles that are "constructed, equipped or loaded as to unduly interfere with the driver's vision to the front and to the sides." Among other definitions, "loaded" is defined as "something carried or to be carried at one time or in one trip; burden; cargo" Webster's New World Dictionary, 792 (3d ed. 1988). Accordingly, "loaded" applies to objects that are carried and placed in a vehicle, including items hung from a rearview mirror, such as the boxing gloves. It is unreasonable to conclude that a statute regulating a driver's vision, such as N.J.S.A. 39:3–74, would not include such an object if, in fact, the object unduly interfered with the driver's vision.

The question then is whether Wittke had a reasonable, articulable belief that the boxing gloves "unduly interfered" with the driver's vision. Defendant contends that the officer never articulated how the boxing gloves actually unduly interfered with the driver's vision and, thus, the statute was not satisfied. Defendant is wrong. Wittke testified that he believed the swaying boxing gloves "obstructed" the driver's view. Although N.J.S.A. 39:3–74 does not define "unduly interfere," "unduly" is defined, in part, as "excessively" and "interfere" is defined, in part as "interposed in a way that hinders or impedes." Webster's Third New International Dictionary, 1178, 2492 (1981). "Obstruct" is defined, in part, as "to cut off from sight: shut out." Id. at 1559.

Other states with statutes such as N.J.S.A. 39:3–74 follow one of three distinct approaches to construing obstruction violations which directly refer to the driver's "vision" or "view." These are: (1) statutes that criminalize the placement of objects that "materially obstruct" the driver's vision (the "materially obstruct" approach); (2) statutes that criminalize the placement of objects that "obstruct" or "obstruct or impair the driver's vision" (the "majority approach"); and (3) statutes that criminalize the placement of any object between the driver and the windshield (the "minority approach").

We do not address whether sufficient proof beyond a reasonable doubt existed that the statute was, in fact, violated. That issue is not before us, given the driver's guilty plea. Our holding is confined to the constitutionality of the stop of the automobile in which defendant was a passenger.

Affirmed.

---

1 What was the initial reason for pulling over the defendant in this case?
2 How does this court define "reasonable suspicion"?
3 Suppose that the officer in this case was merely stopping the defendant on a pretext? Would that make the arrest invalid?
4 Were the officer's actions appropriate in this case?

CASE QUESTIONS

CHAPTER SUMMARY

This chapter examined the concept of arrest. A person who is under arrest is not free to leave. Courts do not leave this determination to the police officer or the defendant. Instead, the courts have created a reasonable, third-person standard. When a reasonable person would believe that the defendant was not free to leave, then the defendant is under arrest, despite what the officer says or the defendant believes. Only licensed police officers can make arrests. Although there is a provision in law that allows citizens to make detentions; these so-called "citizen's arrests" merely allow citizens to detain a suspect so that the police can make an arrest. A police officer who is in fresh pursuit of a suspect may cross over the geographic boundaries of the officer's authority and pursue the suspect into another county or even another state.

There are three types of interactions between individuals and police officers. First, there are voluntary interactions, which do not require any constitutional showing by the police. Second, there are "*Terry*" stops, which were authorized in the case of *Terry v. Ohio*. Under this ruling, an officer may briefly detain a suspect when the officer has reasonable suspicion that the suspect is involved in illegal activity. During a *Terry* stop, police are allowed to frisk a suspect for weapons. Third, there are arrests. An arrest must be support by probable cause, which is a reasonable belief that the suspect has committed crime.

Following arrest, a suspect can be interrogated. When the police decide to interrogate a suspect, they must read him or her the *Miranda* warnings. These warnings are required by the U.S. Supreme Court.

KEY TERMS

Jurisdiction

Venue

Fresh pursuit doctrine

Citizen's arrest

Terry stops

Stop and frisk

Pretextual stops

Interrogation

Miranda rights

Exigent circumstance

REVIEW QUESTIONS

1 How is arrest defined?
2 Explain probable cause.
3 Who is authorized to make arrests?
4 Explain the relationship between jurisdiction and venue.
5 What is the fresh pursuit doctrine?
6 What is the difference between a police officer's arrest and a "citizen's arrest"?
7 Explain the difference between jurisdiction and venue.
8 Why is it important to determine when the suspect is actually under arrest?
9 What test has the court system created to determine when a person is considered to be under arrest?
10 Explain probable cause.
11 What constitutional standard must a police officer show in order to justify a *Terry* stop?
12 How long can a *Terry* stop be? Is there a constitutional time limit on *Terry* stops?
13 What is a "stop and frisk"?
14 Give some examples from this chapter that can establish probable cause for arrest.
15 What is a pretextual stop?
16 Does flight give probable cause for arrest? Explain.

17 How does a police officer's "gut feeling" play into establishing probable cause?

18 Who is normally present during a police interrogation?

19 What are the *Miranda* rights?

20 Why were the *Miranda* rights created?

21 What are some arguments that law enforcement put forth in originally arguing against *Miranda* rights?

22 Provide some examples where police are not required to read a suspect *Miranda* rights.

23 What are exigent circumstances?

24 When and under what circumstances can police use trickery during an interrogation?

25 What is the rule about *Miranda* rights and reinitiated interrogation?

QUESTIONS FOR ANALYSIS

1 Is it time for the American judicial system to do away with *Miranda* rights? There have been several initiatives to get rid of them. Create an argument for or against that position.

2 Is it fair that courts allow pretextual stops? Explain your answer.

HYPOTHETICALS

1 Officer Jan receives an email from a person whom she does not know. In the email, the writer describes the time and place where a cocaine sale will occur. The email is detailed about the location, who will be present, what amount will change hands, and the time it will occur. The email is signed, "Ted." Officer Jan cannot recall meeting anyone named Ted. Based on this email, can she go to the meeting and make an arrest?

2 Javon is home one evening when he hears a knock on his door. When he opens it, he sees a police officer standing there. The officer asks Javon if he will come down to police headquarters to discuss some matters that might concern him. Javon says that he will go and volunteers to follow the officer to headquarters in his own car. The officer agrees. About halfway to headquarters, Javon changes his mind, turns his car around, and starts driving home. The officer follows him, turns on his patrol car lights, then arrests Javon. The officer claims that Javon was fleeing. Does the officer have probable cause?

3 Nora has a deep-seated phobia of anyone in uniform and is especially afraid of police officers. One day, she is pulled over for failing to yield to another car. As the officer approaches her car, Nora jumps out and starts screaming. The officer orders her to get on the ground and to stop screaming. Instead, Nora starts to run away. The officer tackles her and places her under arrest. Is this a constitutional arrest? Why or why not?

Warrants for Arrest, Search, and Seizure

Chapter Objectives

■ Explain the process that law enforcement officers use to obtain arrest warrants
■ Define the role of the magistrate in issuing a warrant
■ Explain the details that a warrant must have to make it legally sufficient
■ Describe situations where search warrants are not required
■ Discuss the various ways that a warrant may be challenged

I   INTRODUCTION TO WARRANTS

The last chapter considered the law of arrest and the procedural steps that occur after arrest, concentrating on arrests that occur without warrants. Many arrests occur after a warrant has been issued. This chapter will examine exactly how such an arrest warrant is issued and also describe how and under what circumstances search warrants may be issued.

A. COURTS HAVE A PREFERENCE FOR WARRANTS

Courts have always preferred that an arrest or a search be conducted with a warrant. The reasoning behind this approach is simple: When a warrant is issued, some third party — specifically a magistrate or other judge — has reviewed the facts and made a determination that probable cause exists. This takes the factual evaluation of probable cause out of the hands of the police and places it in the judiciary. Having a neutral, third-party review the facts is far more likely to result in a ruling that will follow the law. As shown in Chapter 13, an arrest must be supported by probable cause whether or not it is carried out with a warrant. However, in the case where a law enforcement officer applies for a warrant, the determination of whether or not probable cause exists is removed from the officer's discretion and placed into the hands of a magistrate.

A magistrate's determination that probable cause exists does not always mean that probable cause exists, but a judicial determination raises a presumption that this is the case. Warrants are preferred for arrests or searches because those carried out without a warrant are given greater scrutiny.

A police officer who carries out an arrest has greater freedom to operate without a warrant than the same officer would have when in a search.[1] Human beings are mobile, dangerous, and can flee a scene. As such, it doesn't make sense to require an officer to spend an hour or more obtaining an arrest warrant before any arrests could be made. However, the same philosophy applies in the opposite manner when it comes to searches. Structures, places, and secured automobiles have none of the characteristics of a live person. These places can be secured and police will be required to wait until a search warrant has been issued unless the search falls within some narrowly defined exceptions to the search warrant requirement.[2]

Whether or not a warrant has been issued, all arrests and search warrants must be based on probable cause.

 ARREST WARRANTS

Although probable cause to arrest and probable cause to search have generally been considered to be more or less the same thing, the day-to-day experience of police officers reveals a gap between theory and practice. Probable cause to arrest goes to the ultimate issue of the guilt of the defendant. Probable cause to search boils down to the likelihood of finding evidence in a particular place. For arrests, the rule that has been followed for centuries is that police officers can arrest without a warrant for serious offenses or offenses that have been committed in their presence, but must seek arrest warrants in other situations.[3] Some commentators have even suggested that probable cause to arrest is actually a higher standard than the probable cause necessary to justify a search warrant. Certainly the consequences to the defendant are different. In one, he loses his liberty, in another, his property.

A. THE FOURTH AMENDMENT ONLY APPLIES TO GOVERNMENT CONDUCT

It is important to note at the outset that the arrest warrant requirement only applies to the government, or more specifically, law enforcement. Private individuals are not required to seek arrest warrants. They may go before a magistrate or other judicial official to request that the court issue an arrest warrant, but the court is under no obligation to do so.

---

[1] *Mowrer v. State*, 447 N.E.2d 1129 (Ind. Ct. App. 4th Dist. 1983).
[2] *Draper v. U.S.*, 358 U.S. 307 (1959).
[3] *Morrow v. State*, 140 Neb. 592, 300 N.W. 843 (1941).

B. APPLYING FOR AN ARREST WARRANT

When police officers wish to obtain an arrest warrant, they usually appear before a local judge or magistrate. Because the terminology varies considerably from state to state, we will use the term **magistrate** to refer to the judicial position that is authorized to issue **warrants.** The normal practice is for the officer to fill out a warrant application and include an **affidavit** to support the facts contained in the application. An affidavit is a written statement that contains an oath by the person who made the document that it is correct and contains no perjury. For an arrest, the officer must create a sworn statement that lists the actions carried out by the suspect and why these activities establish probable cause to justify the court in issuing a warrant for the suspect's arrest. (Note that this procedure can vary from jurisdiction to jurisdiction.) Affidavits for arrest warrants are often required by state constitutions.[4] When courts review affidavits, they interpret the language contained in a liberal manner. Hearsay and other evidentiary objections are not considered when evaluating the evidence provided in the affidavit.[5] There is no requirement that a police officer put the precise legal wording in the affidavit. The ultimate charge to be brought against the suspect is the province of the District Attorney. An affidavit violates the Fourth Amendment when the officer knowingly includes false statements.[6]

Once the application and affidavit have been given to the magistrate, he or she must evaluate the facts and make a determination that probable cause exists to arrest the defendant. The arrest warrant must be based on the warrant application and the sworn statement that accompanies it, not on information known only to the magistrate or not communicated through the documents. The facts presented must be sufficient to justify a neutral and detached magistrate to reach the conclusion that the suspect has committed a crime. When a judge makes a probable cause determination, it must be based on the facts presented by the officer, not a gut feeling or a personal bias on the part of the magistrate. If the warrant is later challenged by a defendant, appellate courts will only require that the judge had a "substantial basis" for reaching the conclusion that probable cause existed. Courts will only make this ruling when the judge is "clearly wrong." The chances of overturning a warrant on appeal are low. Consider Scenario 14-1.

Magistrate
A judge who has limited power and authority.

Warrant
An order, issued by a judge that authorizes a police officer to arrest a suspect or conduct a search.

Affidavit
A written statement where a person swears an oath that the facts contained are true.

> **Sidebar**
>
> *An arrest warrant is issued by a magistrate after a law enforcement has made a sufficient showing that there is probable cause to believe that the suspect has committed a crime.*

SUSPECT IS GUILTY

SCENARIO 14-1

Danny Detective has applied for a warrant and in his affidavit, he declares, "Suspect John Doe is guilty of selling Schedule II narcotics." Is this language sufficient for a magistrate to determine probable cause?

continued

---

[4] *Harvey v. Commonwealth*, 226 Ky. 36, 10 S.W.2d 471 (1928).
[5] *U.S. v. Ventresca*, 380 U.S. 102, 85 S. Ct. 741, 13 L. Ed. 2d 684 (1965).
[6] *Kerns v. Board of Com'rs of Bernalillo County*, 707 F. Supp. 2d 1190 (D.N.M. 2010).

SCENARIO 14-1

(continued)

Answer: No. When an affidavit simply states that the suspect committed a crime, it is not enough.[7] The affidavit must provide facts that a magistrate can review and then reach a decision about the existence of probable cause.

Unlike other procedural steps discussed in this text, a defendant is not entitled to know that a warrant has been issued for his or her arrest. The obvious reason for this rule is that if a person knew that a warrant had been issued, he or she might flee the area.[8]

C. THE MAGISTRATE

In addition to the requirements placed on law enforcement officers to provide sworn testimony to support a warrant, there are also requirements placed on the magistrate. Magistrates must be neutral and detached from the proceedings. Magistrates cannot have a vested interest in having a person arrested.[9] They cannot, for example, receive a bonus for every warrant that they issue. Although the people who issue warrants are often referred to as magistrates, there is considerable variation among the states for the name of this position. By whatever name, this individual must be legally empowered to issue warrants and must be neutral and detached. Individuals who are authorized to issue warrants include magistrates, judges, or judicial officers. The magistrate cannot be a prosecutor or a police officer. The individual must operate independently from both. In many states, magistrates are not lawyers or judges. These states allow citizens to serve in the capacity of magistrates, once they have received training from the state about the duties and responsibilities of the office.

D. DRAFTING THE WARRANT

The warrant must state the crime that law enforcement maintains the suspect has violated, but there is some flexibility here. Where the wording of indictments (discussed in Chapter 15) must be precise, warrants are held to a more liberal standard. This means that if the officer incorrectly lists the name of the offense or commits some other typographical error in describing the offense, the warrant will not be considered invalid.[10] So long as the warrant closely follows the wording of the statute, it will be considered legally sufficient.[11]

---

[7] *Whiteley v. Warden*, Wyo. State Penitentiary, 401 U.S. 560, 91 S. Ct. 1031, 28 L. Ed. 2d 306 (1971).
[8] *State v. Dabney*, 264 Wis. 2d 843, 2003 WI App 108, 663 N.W.2d 366 (Ct. App. 2003).
[9] *State v. Penalber*, 386 N.J. Super. 1, 898 A.2d 538 (App. Div. 2006).
[10] *Hopper v. City of Prattville*, 781 So. 2d 346 (Ala. Crim. App. 2000).
[11] *State v. Garcia*, 146 N.C. App. 745, 553 S.E.2d 914 (2001).

E. LEGALLY SUFFICIENT ARREST WARRANT

What makes a warrant legally valid? Here are the features of a valid warrant. It must:

- Be prepared in the correct form
- Be issued by a magistrate or other court that has authority to issue warrants
- Be issued by a court that has jurisdiction over the suspect
- Bear the name of the person to be arrested or provide a description that identifies a specific person

A warrant remains legally sufficient even if it contains typographical errors, including incorrect dates and times.[12] Arrest and search warrants are given a certain amount of latitude. If the warrant is sufficient on its face or has an obvious and explainable error, then it will still be considered valid. However, there are some features that must appear in a warrant. For example, applying the list above, if a warrant is issued by a court that has no jurisdiction to do so, it will be invalid. Similarly, a warrant must be signed by the magistrate to be effective. Consider Scenario 14-2.

FRIENDLY JUDGE

SCENARIO 14-2

Danielle Detective knows a "friendly" judge who will issue warrants without inquiring too seriously into the details presented in sworn testimony. Danielle appears before the judge, but before the warrant is officially issued and signed, the judge is called away. Danielle is in a hurry, takes the unsigned warrant, and uses it to arrest Sally Suspect. Is this a legally sufficient warrant?

Answer: No. An arrest based on unsigned warrant is not legally valid.[13]

THE "FOUR CORNERS" TEST

A magistrate must limit his or her review of the warrant application to the materials presented. This is the **"Four Corners" test**, which essentially means that the magistrate's decision must be based on the material presented within the four corners of the application and affidavit. The affidavit and accompanying sworn testimony must be sufficient on its face to authorize the magistrate to issue the warrant. (There are jurisdictions that allow a magistrate to base the warrant not only on the evidence presented, but also the magistrate's personal knowledge, but these are in the minority.[14])

"Four Corners" test
A judicial requirement that a warrant affidavit contain all necessary information in the materials before the warrant was issued.

IDENTIFYING THE PERSON TO BE ARRESTED

A person whose first and last names appear on the warrant can be validly arrested, even if he or she is known by some other name or alias. Courts have even held that

---

[12] *Burke v. Town Of Walpole*, 405 F.3d 66 (1st Cir. 2005).
[13] *State v. Wilson*, 6 S.W.3d 504 (Tenn. Crim. App. 1998).
[14] *State v. Davidson*, 260 Neb. 417, 618 N.W.2d 418 (2000).

warrants that drastically misspell the suspect's name, but are close to his or her name phonetically, will still be considered constitutional.[15] Consider Scenario 14-3.

SCENARIO 14-3

DIFFERENT NAMES

Officer Tate has applied for a warrant. To the best of his knowledge, the suspect in a series of armed robberies is known as Jorge Luis Escobar Henao. However, when the warrant is issued, the judge writes the name as George Louis Escobar Henao. Is this warrant legally valid?

   Answer: Yes. As long as the warrant sufficiently describes the person to be arrested and, although the warrant spells the person's name incorrectly, the names — as they would be pronounced in English — sound the same. The officer may proceed.

Suppose that law enforcement does not know the suspect's name? In such a case, they can draft a warrant that uses the suspect's nickname, as long as the description includes enough detail that the defendant can be identified with reasonable certainty.[16] (See this chapter's Case Excerpt.)

FAMOUS CASES
TED BUNDY

Ted Bundy was smart, on the fast track to a career in both law and politics. Charming and good looking, he attracted women, which made it easy for him to become one of the most prolific serial killers in U.S. history.

   Born in Burlington, Vermont, to an unmarried mother in 1946, Bundy believed until adulthood that his mother was his sister and his grandparents were his true parents. The identity of his father remains a mystery, but many family members suspected that his grandfather — a violent, abusive bully — might have fathered Bundy. His mother eventually moved with her son to Tacoma, Washington, where she married Johnnie Bundy, who adopted young Ted.

   Ted Bundy attended both the University of Puget Sound and the University of Washington (UW), but he was not an accomplished student. After a painful breakup with a girlfriend, he dropped out in 1968, getting by on a succession of minimum-wage jobs. It was around this time he learned of his true parentage and plunged into depression. Before long, however, Bundy met a new girl and, feeling re-energized, returned to UW, from which he graduated in 1972. After college, he joined Governor Daniel Evans' re-election campaign and applied to law school in Utah. He also became assistant to the chairman of the Washington State Republican Party. At the same time, young women began disappearing in the Pacific Northwest.

---

[15] *Fulgencio v. City of Los Angeles*, 131 Fed. Appx. 96 (9th Cir. 2005).
[16] Fed. R. Crim. P. 4(b)(1)(A).

It is unknown exactly who Bundy's first victim was or how many women he actually murdered, but he confessed to 30 homicides in seven states between 1974 and 1978. It is widely suspected that he began murdering as a teenager. But by the time he commenced his rampage in 1974, he had perfected his ability to leave few clues at the scene of the murder. His method for luring women was simple: He would wear a fake cast or feign some other disability and ask for help. His sham helplessness, combined with his good looks, made women trust him and eagerly offer assistance. Once Bundy had them isolated, he overpowered and killed them, usually with blunt force to the head. Twelve of his victims were decapitated. All of the women were young, white, attractive, and had long hair parted in the middle.

Bundy frequently revisited the sites of his murder, performing sex acts on the corpses, combing their hair, and applying makeup until they had decomposed to the point it was no longer possible. Additionally, he kept some of the severed heads in his apartment as mementos. In the fall of 1974, Bundy moved to Utah to attend law school. The series of murders in the Pacific Northwest abruptly ceased, and women then began disappearing in Utah.

In Salt Lake City, Bundy's modus operandi expanded from feigning injury. He picked up hitchhikers and posed as a policeman, using assumed authority to convince young women to leave with him. His girlfriend back in Washington became suspicious when the Pacific Northwest homicides seemed to shift to Utah, appearing to follow Bundy. She alerted police, who added Bundy's name to a list of suspects, but they had no solid evidence to link him to the crimes in either state.

Bundy was first arrested outside of Salt Lake City by a Utah Highway Patrol officer. The officer tried to pull him over for a routine traffic violation, but Bundy sped away. When the officer caught up with him, he saw that the front passenger seat was missing. Upon searching the car he found a pantyhose mask with cutouts for eye holes, a crowbar, handcuffs, and other questionable items. Following further investigation, police felt they had enough evidence, including strands of hair, to charge him with kidnapping Carol DaRonch, one of his victims who managed to escape. DaRonch identified Bundy in a lineup, and he was convicted and sentenced to 15 years.

With Bundy safely in prison, investigators pieced together enough evidence to link him to the murders in Colorado. He was extradited to Colorado, but during his trial in December 1977 he managed to escape from custody, using a smuggled hacksaw to cut a hole in the ceiling of his cell. He fled first to Chicago then to Atlanta, before finally boarding a bus to Tallahassee, Florida, on January 8, 1978. During the next month, Bundy continued his murderous ways, killing two women at a Florida State University sorority house, seriously injuring two other sorority members and another FSU student, and killing a 12-year-old junior high school girl in Lake City, Florida.

Running out of money and fearing that authorities were closing in, Bundy stole a car and drove west across the Florida panhandle. On February 15, a Pensacola police officer stopped and arrested him when a warrants check showed the car was stolen. As the officer transported Bundy to jail, he said, "I wish you had killed me."

In two separate trials, one in 1979 and one in 1980, Bundy was convicted of the sorority house murders and the murder of the 12-year-old girl. He was sentenced to death in Florida's electric chair. After his string of appeals had been exhausted,

Bundy was due to be put to death on January 24, 1989. Before his execution, he gave the details of at least 30 murders, but many believe he could have been responsible for as many as 100. Bundy was electrocuted on schedule, and those who had gathered outside the prison cheered his death.

F. WHAT HAPPENS AFTER THE WARRANT IS ISSUED?

Once a warrant has been issued, it must be served on the suspect as soon as possible or within a reasonable period of time. A warrant to arrest a person may remain active for a much greater period of time than a warrant to search a location. However, this does not mean that an arrest warrant remains valid forever. New evidence might arise in the case that could cause law enforcement and prosecutors to reevaluate the need to arrest a specific person.

SEARCH WARRANTS

Search warrant
A court order authorizing law enforcement to enter, search, and remove evidence of a crime.

A **search warrant** is a warrant issued by a judge that authorizes the police to search a private residence or other area and seize particular kinds of property. To be more precise, a search warrant should be described as a *search and seizure warrant*, because it authorizes police to search a specific area and to seize evidence of a crime. When they have a warrant, police are authorized to enter the private residence of a person, conduct a search, and take away items described in the warrant. When the police arrive at a person's home with a valid search warrant, the homeowner cannot legally interfere with the police. Police officers are not required to wait until the homeowner contacts his or her attorney or calls the magistrate court to make sure that the warrant was issued there.

A. STANDARDS FOR ISSUING SEARCH AND SEIZURE WARRANTS

Police officers have wide latitude to arrest persons without a warrant. However, the opposite situation occurs when law enforcement conducts searches. Here, the courts will presume that a warrant was required unless and until the police and prosecutors can show that warrantless search was valid. The reason behind this is simple: Police can secure a location and obtain a warrant to search it, but they often do not have the same option when it comes to a human being.

Expectation of privacy
The Constitutional standard that a court must determine before issuing a search warrant. If an area has a high expectation of privacy, then a warrant will be required; if low or non-existent, then no warrant is required.

Just as with arrest warrants, before a magistrate can issue a search warrant, he or she must have reviewed all of the sworn testimony and made a determination that there is sufficient probable cause to believe that evidence of a crime will be found in a certain location. For instance, is a warrant to search even necessary? To answer that question, the judge must look at the issue of **expectation of privacy.** When the location to be searched enjoys a high degree of expectation of privacy, then police must obtain a warrant before conducting a search. However, if the expectation of privacy is low, police may not be required to obtain a search warrant at all. What then is expectation of privacy?

The phrase *expectation of privacy* does not appear in the U.S. Constitution. In fact, the Fourth Amendment makes no reference to privacy at all. The interpretation of the Fourth Amendment was left to the courts. Those courts created the expectation of privacy test as a way to evaluate when or if a search warrant is required.

The expectation of privacy test was created in *Katz v. U.S.* The test has both subjective and objective components. What the U.S. Supreme Court did in *Katz* was first to see if the suspect who was searched had a subjective expectation of privacy in the item or place to be searched. The second part of the test was to evaluate the search from an objective, hypothetical third party's perspective. Would this hypothetical third party believe that the area to be searched would have a high expectation of privacy? If the answer to both of these questions is yes, then the police must obtain a search warrant. An expectation of privacy is a person's belief in how secure and private an area should be. For the courts and for most individuals, the place with the highest expectation of privacy is the home. Examples of places with the least expectation of privacy are public areas where a person's actions can be seen by anyone.

Essentially, if a suspect has a high degree of expectation of privacy, then the police have a higher burden to meet before search warrants will be issued. A person has an expectation of privacy in personal papers, his or her residence, and any other private areas. People do not have a high expectation of privacy in the items that can be clearly seen in public. An area with no expectation of privacy would not require a search warrant. This explains why there are very few instances in which courts will allow warrantless searches of a person's home, but frequently find warrantless searches of items fully exposed to view and in public to be constitutionally permissible. Before police may enter your home, a magistrate must issue a search warrant authorizing them to do so. Police and magistrates face these issues every day in trying to determine what areas have a high degree of expectation of privacy and establishing sufficient probable cause for a magistrate to issue a warrant to search that area.

When it comes to interpreting the language of a search warrant, courts follow rules that are similar to the way that arrest warrants are evaluated. Numerous court decisions have established that warrants should be read in a common sense fashion. The U.S. Supreme Court does not impose highly technical rules on search warrants. Common misspellings, for instance, will not invalidate a search warrant. A warrant will not be ruled invalid because of a minor technicality. The U.S. Supreme Court has approved of this more lenient treatment of affidavits and search warrants, reasoning that a highly technical requirement would only work to discourage police officers from applying for search warrants in the first place.

B. THE "GOOD FAITH EXCEPTION"

Several cases have upheld technically faulty warrants when the police officers were obviously acting in good faith. When a police officer has no reason to suspect that a warrant is technically flawed, the courts will not rule that the warrant is invalid. However, the good faith exception is not a panacea for all insufficient warrants. Before they will apply the good faith exception, courts must also look to other features of the case.[17] A police officer must have an objective, reasonable ground to believe that the warrant was validly issued. Where a warrant is so obviously defective that no trained police officer could reasonably believe that the warrant was correct, the good faith exception does not apply.[18] Obviously, if the officer deliberately caused the error, then he or she cannot take advantage of the good faith exception.

C. EXCEPTIONS TO THE SEARCH WARRANT REQUIREMENT

Although courts have a preference for searches conducted with a warrant, there are instances where appellate courts have allowed searches without a warrant, but only in narrow circumstances. Examples of instances where a search warrant will not be required include:

- Plain view
- Open fields
- Dropped evidence
- Abandoned property
- Contraband
- Stop and frisk
- U.S. border searches
- Canine officers
- Consent
- Exigent circumstances

"PLAIN VIEW"

Plain view doctrine
A court principle that allows police to search without a warrant when they see evidence of a crime in an unconcealed manner.

Courts developed the **"plain view" doctrine** in response to a common problem. Suppose that an officer pulls over an automobile and while talking with the suspect, the officer sees an item that is evidence of a crime. Because the officer had a legal reason to be where he or she was at the time that the evidence was observed, the officer is not required to obtain a warrant. A similar problem occurs when police officers execute a search warrant looking for specific items, but come across other items that are clearly illegal. In both cases, the evidence may be seized without a warrant because the items were in "plain view" or available for anyone to see. "It has long been settled that objects falling in the plain view of an officer who has a right to be in the position to have that view are subject to seizure and may be introduced

---

[17] *U.S. v. Leon*, 468 U.S. 897 (1984).
[18] *Lo-Ji Sales, Inc. v. New York*, 442 U.S. 319 (1979).

into evidence."[19] The plain view doctrine does not permit police officers to seize any evidence at any time. The officers must have a legitimate reason to be in position to see the object. Consider Scenarios 14-4 and 14-5.

TWO JOBS

Officer Tango is working his off duty job as a security officer at an apartment building. The apartment complex is built into the side of a steep hill and as Officer Tango walks along a sidewalk, he is actually even with the second floor of the apartment complex. He hears a sound and glances toward an open window. Inside, he sees four people snorting a white, powdery substance off a small mirror and then laughing very loudly. He goes to the door of the apartment and knocks. When a woman answers the door, she is carrying a small mirror in her hand that is smeared with a white, powdery substance. He arrests her for possession of cocaine and then searches the apartment. He finds more cocaine and some marijuana and charges the others present. Is the search valid under the plain view doctrine?

Answer: Yes. Because the officer had a legitimate reason to be where he was when he saw the criminal activity, the subsequent search is constitutional.

KICKING IN THE DOOR

Officer Cash knows that the resident of a certain apartment has been in trouble with the law before. Officer Cash believes that the resident may be in possession of cocaine. He climbs up the back stairs of the apartment and peeks in through the back window through a drape, which almost, but not completely covers the window. He sees the suspect snorting a white, powdery substance. Officer Cash kicks in the back door and arrests the suspect. He subsequently searches the apartment and finds more suspected cocaine and some marijuana. Is the search valid under the plain view doctrine?

Answer: No. Because the officer had no legitimate reason to be on the suspect's back stairs or to be looking into his apartment, the officer's subsequent search was a violation of the Constitution and the evidence cannot be used at trial.

"OPEN FIELDS"

In addition to plain view, there is also a doctrine called *"open fields"* where officers are not required to obtain a warrant before conducting a search. Unlike plain view, the open fields doctrine revolves around expectation of privacy. An open field, fully exposed to view by anyone has virtually no expectation of privacy. "An individual may not legitimately demand privacy for activities conducted out of doors in fields, except in the area immediately surrounding the home."[20] (See Scenario 14-6.)

Open fields doctrine
A court principle that allows police to search without a warrant when the evidence is located in a public setting, such as farmland or beside a road.

---

[19] *Harris v. U.S.*, 390 U.S. 234 (1968).
[20] *Oliver v. U.S.*, 466 U.S. 170 (1984),

| **SCENARIO 14-6** | MARIJUANA GROWING |

Steve has a home in the country, and directly behind his home he has a plowed field. He grows herbs in this field, but also grows marijuana plants. The field is within ten feet of his back door and cannot be seen from the driveway of his home. It is, in fact, surrounded by a high privacy fence. A police officer visiting the neighborhood on an unrelated matter, decided to walk on to Steve's property and peek over his privacy fence. Is this an example of an "open fields" exception to a search warrant requirement?

Answer: No. Because the marijuana was growing close to Steve's home and not a "field" in the traditional sense, the most likely result will be a ruling that the police must obtain a warrant before looking over Steve's fence.

DROPPED EVIDENCE

When police officers are chasing a fleeing suspect and he drops or throws away some evidence, police do not have to obtain a search warrant to seize it. Many courts refer to these cases as "dropsy" cases, since many suspects will drop incriminating evidence when confronted by the police. The inherent problem with these cases is making the connection between the recovered evidence and the suspect. For instance, police chase a suspected drug dealer and see him fling out an arm. The police then retrieve a bag containing three rocks of crack cocaine. How can the police be sure that this bag belongs to this suspect? Generally, a police officer will testify about the circumstances of the arrest, the area in which the item was thrown, and the condition of the item when it was recovered. If it was a rainy night, for example, but the bag was still relatively dry when it was recovered, that would indicate that the bag was not lying on the ground for a long period of time.

ABANDONED PROPERTY

There is no requirement for law enforcement to obtain a warrant to search and seize abandoned property. Garbage is a perfect example. In *California v. Greenwood*,[21] the U.S. Supreme Court held that there is no privacy expectation in garbage. If an item — for example, drug paraphernalia — has been thrown into a communal trash receptacle, or even into a private trash receptacle subsequently taken to the curb for collection, then the person throwing it out has also tossed away any constitutional objections to having the item seized. The U.S. Supreme Court has ruled that there is no reasonable expectation of privacy for discarded garbage.[22] Of course, there are limits to the rule for the police obtaining abandoned property. They cannot, for instance, commit trespass in order to get to a suspect's trash. In that case, they would have to wait until the trash can has been placed on the curb for collection and is off the suspect's property.

---

[21] 486 U.S. 35 (1988).
[22] *California v. Greenwood*, 486 U.S. 35 (1988).

CONTRABAND

The Fourth Amendment does not protect items that are illegal to possess. Contraband encompasses items such as illegal weapons or narcotics, which can be seized by law enforcement without a warrant whenever they are discovered. Under the Fourth Amendment, there is no reasonable expectation of privacy in items that are illegal to possess in the first place.

STOP AND FRISK

The previous chapter discussed the law of stop and frisk. A police officer can briefly detain a person and pat this person down for weapons. If, during that pat down, an officer discovers evidence of a crime, that evidence can be retained and used against the suspect at trial. Stop and frisk does not require a warrant.

U.S. BORDER SEARCHES

U.S. Customs and Border Patrol officers and others who monitor the U.S. borders have much greater freedom to search without a warrant than do police officers. Because these officers are charged with preventing items from coming into the United States, they can search many more items. These searches can be carried out without a search warrant, but they do not give the officers involved complete freedom to search anyone and everything. As a general rule, these officers can perform a cursory search. Any additional or intrusive searches would likely require a search warrant.

CANINE OFFICERS

The U.S. Supreme Court has stated that the use of specially trained dogs to detect narcotics, explosives, or other items does not fall within the protections of the Fourth Amendment. According to the court, there is no expectation of privacy in air, but there are cases pending before the court that will test that maxim. The court recently ruled that these specially trained dogs are not permissible around private residences without a warrant.[23] However, the court ruled that they can be used in open areas.[24]

CONSENT

When a person knowingly and voluntarily gives law enforcement officers consent to search his or her belongings or residence, then there is no longer a need to obtain a search warrant. The consent cannot be coerced. If a suspect does give consent, he or she cannot revoke it once the police have recovered evidence of a crime. However, a

---

[23] *Florida v. Jardines*, 569 U.S. ___ (2013).
[24] *U.S. v. Place*, 462 U.S. 696 (1983).

person who has given consent can withdraw it before police have located such evidence.

In cases where police testify that a suspect gave them consent to search, the issue is often whether or not the consent was given knowingly and intelligently. Consent that is obtained by force or threats is not consent at all and any evidence obtained may be suppressed.

EXIGENT CIRCUMSTANCES

The concept of exigent circumstances was addressed in Chapter 13. Exigent circumstance is some kind of emergency that threatens the lives of people or the existence of evidence. Police are not required to obtain a search warrant if they can show that an emergency (exigent) circumstance existed. An exigent circumstance is one that poses some danger to property or people such that waiting to obtain a warrant might result in the loss of evidence or injury to a person. One example is a situation in which police officers hear two people having a violent fight inside their home. They do not have to wait for a warrant before entering and stopping one person from killing the other.

D. SEARCH WARRANT LIMITATIONS

As Figure 14-1 shows, the Fourth Amendment calls for specific steps before a search can be conducted, including the provision for an oath or affidavit as well as the requirement that the warrant must state with particularity the person or place to be searched. A search warrant must be executed within a reasonable time period after it is issued. If not, it becomes **stale.** A stale warrant is no longer valid. A warrant becomes stale when the circumstances originally involved in issuing it have changed substantially. For instance, a magistrate judge issues a warrant authorizing the search of a home for narcotics. Because drugs tend to be moved or consumed very quickly, a one month delay between the issuance and execution of a search warrant could be far too much time. There are many things that may have changed in the intervening time and the officers who waited such a long period of time would be required to apply for a new search warrant.

Staleness is an issue that is very much dependent on the facts and the items to be searched. Two days between issuance and execution of a search warrant for drugs might be too long, but in one case, a court held that a seven-month wait between the

Stale
When too much time has passed between the application and issuance of a warrant, and the search that it authorizes.

FIGURE 14-1

The Fourth Amendment to the U.S. Constitution

The right of the people to be secure in their persons, houses, papers, and effects, against unreasonable searches and seizures, shall not be violated, and no Warrants shall issue, but upon probable cause, supported by Oath or affirmation, and particularly describing the place to be searched, and the persons or things to be seized (emphasis added).

issuance and execution of a search warrant for child pornography did not make the warrant stale.[25]

In order to avoid this problem, a warrant may have to be executed quickly. Narcotics, for example, are produced for the express purpose of being consumed.[26] Staleness may not be such an issue when the goods are more permanent in nature (illegal automatic weapons, for instance). In some cases, law enforcement may apply for an **anticipatory warrant,** that is, a warrant authorizing a search and seizure of illegal items at some future time.

Anticipatory warrants
Warrants issued for contraband or evidence that has not yet arrived at its final destination.

GENERAL SEARCHES NOT ALLOWED

The Fourth Amendment does not permit a general search. This is the type of search where law enforcement goes through a person's home or other belongings looking for evidence of some crime. The Framers of the U.S. Constitution had some experience with general searches authorized under British law and they wanted to make sure that no such search would be carried out in the United States. This is why they insisted that all search warrants must have probable cause and describe with particularity the place to be searched. Consider Scenario 14-7.

SEARCHING FOR A KILLER

SCENARIO 14-7

A suspect is wanted for detonating a bomb in a large urban area. Someone has reported seeing a person who meets the description in a neighborhood. Police arrive and cordon off the area, then begin searching the front and backyards of everyone in the area. Then, police enter every home in the neighborhood without seeking permission or consent. They do not find the suspect, but they do find a methamphetamine lab in Darryl's house. When Darryl challenges the search on the grounds that it is unconstitutional and qualifies as a general search, how is the judge likely to rule?

Answer: The judge will probably rule that the search that resulted in locating the meth lab was unconstitutional and any evidence seized is not admissible. If this is the only evidence against Darryl, then the case against him will be dismissed.

VAGUENESS

A warrant must state with "particularity" the places to be searched and the items to be seized. If a warrant fails to meet this standard, then the subsequent search may be ruled unconstitutional. A warrant authorizing the seizure of "all suspected items" would be vague to the point of absurdity. Such a warrant would give the police the power to seize anything and everything they wished and would be considered too vague to be enforceable.

---

[25] *U.S. v. Seiver*, 692 F.3d 774, 775 (C.A.7 (Ill.),2012).
[26] *U.S. v. Beltempo*, 675 F. 2d 472 (2d Cir. 1982), cert. denied 457 U.S. 1135 (1982).

OVER BREADTH

Overbroad
When a search warrant allows police far too much discretion in what they may search; similar to the prohibition against general searches.

The requirement of particularity also means that a warrant cannot be **overbroad** in its description of items to be seized. This is another way of restraining police by requiring that they search for specific evidence of a crime. Police are not allowed to engage in a "fishing expedition" that would search for any evidence of a crime. This resembles general searches far too closely.

E. CHALLENGING A WARRANT

Standing
A recognized legal right to bring suit or to challenge a legal decision.

The question of a legal challenge to a search involves the issue of **standing.** Broadly speaking, standing is the requirement that the person making the challenge must have some personal interest in the search. The personal interest has more to do with expectation of privacy than ownership rights. This explains why a renter may have standing to challenge a search where the landlord might not. A renter actually lives on the premises and has an obvious expectation of privacy, whereas the landlord who does not live on the premises may lack such an expectation. Only those who have an expectation of privacy in an area that was searched can challenge the constitutionality of the search.[27]

F. "THE EXCLUSIONARY RULE"

The consequences of an unconstitutional search are simple: The evidence obtained cannot be used at trial. This is the premise of the exclusionary rule, which will be addressed in greater detail in Chapter 16.

CASE EXCERPT

STATE v. DABNEY
264 Wis.2d 843, 663 N.W.2d 366 (2003)

WEDEMEYER, P.J.

Bobby R. Dabney appeals from a judgment entered after a trial to the court where he was found guilty of kidnapping and two counts of first-degree sexual assault while using a dangerous weapon, contrary to Wis. Stat. §§ 940.31(1)(a), 940.225(1)(b) and 939.63 (2001-02). Dabney contends that the complaint and arrest warrant in this case, which initially only identified him by his DNA profile, were insufficient to confer personal jurisdiction. He further claims that the amended complaint, which identified him by name, was untimely and barred by the statute of limitations. Finally, he asserts that his due process rights were violated based on the six-year-plus delay between the criminal act

---

[27] *U.S. v. $40,955.00 in U.S. Currency*, 554 F.3d 752, 756 (C.A.9 (Cal.), 2009).

and the prosecution in this case. Because the complaint and arrest warrant were sufficient to confer personal jurisdiction, because the case was commenced before the statute of limitations expired, and because Dabney has failed to demonstrate that his due process rights were violated by any delay, we affirm.

I. BACKGROUND

On December 7, 1994, an unknown male accosted fifteen-year-old Dawana F. at a bus stop in Milwaukee. He forced her at gunpoint to a nearby lot. There, he tied her hands behind her back, covered her eyes and led her to a car. He pushed her into the car, drove a short distance, and stopped. He then fondled her breasts and forced her to perform fellatio on him, promising not to kill her if she "did that good." The unknown male ejaculated in her mouth. He then drove again for a short time and the sequence was repeated. Finally, the man let Dawana out of the car. She found her mother and called the police.

Dawana was taken immediately to a sexual assault treatment center where "oral swabs and saliva samples," as well as a "blood standard," were obtained from her. The state crime lab found semen present in the saliva and developed a DNA profile for the unknown male suspect.

On December 4, 2000, the State charged John Doe # 12 with kidnapping and four counts of first-degree sexual assault. The DNA profile was included in the caption of the complaint. On that same day, a trial court found probable cause in the complaint and issued an arrest warrant for John Doe # 12.

On March 14, 2001, the State filed an amended complaint substituting Dabney's name for "John Doe." The amended complaint stated that the DNA profile had been run against the databank on December 18, 2000, without finding a match; however, on February 27, 2001, a match was found. This was reconfirmed on March 7, 2001.

On April 12, 2001, Dabney was bound over for trial and an information was filed, setting forth five counts: kidnapping, and four counts of first-degree sexual assault (two hand-to-breast and two mouth-to-penis). In June of 2001, Dabney moved to dismiss the charges, alleging that the original complaint and arrest warrant, based solely on his DNA profile, were insufficient and should not toll the six-year statute of limitations, which otherwise would have expired on December 7, 2000. He also argued that the State's delay in commencing this prosecution violated his right to due process. The trial court denied his motion to dismiss orally in July of 2001, followed by a written decision in August of 2001.

On September 13, 2001, Dabney filed a petition for leave to appeal to this court, which was denied. The supreme court also denied Dabney's request for pretrial review in this case. As a result, the case was tried to the court on February 6, 2002. Dabney waived his right to a jury trial, and agreed to have the case presented by stipulated facts. Because Dabney agreed that the victim, Dawana, did not need to testify in person, the State dismissed the two counts of sexual assault that alleged hand-to-breast contact. Dabney was found guilty on the three remaining counts. He was sentenced to three consecutive forty-year prison terms. Judgment was entered. He now appeals.

II. DISCUSSION

DNA Complaint & Statute of Limitations

Dabney contends that the original complaint and the arrest warrant, which were filed and issued three days before the expiration of the six-year statute of limitations, did not satisfy the "reasonable certainty" identification requirements of Wis. Stat. § 968.04(3)(a)4, thereby depriving the court of personal jurisdiction over him. He also argues that because the original complaint was insufficient, and the warrant was not timely issued, the six-year statute of limitations passed, and therefore bars this prosecution. We reject both arguments for the reasons that follow.

Whether a criminal prosecution is properly and timely commenced by a "John Doe" complaint and arrest warrant which identify the defendant solely by a DNA profile, is an issue of first impression in this state. The issue presented requires an interpretation of statutes and, thus, is a question of law for this court. *State v. Adams*, 152 Wis.2d 68, 73-74, 447 N.W.2d 90 (Ct.App.1989).

Dabney contends that the original complaint and arrest warrant were insufficient to confer personal jurisdiction. Personal jurisdiction in criminal cases involves the power of the circuit court over the physical person of the defendant. The circuit court obtains personal jurisdiction when two requirements are satisfied: (1) a complaint or an indictment must be filed stating probable cause to believe a crime has been committed and that the defendant probably committed it, see *State v. Smith*, 131 Wis.2d 220, 238, 388 N.W.2d 601 (1986); and (2) there must be compliance with the applicable statute of limitations, see *State v. Pohlhammer*, 78 Wis.2d 516, 523, 254 N.W.2d 478 (1977). To satisfy the statute of limitations, an action must be commenced before the statute expires. In a criminal prosecution, an action is "commenced . . . when a warrant or summons is issued, an indictment is found, or an information is filed." Wis. Stat. § 939.74(1).

Here, a complaint and arrest warrant were both issued on December 4, 2000, three days before the six-year statute of limitations expired. Dabney does not dispute this fact. He argues, however, that because the complaint and arrest warrant identified him solely by his DNA profile, the "reasonable certainty" requirement of Wis. Stat. § 968.04(3)(a)4 was not satisfied. Section 968.04(3)(a)4 provides in pertinent part that the arrest warrant shall: "State the name of the person to be arrested, if known, or if not known, designate the person to be arrested by any description by which the person to be arrested can be identified with reasonable certainty."

Although Dabney repeatedly argues that the "reasonable certainty" requirement applies to both the complaint and the arrest warrant, this is not the case. The "reasonable certainty" requirement is specific to the warrant only. The statutory requirements for a complaint require only that the complaint set forth "a written statement of the essential facts constituting the offense charged." Wis. Stat. § 968.01(2). Moreover, case law consistently provides that a complaint must meet certain requirements to be sufficient:

A criminal complaint is a self-contained charge that must set forth facts within its four corners that are sufficient, in themselves or together with reasonable inferences to which they give rise, to allow a reasonable person to conclude that a crime was probably committed and the defendant is probably culpable. . . . To be sufficient, a complaint must only be minimally adequate. This is to be evaluated in a common sense rather than a hypertechnical manner, in setting forth the essential facts establishing probable cause.

The complaint must answer who is being charged and why. Id. at 73-74, 447 N.W.2d 90. Thus, we interpret Dabney's argument with respect to the complaint to suggest that the DNA profile fails to answer the question of who is being charged. Accordingly, in addressing this issue, we refer to both the complaint and the arrest warrant.

The question to be addressed is whether a complaint and an arrest warrant, which identify the defendant/suspect as "John Doe" with a specific DNA profile, satisfies the particularity and reasonable certainty requirements. Our supreme court considered a similar issue more than a century ago in a case where an unknown female was accused of larceny. See *Scheer v. Keown*, 29 Wis. 586, 588 (1872). In Scheer, the court held: "The fact that her name was unknown should have been stated in the complaint and warrant, and the best description of the person prosecuted, which the nature of the case would allow, should have been given therein." Id. Thus, the particularity or reasonable certainty requirements do not absolutely require that a person's name appear in the complaint or warrant. When the name is unknown, the person may be identified with "the best description" available.

One treatise writer advises that a "John Doe" arrest warrant satisfies the particularity requirement if it describes the person's "occupation, his personal appearance, peculiarities, place or residence or other means of identification." 3 Wayne R. LaFave, Search and Seizure § 5.1(g) (3d ed. 1996 & Supp.2003) (footnote citations omitted). The case law suggests that the complaint and warrant satisfy the sufficiency standard when the description clearly demonstrates that the "law enforcement authorities had probable cause to suspect a particular person of committing a crime." *Powe v. City of Chicago*, 664 F.2d 639, 646 (7th Cir.1981).

Here, the complaint and arrest warrant identified the suspect as "John Doe" and set forth a specific DNA profile. We conclude that for purposes of identifying "a particular person" as the defendant, a DNA profile is arguably the most discrete, exclusive means of personal identification possible. "A genetic code describes a person with far greater precision than a physical description or a name." Meredith A. Bieber, Comment, Meeting the Statute or Beating It: Using "John Doe" Indictments Based on DNA to Meet the Statute of Limitations, 150 U. Pa. L.Rev. 1079, 1085 (2002). Thus, we agree with the State's arguments that the DNA profile satisfies the "reasonable certainty" requirements for an arrest warrant and answers the "who is charged" question for a complaint.

We are, however, persuaded by Dabney's suggestion that in addition to the DNA profile, the particular physical characteristics known to police would have further enhanced the completeness of the complaint and warrant. As Dabney points out, an individual would not necessarily recognize the DNA profile as his own. Thus, although the DNA profile satisfies the particularity requirements in identifying a suspect whose name is not known, it would be helpful, for notice purposes, to also include any known physical appearance characteristics. The lack of a more particular physical description in this case, however, does not defeat the State's argument.

Dabney also contends that because a DNA profile is not apparent to the naked eye, the warrant cannot be readily executed. This argument does not alter our conclusion that the particularity requirement was satisfied in this case. Clearly, a police officer with a DNA profile in hand could not walk up to an individual and arrest him or her on that basis. Rather, the officer would need to obtain a DNA sample from the individual to compare it with the one identified in the arrest warrant. This extra step, however, is not unique to a warrant based on DNA. No matter how well a warrant describes the individual, extrinsic information is commonly needed to execute it. If a name is given, information to link the name to the physical person must be acquired. Accordingly, we conclude that an arrest warrant based on a DNA profile can be readily and accurately executed.

Based on the foregoing, we conclude that the complaint and warrant in this case satisfy the statutory requirements; therefore, the documents were sufficient to identify Dabney and were sufficient to confer personal jurisdiction. Accordingly, the trial court did not err when it denied Dabney's motion to dismiss based on this argument.

Due Process

Dabney's last claim is that his due process rights were violated for two reasons: (1) he was not given sufficient notice of the claim because the original complaint and warrant identified him only by his DNA profile; and (2) he was prejudiced by the pre-charging delay. We reject both arguments.

First, the fact that the original complaint and arrest warrant were issued as "John Doe" and contained only a DNA profile does not create any lack of "notice" issues. A defendant is not entitled to specific notice that the state is issuing a complaint and seeking an arrest warrant. "An arrest warrant issues when it is signed by a judge with intent that it be executed and the warrant leaves the possession of the judge." *State v. Mueller*, 201 Wis.2d 121, 129, 549 N.W.2d 455 (Ct.App.1996). Thus, the warrant is issued without any involvement from the defendant and the defendant is not provided with any notice of the underlying charge until the warrant is executed. Here, the warrant was not executed until Dabney's name was substituted for "John Doe." Thus, whether or not Dabney knew his specific DNA profile is irrelevant.

Second, Dabney contends that the prosecutorial delay in filing the complaint violated his due process rights. He argues that the State intentionally delayed this case until it was able to obtain a positive DNA identification. He contends that, as a result, he has been prejudiced because "memories fade" and "witnesses become unavailable." We must reject this claim as well.

In order to demonstrate a due process violation on this basis, Dabney has to establish that he suffered: (1) actual prejudice as a result of the delay; and (2) that the delay arose as a result of an improper purpose, so as to afford the State a tactical advantage over him. *State v. Wilson*, 149 Wis.2d 878, 903-05, 440 N.W.2d 534 (1989). Whether the pre-charging delay violated the due process clause is a constitutional question, which we review independent of the trial court.

Dabney has failed to satisfy his burden. Although he alleges that "memories fade" and "witnesses become unavailable" as time passes, he does not set forth any specific facts to establish actual prejudice. Without any more specific factual allegations, he has failed to sufficiently present a claim of actual prejudice. Rather, he relies primarily on his claim that the statute of limitations expired and, therefore, prejudice is "irrebuttably presumed." We disagree based on our earlier conclusion that the statute of limitations was not violated in this case.

The primary evidence against Dabney was the DNA sample he left in the victim's mouth and the victim's statement. He offered no challenge to the DNA evidence and no evidence challenging the victim's version of events. Based on the foregoing, we are not persuaded by his conclusory assertions of actual prejudice.

Moreover, he also fails to establish that the delay in filing the complaint resulted from an improper prosecutorial motive or purpose. He made no showing as to how the timing of the complaint created a tactical advantage for the State. He argues only that the DNA profile could have been run and discovered earlier. The State refutes this allegation, pointing out that the original complaint states that the DNA sample was tested earlier, but no match was found. Regardless, there is no evidence that the State intentionally delayed the prosecution of this case in order to obtain a tactical advantage over Dabney.

Judgment affirmed.

CASE QUESTIONS

1 What is Dabney's challenge to the warrant in this case?
2 How did the police locate Dabney's DNA?
3 How was Dabney identified as the suspect in the rape case?
4 According to the court, was Dabney particularly and reasonably identified in the warrant as required by law?
5 Is it significant that Dabney's name was not listed in the original warrant?

CHAPTER SUMMARY

This chapter examined the legal implications of arrest and search warrants. In either situation, a magistrate must issue the warrant. A police officer prepares an application and takes sworn testimony from the officer to establish the facts that lead the magistrate to make a determination that probable cause exists either to arrest or to search for evidence for a crime. A legally sufficient warrant must be signed and must describe with particularity the item to be searched for. The greater the degree of expectation of privacy, the more likely that a search warrant will be required. There are exceptions to the necessity for requiring a search warrant, including open fields, plain view, contraband, and exigent circumstances, among others. A warrant may also be considered unconstitutional if it is stale or overbroad. In no circumstances will courts allow general searches.

KEY TERMS

Magistrate	Search warrant	Stale
Warrant	Expectation of privacy	Anticipatory warrants
Affidavit	Plain view doctrine	Overbroad
"Four Corners" test	Open fields doctrine	Standing

REVIEW QUESTIONS

1 This chapter mentions that there is a preference for warrants, but that courts give police officers greater latitude to arrest without a warrant. Explain this difference.

2 What purpose does an affidavit serve in a warrant application?

3 Can a magistrate have a vested interest in the outcome of a criminal case? Explain your answer.

4 Who is authorized to carry out an arrest once an arrest warrant has been issued?

5 What would make a warrant "stale"?

6 Explain how a warrant would be considered vague, as that term is described by courts. Can a valid arrest warrant be issued even though police do not know the suspect's name, but can provide a detailed description of him or her? Explain.

7 What is "standing"?

8 What does "expectation of privacy" mean?

9 What is the "good faith exception" as it applies to search warrants?

10 Explain the difference between "plain view" and "open fields."

11 Does a person have an expectation of privacy in garbage? Explain.

12 What is an anticipatory warrant?

13 Why would a search warrant be invalidated for vagueness?

14 How does a defendant challenge a search warrant?

15 What are the limitations on a magistrate?

16 What are some factors that make a warrant legally valid?

17 What is the "four corners" test?

18 Explain the legal term "overbroad" as it applies to search warrants.

19 List and explain at least three exceptions to obtaining a search warrant.

20 What is a general search and why is it not permitted?

QUESTIONS FOR ANALYSIS

1 Should police officers be bound by the same rules to obtain arrest warrants as they do for search warrants? Why or why not?

2 Why is there a requirement that a magistrate be neutral and detached? Is that a good idea?

HYPOTHETICALS

1 Advances in technology may make it possible for the police, in just a few years, to be able to fly drones the size of insects around residences. Given the ruling concerning the use of drug dogs, how would constitutional rules be applied to drones?

2   Have we as a society moved beyond some of the problems that were faced by the individuals who created the U.S. Constitution? For instance, in the case of suspected terrorism in an American city, wouldn't it make more sense to allow general searches when there is a report of a possible terrorist plot?

3   Leaks from various sources have revealed that the federal government has been monitoring email, Internet access, and the phone numbers dialed by people both inside and outside the United States. Are these activities a violation of the U.S. Constitution? Why or why not?

Post Arrest, Grand Jury, Indictment

Chapter Objectives

- Explain the purpose of the initial appearance
- Describe the role of the preliminary hearing in a prosecution
- Define how a court decides on a bail and bond amount
- Explain the role of the grand jury
- Describe the role of the prosecutor in the charging decision

I   INITIAL APPEARANCE

In some jurisdictions, the **initial appearance** is also called the preliminary examination. Whatever its name, the hearing itself has a specific function. It ensures that the person who has been placed under arrest is made aware of his or her rights under the Constitution.

Initial appearance
A hearing that takes place within days of the suspect's arrest where the suspect is advised of his or her constitutional rights, is given the opportunity to request a court-appointed attorney, and the court can confirm the defendant's identity.

A. PURPOSE OF THE INITIAL APPEARANCE

At the initial appearance, a magistrate or some other court official will notify the accused of his or her rights, as well as any additional information, such as:

 The seriousness of the charge against him or her
 The consequences of the hearing and future hearings
 The right to the assistance of counsel

The initial appearance hearing is specifically designed to ensure that the defendant is aware of his or her constitutional rights as early in the legal process as possible. The person who informs the defendant of his rights is often a magistrate judge, the same position discussed in Chapter 14. The magistrate may appoint an attorney to represent the defendant if the defendant cannot afford to hire his or her own.

At the initial appearance, the judge will advise the defendant of the charge against him. The judge will also inform the defendant that this is a preliminary charge and that additional charges may be brought against the defendant. The defendant will be told if he or she is charged with a felony or a misdemeanor and the maximum possible sentence (although not all jurisdictions follow this last procedure).

The judge will also confirm the defendant's identity, making sure that the person the police have charged and placed under arrest is the same person referred to in the arrest warrant. To that end, the judge may sometimes require fingerprint analysis to confirm that the person in custody is in fact the person whom the police believe him to be. If the defendant contests his identity, then the court may order DNA evidence to be obtained.

B. RIGHT TO AN ATTORNEY AT INITIAL APPEARANCE

Although some initial appearance hearings are conducted by other officials, for the sake of clarity this text will continue to refer to the presiding official at the initial appearance hearing as a magistrate judge. This judge will read the defendant his or her constitutional rights. The rights sound similar to the *Miranda* rights read to the defendant shortly after being placed under arrest and that similarity is by design. The *Miranda* decision, as well as subsequent Supreme Court decisions, requires that the defendant be made aware of his or her rights to be presumed innocent, that the defendant has the right to remain silent, that the defendant has the right to a jury trial and that the defendant has the right to an attorney. If the defendant cannot afford an attorney, the magistrate at the initial appearance hearing may appoint one at that time or advise the clerk's office or other administrator that the defendant's case should be routed to the public defender's office or to the appointed attorney list, depending on the procedure followed in that jurisdiction.

A defendant may hire an attorney at any point following the arrest. The defendant may have contacted an attorney before the arrest warrant was served, assuming that the defendant was aware of the warrant. In any event, as soon as an attorney is hired for the defendant, the attorney's first bit of advice to the client is usually to say nothing to the police. Defense attorneys know that it is far more likely that the defendant, in trying to explain his or her actions, will only give law enforcement and the prosecution more evidence that they can later use against him or her. However, once the defendant has invoked his or her right to remain silent, the police cannot question the suspect any further. If an attorney is either retained to represent the defendant or is appointed to represent the defendant, that attorney will normally handle the defendant's case from that point onward. The attorney will discuss the case with the prosecutor, attend the preliminary hearing and any other hearings, as well as conduct the jury trial, should it come to that. A defense attorney may enter the picture at any of several different steps in the post-arrest process.

One of the first duties of a defense attorney is to attempt to have the defendant released from jail on bond. We will discuss the role of bond in the next section.

BAIL AND BOND

There is wide variation among the states and the federal government regarding *bail* or *bond*. Although criminal defendants cannot be subject to "excessive bail," the Eighth Amendment (as shown in Figure 15-1) does not explain what is excessive. We will begin our discussion with definitions of bail and bond, then discuss how they are used in criminal cases, and finally examine the parameters of the Eighth Amendment as they apply to bail and bond. For the purposes of simplicity, this text will refer only to bail and then later explain the differences between bail and bond.

Bail may be set at the initial appearance hearing, but usually this issue comes up more often at the preliminary hearing stage, discussed later in this chapter. In many jurisdictions, a judge has wide latitude in deciding on bail. The accused is entitled to a hearing where evidence will be presented to determine the amount of bail required. In serious cases, there is no set monetary amount for each case. The nature of the charge will determine the monetary amount of bail. The arresting officer has no authority to set the amount of bail. A judge will often consider the officer's recommendation but is not bound to follow the officer's wishes. Similarly, a prosecutor may make a bail recommendation, but the court may disregard the prosecutor's desires as well. The reason bail is required is to ensure the defendant's appearance at trial or other proceeding.

Posting bail serves two purposes: It releases the defendant and allows him or her to return to gainful employment and to ensure that the defendant has a vested interest in returning for his or her court hearing. If the defendant does not return for court, then his or her bail is forfeited and a warrant will issue for the defendant's arrest. There are several factors that weigh into a bail decision. The concept of bail arises under the presumption in U.S. law that a person is innocent until proven guilty and should, therefore, not be held in jail until trial unless there is some overriding reason for doing so.

The words *bail* and *bond* have been used and misused so often that they have become confused with one another. Bail is a person's assurance that he or she will return to court at a specific date and time. As such, there are some bails that do not involve money or property at all. Bail can mean several different things. A person released on bail might be released with no conditions or might be released on supervised bail, where he or she must check in with a court clerk or other official periodically. Defendants may also receive conditional bail or conditional release, where their release from jail contains specific provisions that, if broken, will land the person back in jail. One of the most common requirements of conditional bail is that the accused stay away from the victim in the case. Bond, on the other hand, is a monetary guarantee by the defendant or someone else that offers the promise that

Bail
The posting of a monetary amount to guarantee the return of the defendant for subsequent court hearings.

Excessive bail shall not be required, nor excessive fines imposed, nor cruel and unusual punishments inflicted.

FIGURE 15-1

Amendment VIII

Property bond
Posting of real estate to guarantee the defendant's return for a subsequent court appearance.

Bond
A promise of specific monetary amount promised to the state and offered as a guarantee for the defendant's return to court at a later date.

the defendant will return for court. If he or she fails to return, the bond will be forfeited. In addition to setting monetary amounts as a condition of release, some judges may turn to **property bonds** in lieu of cash. A property bond is the posting of an individual's title to his home or other land as a guarantee of the defendant's return. If the defendant flees the jurisdiction and does not return for court hearings, then the court has the unenviable task of seizing someone's home as forfeiture of the bond. In such a case, the owners are removed from their home and the house and land become property of the local government.

Because **bond** can involve real estate as well as money or other items of value, the consequences for the person who owns the property, especially if the property belongs to someone other than the defendant, can be disastrous. Consider Scenario 15-1.

SCENARIO 15-1

AUNT TIA'S HOME

Ralph has been arrested, and the court is requiring that someone post a property bond for his release. This means that someone who owns real estate outright can pledge the property as a guarantee for Ralph's return to court. Ralph's grandmother, Tia, posts her own home for Ralph's bond. Unfortunately, Ralph immediately flees the jurisdiction and does not return for his court date. What are the consequences for Grandma Tia?

Answer: She will lose her home. The state will bring a forfeiture action against her, and because she posted her personal residence as bond for Ralph, she will lose it because he failed to appear.

Bail can be set by magistrate judges or trial judges. The appellate courts have said, time and again, that the trial judge is in the best position to review all of the available facts and to know the case "on the ground" better than an appellate court. As such, appellate courts are generally reluctant to overturn a trial judge's decision regarding the amount of bail or even if bail should be set at all.

The ultimate purpose of bail is to prevent or at least discourage people accused of crimes from fleeing the jurisdiction. Having to forfeit a large sum of money is enough to keep most people from running, but there are other forms of bail that serve the same purpose.

 **FAMOUS CASES**
STEVEN STAYNER

Seven-year-old Steven Stayner was walking home from school on December 4, 1972, in the Northern California city of Merced, when he was stopped by a naïve, simple-minded man named Murphy. Murphy asked Steven if he thought his mother might make a donation to Murphy's church. When Steven said yes, Murphy offered to give him a ride home. He led him to a car driven by Kenneth Parnell, a convicted sex offender in his early forties, who had persuaded the trusting

Murphy to assist in his plan to kidnap a young boy to supposedly raise in a religious environment.

It quickly became clear to Steven that Parnell was not taking him to his house; instead, he took him to a cabin in the Yosemite Valley, where within hours he began molesting him. Throughout the first week, Steven told Parnell numerous times that he wanted to go home. But Parnell refused, saying that he had been in contact with Steven's parents, and they had given him custody of Steven because they didn't want him any longer. From that day forward, Steven was to call Parnell "Dad," and his name would now be Dennis Parnell.

The Stayners, meanwhile, had been frantically searching for their son from almost the moment he had disappeared, a search that would endure for seven years. Police had nothing to go on, however, as there were no witnesses, and what clues they had invariably led to dead ends.

Steven adjusted to his new life with Parnell, albeit uneasily. For the next seven years they moved around California a dozen or more times. Steven attended school, made friends, and fabricated a story about himself and Parnell to answer questions that neighbors and schoolmates would ask. By all accounts they appeared to be a normal father and son who got along well. Parnell left Steven alone often, and Steven himself was unable to explain why he never tried to escape. Perhaps the fiction that Parnell had implanted — that his parents no longer wanted Steven — had the desired effect of demoralizing him to the point he no longer harbored a desire to get away.

Parnell allowed — even encouraged — Steven to begin smoking, drinking, and using drugs at a young age. When he was nine years old, a woman name Barbara Mathias moved in with them, along with her son Kenny, a friend of Steven's. She stayed for a year and later claimed to have no knowledge that Steven had been kidnapped. However, she and Parnell brought Steven to bed with them, and he was forced to have sex with her.

As Steven aged, he became less attractive to the pedophiliac Parnell. On Valentine's Day 1980, Parnell kidnapped another boy, five-year-old Timmy White in Ukiah, California, and took him to the remote Mendocino County cabin where he was staying with Steven. When Steven saw how frightened and distressed Timmy was, he made the decision to escape with him and return him to his parents. On March 1st, he found his chance.

Parnell was working at his night security job, so Steven took Timmy and hitchhiked into Ukiah. When they could not find Timmy's house, Steven decided to have Timmy walk into the police station, and then Steven would escape. He had no idea where he might go, but he knew he would not return to Parnell. Before he could fully execute his plan, police officers spotted the two boys and took them into custody. Steven identified Timmy and then began to tell his own story, starting with the statement, "I know my first name is Steven."

Parnell was arrested before daybreak, and both boys were reunited with their families that same day. Steven's homecoming was strained, however, because he returned to his family as a young adult, yet they still saw him as a seven-year-old boy. Furthermore, he had easy access to alcohol, drugs, and cigarettes while he was with Parnell, and he had difficulty adjusting to the stricter rules in the Stayner household.

In two trials, Parnell was convicted of kidnapping both Steven and Timmy, but he was never charged with the multiple sexual assaults on Steven. Most had occurred outside the Merced County jurisdiction, and the statute of limitations had expired on many of the offenses. Furthermore, Mendocino County prosecutors declined to press charges in an attempt to protect Steven from the trauma of a trial. Parnell was sentenced to seven years in prison and was paroled after five. Following his release, Parnell was again convicted in 2004 for trying to purchase a child and attempted molestation. He died in prison on January 21, 2008.

Steven Stayner readjusted to his life, married, and had two children. He spoke to children about the dangers of trusting strangers and to parents about how to protect their children. Nevertheless, he could not escape tragedy. He died in 1989 in a motorcycle accident while driving home from work. Timmy White not only attended the funeral but also served as one of Steven's pallbearers.

In yet another bizarre twist, Steven's brother, Cary Stayner, faced a different set of troubles. Cary led a difficult life, feeling neglected during the seven years that his parents grieved the loss of Steven, descending into drug use, and claiming that he himself had been molested as a child. Currently, he is on California's death row for the murders of four women near Yosemite.

Another purpose of bail is to allow the defendant to help his or her attorney prepare his or her defense. That is considerably easier to do when the defendant is out in the community rather than being held at the local jail. The defendant, while out on bail, can continue to work, which will help him or her pay for legal services, and the defendant can help the attorney to locate witnesses beneficial to the defense. Bail or bond is not intended to punish the defendant before the case has been concluded. It is not, as has sometimes been portrayed in various media, a means for the court to financially cripple the accused before the trial ever occurs. Although there are many situations where the court might deny bail, those reasons must be based on factors independent of the person's supposed guilt.

A. BONDING COMPANIES

Bonding company
A private business that posts bonds for individuals who have been charged with crimes and will be forced to pay the balance of the defendant's bond if the defendant flees the jurisdiction or otherwise does not appear for a court date.

A **bonding company** is in the business of posting monetary bail bonds for people who cannot afford to pay their own bail. Usually, these companies will charge a 10 percent, nonrefundable fee to the defendant for this service. In the case where a judge sets a bond at $20,000, the bonding company will charge the defendant $2,000 in exchange for posting a promissory bond that it will pay in the event that the defendant fails to appear for court. In addition to posting a monetary amount for bail, a judge may impose other conditions, such as:

- Defendant must maintain gainful employment
- Defendant will have no contact with the victim in the case

In states that allow the use of bonding companies, the individuals who work for the bonding company may periodically check up on the defendant before his or her court date to make sure that the defendant has not fled the jurisdiction. States tend to like this arrangement because it keeps a second pair of eyes on the defendant to make sure that he or she will appear for a subsequent court date. On the other hand, there are many critics that point out that bonding companies may take a far more intrusive interest in their clients and may engage in questionable, if not violent, tactics to ensure that the defendant appears for his or her court date.

Some states have eliminated bonding companies entirely. Citing concerns about abusive practices by bonding company employees, some states allow defendants to post bond through the state government, which in many ways acts in the same capacity as a bonding company. In states that continue to allow the use of bonding companies an interesting profession has arisen: the so-called "bounty hunter."

BOUNTY HUNTERS

Bonding companies often employ individuals to hunt down and return defendants who have fled the jurisdiction. State law usually gives a grace period to the bonding company to produce the individual who has not appeared for court. This grace period might be 72 hours to 10 days, depending on the circumstances. If the bonding company is able to locate the defendant and return him to the jail, then the bonding company will not be required to forfeit the defendant's bond. This creates a system in which the bonding company has a strong interest to keep tabs on its client, and also gives law enforcement another tool to help locate defendants who have absconded. This is where the **bounty hunter** enters the picture. The bonding company may pay a flat fee to an individual to find the defendant and bring him back to the jurisdiction. In other cases, the bounty hunter may be paid on a percentage basis, such as 10 percent of the bonding company's fee. In either event, the bounty hunter is employed by the bonding company to locate the defendant, return him to the jurisdiction, and surrender him off bond to the local authorities.

Bounty hunter
An individual hired by a bonding company who works to locate defendants who have absconded and to return these defendants to face their court dates.

The use of bounty hunters has been called into question by several instances where bounty hunters have used excessive force to subdue defendants and return them. In one notable case, a bounty hunter crossed into Mexico, kidnapped a defendant, and returned him to the United States. The Mexican government charged the bounty hunter with kidnapping, causing no end of confusion for all parties concerned.

B. RECOGNIZANCE BOND

Recognizance bond is a type of bond procedure that once was quite common, but is not seen as frequently in modern times. When someone posts a recognizance bond, he or she is simply giving a promise to return and not posting any money to ensure that return. Basically, the person is giving his or her word. In the past, when communities were smaller, such a process worked with reasonable efficiency. The person who posted an OR (own recognizance) bond would simply promise to return to court and then would be released. Because the person was known in the community, tracking him or her down did not involve much effort if the person failed to appear. Recognizance bonds are used with much lower frequency in bigger cities and even in smaller communities where the populace is a more mobile than it once was.

Recognizance bond
The accused simply gives his or her word that he or she will return for a specific court date.

C. FACTORS TO CONSIDER IN SETTING BOND

Before a judge sets bail, he or she must consider several different factors. Obviously, no judge wishes to release a defendant who then commits another crime, such as murdering the witness in the case. On the other hand, the Eighth Amendment prohibits excessive bail. In order to juggle these competing interests, a judge will consider all of the following factors before setting bail:

- Defendant's ties to the community
- Seriousness of the offense
- Defendant's likelihood of flight to avoid prosecution
- Danger of the defendant to victim or community

DEFENDANT'S TIES TO THE COMMUNITY

One important factor in setting bail is the defendant's ties to the community. If the defendant is a stranger or someone simply passing through the area on his way to some other locale, then there is a greater likelihood that the defendant will abscond from the jurisdiction when he is released. However, a defendant with strong ties to the community, such as family members who live in the area, children who attend school in the jurisdiction, or long-term employment in the area is less likely to flee. All of these factors will weigh in the defendant's favor. If the defendant cannot show any of these ties to the area, then the bail amount will undoubtedly be larger than for someone charged with the same offense who can boast of these connections to the community. Consider Scenario 15-2.

SCENARIO 15-2

HISPANIC ORIGIN

Juan has been arrested for shoplifting. At his bond hearing, the judge says that because Juan is Hispanic, it's likely that he will flee the jurisdiction and return to his home country if he is set free on bond. The judge makes no inquiry into what country Juan is from or even his citizenship status. Is this a valid consideration for a bond?

Answer: No. The judge may consider a defendant's ties to the communities, but may not simply assume that because someone is of a particular race that he or she is a flight risk. In this case, the judge did not even determine if Juan was an American citizen.

SERIOUSNESS OF THE OFFENSE

Presumption of innocence
A basic tenet of American law that a defendant enters the criminal process clothed in the assumption that he or she is innocent unless and until the prosecution proves that he or she is guilty beyond a reasonable doubt.

Although a defendant enters all courts with the **presumption of innocence**, a judge may take into account the nature of the charge before setting a bail amount. There are certain offenses, such as rape and murder, where the court may deny bail. In such a situation, the danger to the community, or to specific individuals, may be such that it outweighs the defendant's need for freedom pending trial. There are also certain offenses, including rape and murder, where many states will not allow a magistrate to set bail. In these cases, the bail must be set by a superior or trial court judge.[1] The trial judge has exclusive jurisdiction in these types of cases to set the bail amount. The defendant must remain in custody until he or she is brought before the trial judge for a bond hearing. See Scenario 15-3.

SERIOUSNESS OF THE OFFENSE

Cyril is charged with several counts of first degree murder. There are allegations that Cyril is involved with a gang and that these murder charges were gang-related. When Cyril's defense attorney brings a motion for bond, the trial judge summarily rejects it, stating that given the seriousness of the offense, she will not set any bond. Is this a valid ruling?

Answer: Yes. Although a judge must consider several factors, seriousness of the offense alone may be enough to deny bond, however the judge should also review other factors in the case.

DEFENDANT'S LIKELIHOOD OF FLIGHT TO AVOID PROSECUTION

Closely linked with the consideration of the defendant's ties to the community is the issue of whether or not the defendant is likely to flee the jurisdiction once he or she is released. A defendant who has fled while on bond in previous cases is unlikely to be granted bail at all. It is not always easy for the judge to decide who is or is not a likely candidate to flee the jurisdiction. The defendant's attorney will certainly argue that he will not, while the prosecutor may just as forcefully argue that he might. The judge must make up his or her own mind about this issue.

DANGER OF THE DEFENDANT TO VICTIM OR COMMUNITY

A defendant who has threatened police or victims in a case is unlikely to be granted bail. A judge must consider the danger to the community, to specific individuals, and even to the defendant, if bail is set and the defendant is released pending trial. There have been cases in which a defendant who was released on bond killed the witness against him or otherwise caused bodily injury and property damage. Judges do not have crystal balls; they must rely on their own experiences and the law as they weigh this element in with the other factors that must be considered before setting a bond amount.

DEFENDANT'S BURDEN IN A BAIL HEARING

A defendant requests bail so, unlike in other hearings, he or she will often take the stand to offer testimony on the limited subject of bail. A prosecutor may cross-examine the defendant but will be limited to questions surrounding the four basic

---

[1] *State v. Dodson*, 556 S.W.2d 938 (Mo. Ct. App. 1977).

issues of bail, not issues related to the underlying case. Even with this limited interaction, many defense attorneys prefer testimony from individuals other than the defendant. Defense attorneys are well aware that many bail hearings are transcribed and that the defendant may make some statement that might be used against him or her at a later date — although some jurisdictions do not allow statements made in bail or bond hearings to be used at trial.

Bond forfeiture
A judicial determination that the defendant has violated the conditions of his or her release and that the defendant should be placed into custody pending further hearings.

D. BOND FORFEITURE

Once a defendant has been released on bail, a judge has full discretion to revoke bail and have the defendant returned to jail pending trial. A judge can base this decision on allegations that the defendant has attempted to intimidate or injure witnesses in a case or has committed another offense.[2]

PRELIMINARY HEARINGS

As discussed earlier in this chapter, an initial appearance occurs shortly after the defendant is arrested and processed at a local holding facility. Within a few days of the initial appearance, the defendant will have an additional court hearing: the **preliminary hearing**. The preliminary hearing (also known as a probable cause hearing) is held within days of the defendant's arrest. Unlike the initial appearance hearing, preliminary hearings are adversarial in nature. The prosecutor will be present, as well as the defendant, defendant's attorney, and state's witnesses. The defendant also has the opportunity to testify at the preliminary hearing, although this rarely happens.

Preliminary hearing
A court hearing that determines if there is probable cause to believe that the defendant committed the crime with which he or she is charged.

A. THE PURPOSE OF THE PRELIMINARY HEARING

The preliminary hearing has one purpose: to establish that there is sufficient probable cause for the defendant's arrest and continued detention. At the preliminary hearing, the government, through the prosecutor, is required to present witness testimony to establish probable cause. Normally, a preliminary hearing is held before a magistrate judge. The judge has the responsibility of deciding whether or not the prosecution has met the burden of showing probable cause. The actual procedure for carrying out a preliminary hearing varies somewhat from jurisdiction to jurisdiction, but the basic elements are the same everywhere: the state must present evidence to prove probable cause for the defendant's arrest.

---

[2] *Stiegele v. State*, 685 P.2d 1255 (Alaska Ct. App. 1984).

B. THE PROCEDURE FOLLOWED AT THE PRELIMINARY HEARING

Because the purpose of a preliminary hearing is to establish probable cause that the defendant committed the crime with which he or she is charged, the state must present some evidence to meet its burden. This burden never shifts to the defendant to prove his or her innocence. The state meets its burden by calling witnesses, often police officers, but frequently civilian witnesses as well. These witnesses will testify about the facts surrounding the crime and the defendant's arrest. The prosecutor calls his or her witnesses first, and then the defense attorney has the right to cross-examine the witnesses about their testimony. This cross-examination is supposed to be limited to the issue of probable cause, but many defense attorneys see this as a perfect opportunity to learn more about the case. They will often ask questions outside the scope of the hearing to learn these facts. There is no requirement to prove probable cause beyond a reasonable doubt. Instead, the state must establish probable cause by a **preponderance of evidence**.

Preponderance of evidence
A showing by one side in a suit that its version of the facts is more likely to be true than not.

During a preliminary hearing, the state's burden is simply to show that it is more likely than not that the defendant committed the crime. The state does not have to prove that the defendant committed the crime beyond a reasonable doubt, because that standard is reserved for trials. It is also not required because the defendant will not be sentenced at the conclusion of the hearing, and the defendant continues to enjoy the full spectrum of constitutional protections. However, because the burden of proof at a preliminary hearing is much lower than that required at trial, there are some practical issues that heavily favor the prosecution. One such issue concerns the rules of evidence that are used in preliminary hearings.

C. EVIDENTIARY ISSUES AND RULES DURING PRELIMINARY HEARINGS

The rules of evidence at a preliminary hearing are more relaxed than those used at a trial. For instance, hearsay testimony, which is generally inadmissible during a trial, can be used in a preliminary hearing. The reason that the rules of evidence are not as rigorous goes to the very heart of the preliminary hearing. The defendant will not be found guilty or sentenced at the conclusion. The jury in the defendant's case will never be told about the result of the preliminary hearing. As such, the standard of proof is much lower. Prosecutors routinely win preliminary hearings, and it is rare for a judge to rule that there is insufficient probable cause, given such a low standard of proof.

Preliminary hearings are not difficult to present, and this explains why many new prosecutors are assigned to this duty. The hearing superficially resembles a trial, and inexperienced prosecutors can gain valuable insights into the adversarial process without the prospect of losing a major trial.

D. DECISION AT THE PRELIMINARY HEARING

There are only two decisions at a preliminary hearing: a finding that the state has established probable cause or that it has not. In the vast majority of cases, the magistrate will find that probable cause exists. This result can be explained by various factors including good police work, the prosecutor's preparation, and the very low standard of proof. Beyond that, if a magistrate rules that there is no probable cause and the prosecutor disagrees with this ruling, then the prosecutor may still present the case to the grand jury. That procedure will be discussed later in this chapter.

Binding over
A determination that probable cause exists in a preliminary hearing, triggering a transfer of the case to a higher court, usually superior court.

When a magistrate decides that the state has met the burden of probable cause in a preliminary hearing, the judge issues a ruling **binding over** the case to a higher court. In many states, that means the defendant's case will be transferred to superior court, although not all states use that term to refer to a trial court empowered to hear felony cases.

On the other hand, if the magistrate rules that there is insufficient probable cause, then the defendant will be ordered to be released. Assuming that there are no other charges pending against the defendant, the holding facility will release him or her. Consider Scenario 15-4.

| **SCENARIO 15-4** | ## PROOF BEYOND A REASONABLE DOUBT |

Sandy is charged with aggravated assault and represents herself at her preliminary hearing. The police officer testifies that the victim told him that Sandy hit him with a shovel and then fled the scene. Sandy objects that the victim is not present to testify, but the judge overrules the objection. The officer identifies Sandy as the person he later found running through the neighborhood, holding a shovel. The victim also identified Sandy. The judge allows Sandy to offer testimony and, when she finishes, the judge rules that there is probable cause to bind the case over. Sandy objects that based on this evidence no jury would convict her. She requests that the judge dismiss the case on these grounds. Is she correct?

Answer: No. The standard of proof at a preliminary hearing is not the same as that required in a jury trial. Therefore, a judge can rule based solely on probable cause to believe that Sandy committed the crime and bind the case over.

THE DEFENDANT'S ROLE AT THE PRELIMINARY HEARING

A defendant sits with his or her counsel during the preliminary hearing, and they are allowed to confer with one another as the hearing proceeds. Many defense attorneys will meet with their clients shortly before the hearing to explain what will happen, to discuss the merits of the case, and also to explain that the hearing will not result in the defendant going to prison or being found guilty.

Defendants are permitted to testify at a preliminary hearing, but they are normally counseled to remain silent because establishing probable cause is an easy thing to do and the chances are extremely high that the court will rule against the defendant. Given those facts, having the defendant testify — and then be subject to cross-examination by the prosecutor — could only help the state's case.

E. NEGOTIATIONS BETWEEN PROSECUTORS AND DEFENSE ATTORNEYS AT PRELIMINARY HEARINGS

Even though a case is on the docket for a preliminary hearing, there still may not be a hearing. There is a certain amount of give and take between prosecutors and defense attorneys, and the negotiations between them can become intense. What are they negotiating? On the surface, there may appear to be very little that a prosecutor could offer a defendant or anything that the defendant would want, but appearances can be deceiving. Prosecutors often have dozens of cases pending on a particular day's calendar. It is also the prosecutor's role to make bail recommendations in cases, although the magistrate is not bound to follow those recommendations. The prosecutor and the defense may enter into some hardnosed bargaining about two issues: waiver and bail recommendations.

If a defendant waives the preliminary hearing, then he or she admits that there is sufficient probable cause to bind the case over. This admission cannot be used against the defendant at trial, so there is little danger to the defendant to simply avoid the hearing. However, a defense attorney may negotiate with the prosecutor over the issue of the bail recommendation. The bargaining might go something like this:

> **Prosecutor:** My bail recommendation on your client is $10,000.
> **Defense attorney:** If I get my client to waive the hearing, will you consider lowering that recommendation to $5,000?
> **Prosecutor:** If you can get your client to waive the hearing, I'll go to $7,500.
> **Defense attorney:** I'll talk to my client.

In such a scenario, the prosecutor lowers his or her bail recommendation to the court in exchange for a waiver of the preliminary hearing. The prosecutor will have one less case to worry about and may be able to release one or two witnesses. The defense attorney can tell his client that the prosecutor is lowering the bail recommendation. Of course, both parties realize that a judge is not compelled to follow the prosecutor's recommendation, but in the vast majority of cases, the judge will follow the mutually agreed upon resolution, reasoning that the defense attorney and prosecutor are both in the best position to know the issues in the case. Their compromise saves valuable court time and resources.

For purposes of clarity, this text will continue to refer to the trial court as superior court, keeping in mind that there is some variation among the states, and not all states use the term "superior court" to refer to the trial court. Following the preliminary hearing, when the case is bound over to superior court — and the overwhelming majority will be bound over — the next phase is the charging decision by the prosecutor.

 **CHARGING DECISION**

One might be tempted to think that the next phase of a criminal case would be simply to present the case that was bound over in magistrate court to the grand jury. However, when the case is bound over from magistrate court to superior court, the case also comes under the power and authority of the prosecutor whom this text will refer to as the district attorney (acknowledging that prosecutors can also be known as state's attorneys, people's attorneys, solicitors, and other names). When a case is bound over to superior court, the district attorney is permitted to review the case and to add, change, or dismiss the charges against the defendant. This process is loosely defined as the **charging decision** and involves a review of the facts and the law to decide not only what would be the most successful charge that the state can bring against the defendant, but also what is the most just way to proceed. Prosecutors are not charged with the duty to obtain convictions, but to seek justice. The charging decision involves several steps. Usually, the elected district attorney delegates charging decisions to her assistant district attorneys. In large cities, there could be hundreds of assistant district attorneys, all handing thousands of cases. In small communities, on the other hand, there may only be a few assistants. In either situation, it is up to the prosecution to decide how best to proceed in the case. An assistant district attorney might do some or all of the following:

Charging decision
The process that a prosecutor goes through to determine what is the appropriate and just charge to bring against a defendant based on the law and the facts in the case.

- Ask for additional investigation
- Bring additional charges against the defendant
- Dismiss the case

A. ASK FOR ADDITIONAL INVESTIGATION

A prosecutor is empowered to request additional investigation of the case by the police or through investigators employed directly by the district attorney. Many district attorneys' offices have their own body of investigators and support staff whose sole purpose is to conduct additional investigations into cases brought by the police. Why might such additional investigation be necessary? The simple answer is that the police may have overlooked some important issue, or the prosecutor believes that he or she can add more charges in the case, but must have the facts to support them. The charging decision by the prosecutor always focuses on the facts and law in a case. Without the facts, and the evidence to support them, there can be no case.

B. BRING ADDITIONAL CHARGES AGAINST THE DEFENDANT

Although the police have brought specific charges against a defendant, the prosecutor may add other charges as he or she sees fit. A prosecutor can add, delete, modify, or dismiss the original charges brought by law enforcement. This gives the prosecutor a great deal of authority. A prosecutor often will consult with the police officers involved in the case before taking any of these actions, but the prosecutor is not compelled to do so. The prosecutor acts independently of the police. Just as a prosecutor has no power to hire or fire police officers, law enforcement officials have no right to dictate what charges should or should not be brought against defendants. Having said this, however, a prosecutor who routinely disregards the input of the police will find himself or herself isolated and ignored by the police. Although it is rarely depicted in fictional portrayals of criminal cases, there can be a certain amount of animosity between police and prosecutors. They have different approaches to cases. For example, police officers often consider a case "closed" when an arrest is made, while for the prosecutor, the case has just begun. There are other differences to consider in the approach of police officers and prosecutors to criminal cases. Although fictional portrayals show police and prosecutors working in a harmonious partnership, that is not always the case. Police officers work odd hours and are almost universally poorly paid. They face danger on a daily basis and must often interact with people and situations that most of us would eagerly avoid. Prosecutors, on the other hand, focus on the elements of proof and are not always as aware of the situations that police must face. At its worst, police and prosecutors can despise one another, with police officers believing that prosecutors are pampered law graduates with no sense of the real world, while prosecutors believe that police officers are brutes with little consideration for constitutional principles or the pressures brought to bear on a trial attorney. However, this extreme viewpoint is not common. In the typical scenario there are prosecutors and police who get along very well together and others who do not. However, it would be a mistake to believe that police officers subjugate themselves to the whims of prosecutors or that prosecutors blindly follow the recommendations of police officers. The relationship can often be complicated. Consider Scenario 15-5.

ALTERING THE CHARGES

SCENARIO 15-5

Detective Letisha has brought charges against John Doe for forgery and fraud. The assistant district attorney assigned to the case reviews the file and decides to dismiss those charges and bring entirely different charges. Can Detective Letisha force the prosecutor to bring the original charges?

    Answer: No. The decision about what crimes to charge against the defendant are exclusively the province of the prosecutor and, though the police officer may have strong feelings about a case, it is ultimately the prosecutor's decision about how to proceed.

C. DISMISS THE CASE

Prosecutors have the right to dismiss a case prior to presenting it to the grand jury. They actually have the right to dismiss their case at any point, but after a case has been presented to a grand jury, the dismissal must usually be signed by a judge. However, a prosecutor may seek a dismissal of a case, referred to as a **nolle prosequi**, if the prosecutor does not believe that there is sufficient evidence in the case to prove that the defendant is guilty beyond a reasonable doubt. The prosecutor can take this action against the wishes of the victim in the case, the police officer's desires, and even the community's interest in the case. In most cases, of course, the prosecutor will discuss a dismissal of a case with a victim and also engage the police officer, but there is no requirement that he or she do so. A

Nolle prosequi
An order dismissing a criminal charge.

prosecutor should be guided by conscience and the law, and a prosecutor who believes that a defendant is innocent should dismiss a case. A prosecutor has an ethical duty not to prosecute someone that he or she believes is innocent.

Once a prosecutor has decided what the appropriate criminal charges in a case should be, he or she will draft a charging document. Most states make a strict distinction between misdemeanor and felony cases. As shown in Chapter 2, a felony is any charge where the potential punishment is more than one year in custody. In such a case, the prosecutor would draft an **indictment**. The indictment lists the facts of the charge and the code section that the defendant has violated. When the charge is a misdemeanor, the charges are brought in an **accusation** (referred to as an **information** on the federal level and in some state jurisdictions).

The indictment must give the defendant notice of the charges against him or her, list the crimes committed, and give the defendant details about the circumstances surrounding the charges. Generally, an indictment is sufficient if it answers the question words: who, when, where, and how? (Indictments do not answer the question of *why*). See Figure 15-2 for a sample indictment.

Indictment
A document that charges a defendant with a felony.

Accusation
A document that charges a defendant with a misdemeanor in most state courts.

Information
A document that charges a defendant with a misdemeanor in federal court.

FIGURE 15-2
Sample Indictment

BILL OF INDICTMENT

Grand Jury Witnesses: R. L. Queen, Prosecutor

State of Placid
Placid Superior Court
March Adjourned Term

State of Placid
versus
Mark William Finnegan

Offense (s):

Count 1:	**Kidnapping**
Count 2:	**Aggravated Assault**
Count 3:	**Stalking**
Count 4:	**Simple Battery**
Counts 5-12:	**Stalking**

_____ Bill

This _____ day of _____, 20_____.

_____

Howard D. Purcell, Jr.
Grand Jury Foreperson

==========================

Received in open court from the swc Grand Jury bailiff and filed in office.

This _____ day of _____, 20_____.

Deputy Clerk, Placid Superior Court.

========================

Sean J. Turlow, District Attorney
Placid Judicial Circuit
Special Presentment.

We the jury find the defendant

_____

_____

_____

_____

_____

Foreperson

This _____ day of _____, 20_____.

The defendant herein waives a copy of indictment, list of witnesses, formal arraignment and pleads _____ guilty.

This _____ day of _____, 20_____.

_____
Defendant

_____
Attorney for the Defendant

_____
Assistant District Attorney

STATE OF PLACID, COUNTY OF PLACID
IN THE SUPERIOR COURT OF SAID COUNTY

Count 1 of 12

The GRAND JURORS selected, chosen and sworn for the County of Placid, to wit:

1. Howard D. Purcell, Jr., Foreperson
2. Marion Fred Walden, Jr., Vice Foreperson
3. Teresa Ann Morris, Clerk
4. Wendy Ball, Asst. Clerk
5. Alice V. Banks
6. Kathleen M. Barrett
7. Dennis F. Boyd
8. Lois M. Cragin
9. Charlotte C. Crosland
10. Faye P. Crowe
11. Samuel E. Couch
12. Virginia E. Driskell
13. Dennis Eckman
14. Billie Ellis
15. William B. Francis, III
16. Elizabeth Hawkins
17. Cynthia J. Hope
18. Venita Masters
19. Bennie W. Moorehead
20. Mrs. Martha A. Nunnally
21. Helen Phillips
22. Doris F. Stone
23. Diane Young

in the name and behalf of the citizens of Placid, charge and accuse **Mark William Finnegan** with the offense of **Kidnapping** in that the said accused, in the State of Placid and County of Placid, on the **20th day of April, 2013**, did then and there unlawfully abduct Hilda River, a human being, without lawful authority and hold said person against her will, contrary to the laws of said State, the peace, good order and dignity thereof.

Count 2 of 12

and the GRAND JURORS, aforesaid, in the name and behalf of the citizens of Placid, further charge and accuse **Mark William Finnegan** with the offense of **Aggravated Assault** in that the said accused, in the State of Placid and County of Placid, on the **20th day of April, 2013**,

continued

FIGURE 15-2

Sample Indictment
(continued)

did then and there unlawfully make an assault upon the person of Hilda River, with a knife, a deadly weapon by holding said knife and threatening her with it, contrary to the laws of said State, the peace, good order and dignity thereof.

Count 3 of 12

and the GRAND JURORS, aforesaid, in the name and behalf of the citizens of Placid, further charge and accuse **Mark William Finnegan** with the offense of **Stalking** in that the said accused, in the State of Placid and County of Placid, **between the dates of the 1st day of August, 1993 and the 30th day of September, 1993, the exact date being unknown to the Grand Jurors**, did then and there unlawfully contact Wilma Johnson at a public place, to wit: the Ingles Market, Inc. parking lot, 2850 Gant-Suwanee Road, Suwannee, Placid, without her consent and for the purpose of harassing and intimidating her, contrary to the laws of said State, the peace, good order and dignity thereof.

Count 4 of 12

and the GRAND JURORS, aforesaid, in the name and behalf of the citizens of Placid, further charge and accuse **Mark William Finnegan** with the offense of **Simple Battery** in that the said accused, in the State of Placid and County of Placid, on the **29th day of October, 1993**, did then and there unlawfully and intentionally make contact of an insulting and provoking nature to Chula Smith by grabbing her skirt, contrary to the laws of said State, the peace, good order and dignity thereof.

Count 5 of 12

and the GRAND JURORS, aforesaid, in the name and behalf of the citizens of Placid, further charge and accuse **Mark William Finnegan** with the offense of **Stalking** in that the said accused, in the State of Placid and County of Placid, on the **29th day of October, 1993**, did then and there unlawfully contact Chula Smith at a public place, to wit: the Annexter Wire and Cable Co., 550 Old Peachtree Road, Suwanee, Placid, without her consent and for the purpose of harassing and intimidating her, contrary to the laws of said State, the peace, good order and dignity thereof.

Count 6 of 12

and the GRAND JURORS, aforesaid, in the name and behalf of the citizens of Placid, further charge and accuse **Mark William Finnegan** with the offense of **Stalking** in that the said accused, in the State of Placid and County of Placid, on the **15th day of February, 2013**, did then and there unlawfully contact Silvia Swenson at a public place, to wit: the Ingles Market, Inc. parking lot, 2850 Gant-Suwanee Road, Suwanee, Placid, without her consent and for the purpose of harassing and intimidating her, contrary to the laws of said State, the peace, good order and dignity thereof.

Count 7 of 12

and the GRAND JURORS, aforesaid, in the name and behalf of the citizens of Placid, further charge and accuse **Mark William Finnegan** with the offense of **Stalking** in that the said accused, in the State of Placid and County of Placid, on the **30th day of March, 2013**, did then and there unlawfully contact Jessica Wilhoit at a public place, to wit: the Ingles Market,

Inc. parking lot, 2850 Gant-Suwanee Road, without her consent and for the purpose of harassing and intimidating her, contrary to the laws of said State, the peace, good order and dignity thereof.

Count 8 of 12

and the GRAND JURORS, aforesaid, in the name and behalf of the citizens of Placid, further charge and accuse **Mark William Finnegan** with the offense of **Stalking** in that the said accused, in the State of Placid and County of Placid, **between the dates of the 2nd day of April, 2013 and the 10th day of April, 2013, the exact date being unknown to the Grand Jurors**, did then and there unlawfully contact Nicole Parker at a public place, to wit: the Ingles Market, Inc. parking lot, 2850 Gant-Suwanee Road, Suwanee, Placid, without her consent and for the purpose of harassing and intimidating her, contrary to the laws of said State, the peace, good order and dignity thereof.

Count 9 of 12

and the GRAND JURORS, aforesaid, in the name and behalf of the citizens of Placid, further charge and accuse **Mark William Finnegan** with the offense of **Stalking** in that the said accused, in the State of Placid and County of Placid, on the **10th day of April, 2013**, did then and there unlawfully contact Sasha Sasha at a public place, to wit: the Ingles Market, Inc. parking lot, 2850 Gant-Suwanee Road, Suwanee, Placid, without her consent and for the purpose of harassing and intimidating her, contrary to the laws of said State, the peace, good order and dignity thereof.

Count 10 of 12

and the GRAND JURORS, aforesaid, in the name and behalf of the citizens of Placid, further charge and accuse **Mark William Finnegan** with the offense of **Stalking** in that the said accused, in the State of Placid and County of Placid, on the **between the dates of the 12th day of April, 2013, and the 14th day of April, 2013, the exact date being unknown to the Grand Jurors**, did then and there unlawfully contact Kim Kimberly at a public place, to wit: the Ingles Market, Inc. parking lot, 2850 Gant-Suwanee Road, Suwanee, Placid, without her consent and for the purpose of harassing and intimidating her, contrary to the laws of said State, the peace, good order and dignity thereof.

Count 11 of 12

and the GRAND JURORS, aforesaid, in the name and behalf of the citizens of Placid, further charge and accuse **Mark William Finnegan** with the offense of **Stalking** in that the said accused, in the State of Placid and County of Placid, on the **17th day of April, 2013, said date being a material element**, did then and there unlawfully contact Juana Juan at a public place, to wit: the Ingles Market, Inc. parking lot, 2850 Gant-Suwanee Road, Suwanee, Placid, without her consent and for the purpose of harassing and intimidating her, contrary to the laws of said State, the peace, good order and dignity thereof.

Count 12 of 12

and the GRAND JURORS, aforesaid, in the name and behalf of the citizens of Placid, further charge and accuse **Mark William Finnegan** with the offense of **Stalking** in that the said

continued

FIGURE 15-2

Sample Indictment
(continued)

accused, in the State of Placid and County of Placid, on the **2nd day of May, 2013, said date being a material element**, did then and there unlawfully contact Kim Kimberly at a public place, to wit: the Ingles Market, Inc. parking lot, 2850 Gant-Suwanee Road, Suwanee, Placid, without her consent and for the purpose of harassing and intimidating her, contrary to the laws of said State, the peace, good order and dignity thereof.

Sean J. Turlow, District Attorney

Special Presentment

Once the prosecutor has gone through the charging decision and drafted the indictment, the case is ready to be presented to the grand jury.

V. THE GRAND JURY

No person shall be held to answer for a capital, or otherwise infamous crime, unless on a presentment or indictment of a Grand Jury. — Fifth Amendment

The U.S. Constitution requires a grand jury indictment for a person charged with a capital offense (one punishable by death) or "otherwise infamous crime." This phrase has come to mean any felony offense. However, the U.S. Supreme Court has never held that this provision of the Fifth Amendment applies to the states. In fact, there are some states that do not use grand juries at all, but because most states do, this text will spend some time examining the functions and procedures of the grand jury.

A. HISTORY OF THE GRAND JURY

Sidebar

Cases involving misde-meanors are not presented to grand juries.

Grand juries have been part of both the American and English systems for centuries. The primary reason for the creation of a grand jury was to interpose a barrier between the government and the individual. Prosecutors must present their version of the criminal case to a grand jury and receive its permission to continue with the prosecution. Grand juries were traditionally seen as a way of allowing the community to protect innocent individuals from being persecuted by overzealous government officials and to prevent the government from using its power to bring criminal charges as a way to intimidate and silence those who disagreed with government policy.[3] Grand juries do not exist in civil cases. There are also no grand juries authorized under the Military Code of Justice or in juvenile cases. Misdemeanor

---

[3] *In re Grand Jury Appearance Request by Loigman*, 183 N.J. 133, 870 A.2d 249 (2005).

FIGURE 15-3

**Sample Statute Authoriz-
ing the Prosecution of
Some Felonies through
Accusations Bypassing
the Grand Jury (Georgia)**

TITLE 17.   CRIMINAL PROCEDURE
CHAPTER 7.   PRETRIAL PROCEEDINGS
ARTICLE 4.   ACCUSATIONS

O.C.G.A. § 17-7-70 (2013)

§ 17-7-70. Trial upon accusations in felony cases; trial upon accusations of felony and misdemeanor cases in which guilty plea entered and indictment waived

(a) In all felony cases, other than cases involving capital felonies, in which defendants have been bound over to the superior court, are confined in jail or released on bond pending a commitment hearing, or are in jail having waived a commitment hearing, the district attorney shall have authority to prefer accusations, and such defendants shall be tried on such accusations, provided that defendants going to trial under such accusations shall, in writing, waive indictment by a grand jury.

(b) Judges of the superior court may open their courts at any time without the presence of either a grand jury or a trial jury to receive and act upon pleas of guilty in misdemeanor cases and in felony cases, except those punishable by death or life imprisonment, when the judge and the defendant consent thereto. The judge may try the issues in such cases without a jury upon an accusation filed by the district attorney where the defendant has waived indictment and consented thereto in writing and counsel is present in court representing the defendant either by virtue of his employment or by appointment by the court.

cases are not presented to grand juries and some states even allow specific types of minor felonies to bypass the grand jury system. See Figure 15-3.

Even in states that follow a grand jury system, there are variations in how the grand jurors are selected and how the case is presented. When a state does have a grand jury system, it is authorized and governed by statutes. Often, the grand jury requirement is set out in the state constitution.

Grand juries do not decide whether a person is guilty or not guilty of a crime. Instead, they reach a decision that is partially based on probable cause and partially on the opinions of the individual jurors. It is easy to confuse a grand jury with a regular or petit jury. A regular jury is what is normally portrayed on courtroom television dramas. These jurors decide the guilt or innocence of the defendant. The grand jury does not make that determination. Instead, it simply returns a vote stating whether or not the case against the defendant should proceed. If the grand jury believes that the prosecution has made a sufficient showing, it will return a vote of "true bill." This authorizes the state to bring the defendant to trial. If the grand jury returns a "no bill" the case is dismissed, and the only way that the state can proceed is either by charging the defendant with a misdemeanor or by waiting until a new grand jury is seated and present the case to them.

FIGURE 15-4	Differences Between a Grand Jury and a Regular (Petit) Jury

Grand jury	Regular jury
16–23 members	12 members
Do not determine guilty or not verdicts Do not recommend sentences Meet regularly for a set period of time, ex: every month for six months	Return guilty or not guilty verdicts May recommend sentences Meet only once to consider a specific case

FIGURE 15-5	BILL OF INDICTMENT

Sample Indictment with True Bill Determination

Grand Jury witnesses:
Detective Able

State of Yuma
Gannett Superior Court
March Adjourned Term

State of Yuma
  versus
Christine Lynn Kline
  Offense(s):
Count 1: Murder

True ☐ Bill

This the ___ day of April, this year

[signature]
_____
Seamus Kadirka,
Grand Jury Foreperson
=========================
Received in open court from the sworn Grand Jury Bailiff and filed in office.

This the ___ day of April, this year

[signature]
_____
Irma Friendly, Deputy Clerk
Gannett Superior Court
=========================
Derrick Young, District Attorney
Gannett Judicial Circuit

We the jury find the defendant:
_____
_____
_____
_____
Foreperson
This ___ day of _____, _____

The defendant herein waives a copy of indictment, list of witnesses, formal arraignment and pleads ___ guilty.
This ___ day of _____, _____
_____
Defendant
_____
Attorney for Defendant
_____
Assistant District Attorney

Count 1 of 1

The GRAND JURORS selected, chosen and sworn for the County of Gannett, to wit:

1. Seamus Kadirka, Foreperson
2. Randall Makepeace
3. Mary Manz
4. Jessica Etters
5. Janae Freeman
6. Melodie Sisk
7. Yolanda Price
8. Starla Hoke
9. Debra Holbrook
10. Deborah Bolstridge
11. Sharon Ferguson
12. Lisa Mazzonetto
13. Brenda Timmerman
14. Richard Garrison
15. John Farthing
16. Paul Dellinger
17. Paula Barnes
18. Patsy Dellinger
19. Betsy Bevans
20. Christy Wallace
21. Gayle Hartung
22. Marianne Simpson
23. Star Hand

In the name and behalf of the citizens of Yuma, charge and accuse Christine Lynn Kline, with the offense of Murder in that the said accused, in the state of Yuma and County of Gannett, on or about the 19th day of November, last year, did then and there unlawfully and with malice aforethought, kill Douglas Betters by smothering him to death, contrary to the laws of said State, the peace, good order and dignity thereof.

Derrick Young, District Attorney
Gannett Judicial Circuit

B. THE PURPOSE OF THE GRAND JURY

The grand jury was devised to act as a buffer between the state and the defendant. Developed in England and later transplanted to the New World, the original concept of the grand jury has existed for more than 700 years. The grand jury is composed of citizens who sit in secret session and listen to evidence about specific cases. The essential function of the grand jury is to determine that there is probable cause to believe that a crime has occurred. Once they do, the grand jurors allow the prosecutor to continue with his or her case.[4] The grand jury writes its decision on the indictment. See Figure 15-5 for an example of a case that has been true billed by a grand jury.

---

[4] *State v. Hall*, 152 N.H. 374, 877 A.2d 222 (2005).

C. HOW IS THE GRAND JURY COMPOSED?

A grand jury is selected in various ways in different jurisdictions. The most common method of selecting individual grand jurors is by using the same pool of jurors that would be used for a normal jury trial. Grand jurors must meet the following criteria:

- Must be members of the jurisdiction
- Cannot have been convicted of a felony
- Must be citizens

A grand jury is made up of citizens of the county or federal district. They must be selected from a cross-section of the community, including factors such as race, sex, occupation, etc.[5] Citizens cannot be excluded from a grand jury on the basis of their race, ethnic origin, or their sex.[6] The usual number of jurors is between 12 and 23, again depending on the jurisdiction. Neither the federal system nor any state allows a grand jury to proceed with fewer than 12 members[7], but many states allow a grand jury to convene if some of its members are temporarily absent. Members are selected by the chief judge of the district.

When it comes to the actual composition of the grand jury, the members must represent a fair and impartial cross-section of the jurisdiction, with the percentages of minorities reflected as closely as possible in the composition of the grand jury itself. There is no requirement that the exact percentages of race and ethnicity found in the jurisdiction must be represented in the composition of the grand jury. As long as no minority group is deliberately excluded, a defendant has no claim of improper grand jury composition if it turns out that a specific minority group was not represented on his or her particular grand jury. Beyond that, states vary considerably on who may serve as a grand juror. Most states specifically prohibit the victim from being a grand juror in his or her own case for obvious reasons. Many, but not all, states prohibit actively serving law-enforcement officers from serving on a grand jury, and obviously the arresting officer is not permitted to act as a grand juror in his or her own case.[8]

CHALLENGING THE COMPOSITION OF THE GRAND JURY

A defendant may challenge the composition of the grand jury as not representing a fair cross-section of the community, but unless the defendant can

---

[5] *Campbell v. Louisiana*, 118 S.Ct. 1419 (1998).
[6] *Taylor v. Louisiana*, 95 S.Ct. 692 (1975); *Castaneda v. Partida*, 97 S.Ct. 1272 (1977).
[7] Fed. R. Crim. P. 6(f).
[8] *Stinski v. State*, 281 Ga. 783, 642 S.E.2d 1 (2007).

show a clear pattern of exclusion of individuals on the basis of ethnicity or race, the court is unlikely to rule that the composition was improper. In order to successfully challenge the composition of the grand jury, a defendant must show that there was some irregularity in the way that the grand jury was compiled, such as government officials deliberately ignoring statutory procedures or deliberately excluding individuals on the basis of race, religion, or ethnicity.

D. FUNCTION OF THE GRAND JURY

The grand jury actually has several functions. The primary purpose of the grand jury is to determine if a crime has occurred. If the government can establish probable cause to believe that the defendant committed the crime presented, the grand jury has the power and duty to authorize further prosecution of the case.[9] As such, it is a key element of the criminal justice process. Witnesses appear before the grand jury and are asked questions to establish the basic merits of the case. In many states, an assistant DA is permitted to enter the grand jury room long enough to question the witness and establish the legal basis of the claim; in other states, the prosecutor is not permitted to be present at all, and law enforcement officers present the case. In all states, however, the grand jury votes in secret, with no one else present.

> **Sidebar**
>
> *The grand jury does not determine if the person charged is guilty or not guilty. It simply makes a determination that there is probable cause to believe that the defendant is guilty.*

Beyond its strictly "bill or no bill" role, the grand jury is also empowered to conduct its own investigations into criminal allegations. The grand jury can investigate people or activities to determine if crimes have occurred. To this end, the grand jury can subpoena witnesses and documents and does not have to establish probable cause before doing so. As such, the grand jury has more latitude than police or prosecutors when investigating a case.

In its role as a supervisory body, the grand jury also oversees many local government offices and procedures. The grand jury is often called upon to make a written report about the condition of the buildings and other facilities found in the county.

But grand juries also have limitations on their power. They cannot, for example, randomly subpoena witnesses to determine if some crime has occurred. The grand jury must be focused on a particular crime and does not function as an extension of the police department. The grand jury must confine its investigating and accusatory powers to investigating criminal cases. Grand juries do not involve themselves in civil cases.

---

[9] *State v. Kuznetsov*, 345 Or. 479, 199 P.3d 311 (2008).

E. PRESENTING A CASE TO THE GRAND JURY

Unlike criminal trials, where prosecutors must prove that a defendant is guilty of a crime beyond a reasonable doubt, prosecutors have a much lower standard of proof for a grand jury. After all, the grand jury does not reach a verdict about a defendant's guilt, only whether the case should proceed.

The actual procedure to present a case to the grand jury varies from state to state and on the federal level. In many states, the district attorney may appear before the grand jury and question witnesses and present evidence. In other states, the prosecutor is barred from entering the grand jury room at any time and must wait outside while an investigator or a police officer presents the case to the grand jurors. In still other instances, the grand jurors may initiate their own investigations and obtain legal advice from the district attorney.

Just as we saw with preliminary hearings, the rules of evidence are different than in a criminal trial. In preliminary hearings, the court may consider hearsay testimony. In cases presented before the grand jury, the evidentiary rules do not apply. Grand juries may consider evidence that may or not be ruled unconstitutionally seized as well as consider hearsay testimony. (Hearsay will be covered in Chapter 16.)

Given this wide latitude in what the grand jury may consider, it may come as a surprise that the grand jury has some limitations. The grand jury cannot, for example, decide to investigate anyone for anything. It cannot randomly issue demands for people to appear before it in order to see if a crime has occurred. It cannot issue orders for individuals who are not suspected of a crime to appear before it in an effort to discover if they have committed some crime. The grand jury must focus on a specific investigation or risk having the indictment quashed.

Prima facie
Facts that are considered true as presented until they are disproven by some contrary evidence.

Another limitation on the grand jury is that the government must present enough evidence to justify a vote of true bill. The state must make a **prima facie** showing of the defendant's guilt. The prima facie standard means that the prosecution must present enough evidence to convince the jury that the basic facts of the case are true. The prima facie standard requires the state to present a basic case to the grand jury, showing that the defendant is the person who most likely committed the crime and providing enough evidence to support this contention. Because the grand jury only hears from state's witnesses (in most cases), it is not difficult for the state to make out a prima facie showing of the defendant's guilt.

The grand jury system has come under criticism over the years by groups claiming that it simply functions as a rubber stamp for the prosecutor. Critics claim that the prosecutor has too much control over the grand jury and can obtain indictments on anyone he or she chooses. However, others push back by pointing out that there are frequent examples of grand juries refusing to indict cases brought before it. If the grand jury were a rubber stamp for the prosecution, then a vote of no bill would never occur. Whether the grand jury still functions as a bulwark between the individual and the vast power of the state or simply as a rubber stamp for the prosecutor probably depends on one's point of view. The truth is probably somewhere between these two opposing views.

ONLY THE STATE'S WITNESSES APPEAR BEFORE THE GRAND JURY

Critics of the grand jury system also claim that the jurors only hear the state's version of the case. Defendants do not appear before the grand jury. The defendant has no right to testify before the grand jury or present any favorable evidence. Because the state is not obligated to present the defendant's version of the facts, it is highly likely that, having heard only the state's version of the events, the grand jury will decide that there is sufficient probable cause to continue the case. The defendant's attorney is not permitted to attend or make any statements to the grand jury. In addition, the state is not required to present a balanced account of the case. The U.S. Supreme Court has even held that the prosecution is under no obligation to present evidence that is favorable to the defendant during a grand jury hearing.[10]

Although state law often invests the grand jury with the sole power to drive the investigation, it is not uncommon for a prosecutor to guide a grand jury in such a way that it would appear that the prosecutor is taking the lead. A grand jury is supposed to be independent of the prosecutor's office, but the reality is somewhat different. In order to maintain the separation between prosecution and grand jury, courts have held that a prosecutor must at least inform the grand jury that the defendant wishes to testify.[11] Prosecutors are barred from giving closing arguments before a grand jury to convince them to rule in a particular way.[12]

When there is a question about improprieties in the way that the grand jury conducted its investigation, the defendant has the burden of showing that the grand jury failed to act properly. This is one of the few instances in which the burden is on the defendant instead of the state to prove wrongdoing.[13] The defendant will face some difficult hurdles to meet this standard. The grand jury meets in secret and no one, other than the grand jurors, are allowed to be present when they vote on a case.

F. SUBPOENA POWERS OF THE GRAND JURY

A grand jury has the power to issue a **subpoena**. A subpoena is a court order requiring a person to appear and testify or for a person to appear with specific evidence, such as documents, records, or other tangible objects. Once issued and served on a person, the subpoena cannot be ignored. A person who fails to abide by a grand jury subpoena is subject to a finding of contempt of the grand jury and may be held in custody until he or she complies or until the grand jury's term ends, whichever comes first. This gives the grand jury great power, but this power is subject to some limitations. The party who receives the subpoena may always contest it on the grounds that the subpoena calls for material that is protected by a witness privilege or by invoking the provisions of the Fifth Amendment to the U.S. Constitution.

Subpoena
A court order demanding that a person or item be produced to the court at a specific date and time.

---

[10] *U.S. v. Williams*, 112 S.Ct. 1735 (1992).
[11] *Cameron v. State*, 171 P.3d 1154 (Alaska 2007).
[12] *State v. Penkaty*, 708 N.W.2d 185 (Minn. 2006).
[13] *State v. Francis*, 191 N.J. 571, 926 A.2d 305 (2007).

OBJECTING TO A GRAND JURY SUBPOENA: WITNESS PRIVILEGE

Privilege
A right to refuse to answer questions and to prevent disclosure of information communicated within a legally recognized confidential relationship.

The law has always protected specific types of communications from being revealed in open court and before a grand jury. Some relationships are protected under law by a **privilege**. A privilege is a legal right that protects a person from being compelled to testify about certain matters. Attorney-client discussions are privileged, which means that most discussions between a client and his attorney are protected from disclosure. If an attorney receives a grand jury subpoena and is asked to reveal confidential information shared with him or her by a client, the attorney can refuse to answer the question on the grounds of the attorney-client privilege. There are other privileged communications, including those between:

- Pastor and member of the church
- Doctor and patient
- Psychiatrist and patient
- Spouse and spouse

PLEADING THE "FIFTH AMENDMENT" BEFORE THE GRAND JURY

In addition to refusing to answer a question on the basis of a legally recognized privilege, a person may also raise the Fifth Amendment as a reason not to answer specific questions. Among other rights, the Fifth Amendment to the U.S. Constitution provides that no one *"shall be compelled in any criminal case to be a witness against himself."*[14] The Fifth Amendment guarantees that persons cannot be compelled to give evidence against themselves. This right protects not only defendants but also witnesses who are called to testify before the grand jury. If a person believes that by answering a specific question, he or she may be admitting to a crime, then the person may state to the grand jury, "I refuse to answer on the grounds that I might incriminate myself." The grand jury is not authorized to override the witness's constitutional rights.

MOTION TO QUASH GRAND JURY SUBPOENA

Quash
Do away with, annul, overthrow, cease.

A motion to **quash** a subpoena is filed with the court and describes the material that has been subject to subpoena and the reason that the party objects to producing those documents. In such a case, a judge would quash the subpoena and refuse to allow the grand jury to review the materials.

G. IMMUNITY POWERS OF GRAND JURIES

There are times when federal grand juries wish to hear testimony from individuals who may also be facing charges themselves. To avoid the witness invoking his or her

---

[14] Amendment V, U.S. Constitution.

Fifth Amendment rights, the only way to get necessary testimony is to grant **immunity** to the witness. When a person has been granted immunity, it means that the testimony given before the grand jury cannot be used as the basis to prosecute that person. In some states, the grand jury is empowered to grant immunity as a way of encouraging a witness to give evidence against others. In other states, the prosecutor must bring a motion before a court in order to have immunity granted. No matter how it is granted, once given, the witness may testify about specific criminal activity without fear that the testimony will be taken down and then used against him or her at a later date.

Immunity
A grant to an individual that exempts him or her from being prosecuted based on the testimony that the person gives.

The problem with granting immunity is that if the grand jury confers that benefit on the wrong person, then they are effectively preventing the prosecution from bringing a case. Suppose, for example, that the grand jury is investigating organized crime, and they grant immunity to the person who turns out to be the head of the organization. In that situation, any testimony that the crime boss gave before the grand jury would be immunized, and the state would be unable to use it against him or her.

 ## VI AFTER THE GRAND JURY PROCEEDINGS

The role of the grand jury ends with a return of a true bill. The individual grand jurors are not permitted to sit on the jury that determines the defendant's verdict, and they will not have any input on the judicial decision after the case proceeds to trial. Often, the individual grand jurors have no idea how a particular case was resolved.

The next procedural step after a successful indictment by the grand jury is the arraignment, which will be explored in greater depth in Chapter 18.

CASE EXCERPT

STATE v. BENT
263 P.3d 903, 904-911 (N.M.App.,2011)

KENNEDY, Judge.

Defendant stands convicted of various counts of criminal sexual contact of a minor and contributing to the delinquency of a minor as a result of which he was sentenced to prison. Of the many issues he raises on appeal, one defect in the grand jury proceedings deprives the district court of its jurisdiction and is, accordingly, dispositive of all other issues.

Defendant was indicted by a grand jury, which was convened on October 3, 2007, and whose statutory term would have ended on January 4, 2008, but for an order extending the statutory term issued verbally by a district judge. Defendant's case was presented to the grand jury on May 20, 2008. Since NMSA 1978, Section 31–6–1 (1983) provides that a "grand jury shall serve for a period of no longer than three months," we hold that this statutory term is a mandatory limitation on the grand jury's jurisdiction. An indictment returned after the grand jury's term expires is *void ab initio*. Therefore, Defendant's motion to quash the indictment should have been granted, as the grand jury was without legal authority to consider his case and return an indictment. As a result, the indictment issued by the grand jury was void, and the district court did not have jurisdiction to proceed with the trial in this case.

I. FACTUAL AND PROCEDURAL BACKGROUND

Defendant, the apparent leader of a religious community in northeastern New Mexico, was charged with various crimes centering around what he maintained were religious practices intended to be cleansing ceremonies. The State argued that such practices amounted to criminal sexual contact of minors and contributing to the minors' delinquency. The case was presented to the grand jury of Union County on May 20, 2008. Defendant was indicted and arraigned on the indictment.

There is no dispute in this case as to the facts pertaining to this issue. The grand jury that heard Defendant's case had been convened on October 3, 2007. An almost indecipherable pleading bearing a file stamp from that date appears to have summoned grand jurors for service on November 12, 2007. At the hearing on Defendant's motion to quash the indictment, the prosecutor stated to the court that the grand jury's term had been verbally extended "*sua sponte*" by District Judge Sam Sanchez without the entry of any written order. There is no documentary evidence concerning such an extension, nor does the record contain any explanation as to why the extension was made. We are left to rely on assertions by counsel and the district court that it happened. The parties agree that the grand jury only sat twice, once in November, and again on May 20, 2008. The date in May was beyond three months past the date of any previous grand jury activity.

Defendant's motion to quash the indictment was heard on August 12, 2008, alleging that, under NMSA 1978, Section 31–6–3(A) (2003), the grand jury was not selected and seated in accordance with the law. Specifically, Defendant alleged that the grand jury had been convened on October 3, 2007, and had convened again on May 20, 2008, in violation of Section 31–6–1, which mandates a maximum period of grand jury service of "no longer than three months."

The district court responded to the portion of the motion related to the grand jury term by stating that the statute "doesn't provide for any relief if there's a violation." Defendant responded that the remedy for an illegal indictment is that it be "quashed, and a new grand jury seated properly." The court further inquired as to whether a showing of prejudice to Defendant was required before an indictment may be quashed. Defendant responded that the indictment was deficient on its face and should be quashed because the grand jury exceeded its term, the State denied discovery, and the State did not present exculpatory evidence to the grand jury that had been requested by Defendant. The State responded that the district court had already noted that the statute was only advisory in nature. The State then asserted, without citation to the record, that Judge Sanchez had explained to the grand jury that he extended their tenure *sua sponte* for an additional three months without issuing a written order on the record. The prosecutor, without having them admitted, showed to the court certified pay records indicating the grand jury served on two days.

The State was aware and informed the district court of case law indicating that an indictment handed down by a grand jury after the expiration of its statutory period would in some states render the indictment "*void ab initio*." The State mentioned that there are such things as "*de facto*" grand juries that are allowed to proceed past their terms. At the end of the argument, the district court ruled:

With respect to the first issue, that the grand jury was empaneled or served beyond the three-months time period as provided by Section 31-6-1, it appears that within that section, there is no remedy provided for a jury that serves longer than its term. And at this point in time, there's been no prejudice shown by . . . Defendant with respect to that issue by itself. And so, the motion to quash with respect to that violation or apparent violation of the statute will be dismissed.

II. DISCUSSION

When an indictment is presented by a grand jury in open court, the presumption is that it is legally presented; that the jurors were properly summoned, legally qualified, and competent, and that the required number, at least concurred in the finding. These facts are essential to the lawful finding and presentment.

In this case, the questions are (1) whether the term of the grand jury had expired; and (2) if the term expired, what was the expiration's effect on the validity of the grand jury's indictment of Defendant. Challenges to the validity of the grand jury are specifically limited by statute to three enumerated grounds: (1) the grand jury was not legally constituted, (2) an individual grand juror was not legally qualified to serve as a juror, and (3) an individual juror was a witness against the person indicted. Section 31-6-3. It is to the legal constitution of the grand jury that Defendant directs his appeal.

The Requirement of the Filing of an Indictment or Information is a Constitutional Requirement Upon Which the Jurisdiction of the District Court Depends

"A court obtains no jurisdiction to proceed and render judgment in an action brought without authority." The New Mexico Constitution, Article II, Section 14 and the Fifth Amendment to the United States Constitution require the State to file an indictment or information before commencing a felony prosecution. In such cases, the district court has no jurisdiction to try a defendant without an indictment. The failure of jurisdiction in this regard may not be waived. Nor, in the absence of a proper indictment conferring jurisdiction on the district court, may a defendant be sentenced. Thus, if the indictment in this case is void for having been issued by a grand jury that was not empowered to sit, the indictment cannot confer jurisdiction on the court to consider the case and would require dismissal.

Section 31-6-1 constitutes the statutory framework applicable to grand juries and states: "The district judge may convene one or more grand juries at any time, without regard to court terms. A grand jury shall serve for a period of no longer than three months." The Supreme Court, in adopting the Uniform Jury Instructions, uses this construction. The district court judge swears in a grand jury with an oath, which contains the following instruction: "Your term as members of the grand jury expires _____ unless you are discharged or excused by the court prior to this time." UJI 14-8002 NMRA. Use Note 2 states: "Members of a grand jury may not serve for a period longer than three months." We read the statute and jury instruction as being in parity, establishing and recognizing in turn that a grand jury cannot by law be convened for a period "longer than three months." There is no exception to this mandate contained in the statute, nor provision for an extension of the statutory period. The language is clear and unambiguous.

The clear language of the statute limits the term of a grand jury to not more than three months. There being no statutory language for extending the period of a grand jury's service, we hold that, in the absence of any legislative expression to the contrary, a grand jury may not be empaneled to serve under Section 31-6-1 for a period longer than three months. To ask it to engage in further work on another matter after the end of its three-month term was beyond the power of the prosecutor or district court.

Statutory provisions concerning the nature of what is fundamental in empaneling, convening, and providing structure to the grand jury are generally mandatory, and provisions concerning its administration once empaneled are directory. In *State v. Ulibarri*, 1999-NMCA-142, 8, 15-25, 128 N.M. 546, 994 P.2d 1164, we held that compliance with the statutes, requiring the preparation of a verbatim record of grand jury proceedings, setting the number of concurring jurors necessary to issue an indictment, and requiring instruction of the grand jurors on the record concerning the elements of offenses they were considering, were mandatory preconditions to an indictment. There, statutes mandated the existence of an adequate record of the proceedings and proper instruction on the law and ensured the overall legal adequacy of the process of the grand jury's work as protecting "the very heart of the grand jury system." Id. ¶ 15. When a person appeared to prosecute before the grand jury who was not properly authorized by statute to do so, we held that the violation of the mandatory statute compelled dismissal of the indictment.

Obtaining an Indictment After the Grand Jury's Term Expires Results in an Indictment That is *Void Ab Initio* and Confers No Jurisdiction to Try Defendant

Other jurisdictions that set specific terms for their grand juries have held them to have no power after the expiration of their terms. Under federal law, "an indictment returned by a grand jury sitting beyond its legally authorized time is a nullity. The uniform rule is that in the absence of statute to the contrary the grand jury is discharged by operation of law at the end of the term of court for which it was called."

We therefore construe the statute in this case as unambiguously mandatory in limiting the term of grand juries to not more than three months. We are provided with no legislative history, but note that, in most other jurisdictions, the terms of grand juries are limited by statute, and we impute what we know of their intent in limiting grand jury terms to our situation in New Mexico. The policy considerations employed elsewhere are illustrative of why a limited term of service is considered mandatory elsewhere, and why we have come to regard it as such in this case.

Thus, for a grand jury to act without authorization beyond the term during which it is empowered to sit, is fatal to the indictment. An unauthorized extension of the term of a grand jury beyond its term is a defect which "goes to the very existence of the grand jury itself." There is no statutory provision for extending the term of a grand jury in New Mexico contained in Section 31-6-1 or otherwise and, in that absence, we cannot legislate the existence of one. The jurisdiction of any proceeding in which Defendant is charged with a felony depends on the "presentment or indictment of a grand jury." N.M. Const. art. II, § 14. Without a properly constituted grand jury returning a valid indictment charging Defendant with a crime, we hold that the district court was without jurisdiction to proceed against him.

III. CONCLUSION

The indictment in this case is void because the group of citizens that issued the purported indictment was not a legally constituted grand jury, as it had finished its term some months before and had ceased to exist. Any extension of its term by the district court was undertaken without statutory authority. Legally speaking, there was no grand jury convened in this case. Therefore, there was no indictment under the law in this case to confer jurisdiction on the district court to try, convict, or sentence Defendant. We note that Defendant's acquittal in a court lacking proper jurisdiction did not violate the constitutional prohibitions against double jeopardy and would not in and of itself bar retrial. Therefore, we remand this case to the district court and instruct that the charges and conviction be set aside without prejudice, the indictment be quashed, and Defendant be discharged from custody.

IT IS SO ORDERED.

WE CONCUR: JONATHAN B. SUTIN and TIMOTHY L. GARCIA, Judges.

---

1   When was the defendant indicted in this case, and why is that date important?
2   How was the grand jury's term supposedly extended?
3   Was the statute in this case "advisory" in nature or mandatory? Explain.
4   What presumption normally greets an indictment?
5   What effect did the filing of this indictment have, considering that the term of the grand jury had expired?

CASE QUESTIONS

CHAPTER SUMMARY

This chapter examined the first procedural step that occurs after a defendant has been placed under arrest. An initial appearance is a court hearing where the defendant appears before a judge — often a magistrate — and is advised of his or her constitutional rights. During the initial appearance hearing or at any subsequent time, the judge may also set bail for the defendant. Bail is the posting of money or sometimes real property as a guarantee that the defendant will return for future court hearings. Judges must consider several factors before setting bail, including the seriousness of the offense charged, the defendant's ties to the community and the defendant's likelihood of fleeing the jurisdiction should he or she be released on bail.

Following the initial appearance hearing, the next procedural step is the preliminary hearing. At a preliminary hearing, the prosecutor will present testimony from a witness to establish that there is probable cause to believe that the defendant committed the crime with which he is charged. The defense attorney has the right to cross-examine the witness, and the judge makes a determination whether the state has met its burden. Because the rules of evidence are much more liberal and because the standard of proof is usually preponderance of the evidence — not beyond a reasonable doubt — the state usually wins this hearing, and the defendant's case is bound over to the superior court.

Once the case is bound over, the prosecutor reviews the case to see if any additional investigation is required and also to determine if the original charge should remain in place or if the charge should be changed to something else. The prosecutor is also free to add any additional charges supported by the evidence and to dismiss the case if the prosecutor does not believe that there is sufficient evidence. Once the prosecutor drafts the indictment, it is presented to the grand jury for consideration.

A grand jury is a group of citizens who meet periodically to consider felony cases. They are not required in all states, but in the ones where they are, the purpose of the grand jury is to decide if there is prima facie evidence that the defendant should be charged with the crime. If the grand jury determines that the case against the defendant should continue, they return a true bill. If not, they dismiss the case with a vote of no bill.

KEY TERMS

Initial appearance	Bond forfeiture	Information
Bail	Preliminary hearing	True bill
Property bond	Preponderance of	No bill
Bond	evidence	Prima facie
Bonding company	Binding over	Subpoena
Bounty hunter	Charging decision	Privilege
Recognizance bond	Nolle prosequi	Quash
Presumption of	Indictment	
innocence	Accusation	

REVIEW QUESTIONS

1 What is the purpose of the initial appearance?
2 Explain how an attorney may be appointed at an initial appearance.
3 What are some factors that a court considers when setting bail or bond?
4 What is the difference between bail and bond?
5 How do bonding companies function?
6 Explain the role of so-called "bounty hunters."
7 What is a property bond?

8   Explain how a defendant would receive a recognizance bond.
9   What is bond forfeiture?
10 Explain the purpose of a preliminary hearing.
11 What procedure is followed at a preliminary hearing?
12 How are the evidentiary rules different at preliminary hearings when compared to trials?
13 What is the significance of "binding over" after a preliminary hearing?
14 What negotiations typically occur between prosecutors and defense attorneys before and during preliminary hearings?
15 What is the purpose of the grand jury?
16 Explain the historical background of the grand jury.
17 Describe the composition of the grand jury.
18 How and why would a defendant challenge the composition of the grand jury?
19 Does a grand jury reach a verdict? Explain.
20 Explain how a case is usually presented to a grand jury?
21 What is a prima facie showing?
22 Explain the subpoena powers available to the grand jury.
23 How does a prosecutor decide what crime to charge against a defendant?
24 What is a motion to quash?
25 Explain what it means for a witness to invoke the Fifth Amendment before the grand jury.

QUESTIONS FOR ANALYSIS

1   Given the criticism leveled at grand juries (that they are simply rubber stamps for prosecutors), does the grand jury still serve an important function?
2   Some states have done away with bonding companies. Should all states make bond an issue for the government and not for private enterprise? Explain your answer.

HYPOTHETICALS

1   Barry has been charged with perjury and during his preliminary hearing, he requests that the magistrate set bond at $1,000. The prosecutor responds that the amount is too low given that Barry has no significant ties to the community and has no job in the area. The prosecutor suggests a bond of $10,000. The judge responds, "It's cases like this that show just how despicable you are, Barry. I've known you since we were both children and you beat me up after school. Bond is set at $1 million." You are the defense attorney assigned to Barry's case. How do you respond?
2   Tamara has come up with a computer program that can factor in all of the evidentiary points in a criminal case and can show, with a high degree of

mathematical certainty, whether a specific defendant is likely guilty of the crime with which he is charged. The local magistrate would like to adopt this program as a way of establishing probable cause. Would this be a better system?

3   Detective Dan has charged John Doe with aggravated assault. The prosecutor, Paula, decides that there is no real evidence that John Doe committed the crime. Detective Dan insists that the case continue. The detective is well known in the community and has a great deal of political support. What should Paula do?

Evidence

Chapter Objectives

- Define the differences between direct and circumstantial evidence
- Explain the various types of physical evidence
- Demonstrate your understanding of the use of expert evidence
- Describe how physical and photographic lineups are conducted
- Explain the difference between relevancy and admissibility

I. INTRODUCTION TO EVIDENCE

Although the topic of **evidence** law can, and has, filled multiple volumes, this chapter will address it by examining exactly what evidence consists of and explain how some of the more important types of evidence factor into criminal cases. One of the most important aspects of evidence has to do with how it is used at trial and even whether it can be used at trial. Those preliminary questions begin the consideration of admissibility and relevance.

Evidence
All types of data and information that can be presented at a trial or other hearing that bears on the issues in the case.

II. ADMISSIBILITY AND RELEVANCY

Before discussing what evidence is, the foundational question is whether any particular piece of evidence is both **relevant** and admissible. As shown in Figure 16-1, evidence is relevant if it tends to prove or disprove a point in contention. The threshold question that a judge must consider before considering any evidence revolves around a simple question: Is the evidence relevant? If it is, then the court must then consider the next step: admissibility. Consider Scenario 16-1.

Relevant
Any evidence that makes a fact more or less likely to be true; evidence that tends to prove or disprove a point in contention in the trial.

SCENARIO 16-1

BIAS?

Raul is presenting a defense for his client, John. During cross-examination of the police officer who arrested John, Raul points out that this particular officer has arrested or attempted to arrest John at least six times. In the previous five cases, the charges against John were dismissed, and the officer was sanctioned by the police department and put on probation for unprofessional conduct. Is this evidence relevant in John's current prosecution?

Answer: Most judges would probably allow this testimony as a means of showing that the officer has a clear prejudice or bias against John, and it is relevant to show that the officer may not have been acting based on the facts of this case, but on his clearly demonstrated dislike for John.

Admissible
A judicial ruling that evidence is relevant and that it has been properly submitted for review by the jurors.

Once a determination of relevancy has been made, the next question becomes whether the evidence should be **admissible**. There are times when evidence is relevant, but still may not be admissible. Consider, for example, horrific photographs of a murder victim taken during autopsy. The photos may very well be relevant in showing the cause of death and other factors, but their relevance is outweighed by the fact that they will greatly disturb the jury, and the jurors might give more weight to these photos than they would to other aspects of the case, including the defense offered by the defendant. In such a case, a judge might rule that a photo of the deceased is permissible, but not the gruesome photos showing a full-blown autopsy on the victim's body.

A judge rules on the admissibility of evidence when the evidence is offered during the trial. What usually happens is that one party will offer evidence, the other party will object, either based on relevancy, admissibility or some other factor, and the judge must decide whether or not to admit the evidence. Before the judge makes this ruling, the jury is not permitted to view the evidence. If a judge rules that certain evidence is admissible, the jury will be allowed to hear or see it. When the evidence consists of physical objects, such as the murder weapon or any other physical evidence, a ruling of admissibility means that the evidence will go into the jury room with the jurors when they deliberate at the end of the case. They will be permitted to handle the evidence and examine it for themselves.

However, a judge might rule that particular evidence is inadmissible, meaning that the jury will not be permitted to hear it or see it. Evidence can be ruled inadmissible for a variety of reasons. The judge might decide that the evidence is not relevant to the issues in the case or that the evidence is too prejudicial and would result in an unfair trial if the jury were to know about it. **Admission of evidence** refers to the process through which the attorney establishes the relevancy of the evidence, and the judge then rules that the jury may view it. An attorney is not permitted to testify about the evidence. Instead, the attorney must ask a witness about the evidence. In criminal cases, most evidence is presented to the court through the testimony of a live witness. There are few provisions that allow an attorney to simply present evidence to the court without some witness answering questions to establish the relevance and admissibility of the particular item.

Admission of evidence
The process of tendering evidence to the court and requesting a judge to rule that evidence is admissible and may, therefore, be shown to the jury.

A. FOUNDATION QUESTIONS

One aspect of admitting evidence is the necessity to ask the right series of questions to prove that evidence is both relevant and admissible. The questions that a party might use to **tender** a video recording into evidence are different from the questions that the party might use to tender carpet-fiber analysis. As a result, a large body of scholarly work has gone into developing precise questions that show exactly how and why particular types of evidence are admissible. These questions are called **foundation questions**. Establishing how a piece of evidence is relevant is commonly referred to as **laying the foundation**. Different types of evidence require different kinds of questions.

Tender
Offer to the court.

Foundation questions
A series of questions that show that evidence is relevant, admissible, and that it has not been tampered with or altered in any way.

B. CHAIN OF CUSTODY REQUIREMENTS

Whenever evidence is seized, it must be safeguarded. Police agencies have created evidence rooms, where evidence is stored for later use at trial. Evidence requiring testing by the state crime lab or other agency must also be handled methodically. Before the evidence can be admitted at trial, the state must show that it has not been altered or tampered with in any way. This is called the **chain of custody** requirement. All of the people who handle the evidence must take the stand and account for what they did with this evidence and where they took it. They must all testify that they did not tamper with the evidence. The "chain" is established by first having the crime-scene technician testify to removing the evidence from the crime scene, then placing it into the evidence room. Then the person who removed it from the evidence area testifies and so on until every person who has handled the evidence testifies.

Laying the foundation
The process, often involving the testimony of several witnesses, to show that evidence is reliable, relevant, and admissible.

Chain of custody
The chronological list of those in continuous possession of a specific physical object. A person who presents evidence (such as a gun used in a crime) at a trial must account for its possession from time of receipt to time of trial in order for evidence to be admitted by the judge.

The importance of the chain of custody is demonstrated in the federal government's perjury case against baseball player Barry Bonds. The urine samples that tested positive for steroids were casually passed hand-to-hand by several people, or may have even gone through the mail, which left the possibility for tampering. Even if no tampering took place, the break in the chain of custody was dramatic.

C. EVIDENCE ROOMS

The **evidence room** is a restricted area. The only people permitted into the area are the evidence-room technicians. Police, prosecutors, and judges are all barred from

Evidence room
A secured area, maintained by law enforcement, where evidence in pending cases is kept and guarded until it is needed at trial.

entering the evidence room. When police deposit evidence there, they hand it over to technicians who are responsible for storing it. A break in the chain of custody could result in the evidence not being admitted at trial. If this evidence is crucial to the prosecution's case, then the entire charge might fail. After the case has been concluded — and while it is pending on appeal — the evidence will usually be returned to the same evidence room for additional safekeeping. It will remain in the evidence room as long as the case remains pending on appeal. Eventually, the district attorney will notify the evidence room that a particular defendant has exhausted all appeals and will issue an order allowing the evidence to be destroyed. In some instances, a weapon might be ordered to be destroyed. In that case, it is the responsibility of evidence-room technicians to make sure that the gun, knife, or other instrument is properly disposed of (usually by melting it down). When the evidence involves narcotics, they are usually burned. Some evidence is simply thrown away.

In recent years, advances in DNA evidence have made it important for evidence room technicians to retain bodily fluid evidence. This evidence is now often kept for years after the defendant has been convicted.

CLASSIFYING EVIDENCE: DIRECT AND CIRCUMSTANTIAL

Direct evidence
An object or testimony that establishes a fact.

Circumstantial evidence
An object or testimony that suggests a conclusion.

As we have already seen, evidence refers to anything that helps to prove or disprove a point in contention. However, evidence can be broken down into various sub-categories. The two broadest categories are direct and circumstantial. **Direct evidence** refers to any object or testimony that has an immediate connection with the facts in the case. Eyewitness testimony is direct evidence. Blood spatter on a wall is direct evidence. **Circumstantial evidence**, on the other hand, suggests possible conclusions about the case, but does not necessarily establish an uncontroverted fact.

A. CIRCUMSTANTIAL EVIDENCE

In any trial there is often a mixture of both direct and circumstantial evidence. Of the two, circumstantial evidence is considered to be weaker than direct evidence because circumstantial evidence does not conclusively establish a fact. Instead, it suggests a conclusion. Suppose for example, that a person is preparing breakfast one morning and briefly leaves the kitchen. When the person comes back, she finds a fish floating in her glass of milk. She could not testify to that fact that she saw someone put the fish there, but her testimony certainly suggests a conclusion: Someone put the fish in the glass of milk. Tie this evidence with the fact that her nephew is known for practical jokes, that he recently complained about having too many fish in his tank, and that she saw him peeking through the kitchen window with a devilish grin on his face, and the circumstantial evidence adds up to a powerful conclusion: Her nephew put the fish in her glass of milk. However, there may be several other possible conclusions.

A criminal case can be based entirely on circumstantial evidence, but it must exclude every other reasonable hypothesis. If the state were to prosecute the nephew for the new crime of putting fish in glasses of milk, then the prosecutor would have to show that other possible scenarios do not make sense. Some stranger could have come into the house and put the fish there, but the likelihood of that is low. As long as a prosecutor can exclude all other reasonable hypotheses, he or she can prove a defendant guilty beyond a reasonable doubt based exclusively on circumstantial evidence. Consider Scenario 16-2.

HOMICIDE WITH NO BODY?

Earl was last seen at his cabin, which he was sharing with Bob. Earl's mother stopped by the cabin last week and couldn't find any sign of her son. However, she discovered a tremendous amount of blood soaked into Earl's mattress. Bob was missing and had taken many of Earl's personal items. Earl has not used his credit cards or his cell phone for almost a week. When the blood is tested, it is a match for Earl. Several months go by and Earl never returns. However, police find Bob and charge him with murder. They find a bloody knife in Bob's belongings. The blood is a DNA match for Earl. When the crime lab weighs the mattress containing the blood, they realize that Earl has lost so much blood that there is no way that he could still be alive. Does the prosecution have a circumstantial case of murder against Bob, even though Earl's body has never been found?

Answer: Yes. Although the prosecution would undoubtedly like to have Earl's body, they can still proceed with murder charges against Bob. The quantity of circumstantial evidence against Bob is enough to satisfy proof beyond a reasonable doubt, assuming that the jury sees the case the same way as the prosecutor does.

B. CLASSIFICATIONS OF DIRECT EVIDENCE

There are no sub-classifications of circumstantial evidence, but there are numerous categories of direct evidence which include the following:

- Physical evidence
- Documentary evidence
- Testimonial evidence
- Demonstrative evidence
- Expert evidence

PHYSICAL EVIDENCE

Physical evidence refers to objects and things. As you can imagine, the category of physical evidence can cover an almost infinite variety of objects, from murder weapons to DNA to mud traces to almost anything in between. When detectives and crime-scene technicians gather physical evidence, they usually seal it in plastic bags or other containers to keep it from being contaminated or tampered with until the object can be tested, examined, or later used at trial. Detectives will often label a physical item with a marker or a tag, writing their initials on it, along with other identifying information so that they can identify it at a later date.

DNA
Deoxyribonucleic acid, the basic building blocks of cells that direct the overall appearance and structure of an organism.

DNA. One of the most important examples of physical evidence is **DNA**. It is composed of two strands of molecules arranged in the now famous double-helix configuration. The double helix is like a spiral staircase, where the handrails are composed of sugars and phosphates and the steps are composed of matching pairs of four (and only four) chemical compounds. These bases are adenine, cytosine, guanine, and thymine. Normally abbreviated A, C, G, and T, these bases only combine in the following sequences A–T and C–G and are referred to as base pairs. The human genetic code, which contains all of the information required to develop a human being from a single cell, consists of three billion base pairs. It is the arrangement or sequence of the base pairs that is important. Base pair arrangements determine the ultimate shape of the animal: cat, dog, or human being.

When crime scene technicians examine blood, bodily fluid, or some other tissue, they first break down the cell membranes to get to the DNA strands. These microscopic strands are then treated to separate them from surrounding protein molecules. Once the DNA is separated, the solution is suspended in a gel and an electric current is passed through it. Because DNA strands have different weights, they will travel different distances through the gel. Computers can then code these locations, and technicians can enter the various positions into a computer database that will be available at any future time to check against known or unknown samples. The DNA results are stored in a database and then run against any known samples already contained in the database. Unlike other types of physical evidence, such as blood type, a DNA match can be accurate to one in several billion.

Because DNA is unique to each person (except identical twins who have identical DNA), it makes an excellent tool for identifying suspects who have left blood, bodily fluid, or some other tissue at the scene of a crime. The advances brought about by DNA have been compared to the development of fingerprint databases that revolutionized the way that criminal cases were investigated in the first part of the twentieth century. With DNA, the chances of a successful prosecution increases dramatically. DNA is also helpful in eliminating others as suspects who may have been prosecuted based on other testimony.

State and national agencies now maintain DNA databases that help them try to match evidence gathered at crime scenes or recovered from rape and murder victims in an attempt to get a "hit" in the computer records. A hit matches an unknown sample with one that has already been provided by someone who has been required to submit a DNA sample to the government.

Sidebar

Although identical twins have the same DNA, they do not have identical fingerprints.

● **FAMOUS CASES**
THE FORD HEIGHTS FOUR

On a May evening in 1978, a young woman and her fiancé were abducted from a filling station. The woman was gang-raped in an abandoned house in one of the poorest suburbs in the country, the Ford Heights section of Chicago's South Side. Her attackers then shot and killed both her and her fiancé.

Four black men, residents of Ford Heights, were arrested for the crime: Dennis Williams, Kenneth Adams, Willie Rainge, and Verneal Jimerson. The four men had been placed at the scene by Paula Gray, Dennis Williams' girlfriend and a self-proclaimed eyewitness to the crime. Gray was only 17 years old at the time and borderline mentally disabled. Nevertheless, her testimony secured indictments for the men, who came to be known as the Ford Heights Four. Gray later recanted part of her story, and the charges against Jimerson were dropped.

Despite the fact that there was no physical evidence tying the men to the crime, the remaining three were tried and convicted that same year. Williams was sentenced to death, Adams to 75 years in prison, and Rainge to life without parole. The state's case was based primarily on Gray's eyewitness testimony, which had been secured after intense questioning by police over a two-day period. Her testimony had major inconsistencies about the timing of the crime, but defense attorney Archie Weston failed to point them out. Weston later claimed to have been under unbearable stress because of the trial and couldn't think straight. Subsequently, he was disbarred for committing fraud in another case.

Paula Gray was convicted as an accomplice and also for perjury after her recantation, and was sentenced to 50 years in prison. When Williams won a new trial, she returned to her original story and again implicated Verneal Jimerson. To gain her own release from prison, she agreed to testify against both Jimerson and Williams at his new trial. Williams was convicted once again and sentenced to death; Jimerson was also convicted and sentenced to death.

The four men remained in prison until 1995, when a Northwestern University investigative journalism professor, David Protess, and a team of his students uncovered a shocking piece of information in the case file. Shortly after the Ford Heights Four's arrest, Chicago police had been tipped off to the true killers' identity. The witness who supplied the tip said he knew who committed the crime because he heard shots and saw three men running away from the scene. The next day he saw the men selling items that belonged to the victims. No one knows exactly why the police didn't follow up on the information, but speculation is that there was a pervasive attitude that if the men in custody didn't commit that crime, they probably had done something else.

Protess's discovery led to new DNA testing, which exonerated all four men, and they were released from prison in 1996. The misconduct in the case led to a massive lawsuit by the Ford Heights Four, one that Cook County settled in 1999 for $36 million — the largest civil rights payment in U.S. history. One of the real killers had already died, but the remaining two confessed to the crimes and pleaded guilty in 1997.

Fingerprints. Although the idea of using fingerprints as a means to identify a suspect seems like an obvious, even an old-fashioned idea, when it was first introduced in the early 1900s in the United States and Great Britain, the concept was unpopular. The idea of identifying a person based on the tiny whorls and grooves on the tips of his or her fingers was considered ridiculous. This opinion was not completely based in resistance to change. There were very real time constraints built into identifying anyone by fingerprints. First of all, in order to identify a suspect, law enforcement needed a pre-existing sample or a person whose fingerprints could be taken and compared to the unknown sample. The idea of fingerprinting everyone who was arrested in a large city and then housing all of these fingerprint cards was daunting, as was the prospect of having to train someone to be able to go through all of the cards and identify one set of matching prints from literally thousands of cards.

The advent of computers radically changed the use of fingerprints. Because computers can be designed to — and are quite good at — doing thousands of repetitive actions every second, fingerprint cards could be coded into the computer by identifying specific areas on the print and then using the computer to match these areas to other known samples. Comparing an unknown print to a known print went from weeks or months to seconds. Even today, however, a trained fingerprint analyst still personally views the match provided by a computer.

Fingerprints can be left behind on a wide variety of surfaces, including human skin. Specially trained technicians search for fingerprints in likely places: doorknobs, tabletops, or anywhere a person was likely to put his or her hand. The Federal Bureau of Investigation maintains a nationwide database of fingerprints, which can now be computer matched in a short period of time. The FBI's database of fingerprints is known as the Integrated Automated Fingerprint Identification System or IAFIS.

Blood Tests. Blood tests are commonly performed in order to eliminate a suspect rather than implicate one. The reason for this is simple. Blood testing — or typing — of the victim's or defendant's blood can usually only tell the examiner whether or not the blood is the same type as the unknown specimen found. It will not reveal if the unknown specimen of blood actually belongs to any particular person. As such, if the blood found is not the defendant's blood type, the only conclusion that can be reached is that the blood does not belong to him.

Polygraph Tests. Polygraph machines, or lie detectors, have been around in one form or another for decades. The basic principle behind any "lie detector" is that when a person tells a lie, it causes him or her physical stress. This stress can be measured, in the form of increased heart rate, minute changes in the skin's resistance to electricity, and greater perspiration. However, because of their notorious unreliability, few courts have allowed them to be used as evidence. Occasionally, defense attorneys will attempt to use them to show that the defendant has been telling the truth, but in almost all cases, polygraph results remain inadmissible in criminal trials.

The "CSI Effect." The popularity of shows like *CSI* and others have had an impact on modern jurors. Even though the shows are not realistic when it comes to the technology (and the speed) with which evidence can be tested, more and more jurors are expecting to be dazzled by high-tech evidence gathering and analysis and are often disappointed when the fictional tools of television shows are not used in real-life cases. Prosecutors call this the "CSI Effect." Modern prosecutors find themselves in a strange quandary: They must often explain to jurors that in the real world, many of the tests shown on television shows do not exist. Prosecutors must also cope with the disappointment that jurors manifest when they discover that the real world of forensics is not as exciting or as technologically advanced as television and movies would have them believe.

DOCUMENTARY EVIDENCE

Documentary evidence refers to anything in writing, including contracts, letters, notes, and agreements, among many others. The reason a distinction is drawn between documents and other forms of physical evidence is that a document can be copied, altered, or forged (often in such a way as to make it impossible to tell which was the original). There are special rules about how and when documentary evidence can be admitted at trial. At trial, it is often important to be able to identify the original text of a document and to distinguish it from copies. One way of doing this is to keep the original safe and unmarked. Copies can always be highlighted or annotated, but the original cannot be.

Documentary evidence
Evidence produced or presented in a writing or other type of printed material.

TESTIMONIAL EVIDENCE

The evidence given by the witnesses in the case is testimonial evidence. This **testimony** can involve directly observed facts (thus making it direct evidence), as well as inferences and assumptions (making it fall into the category of circumstantial evidence). When a witness testifies about the facts of the crime and how she personally observed them, this is direct evidence. However, in the same breath, a witness can also embark on circumstantial evidence. For instance, a witness could testify that the defendant left the room and, while he was gone, she heard a loud noise. Later, she saw that a window was broken. This evidence would suggest that the defendant broke the window, but since the witness did not actually see the defendant break the window it is circumstantial evidence. Consider Scenario 16-3.

Testimony
Oral evidence given by a witness under oath.

WHAT TYPE OF EVIDENCE?

During a trial for armed robbery, a witness takes the stand and gives testimony that he reviewed a video tape of the robbery and was able to develop a photograph of the defendant by freezing the video and printing a hard copy of a photo showing the defendant's face. The photo that the witness printed is offered as evidence. What kind of evidence is this?

Answer: The photograph is physical evidence and the man's testimony is testimonial. It is for the jury to determine if the photo matches the defendant.

Evidence Used to Identify the Defendant. One of the most important and dramatic points in a trial comes when a witness identifies the defendant as the person who committed the crime. Because this testimony is so important and can have such devastating consequences for the defendant, courts have imposed strict limitations on the ways that law enforcement can ask a witness to identify a suspect during the course of the investigation. This is especially true in the area of lineups and showups.

Lineups. A **physical lineup** is often shown on television and in movies. In the fictional version, several very different people are lined up against a wall, and a witness is asked to identify the person who committed the crime.

-How a Lineup is Conducted. The people chosen to stand with the suspect at the lineup are selected on the basis of similarity to the suspect: same approximate age, race, build, hair, and skin coloring, and so on. The members of the lineup are allowed to pick where they will stand. Each position has a corresponding number so that no names will be used. Police are not permitted to draw the witness's attention to the suspect in any way, such as dressing him in different clothing or selecting people to serve in the lineup who do not resemble the defendant. The entire procedure in the pretrial lineup should be reliable. Without some indicia of reliability, the identification is useless.[1]

The U.S. Supreme Court has placed strict limitations on how such a lineup can be conducted in the real world. One such restriction is that the lineup cannot be unduly suggestive, for instance, having the defendant as the only member of one race while all of the others are of a different race. In such lineups, the eyewitness would naturally be drawn to the person who was different from the others. The Court has ruled that even putting a person with dark hair in a lineup with others who have lighter hair would also be unduly suggestive. The height and general body appearance of all members of the lineup should be approximately equal. A lineup that suggests the identity of the perpetrator is a violation of a defendant's due process guarantees under the Constitution.[2] The penalty for a suggestive lineup is that the identification of the suspect will be inadmissible at trial.

-Photographic Lineup. In many situations it is not practical to arrange a live lineup. Because of the problems inherent in trying to find four or five people who look more or less like the suspect, police often rely on a **photographic lineup** instead. It is far easier to arrange seven or eight photographs on a piece of paper and present that to a witness than it is to find seven or eight actual persons who resemble each other.

To create a photographic lineup, a police officer will go through mug shot books and arrange a photographic lineup to show the eyewitness. Despite the fact that the lineup is photographic, the same rules apply. The pictures should all look something like the suspect. The photographs are often taped to a file folder and numbered. Like a live lineup, no names are provided. The witness must pick out the suspect from the photographs. The defendant's attorney does not have the right to be present during a photographic lineup.[3]

Physical lineup
Arranging persons of similar appearance as the suspect so that the witness can attempt to identify the person who committed the crime.

Photographic lineup
Arranging photographs of persons of similar appearance to the suspect so that the witness can attempt to identify the person who committed the crime.

---

[1] *Manson v. Brathwaite*, 432 U.S. 98, 97 S. Ct. 2243, 53 L. Ed. 2d 140 (1977).
[2] *Moore v. Illinois*, 434 U.S. 220, 98 S. Ct. 458, 54 L. Ed. 2d 424 (1977); *Foster v. California*, 394 U.S. 440, 89 S. Ct. 1127, 22 L. Ed. 2d 402 (1969).
[3] *Milholland v. State*, 319 Ark. 604, 893 S.W.2d 327 (1995).

Photographic lineups have several advantages over physical lineups. From a purely administrative viewpoint, it is far easier to obtain photographs of people who have a similar appearance than it is to locate five or six other people, on short notice, who have similar features. The disadvantage of a photo lineup is that the witness does not get to see the suspect in three dimensions and a flat photograph of a person is not always the best way to identify someone.

Constitutional Limits on Lineups. One of the most important Supreme Court cases in the area of lineups is *U.S. v. Wade*, 388 U.S. 218 (1967). Wade was placed in a lineup without his attorney's knowledge and identified as the suspect. Prior to the lineup, however, the witness saw Wade standing in the courtroom. The witness knew that Wade was the person charged with the offense before he identified him in the lineup. The Supreme Court held that the subsequent identification was unduly suggestive, and testimony about the identification should not have been allowed.

-Right to Counsel at Lineup. The defendant's attorney should be present for any post indictment lineups. The attorney has the right to observe how the witness responds and to hear anything that the witness says during the identification process. However, the attorney does not have a right to be present when the lineup occurs prior to a formal charge.

The Importance of an Eyewitness Identification. During the course of a trial, the identification of the defendant as the person who committed the crime can have a profound psychological impact on the jury. Once the defendant has been identified, it is difficult for the defense to sway the jurors back to the idea that the defendant did not commit the crime. There is something telling for jurors when they see a person point to the defendant and say, "That's the man."

Just How Accurate Is Eyewitness Testimony? It turns out that the old saying "seeing is believing" has been attacked on many different fronts. Numerous studies have shown that human beings are not accurate in identifying persons and that eyewitness testimony can often be incorrect. Despite this, we all tend to believe what we see and to think that our sense of sight is dependable.

DEMONSTRATIVE EVIDENCE

Demonstrative evidence refers to any charts, diagrams, or other pictorial documents used by the attorneys or witnesses to help illustrate or explain testimony. The parties normally prepare these exhibits themselves, and because of that, this type of evidence is usually not admissible. The attorneys may use these aids during opening statements and closing arguments, but it is rare that such an aid would be admitted during the trial and sent back to the jury room during jury deliberations. The fact that they are prepared by one side makes them suspect. Unlike physical and documentary evidence that was produced through the natural course of events, demonstrative evidence was created specifically to persuade the jury, and therefore most states do not permit it to go into the jury room for fear that

Demonstrative evidence
PowerPoint presentations, diagrams, charts or other aids that are developed by an attorney to persuade the jury to a particular viewpoint.

the jury might give it more weight or credibility than the other forms of evidence. Consider Scenario 16-4.

THE CHART

Ted is a licensed stock broker. He is charged with using his client's funds to fund his personal expenses, including buying a new car for himself. These funds were deposited on account with him in the understanding that they would be used to purchase stocks and other investments. During the trial, the prosecutor prepares an elaborate chart showing when each client's deposit was made and has each victim annotate the chart as he or she testifies, inserting information such as where the meeting with Ted took place and how much money they gave him. By the end of the trial, the chart is filled with information created by the witnesses in the case. Is this chart demonstrative evidence or physical evidence? Put another way, will the chart go back into the jury room during deliberations?

Answer: No. In almost all situations, a chart that has been prepared by one of the attorneys in the case remains demonstrative evidence even when witnesses have made notations on it. The attorneys can refer to the chart during closing arguments, but the judge will most likely rule that the chart cannot go into the jury room.

EXPERT EVIDENCE

Expert witness
A person qualified by training, education, or experience to offer an opinion about a scientific or other process; a person with knowledge that is not available to the normal juror.

At some point in a criminal trial, one or both of the sides may need someone who can explain complicated scientific or other processes to the jury. An **expert witness** is the person called in to do this. The legal definition of an expert is someone who is qualified, either by training, experience, or study (or by all of them) to give an opinion regarding a scientific or other matter.[4] Normally, a witness cannot give an opinion about the facts in a case. A normal, or lay, witness is not permitted to offer a personal opinion about the guilt or innocence of the defendant, for example, or to offer an opinion about the evidence in the case. Those are decisions that the jury must reach. But there are times when the jury, which is composed of regular citizens, has no background on the topic being discussed. We have already discussed the use of DNA testimony in this chapter, and that is an excellent example of the type of evidence for which an expert would be needed. Most people do not understand the advanced chemistry and biology necessary to understand how DNA can match tissue with a specific individual. To explain this, the state would call an expert to the stand, prove that the person has the necessary scientific background, training, and education, then ask this expert to give an opinion about the DNA evidence. An expert can provide an opinion to help the judge or the jury to determine a specific fact that is in issue in the case.[5] At trial, an expert is someone who has knowledge or training that is beyond the normal experience of the average juror and whose testimony will help the jury understand a complex issue.[6] An expert witness is almost always a person who has no personal knowledge about the facts of

---

[4] *Hannah v. Gregg*, Bland & Berry, Inc., 840 So. 2d 839 (Ala. 2002).
[5] *Ficic v. State Farm Fire & Cas. Co.*, 9 Misc. 3d 793, 804 N.Y.S.2d 541 (Sup 2005).
[6] *Haymore v. Thew Shovel Co.*, 116 N.C. App. 40, 446 S.E.2d 865 (1994).

the case. This person was not present when the crime occurred. However, some states allow a person who has personal knowledge to be qualified as an expert witness in a case.[7] Consider Scenario 16-5.

EXPERT WITNESS?

During a trial for driving under the influence of alcohol, the defense attorney calls a fellow defense attorney to the stand to testify as an expert witness. To qualify the witness, the defense attorney reviews the witness's training, education, and background. The witness testifies that although he is a defense attorney and has represented over 100 clients charged with driving under the influence, he has also attended conferences and seminars put on by the state on the use and function of the breath testing machines that determine blood alcohol content. The witness also testifies that he has read extensively on the subject and has been certified as a technician on the Intoxilyer 5000, the most recent model of machine used to test breath samples from suspected drunk drivers. Can this defense attorney be an expert witness in this case?

Answer: Yes. If the test of an expert is someone who with background, training, knowledge, and education attains a level of understanding that is beyond that of a normal juror, then this witness qualifies as an expert, despite the fact that he is also a defense attorney. Of course, a defense attorney who is actively representing someone during a trial cannot also appear as an expert witness in the same case.

 ## THE EXCLUSIONARY RULE

The **exclusionary rule** was created by the U.S. Supreme Court and dictates the punishment for failing to follow the correct procedures in obtaining evidence. Illegal or unconstitutional evidence cannot be used at trial. By providing such a sanction, the U.S. Supreme Court hoped to effectively force all law enforcement agencies to abide by constitutional provisions in seizing evidence. The exclusionary rule is the device used in numerous movie and television dramas as the "technicality" that allows an obviously guilty suspect to go free. However, because the court's ruling actually states that the police violated the Constitution in obtaining the evidence, to allow unconstitutionally seized evidence to be used in one case would invite police to circumvent the Constitution in future cases, too. A ruling that certain evidence was obtained unconstitutionally does not mean that the charges against the defendant are dropped. However, if all evidence against a defendant is ruled illegal, then for all practical purposes there is nothing that the prosecution can use that links the defendant to the crime.

Exclusionary rule
A court-created doctrine that prevents illegally obtained evidence from being used in a criminal trial.

---

[7] *Rogers v. Department of Family and Protective Services*, 175 S.W.3d 370 (Tex. App. Houston 1st Dist. 2005).

It is extremely rare for all evidence against a defendant to be ruled unconstitutional. Even in cases where some of the evidence was obtained illegally, the prosecution may still continue with the case. The government simply cannot use that evidence and will instead rely on other evidence that was obtained constitutionally.

A. "FRUIT OF THE POISONOUS TREE"

Occasionally, when evidence has been obtained in violation of the Constitution, this evidence will often lead to the discovery of additional evidence. What happens when other evidence is located, but this evidence was derived from a constitutionally void source? The courts have said that the exclusionary rule, to have any binding effect, must be applied to this new evidence as well. When new evidence is discovered only through unconstitutionally obtained evidence, this new evidence will be excluded at trial. This is the so-called **fruit of the poisonous tree doctrine**. This doctrine holds that if the original evidence was tainted, any additional evidence obtained from it is also tainted and suffers the same penalty: exclusion at trial. Say, for example, that a key to a safe-deposit box was found during an illegal search. The key itself (the poisonous tree) cannot be admitted into evidence during trial, nor can the contents of the safe-deposit box (the fruit).

Fruit of the poisonous tree doctrine
The rule that evidence gathered as a result of evidence gained in an illegal search or questioning cannot be used against the person searched or questioned even if later evidence was gathered lawfully.

EXCEPTIONS TO THE EXCLUSIONARY RULE: GOOD FAITH

When officers are acting on a reasonable belief that the search warrant they have been given to execute is valid, the courts will not invalidate the evidence that they recover when it turns out the warrant was invalid. This is the **good faith doctrine**, an exception put forth in the U.S. Supreme Court case of *U.S. v. Leon*.[8] As long as there is no reasonable way that the officer would know that the warrant was invalid, the evidence will not be suppressed. Obviously, this exception to the exclusionary rule does not operate when the officer caused the warrant to be invalid in the first place or where the officer could obviously tell that the warrant was invalid.[9]

Good faith doctrine
A court-created doctrine that holds that evidence will not be suppressed under the exclusionary rule when officers were acting in good faith and had no reason to know that the warrant was invalid.

V SELF-INCRIMINATION AND IDENTIFICATION

The Fifth Amendment to the Constitution prohibits criminal defendants from being coerced into giving testimony against themselves. Is it a violation of the Fifth Amendment to force the defendant to stand up in trial and show the jury the facial scar that the victim described as belonging to her attacker? According to the U.S. Supreme Court, the answer is no. Physical traits, especially those that can be

---

[8] 468 U.S. 897, 104 S. Ct. 3405, 82 L. Ed. 2d 677 (1984).
[9] *Green v. State*, 688 So. 2d 301 (Fla. 1996).

seen by ordinary observation, do not fall under the protection of the Fifth Amendment.[10] Making a defendant demonstrate a physical trait, such as a scar or tattoo, is not the same thing as compelling the defendant to admit to a crime.[11] However, there are some states that do not permit this kind of action because of the potential conflict it will cause with the defendant's constitutional rights.

STATE v. HANDY
206 N.J. 39, 54, 18 A.3d 179, 188) (N.J.,2011)

CASE EXCERPT

Justice LONG delivered the opinion of the Court.

Germaine A. Handy was arrested as a result of incorrect information regarding the existence of a warrant, conveyed by a police dispatcher to an officer who had stopped Handy for riding his bicycle on the sidewalk in violation of a city ordinance. At issue before us is whether evidence uncovered in the ensuing search should be suppressed. We answer that question in the affirmative. The dispatcher had, in hand, a ten-year-old warrant for a California resident that did not match the spelling of Handy's name and bore a different date of birth, yet she advised the officer on the scene that there was an outstanding warrant for Handy. That conduct by the dispatcher, an integral link in the law enforcement chain, was objectively unreasonable and violated the Fourth Amendment to the United States Constitution and Article I, Paragraph 7, of the New Jersey Constitution, requiring suppression of the evidence.

I

On September 13, 2005, at approximately 7:40 p.m., Millville Special Officer Anthony Sills stopped a group of individuals for riding their bicycles on the sidewalk, in violation of a city ordinance. Officer Sills called for back-up and Officer Carlo Drogo, who was on routine patrol, responded. Because none of the bicyclists had identification, Officer Drogo asked for their names and dates of birth.

Defendant, Germaine A. Handy, was one of the individuals questioned by Officer Drogo. He provided his name as Germaine Handy, which he spelled out, along with his address — 218 East Broad Street, Millville, New Jersey, and his date of birth — March 18, 1974. Officer Drogo recorded Handy's information and radioed police dispatch with Handy's name and date of birth for a warrant check. The police dispatcher informed Officer Drogo that there was an outstanding warrant for Handy. Based on that information, Officer Drogo placed Handy under arrest and handcuffed him.

A search incident to the arrest led to the recovery of drugs. Subsequently, the police dispatcher informed Officer Drogo that there was a discrepancy between the date of birth Handy had given (March 18, 1974) and the date of birth listed on the warrant (March 14, 1972).

---

[10] *State v. Roy*, 220 La. 1017, 58 So. 2d 323 (1952); *State v. Moore*, 308 S.C. 349, 417 S.E.2d 869 (1992).
[11] *Holt v. U.S.*, 218 U.S. 245, 31 S. Ct. 2, 54 L. Ed. 1021 (1910).

When Officer Drogo arrived at headquarters with Handy he attempted to verify the existence of the warrant himself. In doing so, he ascertained that, in addition to the birth date discrepancy, the warrant, which was about ten years old, had been issued to Jermaine O. Handy with an address on W. 73rd Street in Los Angeles, California.

Officer Drogo then called the Chesterfield Township Municipal Court which had issued the warrant, reached an automated voicemail, left a message, but did not receive a reply. In light of what he had learned, Officer Drogo did not process Handy on the warrant, presumably because he concluded that Handy was not the subject of the warrant; instead, he charged him with the drug offenses and subsequently released him.

Cumberland County Indictment No. 05–12–1153 charged Handy with one count of third-degree possession of a controlled dangerous substance (cocaine) in violation of N.J.S.A. 2C:35–10(a)(1). Handy moved to suppress the evidence against him on the ground that the police acted unreasonably in linking him to the warrant. The State countered that the arresting officer was entirely reasonable in relying on the police dispatcher.

The trial court denied Handy's motion and, in ruling, found, as a matter of fact, that the dispatcher was aware of the discrepancies between the warrant and the information conveyed by Officer Drogo. Although the trial court characterized the dispatcher's actions as unreasonable, it noted that the more important factor was that the arresting officer's actions were entirely reasonable in light of the information presented to him.

Handy ultimately entered a plea to the indictment and to an unrelated indictment. He was sentenced in accordance with the plea agreement to an aggregate three-year term. Thereafter, he appealed the denial of the suppression motion. The Appellate Division reversed. *State v. Handy*, 412 N.J.Super. 492, 494, 991 A.2d 281 (App.Div.2010). In ruling, the panel agreed with the trial court that the police dispatcher acted unreasonably when she conveyed the warrant information to Officer Drogo, despite substantial discrepancies, and that Officer Drogo was entirely reasonable in his response. The panel parted company from the trial court in connection with the ultimate question of whether the reasonableness of the arresting officer somehow insulated the search from suppression and rejected the State's contention that the deterrent effect of suppression based on the dispatcher's conduct would be minimal. Judge Waugh, writing for the panel, said:

> Here, the police were responsible, through the unreasonable actions of the police dispatcher, for conveying incomplete and inaccurate information to the arresting officer. If the citizens' right to be free from unreasonable search and seizure is to be vindicated, then the exclusionary rule must be applied beyond the officer in the field and to the police employee who acts unreasonably in supplying critical, but inaccurate or incomplete, information under circumstances such as those before us.

The State sought certification, which we granted. *State v. Handy*, 203 N.J. 95, 999 A.2d 463 (2010). We now affirm.

II

The State argues that: the conduct of both the arresting officer and the dispatcher was entirely reasonable; even if the dispatcher's conduct is deemed unreasonable, the evidence should not be suppressed because the exclusionary rule is only triggered by police action that is deliberate, reckless, or systemic; and, in this case, the goal of deterrence would not be advanced by suppressing the evidence against Handy.

Handy counters that the Appellate Division was correct in: viewing the police dispatcher as part of the police department family; characterizing her conduct as objectively unreasonable; attributing her unreasonable actions to the department as a whole; and suppressing the evidence under the exclusionary rule.

III

In reviewing a motion to suppress, an appellate court "must uphold the factual findings underlying the trial court's decision so long as those findings are supported by sufficient credible evidence in the record." A trial court's findings should not be disturbed simply because an appellate court "might have reached a different conclusion were it the trial tribunal." However, a trial court's legal conclusions are not afforded such deference; appellate review of legal determinations is plenary. Here, the trial court's factual findings, in particular that the dispatcher was aware of the discrepancies between the warrant and what Officer Drogo had told her, were accepted by the Appellate Division and we adopt them as well. What is before us is purely a legal question: whether those facts warrant suppression.

IV

The Fourth Amendment to the United States Constitution provides:

> The right of the people to be secure in their persons, houses, papers, and effects, against unreasonable searches and seizures, shall not be violated, and no Warrants shall issue, but upon probable cause, supported by Oath or affirmation, and particularly describing the place to be searched, and the persons or things to be seized. U.S. Const. amend. IV.

A consequence for violating the Fourth Amendment is the so-called exclusionary rule, "a judicially created remedy designed to safeguard Fourth Amendment rights generally through its deterrent effect." *United States v. Leon*, 468 U.S. 897, 906, 104 S.Ct. 3405, 3412, 82 L.Ed.2d 677, 687 (1984) In addition to deterrence, the exclusionary rule "enables the judiciary to avoid the taint of partnership in official lawlessness," and "assures the people — all potential victims of unlawful government conduct — that the government would not profit from its lawless behavior, thus minimizing the risk of seriously undermining popular trust in government." As Justice Clark, writing for the Supreme Court in *Mapp v. Ohio*, 367 U.S. 643, 81 S.Ct. 1684, 6 L.Ed.2d 1081 (1961), declared:

> There are those who say . . . that under our constitutional exclusionary doctrine "the criminal is to go free because the constable has blundered." In some cases this will undoubtedly be the result. But, . . . "there is another consideration — the imperative of judicial integrity." The criminal goes free, if he must, but it is the law that sets him free. Nothing can destroy a government more quickly than its failure to observe its own laws, or worse, its disregard of the charter of its own existence. . . .

The ignoble shortcut to conviction left open to the State tends to destroy the entire system of constitutional restraints on which the liberties of the people rest. Having once recognized that the right to privacy embodied in the Fourth Amendment is enforceable against the States, and that the right to be secure against rude invasions of privacy by state officers is, therefore, constitutional in origin, we can no longer permit that right to remain an empty promise. Because it is enforceable in the same manner and to like effect as other basic rights secured by the Due Process Clause, we can no longer permit it to be revocable at the whim of any police officer who, in the name of law enforcement itself, chooses to suspend its enjoyment. Our decision (to apply the rule to the States), founded on reason and truth, gives to the individual no more than that which the Constitution guarantees him, to the police officer no less than that to which honest law enforcement is entitled, and, to the courts, that judicial integrity so necessary in the true administration of justice.

Without an exclusionary rule, the Fourth Amendment "is of no value, and . . . might as well be stricken from the Constitution." *Weeks v. United States*, 232 U.S. 383, 393, 34 S.Ct. 341, 344, 58 L.Ed. 652, 656 (1914).

In parallel language, our own constitution protects our citizens from unreasonable searches and seizures:

> The right of the people to be secure in their persons, houses, papers, and effects, against unreasonable searches and seizures, shall not be violated; and no warrant shall issue except upon probable cause, supported by oath or affirmation, and particularly describing the place to be searched and the papers and things to be seized. N.J. Const. art. I, ¶ 7.

At issue in this matter is the execution of a warrant. In that connection, the basic test under both the Fourth Amendment to the United States Constitution and Article I, Paragraph 7, of the New Jersey Constitution is the same: was the conduct objectively reasonable in light of "the facts known to the law enforcement officer at the time of the search." That standard affords the police necessary latitude to respond to criminality while deterring unreasonable conduct and protecting the citizens from government overreaching.

V

All parties agree that the aforementioned standard of objective reasonableness is the polestar for our inquiry. They differ over how the application of that standard plays out.

A

The State first argues that the conduct of both the arresting officer and the dispatcher was reasonable, and thus, no further analysis is required. Like the trial court and the Appellate Division, Handy disagrees, as do we. Although we cannot quarrel in any way with Officer Drogo's behavior, the dispatcher's actions were plainly unreasonable. Despite the fact that the warrant was over ten years old and referenced Jermaine Handy, a California resident, not Germaine Handy and bore a different date of birth, the dispatcher told Officer Drogo that the warrant was issued for Handy.

There was nothing reasonable about that conduct in light of what the dispatcher actually knew. Indeed, there were two reasonable paths for her: one was to tell Officer Drogo about the information on the warrant she had before her so that he could probe the issue further with Handy, the other was to say that there was no warrant matching the information she had been *48 given. She chose neither course, deciding instead to tell Officer Drogo that there was an outstanding warrant against the errant Millville bicyclist who had been stopped for riding on the sidewalk, thus precipitating the arrest that could not otherwise have occurred in the face of an ordinance violation, and the cascade of events that followed.

When the actions of the dispatcher, given the facts she knew at the time, are tested against the "touchstone of reasonableness," her conduct fell short. Although she had before her every reason to doubt the existence of a warrant for this defendant, she reported the opposite and did not make Officer Drogo aware of the real facts in the matter. Like the courts below, we have no difficulty in concluding that that conduct was constitutionally infirm.

B

Alternatively, the State contends that even if the dispatcher's conduct is deemed unreasonable, suppression is unwarranted. In particular the State, citing *Herring v. United States*, 555 U.S. 135, _____, 129 S.Ct. 695, 702, 172 L.Ed.2d 496, 507 (2009), argues that the conduct was not deliberate, reckless, grossly negligent, or evidential of systemic carelessness and, under those circumstances, the deterrence rationale of the exclusionary rule would not be advanced by suppression.

In Herring, the Supreme Court addressed the application of the exclusionary rule to conduct by one who was not the officer executing a warrant. Id. at _____, 129 S.Ct. at 698, 172 L.Ed.2d at 502. There, a county sheriff's investigator asked the county warrant clerk to check for any outstanding warrants against Bennie Dean Herring who had presented himself at the local impound lot to retrieve some personal items. Ibid. The sheriff's officer, who knew that Herring had had prior criminal involvement, was advised that there were no warrants. Ibid. At the officer's behest, the clerk checked with her counterpart in a neighboring county who responded that there was, in fact, a warrant for Herring. The first clerk conveyed that information to the officer who arrested and searched Herring and his vehicle uncovering drugs and a weapon. As it turned out, however, the warrant had been recalled five months earlier. That information should have been, but was not, entered into the computer database. By the time the clerk realized what had happened, Herring had already been arrested and searched. Id. at _____, 129 S.Ct. at 698, 172 L.Ed.2d at 502-03.

The trial court denied Herring's motion to suppress the evidence against him. Id. at _____, 129 S.Ct. at 699, 172 L.Ed.2d at 503. On appeal, the Eleventh Circuit affirmed that decision declaring that, because the error was not reckless or deliberate, the exclusionary rule was not triggered. In affirming, the United States Supreme Court asserted that an error arising "from nonrecurring and attenuated negligence is . . . far removed from the core concerns" that led to the adoption of the exclusionary rule. Moreover, police conduct must be sufficiently deliberate that exclusion can meaningfully deter it, and sufficiently culpable that such deterrence is worth the price paid by the justice

404 Chapter 16: Evidence

system. As laid out in our cases, the exclusionary rule serves to deter deliberate, reckless, or grossly negligent conduct, or in some circumstances recurring or systemic negligence.

According to *Herring*, because the bookkeeping error at issue was isolated negligence attenuated from the arrest, and because reliance on the errant database by the officer was not objectively unreasonable, the deterrent effect of suppression was minimal, such that the principles underlying the exclusionary rule would not be advanced thereby.

In *Herring*, the Supreme Court expanded on its earlier decision in *Arizona v. Evans*, 514 U.S. 1, 115 S.Ct. 1185, 131 L.Ed.2d 34 (1995). In *Arizona v. Evans*, the defendant was arrested and searched after a computer check during a routine traffic stop indicated, incorrectly, that there was an outstanding warrant against him. The defendant was charged with a possessory drug offense as a result of the search and moved to suppress on the ground that the drugs were the fruit of an unlawful arrest because the warrant had been quashed before he was arrested.

After the Arizona courts split over the issue, the United States Supreme Court declared that where the mistaken conduct that led to the arrest was attenuated — that is, attributable to a judicial employee who had "no stake in the outcome of particular criminal prosecutions" — suppression would not deter police misconduct and thus application of the exclusionary rule would be unwarranted. The difference between *Arizona v. Evans* and *Herring* is the degree of attenuation: the former involved a non-police database and the latter a police-related one. In both cases, the actions of the law enforcement officers in relying on the databases was deemed objectively reasonable.

The State properly concedes that this is not an Arizona v. Evans case in that the dispatcher was not attenuated from the arrest, but was an integral link in the law enforcement chain. The State nevertheless argues that under Herring, the dispatcher's mistake was not such as to warrant suppression.

C

It is axiomatic that our interpretation of our own constitution will not always conform with the view of the federal courts. Indeed, although we look to federal interpretation of the United States Constitution as a guide, we do not view it as requiring lockstep. Thus, we often interpret our own constitution in such a way as to provide greater protections for our citizens than would its federal counterpart.

We make that point in light of the robust criticism that Herring has drawn. Indeed, many scholars and treatise writers fault Herring for unjustifiably watering down Fourth Amendment protections and, in particular, for failing to consider the non-deterrent rationales underlying the exclusionary rule.

We note as well that the parties are sharply divided over whether adopting Herring would violate our decision in Novembrino, rejecting the "good faith" exception of Leon. As might be expected, the State argues that Herring does not run afoul of Novembrino and defendant asserts the contrary.

We need not assess whether Herring can be reconciled with our own constitutional standards for, like the Appellate Division, we conclude that this case would not be governed by Herring, in any event. Herring's focus, and that of Arizona v. Evans, was an attenuated clerical error in a database upon which police officials reasonably relied. In both instances, the Court assessed the deterrent effect of suppression as minimal.

Attenuation is not part of the factual calculus before us. First, the dispatcher was not attenuated from the arrest but was literally a co-operative in its effectuation along with the officer on the scene. Second, as far as we know, the database was entirely accurate and there is, in fact, an outstanding warrant for a Jermaine O. Handy of Los Angeles, California. What occurred here was that the dispatcher, with a presumably accurate database, simply provided Officer Drogo with wrong information when a reasonably prudent person would, at least, have advised him of the discrepancies so that he could verify the information himself.

Third, the minimal deterrent effect that the Supreme Court in Herring and Arizona v. Evans intuited would flow from suppression based on an attenuated "clerical error," is wholly unlike what is before us. Instead, suppressing the evidence garnered from this illegal search would have important deterrent value, would underscore the need for training of officers and dispatchers to focus on detail, and would serve to assure that our own constitutional guarantees are given full effect. As the Appellate Division pointed out:

> The police dispatcher is the crucial link between the officer in the field and police headquarters. The officer depends on receiving the correct information from the dispatcher, information such as whether there is or is not an outstanding arrest warrant for the person with whom the officer is then face to face. Misinformation either way has the potential to leave the officer either unaware that he or she is dealing with a dangerous criminal or arresting the wrong person.

The need to avoid the former is obvious and clearly in the best interest of the police officer in the field, the need to avoid the latter finds its basis in the Fourth Amendment's protection of "the right of the people to be secure in their persons, houses, papers, and effects, against unreasonable searches and seizures." The police officer in the field and the citizen on the street both benefit from a police dispatch system that is free of unreasonable conduct by dispatchers who fail to ensure that they are providing the available information about outstanding warrants as accurately and completely as possible.

What is critical to our analysis is that neither Herring nor Arizona v. Evans dispensed with the standard of "objective reasonableness" that governs the execution of a warrant. To the contrary, those decisions took pains to reaffirm that standard. In ruling as it did, on the effect of an attenuated clerical error in Herring and Arizona v. Evans, the Supreme Court addressed a niche that is simply not present here. Here, the dispatcher's slipshod conduct, which clearly would not have been tolerated had the officer committed it, was objectively unreasonable and thus failed to satisfy the Fourth Amendment or the New Jersey Constitution.

VI

The Fourth Amendment is a bulwark against the government's unwarranted intrusions into the daily lives of our fellow citizens. As interpreted by the dissent, it would provide little or no protection to the people it was intended to serve. First, the dissent's notion that the "urgency" of the situation facing the dispatcher justified her conduct is misguided. Officer Drogo was confronted with persons who had ridden their bicycles on the sidewalk, not suspected armed robbers, burglars, or rapists. If ever there was a case in which the dispatcher had the luxury of time and care — this was it.

Second, the dissent's conclusion that a Fourth Amendment exclusionary rule analysis is limited to the conduct of the arresting officer is wrong. Under that construct, police operatives, like the dispatcher here, are free to act heedlessly and unreasonably, so long as the last man in the chain does not do so. Nothing in our jurisprudence supports that view.

Third, as we have said, the analysis under federal and state jurisprudence focuses on the objective reasonableness of the police conduct. Here, the dispatcher's notion, echoed by the dissent, that a warrant with a wrong name and a wrong date of birth, is close enough to justify the arrest of a citizen, fails to satisfy that standard. To be sure, "room must be allowed for some mistakes by police . . . ," But that principle bears with it an important caveat — that the police have behaved reasonably. The police dispatcher here was plainly unreasonable in failing to take further steps when she recognized that she did not have a match on the warrant check. As such, our own constitution requires suppression. One need not have pristine vision or the benefit of hindsight to know that that is so.

VII

The judgment of the Appellate Division reversing the order denying suppression is affirmed.

CASE QUESTIONS

1   Why was Handy stopped and then arrested?
2   How were the drugs discovered?
3   What actions did the officer take to verify the outstanding warrant?
4   What is the basis for the creation of the exclusionary rule according to this court?
5   According to the court, how valuable is the exclusionary rule?

CHAPTER SUMMARY

Evidence comes in many different types. Before any evidence can be reviewed by the jury, it must be shown to be relevant to the issues in the case and also that the evidence is admissible. A judge rules on the admissibility of evidence. Once admitted, the evidence may go with the jury into the jury room when they deliberate at the end of the case.

There are two broad categories of evidence: circumstantial and direct. Circumstantial evidence suggests a conclusion, while direct evidence establishes a fact. Direct evidence can be further broken down into other subcategories, including physical, documentary, testimonial, and expert. One example of direct, physical evidence is DNA, which has revolutionized law enforcement investigative techniques. When eyewitness testimony is used, it can have a dramatic effect on the case. This is one reason why pretrial identifications of the defendant are strictly monitored. It is common for a witness to identify a defendant from a photographic lineup. These lineups have rigid rules that govern how they may be conducted. The lineup must not be overly suggestive of who the defendant is. When evidence is seized in violation of the Constitution, the courts will often refuse to admit it. The exclusionary rule prohibits the police from using evidence that has been obtained illegally.

KEY TERMS

Evidence	Evidence room	Demonstrative evidence
Relevant	Direct evidence	Expert witness
Admissibility	Circumstantial evidence	Exclusionary rule
Admission of evidence	DNA	Fruit of the poisonous
Tender	Documentary evidence	tree doctrine
Foundation questions	Testimony	Good faith doctrine
Laying the foundation	Physical lineup	
Chain of custody	Photographic lineup	

REVIEW QUESTIONS

1 What is admissibility?
2 Why is relevance important in using evidence?
3 Explain "admission of evidence."
4 What are foundation questions?
5 Explain "laying the foundation."
6 What is the chain of custody?
7 What is the purpose of the evidence room?
8 Explain the difference between direct and circumstantial evidence.
9 What is DNA?
10 How is DNA used in criminal cases?
11 Why are polygraph tests not admissible in court? Explain.
12 What is the "CSI Effect?"
13 What is the difference between a lineup and a showup?
14 Is eyewitness testimony reliable? Explain.
15 What is demonstrative evidence?
16 Explain the exclusionary rule.
17 How does the exclusionary rule interact with the fruit of the poisonous tree doctrine?
18 How does a person qualify as an expert witness?
19 Why are photographic lineups more common than physical lineups?
20 Give some examples of documentary evidence.

QUESTIONS FOR ANALYSIS

1 The text mentions the distinctions between direct and circumstantial evidence. Tell a story about something that happened to you and explain what evidence was circumstantial and what evidence was direct.

2 Should everyone in the United States be required to give a DNA sample? Support your answer.

HYPOTHETICALS

1 Eyewitness testimony, especially the testimony of a victim on the stand who identifies the defendant, can have a dramatic impact on the jury. However, eyewitness testimony is not as reliable as we would like to think. Let's put it to the test: Describe the person who sits next to you in class, without looking at him or her. How well did you do? What does this tell you about what it must be like for a witness, testifying weeks, months, or even years after the event?

2 Rick is being questioned by the police in relation to a narcotics sale. The police sent a confidential informant (CI) into Rick's home and the CI reported buying cocaine directly from Rick. The CI even described Rick, including Rick's tattoo on his right forearm. During questioning, Rick admits that he was home that day, but that he didn't sell anything to the CI. In fact, he says, the CI tried to sell drugs to him. When they point out that the CI identified Rick, even down to his tattoo, Rick tells them the tattoo is on his left forearm and differs in important ways from the details provided by the CI. Suppose that you are a juror on this case: Is this variation in facts between Rick and the CI enough to give you reasonable doubt that Rick committed the crime?

3 Dana has been arrested for attempting to arrange the murder of her husband. The police have her on audio and video talking to a person whom she believed was a hit man, but was actually an undercover police officer. On the audio, Dana can clearly be heard saying, "My life would be so much better with Walter out of it." She then says that she can pay the supposed hit man $5,000 to make the problem "go away." Dana won't get any more specific about what she wants done. She tells the hit man that her husband will be home tomorrow all day. When she leaves her meeting with the hit man, she withdraws $5,000 from her bank account. She makes an appointment with a spa for an all-day treatment on the following day. The following morning, she turns off the alarm system before leaving and leaves a side door unlocked, per her arrangement with the hit man. She is arrested on her way to the spa. Dana claims that all of the evidence against her is circumstantial. Is she right? Which evidence is circumstantial and which is direct? Is there enough evidence here, of either type, to prove beyond a reasonable doubt that she was planning on having her husband killed?

Defenses to Criminal Accusations

Chapter Objectives

- Explain the difference between a simple defense and an affirmative defense
- Describe the defendant's burden of proof in bringing an affirmative defense
- List and describe the various types of affirmative defenses
- Explain the insanity defense
- Define the significance of self-defense and "stand your ground" defenses

I BASIC DEFENSES

This chapter will discuss the wide variety of defenses available to a person who has been accused of a crime. Some of these defenses are provided directly by the U.S. Constitution and statutes, while others are the product of the creativity of defense attorneys.

II CONSTITUTIONAL DEFENSES

The Fifth and Fourteenth Amendments to the U.S. Constitution provide numerous protections to a person accused of a crime, including the following:

 Double jeopardy
- Privilege against self-incrimination
- Due process
- Equal protection

However, there was an interesting (and far reaching) problem that arose after the U.S. Constitution was ratified: Did the provisions of the Bill of Rights actually apply to the individual states? Many states, which had held enormous power under the Articles of Confederation, argued that the provisions of the U.S. Constitution functioned more like guidelines than mandates. That question remained open until the Civil War finally provided an answer. The southern states had always maintained that they could, under a supposed agreement of mutual independence, secede from the various United States when they no longer supported the positions taken by the federal government. Although there were many causes of the Civil War and many outcomes, there is no doubt that it settled some questions of constitutional law. The ratification of the Fourteenth Amendment clearly decided some specific issues that had been left unresolved since the founding of the country. One of the results is that the protections guaranteed in the Fifth Amendment to the U.S. Constitution applied to all of the states, regardless of what their individual constitutions guaranteed. See Figure 17-1 for the text of the Fifth and Fourteenth Amendments to the U.S. Constitution.

FIGURE 17-1

The Fifth and Fourteenth Amendments

The Fifth Amendment

No person shall be held to answer for a capital, or otherwise infamous crime, unless on a presentment or indictment of a Grand Jury, except in cases arising in the land or naval forces, or in the Militia, when in actual service in time of War or public danger; nor shall any person be subject for the same offence to be twice put in jeopardy of life or limb; nor shall be compelled in any criminal case to be a witness against himself, nor be deprived of life, liberty, or property, without due process of law; nor shall private property be taken for public use, without just compensation.

The Fourteenth Amendment, Section 1

All persons born or naturalized in the United States, and subject to the jurisdiction thereof, are citizens of the United States and of the State wherein they reside. No State shall make or enforce any law which shall abridge the privileges or immunities of citizens of the United States; nor shall any State deprive any person of life, liberty, or property, without due process of law; nor deny to any person within its jurisdiction the equal protection of the laws.

Under the provisions of the Fifth and Fourteenth Amendments, we can see that the original list of constitutional defenses available to a criminal defendant expanded to include not only the protections of double jeopardy, self-incrimination, and due process, but also equal protection. This chapter will discuss each of these defenses in turn.

A. DOUBLE JEOPARDY

A person who has been prosecuted for a crime and found not guilty cannot be tried for that offense again. That provision is at the core of the Fifth Amendment and made applicable to the states through the Fourteenth Amendment. The law on this point has been refined over many decades. One of the key points in analyzing

double jeopardy is knowing when it applies. Clearly, a defendant cannot be retried if the jury finds him not guilty. But not all cases end in this manner. There are times when the court may declare a mistrial because of some irregularity that occurred during the trial. Because a mistrial resets the parties and the issues back to a point as though the trial never occurred, does this bar the defendant from being retried? The answer is no. However, the law concerning double jeopardy has some subtleties to it that have come out over time. Suppose that during the trial, the prosecutor realizes that things are going badly and deliberately causes a mistrial. Does this mean that the defendant can be tried again? Conceivably, a prosecutor could cause a mistrial in the subsequent trials as well, retrying the defendant until the prosecutor believed that he or she had finally gotten it right, so, there must be some guidelines about double jeopardy that apply in situations like this.

Courts then have been wrestling with the issue of when the double jeopardy provision applies in cases where the defendant has not been found guilty, but some other irregularity has occurred in the trial.

The general rule is that double jeopardy attaches when the jury is sworn and enters the jury box. A clever defendant, knowing this, might try to cause a mistrial. Many states have addressed this issue by declaring that if the prosecution deliberately causes a mistrial, the case cannot be retried, but if the defendant deliberately causes a mistrial, the case can be retried. On the other hand, double jeopardy as a defense does not apply when a defendant has been found guilty and his or her case goes up on appeal. If the defendant should win the appeal, the state has the right to retry him. Is this a violation of double jeopardy? No. In this situation, the original trial has been vacated and the new trial will take the place of the original. If the defendant is retried and found guilty, then he or she may still appeal that conviction, so the defendant has not lost any rights. Consider Scenario 17-1.

> **Double jeopardy**
> A provision of the Fifth Amendment that forbids the retrial of a person who has already been tried for an offense and found not guilty.

A MURDER WITH NO CONSEQUENCES?

SCENARIO 17-1

Sue has been convicted of murdering her husband. After serving ten years in prison, she discovers that her husband is actually alive. She seeks him out and confirms that he was not killed. However, because she has already been convicted of killing him, she reasons that she can't be tried twice for killing the same man, so she kills him out of revenge for the ten years she spent in prison. Can she be prosecuted for this murder?

Answer: Yes. A person cannot use a legal technicality to commit murder. What will happen in this case is that Sue's first conviction will be vacated because she obviously did not commit the murder. Then she will be tried and no doubt convicted for murdering her ex-husband. She may even serve time in the same prison where she served her first sentence.

B. PRIVILEGE AGAINST SELF-INCRIMINATION

Technically speaking, the privilege against **self-incrimination** is not a defense so much as it is a right of the defendant to refuse to answer questions or to be forced into giving evidence against himself. This right is afforded by the Fifth Amendment. Defense attorneys do not use the right against self-incrimination as a defense so

> **Self-incrimination**
> A provision of the Fifth Amendment that prohibits a person from being forced to give evidence against himself.

much as they use it as a means to suppress the defendant's statement when evidence shows that it was obtained in an unconstitutional manner.

C. DUE PROCESS

Due process
A clause in the Fifth Amendment that guarantees that each and every defendant will receive the same procedural safeguards throughout a criminal case, regardless of the charge.

The **due process** clause requires that the same procedures be used in all criminal cases. The rules do not change when someone is "obviously" guilty as opposed to someone who "may" be guilty. A claim of violation of due process is usually raised on appeal and not during the trial. On appeal, the defendant may claim that specific, required procedures were either not followed or were somehow curtailed or prejudiced in his or her case.

D. EQUAL PROTECTION

The Fifth and Fourteenth Amendments require that all citizens be treated fairly. As far as criminal law is concerned, this means that people falling into different socio-economic, religious, or racial categories cannot be treated differently under the law. Any law that contains classifications based on these factors is immediately suspect and may be found unconstitutional.

E. FIRST AMENDMENT

For certain types of crimes, a defendant may also use the First Amendment as a protection. As we have already seen earlier in this text in prosecutions involving obscenity, a defendant may urge the defense that what the government considers to be obscene, he or she considers to be an expression that is protected under the First Amendment. In such cases, it is the judge who must make a determination whether the Amendment bars the prosecution or if it should proceed.

TECHNICAL DEFENSES

When a defendant raises what could be called a "technical defense," he or she is saying that there is something wrong with the law that makes the action a crime or there is something wrong with the charging document that alleges that the defendant committed a crime. The first category includes defenses such as:

- Vagueness and over breadth
- *Ex post facto*

Under the second category of challenges to the charging documents themselves are defenses such as:

- Statute of limitations
- *Allegata* versus *probata*

A. VAGUENESS AND OVER BREADTH

When a defendant raises the defense of vagueness and over breadth, the defendant is actually challenging the statute that criminalizes the behavior. A defendant may challenge the statute under which he or she has been charged by claiming that the statute is worded in such a vague manner that people of common intelligence would have to guess at its meaning. The underlying principle in criminal law is that people must be able to figure out what is and is not illegal. When a statute fails to make this notice clear, a court may declare it unconstitutional. Consider Scenario 17-2.

CELL PHONE

Because of numerous complaints and a great deal of press coverage, the State of Placid's legislature has decided to take on the issue of cell phone use. The legislature voted on and the governor passed a statute that reads:

> In this state, it shall be illegal for any person to use any electronic device while carrying out any activity that could be deemed unsafe.

Is this statute one that could be challenged for vagueness?

Answer: Yes. If the standard for vagueness is whether a person of average intelligence would have to guess at its meaning, then this statute clearly fails the test. Although it was obviously intended to deal with such things as texting while driving, the wording is so vague that it could also apply to listening to an iPod, using a hearing aid, having a heart pace-maker, and any of a number of other electronic devices, all while doing an activity that is considered "dangerous." There are many activities that people carry out every day that could meet this definition, including mowing a yard, driving a car, and conducting surgery, to name just a few. The statute is too vague to be enforceable.

In a similar vein, a court may strike down a statute if it is overbroad. A statute that is overbroad is one that makes constitutionally protected and *unprotected* activities equally illegal. A statute that criminalizes the homeless, for example, when they carry out inoffensive conduct, is considered overbroad.[1]

B. *EX POST FACTO*

No Bill of Attainder or ex post facto *Law shall be passed.* — Article I, Section 9, U.S. Constitution

A bill of attainder is a legislative action attempting to short-circuit a criminal trial and declare an individual guilty of a crime (usually treason). Bills of attainder are

---

[1] *Pottinger v. Miami*, 810 F Supp. 1551 (S.D. Fla. 1992).

not permitted in the United States. Challenges to a law based on a claim that it is a bill of attainder are extremely rare. Instead, it is far more common to base a claim on *ex post facto* laws.

Ex post facto
An action that is criminalized only after it has been committed.

An ***ex post facto*** law is one that criminalizes behavior or increases punishment for an action *after* it has occurred. In many cases, a person may carry out an activity that is not technically illegal at the time, but one that many people consider to be criminal in nature. When they are surprised to learn that there is no law against the activity, they lobby for one. For instance, when the crime of computer hacking first began, most states had no statute on the books that made this illegal. The prohibition against *ex post facto* laws prevents the legislature from making that action illegal after the fact just to punish that individual. The legislature can, and often does, address the situation by enacting laws, but these laws only apply to people who commit the crime *after* the statute has been enacted.

Ex post facto defenses also apply to sentences. A person's sentence must reflect the law at the time he committed the action. The legislature cannot, in a fit of outrage, seek to enhance the punishment for a particularly gruesome crime. The legislature can only enhance the sentence for others who commit it. The constitutional limit of *ex post facto* means that these new statutes cannot be applied to a defendant who committed the crime before the new law was created.

C. STATUTE OF LIMITATIONS

Statute of limitations
The time period in which a criminal case must be commenced or is barred forever.

Almost all crimes have a statutorily determined time period in which the government must bring charges against an individual or the case cannot be prosecuted. Some people question why the state would impose a limitation on itself to bring a prosecution or have it barred forever. There are some very practical reasons for a **statute of limitations**. First, there is the simple issue that over time, witness memory fades, evidence disappears, and the likelihood of returning a verdict against the correct person for an old crime gets more and more difficult. There is also the issue that for some crimes, there should be a point where all concerned realize that no case can ever be brought against anyone, and all parties concerned can move on with their lives. Generally, less serious crimes have shorter statutes of limitations. For crimes such as shoplifting, the statute of limitations is often two years. For battery, it could be one year. But when we deal with more serious crimes, we find that the statute of limitations increases dramatically. For armed robbery cases, the statute of limitations is between 5 and 10 years, depending on the jurisdiction. In rape cases many states have a 10- or 15-year statute of limitations. When it comes to the worst of crimes, murder, there is no statute of limitations at all. A person can be charged with murder decades after it was committed.

Like constitutional defenses and other technical defenses, a defendant would bring a claim that a particular prosecution was barred by the statute of limitations to the trial court, not the jury. In situations dealing with the law, the judge has the final say. In issues of fact, it is the jury.

D. ERRORS IN CHARGING DOCUMENTS

In addition to bringing a claim that the prosecution is barred by the passage of time, a defendant might also challenge the sufficiency of the charging document. Because this text has used the term indictment to refer to the charging document used in felony cases, it will continue with that use, keeping in mind that a defendant is perfectly free to challenge the sufficiency of a misdemeanor charge in exactly the same way, and can challenge the charging document (which can be an accusation or an information) because it is facially deficient.

ALLEGATA VERSUS *PROBATA*

The terms **allegata** and **probata** are Latin terms for "allegations" and "proof," respectively. Essentially, this defense is based on what the state has alleged is the crime and what the state has proven at trial. There are times when the proof does not match up to the allegations. A motion for directed verdict is often based on the simple premise that the crime charged against the defendant does not match the evidence produced against him or her at trial. In such a situation, the defendant might claim that although the state has produced evidence that the defendant committed a crime, it was not the crime originally alleged in the indictment. In most cases, such claims are not successful. It is rare for the state to bring charges against a defendant and then seek to prove some other crime instead. This is not to say that the state can bring additional evidence against a defendant to support a lesser-included offense. As we saw in a previous chapter, a lesser-included offense is one that has almost all of the same elements as a greater offense. Kidnapping is an example. The elements of kidnapping are:

Allegata
Latin. for "the allegations contained in a charging document."

Probata
Latin. for "the proof elicited in a trial."

- The unlawful
- Restraint
- Asportation
- Of a person
- Against his or her will

The lesser-included offense of false imprisonment consists of the following elements:

- The unlawful
- Restraint
- Of a person
- Against his or her will

In such a case, a defendant's claim that the allegations do not match the proof would fail because false imprisonment contains the same elements (but one) of kidnapping.

TECHNICAL DEFICIENCIES IN CHARGING DOCUMENTS

Similar to a claim of *allegata* versus *probata*, a defendant can also offer the defense that the indictment itself is insufficient. For instance, a defendant might claim that the indictment does not provide sufficient information to show that the defendant committed a crime. Many states require that the indictment must provide sufficient information, on its face, to put the defendant on notice of the crime he or she is alleged to have committed, including dates, persons, locations, and other information that the defendant will need to prepare a defense. As we will see in the chapter on motions, a defendant can file a bill of particulars requesting additional information about the charges in the case. If the state fails to comply, then the judge is authorized to dismiss the indictment.

AFFIRMATIVE DEFENSES

As we have already seen, the state always has the burden of proving that the defendant is guilty beyond a reasonable doubt. A defendant enters a criminal trial with certain defenses already in place. He or she is not required to raise them at the trial. These are the legal or constitutional defenses that all defendants have and are often referred to as **simple defenses**. Among these simple defenses is the right to be considered not guilty until his or her guilt is proven beyond a reasonable doubt. With technical and constitutional defenses, the state must sustain its case by showing that the constitutional provisions were provided and that there were no irregularities. There is little or no burden on the defendant when it comes to offering these defenses. However, the same cannot be said of **affirmative defenses**. As the name suggests, the defendant must put forth some evidence or testimony to affirmatively state these defenses. Affirmative defenses require the defense to make a presentation at trial and produce enough evidence to warrant a serious consideration by the judge and jury. If a defendant wishes to raise the affirmative defense of alibi, for example, then the defendant must present testimony that he or she was somewhere else when the crime occurred. It is not enough for a defense attorney to simply state that the defendant was not present when the crime occurred. The defense attorney must present testimony, either from the defendant or someone else, to substantiate this defense to a preponderance of the evidence. Affirmative defenses do not require that the defendant take the stand, but someone must. An affirmative defense attempts to explain, refute, or excuse the defendant's criminal conduct. If the jurors believe the affirmative defense to a preponderance of the evidence, then they would be authorized to find the defendant not guilty of the charges.

Is a defendant required to prove his or her affirmative defense beyond a reasonable doubt? No. That burden is reserved for the state. But there must be some minimal level that a defendant must meet in order to qualify for the defense. In most jurisdictions it is preponderance of evidence. Preponderance of evidence is a burden of proof that requires a party to simply show that his or her version of facts is more

Simple defenses
Defenses that are automatically triggered when a defendant is charged with a crime. A defendant is not required to submit any evidence or testimony to raise a simple defense.

Affirmative defenses
Defenses that are something more than a mere denial and that require that the defense present evidence or testimony to prove, either by a preponderance of evidence or by clear and convincing evidence, that the defense is true.

likely to be true than not true. Chapter 1 examined preponderance as a standard of proof for civil cases. This is one of the few times that a civil standard of proof enters into a criminal case. Preponderance of evidence is a much lower standard than proof beyond a reasonable doubt, but it does serve as a high enough threshold to prevent the defense from simply stating a defense and providing no evidence to back it up. It should be noted that not all states follow the preponderance of evidence standard for defenses. In those jurisdictions, the standard is **clear and convincing evidence**. In those jurisdictions, defendants have a higher standard than preponderance of evidence and must establish that there is a high likelihood that the defense is true.

One of the more interesting aspects of an affirmative defense is that the defendant is often placed in the unenviable position of having to admit to committing the crime before claiming specific types of defenses. In the case of self-defense, age, or insanity, for example, the defendant must admit that he or she carried out the crime, but that the action was excused in some way. With other affirmative defenses, however, the defendant is not placed in that position. With alibi, a defendant raises the defense that he or she was somewhere else when the crime occurred and therefore could not have committed it.

Once an affirmative defense is presented, it is the duty of the prosecution to disprove the defense beyond a reasonable doubt. The burden in a criminal trial never shifts to the defendant to prove his or her innocence. Instead, the burden of proving the case beyond a reasonable doubt applies both to the state's case and to the defendant's affirmative defense.

In almost all jurisdictions, defendants are required to notify the state in writing when they intend to bring specific types of affirmative defenses such as alibi or insanity. This notice allows the state to prepare additional witnesses to rebut the defense. The idea behind the notification requirement is not limited to giving the state additional time to prepare to attack the defense. When the defendant places the state on notice of a specific type of defense, such as alibi, it also allows the state additional time to investigate the defense to determine if it is accurate. The theory is that if the state should confirm that the defendant's affirmative defense is correct, the state will be saved the expense of taking an innocent person to trial. In the real world, however, the defense presented is not necessarily clear or obvious. If the state received irrefutable evidence that the defendant's alibi was correct, then the state would be obligated to dismiss the case. However, such concrete evidence is not normally forthcoming from the defendant. Instead, the defense produces an *indication* that someone *might* be able to place the defendant at some other location at the approximate time when the crime occurred. This evidence is hardly conclusive.

Just as the state is required to present evidence on specific elements of criminal charges, defendants are obligated to present evidence or testimony to meet the specific elements of their defenses. However, the defendant's burden is never as great as the state's and it is usually left to the jury to determine how much weight and credence to give to the defendant's evidence. Of course, if the defendant fails to present any evidence to support the defense, then the judge can refuse to instruct the jury on the defense and they will not be able to consider it during their post-trial deliberations.

Clear and convincing evidence
The version presented by the party is highly probable to be true and is a higher standard than preponderance of the evidence.

There are a number of ways to present the various affirmative defenses. For the sake of clarity, they are listed here in alphabetical order. Among the affirmative defenses are:

- Age
- Alibi
- Battered Woman's Syndrome
- Coercion
- Consent
- Defending property
- Duress
- Entrapment
- Insanity
- Intoxication
- Mutual combat
- Necessity
- Self-Defense

A. AGE

One affirmative defense that a defendant can raise is age. When the defendant is below a specific age, the law presumes that he or she is incapable of forming *mens rea* and therefore cannot be guilty of a crime. In most jurisdictions, that age is seven or below. Society has made a decision that young children should not be treated in the same manner as adults and that children below a certain age cannot be guilty of crimes. That is not to say that the state cannot intercede. The juvenile justice system is specifically designed to operate in this situation, but the child will not be prosecuted in an adult court. For children between the ages of 7 and 14, the presumption is rebuttable, meaning that the prosecution can present evidence that a particular child could form *mens rea*. Over the age of 14, a child is presumed to be able to form *mens rea*. In some situations, a child between the age of 14 and 18 can be certified as an adult, usually only for purposes of prosecuting a major felony such as rape or murder, and can be tried in adult court.

B. ALIBI

Alibi
A defense that the defendant was not present when the crime occurred.

Complete defense
A defense that would completely exonerate the defendant of the crime charged, assuming the defendant presents sufficient evidence to meet his or her burden of proof (usually preponderance of the evidence).

Alibi is the defense that asserts that the defendant was not present when the crime occurred. Unlike many other affirmative defenses, alibi does not admit to the underlying crime and then seek to mitigate or excuse it. When a defendant raises the defense of alibi, the defendant is claiming that he or she was somewhere else when the crime occurred and therefore cannot be guilty. Alibi is a **complete defense**, meaning that if the defendant presents sufficient proof, the jury is required to reach a not guilty verdict.

C. BATTERED WOMAN SYNDROME

Battered woman syndrome is not recognized as a legitimate defense in all states, but in those where it is, it can be offered as an affirmative defense by a defendant who has committed an act of violence against a husband or intimate partner. Battered woman syndrome developed as a refinement of self-defense. In self-defense (discussed later in this chapter), a person may take violent action to protect himself. Battered woman syndrome takes this analysis one step further. The controversial aspect to battered woman syndrome is that unlike self-defense, where the person being attacked immediately acts violently to protect himself or herself, battered women syndrome allows a battered spouse or significant other to retaliate against repeated abuse at a time when the person is not actually being attacked. The most common example of battered woman syndrome is when a woman who has been repeatedly battered waits until her attacker falls asleep or is otherwise incapacitated and then attacks him, sometimes even killing him. Such an action would not be justified under traditional self-defense, where the response must be contemporaneous with the threat. Advocates of battered woman syndrome point out that it is only when the abuser is vulnerable that the victim can respond in some way to end the abuse. Just as with many affirmative defenses, a person who raises battered woman syndrome must first admit to the act and then seek to mitigate or excuse it because of the surrounding circumstances.

Battered woman syndrome
An affirmative defense that asks the jury to excuse a woman's attack on her supposed long-time abuser or asks the judge to mitigate her sentence in reflection of the fact that she was responding to a long period of abuse at the hands of the victim.

D. COERCION

Coercion is the use of intimidation, physical threats, or psychological pressure to force a person to commit a crime that he or she ordinarily would not commit. In coercion, if the defendant can show that he was physically threatened with violence unless he committed a crime, then a defense of coercion can be sustained. If proven, the jury is authorized to find that the defendant is not guilty because he or she was forced by someone else to commit the crime.

> ## Sidebar
>
> *In states that recognize battered woman's syndrome, a woman who can show that she was the subject of repeated beatings can be found not guilty for retaliating against her abuser, even though he was not a threat when she acted violently.*

Coercion
The direct threat of physical violence to make a person commit a crime that he or she would not ordinarily commit.

E. CONSENT

Consent is a defense that states that the victim agreed to the actions carried out by the defendant. In a case of assault and battery, for example, a defendant might claim that the victim acquiesced to the attack and even encouraged it. If the victim gives voluntary and knowing consent, it is a complete defense to some crimes. However, consent is not a defense to many crimes. A child molester, for example, cannot claim consent as a defense because children are legally barred from giving consent to sexual activity. Consent is also not available in murder convictions. A person cannot consent to being murdered. The most common use of the consent defense is in cases of rape and sexual battery, where the defendant claims that the victim agreed to the sexual contact.

Because consent requires a knowing and voluntary agreement, there are individuals who cannot consent to a crime for the simple reason that they are incapable of doing so. Mentally handicapped individuals and those who have been found to be legally incompetent cannot give valid consent.

Consent is also not a defense in a crime like statutory rape, where one partner is legally incapable of giving consent. Third parties cannot consent for others. A husband cannot give consent to another man to have sex with his wife. People do not have the authority to allow another person to be the victim of a crime. The law requires that consent must be given freely and voluntarily. Without such a showing, consent is not a valid defense

F. DEFENDING PROPERTY

A question that often arises in the context of theft cases is how far a theft victim can go to protect property. A person can take reasonable steps to prevent property from being stolen, but these actions cannot extend to deadly force. Violence, especially deadly force, is not permitted to protect property, only people.

G. DURESS

Duress
Unlawful psychological and mental pressure used on a person to force him or her to commit a crime that the person would ordinarily not commit.

A claim of **duress** is one in which the defendant claims that some other person used intimidation, psychological control, or other means short of outright threats to force a defendant to commit a crime. Unlike coercion where there is a direct correlation between the crime and the threat of physical violence to the defendant, duress operates more as subtle mental manipulation — even what some might term verbal and mental torture. Because of this, duress is often more difficult to prove than coercion. In coercion, a person physically threatens the well-being of another unless they commit a crime, but in duress, the defendant must show that another person used psychological pressure, torment, and manipulation to force him or her to carry out a crime. Because people respond differently to psychological pressure, the jurors are often left with a question as to whether or not the abuse alleged by the defendant was sufficient to cause a reasonable person to respond by committing a crime.

H. ENTRAPMENT

Entrapment
A defense that claims government agents induced a defendant to commit a crime when he or she was not predisposed to do so.

Entrapment is a defense in which the defendant claims that he was tricked or manipulated into committing a crime by the police. Unlike coercion or duress, entrapment can only be carried out by law enforcement officers. When a person is entrapped, he or she has been given both the idea for the crime and the means to carry it out by law enforcement or prosecutors. Essentially, the defendant is saying that the police made him do it. The idea behind making entrapment a valid defense is that we, as a society, do not want the police in the business of thinking up crimes and then encouraging others to carry them out. Because the government should not be in the business of creating crime, jurors are authorized to punish the government for doing so by finding the defendant not guilty.

Entrapment can be a confusing defense. Defendants often claim that they have been entrapped by undercover police officers, sometimes even providing defendants with drugs so that they can continue the illusion that the undercover officer is actually a fellow criminal. The question becomes when do the government's actions cross the line between acceptable police work and entrapment?

There are two ways of testing whether entrapment exists in a particular case. This involves answering two separate questions: 1) Did the idea for the crime originate with the police? 2) Did the police provide the defendant the means to carry the crime out? If the answer to both questions is yes, then there is a solid case for entrapment. If the answer to either question is no, then there is no case of entrapment.

As with all affirmative defenses, the prosecution must disprove entrapment beyond a reasonable doubt, assuming that the defendant has met the relatively low burden of presenting it. When a defense of entrapment is presented, the government must present rebuttal testimony refuting that the idea of the crime originated with the police or that the police provided the means to the defendant to consummate the crime. The most common way to rebut a defense of entrapment is to show that the defendant was already disposed to commit the crime, and the police simply provided the defendant with the opportunity to put his or her wish into action. Some states have a further requirement in order to disprove entrapment beyond a reasonable doubt: The state must prove that it did not overcome the defendant's free will and force him to carry out the crime.[2]

I. INSANITY

The **insanity** defense has been portrayed in movies, books, and television for decades and as a result, there are misconceptions concerning its use. Insanity is an affirmative defense and a defendant must admit to committing the underlying crime before claiming that he or she was legally insane at the time. The reason that the insanity defense can be confusing is that the legal standard to determine when a person is insane is not the same standard used by psychiatrists or medical professionals to make the same determination. At its core, the test for legal insanity is relatively simple: Did the defendant know the difference between right and wrong when he or she committed the crime? If the answer to that question is yes, then the defendant is legally sane, even though he or she may suffer from debilitating mental problems. A person can suffer from any number of different psychological problems, including schizophrenia and multiple-personality disorder and still not meet the legal test for insanity.

A defendant offers the insanity defense by presenting expert testimony during the defense case to show that the defendant did not know or understand the difference between right and wrong when he committed the crime. This requires either a psychiatrist or a psychologist to testify that at the time the defendant committed the crime he met the legal standard for insanity.

Insanity
A defense in which the defendant claims that at the time the crime was committed, he or she did not know the difference between right and wrong.

---

[2] *Quick v. State*, 660 N.E.2d 598 (1996).

There are many misconceptions about the defense of insanity. One common misconception is that people who have a mental illness will automatically be considered not guilty by reason of insanity. This is not true. No matter what form of mental illness the defendant may or may not have, the legal standard remains the same: Did the defendant understand the difference between right and wrong? Another common misconception about the defense of insanity is that if the defense is raised successfully, and a verdict of not guilty by reason of insanity is entered, the defendant is then released. This is also not true. If a defendant has been found not guilty by reason of insanity, the defendant is usually placed in a mental hospital for the criminally insane.

Like alibi, insanity is a complete defense and if the jury finds that the defendant is not guilty by reason of insanity, he or she is relieved of all criminal liability. The defendant is not guilty of the crime for the simple reason that when he or she committed it, the defendant lacked the ability to form *mens rea*. As seen in several contexts throughout this text, there are essentially two basic elements to all crimes: *mens rea* (intent) and *actus reus* (act). A person who cannot form *mens rea* cannot commit a crime.

The ancient Romans recognized that insanity was a valid defense. However, over time under the English and American legal systems, the pendulum has swung far in both directions, with occasional periods where the standard for the determination of insanity was quite liberal and others where it has been extremely difficult to prove. No discussion of the insanity defense would be complete without its most famous example: the M'Naghten case.

In 1843, M'Naghten attempted to kill Sir Robert Peel, the prime minister of England. Instead, he killed Peel's private secretary, a man named Edward Drummond. He was found not guilty by reason of insanity, and this controversial verdict started a national debate in both England and the United States over what the definition of legal insanity should be. The findings of a British court of inquiry into the case established the first conclusive test for legal insanity:

> To establish a defense on the ground of insanity, it must be clearly proved that, at the time of the committing of the act, the party accused was laboring [sic] under such a defect of reason, from disease of the mind, as not to know the nature and quality of the act he was doing; or, if he did know it, that he did not know he was doing what was wrong.[3]

Since M'Naghten there have been many modifications to the insanity defense. Various states have sought their own standards and the Model Penal Code has also weighed in on the issue.

MODERN DEFINITIONS OF INSANITY AFTER M'NAGHTEN

In most states, the modern definition of insanity is either the standard M'Naghten test or some variant on the definition shown in Figure 17-2.

---

[3] M'Naghten's Case, 10 Clark & Finnelly 200, 210, 8 Eng Rep 718, 722 (HL 1843).

A defendant is considered to be legally insane when:

- He or she cannot distinguish between right or wrong
- A person suffers from an irresistible impulse that precludes him or her from choosing between right and wrong
- His or her lawful act is the product of a mental disease or defect (Durham Test)

FAMOUS CASES
BELTWAY SNIPERS

On October 2, 2002 at 6:30 p.m., a 55-year-old program analyst at the National Oceanic and Atmospheric Administration was shot and killed in the parking lot of a grocery store in Glenmont-Wheaton, Maryland, north of Washington, D.C. The next day, five more people were shot and killed, all in locations either in or around the District of Columbia. In every case, a single bullet felled the victims. Fear spread quickly throughout the community. Schools locked down, refusing to allow students outside. Residents of the D.C. area began avoiding going anywhere in public for fear of being the next victim. There was no pattern to be found among the victims, no discernible reason for the killings.

During a three-week period, from October 2 until October 23, ten people were gunned down while engaging in the most mundane tasks: mowing the lawn, getting gas, shopping. Another three people were seriously injured, including a 13-year-old boy at a middle school. One victim, who was fatally shot outside a home improvement store, was an FBI intelligence analyst. Because all the shootings took place in the same general area, they were referred to as the Beltway shootings, in reference to the interstate highway that surrounds Washington D.C.

Maryland's Montgomery County Police Department led the investigation, with the FBI and other law enforcement agencies lending a hand. With the help of forensics, by the evening of October 4, the shootings had been linked, and investigators realized they were dealing with a spree killer. Eyewitness reports from the sites of the shootings were confusing. At one point police searched for a boxy white van; later they looked for a gray sedan. News about the shootings traveled quickly, and soon much of North America anxiously awaited either the next shooting or the apprehension of the sniper.

The sniper occasionally left cryptic messages at the scenes of the murders: Tarot cards with the words "Call me God" written on them, long handwritten notes, a $10 million ransom demand, and a message that read, "Your children are not safe, anywhere, at any time."

Publicly, the investigation seemed to be producing no results, but behind the scenes police were making progress. The shooter made a telephone call to police that was traced to a pay phone at a gas station. Although the police missed the suspect by a matter of minutes, during the phone call a reference was made to an unsolved murder at a liquor store in Montgomery, Alabama. A fingerprint from that murder scene matched one from the scene of one of the Beltway shootings. It was identified as belonging to Lee Boyd Malvo, a juvenile from Jamaica who had a record for shoplifting and for being in the country illegally.

As police looked more deeply into Malvo's background, they discovered that he was closely associated with John Allen Muhammad, a twice-divorced veteran of the Gulf War. Muhammad at one point had kidnapped his three children and taken them to Antigua. There he met Lee Boyd Malvo, and the two formed a close friendship. Back in the United States, the two lived together in a homeless shelter in Washington State for a while before setting out across the country.

Midway through the investigation, police learned that a dark blue 1990 Chevrolet Caprice had been checked by patrol cars near several of the shooting sites. Authorities issued a media release, alerting the public to be on the lookout for such a car. At 11:45 p.m. on October 24th, the car was spotted at a rest stop off Interstate 70 in Maryland. Within the hour, police had blocked off the rest stop so that there could be no escape. SWAT officers and agents from the FBI Hostage Rescue Team swarmed the car, found Muhammad and Malvo sleeping inside, and arrested them without incident. When they inspected the car, they found a hole had been cut out of the trunk near the license plate. It was, in effect, a mobile sniper's nest. While one drove, the other fired shots while safely hidden in the trunk. Also found was the gun responsible for all the shootings.

Muhammad and Malvo's motive for the shootings was never made clear, although Malvo, during his confession, said that they had planned to kill six people a day for a month in order to terrorize the nation. Muhammad was tried and convicted in a Virginia court in 2003 on four counts of capital murder and conspiracy. Upon the conclusion of that trial, he was extradited to Maryland, where he was convicted on six counts of murder. Following that trial, he was returned to Virginia, where he was executed by lethal injection on November 10, 2009.

Malvo pleaded not guilty to all charges against him by reason of insanity, claiming that he was under Muhammad's complete control. His Virginia trial concluded with a finding of guilty, and because he was a juvenile, he was spared the death penalty and sentenced instead to life in prison without parole.

A growing dissatisfaction with the plea of not guilty by reason of insanity brought about legislative initiatives in many jurisdictions that modified this defense. Some of these initiatives included creating new verdicts in criminal cases, such as guilty but mentally ill. When the jury returns this verdict, the defendant will be incarcerated in a regular prison facility but must have some access to psychiatric or psychological services and treatment.

DETERMINING THE MOMENT OF INSANITY

There are two points at which the defendant's sanity can become a factor in the trial. A defendant can be found legally insane at the time that he or she committed the crime or at the time of the trial. When a defendant claims that he or she is insane at the time of the trial — and not when the crime occurred — the defendant may raise the "special plea" of insanity at the time of the trial. Although these two defenses sound similar, in practice they are quite different. When a defendant pleads insanity at the time of the trial, he is alleging that he is not competent to understand the legal process and cannot assist in his defense. However, when a defendant raises the defense of insanity at the time that the crime was committed, the defendant is maintaining that he or she cannot be guilty of a crime. Defendants who claim that they are insane at the time of trial do not get the benefit of the insanity defense. The jury is not authorized to find them not guilty by reason of insanity, because they are not alleging that they were insane at the time that the crime was committed. A defendant who is not competent to stand trial may be remanded into a state facility until such time that he or she is able to stand trial. In many cases, a defendant may claim both forms: insanity at the time of the crime and insanity at the time of the trial. If it is proven that the defendant is incompetent to be tried, the court will wait and make further determinations in the future. If, at some time, the defendant is declared to be fit for trial, then the trial will proceed. The defendant can then raise any affirmative defense he or she wishes, including legal insanity.

RAISING THE INSANITY DEFENSE

The defendant who wishes to use the defense of insanity must serve notice on the state prior to trial that he or she plans to do so, usually a minimum of ten days prior to trial. This notice allows the state to bring in its own experts to evaluate the defendant and offer their own opinion about the state of the defendant's sanity at the time that the crime occurred. At the trial, the defense will present its own expert witnesses to testify that the defendant was not legally sane at the time that he or she committed the crime, and the state will then, in rebuttal, present evidence that the defendant was legally sane when the defendant committed the crime. In the end, it becomes a battle of the experts, and the jurors are left to decide which expert to believe. If they believe the defense expert, then they must find the defendant either not guilty by reason of insanity or, in the states that have this verdict alternative, guilty, but mentally ill.

Having said this, the insanity defense is rarely used and is even less likely to be successful. Part of this rests with the burden placed on the defense to present believable evidence that the defendant did not know the difference between right and wrong when the crime occurred. Any action that a defendant took to conceal the crime, dispose of evidence, or flee indicates that the defendant understood that what he or she did was wrong. Consider Scenario 17-3.

INSANITY?

Rob believes that the CIA has inserted a radio into his head and this radio instructs him to kill other people. One afternoon, he arms himself with a pistol and a rifle and goes to a local mall. He opens fire on several people, killing two. He then flees the scene and disposes of both weapons. Rob returns to his home, washes off any gunpowder that might be on his skin, and burns the clothes that he was wearing. When he is questioned later about his actions, he says that the radio in his head told him to take these actions. Does Rob meet the standard for legal insanity?

continued

Answer: Probably not. Although it is up to the jury to determine if Rob is insane, none of his actions indicate that he did not understand the difference between right and wrong. In fact, his actions clearly demonstrate that he knew his actions were wrong and that he was attempting to avoid being captured for carrying out the killings.

BURDEN OF PROOF FOR THE DEFENDANT WHEN RAISING THE INSANITY DEFENSE

As is true with many other affirmative defenses, the defendant who raises the defense of insanity must present enough evidence to establish by a preponderance of evidence that he or she is legally insane. In some jurisdictions the standard the defendant must meet is "clear and convincing" evidence of legal insanity. Once the defendant has presented this evidence, the prosecution must rebut the defendant's evidence. The government must show that the defendant was legally sane at the time of the crime.

DIMINISHED CAPACITY

Diminished capacity
Inability of the defendant to understand the actions that he or she took and why his or her actions constituted a crime.

The defense of **diminished capacity** is a form of insanity defense. Although it is not recognized in all jurisdictions, the defense of diminished capacity allows a defendant to offer testimony and evidence about his or her mental condition. This evidence is intended to mitigate or excuse the defendant's guilt in the crime. Often, diminished capacity defenses focus on the *mens rea* element of a crime. A defendant presents evidence of lower-than-normal IQ or slow mental development as a way to show the jury that he lacked the ability to form *mens rea*. In specific intent cases, such as murder, diminished capacity may be used as a defense to show that the defendant lacked the ability to form specific intent and therefore could not be guilty of first-degree murder.[4] The problem with diminished capacity defenses is defining exactly what diminished capacity is. For instance, courts have held that a defendant does not fall under the category of diminished capacity if he suffers from mood swings, feelings of insecurity, overwhelming fear of disease, or inability to care about others.[5]

J. INTOXICATION

Intoxication
When a person is acting under the influence of alcohol or other drugs to the extent that judgment and motor reflexes are impaired.

Voluntary **intoxication** is not a defense to most crimes. Permitting a defendant to avoid responsibility for a crime by getting drunk would not serve society's interests. However, there are times when voluntary intoxication does affect criminal liability. For example, voluntary intoxication might help reduce a crime from the most severe to a lesser-included offense. In the crime of murder in the first degree, for example, the state must prove that the defendant specifically intended to cause the

---

[4] *State v. Warden*, 133 Wash. 2d 559 (1997).
[5] *State v. Wilburn*, 249 Kan. 678, 822 P.2d 609 (1991).

death of another human being with malice and premeditation. A defendant who is intoxicated, even if this intoxication is the result of his or her own actions, may be unable to form specific intent or premeditation to murder. This does not mean that the defendant cannot be charged with murder; it simply means that it might reduce a charge of first-degree murder to second-degree murder. Except for this narrow exception, voluntary intoxication is not a defense to a crime and will neither lessen the defendant's culpability or the ultimate sentence.

However, there are situations where a form of intoxication can be a defense. Involuntary intoxication can be an affirmative defense. The defense of involuntary intoxication results when a person is overcome by fumes or chemicals to such an extent that he is no longer capable of rational thought. When the defendant is overcome with these substances, and has not voluntary submitted to the condition, he or she may not be criminally liable. Situations that bring about involuntary intoxication are rare and might include a worker in a factory where dangerous chemicals have been accidentally released or the defendant who has been unknowingly exposed to fumes or toxins.

K. MUTUAL COMBAT

The affirmative defense of **mutual combat** arises when the defendant and the victim agree to fight one another. Similar to consent, when a victim agrees to enter into a fight, he essentially surrenders his right to bring charges for battery against the other fighter. However, mutual combat has some strict limitations. If the defendant exceeds the understanding of what weapons will be used in the fight, or uses excessive force, then mutual combat as a defense may not be available. Consider Scenario 17-4.

Mutual combat
A defense that claims that the defendant and the victim voluntarily entered into a physical confrontation.

MUTUAL COMBAT?

Sisters Kim and Khloe are at a party and get into a disagreement. They begin shoving each other and Kim says, "Let's take it outside." Khloe agrees and they get into a fight next to their limousine in the parking lot. During the tussle, Kim pulls a knife and cuts her sister. The police are called and Kim is charged with aggravated battery. Will she have the defense of mutual combat?

Answer: No. Mutual combat assumes that both parties have the same weapons and defenses. There was nothing to indicate that either Kim or Khloe had a knife when they left the party to go the parking lot. When Kim pulled the knife, she went beyond the implied ground rules of the fight. As a matter of law, Kim is not allowed to raise the defense of mutual combat.[6]

---

[6] *Martin v. State*, 258 Ga. 300, 368 S.E.2d 515 (1988).

L. NECESSITY

Necessity
The defense that a defendant committed a crime in order to avoid an act of nature or of God.

The affirmative defense of **necessity** is similar to duress. When a defendant claims necessity, he admits that he committed the crime, but in this case, he did so in order to avoid some catastrophe or force of nature. A common example of necessity is when someone breaks into a cabin to avoid a blizzard. Normally, he would be guilty of trespass or criminal damages to property; however, the offense is excused by his need to stay alive. In this case, breaking into the cabin was the lesser of two evils: committing a crime or dying. In applying the defense of necessity, most jurisdictions require that the danger to the defendant outweigh the damage he does in committing the crime. A defendant could not use the defense of necessity in attempting to excuse a murder, for example, because all jurisdictions have held that no danger outweighs the value of another person's life. See Scenario 17-5.

SCENARIO 17-5

A CASE OF NECESSITY?

Kevin works at a jewelry store. One evening, he comes home to find that a man is threatening his girlfriend. The man demands money and Kevin says that he works at a store that has valuable jewelry. He drives to the store with the man and breaks in. He gives jewelry to the man. The man flees the scene. When the police arrive, they arrest Kevin for arrest. Is this a case of necessity?

Answer: No. Kevin probably has a valid defense, but it is not necessity. This defense is reserved for situations involving natural disasters or other acts of God. In this case, Kevin was responding to a threat by a man to injure or kill Kevin's girlfriend. Assuming that Kevin can make out a case for the existence of this man, he may have a valid defense of duress, but not necessity.

M. SELF-DEFENSE

Self-defense
The defense that the defendant injured or killed another, but only as a direct threat to the defendant's well-being.

Self-defense is, perhaps second only to insanity, the most misunderstood of defenses. Under the law, a person always has the right to defend himself or herself against a physical threat. However, there are severe limitations on this affirmative defense. In most situations, the response of the person raising the claim of self-defense must be comparable to the threat. This means that when someone is threatening the defendant with bare fists, the defendant is not permitted to retaliate with a weapon. The claim of self-defense seeks to excuse the defendant's actions by showing that they were necessary to keep the defendant alive. In order to use self-defense, the defendant must admit that he used force, but only for protection. When self-defense is raised, most jurisdictions require the jury to make a determination as to whether or not the defendant acted reasonably when he used force. If the jury finds that the defendant did not act reasonably, the jury could refuse to take self-defense into account.[7]

---

[7] *State v. Adams*, 52 Conn. App. 643, 727 A.2d 780 (1999).

What if the victim had a reputation for being a violent and aggressive person? Could the defendant present such evidence to prove that the he or she acted reasonably? Maybe. In most jurisdictions, if the defendant was aware of the victim's violent history, then it may be admissible. However, if the defendant did not know the victim's history, it probably would not be admissible. The reason for this discrepancy is simple. Self-defense has a great deal to do with what was in the defendant's mind at the time of the attack. If the defendant didn't know that the victim was a violent person, then he couldn't have based his actions on this fact.

DEFENDANT AS AGGRESSOR

A defendant cannot use the defense of self-defense when he or she is the person who started the fight. Aggressors are not permitted to raise the claim of self-defense when they attack a person and that person fights back. There are other times when a defendant cannot use self-defense. Individuals who are trained in the martial arts or are professional fighters or have advanced military training may be considered to use deadly force even when they respond with their bare hands. These individuals must be much more cautious before they engage in physical confrontations because their greater skill and training makes their hands and feet "deadly weapons" as far as self-defense is concerned.

DEFENSE OF OTHERS

Does self-defense apply to protecting other people? Under the common law, a person could only defend another person with whom he had a close, legally recognized relationship. Parents could defend children; husbands could defend wives. But in common law, a stranger could not use force to defend another stranger. That rule is no longer followed in most jurisdictions. Like self-defense, however, the other person must be faced with the immediate threat of bodily injury before the stranger acted to defend him. The threat must be one that a reasonable person would perceive as a threat.

"STAND YOUR GROUND" LAWS

Some recent cases have highlighted an interesting — and some would argue, dangerous — change in the law of self-defense. Traditionally, states followed the retreat doctrine. Under this doctrine, a person who is presented with violence, even deadly force, must retreat if he or she can reasonably do so. The reasons for the retreat doctrine are easy enough to understand: If a person can avoid being injured by a simple action, then he or she should. However, the doctrine has never required a person to retreat in all circumstances, only when it was reasonable to do so. If a person would put himself in greater jeopardy by retreating, then the doctrine did not apply. In recent years, some states have decided to repeal the retreat doctrine and replace it with "stand your ground" laws. Under these new laws, a person who is presented with violence, including deadly force, is not obligated to retreat, even when it is reasonable to do so. In these states, if a judge makes a determination that

the person was under a threat, and the person responds with deadly force to a perceived deadly force attack, the person is protected under the laws of self-defense.

REBUTTING A CLAIM OF SELF-DEFENSE

Like all affirmative defenses, the state has the burden of disproving one or more of the elements of the self-defense beyond a reasonable doubt. To do this, the state must present evidence in rebuttal showing that the defendant's actions were not justified, either because the defendant used excessive force or because the defendant was the aggressor, or because of some other reason.

N. OTHER DEFENSES

The variety of defenses presented in criminal cases is almost as varied as the crimes and the people who are charged with committing them. Over the years, defendants and defense attorneys have presented legions of unusual, even bizarre, defenses to crimes including defendants driven to violent actions by telephone shows or video games to imbibing certain drinks or foods that cause defendants to supposedly act in criminal ways. Among the more unusual and generally ineffective defenses are claims that antidepressant drugs caused the defendant to black out and commit murders.[8] Although these defenses are interesting to note and watch unfold, most of them are unsuccessful.

CASE EXCERPT

FOSTER v. STATE
283 Ga. 47, 50, 656 S.E.2d 838, 841) (Ga.,2008)

HUNSTEIN, Presiding Justice.

A jury found appellant Calvin Wayne Foster guilty of malice murder, felony murder, and possession of a firearm during the commission of a crime in connection with the shooting death of his estranged wife. The trial court denied Foster's motion for new trial and he appeals.

The crimes occurred on September 27, 2005. On December 20, 2005, Foster was indicted in Richmond County on charges of malice murder, felony murder with aggravated assault as the underlying felony, and possession of a firearm during the commission of the crime of felony murder. He was convicted on all counts and sentenced on November 21, 2006 to life imprisonment for murder and a five-year consecutive term for firearm possession. Foster's motion for new trial was filed on December 15, 2006, amended on June 12, 2007, and denied on July 9, 2007; his notice of appeal was timely filed. The appeal was docketed in this Court on August 3, 2007 and submitted for decision on the briefs.

---

[8] *State v. Clemons*, 82 Ohio St. 3d 438, 696 N.E.2d 1009 (1998).

1. On the morning of the shooting, Foster and the victim argued at Foster's home. The victim ran to a neighbor's house for help and was shot on the neighbor's front porch. Foster was seen driving away from his home soon thereafter. He called the victim's brother and confessed to the shooting, then called police and asked that they meet with him regarding the events of that morning. After Foster was located and taken into custody, he confessed.

At trial, Foster contended that he was temporarily insane at the time of the crimes. He offered the testimony of forensic psychologist James Stark, who opined on the stand that Foster likely had a "transitory psychotic episode" during the event in question and did not know the difference between right and wrong at the time. On cross-examination, Stark's July 2006 evaluation of Foster, in which he stated that Foster "probably knew the difference between right and wrong at the time of the shootings," was admitted into evidence. The State also offered rebuttal testimony from the forensic psychologist who conducted a court-ordered evaluation in September 2006 and found that Foster was able to determine right from wrong at the time of the crimes. Neither expert believed that Foster was acting on a delusional compulsion.

A person who is legally insane at the time of a crime, i.e., one who does not have the mental capacity to distinguish between right and wrong or who acts because of a delusional compulsion, is not guilty of that crime. OCGA § § 16-3-2, 16-3-3. A defendant claiming insanity has the burden of proving this affirmative defense by a preponderance of the evidence; unless the evidence of insanity is overwhelming, a jury determination that the defendant was sane at the time of the crime will be upheld. *Whitner v. State*, 276 Ga. 742(6), 584 S.E.2d 247 (2003). Here, the evidence regarding Foster's mental state at the time of the crimes was conflicting and the jury was authorized to find that Foster failed to prove his insanity by a preponderance of the evidence. In addition, the evidence was sufficient for a rational trier of fact to find Foster guilty beyond a reasonable doubt of the crimes charged. *Jackson v. Virginia*, 443 U.S. 307, 99 S.Ct. 2781, 61 L.Ed.2d 560 (1979).

2. Foster claims that the trial court erred by failing to fully charge the jury on his defense of insanity. The trial court gave a pattern charge based on OCGA § 17-7-131, which instructed the jury to determine whether Foster was: (1) not guilty; (2) not guilty by reason of insanity; (3) guilty beyond a reasonable doubt; (4) guilty but mentally ill; or (5) guilty but mentally retarded. See id. at (b)(1), (c). This charge also instructed the jury that because the law makes a distinction between being insane at the time of the crime and being mentally ill or mentally retarded, an understanding of these terms is necessary. Although the trial court proceeded to give the pattern jury instruction that defines insanity as the inability to distinguish between right and wrong at the time of the act, it failed to define the terms "mentally ill" and "mentally retarded." And although it advised the jury that if it found Foster not guilty by reason of insanity at the time of the crime he would be committed to a state mental health facility, see OCGA § 17-7-131(b)(3)(A), it failed to advise the jury of the consequences of a verdict of guilty but mentally ill or guilty but mentally retarded, i.e., that Foster would be incarcerated. See OCGA § 17-7-131(b)(3)(B), (C).

When a defense of insanity has been interposed, OCGA § 17-7-131(c) requires that the jury be instructed to consider all five verdict options set forth therein. FN2 The failure to charge on all five options is harmless error if there is no evidence to support the verdict option or options omitted. Here, however, Foster's expert did provide some evidence that was relevant to the issues of mental illness and mental retardation, i.e., that Foster suffered from depression and anxiety, that he appeared to have learning disabilities, and that he had a mental age of approximately 14 years. Thus, the trial court did not err in giving the jury all five verdict options.

> OCGA § 17-7-131(c) provides:
>
> In all criminal trials in any of the courts of this state wherein an accused shall contend that he was insane or otherwise mentally incompetent under the law at the time the act or acts charged against him were committed, the trial judge shall instruct the jury that they may consider, in addition to verdicts of "guilty" and "not guilty," the additional verdicts of "not guilty by reason of insanity at the time of the crime," "guilty but mentally ill at the time of the crime," and "guilty but mentally retarded."

Whether the evidence was sufficient to establish that Foster was mentally ill or mentally retarded was for the jury to decide. OCGA § 17-7-131(c)(2), (3). Without the statutory definitions of mental illness and mental retardation, however, the jury was unable to make this assessment and thus to give proper consideration to the potential verdicts of guilty but mentally ill or guilty but mentally retarded. Compare *McDuffie v. State*, 210 Ga.App. 112(1), 435 S.E.2d 452 (1993) (failure to charge on definition of or criteria for returning alternative verdicts harmless because no evidence to support such verdicts). Moreover, the failure to advise the jury of the consequences of rendering either of these verdicts in accordance with OCGA § 17-7-131(b)(3)(B) and (C) is presumptively harmful. *Spraggins v. State*, 258 Ga. 32(2), (3), 364 S.E.2d 861 (1988) (decided under previous version of OCGA § 17-7-131(b)(3)). The State has not shown that the jury's lack of knowledge that Foster would be incarcerated following a verdict of guilty but mentally ill or guilty but mentally retarded did not contribute to its verdict of guilty. See id. at (3).

> "Mentally ill" means having a disorder of thought or mood that significantly impairs judgment, behavior, capacity to recognize reality, or ability to cope with the ordinary demands of life. OCGA § 17-7-131(a)(2).
>
> "Mentally retarded" means having significantly subaverage general intellectual functioning resulting in or associated with impairments in adaptive behavior that manifested during the developmental period. OCGA § 17-7-131(a)(3).
>
> OCGA § 17-7-131(b)(3) provides in pertinent part:
>
> In all cases in which the defense of insanity is interposed, the trial judge shall charge the jury, in addition to other appropriate charges, the following: . . .
>
> (B) I charge you that should you find the defendant guilty but mentally ill at the time of the crime, the defendant will be placed in the custody of the Department of Corrections which will have responsibility for the evaluation and treatment of the mental health needs of the defendant, which may include, at the discretion of the Department of Corrections, referral for temporary hospitalization at a facility operated by the Department of Human Resources.
>
> (C) I charge you that should you find the defendant guilty but mentally retarded, the defendant will be placed in the custody of the Department of Corrections, which

will have responsibility for the evaluation and treatment of the mental health needs of the defendant, which may include, at the discretion of the Department of Corrections, referral for temporary hospitalization at a facility operated by the Department of Human Resources.

A trial court's instructions, considered as a whole, must not mislead or confuse the jury. *Laster v. State*, 276 Ga. 645(5), 581 S.E.2d 522 (2003). Here, the jury was required to understand the legal distinctions between insanity, mental illness, and mental retardation, but never given the guidance necessary to reach such an understanding. Because we cannot conclude that the jury was not misled or confused under these circumstances and because the instructions given failed to comply with statutory directives, Foster's conviction must be reversed.

Judgment reversed.

All the Justices concur.

CASE QUESTIONS

1 What crimes are alleged in this case?
2 What was the defense offered at trial?
3 What burden of proof does a defendant have when bringing a defense of insanity?
4 When the defense of insanity is brought, there are actually five possible verdicts allowed in this state. What are they?
5 Why was this case reversed on appeal?

CHAPTER SUMMARY

Defendants have a wide variety of defenses available to them. A defendant is not required to present any evidence to support a simple defense. These types of defenses are available to all defendants and include the presumption of innocence and various constitutional defenses. However, if the defendant decides to present an affirmative defense, he or she must present evidence to support the claim. Affirmative defenses include alibi, consent, coercion, duress, and insanity, to name just a few. When a defendant raises the defense of alibi or insanity, he or she must give notice to the state of the intent to do so. Insanity is one of the more controversial defenses and requires that the defendant establish, by a preponderance of the evidence, that he or she did not know the difference between right and wrong when the crime was committed. A defendant must present expert testimony to this effect and the state must rebut this evidence with its own expert testimony showing that the defendant understood the difference between right and wrong. Ultimately, the question of the defendant's sanity, like all affirmative defenses, rests with the jury.

KEY TERMS

Double jeopardy	Statute of limitations	Affirmative defenses
Self-incrimination	*Allegata*	Clear and convincing
Due process	*Probata*	evidence
Ex post facto	Simple defenses	

REVIEW QUESTIONS

1. What is the defense of double jeopardy?
2. What U.S. Constitutional Amendment provides that a person cannot be compelled to testify against himself?
3. When does double jeopardy "attach"?
4. What is the due process clause?
5. Explain the equal protection provision of the Fourteenth Amendment.
6. Explain a situation where a statute would be considered void for vagueness?
7. What is an *ex post facto* law?
8. Why do statutes of limitation exist?
9. What is the statute of limitations for murder?
10. Explain the difference between *allegata* and *probata*?
11. Describe simple defenses as compared to affirmative defenses.
12. What standard of proof must a defendant meet in presenting an affirmative defense?
13. What is "clear and convincing evidence" and how does it differ from "preponderance of the evidence"?
14. Explain the defense of alibi.
15. What is battered woman syndrome?
16. What is the difference between coercion and duress?
17. When can a person's age be considered a defense?
18. Define "complete defense."
19. Can a victim consent to murder? Why or why not?
20. Is it possible to use deadly force to protect property? Explain.
21. What are "stand your ground" laws?
22. List and explain the two elements of entrapment.
23. What is the legal test for insanity?
24. How does a defendant raise the defense of insanity?
25. What is the "Durham" test as it applies to the defense of insanity?

QUESTIONS FOR ANALYSIS

1   Should the insanity defense be modified or even eliminated? Why or why not?

2   This chapter has listed numerous defenses. Should the defenses available to a criminal defendant be limited or expanded? Justify your answer.

HYPOTHETICALS

1   Danny has an overwhelming fear of reptiles. As he is driving home one night, he sees a large alligator in the road. Danny is particularly afraid of alligators. He sees a car coming in the opposite direction and is faced with a choice: He can run over the alligator or enter the oncoming lane and hit the approaching car. He chooses to hit the car, killing the driver. At trial for vehicular manslaughter, Danny claims necessity. You are a juror on the case. How do you vote?

2   Troy enters a department store and a strange man begins following him around. The man continually stares at Troy, making Troy feel very uncomfortable. As Troy approaches the register to pay for his belongings, the man steps forward and Troy punches him. At trial, Troy claims self-defense. Has Troy met his burden for this defense?

3   The law recognizes that children under a certain age cannot be guilty of a crime because they cannot form *mens rea*. Charlie is 95 years old and commits a shoplifting. He claims that he should also be allowed to use the defense of age because he cannot form *mens rea* because of his age. Is he right? Why or why not?

Arraignment and Discovery

 ARRAIGNMENT

When a defendant has been indicted by the grand jury in a felony case, the next important procedural step is the **arraignment**. In some jurisdictions, initial appearances and arraignments are held at the same time (usually when a person is charged with a misdemeanor), but for our purposes, we will continue our discussion for the procedures followed in felony cases. The arraignment is normally scheduled several weeks after a true bill of indictment has been returned by the grand jury. In some jurisdictions, a defendant can be arraigned the day of the trial, but most follow a pattern that sets the arraignment several weeks before the next scheduled trial date. At the arraignment, the defendant is told exactly what the charges are against him and is given an opportunity to plead either guilty or not guilty. If the defendant has hired his or her own attorney, the attorney will respond for the defendant. Many defendants appear at the arraignment without an attorney and request that the judge appoint one for them. The court is authorized to appoint an attorney when the defendant's financial status indicates that the defendant is not able to afford one.

The arraignment is important for several reasons. At the arraignment, the defendant and his attorney are given a copy of the formal charges pending against the defendant; in felony cases the formal charge is embodied in the indictment. Traditionally, the indictment and the state's list of witnesses were the only items that the state was required to serve on the defendant at the arraignment. However,

Arraignment
A court hearing where the defendant is informed of the charge against him or her and given the opportunity to enter a plea of guilty or not guilty.

the traditional rules have been changed, and the state is not only often required to present additional discovery materials to the defendant, but also must do so at the arraignment.

A. PURPOSE OF THE ARRAIGNMENT

Calendar or docket
A listing of the cases currently pending before the court, usually by the defendants' names, case file number, and charges brought against them.

The procedure followed at an arraignment is simple. A list of cases, called a **calendar** or **docket**, is published. This docket contains the names of all the defendants who will be called on a particular day's arraignment calendar. The cases are normally announced according to their case file number or sometimes in alphabetical order based on the defendant's last name. "Calling" the calendar refers to the process of simply calling out the names of the defendants. This case file number or docket number has been assigned by the clerk's office after the grand jury returned a true bill of indictment. Defendants are instructed that they must respond when their names are called. Failure to appear for the scheduled arraignment can have severe consequences for the defendant, which will be discussed later in this chapter.

At the arraignment, once the defendant's case has been called, the defendant is brought before a judge and officially informed of the charges pending against him or her. This hearing might seem redundant, but for important reasons it is not. The defendant has already been arrested, so why does he or she need to be informed of the charges? The simple answer is that the prosecutor may have amended those charges during the prosecutor's charging decision. The arraignment is the point during the case when the defendant receives the final word about the pending charges. The defendant is given a copy of the indictment (for felonies) or an accusation (for state-level misdemeanors). The judge will also use the arraignment as an additional opportunity to inform the defendant of his or her rights and to inquire whether or not the defendant has an attorney. If the defendant cannot afford an attorney, the judge may appoint one or have the public defender review the defendant's status to see if he or she qualifies for their services. In some jurisdictions, the judge also informs the defendant of the maximum sentence possible for each of the charges pending against him or her.

The defendant is required to enter a plea at the arraignment. If the defendant pleads not guilty, he or she will be scheduled to return at a later time for a trial. If the defendant chooses to plead guilty, the judge may impose a sentence that day or defer sentencing for a later date.

B. FILING MOTIONS AT ARRAIGNMENT

In the past, the arraignment procedure had greater significance than it has today. For instance, it was common for defendants to request *formal arraignment*. A formal arraignment consists of either the judge or the prosecutor reading the entire indictment, out loud, before the defendant and the others present in the courtroom. The defendant would then have the opportunity of challenging the sufficiency of the indictment. However, modern practice has tended away from formal arraignment to a more informal procedure where the defense counsel expressly waives formal arraignment, requests a copy of the indictment and discovery and reserves the right to file an additional **motion**, including those challenging the sufficiency of the indictment at a later time. The defendant may also reserve the right to file additional motions after going through the indictment and whatever discovery the state may have served on him or her at the arraignment.

Motion
An oral or written request to a court to take some action.

C. WAIVING ARRAIGNMENT

A defendant is always free to waive both formal and informal arraignment through his or her counsel or by filing a written notice waiving arraignment and filing motions about specific issues in the case.[1] As noted, formal arraignment refers to the prosecutor or the judge actually reading the indictment aloud in court. This practice dates back for centuries and was probably instituted in a time when most people could not read. These days, it is common for a defense attorney to announce that the defendant waives formal arraignment (or the full reading of the indictment) and agree to proceed with an informal arraignment.

D. BENCH WARRANTS

When a defendant has been officially notified of his arraignment date and fails to appear, the judge is empowered to issue a **bench warrant** for his arrest. When a defendant makes bond after his arrest, one of the notifications he receives is the date of his arraignment. The jail personnel usually give this notification to him. However, the prosecutor's office may also send him a certified letter, informing him of his arraignment date, along with a letter informing the defendant of the consequences should he fail to appear. Consider Scenario 18-1.

Bench warrant
A warrant issued for the arrest of a person who was scheduled to appear in court but failed to do so.

BENCH WARRANT

SCENARIO 18-1

Allen was given a notice for his arraignment when he bonded out of jail. However, in the meantime, he has done some of his own research into the law and has decided that his arrest was unconstitutional. He sends the judge a letter disputing his arrest and stating that he cannot be compelled to appear for trial because this arrest was clearly the result of illegal tactics used by the police. Furthermore, he asserts that by appearing before the court, he will waive these important constitutional rights and therefore asks the court to enter a not guilty verdict on his behalf. What is the court likely to do in this situation?

Answer: The court will issue a bench warrant for Allen's arrest. Despite his claims, Allen had a clear directive from the court for a specific day and time to appear and even though he claims that his appearance will waive some kind of defense that he has, Allen must abide by the court's order.

---

[1] *Shivers v. State*, 188 Ga. App. 21, 372 S.E.2d 2 (1988).

In the past, a defendant was always required to be physically present for an arraignment, but some jurisdictions have softened this requirement, either by allowing an attorney to appear on behalf of the defendant or by conducting arraignments through closed-circuit television.[2] Defendants may not actually be in the courtroom during a video arraignment. Instead, they may be several miles away at the local jail, and they "appear" in court by stepping before a camera and answering the judge's questions.

If a defendant fails to appear for an arraignment at all, the judge is authorized to issue a bench warrant for the defendant's arrest. A bench warrant permits any law enforcement officer to arrest the defendant and place him in custody pending a new court date. The defendant's bond is revoked, and if a bonding company posted bail for the defendant, the bond amount is forfeited to the state. Many states allow a grace period after arraignment for a bonding company to locate and surrender the defendant to the authorities without forfeiting the entire bond amount. Although the amount of time varies, 72 hours is common. During that time, if the bonding company can locate the defendant, they can save themselves the entire bond amount, which gives them a strong interest in locating the defendant.

FAMOUS CASES
UNABOMBER

For a period spanning 17 years, from 1978 to 1995, Theodore John "Ted" Kaczynski sent packages containing homemade bombs to various universities, airlines, and computer stores. Lacking a suspect, the FBI coined an acronym to identify the then-unknown Kaczynski during the investigation: UNABOM, for **UN**iversities, **A**irlines, and **BOM**bings, inspiring the media to dub him the Unabomber. During his crime spree, the Unabomber's 16 bombs killed three people and injured 23.

Kaczynski, born May 22, 1942, was considered an intellectual prodigy. At the age of 16 he was awarded a scholarship to study mathematics at Harvard University. He later earned a PhD from the University of Michigan and by the age of 25 had secured a prestigious teaching position at the University of California, Berkeley. Kaczynski, however, lacked social skills and suffered from emotional problems. He abruptly resigned from Berkeley after two years and moved to a small, remote cabin in Montana. There he learned survival skills and strove to become self-sufficient.

Living in the wilderness, Kaczynski evolved into a radical environmentalist and opponent of technology. He tried to publish several academic papers on his pet subjects, and the theory is that the rejection of his work led to his first bombing. A package delivered to Northwestern University in Chicago in 1978 exploded when a security guard opened it, seriously injuring him. The following year, he sent another bomb to the Technological Institute at Northwestern, which injured a student who opened it. In that same year, one of his

---

[2] *State v. Phillips*, 74 Ohio St. 3d 72, 1995-Ohio-171, 656 N.E.2d 643 (1995).

bombs exploded in the baggage hold of an American Airlines flight, causing smoke-inhalation injuries to a dozen passengers. In the years that followed, Kaczynski sent bombs to numerous university professors and airline executives, injuring all those who opened the packages.

The first death resulted from a bomb sent to a computer store in Sacramento, California. The owner, Hugh Scrutton, spotted a block of wood with nails protruding from it in the parking lot of the store. Probably thinking that it was the sort of thing that could damage tires, Scrutton bent to retrieve it and toss it in the trash bin. As soon as he disturbed the block of wood, it exploded, blowing off his hand and sending shrapnel throughout his body, killing him almost instantly.

Two years later, in 1987, a woman spotted a man wearing aviator glasses and a hoodie sweatshirt placing what turned out to be a bomb outside another computer store in Salt Lake City. The FBI finally had a witness, and a composite drawing was released and widely publicized. Fearing capture, Kaczynski pulled back from his reign of terror for six years. Nevertheless, he picked up his activities once again, in 1993, sending mail bombs to a University of California geneticist and a Yale computer science professor, seriously injuring both.

In 1994, Kaczynski mailed a bomb to an advertising executive in New Jersey, killing him. Kaczynski mistakenly thought the man had orchestrated the public relations campaign for Exxon following the *Exxon Valdez* oil spill. His final attack occurred in April 1995, when a bomb killed the president of a timber-industry lobbying group.

That same year, Kaczynski sent a lengthy manifesto to the *New York Times* and the *Washington Post*, a 35,000-word document detailing what he perceived as serious problems with an industrial-technological system. Kaczynski promised that if the manuscript was published verbatim, he would cease the bombings. The FBI persuaded the *Washington Post* to publish it, hoping that someone would read it and be able to offer clues about its author. Sure enough, Kaczynski's younger brother, David, read it and recognized his brother's ideas and language patterns. David Kaczynski informed the FBI in early 1996 that he suspected his brother might be the Unabomber. On April 3, Kaczynski was arrested at his Montana cabin, and extensive evidence was also recovered — including bomb-making materials and a copy of the manifesto. He was charged with three counts of murder and ten counts of illegally transporting, mailing, and using bombs.

For the next year and a half, Kaczynski fought with his defense lawyers, who wanted to mount an insanity defense to try to save his life. Kaczynski, however, maintained that he had a defensible case on the basis of his legitimate political motives and philosophy. In January 1998, the judge rejected Kaczynski's request to dismiss his defense team and represent himself. Consequently, he pleaded guilty to all charges on January 22 and was sentenced to four life terms plus 30 years.

The FBI used more than 500 investigative agents over the span of the 17 years it took to track down Kaczynski. His 10x12-foot Montana cabin was transported to a storage facility outside of Sacramento. It ultimately became part of an exhibit about the FBI at the Newseum, in Washington D.C.

DISCOVERY

Discovery refers to the process through which both sides in a case exchange information. In civil cases, the rules of discovery are quite liberal and the parties exchange a great deal of information. Both the civil plaintiff and defendant know the identities of each side's witnesses, what documents will be relied upon, and what evidence will be presented. In addition to this wealth of information, civil litigants can also depose witnesses. In a civil deposition, the attorneys are allowed to question witnesses prior to trial, under oath, and to have this testimony recorded or transcribed. Later, at the trial, the attorneys may rely on transcripts of these depositions when questioning the witness.

This extensive exchange of information is not mirrored in criminal cases. Traditionally, very little discovery was allowed in criminal cases. Trials were conducted in the past by surprise and ambush. Where a civil litigant will know virtually every aspect of the case before the trial ever starts, a modern-day prosecutor may not know who the defense is going to call as a witness or even what the defense to the crime may be until the defense attorney gives his or her opening statement. Modern changes to criminal discovery rules have attempted to change this age-old pattern.

Under the traditional criminal law system, where pretrial discovery procedures common to civil cases were not permitted in criminal trials, both the prosecutor and the defense attorney often began a trial with no clear idea of what the other side's witnesses would say. No doubt it made for an exciting trial, but it was not the most efficient use of court time. In many states, this traditional approach to discovery still exists.

The trial by "surprise" aspect of criminal cases has been modified in recent years with some changes in discovery rules that force the prosecutor to give the defendant far more information than the prosecutor was ever required to provide in the past. But these changes in discovery rules also now put some burden on the defense to produce information for the prosecutor. In the past, except in rare circumstances, this was unheard of. Historically, the defendant was not required to provide any discovery to prosecutors, and only in cases of insanity or alibi were they even required to tell the prosecution what the defense would be.

Under traditional rules of discovery, the state had to produce certain items for the defendant, but there was no requirement for the defendant to produce anything. The result of this limited discovery was that a prosecutor often began a trial with no clear idea of what the defense would be, who the defense witnesses would be, what they would say or what evidence the defense would seek to admit. The information that the state provided to the defense attorney was little better. The defense attorney would know the names of the state's witnesses but would not know what these witnesses would say.

A. PURPOSE OF DISCOVERY

The purpose of discovery in criminal cases is similar to that in civil cases: to provide information to the opposing side that will ensure better and more efficient use of court time. The more the parties know about the facts of the case before they come to trial, the less time they will need during the trial for discovery of important information. However, there has always been an enormous difference between discovery in civil cases and discovery in criminal cases. Part of this has to do with the nature of a criminal case itself, but the rules of discovery are different in criminal cases for other reasons. Even though there was very little statutory guidance about what a prosecutor should produce for the defense, there were at least two guiding principles that compelled prosecutors to act, even in the absence of statutes mandating certain actions. These two principles are a prosecutor's ethics and U.S. Supreme Court cases.

A prosecutor is not merely an advocate for a client. Prosecutors have moral and ethical duties to seek justice, not simply to convict as many people as possible. Some courts have stated that a prosecutor has a moral, if not a legal, obligation to produce evidence for the defendant prior to trial to allow the defendant to present an adequate defense. This often placed the prosecutor in the position of having to decide how much evidence to give to the defense to make sure that the prosecutor has met his or her obligation. It is the prosecutor's duty to ensure that full discovery, at least to the extent required by statute, is met. Courts have held, time and again, that the prosecutor's duty is to seek justice, not to guarantee convictions. See Scenario 18-2. Faced with this dilemma, most prosecutors decided, and continue to do so, to give more rather than less information in the discovery process. Some prosecutors even realize that by providing more information than is actually required by statute, they may convince the defense that it would be better to plead guilty than face trial, given the sheer volume of evidence against the defendant.

EVIDENCE HELD BY THE PROSECUTION

SCENARIO 18-2

Maria is a prosecutor in a state that has minimal requirements in criminal discovery. She discovers evidence that clearly indicates that the defendant was not present when the crime occurred. Is she obligated to give this evidence to the defense?

Answer: Absolutely yes. Setting aside whether or not the evidence comes under the definition of material that must be provided under *Brady v. Maryland*, (discussed later), Maria is a prosecutor and she has legal and ethical duties to ensure that a miscarriage of justice does not occur.

The prosecutor has both legal and ethical obligations to ensure a fair trial and cannot pick and choose among the evidence that he or she will provide to the defendant in order to make sure that the prosecutor secures a guilty verdict.[3] Balanced against that ethical and legal responsibility is the concept that there is no general right to discovery in criminal cases at all.[4] There is considerable variation among states about how much information the defendant should be provided with prior to trial. Some Supreme Court cases have preempted state law and require the

Sidebar

The prosecutor should always err on the side of giving the defense too much information, rather than too little.[5]

---

[3] *U.S. v. Consolidated Laundries Corp.*, 291 F.2d 563 (2d Cir. 1961); *State v. Spano*, 69 N.J. 231, 353 A.2d 97 (1976); *State v. Reiman*, 284 N.W.2d 860 (S.D. 1979).
[4] *Weatherford v. Bursey*, 429 U.S. 545, 97 S. Ct. 837, 51 L. Ed. 2d 30 (1977).
[5] *State v. Reiman*, 284 N.W.2d 860 (S.D. 1979).

state to produce certain types of information whether they are required by state law or not. The famous *Brady* case is a perfect example, and we will address that case in depth later in this chapter.

B. MATERIAL PROVIDED IN DISCOVERY

Although many states have modified their criminal discovery rules in recent years, this is certainly not true in all states. In states that have not changed their discovery rules, a defendant must request discovery before he will receive most items from the prosecution. In such states, if the defendant fails to file discovery motions, then the prosecution is under no obligation to give him anything, except for *Brady* material, which will be discussed later in this chapter.

C. CHANGES TO DISCOVERY RULES

Many states have recognized the discrepancy between civil and criminal discovery and have made changes in their criminal discovery statutes. For instance, many states have amended their rules about what information a prosecutor must serve on a defendant. These statutes were amended to protect defendants from the consequences of unfair surprise at trial and to assist them in locating evidence that they could offer in their defense.

These new discovery statutes are designed to encourage voluntary disclosures of information like the information exchange that takes place in civil cases every day. These statutes also give the court the power to compel either side to disclose relevant facts to the other side. The judge may order such disclosure prior to trial. Many of these new changes require the state to turn over far greater portions of its prosecution and police files to the defendant than was ever required before. This means that the state is now compelled to give the defendant copies of witness statements, police reports, and many other items traditionally withheld by the state.

Among the changes to the discovery rules is the requirement that the defense provide some information to the state. Traditionally, discovery in criminal cases was almost always one-way. In some very limited circumstances, discussed below, a criminal defendant might have to provide some minimal information to the state, but in most situations, the criminal defendant was not compelled to provide any discovery whatsoever. That rule changed under the new discovery statutes.

A criminal defendant does not have to produce the same amount of material, nor to such an extent as the state, but requiring the defendant to produce any information at all is a novelty in criminal law. Here is a sample of the kind of information a defendant must produce prior to trial:

- Specifics about alibi or other legal defenses, especially insanity defense
- List of defense witnesses, known addresses, and telephone numbers

In redrafting their criminal discovery statutes, many states have followed the model set out in the federal rules of criminal procedure.

When the defendant makes a discovery request under the new rules, the state normally produces the following kinds of information:

- Witness list
- Statement of defendant (both written and oral)
- Statement of a codefendant
- Defendant's criminal record
- Documents and tangible objects (books, papers, documents, photographs, motion pictures, mechanical or electronic recordings, buildings, and places or any other crime scene, etc.)
- Scientific reports
- Statements of witnesses

WITNESS LIST

State and federal prosecutors are required to give the defendant a list of the witnesses that the government intends to call during the trial. This list consists of not only the names of each witness but also their addresses and phone numbers (if known). Witnesses are often troubled by the fact that the defendant will know his or her complete name, residence, and telephone number. This would seem to ensure that the defendant will take retribution against the witness, especially now that he or she knows exactly where to find the people who will testify in the case. Although witnesses have been harassed and even murdered prior to trial, in most cases the defendant does not contact the witnesses or try to intimidate them. Defense attorneys will certainly attempt to contact these witnesses to find out their version of the facts, but it is rare for a defendant to attempt to do so. Witnesses are under no compulsion to actually speak with the defense attorney prior to trial.

STATEMENT OF DEFENDANT

If the police have questioned the defendant, then the written statement they made of that interrogation must be provided to the defense. One might wonder, because the defendant was present when he made his statement, why he would need a copy of it. The answer is that it is really for the defendant's attorney. One of the defense attorney's obligations is to review police actions to make sure that the defendant was not coerced, promised, or threatened into giving a confession. If a video or audio recording of the interrogation was made, then the defense gets a copy of that, too.

STATEMENT OF CODEFENDANT

The rule about providing defendant's statements to the defense team also applies to statements by codefendants. It is important to note that the prosecution may not be able to admit the statement of codefendant A in the trial of codefendant B.[6] The statement by codefendant B might unfairly prejudice defendant A's case, so a court might rule that the state cannot use it.

DEFENDANT'S CRIMINAL RECORD

In the past, the defendant's own criminal record was not provided to the defense attorney. However, that rule has changed in many jurisdictions. It is now common for a state's discovery package to contain the defendant's statement, any statements by codefendants, and a complete breakdown of the defendant's criminal record. This information may help the defense to do a better job in advising his or her client, especially if the client has not been forthcoming with information. Providing the criminal history also factors into the state's decision to file a similar transactions motion, which will be discussed later.

DOCUMENTS AND TANGIBLE OBJECTS

In addition to receiving a copy of the defendant's statement and his or her criminal history, the defense also has the right to see and inspect the state's evidence prior to trial. This includes weapons, documents, photographs, even scenes of the crime, depending on the nature of the case. The defense can inspect any piece of evidence before the trial occurs. If the state attempts to bar the defense from visiting a scene or viewing evidence, the defendant can file a motion requesting the court give the defense team permission to do so. The defense also has the right to request independent testing of certain items, including blood samples, DNA, and other scientific evidence.

SCIENTIFIC REPORTS

All states require the prosecution to give the defendant copies of any and all scientific reports prepared by prosecution witnesses. These scientific reports must be produced at least ten days prior to trial in most jurisdictions. This ten-day rule allows the defense time to hire its own experts to review the tests and also to request permission to conduct tests on physical evidence. In an era where shows like *CSI* dominate nightly television schedules, it is surprising to note that in many cases there are no scientific reports to turn over at all. In many cases, there are no scientific tests even conducted. Crime scene technicians may be unable to lift fingerprints from various objects, and there is no other evidence to test. In that situation, there is no scientific report to pass along to the defendant. However, it must also be said that in high-profile cases, usually murder cases, law enforcement often pulls out every tool in their arsenal, and they conduct DNA tests, carpet-fiber analysis, blood-spatter pattern analysis, and fingerprint testing, to name just a few. Furthermore, if the defendant has

---

[6] *Bruton v. United States*, 391 U.S. 123 (1968).

received a mental evaluation, a copy of the report of this evaluation will also be given to the defendant. All of these tests must be copied and made available to the defendant.

STATEMENTS OF WITNESSES

Traditionally, the defense was not permitted to obtain statements of witnesses from the police or prosecutors' files. That rule has been eliminated with modern changes to discovery rules. Now, all states that have revised their discovery laws require the prosecution to provide witness statements to the defense. This is true even if the statement was given to a prosecutor instead of a police officer. In the past, the rules made no such provisions, and defense attorneys were left to their own devices to find out what the state's witnesses said to the police. Even though modern discovery rules require the prosecution to provide these statements, many defense attorneys still make the request in their motions for discovery. See Figure 18-1 for an example.

D. OPEN FILE POLICY

Although discovery rules have changed over the years, many prosecution offices have maintained a separate system from what is required under discovery statutes. Some prosecutors' offices have made standard procedure out of their "open file" policy. Under this approach, the prosecution provides the defense complete access to its files, including witness statements, police reports, detectives' reports, and any other information that might be relevant to the case. The advantage of such a system is that it completely sidesteps any claim that the prosecution is attempting to hide information. Open-file policies are not mandated by law but are set up by individual district attorneys. Some prosecutors favor these policies, while some do not. The fact that one district attorney's office operates under an open file policy cannot be used to force a district attorney in another county or state to open up his or her files.[7]

E. VARIATION AMONG STATES IN DISCOVERY RULES

The discussion in this chapter had made an assumption that all states follow basically the same discovery rules. That is not actually true. There is considerable variation among the states in what they typically provide to the defense and even what information is required to be handed over to the prosecution by the

---

[7] *State v. Moore*, 335 N.C. 567, 440 S.E.2d 797, cert. denied, 513 U.S. 898, 115 S. Ct. 253, 130 L. Ed. 2d 174 (1994).

FIGURE 18-1

Defendant's Motion for Discovery

NOW COMES the defendant in the above criminal action and files this MOTION FOR DISCOVERY AND INSPECTION OF PHYSICAL EVIDENCE. Pursuant to the State of Grace's Rules of Criminal Discovery, 4-102, defendant prays for discovery and inspection of the following items:

I.

1. The Defendant moves the Court to order and require the District Attorney to produce and permit by the Defendant or Defendant's counsel the inspection of and the copying and/or photographing of the following:

- Any and all documents, papers, books, accounts, letters, photographs, objects, digital recordings in any format or other tangible things not protected by a recognized legal privilege, which constitute, contain or could be construed as evidence relevant and material to any matter involved in the above-styled criminal action and which are in the possession, custody or control of the State or any of its agencies, including police departments and civilian witnesses acting on behalf of the State;
- Any written or oral statements of the Defendant;
- The Defendant's criminal record consisting of any criminal conviction in this or any other state, territory or other recognized jurisdiction of the United States.
- Criminal records of each and every of the State's witnesses;
- Personnel records and internal memoranda relating to disciplinary actions taken by the lead police officers and/or detectives in this case.
- Any evidence that could be construed under *Brady v. Maryland* as exculpatory or mitigating for the defendant's benefit
- All statements made by any witness intended to be called by the state, whether reduced to writing or recorded in an audio or video format.

WHEREFORE, the Defendant respectfully prays and submits that this Court grant the Defendant's Motion for Discovery and Inspection.

Respectfully submitted,
Clarence D. Arrow, Esq.
Attorney for Defendant Sal Suspect
State Bar No. 006640

defense. This discussion has focused on the minimum material that a state must provide, but there are states that require the prosecution (and the defense) to produce considerably more information. In states that have not changed their discovery rules, a defendant must request discovery before he or she will receive most items from the prosecution. In such states, if the defendant fails to file discovery motions, then the prosecution is under no obligation to give him anything, except for material that the U.S. Supreme Court requires in all criminal cases.

F. INFORMATION THAT IS NORMALLY NOT DISCOVERABLE BY THE DEFENDANT

The defendant is not allowed to use the discovery process as a fishing expedition, that is, as a means to go through all of the prosecution's files, hoping to find something useful. The defendant can request specific items, or any exculpatory information (see *Brady* material below), but is not permitted to submit a general request for "all information." In fact, the following are not generally provided by the state in discovery:

- Work product
- Criminal records of state witnesses

WORK PRODUCT

The prosecuting attorney's mental notes and strategy ideas about the case are not discoverable. The prosecuting attorney's ideas and mental impressions about a case are referred to as **work product**. As a general rule, work product is not discoverable, either in criminal or civil cases. This is based on the premise that mental notes, ideas, and impressions form the very core of the service provided by an attorney, and requiring the disclosure of such information would severely limit the attorney's effectiveness (see Scenario 18-3). The general exception to this rule, however, comes when these notes focus on witness testimony that may be exculpatory to the defendant, which would bring it within the scope of *Brady*.

Work product
The principle that a lawyer need not show the other side in a case any facts or things gathered for the case unless the other side can convince the judge that it would be unjust for the thing to remain hidden and there is a special need for it.

WORK PRODUCT?

SCENARIO 18-3

Maria is the prosecutor assigned to a case and as part of her preparation, she has prepared a timeline of the events that includes information provided in written statements by witnesses and the defendant's written confession. Is she obligated to turn this material over to the defense as part of discovery or does this qualify as work product?

Answer: A court will almost certainly rule that Maria's timeline is work product. She prepared it to help prepare herself for trial and it is based on statements provided by witnesses (and the defendant) that are already in the file. As a result, it is work product and protected from being turned over to the defense through discovery.

CRIMINAL RECORDS OF STATE WITNESSES

In most states, the criminal records of the witnesses, other than the defendant, are not made discoverable. This means that prosecutors do not make a habit of running criminal records on all of their witnesses and then making them available to the defendant. However, this rule can have several major exceptions, not the least of which comes when this information falls under *Brady*. Consider Scenario 18-4.

SCENARIO 18-4	WITNESS WITH A RECORD

In a trial for burglary, it turns out that the state's main witness, and the person who saw the defendant at the scene coming out of the house with stolen goods, is also a convicted burglar. Should this witness's criminal history be turned over to the defendant?

Answer: Yes. Most interpretations of *Brady* would require that this information be provided to the defense.

The situation outlined in Scenario 18-4 is not all that unusual. It is quite common for one or more of the state's witnesses to have a criminal record. In fact, this person may have been a codefendant or be someone who is facing unrelated criminal charges and has agreed to testify for the state in exchange for a more lenient sentence recommendation. As we will see in the section on motions filed by the defense, such an arrangement must be made known to the defense.

In the real world of prosecutions, the prosecutor might not only voluntarily hand over this information to the defense, but also will make the jury aware of the witness's criminal history at the beginning of the trial. Why would the state volunteer this information to the jury? The primary reason is because the jury is going to hear about it anyway. Because the defense attorney is aware of the witness's criminal history, he or she will bring the state's witness's criminal record up at every opportunity. It is better that the jury hear about this from the prosecution first.

The topic of the state's witness's criminal records has been controversial for years. Many states have never required the state to produce any criminal records of its intended witnesses for the defense, while others have required it for decades. Even in the states that require the state to hand over any criminal records of its witnesses, there is no uniformity about how much information is provided to the defense. For instance, in some states the defense must be given a copy of the witness's criminal history, showing any convictions but not necessarily any arrests. In other states, all arrests and convictions must be produced.

G. *BRADY* MATERIAL

Exculpatory

Evidence that tends to provide an excuse or a justification for the defendant's actions or that shows that the defendant did not commit the crime charged.

Regardless of whether or not a particular state has changed its discovery rules in criminal cases, the U.S. Supreme Court has mandated that certain kinds of information must be turned over to the defendant prior to trial in all criminal prosecutions. In the *Brady v. Maryland*[8] decision, the Court ruled that when the state has **exculpatory** evidence or information tending to show the defendant is not guilty of the crime, the state must produce such evidence for the defendant, whether or not the defendant has requested it. The Supreme Court reasoned that because the role of the prosecutor was not simply to convict a defendant but to seek justice, it was only proper that the state turn over such evidence to the defense in order for the defendant to have a fair trial.

---

[8] *Brady v. Maryland*, 373 U.S. 83, 83 S. Ct. 1194, 10 L. Ed. 2d 215 (1963).

The *Brady* decision has been expanded over the years to include not only exculpatory information but also any evidence or information that might mitigate the defendant's guilt. *Brady's* effect has been far-reaching. Most prosecutors now serve on the defendant a *Brady* notice, including all **Brady material** detailing any evidence that has come to light during the state's investigation that might arguably tend to mitigate the charges against the defendant. Consider Scenario 18-5.

Brady **material**
Information available to the prosecutor that is favorable to the defendant, either because it mitigates his guilt or his sentence. This material must be provided to the defense prior to trial.

DISCOVERY

As Keisha is preparing to defend Sam for armed robbery of a jewelry store, she finds an indication that the entire armed robbery was recorded on a computer hard drive. The only items that she has received through discovery from the state are still photographs showing her client waiving a gun around and pointing it at people inside the jewelry store. The note in her file indicates that the video showed the defendant actually striking several victims inside the jewelry store. Keisha files a motion alleging that the state has violated *Brady*.

In the hearing on her motion, Keisha learns from a witness that the hard drive on the computer crashed shortly after the photos were downloaded and no one has been able to retrieve the entire video. Is this a violation of *Brady*?

Answer: No. *Brady* was designed to force the state to produce any evidence that might tend to exculpate or mitigate the defendant's guilt. The DVD, in contrast, would have actually further incriminated the defendant. There is no *Brady* violation.[9]

IN CAMERA INSPECTIONS

When a judge receives a request by a defense attorney under *Brady*, the judge must conduct an **in camera** inspection of the state's file. An *in camera* inspection is carried out by the judge in his or her chambers. The state provides the judge with its entire file, and the judge goes through all of the witness statements, police reports, and other material looking for anything that might be construed under the *Brady* decision to be exculpatory. If the judge finds some material, he provides it to the defense. In this manner, the defense can be assured that an impartial party has reviewed the state's file, and the defense attorney does not have to take the prosecutor's word that all exculpatory information has been provided. The judge must make appropriate findings of fact, detailing that he or she has reviewed the state's file and found nothing that might be exculpatory to the defense that has not been already provided to the defendant.

The U.S. Supreme Court in Brady *held that "the suppression by the prosecution of evidence favorable to an accused upon request violates due process where the evidence is material either to guilt or to punishment, irrespective of the good faith or bad faith of the prosecution."*[10] *This evidence must be revealed to the defendant even if the defendant does not request it.*[11]

In camera
Latin for "in chambers"; a review of a file by a judge carried out in his or her private office.

---

[9] *U.S. v. Drake*, 543 F.3d 1080 (9th Cir. 2008).
[10] *Brady*, 373 U.S. at 87.
[11] *State v. Hunt*, 615 N.W.2d 294, 296 -302 (Minn., 2000).

DEFENSE MOTIONS BASED ON DISCOVERY

Defendants may raise a wide variety of motions before trial. These motions may involve evidentiary issues but can also involve many other issues. Some defense attorneys will file dozens of motions before trial and insist that each motion be argued. Some of these motions might include motions to suppress and motions *in limine*.

A. MOTIONS TO SUPPRESS

Motion to suppress
A motion that requests a court not allow the jury to hear specific information, such as the defendant's confession or other statements based on improprieties in obtaining the information.

A **motion to suppress** is a motion requesting the judge to rule that certain evidence is inadmissible at trial. The most common reason for this request is that the evidence was seized in violation of the defendant's constitutional rights. In situations where evidence has been seized illegally, the judge is authorized to rule the evidence inadmissible and therefore unusable at trial. This is the famous Exclusionary Rule, first enunciated in the early 1900s and expanded by later U.S. Supreme Court decisions. Under the Exclusionary Rule, if law enforcement officials violate constitutional principles in obtaining evidence, their punishment is that they cannot use it at trial.

Defendants often file motions to suppress evidence in cases even when there is no clear constitutional violation. Many defense attorneys believe that there is nothing to lose by filing such a motion. If the judge denies the motion, the defendant is in no worse a position than he was already. If the judge grants the motion, a crucial piece of evidence will be excluded from the trial. However, if the judge rules against the government on a motion to suppress, the government is permitted to appeal that decision.

A motion to suppress can be focused on any of a number of issues raised in the case, from the defendant's confession to the photographic lineup used to identify the defendant as the person responsible for the crime. Defense attorneys routinely file motions to suppress the following:

- Physical evidence
- Defendant's statement
- Photographic lineup
- Warrantless searches
- Searches with warrants
- Wiretaps

MOTION TO SEVER

Sever
Separate or cut off into constituent parts.

In some cases, the defendant may request a motion to **sever** offenses or parties. A motion for severance asks the court to try different counts of an indictment as separate trials or different codefendants in separate trials. A defendant requests severance when he or she believes that being tried together with several other defendants will unduly prejudice the case and prevent the defendant from receiving a fair trial. In a similar fashion, a motion to sever offenses requests a separate trial for offenses that may be unrelated in time or action from each other. The jury might not separate out the proof of one offense from the other but might instead be more likely to assume that the defendant is guilty simply by the sheer number of offenses against him.

MOTION *IN LIMINE*

In addition to motions to suppress, a defendant will also file numerous motions *in limine*. A motion *in limine* is a motion requesting a ruling on the use of a particular piece of evidence or a limitation on the kind of testimony that a witness may give on the stand. For instance, if a defense attorney has reason to believe that a particular state's witness will refer to the defendant's criminal history during her testimony, the defense attorney may file a **motion *in limine*** requesting the judge to order the witness to make no such references. Since a defendant's prior criminal record is normally not admissible at trial, such a motion will usually be granted. The defense may also file a motion *in limine* to restrict the use of other kinds of evidence or testimony. Each such motion will be argued by the attorneys and may involve the testimony of a witness at a motion hearing prior to trial. These motion hearings are often days or even weeks before the actual trial. Some motions may also be argued shortly before the trial begins. Still other motions may also be raised during the course of the trial.

Motion *in limine*
Latin for "at the beginning." A motion *in limine* is a motion by one party that requests specific judicial rulings at the outset of the trial.

MOTION TO REVEAL THE DEAL (GIGLIO)

When a defense attorney suspects that a prosecution witness has been offered a deal for his testimony at trial, he or she can file a motion requesting the details of the arrangement. When a defense attorney requests information about any arrangements between the prosecution and a witness, it is commonly referred to as a **motion to "reveal the deal."** This is a motion asking that the state be ordered to reveal any deal entered into with any witness in which the state has offered immunity or some other benefit in exchange for testimony. It is fairly common for a state's witness to be granted some form of immunity or the promise of a light recommendation on sentencing in exchange for the witness's testimony against another codefendant. Defense attorneys rightly assume that such promise could have an effect on the witness's performance on the stand. Although a prosecutor would probably feel that any such promise would have to be revealed to the defense attorney because of the *Brady* decision (see above), a defense attorney might decide to cover his bases by filing a motion anyway.

Motion to "reveal the deal"
A defense motion seeking any information that a state's witness has negotiated an arrangement with the prosecution to testify in exchange for a lower sentence.

MOTION TO REVEAL IDENTITY OF CONFIDENTIAL INFORMANTS

Defense attorneys may file a motion to reveal the identity of a **confidential informant** (CI) who was involved in the case. Generally, police and prosecutors protect confidential informants because to release their names to the defendant might put the CI in danger of being killed. Discovery rules allow a prosecutor to

Confidential informant
A person who works with the police, providing them information about illegal activities.

conceal the identity of a CI, but this right is not absolute. The court is allowed to weigh the right of the government to protect its confidential informants from retribution against the right of the defendant to receive a fair trial. If a judge decides that the only way to make sure that the defendant receives a fair and proper trial is to release the name of the confidential informant to the defense, then the judge is authorized to do so.[12] This is another example where the judge would review the state's file *in camera* before making a decision on whether or not to reveal the CI's name.

OTHER DEFENSE MOTIONS

In addition to bringing motions to suppress and motions to reveal any deal between a witness and the state, defense attorneys are free to file as many motions as they see fit. In high-profile cases, the defense may file literally dozens of motions. One of the most common in such a case would be a motion for change of venue.

A. MOTION TO CHANGE VENUE

A defendant who wants to move the location of the trial will request a change of venue. Generally, a defendant must show that his chances of receiving a fair trial in the original area have been diminished or completely negated, usually by intensive pretrial publicity. Defendants will often present evidence of newspaper or other media reports that have focused on the case in a negative way. Since the potential

Motion for change of venue
A motion to transfer the location of the trial to another area, often brought when there is extensive pretrial publicity.

jurors for the trial will be drawn from the same area, a **motion for change of venue** alleges that the jury pool for this case has been influenced before they ever hear any testimony. If the judge grants a change of venue motion, it usually means that the trial will be moved to some other jurisdiction. The jury will be selected from the new area, but the prosecutor, judge, and defense attorney remain the same.

B. MOTION FOR CONTINUANCE

Motion for continuance
A request by one party to postpone a trial or other hearing for a future date.

A **motion for continuance** is a motion that can be made by either side in a criminal case, the prosecution or the defense. When the party moves for a continuance, it is requesting that the case be taken off the current calendar and rescheduled for a later date. There are many reasons why a party might request a continuance. The party might not be prepared for the trial, a key witness might not be available, or some other factor weighs heavily against trying the case now. A judge must approve the motion for a continuance, but if the opposing side does not object to the continuance, more often than not the judge will grant it.

---

[12] *Drouin v. State*, 222 Md. 271, 160 A.2d 85 (1960).

C. PLEA OF FORMER JEOPARDY

A **plea of former jeopardy** is a motion filed by a defendant that states that he or she was prosecuted in a former case and that prosecution also was involved in the current charges. Essentially, the defendant is saying that the state is barred from prosecuting the defendant because the defendant has already been sentenced on a related charge and because the Fifth Amendment bars a person from being tried twice for the same offense. Pleas of former jeopardy are often seen in cases where a defendant is charged with a traffic offense and also with some other offense, such as transporting narcotics. The defendant enters a plea to the underlying traffic offense and then brings a plea of former jeopardy attempting to claim that the first prosecution bars the charge on the narcotics. Occasionally, these pleas are successful, but in many cases they are not.[13]

Plea of former jeopardy
A defendant's motion stating that he or she has already been prosecuted for the underlying offense, and any further prosecution is barred by the Fifth Amendment.

D. BILL OF PARTICULARS

Another tool available to a criminal defendant is a motion for a **bill of particulars**. A bill of particulars requests additional information about the counts of the indictment. For instance, a defendant might request in his or her bill of particulars "information concerning any oral statements of the defendant relied upon by the government to support the charge in the indictment." In the alternative, a defendant's bill of particulars might request additional information about the evidence relied upon to support specific allegations in the indictment. In essence, the defendant is requesting that the government provide background information on specific charges to enable the defendant to better prepare his defense. However, a defendant might also file a bill of particulars simply to gather any additional information, whether pertinent to the defense or not.

Bill of particulars
A defendant's motion requesting dates, names, locations, and addresses for the charges set out in the indictment.

E. SPEEDY TRIAL DEMAND

The accused shall enjoy the right to a speedy and public trial. — Sixth Amendment

The right of an accused to a **speedy trial** has a long history. Originally mentioned in the Magna Carta in the year 1215, the defendant's right to a speedy trial was considered to be an important, if often ignored, right. The right to a speedy trial was embodied in the Virginia Declaration of Rights of 1776, then incorporated into the later U.S. Constitution and then all state constitutions. In *Klopfer v. North Carolina*,[14] the Supreme Court declared that the right to a speedy trial was as important as any other right guaranteed in the Sixth Amendment, calling it "one of the most basic rights preserved by our Constitution."

Speedy trial
A constitutional guarantee that a person must receive a trial within a reasonable period of time after being arraigned.

---

[13] *United States v. Sabella*, 272 F.2d 206, 207 (C.A.2 1959).
[14] 386 U.S. 213, 87 S.Ct. 988, 18 L.Ed.2d 1 (1967).

Term of court
The period of time slated for court hearings; it can be as short as a week or as long as a year.

All states have laws that are commonly referred to as "speedy-trial-demand statutes." Speedy-trial statutes seek to enforce the Sixth Amendment guarantee of a speedy trial. These statutes allow a defendant to serve on the state a demand that the defendant be tried in this or the next **term of court**. If the trial is not held, then the defendant's case must be dismissed.

DISMISSING A CASE FOR FAILURE TO RECEIVE A SPEEDY TRIAL

If the defendant serves a speedy-trial demand and is not tried in the specified time, then the charges against the defendant must be dismissed and the defendant released from confinement. Serving a "speedy" on a prosecutor often has a galvanizing effect on the state. Since a prosecutor knows that if the defendant is not tried, he must be released, the practical effect of serving a speedy-trial demand is usually that the defendant's case is moved up to the number one trial in the next trial week. Even when the defendant is already in prison serving a sentence on an unrelated offense, he is still entitled to receive a speedy trial on another charge.[15]

While this right is considered one of the fundamental rights guaranteed in the Constitution, defining what exactly constitutes a "speedy" trial has been difficult to quantify. The U.S. Supreme Court has grappled with this issue in many different cases.

HOW SPEEDY MUST A "SPEEDY TRIAL" BE?

The Supreme Court has held that a delay of eight years between indictment and trial is too long[16]; five years may also be too long.[17] The problem is that each case must be considered on its own facts. The Supreme Court has been reluctant to state a maximum period that will always mean a violation of the Sixth Amendment. Despite the Court's reluctance to name a specific period of time in which a defendant must always be tried, the Court has been specific about the sanction imposed for failing to try a defendant. Where the defendant's right to a speedy trial has been violated, only one sanction is allowed: dismissal of the state's case. This drastic remedy was authorized in *Strunk v. United States*.[18]

WHEN THE DEFENDANT MAY NOT WANT A SPEEDY TRIAL AFTER ALL

Although each state has a statute authorizing the filing of a speedy-trial demand to enforce the Sixth Amendment guarantee, a speedy trial may actually work against the defendant. Often, a delay in bringing the case to trial will help the defendant. Memories fade over time. Evidence may be lost. In fact, taking a case to trial sooner

---

[15] *Smith v. Hooey*, 393 U.S. 374, 89 S.Ct. 575, 21 L.Ed.2d 607 (1969).
[16] *Doggett v. United States*, 5 U.S. 647, 112 S.Ct. 2686, 120 L.Ed.2d 520 (1992).
[17] *Barker v. Wingo*, 407 U.S. 514, 92 S.Ct. 2182, 33 L.Ed.2d 101 (1972).
[18] 412 U.S. 434 (1973).

rather than later may only be helpful to the defendant when the prosecution is not prepared. Otherwise, a quick trial may actually work against the defendant. The defense team should evaluate these potential difficulties before filing a statutory speedy-trial demand.

WHEN IS THE RIGHT TO A SPEEDY TRIAL TRIGGERED?

A question often arises in the context of speedy-trial demands: When is the right triggered? Put another way, at what point during the proceedings does the prosecution pass the point of no return, where the state fails to prosecute the defendant and the provisions of the speedy-trial demand will necessitate dismissing the case? Courts have wrestled with that question for many years and have finally settled it at a specific point during the case. The right to receive a speedy trial is triggered when an indictment has been lodged against the defendant.[19] The right to a speedy trial also attaches when a defendant has been *accused* — that is, when he is charged with a misdemeanor. Of course, this assumes that the defendant has not filed for a motion for continuance. If the defendant files such a motion, he or she waives the right to a speedy trial. After all, the defendant is requesting a trial to be held immediately and then, by his or her own request, wishes to put the trial off.

 ## PROSECUTION MOTIONS

Though there are a wide array of motions that a defendant may raise in a case (discussed in Chapter 19), there are relatively few motions that a prosecutor may file against the defendant. A motion is a request filed with a judge requesting that some action be taken. The defense routinely files a motion to suppress evidence in the case, but defense attorneys are not the only party that is permitted to file motions. The state may also bring motions against the defendant. The prosecutor, however, has much greater limitations on the types of motions that he or she can file. The relatively few motions that a prosecutor can bring are the following:

- Similar transactions
- Aggravation of sentence
- Motion to join

A. SIMILAR TRANSACTIONS

In many states the prosecution is allowed to bring a **similar transactions motion** so that the jury can hear evidence of the defendant's prior crimes. Although the defendant's prior criminal record is normally inadmissible at trial, similar transaction laws allow a limited use of such prior convictions. In situations where the

Similar transactions motion
A motion brought by the state showing that the defendant has committed similar offenses, and this shows his bent of mind, motive, or course of conduct.

---

[19] *Unites States v. Marion*, 404 U.S. 307 (1971).

current charge against the defendant is similar to a previous conviction, the state is permitted to present evidence of the prior conviction to show a common method, plan, or scheme by the defendant to carry out certain kinds of crimes. "If the defendant is proven to be the perpetrator of another . . . crime and the facts of that crime are sufficiently similar or connected to the facts of the crime charged, the separate crime will be admissible to prove identity, motive, plan, scheme, bent of mind, or course of conduct."[20]

However, before the state is allowed to present any such evidence to the jury, the court must rule on the evidence. A similar transactions hearing must be held in which the witnesses from the prior conviction testify, and the state builds a case showing how the prior conviction has many of the same features as the current charge. If the judge rules that there is sufficient similarity between the two offenses to establish the defendant common motive, plan, or conduct, the evidence of the prior conviction can be used in the current case. The judge must give a limiting instruction to the jury, telling them that this evidence is only being admitted for the limited purpose of showing the defendant's common approach to similar crimes. Under this limitation, a prosecutor can only admit evidence of crimes substantially similar to the current charge. A similar transactions motion does not allow the prosecutor to put the defendant's entire criminal record into evidence.

A prosecutor will often file a notice that he intends to use similar transactions in any case where they might possibly apply. The practical effect of similar transactions testimony is to taint the defendant in the eyes of the jury. When a defense attorney learns that the prosecutor intends to use similar transactions, this puts even greater pressure on the defendant to plead guilty to the charge. The defense reasons that if the jury should learn that the defendant has been convicted of a similar crime before, they will be far more likely to convict him of the present crime.

B. AGGRAVATION OF SENTENCE

Motion in aggravation of sentence
A motion filed by the state that seeks to enhance the defendant's sentence based on his or her prior convictions.

In addition to filing a motion for similar transactions, a prosecutor may also file a **motion in aggravation of sentence**. The prosecutor may file this motion prior to the trial or may wait and file it after the defendant has been found guilty. A motion in aggravation of sentence is a document that shows that the defendant has a lengthy criminal record or has a history of violence or harming others. In addition to filing the written motion, the prosecutor will also provide certified copies of the defendant's prior convictions. The judge may or may not take the convictions into account when sentencing the defendant. Generally, when a defendant has a lengthy criminal record, he or she will receive a longer sentence on conviction than someone who has no prior record. One way of ensuring that the court is aware of the defendant's criminal record is for the prosecution to file a motion in aggravation of sentence.

---

[20] *Hatcher v. State*, 224 Ga.App. 747, 752(3), 482 S.E.2d 443 (1997).

The court may order that separate cases be tried together as though brought in a single indictment or information if all offenses and all defendants could have been joined in a single indictment or information.[21]

C. MOTION TO JOIN

A motion to join is exactly the opposite of the defendant's motion to sever. In a motion for joinder, the state requests that a series of crimes or multiple defendants be tried together. State and federal rules allow a prosecutor to move the court to combine several cases into a single prosecution under specific circumstances. If there is one crime or a series of crimes committed by the same individuals, it may make more sense both in terms of time and economy to try all of the individuals at the same time, rather than try them one by one. In situations where the government has separately indicted individuals for the same crime, a prosecutor can file a motion to join the defendants together and have them tried in one trial. Of course, the defense will often fight this motion, reasoning that if a jury sees a group of people charged, it will be harder for a single defendant to stand out as an innocent party.

HATCHER v. STATE

224 Ga.App. 747, 482 S.E.2d 443 (Ga.App.,1997)

CASE EXCERPT

BEASLEY, Judge.

Hatcher was convicted of violating the Georgia Controlled Substances Act, OCGA § 16–13–30, by possessing less than a gram of methamphetamine or "crank."

Narcotics agent Hudson was on patrol around 1:00 a.m. when he spotted a vehicle exceeding the speed limit and stopped it. Driver Hatcher immediately jumped out of his car and approached the officer quickly. He appeared nervous, which made Hudson nervous because Hatcher's behavior cautioned the officer that he might have a weapon or have something surreptitious in mind. Hudson asked Hatcher if he had any prior tickets or had recently been jailed. Hatcher responded he had been locked up for violating the Georgia Controlled Substances Act. Hatcher refused consent to search his vehicle.

Hudson read Hatcher his Miranda rights and told him if he had any misdemeanor amounts of marijuana in the vehicle he would issue only a citation for it. Hatcher admitted there was a small amount of marijuana and offered to get it but again refused consent to search. The officer rejected Hatcher's offer because of the risk he had a weapon in the car.

---

[21] Rule 13. F.R.C.P.

Hudson retrieved his drug dog which, in its second pass around Hatcher's car, alerted to the presence of drugs. Hudson left Hatcher in the custody of another officer and went for a search warrant. When he returned with the warrant, Hatcher admitted both marijuana and "crank" were in a side pouch of the car, and Hudson found the drugs there.

A defendant aggrieved by an unlawful search and seizure pursuant to a warrant may make a motion to suppress the evidence, which must be in writing and state facts showing the unlawfulness of the search and seizure. OCGA § 17–5–30. The motion must be made at or before the defendant's arraignment and if not made at the proper time is waived unless the time for filing is extended by the judge in writing. The purpose of the time requirement in USCR 31.1 is fundamental fairness to all parties and those who must attend trial. Failing to file a timely motion to suppress amounts to a waiver of even constitutional challenges.

Hatcher had several options. He could have timely filed the motion and moved for leave to amend it when the affidavit was obtained. He could have sought an extension of time. He could have moved for leave to file late when he had the affidavit. He was not denied a meaningful opportunity to challenge the search and seizure. Accordingly, it was not an abuse of discretion to dismiss the motion to suppress, even though trial did not transpire for three months.

The challenge to the court's other basis for dismissal of his motion to suppress is moot.

The next enumeration of error is the imposition of a 30–year recidivist sentence.

Hatcher's first ground is that the court failed to determine if he received affirmative and unmistakable advance warning of the State's intention to use prior offenses for recidivist purposes. He seeks remand for the court to make that determination. If the State intends to introduce evidence that defendant is a recidivist for sentencing purposes, it "must notify defendant of any conviction it intends to use in aggravation of punishment pursuant to OCGA § 17–10–2(a). . . . The purpose of § 17–10–2 is to give defendant a chance to examine his record to determine if the convictions are in fact his, if he was represented by counsel, and any other defect which would render such documents inadmissible during the pre-sentencing phase of the trial."

Hatcher was convicted and sentenced on May 10, 1995. The record contains the State's notice of its intent to ask for Hatcher to be treated as recidivist under OCGA § 17–10–7, based on four described prior convictions. The notice is signed and dated May 8, 1995, but is stamped as filed on November 23, 1995. It is unaccompanied by a certificate of service, although all other record documents have certificates indicating Hatcher was served. The record contains no affirmative indication that the State provided Hatcher with the required notice of aggravating circumstances as required by the statute. The State failed to fulfill its duty under OCGA § 17–10–2(a).

At the presentence hearing, the State introduced four, and the court admitted three, of Hatcher's prior convictions into evidence. Hatcher's counsel did not object to the admission of the convictions and affirmatively stated he did not contest their admission, thereby waiving error.

The court permitted the State to introduce three prior violations of the Georgia Controlled Substances Act transactions, one for possession of methamphetamine and two for selling small amounts of the drug, as evidence of similar transactions. Error is enumerated in the admission of the two prior convictions for drug dealing in the trial for simple possession. Assuming but not deciding that Hatcher's objection was timely under USCR 31.3(B), the evidence was properly admitted.

Hatcher concedes on appeal that the court properly admitted evidence of his prior conviction for possession of methamphetamine, since his sole defense at trial was that the drugs had been left in the car by his brother who had recently died of an overdose. His entire defense turned on his credibility as a witness, and he acknowledges the relevancy of his possession of the drug on prior occasions. He argues that his convictions of drug sales were improperly admitted because they raised a character inference that he was a drug dealer and not just a user. He contends that the impact of this evidence, particularly when his sole defense turned on his credibility, was highly and inherently prejudicial.

Under *Williams v. State*, 261 Ga. 640, 642(2)(b), 409 S.E.2d 649 (1991), the trial court is required to determine if the probative value of the evidence outweighs its prejudicial effect, but the court failed to do so on the record. Nonetheless, "it is clear in this case that based upon defendant's denial of the commission of the subject crime (possession of methamphetamine), a past conviction involving the intent to commercially distribute methamphetamine would be most helpful to the jury, and therefore the State's need would have outweighed the prejudice to the defendant. Any error by the trial court in failing to apply the balancing test was harmless under the facts of this case."

As to similarity, "there is no requirement that, to come within the 'other transaction' exception, the 'other transaction' must be identical in every respect. 'The test of admissibility of evidence of other criminal acts by the defendant is not the number of similarities between the two incidents. Rather, such evidence" may be admitted if it' "is substantially relevant for some purpose other than to show a probability that (the defendant) committed the crime on trial because he is a man of criminal character. . . . Drug cases are no different from any other cases. If the defendant is proven to be the perpetrator of another drug crime and the facts of that crime are sufficiently similar or connected to the facts of the crime charged, the separate crime will be admissible to prove identity, motive, plan, scheme, bent of mind, or course of conduct."

The State met the criteria established in Williams. It made an affirmative showing that it sought to introduce evidence of the similar transaction for the purpose of showing course of conduct, intent and bent of mind. There was ample evidence that Hatcher committed the independent acts within five months of each other, and there was a sufficient similarity between the transactions and the crime charged so that proof of the former tended to prove the latter. First, all of the transactions occurred in the metropolitan Atlanta area, specifically within 15 miles of Hatcher's residence. Second, in each situation, Hatcher was in his car. Third, possession, and in some cases sale, each time involved less than a gram of methamphetamine contained in a small clear plastic bag. In its instructions to the jury, the court gave appropriate limiting instructions.

No reversible error is shown.

Judgment affirmed.

BIRDSONG, P.J., and HAROLD R. BANKE, Senior Appellate Judge, concur.

CASE QUESTIONS

1 Why did the officer search Hatcher's car?
2 According to the court, what must a defendant do in order to challenge the constitutionality of a search, and when must he do it?
3 How "similar" must a previous crime be in order to qualify as a similar transaction?
4 As far as this defendant is concerned, what were the facts that made his previous convictions similar to his current charge?

CHAPTER SUMMARY

The arraignment is the court hearing where a defendant is brought before the court and officially informed of the charges against him or her. At the arraignment, the defendant has the opportunity of entering a plea: either guilty or not guilty. If the defendant pleads not guilty, he or she is given a trial date and told to return for trial. If the defendant pleads guilty, then he or she will usually be sentenced that day.

Discovery is often provided at arraignment, or at least ten days prior to trial, depending on the custom found in the jurisdiction. Traditionally, very little information was exchanged between the state and the defendant in discovery; however, that has changed in recent years. These days, it is common for the state to produce numerous documents, including the defendant's and witness's statements, physical evidence, and scientific reports, among others. Whether a jurisdiction has updated its discovery statutes or not, all states must abide by the decision in *Brady v. Maryland*, which requires states to turn over any exculpatory or mitigating information to the defense. Defense attorneys routinely file motions in cases, requesting that specific evidence be suppressed or making other requests of the court. Although it is not as frequent, the state may also file its own motions, such as alerting the defense to the fact that it intends to seek a longer prison term against the defendant or a similar transactions motion, which will show that the defendant has committed similar crimes in the past.

KEY TERMS

Arraignment	Motion to suppress	Plea of former jeopardy
Calendar or docket	Sever	Bill of particulars
Motion	Motion *in limine*	Motion to sever
Bench warrant	Motion to "reveal the deal"	Speedy trial
Discovery	Confidential informant	Term of court
In camera	Motion for change of venue	Similar transactions motion
Exculpatory	Motion for continuance	Motion in aggravation of sentence
Brady material		
Work product		

REVIEW QUESTIONS

1   What is arraignment?
2   What is a court docket?
3   What motions might a defense attorney file at or before arraignment?
4   What is the difference between formal arraignment and arraignment?
5   Explain bench warrants.
6   Provide a brief overview of criminal discovery.
7   Explain the basic information provided by the state in discovery.
8   What is an open file policy?
9   When would a judge conduct an *in camera* inspection?
10 What is exculpatory evidence?
11 How have discovery rules changed over the years?
12 What is *Brady* material?
13 What is work product?
14 When would the state provide criminal records of its witnesses?
15 What is a motion to suppress?
16 Explain motions to sever.
17 Why would a defendant bring a motion *in limine*?
18 Explain the function of a motion to "reveal the deal."
19 When would a defendant bring a motion to change venue?

QUESTIONS FOR ANALYSIS

1   Should criminal discovery be made the same as civil discovery? Can you think of reasons why they should remain different?
2   Can you construct an argument for the premise that everything in the state's file should be available to a criminal defendant, no matter what?

HYPOTHETICALS

1   Because there have been many cases where a conviction was later overturned on appeal because of DNA evidence, should the state be required to take DNA samples from all of its witnesses and provide these to the defense so that the defendant's attorney can run independent DNA tests to ensure that it was not one of the state's witnesses who actually matched the DNA recovered?
2   Should there be categories of cases where regular procedures, such as preliminary hearings and grand jury proceedings are not available? Would this law be Constitutional? Would be it fair? Why or why not?

3 In many cases, defense attorneys file dozens of defense motions that sometimes have nothing to do with the issues in the case. As a way to streamline the judicial system, suppose that Judge A in your jurisdiction creates a rule that states that no such motions will be allowed in "routine, misdemeanor cases." The judge includes a range of crimes on this list that include public indecency, theft by shoplifting, and driving under the influence. Would such a rule be constitutional, enforceable, and practical?

The Defendant's Rights Before and During Trial

I. THE DEFENDANT'S RIGHTS BEFORE AND DURING TRIAL

This chapter will examine the rights that follow a defendant at the beginning and throughout the trial of a criminal case. We will begin with the rights that protect a defendant before the trial begins, then examine those rights that are particular to a trial.

II. DEFENDANT'S RIGHTS PRIOR TO TRIAL

The rights that protect a defendant prior to trial include the following:

 The right to an attorney
 The right to be presumed innocent

A. THE RIGHT TO AN ATTORNEY

In all criminal prosecutions, the accused shall enjoy the right . . . to have the Assistance of Counsel for his defense. — Sixth Amendment

For decades the Sixth Amendment's guarantee of the right to assistance of counsel was narrowly interpreted to mean that a defendant could hire any attorney he or she could afford, but the state was under no obligation to provide one free of charge. If defendants could not afford one, then they would have to represent themselves. The first change to this area of law came in a recognition that in cases where the defendant faced the death penalty, not allowing him or her an attorney was tantamount to an automatic guilty verdict. Then in a series of decisions, the U.S. Supreme Court, especially the Warren Court in the 1960s, addressed the issue of when a person should be allowed to have an attorney and, more importantly, when the state must provide counsel if the defendant could not afford to hire one. The most famous case in this field is *Gideon v. Wainwright*, which will be examined in greater detail later in this chapter.

Before beginning a discussion of the rights of a defendant during and after the trial, an important question must be answered: At what point do suspects have the right to have an attorney represent them? Much of the case law about this question focuses on a discussion of whether or not a particular stage is "critical." If the stage of the prosecution is critical, then the defendant should have an attorney representing his or her interests. But what is a critical stage? In most prosecutions, a critical stage is a hearing where the prosecutor, judge, and possible witnesses appear. One such hearing is the preliminary hearing. However, this is not the first point in a criminal proceeding where a defendant has the right to request an attorney.

This text has already discussed *Miranda* rights and how they are critical to interrogating a suspect. One of the rights provided for in *Miranda* is that a defendant must be told that he or she has the right to an attorney and can refuse to answer any questions until the attorney appears. So, a defendant has the right to an attorney at any critical stage in a criminal case and during interrogation — whenever his or her legal rights are in jeopardy or during any adversarial hearing. This essentially means that a defendant has the right to an attorney beginning at interrogation and proceeding forward. In some jurisdictions, the right is triggered even earlier. In those jurisdictions, a defendant has the right to an attorney the moment that the investigation focuses on him or her.[1]

HIRING AN ATTORNEY

Before discussing the implications of the *Gideon* decision, it is important to note that a defendant who can afford to hire a private attorney is always free to do so. One might wonder how a person who is incarcerated can contact an attorney. The defendant might ask a friend or a family member to contact a specific attorney, but some attorneys who are already visiting a client at the local jail might meet with a

---

[1] *State v. Armfield*, 214 Mont. 229, 693 P.2d 1226 (1984).

defendant who is currently unrepresented. Attorneys who handle criminal cases usually charge a **retainer** — an upfront fee to represent a defendant. The amount of the fee varies with the complexity and seriousness of the case. Some attorneys have also been known to accept private property as payment instead of cash, but there are problems with this practice. The attorney must avoid receiving any merchandise that is stolen. Because of this, most attorneys prefer to deal on a currency basis.

Retainer
A fee charged at the beginning of a case to pay an attorney for all actions carried out.

GIDEON v. WAINWRIGHT

Clarence Earl Gideon was charged with felony burglary in the state of Florida. He was forced to represent himself at the trial because he could not afford to hire his own attorney. At that time, Florida only appointed counsel in death penalty cases, not in felony cases. Gideon represented himself throughout the trial. When it concluded, he was found guilty. The judge sentenced Gideon to five years in prison.

Gideon appealed his case all the way to the U.S. Supreme Court. The basis of the appeal, which he brought himself, was that a felony sentence, by itself, is serious enough to warrant the application of the Sixth Amendment. The Supreme Court agreed with him and created a ruling that radically changed the way that attorneys were appointed throughout the United States.

In ruling in favor of Gideon, the court said that the "assistance of counsel is one of the safeguards of the Sixth Amendment deemed necessary to insure fundamental human rights of life and liberty. . . . The Sixth Amendment stands as a constant admonition that if the constitutional safeguards it provides be lost, justice will not . . . be done."[2] The Court ruled that Gideon should be retried and that this time the state of Florida should provide him with an attorney, paid for by the state. Interestingly enough, when he was retried, this time with an attorney appointed by the state, he was found not guilty and set free.

Gideon was the first in a series of U.S. Supreme Court decisions that expanded the guarantees of the Sixth Amendment's right to counsel and helped expand the public defender system in places that already had it and to create other systems of providing attorneys, free of charge, to those who could not afford them and were facing felony charges anywhere in the United States. As the law now stands, any person facing a potential maximum sentence of greater than six months in prison must have representation. If the person cannot afford to hire an attorney, then the state must provide one for him or her. Consider Scenario 19-1.

MUST THE STATE PROVIDE AN ATTORNEY?

SCENARIO 19-1

Theo is charged with a misdemeanor count of theft by taking an item that is less than $500 in value. However, after he makes bond, the case is reinvestigated and the police and prosecutors determine that the value of the item that Theo is alleged to have taken is actually worth more than $1,000. They present the case to the grand jury and Theo is

continued

---

[2] *Gideon v. Wainwright*, 372 U.S. 335, 343, 83 S.Ct. 792, 796 (U.S.Fla.,1963).

SCENARIO 19-1

(continued)

indicted for a felony. Does he qualify to have an attorney represent him if he cannot afford one?

Answer: Yes. Even though Theo was originally arrested for a misdemeanor — which would not qualify him for attorney representation in most states — the fact that the charge was changed to a felony would mean that he is now entitled to an attorney.

COURT-APPOINTED ATTORNEY VERSUS PUBLIC DEFENDER SYSTEMS

Court-appointed attorney
A private, local attorney who is selected by a judge to handle a criminal case; this attorney is paid by the state, usually an hourly basis.

Public defender attorney
A government attorney who works for an office in the court system whose sole responsibility is to provide legal representation to those individuals who are charged with crimes.

There are essentially two systems for providing legal representation for those who cannot afford it. Although some jurisdictions take a different approach, the most common arrangement is a **court-appointed attorney** or a **public defender attorney**.

States use different systems in different counties. The reason that there are variations is that in smaller counties, with a correspondingly lower tax base, there may not be sufficient funds to hire and staff a public defender's office. In those situations, courts often turn to local attorneys who already have their own offices and staffs and appoint them to criminal defendants on a case-by-case basis. The private attorneys in the court-appointed system are usually paid on an hourly basis by the court system. The money that the government pays to these local, private attorneys is usually far less than they make in other types of cases. Why, then, would a local attorney agree to serve on a court-appointed list? The answer is deceptively simple: An attorney on the court-appointed list will get a great deal of experience in trials. Most people are not aware of the fact that private attorneys actually spend very little time in courtrooms. They do most of their work in their offices, but in order to become good at anything, a person needs practice and for a trial attorney, experience inside the courtroom is valuable. Another reason may be economics. An attorney, especially one who is recently out of law school, has a lot of bills to pay (including student loans), and a ready source of income is always welcome. Finally, there is political pressure. A local judge may ask attorneys to take cases on the appointed list, and when a judge makes such a request, it is difficult to turn down.

The other side of the equation from court-appointed lawyers is the public defender. A public defender is a government employee, just like an assistant district attorney. In fact, both are often paid the same wage. The sole duty of the public defender is to represent persons who have been charged with a crime and who cannot afford to hire their own attorneys. Where public defenders exist, there is no need for an extensive court-appointed attorney system. However, this is not to say that court-appointed cases are never arranged in counties that have public defender offices. There are times when the public defender is overwhelmed with cases, or when the public defender has a conflict of interest, and in those situations the judge may seek a local private attorney to act in a particular case. However, in counties that have public defender offices, very few cases are ever handled by court-appointed attorneys.

WHEN THE DEFENDANT CANNOT AFFORD AN ATTORNEY

Before a judge will appoint an attorney to represent a defendant, he must inquire about the defendant's finances. The state has specific financial guidelines that a person must meet before an attorney will be appointed to represent him. Generally, if the defendant is in custody and cannot afford to make bail or bond, an attorney will be appointed to represent him. Defendants who are not in custody must often complete a questionnaire, providing details about how much money they make. Different states have different guidelines that a defendant must meet. If the defendant does not meet the financial criteria — because he or she makes too much money — then the defendant may not qualify for a court-appointed attorney or a public defender. A great many people have well-paying jobs but huge debt loads that prevent them from raising the up-front retainer for a skilled criminal defense attorney. They find themselves unable to pay for an attorney while making too much money to qualify for a public defender or court-appointed attorney. Defendants who are charged with felonies will get attorney representation, although they may be required to pay back some of the money if their income is too large to initially qualify. Defendants who are charged with a misdemeanor may not have any options: If they cannot afford to hire an attorney, cannot negotiate some payment plan with a local attorney, and do not meet the financial criteria for the public defender's office, they may end up having to represent themselves.

THE RIGHT OF A DEFENDANT TO REPRESENT HIMSELF

Even after the safeguards of *Gideon* and other cases became bedrock law in the U.S. legal system, there was nothing that required a defendant to accept an attorney provided for free by the government. Defendants always have the right to represent themselves. When a person conducts a trial and acts as his or her own attorney, this is referred to as **pro se** representation. However, such an approach is rarely successful. In fact, a *pro se* defendant often does himself more harm than good. A person might, reasonably enough, conclude that no one could better represent his or her interests than himself, but in law, that conclusion is faulty. *Pro se* defendants are not familiar with the rules of evidence or the proper way to subpoena witnesses and evidence. He or she does not know the correct way to give an opening statement or how to conduct a case. The *pro se* defendant also has a very skilled and experienced opponent in the person of the prosecutor. This mismatch usually results the way one might expect: The *pro se* defendant is found guilty. Consider Scenario 19-2.

Pro se
Latin for "by oneself"; a person who chooses to represent himself or herself in a legal proceeding.

PRO SE REPRESENTATION

SCENARIO 19-2

David is charged with first degree murder and the state is seeking the death penalty. The judge in the case has appointed an attorney to represent David but David does not want to be represented. He wants to represent himself. The judge reminds David that he is facing

continued

a possible death sentence. Can the judge force David to have an attorney represent him in this case?

Answer: No. A person has the absolute right to represent himself. In this case, the judge may appoint an attorney to sit with David in case he has some questions, but David can represent himself if he so chooses.

B. RIGHT TO BE PRESUMED INNOCENT

Presumption
A conclusion about a fact that must be made unless and until refuted by other evidence.

Acquit
Finding the defendant in a criminal case not guilty.

In addition to the right to an attorney, another important right protects the defendant from the moment that he or she is arrested: the **presumption** of innocence. In any prosecution, there is a presumption that a defendant is innocent until proven guilty. This is a very powerful presumption. What this means is that, barring any evidence showing the defendant's guilt, the jury must **acquit** the defendant. This presumption follows the defendant throughout the trial. Judges inform the members of the jury about this presumption, telling them they must find the defendant not guilty unless the state proves its case beyond a reasonable doubt. The presumption of innocence can only be overcome by evidence produced against the defendant. If there is insufficient evidence, then the defendant must be set free. The presumption of innocence is one of the cornerstones of the American legal system. Consider Scenario 19-3.

SCENARIO 19-3

QUESTIONING A JUROR IN A CASE

Andy has been called for jury duty. During jury selection, the judge advises the entire panel that the defendant is presumed to be innocent unless and until the state has proven the charges against him. As jury selection proceeds, the judge asks David, "What is your opinion about the defendant's guilt or innocence?"

David responds, "I don't have one, Your Honor. I haven't heard any evidence in the case yet."

The judge responds: "You are dismissed from this jury panel. A juror must always believe that a defendant is not guilty."

Is this action proper?

Answer: Yes. Although this a more literal interpretation of the presumption of innocence than most judges follow, it is a correct statement of the law and a juror is supposed to take this presumption very seriously.

PRESUMPTIONS VERSUS INFERENCES

We have said that a criminal defendant is always presumed innocent. A presumption is a conclusion that a judge or jury *must* make in certain situations. For instance, when a defendant is charged with a crime, the jury has no choice in the matter: They must presume that the defendant is not guilty. If, during jury selection, a potential juror states that he or she cannot make this presumption, then that person will be dismissed from the panel.

An **inference** is an assumption that may be made from the facts. If your friend comes to visit you and he has severe sunburn, you can infer that he has spent too much time outside. Even though a criminal defendant is protected by numerous presumptions, these presumptions can be overcome by the state's case. The jurors are told that they can make inferences based on the facts presented. But they are also told that they are never to presume that the defendant is guilty until the state proves it.

Inference
A fact that a person can believe is probably true.

 # RIGHTS DURING THE TRIAL

There are several critical rights that protect a defendant during a criminal trial. We will examine each of these in detail. They include the right to:

- A fair trial
- A jury trial
- A public trial
- Confront witnesses
- Be present
- Wear civilian clothing during the trial
- Present evidence
- Present a defense

A. RIGHT TO A FAIR TRIAL

In all criminal prosecutions, the accused shall enjoy the right to a speedy and public trial, by an impartial jury of the State and district wherein the crime shall have been committed, which district shall have been previously ascertained by law, and to be informed of the nature and cause of the accusation; to be confronted with the witnesses against him; to have compulsory process for obtaining witnesses in his favor, and to have the Assistance of Counsel for his defense. — Sixth Amendment

One of the most basic rights granted in the American criminal justice system is that a defendant must receive a fair trial. The judge is the person who must ensure this right, and a conviction can be overturned on appeal if the judge or the prosecutor acts in an unfair manner or does something to unfairly prejudice the jury against the defendant before or during the trial.

B. THE RIGHT TO A JURY TRIAL

The Sixth Amendment guarantees that individuals who are charged with certain crimes must be given a **jury trial**. This does not mean, however, that everyone charged with any type of criminal offense must receive a jury trial. Instead, the U.S. Supreme Court has interpreted this amendment to mean that jury trials are warranted in some types of cases, but not in others. For instance, there are no jury trials

Jury trial
A trial with a judge and jury, not just a judge.

in juvenile cases, primarily because the hearings are not considered to be adversarial or criminal. The entire juvenile court system is built around a different concept than the focus of the rest of criminal law: the rehabilitation of the juvenile.

Trials are also not guaranteed under the Sixth Amendment for petty offenses. The U.S. Supreme Court has interpreted that amendment to be reserved for "serious offenses." What the Court means by this phrase is that a defendant is entitled to a jury trial when he or she faces a potential sentence that is more than six months in custody.[3] If the potential punishment for an offense is less than six months, a state does not have to provide a jury trial for the defendant.[4] This ruling applies even in situations where the defendant is charged with several crimes, none of which can be punished by more than six months in custody but, taken as consecutive sentences, could result in the defendant serving more than six months in prison.

To determine whether a defendant's charge is considered a serious offense and therefore one in which he or she must receive a jury trial, the court will consider the maximum sentence allowed by law. Almost all statutes that criminalize behavior list not only the elements of each offense, but the range of punishments for those offenses. In that situation, the judge would simply refer to the applicable statute to decide if a jury trial is warranted. However, there are situations in which the state legislature has made a certain action criminal but has failed to provide a maximum sentence for the offense. In that case, the judge must determine what the possible maximum sentence is by researching similar offenses or by referring to common law. Consider Scenario 19-4.

SCENARIO 19-4

STEALING WIRE

Helen is charged with theft of copper wire. There is no maximum sentence stated for the offense, and the trial judge rules that the charge is a misdemeanor punishable by a maximum of three months in custody and therefore Helen has no right to a jury trial. Helen is given a bench trial, where the judge acts as the fact finder instead of a jury. After her conviction, Helen is sentenced to twelve months in the prison system. She appeals her conviction on the grounds that she should have been given a jury trial. How is the appellate court likely to rule?

Answer: The appellate court will almost certainly rule that Helen's conviction should be overturned and that she should be retried, this time with a jury. The fact that there was no maximum sentence stated in the statutes does not allow a judge to arbitrarily decide to exclude the possibility of a jury trial, especially where the judge by his or her own actions demonstrates that the maximum sentence is clearly beyond the six-month threshold.[5]

NUMBER OF JURORS USED IN THE TRIAL

Everyone knows that the jury is composed of twelve persons. Many would be surprised to learn, however, that this number is not mentioned in the U.S.

---

[3] *Lewis v. U.S.*, 518 U.S. 322, 116 S.Ct. 2163, 35 L.Ed.2d 590 (1996).
[4] *Baldwin v. New York*, 399 U.S. 66 (1970).
[5] *Codispoti v. Pennsylvania*, 418 U.S. 506, 94 S.Ct. 2707 (1974).

Constitution nor is guaranteed in the Bill of Rights. There is, in fact, no constitutional requirement for 12 people to sit on a jury. The U.S. Supreme Court has stated that, "the 12-person requirement . . . is not an indispensable component of the right to trial by jury."[6] Many states allow six-person juries to hear misdemeanor cases. Despite the fact that 12-person juries are not a constitutional requirement, most states have opted for that number and require 12 people to sit as the jury in felony cases. Having 12 jurors has been a tradition for so long, at least in felony cases, that changing the number is unlikely.

Why was the number 12 originally chosen? The simple answer is that the U.S. court system is based on the English system, and that system used 12 as the number of jurors. Why the English adopted this number is more difficult to answer.

As early as 1164 an English king required juries to be composed of 12 men.[7] Twelve has always been a number of special significance. There are 12 months in the year. Roman law, which forms an important foundation of our own legal system, was first promulgated in the Twelve Tables.[8] Because 12 was the original number, the tradition has held and will likely continue to do so for the foreseeable future.

TIMES WHEN NON-UNANIMOUS VERDICTS ARE PERMITTED

It is widely believed, but not always true, that juries must reach unanimous (agreed to by all) verdicts. There are many states that do not impose that requirement. In those states, if eleven out of the 12 jurors reach a specific verdict, then that will be the verdict for the entire jury. Of course, there are also many states that require unanimous verdicts. In states that require unanimous verdicts, jurors who cannot reach unanimity and declare themselves unable to ever reach a unanimous verdict are referred to as a **hung jury**, and the case is declared to be a **mistrial**. However, in states that do not require unanimous verdicts in all of their cases, the majority vote will be the outcome of the case. The U.S. Supreme Court held that there is nothing in the Sixth Amendment that requires unanimous verdicts and has allowed states, such as Oregon, to keep their statutes permitting juries to convict when the ratio is 11:1 or even 10:2.[9] However, most state statutes require that a defendant be convicted by unanimous verdict of the jury.

Hung jury
A jury that is unable to reach a unanimous verdict.

Mistrial
A trial that the judge ends and declares will have no legal effect.

Six-Person Juries. The Supreme Court's view on non-unanimous verdicts changes when dealing with six-person juries. In *Burch v. Louisiana*[10] the Court held that non-unanimous verdicts by six-person criminal juries pose a threat to constitutional principles and will not be allowed.

---

[6] *Williams v. Florida*, 399 U.S. 78, 90 S.Ct. 1893, 26 L.Ed.2d 446 (1970).
[7] *Foundations of Modern Jurisprudence*, William Seal Carpenter, 1958, page 114.
[8] *The Grandeur That Was Rome*, J.C. Stobart, 4th Edition. 1961.
[9] *Apodaca v. Oregon*, 406 U.S. 404, 92 S.Ct. 1628, 32 L.Ed.2d 184 (1972).
[10] 441 U.S. 130, 139, 99 S.Ct. 1623, 60 L.Ed.2d 96 (1979).

EXCEPTIONS TO THE RIGHT TO A JURY

Although there is no right to a jury trial for minor offenses or any offense where the possible sentence is less than six months, there are other types of prosecutions where defendants do not have the right to jury trials. In juvenile cases, for example, juries are not used. Instead, a juvenile court judge hears all evidence and reaches a decision in the case.[11] Traffic-citation cases are another example. In most cases where the possible punishment is only a fine, there is no requirement or authorization for a jury trial.

Criminal Infractions Where the Sentence Is Six Months or Less. Despite the fact that they are not required to do so, many states provide jury trials for people charged with minor offenses. In some states, the defendant is tried first without a jury, and only if he is convicted does he have the right to a jury trial.

To determine the maximum sentence for a particular offense, the criminal sentencing statute should be reviewed. The state legislature sets the maximum sentence for an offense. The legislature generally includes the nature of the punishment in the statute making a certain action illegal. Where the maximum sentence is set at six months or greater, a jury trial would be required. Consider Scenario 19-5.

SCENARIO 19-5

JURY TRIAL REQUIRED?

Cary is charged with several offenses. They are all misdemeanors, and the maximum sentence on each is only four months in custody. However, there are ten such counts and the maximum sentence adds up to 40 months of a possible sentence. Is Cary entitled to a jury trial because of the maximum possible sentence?

Answer: No. A jury trial is based on the maximum sentence for each charge, not the total charges. If any of the charges had a maximum possible sentence of more than six months, then Cary would be entitled to a jury trial.

 **FAMOUS CASES**
HILLSIDE BURGLAR

The lush hillsides and canyons of Los Angeles are home to pricey enclaves such as Brentwood, Beverly Hills, and Pacific Palisades. The multimillion-dollar mansions in those exclusive communities tend to be gated and tucked behind high walls and thick hedges. As a result, the very qualities that make them so desirable also make them vulnerable.

The secluded nature of the homes appealed to a notorious burglar — dubbed the Hillside Burglar — who, along with his ring of helpers, stole more than $10

---

[11] *McKeiver v. Pennsylvania*, 403 U.S. 528, 91 S.Ct. (1976).

million in cash and property from wealthy and well-known residents. During a three-year period between 2006 and 2009, Troy Corsby Thomas and his sophisticated gang of thieves invaded the homes of celebrities, sports stars, and executives. Police detectives, who mounted an intensive and painstaking investigation, were baffled by the lack of clues.

Thomas and his cohorts managed to evade security systems and cameras in all but one of their burglaries. In that particular one, a camera captured an image of two men, but their faces were blurred and difficult to see. The burglars used refined methods. They typically waited until no one was at home, either out for the evening or away on vacation. Using lawn furniture and ladders, they entered the homes on the second floor, which often lacked alarms. Within minutes they were in and out.

For three years Thomas and his ring operated untouched and unchallenged, until he inadvertently left some DNA at five of the crime scenes. Investigators finally held something tangible. An informant's tip had already led police to consider Thomas as their prime suspect. The problem was how to get a DNA sample from him to compare to their evidence without violating the Fourth Amendment.

Police had placed Thomas under surveillance once he became a suspect, and one evening he committed a minor traffic violation. When pulled over, his eyes appeared watery and bloodshot. This gave police a reason to test him for drunk driving. During the sobriety test, Thomas agreed to breathe into a breathalyzer, a device that required him to place his mouth over the tip and blow into it. Although Thomas passed the breathalyzer test and was sent on his way, police now had a saliva sample. The DNA from that sample linked Thomas to two of the burglaries, and additional DNA obtained after his arrest linked him to several more.

Thomas was charged with six counts of felony first-degree residential burglary. In pretrial motions, he tried to suppress the DNA evidence, claiming that the sample taken from the breathalyzer constituted an illegal search. The judge denied the motion, and Thomas subsequently pleaded guilty to a single burglary count in 2010. Since he had previous felonies on his record, he was sentenced to 17 years in prison.

On appeal, Thomas again raised the issue of an unreasonable search under the Fourth Amendment of the Constitution. The California Court of Appeal decided that Thomas had abandoned his expectation of privacy when he failed to wipe his saliva off the breathalyzer after taking the test. The court upheld his conviction.

All around Los Angeles, wealthy residents of posh neighborhoods breathed a collective sigh of relief. The Hillside Burglar had not struck again once Thomas was arrested. Other members of the ring had not been apprehended, but without their leader, they did not burglarized Hillside again.

C. THE RIGHT TO A PUBLIC TRIAL

The Sixth Amendment also provides that a trial must be conducted in public. The Supreme Court has stated that the right to a public trial is one of the most important guaranteed to a criminal defendant. "Without the freedom to attend such trials, which people have exercised for centuries, important aspects of freedom of speech and of the press could be eviscerated."[12] Secret trials are the staple of totalitarian governments around the world. Opening a criminal trial to the public is a simple and efficient way to ensure that justice is served. When judges and prosecutors know that their actions can be monitored by any member of the public or the press, they tend to behave more responsibly. Even though a trial is open to the public, the trial judge may bar specific people from attending if they prove to be disruptive or dangerous to the proceedings.[13]

WHEN CAN A JUDGE CLOSE A TRIAL TO THE PUBLIC?

There are only a few instances in which a trial judge is allowed to close a jury trial to the public, and even in these instances the judge may only do so for a brief period of time. The judge must show a "compelling interest" to close a portion of the trial from the public. The two most common instances involve testimony by rape victims or testimony by children about sexual acts committed on them. There is no standing rule that requires a case to be closed at a certain point in any trial. In fact, the government must show a compelling reason to close the trial before the judge will authorize it. The preference under American law is for all trials to remain open. For instance, in a case where a state passed a statute that required a trial to be closed whenever a child sexual assault victim testified, the U.S. Supreme Court ruled it an infraction of the defendant's right to a public trial, and before any such closing is made, the judge must weigh the state's compelling interest (in this case, protecting the identity of the child) against the defendant's constitutional right to have an open and public trial. In the case of the mandatory statute, the rule that required closure in all such cases was ruled to be unconstitutional. There is no one factor that will always justify the closing of a trial. The trial judge must weigh the defendant's rights against other factors and there is no one right that always outweighs another. The judge must make some accommodation short of closing the trial if at all possible. Consider Scenario 19-6.

| SCENARIO 19-6 | CLOSING THE TRIAL TO THE PUBLIC. |

There is a trial pending before Judge S in which ten different defendants are charged with child molestation of dozens of children. Each of these children will testify, essentially meaning that there will be days and days of testimony by underage children who will be testifying about intensely personal, sexual, and humiliating acts perpetrated on them. Can the judge rule that the trial will be closed during the entire phase where witnesses will be testifying?

Answer: No. A judge can choose to close the trial each time a child testifies, but a judge cannot close most of a trial to the public because of the nature of the charges. The

---

[12] *Richmond Newspapers, Inc. v. Virginia*, 100 S.Ct. 2814 (1980).
[13] *Estes v. Texas*, 381 U.S. 532 (1965).

judge must weigh the rights of the defendants against the rights of the children and come up with some alternative to closing the entire witness testimony phase of the case.

Jury Selection. It is not simply the trial that must remain open to the public, but also the jury selection process as well.[15] If jury selection involves some sensitive issues, the jurors can be questioned in the judge's chambers. Although jury selection must remain a public affair, there are some practical issues to be considered. When a large jury pool is summoned for a case, there may not be any additional seating left over for anyone to sit and view the selection process. In some instances, the size of the courtroom itself is the limiting factor, not the parties' intention of closing an otherwise open trial.

Preliminary Hearings. The rule about open trials also applies to preliminary hearings and many other hearings, including motions, where important issues are decided. The only time the Supreme Court has allowed a preliminary hearing to be closed to the public is when the hearing may actually impinge on the defendant's right to a fair trial, such as when the case involves intensive pretrial publicity.[16]

Sensitive or Underage Witnesses. There are provisions that allow the judge to close a public trial, briefly, while a child or sexual assault victim testifies. However, even then, the prosecution must show a compelling reason to do so. Despite the fact that the testimony in such cases is of a sensitive nature, it is not common for a prosecutor to request that the trial be closed during the entire testimony of a rape or child abuse victim. Instead, they conduct the trial in public, despite the fact that sensitive or embarrassing details may emerge. Prosecutors do not do this to make the victim even more uncomfortable, but to emphasize just how serious the case is and how everyone should know what the defendant is accused of doing. Leaving a trial open to the public, even when it involves extremely sensitive information and a sensitive victim helps to educate not only the jurors, but also the public at large that the state will not shirk its duties to protect victims and hopefully sends a message to those considering such a crime that they will not avoid prosecution. However, the decision to request closing a portion of a trial is a question left to each individual prosecutor and some may routinely request closure while others never do.

Sidebar

Closing a trial to the public is only allowed in limited circumstances. A trial can only be closed for a "compelling interest."[14] In order to close a trial, the state must show that some overriding interest is at stake.

D. RIGHT TO CONFRONT WITNESSES

The right of a criminal defendant to confront witnesses and also to cross-examine them is considered to be one of the fundamental rights guaranteed by the U.S. Constitution. Without the ability to confront witnesses and ask them questions, there can be no due process.[17] Consider Scenario 19-7.

---

[14] *Globe Newspaper Co. v. Superior Court*, 457 U.S. 596, 102 S.Ct. 2613 (1982).
[15] *Press Enterprise Co. v. Superior Court (Press Enterprise I)*, 464 U.S. 501 (1984).
[16] *Press Enterprise Co. v. Superior Court (Press Enterprise II)*, 478 U.S. 1 (1986).
[17] *Chambers v. Mississippi*, 410 U.S. 284, 93 S. Ct. 1038, 35 L. Ed. 2d 297 (1973).

DISCOVERING THE DEAL

During the defendant's trial for armed robbery, Juan, the defense attorney, learns that one of the other codefendants has struck a deal with the prosecution where he will testify against Juan's client. When the codefendant takes the stand, Juan begins to question the codefendant about whether or not he has made a deal with the state. The prosecution objects and the judge sustains the objection, preventing Juan from asking any questions along these lines. Is this an unfair restriction on the defendant's right to cross-examine?

Answer: Yes. Juan must be allowed to confront the state's witnesses, especially with information that so intimately affects his possible testimony.[18]

The provisions of the Sixth Amendment, especially the right to confront witnesses in a criminal trial, have been made applicable to the states through the passage of the Fourteenth Amendment.[19] It is common for courts to say that the right of the defendant to face-to-face confrontation of a witness is one of the most important rights guaranteed under the U.S. Constitution, but this right is not absolute. Like many other rights, it must be balanced against other interests. There are several situations in which a defendant does not have the right of face-to-face confrontation. Many states allow rape and child abuse victims to testify through closed-circuit television as the witness testifies from another room. In other situations, a child victim may not be seated at the actual witness stand, but may testify at a smaller (and child-sized) table in front of the jury box, where he or she faces the jury and does not speak directly to the defendant.

The confrontation clause of the Sixth Amendment provides two rights: 1) the right of the defendant to confront witnesses against him or her, and 2) the right to **cross-examine** these witnesses to show bias or prejudice.[20] Included in this concept is the idea that a defendant can use cross-examination to develop evidence of a witness's biases or even a motive that the witness might have to lie about the events.[21] Cross examination is used to show that a state's witness does not know what he or she claims to know, that the witness lacks personal knowledge, that the witness is biased or prejudiced against the defendant, or that the witness has been coached.[22]

Although the defendant has the right to a cross-examination, this does not mean that the defendant (or defendant's attorney) has the right to ask any question about any topic. Instead, the defendant is guaranteed the opportunity to a full and effective cross-examination. What he or she does with that opportunity is left to the defendant and the defense attorney. Defendants are not given free rein to ask any question that they wish. Their questions must be limited to the issues pending in the case and must still survive the test of relevancy that we

Cross-examine
To question a witness for the opposition about his or possible bias, prejudice, or lack of knowledge about the issues in the case.

---

[18] *Burbank v. Cain*, 535 F.3d 350 (5th Cir. 2008).
[19] *Shorter v. U.S.*, 792 A.2d 228 (D.C. 2001).
[20] *U.S. v. Eagle*, 498 F.3d 885, 74 Fed. R. Evid. Serv. 257 (8th Cir. 2007).
[21] *Commerford v. State*, 728 So. 2d 796 (Fla. Dist. Ct. App. 4th Dist. 1999).
[22] *Com. v. Avalos*, 454 Mass. 1, 906 N.E.2d 987 (2009).

discussed in the chapter on evidence. The judge has the final say about when the defendant has exhausted all relevant questions and can even stop the defense from asking any more questions about a particular topic, once the issue has been thoroughly examined.[23]

Finally, the right to confront witnesses changes with the status of the defendant. During a jury trial, the defendant has the right to confront witnesses as part of the guarantees of the due process clause of the Constitution. However, when the defendant is convicted, and the status of the person charged changes from defendant to probationer or convict his or her constitutional right of confrontation is considerably less. During a probation-revocation hearing, for example, the state has a relaxed standard and can use witness statements, hearsay, and other documentary evidence that might not be admissible during trial but is admissible during a probation-revocation hearing. The defendant's right of confrontation is considerably curtailed after being found guilty.

E. RIGHT TO BE PRESENT

In addition to a fair and public trial, the right to a jury trial and the right to confrontation, the defendant also has the right to be present during the trial. Although this might seem obvious, there are many countries that prosecute individuals but do not allow them to be present for the proceedings. Fortunately, the U.S. legal system requires the defendant to be present, unless certain specific circumstances are present.

TRIALS *IN ABSENTIA*

Although there are instances where a trial may be conducted against an individual when he or she is not present, or ***in absentia***, it is much more common and often required for the defendant to be present during all phases of a jury trial. What happens in situations where the defendant absconds before the trial begins? In that situation, the court will continue the defendant's case until such time as the defendant is arrested and brought back before the court. There will be no trial until the defendant is located.

CONTINUING A TRIAL AFTER THE DEFENDANT FLEES

Once the trial is underway, a defendant who is out on bond is free to come and go, just like the witnesses and attorneys. What happens when a defendant abuses this privilege and flees the jurisdiction after the trial begins? Is the judge required to declare a mistrial? The answer depends on the nature of the case. When the case is a misdemeanor, the judge may opt to continue the case against the defendant, even though he or she is no longer present. This would be a classic case of a trial *in*

> ### Sidebar
> *The right of cross-examination is "beyond any doubt the greatest legal engine ever invented for the discovery of truth."[24]*

In absentia
Latin for "the defendant is not present."

---

[23] *U.S. v. Orisnord*, 483 F.3d 1169 (11th Cir. 2007).
[24] 5 J. Wigmore, Evidence § 1367, p. 32 (J. Chadbourn rev.1974).

absentia. However, if the defendant absconds during a felony case, the court may call a recess to see if the defendant can be arrested and brought back to the courtroom. If the defendant cannot be located, the most common result is for the judge to declare a mistrial and wait for the defendant to be rearrested and a new trial scheduled. In such a situation, the judge would issue a bench warrant for the defendant's arrest, and that would authorize any law enforcement officer to seize the defendant and bring him back to the courtroom so that the trial could continue. A bench warrant will often contain a "no bond" provision, which prevents the defendant from obtaining a bail bond before the next trial date. It would not make much sense to allow a defendant who has absconded on his first bond to be able to make bail again.

WHEN THE DEFENDANT WAIVES HIS OR HER RIGHT TO BE PRESENT

In minor cases, such as misdemeanor charges, the defendant can waive his or her presence during the trial, but only with the judge's permission. Most states have statutes or court rules that allow this for certain minor offenses. However, this rule does not apply to felonies and certainly never to capital murder cases (where the death penalty can be imposed). Although a defendant cannot waive his presence at a felony jury trial, some states do allow the defendant to waive his or her presence during earlier stages in the prosecution, such as preliminary hearing or arraignment.

If the defendant is not available when the trial is scheduled to begin–for example, because he is hospitalized — the court must wait until the defendant is able to be present before the jury trial can commence. Although many foreign countries allow defendants to be tried *in absentia*, it is rare in the U.S. court system.

WHEN THE JUDGE MAY REMOVE THE DEFENDANT FROM THE COURTROOM

In situations where the defendant disrupts the order and propriety of the courtroom setting, a judge may remove the defendant from the courtroom. In situations where the defendant continually interrupts the proceedings or acts out in a violent way, the judge is authorized to bind and gag the defendant or to remove the defendant and keep him someplace nearby.[25] The defendant can be informed about the various stages of the trial by his attorney or can listen (or watch) the trial through a closed-circuit system. This is a better alternative to gagging or binding the defendant to prevent him from acting out in court. In fact, if the defendant is put in chains or handcuffs, he or she must be restrained in such a way that the jury cannot see that the defendant is shackled. Given the choice between handcuffing the defendant to his chair and simply removing him to a nearby cell where he

---

[25] *Illinois v. Allen*, 397 U.S. 337, 90 S.Ct. 1057, 25 L.Ed.2d 353 (1970).

can listen to the proceedings over an intercom, most judges would opt for the latter choice.

F. RIGHT TO WEAR CIVILIAN CLOTHING DURING THE TRIAL

One of the more important rights for a defendant is to be tried in regular or civilian clothes during the trial. A defendant who appeared before a jury in a prison tunic might give the jury the impression that his or her guilt has already been determined.

PRISON ATTIRE NOT PERMITTED

It is common practice for jails to confiscate all of a defendant's personal items, including his or her clothing, and hold it in safekeeping. In such situations, defendants are issued uniforms, often brightly colored so that they may be identifiable at a distance. However, a defendant has the right to appear before the jury without a prison uniform. In fact, numerous appellate court decisions have held that putting a defendant on trial in prison attire would jeopardize his or her right to a fair trial.[26] Instead, the state must provide the defendant with suitable clothing if he has none of his own. A defendant may not appear at a jury trial in a prison uniform. In many cases, the defense attorney often provides his or her client with suitable clothing for the duration of the trial.

G. THE RIGHT TO PRESENT EVIDENCE

Our discussions so far have focused on the rights that protect the defendant, but in this section, we will examine the right of a defendant to be proactive in his or her defense. The ability to present evidence during the trial is probably as important as the right to cross-examine the state's witnesses. If a defendant decides to present evidence, then he or she is bound by the same rules that bind the prosecutor. The defendant must follow the same rules of evidence. A defendant has the right to take the stand and tell his or her side of the story even if the defendant refused to speak to the police after being arrested.

The defendant also has the right to subpoena other witnesses to testify, and this subpoena carries the same weight as the subpoena issued by the government to compel witness testimony on its behalf. A defendant can subpoena both people and records and once issued, it must be obeyed. However, just as with the state, a defendant who requests information to which he or she is not entitled may be subject to having the subpoena quashed. When a defendant issues a subpoena,

---

[26] *Estelle v. Williams*, 425 U.S. 501 (1976).

the prosecutor is allowed to challenge it and ask for a court ruling on whether or not the material should be produced. For instance, if the defendant's subpoena is too broad or calls for violating an evidentiary privilege, the defendant can no more receive this information than can the state.

Although the right to present evidence means that the defendant is permitted to take the stand and to testify in his or her own behalf, most defendants choose not to do so for several reasons. The most obvious is that if the defendant takes the stand, he or she will be subject to cross-examination by the prosecutor. These attorneys are skilled in cross-examining witnesses, and few defendants bear up well to a blistering cross-examination.

Placing character into evidence
When a criminal defendant testifies and his previous criminal record is allowed into evidence through the cross-examination of the defendant.

Another reason is that in some jurisdictions, and in the federal system, a defendant who takes the stand in his or her own defense is **placing character into evidence**. This deceptively simple phrase conceals a complex procedure. Normally, a prosecutor is not allowed to tell the jury about the defendant's criminal record. The prosecutor cannot, for example, tell the jury that the defendant has been convicted of other crimes. The reason for this is that it would prejudice the jury. (They might well decide that a person who has been convicted of a crime similar to the one for which he is currently being tried is probably guilty and might be tempted to ignore the evidence. As seen many times in this text, criminal cases must stand on their own.) However, in jurisdictions that follow the character into evidence rule, when defendants take the stand in their own trials, the prosecutor is allowed to question the defendants about their previous convictions. The jury will then hear that the defendant has a criminal past. (Some jurisdictions modify this rule, and the prosecutor must wait until the defendant says something about his previous criminal record before being allowed to introduce this evidence.)

If a defendant chooses not to take the stand during the trial, then the prosecutor is barred from bringing up the defendant's criminal history. The prosecutor certainly cannot tell the jury in either opening statements or closing arguments that the defendant has a long criminal history–this would result in a mistrial and perhaps even sanctions against the prosecutor by the State Bar. It is up to the judge, defense attorney, and prosecutor to ensure that no witness attempts to bring up the defendant's criminal history.

A defendant is under no obligation to present evidence and is certainly not obligated to take the stand and deny the charge before the jury. Defendants are not even under an obligation to present a defense and may actually remain silent during the entire trial, although that is unusual. When a defendant exercises the right to remain silent, the jurors are instructed that they are to draw no negative inference from this and that they must, in fact, presume that the defendant is innocent until proven guilty. The right to remain silent is so central to the constitutional rights guaranteed to those accused of a crime that a prosecutor is not even permitted to comment to the jury that the defendant invoked it. A prosecutor cannot even imply that if the prosecution's version is not correct, then the defendant should have refuted it. Consider Scenario 19-8.

PROSECUTOR'S MISTAKE?

During Phil's trial, he chose not to take the stand and testify. Phil's attorney presented some other witnesses and some evidence, but the jury never heard from Phil. During the prosecutor's closing argument, she says to the jury, "If the state is wrong, then why hasn't the defendant said so? Why hasn't he taken the stand and told you what he says is the real truth? You want to know why? Because we are right. He is guilty and he knows it."

Phil's attorney immediately objects and moves for a mistrial. Is he likely to get it?

Answer: Yes. The defendant's right to remain silent is one of the bedrock principles of U.S. law. The fact that the prosecutor violated that principle will almost certainly mean that the judge will declare a mistrial.

H. RIGHT TO PRESENT A DEFENSE

Although we have seen that the defendant's constitutional guarantees are so profound that he or she may choose to remain silent throughout the entire trial, most defendants present some kind of a defense, even if it is simply to suggest alternative explanations for the crime by cross-examining the state's witnesses. If a defendant chooses to present a defense, there are a variety available to him or her, many of which were discussed in Chapter 17.

PROVING THE DEFENDANT GUILTY

While discussing the rights of the defendant, it is important to point out that there are burdens on the state. One of the biggest is that the state must always prove that the defendant committed the offense beyond a reasonable doubt.

A. PROOF BEYOND A REASONABLE DOUBT

Under the U.S. legal system, the defendant is never under any burden to prove his or her innocence. Instead, that burden remains on the state throughout the trial. As we have already seen, the defendant is protected by many different rights, including the presumption of innocence. That presumption requires that the state prove every material allegation against the defendant beyond a **reasonable doubt**. Failure to meet this burden means that the case against the defendant will fail. Reasonable doubt can be a difficult term to quantify. Beyond a reasonable doubt is a much higher standard than is used in civil cases. Proving a case beyond a reasonable doubt does not mean that the state has to prove the case beyond all doubt, or beyond a shadow of a doubt. Reasonable doubt means a doubt based on a common sense reason, not some capricious or ill-advised

Reasonable doubt
The standard of proof that the prosecution must meet in order to prove that a defendant committed a crime.

Sidebar

The standard the prosecutor must meet in all criminal trials is proof beyond a reasonable doubt.

opinion. If, at the end of the trial, a juror is still unsettled in his mind, or has qualms about the proof, this is a reasonable doubt. The judge's instruction to the jury leaves little doubt about what should happen if a juror has a reasonable doubt. In any situation where a reasonable doubt exists, the juror must vote to acquit the defendant.

Jurors are repeatedly instructed, during the course of the trial, that the state's burden is proof beyond a reasonable doubt and are even told that if they believe that the defendant committed the crime, but the state did not prove it beyond a reasonable doubt, it is their duty to acquit the defendant.

EXPLAINING THE STATE'S BURDEN OF PROOF

If a defendant presents a defense, such as alibi or insanity, it continues to be the state's obligation to disprove the defense beyond a reasonable doubt. The burden in a criminal case never rests on the defendant to prove that he is not guilty. In cases where the defense is insanity, for instance, the state must present rebuttal evidence establishing that the defendant was legally sane at the time of the crime.

V   CRIMINAL TRIALS AND THE PRESS

Congress shall make no law abridging the freedom of speech, or of the press. — First Amendment

Because criminal trials are open to the public, they are also open to the press. But press coverage brings with it a whole host of other issues that are not seen when members of the general public are in attendance at a public trial. It is not uncommon for intensive press coverage to make it difficult for a defendant to receive a fair trial. As a result, there is an inherent conflict between two constitutional values: the right of the defendant to receive a fair trial and the freedom of the press. Neither of these rights outbalances the other. They must be weighed, one against the other. In each case, the judge must weigh the constitutional values and reach some type of accommodation and balance the freedom of the press with the defendant's right to a fair trial. A judge cannot, for example, bar any press coverage of the trial, but a judge can prevent news organizations from bringing in cameras to televise or photograph the trial.[27] The defendant's right to a fair trial does not always outweigh the freedom of the press, so a judge must take both concerns into account in conducting the trial.

The U.S. Supreme Court confirmed the right of the press and public to attend criminal trials in *Richmond Newspapers Inc. v. Virginia*[28]

---

[27] *Bridges v. California*, 314 U.S. 252 (1941).
[28] 448 U.S. 555 (1980).

SHORTER v. U.S.
792 A.2d 228, 229 -236 (D.C.,2001)

CASE EXCERPT

REID, Associate Judge:

Appellant Richard A. Shorter challenges his convictions for child sexual abuse of and threat to injure T.J. He claims, primarily, that the trial court violated his constitutional Sixth Amendment right of confrontation by refusing his request to cross-examine T.J., or to conduct a voir dire of T.J. and her mother, about T.J.'s alleged prior allegation of sexual abuse which she later recanted. He also contends that the trial court erred by: 1) denying him the right to examine psychological reports regarding the complaining witness and her siblings; 2) failing to grant a mistrial during the complaining witness' testimony; 3) allowing the government to introduce photographs of rooms in his home that were in disarray; and 4) denying his D.C.Code § 23-110 motion (ineffective assistance of counsel) without a hearing and without appointing counsel for him. We remand this case for further proceedings with respect to appellant's primary contention, but reject his remaining arguments.

FACTUAL SUMMARY

The government's trial evidence showed the following facts. Between September 2, 1996 and May 14, 1997, T.J., who at the time was seven years of age, complained that Shorter, her mother's fiancé, whom she called "Uncle Rick," and who is the appellant in this case, had sexual contact with her on three different occasions. On one of those occasions, he threatened to injure her.

ANALYSIS

We turn to Shorter's contention that the trial court erred by denying him the opportunity to cross-examine T.J., or to conduct a voir dire of T.J. and her mother, concerning a recanted allegation of a prior sexual assault against her by Shorter. Shortly before trial, the government filed a motion in limine to exclude irrelevant evidence, including "evidence of prior reports of sexual abuse made by T.J. . . . ." The government stated, in pertinent part: "The defendant may seek to cross-examine T.J. on a prior report of sexual abuse made to her mother. . . ." The issue of cross-examination concerning T.J.'s alleged prior report of sexual abuse was joined late on a Friday evening during the cross-examination of T.J. Defense counsel advised the trial judge that:

> Last year, T.J. accused Shorter of doing something similar in the nature of sexual molestation or abuse, and after she made that report to her mother — I believe the same day — she recanted and said that's not true.
>
> What I would like to do is cross-examine her about that, ask her if there was a time apart from the three times that she's talked about that she accused her uncle and then said it wasn't true.

When the trial court pointed out that a recantation did not establish falsity of the prior sexual assault allegation and that Shorter would have to show convincingly its falsity, his counsel asked for a voir dire of T.J. and her mother. In response to the trial court's request for the government's view regarding voir dire of T.J. and her mother, the prosecutor gave a proffer of what T.J. would say about the prior allegation:

The trial judge made a tentative ruling, allowing Shorter to "cross -examine T.J. about the particulars of the charged sexual assaults and whether T.J. previously made any statements that were different than the particulars that she testified to today." On the other hand, the judge explained her reasons for proposing to deny the defense request to conduct a voir dire of T.J. and her mother: 1) the mother did not witness the recanted incident; and 2) "given the Government's proffer, and the fact that this is a child, I think it would be both not necessary and arguably detrimental to the child were the Court to conduct a voir dire on the matter that is not going to be the subject of the trial." The trial judge was convinced that "the voir dire would not establish the falsity of the prior accusations," and that a mini-trial during the trial would be "confusing" to the jury, whether conducted in or outside the jury's presence.

On the Monday morning following the exchange between counsel and the trial judge regarding the prior allegation of sexual molestation that T.J. recanted, Shorter filed a written memorandum, citing his constitutional Sixth Amendment right to confrontation, and claiming that the prior allegation was admissible: "(a) as substantive evidence of his defense theory that T.J. had fabricated these allegations of other sexual assaults; (b) to show T.J.'s state of mind, credibility and bias against Mr. Shorter; and (c) to rebut the inference that T.J.'s mother, a defense witness, disbelieved T.J.'s allegations without reason and to rehabilitate T.J.'s mother as a defense witness." The trial judge decided that "this issue of alleged prior false accusations will not be admitted"; in part because: 1) T.J.'s mother's disbelief of her daughter's allegation "had not been introduced as substantive evidence"; 2) "even if T.J.'s recantation is shown convincingly, it is not convincing evidence that the underlying accusations were false"; and 3) T.J. could be cross-examined about "prior inconsistent statements about what happened in the kitchen the day before the report in school. . . ."

When defense counsel continued to press the recantation issue, the trial judge asked for a proffer as to her cross-examination of T.J. Defense counsel attempted to link the alleged October recantation incident to the kitchen incident about which T.J. had testified, and to show that T.J.'s report of the kitchen sexual molestation was false, in part because of an alleged inconsistency as to whether there had been a touching or a penetration. As defense counsel put it:

> It is our belief that it is an October report that she made to her mother and then recanted. And I think it would be appropriate for me to cross-examine her by asking something along the lines of what you say happened in the kitchen and you told your mother about that and then later told her that wasn't true. And I'm asking the Court whether that falls into the Court's ruling of appropriate examination.

The trial court responded: "It does not." When defense counsel asked why, the judge explained:

> You are trying to slip in a prior false allegation that has not been demonstrably shown to be false. . . .

> If you simply want to cross-examine her about the timing you may. But to try to bring before the jury a claim of a prior false allegation cannot be done in this case given my ruling as to the lack of substantial evidence of . . . falsity and the balancing issue of it being a mini-trial on another issue.

In reaction to the trial judge's statement, defense counsel reiterated her request for a voir dire of T.J. or her mother, based on a good faith basis to question one or the other about the recantation. The government opposed the voir dire of both, pointing out, first, that: T.J.'s mother was not present when the alleged sexual molestation took place; and second, proffering what T.J. would say. When defense counsel continued to link the kitchen incident with the alleged October recantation, the trial judge made her final ruling: "You may cross-examine about the particulars and whether she previously made any statements that were different than the particulars that she testified to today. You may not base on what's been said so far ask anything about a prior recantation. . . ." The judge also denied the request for the voir dire of the mother because she was not present during the kitchen incident. She also refused to permit the voir dire of T.J. on the grounds that it was unnecessary, and "arguably would be detrimental to the child. . . . and would not establish the falsity of the accusations." Following the bench conference, defense counsel conducted rather extensive cross-examination of T.J.

On appeal, Shorter contends that the trial court violated both his Sixth Amendment right of confrontation and his Fifth Amendment right to present a defense by excluding evidence of the prior sexual abuse allegation. It is beyond dispute that a defendant has a constitutional right to be confronted with the witnesses against him. Indeed, "prejudicial error may result from limiting a defendant's right to cross-examine a crucial government witness, especially a witness without whose testimony the government could not prove guilt." Moreover, "although the extent of cross-examination is within the discretion of the trial court, the trial court's wide latitude in the control of cross-examination . . . cannot justify a curtailment which keeps from the jury relevant and important facts bearing on the trustworthiness of crucial testimony." We recognized these fundamental principles both in *Roundtree v. United States*, 581 A.2d 315 (D.C.1990) and *Lawrence*, supra, cases which the government and Shorter, respectively, advance as controlling the outcome of this case. *Roundtree* affirmed the trial court's preclusion of the cross-examination of the complaining witness about prior allegations of sexual assaults, and Lawrence concluded that the trial court violated the appellant's Sixth Amendment confrontation right by disallowing such cross-examination.

In claiming trial court error, Shorter relies primarily upon Lawrence, supra, and distinguishes *Roundtree*, supra, on the ground that in *Roundtree*, there was corroborating evidence to show that the prior allegation was true; the prior allegation involved others rather than the defendant; and the trial court conducted a voir dire examination. Further, Shorter insists that T.J.'s recantation itself establishes the falsity of her prior allegation, and that, "the failure of the trial court to allow examination of this issue at least through a voir dire of T.J. and her mother . . . deprived him of a fair trial." In response, the government argues that there was no violation of Shorter's constitutional rights, and the trial court did not abuse its discretion in excluding evidence of the prior assault allegation. Relying on *Roundtree*, supra, the government maintains that Shorter failed to show convincingly that the allegation of a prior sexual assault was false; that the government's proffer as to what T.J. would say about the prior assault allegation showed that it was not false; and that the "barebones" defense proffer was inadequate to show falsity of the prior allegation.

Roundtree, supra, is a case involving a conviction for sodomy under a District statute that has since been repealed. There, the defendant, a correctional officer at the D.C. Jail, sought to cross-examine the seventeen-year-old complaining witness, who was an inmate at the jail when the officer sexually molested her, about her prior allegations of sexual abuse by other men, including her brother, in the State of Minnesota. After examining Minnesota documents, "the trial court indicated that there was 'no basis for inquiry into prior accusations' because there had been no 'firm determination' as to whether any of the complaining witness's allegations 'were false or true.' Id. at 319. However, the trial judge decided, apparently without the request of either party, to conduct a voir dire of the complaining witness before reaching a final conclusion. During the voir dire, the complaining witness explained her recantation and reasserted her allegations of prior sexual molestation by others. After the voir dire, and based on the Minnesota documents and the trial judge's assessment of the complaining witness's testimony . . . ," id. at 320, the judge stated: "'there is no substantial basis for concluding that these assaults are fabrication.'" Id. Thus, cross-examination about the prior allegations was precluded, because "appellant had failed to 'show convincingly' that the complaining witness's allegations were false." Id.

On appeal, this court explained that, with respect to credibility, the complaining witness's allegations of prior sexual molestation "would be probative . . . only if they were fabricated." Id. at 321. We stated:

> Where an accused seeks to impeach the credibility of a witness by offering evidence that the witness has made a false claim under similar circumstances, the confrontation clause mandates that the trial court give defendant leave to cross-examine about the prior claim only where it is "shown convincingly" that the prior claim is false.

The *Roundtree* court recognized that in Lawrence, supra, we had "found reversible error in a trial court's refusal to permit the defendant to cross-examine a witness to a sexual assault on a minor about 'prior false accusations of sexual activity made by the witness against other family members.'" That decision, however, had been premised on an apparent assumption — shared by the parties — that the prior allegations were indeed false. No such assumption prevailed in *Roundtree*, where the trial court had conducted a voir dire and "observed the complainant's testimony first hand" before concluding that the defense had failed to show the falsity of the accusations convincingly.

In applying the foregoing principles and cases to Shorter's situation, we are first mindful of the fact that T.J. was a "crucial government witness." Moreover, when the trial judge considered the defense request for a voir dire examination of T.J. and her mother about the prior alleged sexual assault which T.J. recanted, T.J.'s mother was a potentially critical defense witness. The jury's determination of Shorter's guilt or innocence would rest primarily on its perception of the credibility of T.J.'s testimony, as well as the later testimony of T.J.'s mother and Shorter. Equally important, whether T.J. had made a prior false accusation of sexual abuse against Shorter, in October of 1996, which T.J. later recanted, as alleged in Shorter's motion, was also probative of T.J.'s bias against Shorter.

Second, Shorter's proposed cross-examination pertaining to T.J.'s alleged October 1996 recantation of a prior false report of his sexual abuse would be, if the falsity were established, neither "'repetitive nor marginally relevant.'" If Shorter could show convincingly that T.J. fabricated a prior charge of sexual abuse against him, a jury arguably could question her credibility regarding the three charged incidents of child sexual abuse by Shorter, and could deem T.J. to be a biased witness. Third, unlike in Sherer, supra,

Shorter's proffer of facts supporting the claimed false allegation in the past was not "scanty," "conclusory," or supported only by "inadmissible hearsay." The government did not dispute that the child had made and then withdrawn the prior claim of sexual abuse; its counter-proffer was an explanation for why she had made the about-face. Finally, the trial court's concern about a mini-trial and jury confusion could have been alleviated through a limited voir dire examination outside the presence of the jury, and depending upon the results of the voir dire, limited cross-examination of T.J. about the October 1996 alleged incident and her recantation. The trial court's understandable worry about T.J. could not defeat Shorter's Sixth Amendment right to confrontation, in the absence of some objective indication that T.J.'s safety would be compromised, or that she would be harassed because of her trial testimony about the October 1996 incident and her recantation. See Roundtree, supra.

At the same time, contrary to Shorter's position and based on Roundtree, supra, we agree with the trial judge that a complaining witness's recantation of an alleged prior sexual assault, by itself, is insufficient to show convincingly that the accusation is false. Indeed, in this case, the government's proffer concerning T.J.'s testimony about the alleged prior sexual assault indicated that T.J. recanted, not because her accusation was untrue, but because she was afraid of her mother and Shorter, and because her mother threatened to punish her when she made the prior allegation.

Nevertheless, on the record before us, which contains no precise dates for two of the three charged instances of child sexual abuse, we cannot say as a matter of law that, as a result of a voir dire of T.J. and her mother, Shorter would be unable to show convincingly that T.J.'s allegation of a prior, October 1996, sexual assault by him was false, and thus, that T.J. was neither a credible witness nor without bias against him. In contrast with Roundtree, supra, where "exploration into prior false accusations made by a witness . . ." was permitted through the voir dire process, id. at 322, in Shorter's case, no direct exploration of the witnesses into the prior, October 1996 allegation of sexual assault, and the subsequent recantation, was allowed. Our decisions discussed above lead us to conclude that the government's proffer of T.J.'s testimony, by itself, could not establish the truth or the falsity of the uncharged October 1996 allegation of sexual misconduct; nor could the trial court assume its truth or falsity based solely on the government's proffer. Thus, we hold that Shorter had a good faith basis for at least a limited voir dire examination of T.J. and her mother about the alleged and recanted prior sexual abuse in October 1996.

Since "prejudicial error may result from limiting Shorter's Sixth Amendment right to cross-examine a crucial government witness, especially a witness without whose testimony the government could not prove guilt . . . ," Wright, supra, 508 A.2d at 923, we are constrained to "remand this case for the trial court to exercise proper discretion . . . ," by conducting a limited voir dire of T.J. and her mother concerning the alleged prior assault of October 1996. If, following the voir dire, "the court concludes that cross-examination about the prior sexual abuse allegation should have been permitted at trial, the court shall order a new trial, for we cannot say that the omission of relevant cross-examination of T.J. relating to her credibility and bias . . . would be harmless." Should the court determine that the falsity of the prior allegation has not been shown satisfactorily under the Roundtree standard, Shorter's "conviction . . . shall stand affirmed — subject to the right to appeal the trial court's ruling."

Accordingly, we remand this case to the trial court for further proceedings consistent with this opinion.

Second, Shorter argues that the trial court erred in failing to declare a mistrial when T.J. made comments pertaining to her sister's role in telling their mother about Shorter's sexual abuse incident in the kitchen. The denial of a motion for a mistrial is committed to the sound discretion of the trial judge. The challenged comments were inadvertent and the trial court promptly, and also during final jury instructions, told the jury to disregard them. Under the circumstances, there was no abuse of discretion.

Third, Shorter contends that the trial court abused its discretion by denying his motion to exclude prejudicial photographs of his home that had "little probative value." The record shows that the trial court spent time reviewing each of the government's proposed photographic exhibits before deciding whether a photograph, which reflected a dirty room, would be admitted into evidence. The court determined that some of the pictures would be useful in "illustrating the testimony" of T.J. "It is well settled that a decision to admit or exclude photographs as demonstrative evidence is within the trial court's sound discretion." We see no abuse of discretion.

Fourth, Shorter asserts that the trial court committed error by denying his D.C.Code § 23-110 pro se motion to vacate his conviction and sentence, without holding a hearing or appointing counsel. The judge who decided Shorter's § 23-110 motion was the trial judge in his case, and thus, was "'in a far better situation, than an appellate court to determine whether there is any appreciable possibility that a hearing could establish either constitutionally defective representation or prejudice to the defendant. . . .'" Moreover, a hearing is not "automatically required. . . . ," especially "where the existing record provides an adequate basis for disposing of the § 23-110 motion. . . ." Nor is the appointment of counsel required where the appellant fails to state adequate grounds for relief under § 23-110. Our review of the record in this case, as well as the trial court's order denying Shorter's § 23-110 motion (which responds to each of the points raised by Shorter), convinces us that Shorter has not met his burden to show deficient trial counsel performance and prejudice under *Strickland v. Washington*, 466 U.S. 668, 687-88, 104 S.Ct. 2052, 80 L.Ed.2d 674 (1984).

CASE QUESTIONS

1 What was the defendant's claim concerning the confrontation clause in his appeal?
2 How did the trial court rule about TJ's supposed prior recantation?
3 How did the appellate court decide this issue?
4 What was the basis of the defendant's claim regarding a request for mistrial based on statements by TJ's sister?
5 What type of *pro se* motion did the defendant make in this case?

CHAPTER SUMMARY

Among the important rights that protect a defendant before and during a criminal trial are the right to an attorney and the right to the presumption of innocence.

After the decision in *Gideon v. Wainwright*, the U.S. Supreme Court requires that any person facing a felony charge must be provided with an attorney if he or she cannot afford to hire one. States have created two basic systems to deal with the standard created in *Gideon*. Some areas have created a public defender system, where attorneys who work for the government have the job of representing people charged with crimes. In other areas, there is a court-appointed list, where private attorneys take on criminal cases and are paid hourly. A defendant can still choose to represent himself, called *pro se*.

During the trial, the defendant has the right to fair and public trial and to confront the witnesses against him. A defendant cannot be tried before a jury while he or she is wearing prison clothing. Civilian clothing must be provided. In most cases, the defendant must be present for his trial. If a defendant absconds after the trial begins, there are times when he or she can be tried *in absentia*. The burden on the government is to prove that the defendant is guilty beyond a reasonable doubt, and this burden never shifts to the defendant. During the trial, members of the press have as much right to be present as any other member of the public, and the rights of the press do not outweigh the rights of the defendant to receive a fair trial.

KEY TERMS

Retainer	Acquit	*In absentia*
Court-appointed attorney	Inference	Placing character into evidence
Public defender attorney	Jury trial	Reasonable doubt
Pro se	Hung jury	
Presumption	Mistrial	
	Cross-examine	

REVIEW QUESTIONS

1 How are most private criminal attorneys paid?
2 Explain the importance of the *Gideon* decision.
3 What is the difference between court-appointed and public defender systems?
4 What financial restraints are placed on defendants who wish to obtain court-appointed attorneys but are charged with misdemeanors?
5 What is pro se representation?
6 Explain the presumption of innocence.
7 What is the difference between a presumption and an inference?
8 Are twelve people always required to sit on a jury? Why or why not?
9 When are six-person juries permitted?
10 What types of cases do not allow jury trials?

11   Are juries permitted in juvenile cases? Why or why not?

12   When can a trial judge close a trial to the public?

13   Is it permissible to try a defendant while he or she is wearing prison clothing? Why or why not?

14   Under what circumstances can a trial that began when the defendant was present continue without him?

15   What has been called the "greatest legal engine ever invented for the discovery of truth"?

16   What is the confrontation clause?

17   Can a prosecutor comment on a defendant's failure to testify in his or her own defense?

18   Does the right of the press to see a trial always outweigh the defendant's right to a fair trial? Explain your answer.

19   Explain what proof beyond a reasonable doubt means.

20   What does the phrase "placing character into evidence" mean?

QUESTIONS FOR ANALYSIS

1   Should the state's burden in criminal cases be lowered? Is "beyond a reasonable doubt" too high a standard to meet? Explain your answer.

2   Some have said that criminal defendants in the United States have too many rights. What is your view? Provide examples to support your argument.

HYPOTHETICALS

1   Danny is charged with burglary and faces a possible maximum sentence of twenty years. He does not qualify for representation by the public defender because he makes too much money per year, however he claims that he does not have any savings and no equity in his home to borrow against. Essentially, he has no way to pay for an attorney and no local attorney is willing to take his case. What is the judge likely to do in this situation?

2   Tonya is in the state legislature and decides to introduce a bill making all 12 person juries into 15 person juries. Is there a constitutional argument against this proposal? Is there a practical argument against this proposal? Is it a good idea?

3   During the trial of an alleged child sexual assault, the prosecutor asks that the trial be closed to the public from the point of his first statement to the jury until the defense rests its case. Is the judge likely to grant that request? Why or why not?

The Trial

I. THE COURTROOM

When it comes to a discussion of the layout of the trial courtroom, it is important to keep in mind that there are many different types of courthouses, all with their own styles of architecture and peculiarities. However, when it comes to the trial courtroom, there are some basic features that will always be present, even if they are in different locations in each courtroom. There is a distinction between a trial courtroom and other types of courtrooms. A room that has been designed for jury trials is different from other judicial rooms. There are features that all trial courtrooms have in common. All jury trial courtrooms have judge's benches, witness stands, tables for attorneys, and son. For a jury trial, certain additional elements must be present. The most obvious of these is the jury box.

A. THE JURY BOX

The **jury box** is the area where the jurors who have been selected in the *voir dire* process are seated during the trial. (Some jurisdictions may use a term other than "jury box" to refer to this area, but this term will be used throughout the chapter.) The jurors are restricted to this area during the trial and they are not allowed to leave it, unless directed to do so. Jurors cannot, for example, leave the jury box to get a better look at evidence or to sit in a more comfortable chair. When the judge calls a

Jury box
An area that is separated from the rest of a courtroom and is reserved exclusively for jurors during a trial.

Recess
A short break in the
proceedings in a trial.

recess or the trial has finished for the day, the bailiff will guide the jurors back to a jury room. If they are on a recess, this is the area where they can relax and talk. They are forbidden to discuss the case until the end of the trial, so they must discuss other matters. Although all felony cases require 12 jurors, there are usually extra seats in the jury box. These extra seats are for alternate jurors. It is common in any jury trial that may last for a few weeks to have alternate jurors (this will be discussed later in the chapter). Alternate jurors are not allowed to deliberate at the end of the trial, but they do sit and hear all evidence and arguments.

JURY'S DELIBERATION ROOM

The jury room, sometimes called the jury deliberation room, is usually a small room adjacent to the courtroom where the jury will go on recesses and where they will retire to decide the verdict when the trial is over. Jury rooms are not known for their comfort or luxury. This is done purposefully. No one wants the jurors to enjoy the jury room too much; they might be tempted to stay in there longer. Instead, if the room is cramped, with no window and uncomfortable seating, there is a good chance that the jurors will reach a quick verdict and conclude the case. Televisions, cell phones, media players, and other electronic devices are all barred from the jury room. The jurors are not permitted access to outside media for fear that they might base their verdict on coverage in the news and not what they heard in the courtroom. The room is private, and no one but the jurors and the bailiff is permitted to enter.

B. WITNESS STAND

Returning to our tour of the courtroom and using the jury box as the beginning point, the next most obvious feature is the witness stand. It is always located fairly close to the jury box so that the jurors can see and hear the witness without difficulty. The witness stand is often a seat inside a closed area with one side open to admit the witness. Most modern courtrooms have microphones set up at face level for the witnesses, even though the witness stand is close to the jury box. The microphone enables everyone in the courtroom to hear the witness testify and also to record the testimony. The witness may be requested to step out of the witness stand to point out some feature on a diagram or to address some other piece of evidence, but the vast majority of the witness's remarks will be made while seated in the witness stand.

C. JUDGE'S BENCH

Bench
The place in the courtroom
reserved for the judge.

The judge sits on an elevated platform called the **bench**. It is always the highest position in the courtroom and helps to emphasize the judge's power and authority. The judge's bench is always positioned so that the judge can get a clear view of the entire courtroom, including the jury box, witness stand, and attorney tables. In modern courtrooms, the judge may have a laptop available at the bench with real-time transcription of the testimony as it is being taken down by the court reporter. The judge may also use the laptop to access legal databases should a question of law come up during the trial. When the judge calls the attorneys to the bench during the trial, it is called a **bench conference**. In situations where a defendant waives a jury trial, then the judge will act as both the judge and jury and will reach a verdict on his or her own. This type of trial is referred to as a **bench trial**.

Bench conference
A private conference, held at the judge's bench between the attorneys and the judge.

Bench trial
A trial where the judge decides both questions of law and the final verdict in the case; no jury is present.

D. LOCATION OF DEFENSE AND PROSECUTION TABLES

There are usually at least two tables set aside for the attorneys. One table is used by the prosecution, while the other is reserved for the defense. These tables are positioned so that they face the judge's bench and also so that both sides can get a clear view of the witness stand and the jury. In many jurisdictions, there is an old tradition that the prosecutor always uses the table closest to the jury box and the defendant gets the table furthest from the jury box. However, like many traditions, practical issues might dictate a different setup in a courtroom.

Just like the judge's bench, modern courtrooms have wireless hot spots that allow attorneys to access the Internet through their laptops or other devices. This not only gives the attorneys the ability to do real time legal research, but also gives them access to a real time transcription of the witness testimony, as well as access to any other technology available in the courtroom, including a projector in case they wish to display photos, diagrams or PowerPoint presentations during closing argument.

E. CLERK OF COURT

Usually located in front of or on the far side of the bench are spaces for the court reporter and the **clerk** of court. The clerk is usually only present during calendar calls where he or she notes dispositions in cases that day. The clerk will return to the court if the defendant is found guilty. At that point, the clerk will make notes in the public record about the verdict and the sentence that the defendant received. The notations about the outcome of the case will become a part of the public record where anyone may see the results.

Clerk
A court official who maintains records of dispositions in both civil and criminal cases.

F. COURT REPORTER

A **court reporter** is the person is responsible for taking down every spoken word in the courtroom. Court reporters are trained to use various types of technology, including computerized stenographic machines. In the past, court reporters wrote out everything that was said in shorthand, but that has given way to advanced technology. Nowadays, court reporters use a machine that allows them to type as fast 200 words per minute. However, when a court reporter types in a courtroom, he

Court reporter
A trained professional who is responsible for taking down every spoken word in the courtroom during a hearing and reproducing those words as a transcript.

or she is actually recording the spoken words phonetically. Someone who is not trained to be a court reporter would find it impossible to read the print out. A computer chip inside the machine automatically converts the phonemes into English and this written transcript is made available to the attorneys and the judge within seconds of the person having testified on the witness stand. A court reporter takes down everything that anyone in the courtroom says. It is a challenging and repetitive occupation that can be financially rewarding, but it is clearly not a profession for everyone. It takes a certain amount of dedication and concentration to work as a court reporter.

FAMOUS CASES
NIGERIAN SCAM

Nigerian scams, grouped under the umbrella name of "419 Scams," have been defrauding people since the early 1990s. The 419 number refers to the section of the Nigerian criminal code dealing with fraud. The scams have many variations and sometimes originate in countries other than Nigeria; however, the bulk of them have been linked to that country. In the early days of the scam, recipients would receive mailed letters. As technology evolved, the transmission method changed to faxes and then to email. Despite all of the attention brought to these scams, very few of the people who have engaged in them have ever been brought to trial.

The most common Nigerian scam involves the advance fee. You receive an unsolicited email, for example, from a Nigerian citizen stating that a petroleum contract has been overpaid. The email goes on to say that the funds — usually tens of millions of dollars — are ready to be transferred overseas, but the person sending the email is a civil servant and legally prohibited from operating a foreign account. If you would be so kind as to deposit a large sum of money in a Nigerian bank, as supposedly required by Nigerian law, you will be given a percentage of the transfer for his trouble, anywhere from 10 percent to 25 percent. Anyone foolish or trusting enough to make such a deposit will never hear from the sender again.

Another variation is an email from a supposed Nigerian dignitary who is being held under house arrest. He has millions of dollars in Nigerian bank accounts, and he needs your help to transfer the money to an offshore account. To do this, he is asking you to sign a document stating that you are his next of kin. Oh, and by the way, he also needs $200 per day to ensure his safety until he can escape. To prove your trustworthiness, you must wire 30 days' worth of this fee. Once he receives the wire transfer, he will find a way to escape to Korea, and you will receive 10 percent of his millions. Of course, once you wire the $6,000, all contact evaporates.

Yet another variation resulted in a devastating conclusion for an Oregon woman in 2008. Janella Spears received an email promising a $20.5 million inheritance from a deceased relative, J. B. Spears. She was required to advance some funds to make it happen. What hooked her was the scammers' ability to identify her relative by name.

Over the course of two years, she mortgaged her home, refinanced her car, and depleted her husband's retirement account. Family members and bank officials assured her that it was a scam — they begged her to stop — but she became obsessed with the idea of such a lucrative payoff and wouldn't stop until she got it. Her first action was to send $100 through an untraceable wire service. Once that hook was set, more promises of multimillion-dollar payoffs followed. The catch was, she had to keep sending money.

Spears received numerous documents that looked official, many claiming that President George Bush was involved and needed her help. Every communication convinced her that this was a legitimate transaction, so she kept sending money. By the time the scam had played out, Spears had lost $400,000.

Another victim, San Diegan James Adler, lost approximately $5.2 million between 1992 and 1994 in a Nigerian scam. Adler received a letter from a Nigerian official claiming that a military coup had disrupted business. The official needed Adler's help in withdrawing $130 million from an oil-field modernization contract. In exchange for Adler using his name to set up an offshore account, he would receive 40 percent of the funds. When it proved to be a scam, Adler appealed to a federal court to help get his money back. However, the judge ruled that Adler had voluntarily participated in a proposition that in itself was illegal. He had no recourse.

The scams are easy to spot. The emails never come to a specific person; instead, they are addressed to "CEO," "President," or "Kind Friend." They typically are rife with spelling and grammatical errors and frequently are written in all capital letters. They say that you have been recommended because of your honesty and business acumen. The sender can be anyone from a government official or a member of Nigerian royalty to the relative of a deposed leader or a religious figure.

Despite the multitude of red flags these messages should raise, hope is a powerful motivator and what spurs recipients to act. These scams have endured for more than two decades for one reason: they work. The U.S. Secret Service, which investigates such crimes, estimates that the average loss is $50,000. Because of the international aspect of the crimes — and the fact that the Nigerian government itself is often involved — very few arrests and prosecutions ever occur.

 JURY SELECTION

A trial begins in a formal fashion. The judge will call the case and ask the parties if they are ready for trial. If they answer that they are, then the judge will ask the parties to **join issue**. To join issue is similar to boxers touching gloves before a bout and probably predates that custom. When the parties join issue, they are signifying that they are ready to start the trial. The defendant will sign the indictment under the plea: not guilty. Once issue has been joined, the next step is to select a jury.

Join issue
The parties officially submit the case to a jury for a determination and verdict.

The process of selecting a jury is also known as ***voir dire***. This is a French phrase meaning "look-speak." The term is quite expressive of the process of selecting a jury. The attorneys in the case look over the prospective jurors, ask them questions and then eliminate the ones that they believe will not be favorable to their case. It is not an exact science. Prospective jurors are questioned by both the prosecutor and

Voir dire
French for "to see, to say"; the questioning of a jury panel member to determine if the person is competent to serve on a jury.

Venire
The group of local citizens who are summoned for jury duty and from whom a jury will be selected.

defense attorney. Their responses are noted and used to determine which members of the panel will be removed from the panel and which ones will stay. For the sake of clarity, this text will refer to this group of citizens from whom a jury is selected as the *panel*. The term *venire* is often used as well, but panel will serve just as well. The attorneys listen to the responses and take this opportunity to look the panel members over and decide which ones they wish to strike from the panel and which ones they would like to keep.

Although in the past there were many restrictions to jury service, including the deliberate exclusion of women and minorities from panels, modern practice allows almost anyone to serve on a jury. The only people who are barred from jury duty are those who have been convicted of a felony, minors, non-citizens, or anyone who cannot or will not follow the judge's orders and the law.

Panel members are selected from a wide variety of sources. Although it was true that past jury administrators would cull voter registration rolls for names of people to be summoned for jury duty, modern practice has expanded this to DMV records, tax rolls, and other public records.

The actual process of selecting a jury varies from state to state and even county to county, but there are some general provisions that occur in all jury selection. For instance, there is always a general question session.

General questions are asked of the entire panel and often consist of questions designed to make sure that everyone who is present is legally qualified to serve on the jury. The judge or the prosecutor might ask the panel if there are any convicted felons seated in the panel or anyone under the age of 18. Beyond that, general questions might include more nuanced ones about whether panel members can follow the judge's directions and the law. Panel members will also be asked a series of broad-based questions to make sure that all members are not biased or prejudiced against one side or the other. In some states, attorneys question the potential jurors; in others, and in federal court, the judge asks all of the questions. In most courts, the judge will explain what the jury selection process is and how it will proceed. Following that explanation, the prosecutor usually goes first with his or her general questions. Then the defense attorney will to the same.

Prosecutors and defense attorneys have different general questions for the panel. The prosecutor will focus on issues such as seeking jurors who will follow the law, while the defense attorney may ask the panel members if they have had bad experiences with police officers or whether they would tend to put more faith in police officers than in other witnesses. The purpose of these questions is two-fold. First, the attorneys want to know if there are panel members who clearly side with the prosecution or the defense. Secondly, because the attorneys know that the twelve people who will sit on the jury are seated somewhere in the room, they take the opportunity to make a good impression on them and to get them thinking about specific issues.

In recent years, many of the most common general questions asked by attorneys have been reduced to juror questionnaires and given to the panel members when they are summoned for jury duty. Each panel member's answers are provided to the prosecutor and defense attorney, which frequently helps speed up the jury-selection process. One common question is: Have you ever been the victim of a crime? Both attorneys will want to know the answer to that question. The prosecutor would like to know because a person who has been a victim of a crime might be more willing to return a guilty verdict than someone who has not. The defense attorney might wish to strike that person during selection for the same reason.

Once general questioning is over, the attorneys are then allowed to move on to individual questions. Here, they follow up on any indications or answers that panel members gave in general questioning. The attorneys may wish to know more specifics about the panel member's response to a general question and also to try to evaluate the person more closely to see if he or she would make a good juror for the prosecution or defense. Just as with general questioning, the prosecutor goes first in asking individual questions. Attorneys often see this as an opportunity for establishing a personal rapport with the panel members. This rapport may carry over to the trial if this panel member ends up as a juror on the case. Attorneys also wish to see how interested the panel members are, whether they make eye contact and myriad other body language clues that people give off. Jury selection often boils down to an intuitive feeling about a panel member instead of a mathematical appraisal. Barring any openly hostile panel member– who will undoubtedly be eliminated–in the end the attorney removes people often based on nothing more than a negative feeling about a particular panel member.

The phrase *jury selection* is not entirely accurate because attorneys do not select the jurors that they want. Instead, they remove panel members that they do not want until they have 12 remaining. The process of removing panel members is called **striking a jury**. When a panel member is struck, this person will not serve on the jury. In many jurisdictions, the panel might consist of 48 persons. The defense has the right to remove 24 and the prosecutor 12, leaving 12 people who will serve on the jury. In many jurisdictions, the parties have an equal number of strikes. In those jurisdictions, for example, the jury administrator might bring in 36 people on a panel. Both sides have the right to remove or strike 12, for a total of 24 strikes. The remaining 12 would then serve on the jury. Panel members may be struck in two different ways: 1) challenge for cause, and 2) peremptory strike.

> **Striking a jury**
> The process of questioning and removing panel members until twelve jurors are left; these twelve will serve on the jury.

A. PEREMPTORY CHALLENGES

A **peremptory challenge** is the right of a party to strike a panel member for almost any reason. One of the attorneys may not like the way that the person answers a question, or the attorney just has a gut feeling about the panel member (see Scenario 20-1). Peremptory strikes do not have to be justified, except in certain instances (set out below). Both sides are given a specific number of peremptory strikes as we outlined above. In some jurisdictions, the defendant is given twice as many peremptory strikes as the state, while in other jurisdictions, they receive the same number. When either side has used up their allotted number of peremptory strikes, they are not permitted to strike any additional members of the panel.

> **Peremptory challenge**
> A strike of a juror for any reason, except based on race or sex.

JURY SELECTION

During the jury selection process, Paula Prosecutor asks the general question, "Is there anyone here who believes that the drug cocaine should be legalized?" One person, Dale, raises his hand. Paula decides to strike him from the panel because of that answer. Can she do so?

Answer: Yes, peremptory strikes can be used for almost any reason.

B. CHALLENGES FOR CAUSE

A member of the panel may be removed or challenged for "cause." A challenge for cause is the process of removing a panel member because the person has demonstrated some prejudice to one of the parties or has indicated that he or she will not follow the judge's instructions. When either the state or the defense uncovers any of these attitudes, that party normally moves to have the panel member dismissed for cause. A **challenge for cause** does not count against a side's number of peremptory strikes. Consider Scenario 20-2.

Challenge for cause
A formal objection to the qualifications or attitude of a prospective juror.

CHALLENGE FOR CAUSE

During jury selection, Paula Prosecutor asks the following question: "Is there anyone here who for cannot sit on a jury for religious or other reasons?"

Diana raises her hand. In follow up, Diana responds that it is against her religious principles to judge other human beings and no matter what the judge tells her to do, she will not participate in the jury and will not vote to return either a guilty or a not guilty verdict. Can she be removed for cause?

Answer: Yes. Her answer clearly indicates that she will not follow the rules or obey the judge's instructions. She can be removed for cause and this removal will not count against Paula's peremptory strikes.

C. *BATSON* CHALLENGES

In recent decades, the power to use a peremptory challenge for any reason has been substantially curtailed. In the past, a prosecutor might use a peremptory challenge to remove members of a specific race in the mistaken belief that jury members who are the same race as the defendant will not return a guilty verdict against him or her. Eventually those types of practices were dealt with by the U.S. Supreme Court. In the case of *Batson v. Kentucky*, 476 U.S. 79 (1986), the Court ruled that peremptory strikes could not be used by a prosecutor to remove all African-American panel members simply because of their race. The Court reasoned that because the court system is a function of the government, it could not be used to further discriminatory practices. The *Batson* decision has been extended to other types of discriminatory peremptory strikes. For instance, Batson-type decisions have forbidden striking panel members on the basis of any racial affiliation, as well as gender-based discrimination. In the past few years, so-called reverse-Batson challenges have been made as well. In a reverse-***Batson*** **challenge**, the state challenges the defense for striking panel members for a discriminatory reason. See this chapter's Case Excerpt for an example of a reverse-Batson challenge.

Batson **challenge**
A challenge to the strikes used by a party during jury selection that claims the party used discriminatory practices in removing members of the panel.

D. STRIKING THE JURY

When the questioning of the panel has concluded, striking the jury is the next phase. Courts handle this process in different ways, but there are two generally accepted procedures to strike a jury. In the first scenario, the clerk of court reads off the panel member's name, and he or she stands. The prosecutor will either strike this juror (using one of his or her peremptory strikes) or accept the juror. This is done out loud. The prosecutor may say, "The state strikes this juror" or, a little more politely, "The state excuses this juror." This eliminates the panel member from serving on the jury. If the state accepts the juror, then the defendant has the right to strike the panel member. If the defendant accepts, this person becomes a member of the trial jury. Each panel member's name will be called until 12 jurors have been selected. If either the prosecutor or the defendant uses all of his allotted peremptory strikes, he has lost the right to strike any more panel members.

SILENT STRIKES

In some jurisdictions, striking the jury is done on paper with "silent strikes." Under this system, the attorneys do not announce their acceptance or rejection of the panel member out loud. Instead, they simply mark the panel list with their strikes. The list is handed back and forth between each attorney until 12 jurors have been selected. Many judges prefer the silent strike because it moves the jury selection along at a faster pace and causes less inconvenience for the panel members. One might argue that it also creates less discomfort jurors because they do not have to stand and then either be accepted or rejected.

There are times when, in addition to selecting 12 members of the jury, the court may select one or more **alternate jurors**. Although alternates are not used in most trials, there are times when a trial is projected to last several days or even weeks. In that situation, it is wise to select one or two alternate jurors who would take the place of one of the 12 jurors, should he or she become sick or otherwise be unable to carry on in the trial. Alternate jurors sit in the jury box during the trial, but do not retire with the jury at the end to deliberate. Only the main 12 jurors are allowed to deliberate. Alternate jurors are normally released when the case is over and the jury retires to the jury room to reach a verdict. The process of selecting alternate jurors is exactly like the process for selecting the 12 main jurors. Once the 12th juror has been selected, the judge will announce that selection will continue for one or two alternates. The prosecutor and the defendant have the right to use peremptory strikes to eliminate panel members, just as they did when selecting the main jury. Once accepted, these alternate jurors join the main group in the jury box. Jury selection has now concluded.

Alternate juror
A person selected to sit on the jury, but who will have no right to participate in the deliberations and will not be able to vote to return a verdict.

When a jury has been selected and seated in the jury box, the rest of the panel is excused. The people who were not selected to serve on the jury return to the jury administration area, where they may be released from any further jury duty or be called to sit on another panel in a different case. The jurors who have been selected to sit on the trial will now be given badges identifying them as jurors in an ongoing trial. They will be given pads and pencils to take notes. The judge will also give them some preliminary instructions, such as informing them about their duties in the trial. One of the most important instructions that a judge gives the jurors is that they must wait until the end of the case before they reach a decision about the defendant's guilt or innocence. The judge tells the jurors that they will hear testimony from witnesses and will also see physical and other evidence that is admitted during the trial. They are not to make up their minds about the guilt or innocence of the defendant until all evidence and testimony has been tendered. Whether jurors actually follow that admonition has come under a great deal of debate in recent years, with studies showing that many jurors begin to make up their minds as early as opening statements and most have reached a conclusion about the case before the closing argument phase.

The judge will also tell the newly sworn-in jurors that they are forbidden to discuss the details of the case with anyone, even each other, while the case is pending. They may not talk about the case with friends or family and may not discuss the case with the media or anyone else. In fact, most judges tell the jurors that if anyone approaches them and questions them about the case or tries to persuade them, they should report that fact to the judge immediately and the judge will launch an investigation into the possibility of jury tampering.

Jurors are also told to avoid watching media accounts of the trial (if any) and reading anything about the case in newspapers or online. (In the majority of cases, there will be no media attention at all.) In addition to these instructions, the judge will also tell the jury that neither the attorneys nor the witnesses in the case are allowed to speak with them outside the courtroom. Most attorneys take this instruction so seriously that they will not even greet a juror if they should see one in the hallway during a break in the trial.

OPENING STATEMENTS

Once jury selection has been completed and the jurors who preside in the trial are seated in the jury box, the trial can actually begin. The first phase of a criminal trial is the opening statements.

A. WHAT IS AN OPENING STATEMENT?

Opening statement
A preliminary address to the jury by the prosecutor and defense attorney, outlining the general facts of the case.

Opening statements are made by both the prosecutor and the defense attorney. They are short speeches to the jury where the attorneys outline the facts and evidence of the case — as they see them. Attorneys cannot testify or offer opinions during an opening statement. Instead, they often explain what will happen during the course of the trial. After all, most jurors have no idea what to expect so telling them can alleviate some tension. Some attorneys go so far as to explain who will testify and what they expect that witness to say. They cannot show the jury any evidence (because it has not yet been admitted), but they can certainly state what evidence they believe will be admitted during the trial.

An opening statement is not a persuasive argument and a judge will admonish an attorney who attempts to argue that the defendant is or is not guilty during the opening statement. Such persuasion is reserved for the closing argument. The opening statement is only intended as a mechanism for the attorneys to explain the trial process. Instead, the attorneys will outline each of their cases and ask the jury to return a verdict. For the prosecutor, the verdict requested will always be a finding of guilty on all counts against the defendant. After the prosecutor has given his or her opening statement, the defense attorney will give one as well. Defense attorneys often ask the jurors to keep an open mind throughout the case and to remember that there are two sides to every story. Because the state will go first, the defense attorney will remind the jurors that they should not reach a conclusion in the case until they have heard from the defense in the case.

Opening statements are supposed to be short statements that outline the general facts of the case, but this is also the first time that an attorney has to speak to the jurors, so within the confines of the structure of the opening statement, the attorneys will do what little they can to persuade the jurors to their viewpoint. Attorneys are not allowed to give impassioned speeches or to plead with the jury; they must limit their remarks to the evidence, but within that framework a clever attorney can attempt to both deliver a factual overview and also slip in a few remarks intended to persuade the jury. Consider Scenario 20-3.

OPENING STATEMENT

During defense attorney Tamara's opening statement, she makes the following remarks:

"Ladies and gentlemen, the evidence in this case will show that the defendant did not participate in the robbery. The evidence will show that he is a good and decent man who was at home when the robbery occurred, surrounded by his five children and his loving wife. The evidence will also show that because he is gainfully employed as a city worker for twenty years, he had no need of any money and that none of the money from the robbery was ever traced to him. We will also show that as a volunteer member of Habitat for Humanity who has built over twenty homes for indigent people, he has sustained an injury to his right shoulder that would make it impossible for him to aim a shotgun, as the state has alleged."

Is this an improper opening statement?

Answer: Probably not. Although Tamara has inserted several points in her opening statement that should not be there, such as telling the jury about what a good and decent man her client is, she has cleverly couched these terms as an expression of what the evidence will show. As a result, the judge will be hard pressed to say that she is going outside the purpose of an opening statement, although she is certainly coming close to crossing the line.

DIRECT EXAMINATION

Once opening statements have been concluded, the judge will turn to the prosecutor and ask him or her to begin the case. The prosecutor always goes first in the U.S. system because the state has the burden of proving that the defendant is guilty beyond a reasonable doubt. This stage of the trial is often referred to as the state's **case in chief**. This is where the prosecution presents its entire case, including all witnesses and evidence to show that the defendant committed the crime. The phrase, "case in chief" refers to the entire state's case against the defendant. Although there are times when the state may present additional evidence at the end of the trial, in most cases, the state gets a single shot to make its case. Testimony from witnesses will come in the form of **direct examination**.

When prosecutors begin their cases, they do so by calling witnesses. Like all attorneys in criminal and civil cases, prosecutors are not allowed to make their own statements to the jury about evidence or offer opinions about the truth of a witness or the quality of the evidence. Those are decisions that must be made by the jury. In most cases, the only way for an attorney to present evidence and prove the allegations in a case is by calling live witnesses to the stand. In order to do so, the prosecutor will call a witness to the stand and the witness will be sworn. Then the witness takes the stand and is asked questions by the prosecutor in what is referred to as *direct examination.* The questions that the prosecutor asks on direct examination attempt to prove the elements of the offense, establish the basic facts of the case and also provide a platform for the prosecutor to introduce evidence that also establishes the defendant's guilt beyond a reasonable doubt.

Case in chief
The body of evidence and testimony offered by a party during its presentation of a jury trial.

Direct examination
The questions asked of a witness by the attorney who has called him or her to the stand.

A. QUESTIONING WITNESSES

The witnesses who testify on direct examination are generally considered to be friendly to that side. State's witnesses often include police officers, coroners, victims, and others who have knowledge of the case. The rules about direct examination are strict: An attorney is not allowed to ask leading questions. A leading question is one that suggests an answer. For instance, an attorney cannot ask a witness, "The man sitting over there, he was the one who hit you, wasn't he?" That question is not permissible because it leads the witness to the answer. Instead, the attorney who conducts direct examination must stick to general questions, usually ones that begin with the standard question words: who, what, when, and where. (Attorneys usually do not ask why because a witness cannot testify what the defendant was thinking.)

As the prosecutor questions each witness on direct, he or she may also introduce evidence during the examination. As explained in earlier chapters, there are specific foundation questions that an attorney must ask a witness that establish the relevance and admissibility of particular evidence. These questions must be asked before the evidence is tendered to the court for admission into evidence. Just as with opening statements, an attorney cannot simply produce evidence and begin waving it about in front of the courtroom. A witness must be questioned to establish the relevance of the evidence and then the judge must rule that the evidence is admissible, often over the objection of the opposing attorney.

When the attorney who is questioning the witness has asked all the questions necessary, he or she usually announces, "No further questions." This is the signal to the judge and the other attorney that cross-examination is to begin.

 ## CROSS-EXAMINATION

The prosecution always goes first in a criminal trial and presents its witnesses and evidence, but that does not mean that the defense attorney has no role to play. In fact, the defense attorney is involved in every part of the state's case. The defense attorney may object to a particular question of a witness, such as objecting to a leading question. The attorney will almost certainly object to the admission of specific types of evidence and the judge must make a determination if the evidence should be admitted over the defense attorney's objection. But the defense attorney has one other major role to play during the state's case: He or she will cross-examine each of the state's witnesses.

Although there is no requirement that all witnesses must be cross-examined, most of the state's witnesses will face **cross-examination** by the defense counsel. Once direct examination has been completed, the judge will give the defense attorney the opportunity to cross-examine the witness. A judge may not bar or otherwise prevent a defense attorney from conducting a cross-examination, but the judge may prevent the attorney from asking certain types of questions. For instance, if the judge does not believe that a particular question on cross is relevant, the judge may instruct the defense attorney to move on to another question. The prosecutor may object to a question, in which case the judge will rule on the question before allowing the witness to answer it. However, within these guidelines, an attorney has wide latitude on cross-examination. If the attorney can show relevance, then he or she can ask virtually any question.

Cross-examination
Asking questions of a witness to determine bias, lack of knowledge, prejudice, or some other failing.

Attorneys are also not constrained on cross-examination the way that they are on direct examination. As we have already seen, an attorney who asks questions during direct examination cannot ask leading questions. But an attorney who is carrying out a cross-examination is actually encouraged to ask leading questions. An excellent attorney can almost always bring up some serious issues on cross-examination or at least some questions for the jury to consider.

Attorneys often use cross-examination as a way of developing a particular theme of the trial. The defense attorney may emphasize the fact that there is some question about the eyewitness identification of the defendant, for example, or establish some evidence of alibi. Defense attorneys rarely use the tactics portrayed on television or in movies, such as screaming at witnesses or physically intimidating them. These tactics seldom work and often turn the jury against the defense attorney and, by extension, the defendant. Instead, most attorneys focus on the details of the question, not the loudness of the delivery. However, there are times when an attorney may take a more aggressive approach to a witness, such as impeaching the witness.

Sidebar

Cross-examination is both an art and a skill. Attorneys spend many years developing good cross-examination skills.

A. IMPEACHMENT

Impeachment
To show that a witness is not worthy of belief.

Impeachment of a witness is to show that he or she is not worthy of belief. The most common way to impeach a witness is to show that he or she has a criminal record or has no personal knowledge of the case. Calling the witness's credibility into question is a tried and true tactic of both prosecutors and defense attorneys to discredit a witness. A witness may be impeached for any of the following reasons:

- Bias
- Inconsistent statements
- Previous conviction
- Not competent to testify

REDIRECT EXAMINATION

Redirect examination
The process of questioning a witness who was originally called on direct examination to clear up any issues raised during cross-examination.

At the conclusion of each cross-examination, the attorney who originally presented the witness on direct examination has the right to ask question on **redirect examination**. Such questioning is usually limited to points raised on cross-examination and is not designed to allow the attorney to repeat the entire direct examination. The attorney will ask questions to help clear up any apparent contradictions the witness may have made during the cross-examination and then conclude redirect.

DIRECTED VERDICT

Directed verdict
A ruling by a judge that there is not sufficient evidence of the defendant's guilt to present to the jury.

At the conclusion of the state's case, once the prosecutor has presented all the witnesses and evidence that he or she believes has proven the defendant's guilt beyond a reasonable doubt, the state announces to the court, "Your Honor, the State rests."

This announcement signals the next phase of the trial: the defense. However, before the defendant puts up any evidence or witnesses, if any, the defendant will first make a motion for a **directed verdict**. A motion for directed verdict requests the court to enter a verdict of not guilty on some or all of the charges against the defendant. The basis of the motion is that the state has failed to meet its burden of proof on the charges and that there is not sufficient evidence for the jurors to even consider the case in their deliberations at the end of the trial. The defense attorney is essentially asking the court to dismiss the case because of lack of proof. Normally, the court will only grant such a motion when the prosecution has failed to present any evidence to support the various charges against the defendant. If it is a question of the sufficiency or how much weight to give the evidence that has been presented, then the court will usually defer to the jury to make those determinations. The judge will, in that event, deny the motion for directed verdict and allow the jury to decide the issues in the case.

In most cases, the motion for directed verdict fails, but that does not stop defense attorneys from bringing it. In fact, in almost any criminal trial, a defense attorney would be considered remiss–and perhaps ineffective in his or her representation–if the motion were not brought. After all, the defense has nothing to lose and a lot to gain by bringing the motion. If the judge denies the motion, then the defense is in no worse a position than it was before the motion was made. If the judge grants the motion, then some or all of the charges against the defendant will be dismissed. Assuming the defendant's motion for directed verdict is denied, the next phase of the trial begins: the defense.

VIII DEFENSE CASE-IN-CHIEF

The defense is under no obligation to present any evidence or testimony. In fact, there are very good reasons for the defense to stand mute. The defendant may not make a very good witness. Other defense witnesses also may not make a good impression on the jury. Despite the judge's instructions to the jurors that they may not make any negative inference against the defendant for failing to testify, it is human nature that they would like to hear the defendant proclaim his innocence. However, in most situations, the defense attorney counsels the defendant not to take the stand. If the defendant takes the stand, he will be subject to cross-examination.

In addition to whether or not the defendant will do well during direct and cross-examination, the defense must also consider an issue that has already been discussed in this text: placing the defendant's character into evidence. As shown in chapter, in the federal system and in many state systems, the defendant opens himself up to questions about his criminal convictions if he takes the stand. Answering these questions could have a devastating effect on the defense. The defense attorney must weigh all of these factors before deciding to put the defendant on the stand. If the defendant has an unpleasant personality, or could easily be lead astray on cross-examination, the best course is not to put the defendant on the stand.

If the defense decides to put up witnesses and admit testimony, the defense attorney must follow the same rules as the prosecutor. Witnesses must be sworn in. The defense attorney must conduct direct examination with the same limitations placed on the state during its direct examination. After each witness for the defense testifies, the prosecutor has the right to cross-examine that witness. In addition to direct and cross-examination, a defense attorney who wishes to admit evidence must ask the correct foundation questions and deal with any objections raised by the prosecutor.

In many ways, the defense case is a mirror image of the state's version. Witnesses will be called, testify on direct and the defense attorney will admit evidence during that testimony. When the defense attorney has presented what he or she believes is sufficient evidence to create a reasonable doubt with the jury, the defense will rest its case in exactly the same way that the prosecution did. There is one important difference, however. The state is not allowed to move for a directed verdict at the end of the defense case. Instead, the case must be submitted to a jury for their decision. There are some rare instances where the state can present additional evidence at the conclusion of the defense case. This is referred to as rebuttal.

REBUTTAL

Rebuttal
To deny or take away the effect of the other party's presentation; a rebuttal attacks claims made by one party with evidence presented by the other.

At the conclusion of the defense case, the prosecutor has a decision to make. The rules of court allow the prosecutor to make a **rebuttal** to the defense. Rebuttal is used to attack a point raised during the defense. If the defense presents no evidence and raises no new issues, there is little need for the prosecutor to go back over its testimony and present the same witnesses who testified during the prosecution's case-in-chief. In fact, a judge would not allow this. However, there are times when the prosecution must present a rebuttal, such as when the defense is insanity or alibi. These defenses were discussed in Chapter 17, but when such defenses are raised, the jury will be instructed that as long as the defense team has raised some evidence to support its defense, the prosecution must rebut the testimony or the jury will be compelled to find the defendant not guilty. Rebuttal, then, is testimony that directly refutes the defendant's claims made in his or her case-in-chief. Even in situations where the defense has raised several issues, the judge may still restrict the state to rebutting specific points only and prevent the state from presenting evidence on other issues.

MISTRIAL

Mistrial
An invalid or null trial; a trial without any verdict or legal consequence.

There are many events that may cause a **mistrial**. Declaring a case to be a mistrial means that the judge has determined that the case cannot go on, either because the jury cannot reach a decision or because something has occurred in the case that is prejudicial to the defendant. An order of mistrial simply means that all of the parties act as though the trial never occurred. The state is free to try the case all over again. This means that all of the witnesses must testify again, all evidence must be admitted again. In fact, everything must be repeated as though it never happened.

CHARGE CONFERENCE

Charge conference
A meeting held after the close of evidence in a trial and before the closing arguments where the attorneys and the judge discuss what jury instructions will be given to the jurors.

When the evidentiary part of the trial is over, the next phase consists of the closing arguments. However, before those arguments can be made, the attorneys and the judge will meet to discuss the jury charges.

During the **charge conference**, the attorneys will request that specific charges be read and may oppose charges proposed by the other side. A charge is a statement about the law. The most common one used in criminal cases is: "Ladies and gentlemen, I charge you that the defendant in this case is presumed innocent unless and until the state has proven his guilty beyond a reasonable doubt." But there are many

FIGURE 20-1

Standard Jury Charge on
Reasonable Doubt

I hereby charge you that the state must prove each and every material allegation against the defendant by proof beyond a reasonable doubt. The burden in this case never shifts to the defendant to prove his or her innocence. The defendant has presented a defense in this case. It is not the duty of the defendant to prove the defense beyond a reasonable doubt; it is the state's burden to disprove the defense beyond a reasonable doubt.

other statements of the law that the judge will read to the jury to help guide them in their deliberations. Because this is the last thing that the jurors will hear before they go into the jury room to deliberate, the attorneys are concerned about what they hear. Both attorneys are permitted to offer their own versions of particular charges, and there are often objections by one side to the other's jury instructions. In a major case, there may be dozens of different statements about the law that the judge will either read to the jury or provide to them in written form. In addition to the parties' suggested jury charges, there are also standard jury instructions that a judge must give in every jury trial. Eventually, the judge will rule on proposed charges and also inform the attorneys about the standard charges that he or she will read to the jurors. See Figure 20-1 for an example. At the conclusion of the charge conference, the judge will allow the attorneys a brief recess to review the instructions. The attorneys need to know what instructions the judge plans to give because they will refer to some of these statements of the law during their closing argument.

CLOSING ARGUMENTS

When all testimony has been heard and all evidence admitted, including any rebuttal and the charge conference is concluded, the trial moves to the **closing argument** phase. In a closing argument, each attorney will urge the jury to return a verdict in their favor. The prosecutor will argue that each of the elements of the crime has been proven and that the defendant is guilty beyond a reasonable doubt. The defense attorney will argue, just as forcefully, that the state has failed to meet its burden, either because they have prosecuted the wrong person or because the defendant is legally insane or that he had an alibi or is not guilty by virtue of some other reason. The defense attorney will inevitably ask the jury members to carefully consider the case and to consider that the state has failed to prove the case to the high standard of proof beyond a reasonable doubt.

Closing argument
An attorney's summation of his or her case during which the attorney seeks to convince the jury to a return a verdict favorable to his or her side.

Unlike the fictional portrayals of closing arguments that often seen in movies and television shows, real life closing arguments are not conducted in the span of a few minutes. In previous decades, a closing argument might last for hours. Some famous cases had closing arguments that lasted for *days*. Nowadays, the attorneys are usually limited to one or two hours for a closing argument. (Death penalty cases frequently allow greater time for closing arguments.) One hour is a considerably long time for any one person to speak about any topic and attorneys are aware of this. Many of them have become as technologically savvy as any other profession. Instead of simply speaking to the jurors–and risk boring them or, even worse, losing their attention–attorneys now routinely rely on PowerPoint presentations, graphics, videos, computer simulations, and almost any other type of visual media available.

Despite the advances in technology and presentation, studies continue to show that jurors have almost always made up their minds about the verdict in the case before the closing arguments ever start. A closing argument, no matter how brilliantly delivered or flawlessly performed is more often than not ignored by the jurors who have decided to return a different verdict. This is not to say that a brilliant closing argument cannot win a case. In some situations, it probably does. However, the idea that the jurors have not thought through the facts of the case prior to the closing argument and reached some type of conclusion, even tenuous, defies both research and common sense.

Unlike the opening statement and direct and cross-examination, attorneys are given considerable latitude in how they present their closing arguments. They cannot introduce evidence or facts that were not brought out in trial; they cannot offer their personal opinion that the facts in the case are true, but beyond that, an attorney has an enormous range of activities that he or she can do during a closing argument. An attorney can make a logical, consistent argument, but is also permitted to offer a completely illogical and inconsistent position. Attorneys can appeal to emotions, to logic, to altruism; they can appeal to the worst or best in us all.

One practical issue that often comes up is which party gets to give the closing argument first? The general answer is that the prosecution goes first and the defendant goes second, mirroring the opening statement. But this arrangement can be affected by several factors. In some jurisdictions, for instance, if a defendant presents no evidence or testimony, then the defendant has the right to go first. After the state presents its closing argument, the defense attorney is permitted to give a final summation, commenting on the points raised by the state. However, this rule is not followed in all jurisdictions and the exact order of who goes first can vary depending on local court rules.

Regardless of who goes first or second in the closing argument, both sides will ask the jury to do the one thing that they are required to do: return a verdict. The prosecution will obviously ask the jury to return a guilty verdict, while the defense will just as forcefully ask the jury to return a not guilty verdict.

JURY INSTRUCTIONS

Jury instructions
A judge's directions to the jury about the law that pertains to the issues in the trial and the jury's function once they retire to the jury room.

During the charge conference, the judge and attorneys will meet and discuss the jury instructions (referred to as "charges" earlier) that the judge will provide to the jurors. A jury instruction is a statement about the law in the case. **Jury instructions** give the jurors the statutory guidelines and elements of the offense with which the defendant is charged and also direct them in practical matters, such as how to select a foreperson and how to complete the verdict. Among the charges that the judge will provide to the jurors is an explanation that the state has the burden of proof in the case and must prove the case beyond a reasonable doubt. The tradition has been, for hundreds of years, for the judge to read all of these instructions to the jury, probably stemming from a time when most people were illiterate. However, in the days of modern technology (and limited attention spans) sitting through an hour or two of someone reading the law is an excruciating experience. That is why many judges have begun to defy convention and provide copies of the entire charge to the jury. However, there are still courtrooms across the country where the judge reads the entire set of charges to the jury, despite the fact that the process may take several hours.

 ## DELIBERATIONS

All of the evidence and testimony have been presented. The closing arguments are over. The judge has either read or provided the jurors with written copies of the instructions. The final act of the trial is about to commence: jury deliberations.

When the jury begins its deliberations, the jurors are escorted from the courtroom to the jury room. The evidence that has been admitted during the trial is brought to them and the bailiff then leaves the jurors alone to consider the case. The jury deliberation process consists of the jurors reviewing the evidence, discussing the case, and deciding on a verdict. One of the first things that the jury does is to elect one of the members to act as the foreperson. This person will generally keep things organized and will act as the jury's spokesperson when dealing with the judge. The jury deliberation time period can last for a few minutes or can go on for days. There are numerous instances where the jury deliberation actually takes longer than it took to try the case.

What actually happens in the jury room? The attorneys for the case would desperately like to know, but the only people allowed to be present while they deliberate are the jurors themselves. No doubt they discuss the case and sometimes have heated arguments with one another. In most jurisdictions, the jurors are compelled to reach a unanimous verdict. In fact, one of the judge's first instructions to the jurors is that they should select a jury foreperson and then decide on a verdict. If the jurors can reach a unanimous verdict, they will write it down and then tell the bailiff they have reached a decision. They do not tell the bailiff what their decision is. Instead, they must come back into the courtroom for the announcement.

 ## VERDICT

Juries are charged with the duty of reaching a **verdict** in the case. A verdict is what the jury has determined to be the facts in the case. In criminal cases, there are several different versions that a jury may return, including:

Verdict
The jury's finding in a trial.

- Guilty
- Guilty but mentally ill
- Not guilty
- Not guilty by reason of insanity

Reading the verdict in open court is one of the most dramatic moments in a trial. The format is often, "In case of State v. John Doe, we the jury find the defendant. . . ." If the defendant is found not guilty, the jury will be dismissed and assuming that the defendant has no other charges pending against him, he or she will be immediately released. If the verdict is guilty, then the trial moves into the final phase–sentencing.

A. VARIOUS TYPES OF VERDICTS IN CRIMINAL CASES

Traditionally, there were only three possible verdicts in a criminal case: guilty, not guilty, and not guilty by reason of insanity. However, some states have expanded by one the possible verdicts in a criminal case to add "guilty but mentally ill."

GUILTY

If the verdict is guilty, then the judge will enter a judgment that the defendant was found guilty and will either sentence the defendant immediately or defer sentencing to some later date.

GUILTY BUT MENTALLY ILL

As explained in Chapter 17 on defenses, when a defendant raises the claim of insanity, many jurisdictions allow a jury to return a verdict of guilty, but mentally ill. The only difference between these two verdicts is that with a guilty, but mentally ill decision the defendant must be sentenced to some facility that provides counseling or psychiatric services. The defendant is still convicted and will serve a sentence.

NOT GUILTY

A not guilty verdict is the jury's determination that the state has failed to prove the defendant's guilt beyond a reasonable doubt. Once a jury returns a not guilty verdict, the state is barred by the provisions of the Fifth Amendment from retrying the defendant. The Double Jeopardy clause of that amendment forbids retrying a person who has been found not guilty.

NOT GUILTY BY REASON OF INSANITY

When a defendant raises the defense of insanity, a jury is authorized to return a verdict of not guilty by reason of insanity. In such a situation, the defendant is not convicted of a crime because the jury has determined that he or she lacks the ability to distinguish right from wrong and therefore cannot form the necessary *mens rea* to commit a crime.

B. POLLING THE JURY

When the jury reaches a verdict of guilty, the defense attorney has the right to ask that the jurors be polled. **Polling** means that each juror will be asked if this verdict is their personal decision in the case. The judge will ask each and every juror the following series of questions: "Mr. Juror, was this your verdict in the jury room? Is this your verdict now?" Assuming that everyone answers "yes" to that question, then the judge will excuse the jury from any further attendance in the case.

Polling
Requesting the jurors to provide a verbal assurance that the verdict each person reached in the jury room is the still the verdict that they maintain when they return after deliberations.

C. EXCUSING THE JURY

Once the verdict has been returned, the jury is told that they are now free to discuss the case with anyone. The prohibitions on talking about the case are lifted. The attorneys who tried the case will, in many instances, talk to the jury so that they can learn what the jury thought was important in the case. This is a great way for young attorneys to learn how to improve their performance in the courtroom, assuming that they get forthright answers from the jury.

PEOPLE v. MURPHY
79 A.D.3d 1451, 1454, 913 N.Y.S.2d 815, 818) (N.Y.A.D. 3 Dept., 2010)

CASE EXCERPT

CARDONA, P.J.

Appeal from a judgment of the County Court of Albany County (Breslin, J.), rendered May 18, 2009, upon a verdict convicting defendant of the crime of manslaughter in the second degree.

On the night of April 29, 2006 and into the early morning hours of April 30, 2006, defendant was engaged in two incidents with Joseph Jerome on Hudson Avenue in the City of Albany. Jerome's companions, Hector Perez and Rob Desantola, were also present. During the first encounter, defendant exchanged words with the group on the sidewalk outside his home. Perez then punched defendant twice, knocking him down and injuring his lip. The second encounter occurred shortly thereafter when Jerome, Perez and Desantola returned to the area outside defendant's home. During that encounter, defendant fatally stabbed Jerome. The details surrounding both incidents are sharply disputed.

Defendant was convicted of murder in the second degree. Subsequently, this Court reversed that conviction on the ground that the admission into evidence of certain tape-recorded statements by defendant, in conjunction with other circumstances at the trial, violated defendant's right against self-incrimination and right to counsel, and we remitted the matter for a new trial. Following a retrial, defendant was convicted of manslaughter in the second degree and sentenced to 5 to 15 years in prison. He now appeals, and we affirm.

Initially, we are not persuaded by defendant's contention that County Court should have denied the People's reverse-Batson objection to his peremptory challenge of an

African–American juror. While defense counsel offered a race-neutral explanation for the challenge — specifically, that the juror indicated that one of the reasons she kept a dog was for security — our review of the record supports the court's factual finding that the reason was pretextual In particular, we note that defense counsel had stricken every other African–American juror up to that point, and the court had previously put counsel "on notice" and warned him that his proffered explanation as to one of those jurors was only "marginally acceptable." Under these circumstances, and mindful that the court's evaluation of counsel's motivation in making the specific challenge at issue herein turned largely on its assessment of counsel's credibility, which is entitled to great deference, we find no error in the court's decision to strike the peremptory challenge.

Defendant next argues that County Court erred in excluding both the testimony of a mental health counselor who would have testified that defendant exhibits two symptoms of posttraumatic stress disorder (hereinafter PTSD), and the testimony of a psychiatrist who diagnosed defendant with "sub clinical PTSD" based upon his opinion that defendant exhibits three symptoms of PTSD. Defendant argues that such expert testimony was necessary to assist the jury in understanding his state of mind at the time of the stabbing, which was crucial to his justification defense.

"'It is for the trial court in the first instance to determine when jurors are able to draw conclusions from the evidence based on their day-to-day experience, their common observation and their knowledge, and when they would be benefitted by the specialized knowledge of an expert witness'" (*People v. Lee*, 96 N.Y.2d 157, 162, 726 N.Y.S.2d 361, 750 N.E.2d 63 (2001)). Here, after extensive oral argument and written submissions by both parties, County Court excluded the testimony based upon its conclusions that subclinical PTSD is not a recognized syndrome, disease or mental defect, and that the specific symptoms at issue — hypervigilance, emotional numbing, and a sense of helplessness in the face of stress — were within the jury's range of knowledge and intelligence, particularly since defendant himself would be able to testify about his military experience and other events purportedly underlying his symptoms. Under the particular circumstances presented, we find that the court did not abuse its discretion in this regard.

Defendant next contends that the testimony of a police detective briefly noting that defendant "refused to talk about the fight," as well as the People's fleeting reference to that testimony during summation, violated defendant's right against self-incrimination. Notably, however, counsel raised no objection to the summation. Furthermore, when objecting to the testimony, counsel did not contend that the offending testimony impermissibly implicated defendant's invocation of his right to remain silent. Rather, counsel stated that his objection was based upon his belief that the line of questioning being pursued by the prosecutor would "ultimately" result in testimony that defendant invoked his right against self-incrimination and his right to counsel. When the prosecutor assured him that he would take the questioning in another direction, counsel stated, "That is fine," and no curative instruction was requested. Accordingly, the arguments made herein are not preserved for appellate review. In any event, in light of the evidence presented, we find that any such errors were "harmless beyond a reasonable doubt" inasmuch as there is "no reasonable possibility that the errors might have contributed to defendant's conviction" (*People v. Crimmins*, 36 N.Y.2d 230, 237, 367 N.Y.S.2d 213, 326 N.E.2d 787 (1975)).

We are also not persuaded by defendant's claim that the prosecutor violated his rights by noting during summation that defendant failed to provide an exculpatory version of events. Not only did defendant fail to object, rendering the issue unpreserved, but the prosecutor's comments in that regard referenced defendant's tape-recorded conversation with his father and sister, not his interaction with police. Finally, with respect to defendant's challenge to the redacted version of the tape-recorded conversation that was admitted at the retrial, we note that defendant asks this Court to reverse its previous holding that his statements were spontaneous (see *People v. Murphy*, 51 A.D.3d at 1057–1058, 856 N.Y.S.2d 713), which we decline to do.

ORDERED that the judgment is affirmed.

PETERS, SPAIN, KAVANAGH and EGAN JR., JJ., concur.

1   With what crime is the defendant charged?
2   Is this the first time that the defendant was tried on this charge?
3   What is the "reverse-Batson" claim brought by the defendant?
4   What pattern had defense counsel followed during jury selection?
5   Did the prosecutor violate the defendant's rights during the prosecutor's closing argument (or summation)?

CASE QUESTIONS

CHAPTER SUMMARY

There are many phases of a criminal trial. Jury selection is the first phase. Attorneys are allowed to strike or remove members of the panel until twelve jurors remain. An attorney can use a peremptory strike to remove a panel member for almost any cause. However, in the U.S. Supreme Court decision, *Batson v. Kentucky*, the Court barred attorneys on either side from removing jury members for discriminatory reasons. Once the jury is selected, the attorneys address the jurors in a short speech called an opening statement. Following the opening statement, the state must proceed first, calling witnesses and introducing evidence to prove that the defendant is guilty beyond a reasonable doubt. After each of the state's witnesses are questioned on direct examination, the defense attorney has the right to conduct cross-examination.

When the state's case is concluded, the defense will almost always move for a directed verdict. A motion for directed verdict asserts that the state has failed to present enough evidence to sustain the charges. If the judge rules in favor of the defendant's motion, the charges against the defendant are dismissed. If the judge denies the motion, the case continues. At this point, the defense must decide to put up witnesses or evidence of its own. The prosecutor is entitled to cross-examine any defense witnesses who take the stand. When the defense concludes, the attorneys and the judge meet briefly to discuss the jury instructions that the judge will give to the jury members. The attorneys are then allowed to give a closing argument to the jury. At the conclusion of the closing arguments, the judge will provide instructions to the jury and the jurors will retire to the jury room to deliberate and reach a verdict in the case. In most states, jurors must vote unanimously and their verdict can be guilty, not guilty, not guilty by reason of insanity, or guilty, but mentally ill. Once a verdict has been returned and if the defendant has been found guilty, the judge will sentence the defendant.

KEY TERMS

Jury box	Striking a jury	Redirect examination
Recess	Peremptory challenge	Directed verdict
Bench	Challenge for cause	Rebuttal
Bench conference	Batson challenge	Mistrial
Bench trial	Alternate juror	Charge conference
Clerk	Opening statement	Closing argument
Court reporter	Direct examination	Jury instructions
Join issue	Case-in-chief	Closing argument
Voir dire	Cross-examination	Verdict
Venire	Impeachment	Polling

REVIEW QUESTIONS

1   What is the jury box?
2   What is the function of the jury deliberation room?
3   Explain where the witness stand is in relation to the judge's bench.
4   Explain the function of the judge's bench.
5   Where are the defense and prosecution tables located in the courtroom?
6   What functions does the clerk of court carry out?
7   What is the purpose of the court reporter?
8   Explain how a jury is selected.
9   What does it mean to join issue?
10   What is *voir dire*?
11   What is the *venire*?
12   What is a peremptory charge?
13   Explain a challenge for cause.
14   What is a Batson challenge?
15   Explain the process for striking a jury.
16   What is the opening statement?
17   Explain how a direct examination is carried out.
18   What is a cross-examination?
19   What is a redirect examination?
20   What is a directed verdict?
21   What is the purpose of rebuttal?
22   Explain the function of the jury charge.
23   How is a charge conference carried out?
24   How is a typical closing argument carried out?
25   Explain the possible verdicts that a jury may reach.
26   What is polling a jury?

QUESTIONS FOR ANALYSIS

1   Should all peremptory challenges to juries be eliminated? If a jury qualifies for jury service, is it necessary to ask them a lot of personal questions to see if they might be a good juror for one side or the other?

2   Have court rulings gone too far in regard to Batson challenges? Or should the philosophy of anti-discriminatory practices in striking jurors be expanded to other categories? Explain your answer.

HYPOTHETICALS

1   During an opening statement, attorney Matt Lock takes a bloody knife out of his coat pocket and displays it to the jury, telling them that this is the *real* murder weapon and that the prosecutor has the wrong knife. Is this an improper opening statement? Why or why not?

2   During a closing argument, attorney Matt Lock argues to the jury that the murder victim in this case "deserved to die and whoever killed him did the world a great service." Based on what you have learned in this chapter, is this a proper closing argument? Why or why not?

3   It is the middle of a trial for armed robbery and the judge learns that one of the jurors has been talking with the defense attorney and even helping the defense attorney investigate the case. What should the judge do?

Sentencing and Appeal

Chapter Objectives

- Explain the basic procedure involved when a defendant enters a plea
- Describe the various types of pleas available to defendants
- Define the purpose of plea bargaining
- Explain the role of victim impact statements in sentencing
- List and explain the types of actions available to an appellate court

I. INTRODUCTION TO SENTENCING

This chapter will focus on sentencing issues, including how and under what circumstances a defendant enters a plea of guilty and what happens on appeal following a conviction. We will begin by addressing the issue of procedures involved in entering a guilty plea.

A. PROCEDURE

Before addressing the process involved in entering a guilty plea, it's important to understand the significance of pleading guilty. At its simplest, a plea of guilty is the defendant's admission that he or she committed the crime.[1] Once the plea is made and accepted by the court and the defendant begins serving his or her sentence, the defendant is barred from retracting it. A person accused of a crime always has the right to plead guilty to it, even when the crime is capital murder and the defendant is facing a possible death sentence. (Some states do not allow a defendant to enter a plea of guilty in capital murder cases.)[2]

---

[1] *State v. Merino*, 81 Haw. 198, 915 P.2d 672 (1996).
[2] *People v. Coates*, 337 Mich. 56, 59 N.W.2d 83 (1953).

Even though a defendant has the right to plead guilty, it does not mean that the judge is compelled to accept the plea. Why would such a rule exist?

A judge may reject a defendant's guilty plea if the defendant claims that he or she did not commit the activity. A defendant cannot have it both ways: He or she either admits guilt and accepts the sentence of the court or pleads not guilty and goes to trial. With the sole exception of *Alford* pleas (discussed later), a defendant cannot, on the one hand, maintain his innocence while on the other plead guilty to the infraction.

Before a judge can accept a defendant's plea, the judge must make a determination that the plea is given voluntarily and not as the result of coercion, threats, or other inducements.[3] A guilty plea must be given knowingly and voluntarily. To establish the voluntary nature of the plea, the judge (or the prosecutor) will question the defendant on the record to determine that the plea has not been forced. (In some misdemeanor cases, the defendant may simply initial statements on a plea form that state, "This plea is not the result of force, threat, or coercion.") In felony cases, the traditional method of accepting a guilty plea is to do so in open court, with the entire proceeding taken down by a court reporter and subsequently made part of the record. To establish that a guilty plea is voluntarily and knowingly given, many courts have established a standard set of questions that defendants must answer, out loud, in open court. If a defendant refuses to respond to any of the questions or retracts any statement, the court will reject the defendant's guilty plea and set the case for a trial. Defendants are not railroaded into pleading guilty by overzealous judges or prosecutors, despite what may be portrayed on television and in movies. See Figure 21-1 for a list of questions that the defendant must answer.

VOLUNTARY PLEA?

Dora has been charged with larceny and when her case is called for trial, she tells the court that she wants to plead guilty. When the court goes through the standard questions with her, she tells the judge, "I really don't want to plead guilty, but my boyfriend says that if I don't, he'll run off with my children." Is this a valid guilty plea that the judge can accept?

Answer: No. The answer indicates that the defendant is not giving her plea freely, voluntarily, and without intimidation.

Sidebar

Before a defendant is permitted to enter a plea of guilty, the judge must determine that the defendant has done so freely, voluntarily and without any duress, threat, or intimidation.

VOLUNTARINESS OF THE PLEA

The judge must always consider any statements made by the defendant during the questioning process to determine that the plea was made voluntarily, knowingly, and without coercion. If a defendant gives an equivocal answer to one of the plea interrogatories set out in Figure 21-1, then the judge will be required to

---

[3] *Woods v. Rhay*, 68 Wash. 2d 601, 414 P.2d 601 (1966).

FIGURE 21-1

Interrogatories of
Defendant During Plea

1. Please state your name for the record.
2. What is your age?
3. Are you now under the influence of alcohol, medicine, drugs, or any other substance?
4. Can you read and write?
5. Have you read and examined the indictment charging you in this case?
6. Do you understand that you are charged with the following offenses?
7. Do you understand that there are certain rights that you would have at trial and that by pleading guilty you give up those rights? Do you understand that you are giving up the right to:

   - A trial by a jury
   - Be presumed innocent
   - Confront the witnesses against you
   - Subpoena any witnesses to appear on your behalf
   - Testify yourself and offer other evidence
   - Have an attorney represent you during your trial?

8. Do you understand that if you plead not guilty or if you remain silent and enter no plea at all you will have the right to a trial by jury?
9. Do you understand that for the offense of _____ you can be sentenced to a maximum sentence from _____ to _____ years and a fine of $_____?
10. The State has recommended a sentence to the judge of _____. Other than this recommendation, has anyone made any promises to cause you to plead guilty?
11. Do you understand that the judge is not required to follow this recommendation but can give you any sentence allowed by law?
12. Has anyone used any force or threats against you to cause you to plead guilty?
13. Are you satisfied with the services of your attorney in this case?
14. Do you understand all of the questions that you have answered so far?
15. Understanding all of your rights, do you want to enter a plea of guilty to the offense(s) listed in the indictment?
16. Is your decision to plead guilty made freely and voluntarily?
17. Did you in fact commit the offense of _____ as it is stated in the indictment?

suspend the sentencing. During the suspension, the defendant will have the opportunity to speak to his or her counsel and restart the sentencing phase. If the defendant continues to make statements that seem to indicate he or she is not guilty of the crime, then the judge must halt the sentencing process, enter a plea of not guilty, and place the defendant's case back on the active trial roster.

B. *ALFORD* PLEA

Alford plea
A plea, authorized by the U.S. Supreme Court, that allows a defendant to enter a guilty plea, but basing the plea on the amount and quantity of evidence against him instead of the defendant's belief in his actual guilt.

An ***Alford*** **plea** allows a defendant an alternative to pleading either guilty or not guilty. Under an *Alford* plea, a defendant can continue to maintain his innocence but tender a guilty plea and be sentenced as though he had said he was guilty. A defendant might decide to use an *Alford* plea when the government's case against him seems strong and his possible defenses weak. The Supreme Court first recognized the possibility of a defendant choosing to plead guilty while protesting his innocence in the case of *North Carolina v. Alford*, 91 S.Ct. 160 (1970), and it has since been referred to as an *Alford* plea.

Alford pleas are common, although there are no statistics that reveal exactly how commonly they are used. Judges and legal scholars alike support the use of the *Alford* plea as an efficient, constitutional way of resolving cases. Furthermore, when defendants enter an *Alford* plea, it can be a benefit when they seek future employment. They can explain to their potential employer that they were innocent, but the evidence was stacked against them.

C. *NOLO CONTENDERE*

Nolo contendere
Latin for "I do not contest"; a plea offered in a criminal case where the defendant does not contest his or her guilt and asks for the court's mercy.

A plea of ***nolo contendere*** literally means, "I do not contest." For purposes of sentencing, a plea of nolo contendere has the same requirements and the same implications as a guilty plea. If that is the case, why would a person bother to present such a plea? In some instances, a plea of *nolo contendere* can prevent points from being assessed against the defendant's driver's license. Pleas of *nolo contendere* are routinely accepted in first-offense DUI cases for that reason. Because a plea of *nolo contendere* does not admit guilt, a defendant may also wish to use this plea instead of a plea of guilty because of a pending civil case. Because a *nolo* plea does not admit guilt, this plea cannot be used against the defendant in a civil case the same way that a guilty plea can. A certified copy of a defendant's guilty plea to a traffic violation may be the only thing that a plaintiff in a civil case needs to prove that the defendant is liable for medical and property damages. A *nolo* plea cannot be used in that manner.

It should be noted that many states do not allow a defendant to use the plea of *nolo contendere* or, if they do, limit its use to specific types of offenses, usually minor ones like traffic violations or a first-offense DUI. The judge always has the option to accept or reject a *nolo contendere* plea. If the judge rejects the plea, then the defendant must either change the plea to guilty or proceed to trial on a plea of not guilty.

D. CONDITIONAL PLEA

Conditional plea
A plea entered by the defendant who maintains his or her innocence but states that the evidence against him or her is overwhelming.

In some states, a defendant is allowed to enter what is referred to as a **conditional plea**. This is an alternative to an *Alford* plea, and in many ways they are similar. A defendant enters a plea of guilty, including a condition that although he continues to maintain his innocence, the facts and the law are such that the chances of him actually winning at trial are virtually non-existent. In the face of such overwhelming evidence, the defendant enters a conditional plea of guilty. The practical consequences between a conditional plea, an *Alford* plea, and a guilty plea are identical. For purposes of crime records, employment applications, security clearance and any other jobs that require someone without a criminal record, the person who has entered a conditional plea is considered to have pleaded guilty — exactly as the person who offered an *Alford* plea of guilty.

E. FIRST OFFENDER TREATMENT

Another possible outcome for a defendant who decides to plead guilty is a request to be enrolled in the state's First Offender Program. All states have some form of this program, although it is not available for all types of crimes. Generally, First Offender Programs are reserved for youthful offenders for relatively minor crimes. Rather than have these people carry a criminal conviction for the rest of their lives, a judge might decide to enroll them into the First Offender Program. Under the terms of the program, a defendant must sign an agreement to complete various activities. If he or she is successful, at the completion of the First Offender Program, the judge will rescind the defendant's guilty plea. At this point, a defendant can truthfully say that he or she has not been convicted of a crime. The judge will order that the defendant's conviction be expunged from the record. However, in order to earn this generous benefit, a defendant will have to complete some or all of the following:

- Attend education classes
- Complete substantial amounts of community service
- Pay all fines and restitution to victims
- Attend psychological, drug, or narcotics counseling on a regular basis
- Commit no further crimes during his or her time in the First Offender Program

 PLEA BARGAINING

The vast majority of criminal cases end in some kind of negotiated plea of guilty. The process of plea bargaining has been going on for hundreds of years in this country, although it has not always gone by that name. A plea bargain is essentially an agreement between the defendant and the state. The prosecutor promises that he or she will recommend a lower sentence than what the defendant might ordinarily receive in exchange for the defendant's promise to plead guilty. Plea bargaining works differently in different jurisdictions. In some states and on the federal level, prosecutors cannot recommend a specific sentence, because sentencing guidelines demand specific sentences for specific crimes, but prosecutors can negotiate the number and type of charges that they will bring against a defendant. In other states, a plea bargain is as simple as first stated: The state (in the person of the prosecutor) makes a promise to the defendant to recommend a sentence in exchange for a guilty plea.

In most jurisdictions, the judge has specific restrictions on the ultimate sentence that he or she can impose on the defendant. For instance, all crimes carry maximum sentences. In some states, a conviction for armed robbery could carry a maximum sentence of 20 years. Following a conviction for this crime, the judge could not sentence a defendant to any sentence that exceeds this period, even if the judge wanted to set an example for the community and impose a harsher sentence than allowed by law. There are also additional constitutional prohibitions that a judge faces when imposing a sentence that will be addressed later in this chapter.

Although the prosecutor can make a recommendation to the judge about the defendant's **sentence** — at least in those states that do not follow mandatory sentencing guidelines, the judge is the final authority on the sentence that the defendant receives. If the state's recommendation seems inadequate to a judge, then the judge will announce to the defendant that he or she does not intend to follow the recommendation. The judge is not compelled to tell the defendant what sentence he or she is inclined to give. However, the defendant has one option: When the judge announces an intention not to follow the recommendation, the defendant is free to withdraw his or her guilty plea and proceed to trial instead. The defendant's attorney may meet with the prosecution again to determine a new plea bargain in hopes that the judge will accept a different arrangement.

Sentence
The punishment, such as a prison sentence or fine that is imposed on a convicted defendant by a judge.

The vast majority of criminal cases are disposed of through some type of plea bargaining.

A. FEDERAL SENTENCING NEGOTIATIONS

Many states and the federal government have imposed sentencing guidelines for individuals convicted of crimes. These sentencing guidelines have been imposed, in many situations, as a way of reaching more uniform results in sentencing. Essentially, these statutes take away some of the judge's discretion in imposing a sentence and require specific sentences for specific crimes.

The rationale for sentencing guidelines is that they provide more consistent sentences. When a judge has wide discretion in the sentence to be meted out, the judge may give a sentence that is considerably less or considerably more than the sentences other individuals have received for the same offense. This gives the criminal justice system the appearance of being arbitrary and capricious. Under sentencing guidelines or "structured sentencing" as it is sometimes called, judges have far less discretion in the sentence imposed on the defendant. When the judge is confronted with a defendant convicted of a crime, the judge must refer to a schedule that determines the sentence, based on the kind of infraction and the defendant's prior criminal record. In many cases, the guidelines were imposed by legislatures eager to show a "get tough on crime" stance.[4]

---

[4] *Fear of Judging: Sentencing Guidelines in the Federal Courts*, Kate Stith and Jose A. Cabranes. Chicago: The University of Chicago Press, 1998.

FEDERAL SENTENCING GUIDELINES

The U.S. Congress, after making findings that there were large discrepancies in the length of sentences that defendants received for the same crime in different parts of the country, enacted the Federal Sentencing Guidelines. The U.S. sentencing commission was created by Congress in 1984. The commission's job was to develop guidelines for sentencing all federal offenders. These guidelines became the law of the federal courts in 1987 and withstood a constitutional challenge in 1989.[5] One can hardly claim that the Federal Sentencing Guidelines were a success. They have been attacked from all sides, by defense attorneys and prosecutors and even by federal judges.

A big change came in the use of Federal Sentencing Guidelines in the Supreme Court case of *U.S. v. Booker*, 543 US 220 (2005). That case held that the mandatory provisions of the Federal Sentencing Guidelines were unconstitutional because they took power away from juries to determine key facts in a case and gave that responsibility solely to the federal judge. However, the Supreme Court did not rule that the Federal Sentencing Guidelines are unconstitutional in all ways. They may be used as guidelines for judges when they impose sentences. The basic claim raised in the *Booker* case was that the judge made additional factual findings during Booker's sentencing phase concerning facts that the jury had not considered in the case in chief. This put the judge in the impermissible position of being both fact finder and judge in a jury trial. In the aftermath of the *Booker* case, the Federal Sentencing Guidelines are no longer considered mandatory but do provide guidance for federal prosecutors and judges.

B. STATE PLEA NEGOTIATIONS

On the state level, prosecutors face the same pressures as federal prosecutors. As discussed later in this section, there is a genuine need to reduce caseloads on both the state and federal level. States have addressed this problem in different ways. Some states allow a judge great latitude in the sentence that he or she may impose, risking a claim of disproportionate sentencing. Other states have attempted to follow the federal model and enacted their own state sentencing guidelines.

STATE SENTENCING GUIDELINES

Many states have followed the federal model by enacting sentencing guidelines for individuals convicted of crimes. These sentencing guidelines have been imposed, in many situations, as a way of reaching more uniform results in length of prison term and fine imposed. Essentially, these statutes take away some of the judge's discretion in imposing a sentence and require specific sentences for specific crimes.

---

[5] *Mistretta v. U.S.* 488 U.S. 361 (1989).

The rationale for sentencing guidelines is that they provide more consistent sentences. When a judge has wide discretion in the sentence that he or she can impose, the judge may give a sentence that is considerably less or considerably more than the sentences other individuals have received for the same offense. Under sentencing guidelines, or *structured sentencing* as it is sometimes called, judges have far less discretion in the sentence imposed on the defendant. When the judge is confronted with a defendant convicted of a crime, the judge must refer to a schedule that determines the sentence, based on the kind of infraction and the defendant's prior criminal record.[6]

C. THE CONTROVERSY SURROUNDING PLEA BARGAINING

Many claim that allowing defendants to plead guilty to lesser sentences does nothing to advance the cause of justice and merely sets up a system in which an offender is doomed to become a repeat offender. Prison should be made more difficult, the conditions worsened, critics argue, so that no one would want to risk becoming a recidivist. However, others argue that without plea bargaining, the criminal justice system in the United States would grind to a halt. There are simply too many cases for every defendant to receive a jury trial. If prosecutors did not offer some incentive to defendants to get them to plead guilty, then they would all opt for a jury trial. There is already considerable delay between a defendant's arrest and his or her trial, and this gap would only become longer as more and more defendants requested jury trials. There is also the question of economics. All of those jurors must be paid, even if it is only $25 per day. Moreover, in high-profile cases, jurors may be sequestered, meaning that they are sent to hotels at night during the trial instead of being allowed to go home and possibly see news coverage of the trial that could affect their verdict.

Despite the naysayers, plea bargains are a daily fact of every prosecutor's life, and through skillful negotiation, a prosecutor might reduce his or her monthly trial docket by as much as 90 percent by using them.

Of course, there are some cases where plea bargains are simply not appropriate. In states that have enacted "three strikes and you're out" provisions (discussed below), a defendant faces a mandatory life sentence on a third felony conviction. There is no offer that a prosecutor can make to induce the defendant to plead guilty. The sentence is mandatory and the prosecutor cannot alter it. In other cases, such as capital murder cases where a defendant is facing a possible death sentence, there is also very little room — and often very little inclination — for a prosecutor to offer a deal to a defendant.

---

[6] *Fear of Judging: Sentencing Guidelines in the Federal Courts*, Kate Stith and Jose A. Cabranes. Chicago: The University of Chicago Press, 1998.

 **SENTENCING**

The judge sentences defendants who are found guilty at trial. Since there are no further proceedings in cases where defendants are found not guilty, this chapter will concentrate on the sentencing and appeals phase of criminal prosecutions. In most jurisdictions, the judge has specific restrictions on the ultimate sentence that he or she can impose on the defendant. The statute that criminalizes the behavior usually includes a provision for a minimum and maximum sentence and a judge is bound to impose a sentence within those limits.

A. JUDICIAL DISCRETION

Sentencing guidelines were imposed as a way of curbing a judge's discretion. In jurisdictions where sentencing guidelines do not exist, the judge has broad discretion. The judge can take a wide range of factors into account in fashioning a sentence, including the maximum sentence permissible under the statute, the defendant's prior history, and any aggravating or mitigating factors.

JUDICIAL PROCEDURE IN IMPOSING SENTENCES

In most situations, it is the judge's sole responsibility to impose the sentence on the defendant. However, there are jurisdictions that allow the jury to have some input on the sentence. This is especially true in death penalty cases where the jury must actually recommend a death sentence to the judge.[7]

When it comes time to sentence, the judge must address the defendant and also allow the defendant the opportunity to make any statements that he or she wishes, as long as these statements do not cross the line into verbal abuse or disrupt the court proceedings.[8]

STATUTORY MINIMUM AND MAXIMUM SENTENCES

In most situations, when a defendant is convicted of a crime, the statute will provide the maximum, and in some cases the minimum, sentence permissible under law. A judge may not exceed the maximum sentence. In the absence of mandatory sentencing guidelines, a judge has the power to impose any sentence between the minimum and the maximum.

CONCURRENT SENTENCING

A **concurrent sentence** is one that will be served at the same time as any other prison term. When the sentences run concurrently, a defendant serves time for two

Concurrent sentencing
One or more sentences that are served at the same time.

---

[7] *U.S. v. Bishop*, 412 U.S. 346, 93 S. Ct. 2008, 36 L. Ed. 2d 941 (1973).
[8] *Ross v. State*, 676 N.E.2d 339 (Ind. 1996).

or more offenses at the same time. Obviously, a defendant would prefer to be sentenced to a concurrent sentence instead of a consecutive sentence.

CONSECUTIVE SENTENCING

A consecutive prison term is one that is added to a current prison term. If a defendant has been sentenced to a five year prison term on one offense, then his new sentence will begin when the first prison term has ended. Judges often sentence defendants to **consecutive sentences** in order to increase the overall time that a defendant will serve in custody.

Consecutive sentencing
One or more sentences that are served on after the other.

B. PRESENTENCE INVESTIGATION

Once the judge has accepted the plea of guilty, sentence may be imposed. In most situations, the sentence will be entered immediately. In other situations, a sentencing hearing may be scheduled. This is especially true if the judge orders a **presentence investigation** or PSI. A PSI is a report prepared by the defendant's probation officer. This report will detail the defendant's circumstances, including the details of the crime, the defendant's upbringing, his or her criminal history, and any other factors in mitigation or aggravation of sentence. Defense attorneys are given an opportunity to supplement the probation officer's materials with anything they believe relevant. However, the judge still has the final decision on sentencing.

Presentence investigation
An investigation by court-appoint social workers, probation officers, and others, into a criminal's background to determine the criminal's prospects for rehabilitation.

C. SENTENCING HEARING

At the conclusion of a trial, or as part of the defendant's guilty plea, the judge may hold a sentencing hearing to determine what sentence the defendant should receive. A sentencing hearing allows the prosecution to present evidence to justify a harsher sentence. The defense also has the opportunity of presenting any evidence that might mitigate the sentence. This hearing is like a mini-trial. Witnesses may testify and both sides may introduce evidence to support their positions.

VICTIM IMPACT STATEMENTS

A victim is permitted and often encouraged to file a statement that can be read at the hearing and is made a part of the defendant's file. A **victim impact statement** allows the victim to tell the judge what effect the defendant's crime has had on the victim's life. Victim impact statements are often an important part of the healing process that occurs in the aftermath of a crime, especially a violent crime. The victim is permitted to read the statement in open court or the statement may be read by a prosecutor for a victim who does not wish to appear in court on the sentencing day.

Victim impact statement
The right of a victim of a crime to address the court during the defendant's sentencing and to testify about the effect that the defendant's crime has had on the victim.

AGGRAVATION OF SENTENCE

During a sentencing hearing, the prosecutor may seek **aggravation of sentence** and introduce a wide range of evidence to justify a harsher sentence for the defendant. For example, the prosecution might show that:

Aggravation of sentence
Evidence offered by the state to enhance or lengthen the defendant's sentence.

- The defendant has prior criminal convictions
- The defendant's actions have had an adverse impact on the victim or victim's family
- The defendant poses a significant threat to the community or is likely to commit more crimes in the future

Many states have enacted statutes that allow victims of specific kinds of crime to recover money from state or federal funds. These funds are designed to help defray some of the costs associated with obtaining replacement goods (or to meet insurance deductibles when insurance coverage exists). In these states, a victim must file a claim under the applicable legislation and show how the defendant's actions affected the victim's life and also prove any monetary losses that were not covered by insurance.

In general, when the state seeks to enhance a defendant's sentence, it must bring out the underlying aggravating factors during the trial so that they can also be proven beyond a reasonable doubt. In that way, the judge can consider them in the sentencing phase.[9]

MITIGATION OF SENTENCE

The defense may also present evidence in **mitigation of sentence**. For instance, the defense may show that the defendant has a poor education or a bad childhood to help explain why the defendant resorted to crime. In addition to family life and education, the defense might introduce evidence of the defendant's mental stability or intelligence. In addition, the defendant may take the stand and testify about the circumstances of his life as a way to explain why he committed the crime.

Mitigation of sentence
Evidence offered by the defense to lessen or shorten the defendant's sentence.

D. POSSIBLE PUNISHMENTS

There are a wide range of punishments that a defendant can receive at the conclusion of a trial, including:

- Death
- Life in prison without parole
- Life in prison
- Sentence for years
- Probation or parole

---

[9] *Southern Union Co. v. U.S.*, 132 S. Ct. 2344 (2012).

- Fines
- Community service
- Restitution

DEATH

Originally, the prohibition of cruel and unusual punishment was enacted to prohibit torture, but not the death penalty. The Founding Fathers had seen enough of practices such as "pressing" or putting someone in a stock in the village square. The Eighth Amendment forbids these types of corporal and psychological torture, but does not forbid a sentence of death; it simply means that the sentence must be carried out with as little pain as possible. Most "innovations" in the mechanisms of executing a human being have been based on making the death as painless as possible. The invention of the electric chair was originally put forward as a "painless" way to carry out a death sentence.

Procedures in Death Penalty Cases. Issues surrounding the imposition of the death penalty could fill an entire volume. Sentencing a person to execution at the hands of the state has always been considered to be the most extreme sanction in law. As such, death penalty cases or "capital murder" cases have different safeguards and procedures than are seen in other prosecutions. As we have seen, a death sentence itself is not necessarily "cruel and unusual" punishment, but the manner in which it is carried out could be. Many jurisdictions limit the possible methods of execution to proven methods. For instance, some states no longer permit the use of hanging or the use of the electric chair.[10]

Bifurcated trial
Separate hearings for different issues in the same case; for example, for guilt and sanity or guilt and punishment in a criminal case.

Sentencing in Death Penalty Cases. Sentencing in death penalty cases raises a whole host of crucial issues. Death penalty cases are always a **bifurcated trial**, meaning that there are two trials. When a defendant is charged with capital murder and the government announces its intention to seek the death penalty, special rules are triggered to protect the defendant. The bifurcated trial consists of the guilt phase, where the jury decides whether or not the defendant is guilty of the crime, and the sentencing phase where the judge or jury is called upon to decide if the defendant's actions warrant a death sentence. In most jurisdictions the only crime that warrants a death sentence is murder. Although in the past it was possible to be sentenced to death for crimes such as rape, most jurisdictions limit a death sentence to cases involving homicide. In some states only a jury can decide to impose a death sentence. In other jurisdictions, the judge decides to impose death. In either situation, the fact-finder must not only decide that the defendant is guilty of the crime, but also decide that the defendant's actions warrant a death sentence. The only way to reach this conclusion is to find that certain aggravating factors were present. Simply killing another person is not enough to warrant a death sentence. To be sentenced to death, the murder must

---

[10] *Woodson v. North Carolina*, 428 U.S. 280, 96 S. Ct. 2978, 49 L. Ed. 2d 944 (1976).

have been committed during the commission of another crime (such as rape) or in a particularly gruesome way.

Aggravating Factors. In order to put a convicted murderer to death, the defendant must have committed the murder under special circumstances, often referred to as "aggravating factors." These factors authorize the use of the death penalty, and include murders that were:

- Done in a particularly heinous, cruel, or depraved manner, including torture
- Committed during the course of a felony, such as rape or kidnapping
- Carried out for money
- Killed two or more people
- Committed when the defendant was escaping from legal confinement
- Committed against a child
- Acts of terrorism
- Committed by a defendant who had a prior conviction for first degree murder
- Committed against a victim who was an elected official or a police officer

In states that formally punished other types of offenses — such as the rape of a child — with the death penalty, the U.S. Supreme Court has ruled that the death penalty can only be used in cases where the victim died.[11]

LIFE IN PRISON WITHOUT THE POSSIBILITY OF PAROLE

The U.S. Supreme Court has also held that sentences of life without **parole** do not violate the Eighth Amendment for certain offenses. These include murder, kidnapping, bank robbery, narcotic offenses, and aggravated rape. Except for murder, life sentences without parole are only authorized when the other listed crimes (kidnapping, rape, and so on.) involve violence or repeated convictions. A life sentence without the possibility of parole means that the defendant will never be released. Such a sentence is often the alternative for a person who is facing a potential death sentence. In states that allow a person facing a capital murder charge to plead guilty, this is usually the sentence that they receive. The defendants give up the possibility of ever being released from prison in exchange for not facing the death sentence at trial. In most situations, life without parole means exactly what it says and the defendant will never leave the correctional system alive.

Parole
A release from prison, before a sentence is finished, that depends on the person's "keeping clean" and doing what he or she is supposed to do while out.

LIFE IN PRISON

For serious crimes–including murder, kidnapping with violence and cases where the defendant has a long criminal history–he or she may be sentenced to life in prison. Although there is a well-known (and incorrect) saying that a life sentence

---

[11] *Kennnedy v. Louisiana*, 128 S. Ct. 2641, 171 L. Ed. 2d 525 (2008).

simply means a maximum of seven years in custody, the facts are more complicated. For instance, it makes a great deal of difference in what state the defendant is sentenced to life. In some states, for instance, a life sentence may actually mean that the defendant serves the rest of his or her life in prison, while in other states it means that the although the defendant has received a life sentence, his or her first parole hearing will not be scheduled until the seventh year of incarceration, at which time the defendant could be released or could be held for a longer period of time.

● FAMOUS CASES
BAPTIST CHURCH BOMBING

In the early morning hours of Sunday, September 15, 1963, four members of the Ku Klux Klan prepared to plant a box of dynamite equipped with a time-delay device, near the basement of the 16th Street Baptist Church in Birmingham, Alabama, whose congregation was African-American. One of the Klansmen was spotted getting out of a turquoise and white Chevrolet and placing a box beneath the steps at the side of the church. The bomb exploded midmorning during services, killing 4 young girls and injuring 22 others.

The KKK targeted the church specifically because it was the largest black church in Birmingham, and it served as the location for many civil rights meetings, drawing prominent leaders like Martin Luther King Jr. and Ralph David Abernathy. Civil rights activists would gather at the church and march together to demonstrate at a park across the street, where they frequently clashed with police. In the aftermath of the bombing, more than 8,000 mourners attended the funeral services, including 800 clergy of all races. Not a single Birmingham city official attended.

The bombing outraged the nation and ultimately generated support for the passage of President Lyndon Johnson's Civil Rights Act of 1964. However, public outrage and an intensive FBI investigation failed to bring justice to the victims. An eyewitness had identified the man in the turquoise and white Chevrolet as Robert Chambliss, a notorious racist and member of the KKK who went by the name "Dynamite Bob." Chambliss was arrested and tried for murder and possession of dynamite without a permit in October 1963. He was found not guilty of the murder charge and received a $100 fine and a six-month jail sentence for the dynamite-possession charge.

By early 1965, the FBI had identified the other three KKK participants — Bobby Frank Cherry, Herman Frank Cash, and Thomas E. Blanton Jr. — but Director J. Edgar Hoover blocked their prosecution. Hoover was ardently opposed to the civil rights movement, and he eventually halted the investigation in 1968 without filing charges. Hoover refused to give federal prosecutors the testimony that identified the suspects, including a tape recording of Blanton speaking about his role in the bombing.

Bill Baxley was a law student at the time of the bombing, and his hope was that he might one day bring the perpetrators to justice. Within a week of taking office as attorney general of Alabama in 1971, Baxley reopened the case. He secured withheld evidence from the FBI and worked to build trust with witnesses who were reluctant to testify, fearful of the wrath of the Klan. During his investigation, he received a letter from the KKK, protesting his continued involvement in the case and containing a veiled death threat. Baxley replied on official state letterhead, ""My response to your letter of February 19, 1976, is — kiss my ass.""

In 1977 Baxley indicted Robert Chambliss for the murders of all four girls. Chambliss was tried, found guilty, and sentenced to life in prison. He died in prison eight years later. Blanton was tried and convicted in 2001, Cherry in 2002. Cash died in 1994 without ever being tried, and Cherry died in prison in 2004.

SENTENCE FOR YEARS

When the judge sentences a defendant to a term in prison, he or she may order that the sentence be served consecutively to other prison terms or concurrently with other terms. A sentence for years can be as low as a few days in the local jail or decades of life spent behind bars. Usually, a sentence short of life in prison without the possibility of parole always gives the prisoner the right to gain credit for good behavior that will shorten his or her sentence. Similarly, negative or disruptive behavior may see additional time added to the balance of the sentence.

When a defendant is sentenced to prison, it is important to keep in mind that there are many different types of prisons. The Federal Bureau of Prisons lists five distinct categories:

- Administrative
- Minimum Security
- Low Security
- Medium Security
- High Security

Administrative facilities house individuals who have been charged, but not yet processed by the criminal justice system. Minimum security prisons are usually dormitory-style facilities, with relatively little security or guards. Low security prison facilities have double-fenced perimeters surrounding the unit, dormitory housing, and work programs. High security prisons are what most people think of as prisons, with barred doors on the cells (or thick doors), numerous security guards, thick walls, and often double layers of fencing around the entire outside of the facility, usually topped with razor wire.

Alternative Prisons. In some situations, a judge may consider an alternative form of punishment. For instance, in appropriate cases, a judge may order that a defendant be held under "house arrest." There are several private companies that specialize in monitoring services, some of which use advanced technology such as electronic ankle bracelets and computer terminals to confirm that a defendant remains within the confines of the home.

Other alternative forms of punishment include boot camps and shock incarceration. Someone who has been sentenced to a boot camp is normally sent there for a maximum period of 90 days. The conditions are stricter than those found in typical prisons. Modeled on military boot camps, prisoners at such facilities must abide by a strict code of conduct. The advantage for a prisoner is that with successful completion of the boot camp program, the prisoner will be released much sooner than he would have been normally. Of course, if the defendant cannot abide by the limitations of the boot camp, his sentence will convert to a more conventional prison sentence.

PROBATION AND PAROLE

Probation
Allowing a person convicted of a criminal offense to avoid serving a jail sentence imposed on the person, so long as he or she abides by certain conditions (including being supervised by a probation officer).

When a defendant is released from prison, he will often continue to serve the balance of his sentence on **probation** or parole. Probation officers ensure that the defendant follows the conditions of his sentence. For instance, if the defendant has been ordered to pay fines or restitution, the probation officer is the person who monitors these payments. In addition, the probation officer also makes sure that the probationer obtains employment, refrains from drug use, and follows other rules. If the probationer commits another crime while serving probation, the probation officer can seek to have the original probation revoked and the defendant returned to prison. Although this text has used the terms "probation" and "parole" interchangeably, they actually describe two different phases of supervision.

Probation is usually given in place of a prison sentence. When a convict is placed on probation, it means that he will be monitored to see that he does not commit any new crimes, doesn't engage in the use of drugs or other harmful practices, and is gainfully employed. Probation is often seen as a benefit to the defendant who can remain in society and avoid serving time in custody. Parole, on the other hand, is the term used when a person is released from prison before serving his full sentence. The balance of his sentence will be served on parole. While he is on parole, he will be subject to many of the same conditions that the probationer has faced: supervision, employment requirements, and so on.

Probation and parole are both confinement sentences. For example, suppose that a person receives a five-year sentence. If he is released from prison early because of good behavior, he will serve the balance of his sentence on parole. Probation is usually given to people who are not sentenced to confinement. It is important to note that the use of these terms varies from state to state. In some states, parole has been completely eliminated and all non-custody sentences are simply referred to as "probation."

When a probationer violates one or more conditions of his probation, the probation officer is authorized to file a petition with the original sentencing judge, asking that the probation be revoked. In many states, prosecutors can also file such petitions. Probation revocation hearings are similar to trials. The state presents evidence to justify revoking the defendant's probation and the defense is permitted to present evidence to show that the defendant show be allowed to continue on probation. The judge makes the final determination about whether or not the defendant has violated his terms of probation and the judge may then re-sentence the defendant to his original sentence or modify the sentence in other ways. The one thing that a judge cannot do is to re-sentence the defendant to more time in custody than he originally received. The judge can order the defendant returned to prison to serve out the balance of his sentence, but cannot sentence him to a new term in custody as though the first sentence was never imposed.

FINES

The Eighth Amendment to the U.S. Constitution not only forbids cruel and unusual punishment; it also prohibits excessive fines. Many states have enacted minimum fines that a convicted defendant must pay as part of his sentence. For instance, some states require a minimum fine of $1,000 on a third conviction for driving under the influence of alcohol in a five-year period. Other offenses, such as trafficking in narcotics, carry much stiffer fines. Fines for some narcotics offenses are as high as $250,000 and in some states may be even higher. However, the fine must be proportional to the nature of the offense. A minor offense should not be assessed a huge fine.

Once a defendant is sentenced and begins serving his sentence on probation, he must make regular payments on his fine to the probation office. When a probationer fails to make payments on his outstanding fine, his probation can be revoked and he can be placed back into incarceration. A person serving time in custody does not have to make any payments on fines, court costs, or restitution.

COMMUNITY SERVICE

For misdemeanors and some types of minor felonies, a court may sentence a defendant to community service. A sentence served on community service usually puts the defendant to work picking up trash on roads around the county, working in local government offices, or carrying out light labor, such as trash collection or processing materials at a state-run recycling plant. Community service is frequently required in driving under the influence cases and for some first time offenders.

RESTITUTION

In addition to fines, a defendant may also be ordered to compensate the victim for damages or items taken. **Restitution** acts like damages in civil cases, where the defendant pays money to compensate the victim for injuries. The restitution amount must normally be proven during the sentencing hearing, unless the defendant agrees to pay the restitution as part of a plea agreement. As the defendant makes payments to his probation officer on his fines and fees, the probation department will also collect restitution for the victim. In many cases, the victim will receive the final restitution amount as one lump payment.

Restitution
Restitution programs in some states make a convicted criminal pay back the victim in money or work.

IV CONSTITUTIONAL ISSUES IN SENTENCING

Excessive bail shall not be required, nor excessive fines imposed, nor cruel and unusual punishments inflicted. — Eighth Amendment

A judge is permitted to sentence a defendant who has either pled guilty or been found guilty, and the judge often has broad discretion in the sentence that can be imposed, but there are some constitutional limits that a judge may not exceed. When it comes to sentencing in criminal cases, the most important consideration is the Eighth Amendment, which prohibits cruel and unusual punishment.

A. CRUEL AND UNUSUAL PUNISHMENT

One of the most important restrictions placed on the kind of sentence that can be imposed on a defendant is set out in the Eighth Amendment to the U.S. Constitution. In very few words, that amendment prohibits any punishment deemed "cruel and unusual." This Amendment was made applicable to the states through the Fourteenth Amendment. Many state constitutions have similar provisions. Because the amendment does not define exactly what constitutes cruel and unusual punishment, the U.S. Supreme Court has been called on to interpret it. The Court's decisions have established that a sentence cannot involve torture, and that the sentence must be "proportional" to the crime.[12] **Proportionality** means that all states are prohibited from engaging in practices that are considered to be cruel and unusual punishment, including torture, whipping, and corporal punishment.

Proportionality
The U.S. Supreme Court has mandated that a sentence must be proportional to the crime to satisfy the Eighth Amendment. For instance, without some other aggravating circumstance, a life sentence for a petty infraction would be out of proportion and would be a violation of the Eighth Amendment.[13]

B. "THREE STRIKES AND YOU'RE OUT"

So-called three strikes statutes generally require a lengthy prison sentence (sometimes even life in prison) for a third felony conviction. These statutes have been deemed constitutional by the Supreme Court because they place conditions on imposing such a severe sentence (namely, two prior felony convictions before the statute is triggered).[14] In practice, this could mean that a defendant's third felony conviction could be for a relatively minor felony, yet still satisfy the minimum requirements of the statute and trigger a mandatory life sentence.

SCENARIO 21-2

THREE STRIKES?

Leonard has two previous convictions for theft and burglary in a state that has the three strikes law. This time he is charged with possession of five pounds of marijuana, another felony. Is he facing life in prison if he is convicted?

Answer: Yes. Most states do not make a distinction between the types of felonies needed to qualify for the three strikes laws and Leonard will almost certainly face a life sentence.

---

[12] *Miller v. Alabama*, 132 S. Ct. 2455 (2012).
[13] *Solem v. Helm*, 463 U.S. 277, 103 S. Ct. 3001, 77 L. Ed. 2d 637 (1983).
[14] *Ewing v. California*, 538 U.S. 11, 123 S. Ct. 1179, 155 L. Ed. 2d 108 (2003).

 # THE APPELLATE SYSTEM

A defendant who has been found guilty always has the right to **appeal** the conviction. The precise rules and procedures for bringing a criminal appeal vary from state to state. For the sake of clarity, we will assume that a defendant has been found guilty in a state court of a major felony (sexual assault, for example), because there is more uniformity from state to state in such cases than in other types of charges.

At the conclusion of the trial, and assuming that the defendant has been found guilty, he or she is permitted to appeal the conviction. All states allow defendants to appeal their felony convictions. The same cannot be said for the prosecutor. Barring an adverse ruling on a pretrial motion, the government is not permitted to appeal a finding of not guilty by a jury.

After the verdict has been returned and the defendant has been sentenced, he or she usually has only a small window of opportunity to bring an appeal. In most jurisdictions, for example, a defendant must bring the appeals process within ten to thirty days following the entry of sentence. Failure to bring an appeal essentially waives it forever. How the defendant begins his or her appeal is the subject of the next section.

Appeal
Asking a higher court to review the actions of a lower court in order to correct mistakes or injustice.

A. MOTION FOR NEW TRIAL

A **motion for new trial** states specific irregularities that occurred in the trial that justify a new trial for the defendant. In most jurisdictions the same judge who heard the trial also hears the motion for new trial. If the judge grants the request, then a new trial is ordered and everything starts over as though the first trial never occurred. If the judge denies the request, then the defendant's appellate rights are triggered. In most situations, the motion for new trial is denied. At this point, the defendant would then docket his or her appeal in the appellate court, called the Court of Appeals in many states. We will continue to use that name to refer to this first level of the appellate courts, keeping in mind that not all states call this court by that name.

Motion for new trial
A motion, filed by the defendant after sentencing, that requests a new trial based on errors or irregularities in the trial; if denied, it begins the appellate process.

B. NOTICE OF APPEAL

Once the motion for new trial has been denied, a defendant files a **notice of appeal**. This places the state on notice that the defendant intends to appeal his conviction to the Court of Appeals. The filing of a notice of appeal with the Court of Appeals triggers the deadlines that both the state and the defense must follow in order to have a legal appeal. The time limits vary from state to state, but most states have a specific time period from the time of filing of a notice of appeal until the time that the appeal must actually be docketed with the Court of Appeals. Once the defendant files his brief the state will have a set period of time in which to respond to that filing.

Notice of appeal
The official docketing and commencement of the appeals process.

C. APPELLATE PROCEDURE

Once a case has been docketed in the State Court of Appeals, the appellate process has officially begun. From this point forward, many of the terms and procedures associated with a criminal case change dramatically. First, there is the issue of establishing the appellate court's jurisdiction. As we have already seen, jurisdiction refers to a court's power and authority. An appellate court does not have the jurisdiction to make rulings in any prosecution until the jury has returned a verdict, the judge has entered a judgment, the defendant has been sentenced, a motion for new trial has been denied, and a notice of appeal has been filed. More importantly, before an appellate court will accept a case for review, the party bringing the appeal must establish that a final ruling has been made in the trial court and that there are no additional issues to be resolved in that court. The party must also establish that the ruling has an adverse impact on his life, liberty, or property. A criminal conviction qualifies in all of these areas.

Along with establishing jurisdiction for the State Court of Appeals, there are some additional changes that occur on appeal. One such change is that the parties are renamed. In the trial court, the state prosecuted the defendant. The parties were referred to as simply *the government* or *the state* versus *the defendant*. But appellate courts do not use that terminology. Instead, the party bringing an appeal is referred to as the **appellant**. The winning party in the lower court is referred to as the **appellee**.

Appellant
The party bringing the current appeal from an adverse ruling in a lower court.

Appellee
The party who won in the lower court.

THE BRIEF

Cases are appealed by the filing of a written **brief** in a case. Although the parties can request an oral argument before the court, in the vast majority of appeals there is no such argument, only a brief prepared by both sides of the case that argues their positions and asks the court to rule in their favor. A brief is often dozens of pages long and contains an exhaustive discussion of the facts of the case and how legal precedent applies to those facts. The appellant's brief (the original defendant) would list the evidence, testimony, and rulings in the trial court and state why some or all of these were wrong, prejudicial, or counter to prevailing case law. The appellant will make a claim for **reversible error**, showing that some action taken by the trial court so prejudiced his or her case that the only valid remedy is reversal and a new trial. In a similar vein, the appellee's brief (the prosecutor) will also provide details about the trial and just as conclusively attempt to show that all actions taken by the trial court were correct and do not warrant a reversal.

Brief
A written statement prepared by one side in a lawsuit to explain its case to the judge.

Reversible error
A mistake made by a judge in the procedures used at trial, or in making legal ruling during the trial.

MOVING THROUGH THE APPELLATE SYSTEM

It is quite common for appeals in criminal cases to last for years. Although the process outlined above sounds relatively straightforward, in daily practice each of the steps takes months, sometimes years, to complete. Once a defendant is sentenced, he or she will file a motion for a new trial. It may be weeks before that motion is heard. If the motion is denied, then the defendant can file a notice of appeal. Pulling together all of the necessary information can take months. Once filed, the docketing process can also take months. So, before even the first appeal in the case is heard, these time periods often have already added up to a year or more. After the State Court of Appeals receives the briefs, it may take up to a year to make a decision. The Court has hundreds of other cases pending and it decides the cases in the order that they were received. Patience is a virtue in appellate work.

When the State Court of Appeals reaches its decision, whatever it may be, either party may appeal the decision to a higher court. This adds additional time to the course of an appeal. Unlike the original verdict, if the defendant wins a reversal on appeal, the state is permitted to appeal that decision to the next highest court. In most states, that court is referred to as the State Supreme Court. The defendant is also free to appeal to this court, assuming that he or she loses at the State Court of Appeals. However, the rules change again at this point. The State Supreme Court (again, this text will use this name because it is the most common name for this court, but it can be called by another name in some states) has the right to decide which cases it will hear. Unlike the State Court of Appeals which must hear all appeals brought to it, the State Supreme Court, like the U.S. Supreme Court has the power to choose which cases it will accept for appeal. This power is referred to as *certiorari*.

CERTIORARI

State Supreme Courts have the right to decide which cases they will hear. All litigants must pass an administrative hurdle before the court will consider the case. This hurdle is *certiorari*. Certiorari is almost universally referred to as *cert*, not only because the word itself is difficult to pronounce but also because appellate courts commonly abbreviate the term that way in reporting decisions, as in "petition for cert. denied."

State Supreme Courts mirror the U.S. Supreme Court in that they all have the power to grant or deny cert, and in the vast majority of cases that petition for cert, the Court refuses to grant it. Ninety-five percent or more of the cases that apply for cert in both the State and U.S. Supreme Courts are denied.

Certiorari (Cert)
Latin for "to make sure." Cert is a court's authority to decide which cases it will hear on appeal and which it will not.

Standards Used to Determine Granting Cert. A **petition for cert** is filed by the party wishing the court to hear the appeal and sets out why this case is important. In order to be granted cert, a party must show that the case involves a matter that falls into one of three categories, such as:

Petition for cert
A petition filed by a party on appeal requesting a court to consider its appeal and grant cert.

- The issues presented have been interpreted differently in various courts, causing a conflict among the federal circuits.
- The case involves an interpretation of the U.S. Constitution.
- One state has ruled a particular action legal, while another has ruled it illegal.
- The case involves issues of national importance.

Nowhere on the list of issues to be considered in granting cert is a discussion of why the case is important to the individual parties. That is not one of the considerations that courts use in deciding whether or not to grant cert. The U.S. Supreme Court, like state Supreme Courts, does not grant cert simply because the case has vital importance to the defendant or the state in an individual prosecution. In fact, the case must present issues that are important to the community at large, not just the litigants, for the court to grant cert.

The U.S. Supreme Court follows the "rule of four" in deciding whether or not to grant cert. If four out of the nine justices believe that cert should be granted, then the case will be heard. If that minimum is not reached, then the case is denied cert and the decision in the most recent appeal stands as the final decision in the appeal.

Granting Cert. When the State Supreme Court grants cert, it means that the court has agreed to hear the case. The appeal will now proceed in an almost identical fashion as it followed in the State Court of Appeals. The parties will submit written briefs and again ask the court to rule in their favor. However, there are some important differences between the State Court of Appeals and the State Supreme Court. For one thing, oral argument is more common. The justices of the State Supreme Court, like those who serve on the U.S. Supreme Court, may wish to question the litigants in person and the only way to do that is through oral argument before the court.

It is important to note that the decision to grant cert has no bearing on the court's ultimate decision. A court might grant cert to a party and then rule against him or her. A grant of cert simply authorizes the continuation of the appeal. The Court is free to rule any way that it sees fit once it considers the merits of the case.

Denial of Cert. When the state Supreme Court denies cert, it means that the Court has refused to hear the appeal. At this point, the appellate process is essentially over. The appellant can file a motion for rehearing requesting the Court to reconsider its ruling, but that is highly unlikely. If the party has been denied cert before the state Supreme Court, then he or she has one more option: the U.S. Supreme Court. Appeals from State Supreme Courts go to the U.S. Supreme Court. However, if the State Supreme Court has denied cert, it is unlikely that the U.S. Supreme Court will grant it.

D. THE POWERS OF THE APPELLATE COURTS

Record
The actual evidence (testimony, physical objects, etc.) as well as the evidence that refused admission by the judge.

Appellate courts can only review the **record** of the case on appeal. No witnesses testify before the Court of Appeals or Supreme Court. An appeal is not a new trial. Appeals consist of a review of the record and then an in-depth examination of applicable case law. An appellate court reviews the actions of a lower court in order to determine if the court has committed reversible error. If the court finds no error, then no action is taken. Appellate courts are important because they evaluate the precedents in law and explain, enlarge, or reverse those precedents. Occasionally, an appellate court, especially one as important as the U.S. Supreme Court may come out with an interpretation of law that creates entirely new procedures. Consider the earlier discussion of the Miranda rights as only one of many such examples. Although some people are tempted to think that appellate courts have enormous power, their authority is actually limited. There are only a few actions that an appellate court may take. Essentially, an appellate court can only take some combination of the following actions; it can:

- **Affirm**
- **Reverse**
- **Remand**

When an appellate court affirms a decision, it enters a judgment in favor of the finding in the lower court. Whatever the decision may have been in that lower court, a higher court's finding that it affirms that decision will leave the previous decision in place.

However, the opposite occurs when a court reverses. An appellate court issues a reversal when it finds that some improper action occurred in the trial court or when the higher court simply disagrees with the reasoning of a lower court. When a case has been reversed, the defendant's conviction is also overturned. But this is not quite the great news for a defendant that one might think. When a case has been reversed it means that the state is free to retry the defendant. This is not a violation of the Fifth Amendment's prohibition against Double Jeopardy because the appellate court has vacated the defendant's conviction and the state is free to bring the case all over again.

There are occasions when an appellate court requires additional information on a case. In such a situation, it orders a remand. The court is not in a position to make a ruling without this additional information and because appellate courts do not hear witness testimony or consider new evidence, the case is sent back to the trial court. The appellate court directs the trial court to hold a hearing, take specific testimony or consider some evidence, transcribe the hearing, and then send the material back to the appellate court. This is the substance of a remand.

Affirm
When a higher court declares that a lower court's action was valid and right.

Reverse
Set aside; when an appellate court decides that the actions of a lower court were incorrect.

Remand
Send back. For example, when a higher court requires additional information about a case, it returns it to the trial court.

When the defendant loses at trial, he or she is permitted to appeal the conviction to a higher court.

E. *HABEAS CORPUS*

Although an appeal essentially ends when a higher court refuses to grant cert, there is one other avenue of appeal open to a person convicted of a crime: *habeas corpus*. A *habeas* petition is an appeal that goes through the federal court system, regardless of where the original prosecution occurred. A defendant files a writ of *habeas corpus* under the authority of the U.S. Constitution. The Constitution requires that a criminal defendant must be held for reasonable grounds and the writ of *habeas* requires the government to prove that the defendant is being held for valid reasons. Although not originally designed to give a criminal defendant a second round of appeals, many criminal convictions are now routinely appealed using *habeas corpus*. In fact, a current issue is whether or not terrorists taken on the field of battle or seized overseas enjoy this right in the U.S. Court system. An action for *habeas corpus* is based on centuries of legal tradition, extending back through the English system and is an integral part of the U.S. court system.

Habeas corpus
Latin for "you have the body"; a judicial order to a prison system ordering that the incarcerated person be brought to court for a hearing; a constitutional mechanism that allows convicts to challenge their sentences.

In a *habeas corpus* action a criminal defendant requests the federal court system to remove the defendant from a state prison system based on some alleged unconstitutional action that occurred in the trial. Because a *habeas corpus* action is brought in federal court, it will follow the federal appellate court system on subsequent rulings. For instance, once filed in U.S. District Court, it would then move up to the U.S. Circuit Court of Appeals for that part of the country. It is even possible that a case that began in the state trial court and was eventually denied cert by the U.S. Supreme Court, may find itself at the Court again, this time after following a *habeas* appeal.

Considering the time periods involved in bringing a standard state-based appeal and then factoring in the additional time necessary to bring a *habeas* petition, it is easy to see how various criminal appeals in a single case can last for more than a decade. That is especially true in death penalty cases.

CASE EXCERPT

PEOPLE v. ADAMS
198 Ill.App.3d 74, 555 N.E.2d 761, 144 Ill.Dec. 402 (Ill.App. 2 Dist.,1990)

Justice REINHARD delivered the opinion of the court:

Defendant, Daniel Adams, was indicted in the circuit court of Du Page County on one count of criminal sexual assault (Ill.Rev.Stat.1987, ch. 38, par. 12-13(a)(3)), and following defendant's plea of guilty, the court sentenced him to three years' imprisonment on December 2, 1987. On August 18, 1988, the trial court entered an order finding defendant to be a habitual child sex offender and certifying defendant to be such a habitual child sex offender pursuant to the Habitual Child Sex Offender Registration Act (Act) (Ill.Rev.Stat.1987, ch. 38, par. 221 et seq.).

Defendant raises the following issues on appeal: (1) whether the trial court lacked jurisdiction to enter the August 18, 1988, order certifying him as a habitual child sex offender; (2) whether the Act violates the eighth amendment to the United States Constitution; (3) whether the Act violates article I, section 11, of the Illinois Constitution; (4) whether the Act violates the equal protection clause of the Federal and State Constitutions; and (5) whether the Act violates the due process clause of the Federal and State Constitutions.

Defendant appeared before the court on December 2, 1987, to plead guilty to criminal sexual assault. Prior to accepting the plea agreement, the trial court inquired as to defendant's criminal history. The State told the court defendant was placed on probation July 31, 1985, for aggravated criminal sexual abuse against the same daughter who was the victim of the instant case. Defendant's counsel acknowledged that this was correct. The court then admonished defendant and listened to a factual basis for the plea that stated, among other things, that defendant's daughter would have testified that she was 12 years old when her father entered her bed, removed her clothing, and placed his penis into her anus.

Just after the court sentenced the defendant, the prosecutor informed the court that by statute the State was required to file a habitual child abuse offender form which required defendant's signature. The court ordered defendant to sign the form. This form is not contained in the record. There are no written findings indicating that the trial court determined defendant to be a habitual child sex offender or that the trial court certified defendant as such.

On May 3, 1988, the State filed a motion in the circuit court to have defendant certified pursuant to the Act. Defendant objected on grounds of equal protection and on the basis that the trial court was without jurisdiction because 30 days had passed since entry of judgment. The trial court found no violation of equal protection and ruled that it could certify defendant at this date because it was a ministerial function. The August 18, 1988, order states that defendant is found to be a habitual child sex offender and is so certified based upon findings made on December 2, 1987.

The Act, enacted in 1986, requires that anyone convicted of a second offense in Illinois of criminal sexual assault, aggravated criminal sexual assault, criminal sexual abuse, or aggravated criminal sexual abuse when the offense is a felony, against a victim under 18 years of age, shall be certified as a habitual child sex offender. A habitual child sex offender must register with the chief of police in the municipality he resides or moves to for up to 10 years after his conviction or the time he is released from prison or other confinement. Registration consists of a statement in writing by the offender giving information required by the State Police which may include fingerprints and photographs. An offender must notify the law enforcement agency of any change of address within 10 days. Violation of the Act is a Class A misdemeanor.

We first address defendant's contention that the trial court lacked jurisdiction on August 18, 1988, to enter an order finding him to be a habitual child sex offender and certifying him as such because more than 30 days had passed since judgment was entered in the case. We begin by noting that defendant only raises a jurisdictional challenge to the timeliness of the entry of the order and does not raise any other basis for setting the order aside regarding the procedures used in determining he was a habitual child sex offender. As such, we will limit our review to the jurisdictional issue presented on appeal.

The State responds that the statute sets no time limit for the certification and, as the certification is a mandatory act, the certification may be entered at any time. The State also contends that, as the trial court retains jurisdiction over its records and retains the power to correct them, such residual jurisdiction pertains to the entry of mandatory findings, as here. As we agree that the trial court under the circumstances here retained jurisdiction to correct its record, we need not address the alternate basis suggested by the State.

When a defendant has been convicted, sentenced and placed into the custody of the Department of Corrections, the court rendering judgment and imposing sentence loses jurisdiction over the case and is without power to vacate, set aside or modify the judgment. Even though the trial court may lose jurisdiction of a case, it does not lose jurisdiction over its own records and may correct those records to reflect accurately the judgment that was in fact entered.

In this case, the parties agreed at the sentencing hearing on December 2, 1987, that defendant had been convicted of criminal sexual abuse in 1985 in Stephenson County. Additionally, the assistant State's Attorney requested, and the court directed, defendant to sign a "Habitual Child Abuse Offender form." The written order evidencing judgment does not, however, contain any finding regarding defendant's status as a habitual child sex offender or any reference to a certification of such. On the other hand, the order of August 18, 1988, expressly finds defendant to be a habitual child sex offender and certifies him as such by referring to the court's findings of December 2, 1987.

Section 2(A) of the Act provides, in pertinent part, as follows:

"Upon such conviction the court shall certify that the person is a 'habitual child sex offender' and shall include the certification in the order of commitment." Ill.Rev. Stat.1987, ch. 38, par. 222(A).

While the procedure employed at the December 2, 1987, sentencing hearing should have included an express written finding of habitual child sex offender status and certification thereof by the trial court, the report of proceedings does indicate that the trial court was aware that defendant was a habitual child sex offender based on his prior conviction in 1985 and that some effort was made to comply with the Act, albeit less than ideal. Under these particular circumstances, any lack of such finding or certification in the written judgment must be viewed as an oversight or inaccuracy in the record. Thus, the trial court retained jurisdiction to correct the record to reflect accurately its determination on December 2, 1987, that defendant was a habitual child sex offender under the Act.

We next address defendant's contention that the Act's registration requirement constitutes cruel and unusual punishment. In this regard, defendant initially relies on *Kennedy v. Mendoza-Martinez* (1963), 372 U.S. 144, 83 S.Ct. 554, 9 L.Ed.2d 644, in arguing that the registration requirement constitutes punishment thereby implicating the eighth amendment to the United States Constitution.

We believe defendant's reliance on Kennedy is misplaced. Kennedy sets forth the various factors for determining whether a disability constitutes punishment in the context of a fifth amendment due process analysis and did not reach the eighth amendment issue in that case.

Moreover, in *Ingraham v. Wright* (1977), 430 U.S. 651, 97 S.Ct. 1401, 51 L.Ed.2d 711, the Supreme Court noted that an eighth amendment analysis is appropriate in determining the constitutionality of an alleged punishment where the underlying conduct has already been established through formal criminal proceedings, whereas it is inappropriate to reach an eighth amendment analysis where the alleged punishment has been invoked absent a formal criminal process. The Court further pointed out that the State does not acquire the power to punish with which the eighth amendment is concerned until after it has secured a formal adjudication of guilt in accordance with due process.

Where, as here, the alleged punishment is invoked after a defendant is found guilty, the appropriate analysis to apply in challenging the relevant statutory provision is that under the eighth amendment and not due process. This is equally true in addressing the initial question of whether the challenged provision constitutes punishment. Accordingly, we apply the analysis set forth in *Trop v. Dulles* (1958), 356 U.S. 86, 78 S.Ct. 590, 2 L.Ed.2d 630, an eighth amendment case, rather than that provided in Kennedy, a due process case, to the eighth amendment issue in this case.

In applying the analysis set out in Trop to the registration requirement at issue here, we conclude that the registration requirement does not constitute punishment, and therefore, the eighth amendment is not implicated in the first instance. In Trop, the Court stated that in deciding whether a law is penal a court must look to the purpose of the statute. If a statute imposes a disability for the purpose of punishment then it is penal, but if it imposes a disability, not to punish, but for some other legitimate governmental purpose then it is nonpenal. While any statute that creates a disability as a consequence of certain conduct may have both a penal and nonpenal effect, the controlling nature of such statutes normally depends on the evident purpose of the legislature.

The statute at issue here requires a person who meets the definition of a habitual child sexual offender to register with the appropriate local police agency. The pertinent issue, applying the Trop analysis, is whether the legislative purpose of this provision is to punish persons who have been convicted twice for certain child sex offenses within the appropriate time frame or whether the statute accomplishes some other legitimate governmental purpose. We find the legislative debates to be instructive on this issue.

Representative Parke, the House sponsor of this legislation, characterized it as "one of the most important Bills . . . in regards to protecting our children." (84th Ill.Gen.Assem., House Proceedings, June 23, 1986, at 208.) He further emphasized that "this kind of legislation will help our law enforcement agencies stop this kind of carnage on our children. Society demands that we protect our children." Such statements are a clear indication that the purpose of the statute is to aid law enforcement in preventing future sex offenses against children. On the other hand, there is no indication in the legislative history that the registration requirement was intended to serve the purpose of deterrence or retribution, two goals of punishment. Protection of children from sex offenses is very much part of the State's unquestionable interest in protecting the health, safety and welfare of its citizens. As such, the registration requirement at issue here clearly serves a legitimate governmental purpose.

Furthermore, the purpose served by the registration requirement is so fundamental as to far outweigh any penal effect that the statute might have. The statute places no more constraint on the liberty of someone required to register with the local police authority than do many of the well-established civil disabilities associated with felony convictions in Illinois, such as limitations on possession of firearms, the right to vote or the right to hold public office. Although defendant suggests that he will be subject to being hauled before police authorities whenever a child in his chosen community claims to be a victim of a sex offense, such an argument is purely speculative and without any basis in the record. Nor do we perceive the Act to limit or dilute in any way well-recognized constitutional protections ordinarily afforded to anyone who becomes the subject of a police investigation.

Additionally, the statute does not burden defendant's privacy interests as his convictions will be a matter of public record. Although the statute provides that defendant, as a habitual child sexual offender, register with the local police chief or, if appropriate, the sheriff, it is an offense to make public such registration. Under these circumstances, it cannot be said that the registration requirement will have any significant impact on defendant's liberty or privacy interests.

In light of the legitimate governmental purpose that the statute was intended to serve and the negligible impact on defendant's liberty or privacy interests, we hold that the registration requirement is not punishment under the eighth amendment.

Even were we to hold that the registration requirement constitutes punishment, it does not rise to the level of cruel and unusual punishment. As to whether the registration requirement is cruel and unusual, defendant maintains that it is cruel because it provides for punishment after a defendant has served his sentence and because it fails to take into consideration the underlying factual basis for conviction of the specified offenses. He further contends that it violates the proportionality requirement of the eighth amendment.

The eighth amendment prohibition against cruel and unusual punishment "'is not fastened to the obsolete but may acquire meaning as public opinion becomes enlightened by a humane justice.'" The basic concept underlying the eighth amendment is that the penalty must accord with the dignity of man. Additionally, the punishment must be proportional to the offense.

In the present case, there is simply nothing about the registration requirement that fails to comport with humane justice. Nor does the registration requirement affront the dignity of man. It merely requires an offender who has twice been convicted of a sex offense against a child to register with the appropriate police authority. Such registration is kept confidential and is limited to a 10-year period following either defendant's sentence or release from custody if he is incarcerated. Further, there is nothing in the Act that would allow local police authorities to use such information to deny defendant his constitutional rights, nor does the Act in any way dilute or impair the well-established constitutional protections afforded a citizen who becomes the subject of a police investigation. It cannot be said that the registration requirement even remotely approaches the outer fringes of inhumane or undignified punishment.

Furthermore, the registration requirement is not disproportionate to the offense. We begin by emphasizing that, outside the context of capital punishment, successful challenges to the proportionality of a particular sentence are exceedingly rare. Moreover, reviewing courts should grant substantial deference to the broad authority that legislatures necessarily possess in determining the types and limits of punishments for crime. In assessing whether a particular sentence is proportional to an offense, we are guided by three objective criteria: (1) the gravity of the offense and the harshness of the penalty; (2) the sentences imposed on other criminals in the same jurisdiction; and (3) the sentences imposed for commission of the same crime in other jurisdictions. Applying these factors, and keeping in mind our obligatory deference to the legislature, we believe the registration requirement is not disproportionate under the eighth amendment.

First, for an offender to qualify as a habitual child sex offender under the Act he must have committed, not once but twice, a felony sex offense against a child. There can be no doubt that commission of one such offense, let alone two, is serious as the four qualifying offenses carry severe penalties. More importantly, we can identify no reasoned basis to conclude that someone who twice commits one of the qualifying offenses does not present a very serious threat to society. We can perceive of no group who is deserving of more protection against this type of offender than our children. In contrast to the seriousness of repeated sexual offenses against children, the Act merely requires a repeat offender to register with the local authorities where he lives. As we have repeatedly noted already, concerns of privacy and loss of constitutional protections under the Act are unfounded and speculative.

Second, we compare the sentences imposed on other criminals in Illinois. If more serious crimes are subject to the same penalty, or to less serious penalties, that is some indication that the punishment at issue is excessive. In applying this part of the Solem test, we find the habitual criminal statute to be instructive. That statute provides for a mandatory life sentence upon conviction of a third offense, either a Class X felony, criminal sexual assault or first degree murder, under the appropriate circumstances. Obviously, in the narrow context of habitual offenders, the Act under consideration provides a far less serious penalty than that provided for under our other habitual criminal statute. Moreover, if we consider other offenses generally, we cannot say that more serious offenses in Illinois are punished equally or less seriously than that provided for in the Act. Clearly, any length of prison term is more serious a penalty than mere registration with local police authorities.

Finally, we consider the sentences imposed in other jurisdictions for repeat child sex offenders. Our research indicates that seven other States currently have some version of a habitual child sex offender or sex offender registration statute. While a clear majority of States do not presently require sex offenders to register, we think that the number that do is significant. While the defendant here may have been treated less severely in some States, he would have been comparably treated in others. We cannot say that the registration requirement in the Act is so unique as to render it cruel and unusual. More importantly, when we consider all three objective factors, we are compelled to hold that the registration requirement is not disproportional to the underlying offense and does not, therefore, violate the eighth amendment.

We next consider defendant's contention that the registration requirement is inconsistent with the objective of restoration to useful citizenship contained in article I, section 11, of our State Constitution (Ill. Const.1970, art. I, § 11). We find no merit to this argument, however. We cannot perceive how requiring a habitual child sex offender to register with local police authorities will detract from his rehabilitation, particularly where such registration is required to be kept confidential. In fact, registration is far less of a hindrance to defendant's restoration to useful citizenship than would be the imposition of a lengthy prison sentence as the consequence of his habitual status. The registration requirement does not violate article I, section 11, of our constitution.

We next address defendant's equal protection claim under the Federal and State Constitutions. We note at the outset that statutory enactments carry a strong presumption of constitutionality, and all doubts must be resolved in favor of the Act's validity. In considering an equal protection claim, we generally employ a two-step analysis to determine whether a legislative classification deprives an individual of equal protection. Initially, we must determine if the statute under consideration affects a fundamental right or discriminates against a suspect class. If it does, we subject the legislation to strict scrutiny and uphold it only if it serves a compelling State interest. Here, it is clear that no suspect class is involved. Nor does the registration requirement affect any fundamental right. It does not implicate any right of privacy as it mandates confidentiality, nor does it affect defendant's liberty beyond mere speculation. Although defendant suggests in a footnote in his brief that it impacts on his fundamental right to travel, he fails to identify how registration under the Act affects such a right. As we cannot identify how the registration requirement affects defendant's right to travel, or any other fundamental right, we need not apply strict scrutiny in assessing defendant's equal protection claim.

Because the classification challenged here does not affect a fundamental right or discriminate against a suspect class, the proper standard for judging the statute is the rational basis test. Under this test, a statutory classification must bear a rational relationship to a valid legislative purpose, and the classification created by the statute will be set aside as violative of the equal protection clause only if based on reasons totally unrelated to the pursuit of a legitimate State goal. The equal protection clauses of the Federal and State Constitutions do not prohibit our legislature from enacting legislation which affects different classes of persons differently, and, in the absence of involvement of a fundamental right, the legislature may even differentiate between persons similarly situated if there is a rational basis for doing so.

The legislative purpose in enacting this Act was to protect children from sex offenders and aid law enforcement in doing so. That such a purpose is legitimate is without question. Furthermore, the means chosen by the legislature is rationally related to that legitimate purpose. Requiring habitual child sex offenders to register with local police authorities will allow those authorities to keep abreast of potential threats to the children of a particular community which might be posed by the presence of a habitual child sex offender. While the Act does little more than provide police with the fact that a habitual child sex offender resides within the community, it clearly serves the purpose of protecting our children. The rationality of a particular statute does not depend on its purported effectiveness, but, rather, is determined only by whether it reasonably serves the purpose of the legislature in enacting it. Accordingly, we hold the Act does not violate the equal protection clause of our Federal and State Constitutions.

Finally, we address defendant's contention that the registration requirement violates due process under the Federal and State Constitutions. (U.S. Const., Amend. XIV; Ill. Const.1970, art. I, § 2.) In doing so, we are mindful that legislative enactments carry a strong presumption of constitutionality, and the party challenging the statute has the burden of clearly establishing its invalidity. We also note that defendant's due process challenge to the Act is based on substantive rather than procedural due process grounds. In such a case, if the challenged statute does not affect a fundamental right, the appropriate standard of review is the rational-basis test. As we have already determined that no fundamental right is involved, that the legislature had a legitimate purpose in passing the Act, and that the Act rationally serves that purpose, we must conclude that the Act does not deny defendant due process.

For the foregoing reasons, the order of the circuit court of Du Page County is affirmed.

Affirmed.

CASE QUESTIONS

1   What issue does this defendant raise in regard to the Eighth Amendment's prohibition against cruel and unusual punishment?
2   How did the court respond to this allegation?
3   According to the court, what is the purpose of this registration?
4   Does the statute place a restraint on the defendant that would amount to punishment?
5   Does the registration requirement unduly burden the defendant's privacy interests?

CHAPTER SUMMARY

When a defendant opts to plead guilty, a judge may impose sentence on him or her, but only after the judge is convinced that the defendant has done so freely, knowingly, and voluntarily. Defendants often plead guilty as part of a plea bargain, where the state offers a lower sentence recommendation in exchange for the defendant giving up his or her right to a jury trial. Although plea bargaining has been controversial, it is an integral part of the criminal justice system. The judge has broad discretion to sentence a defendant who has been found guilty after a trial. In states (and in the federal system) that have sentencing guidelines, a judge's discretion is substantially curtailed. During the sentencing hearing, a judge must allow the defendant the opportunity to address the court and also to allow a victim to give a victim-impact statement. The Eighth Amendment prohibits cruel and unusual punishment. The death penalty is not considered to be cruel and unusual punishment.

When a defendant is found guilty, he or she is allowed to appeal the verdict and sentence to a higher court. Appellate courts are courts of limited jurisdiction and can only take the following actions: affirm a decision, reverse a decision, or remand a case to the trial court for additional hearings. Some appellate courts, like the U.S. Supreme Court have the authority to decide which cases they will consider on appeal. This authority is referred to as cert.

KEY TERMS

Alford plea	Bifurcated trial	Motion for new trial
Nolo contendere	Parole	Notice of appeal
Conditional plea	Probation	Appellant
Sentence	Restitution	Appellee
Concurrent sentencing	Proportionality	Brief
Consecutive sentencing	Appeal	Reversible error
Presentence investigation	Record	*Certiorari*
Victim impact statement	Affirm	Petition for cert
Aggravation of sentence	Reverse	*Habeas corpus*
Mitigation of sentence	Remand	

REVIEW QUESTIONS

1 What is an *Alford* plea?
2 What are the Federal Sentencing Guidelines?
3 Why is plea bargaining so important to the criminal process?
4 How is a defendant sentenced?
5 What is the difference between concurrent sentencing and consecutive sentencing?
6 What is a presentence investigation?
7 What is a sentencing hearing?
8 What is mitigation of sentence?

9   What is the purpose of the victim impact statement?

10 Explain how the sentencing is carried out in death penalty cases.

11 Why are death penalty sentences bifurcated?

12 What is parole?

13 What is an alternative sentence?

14 Explain probation.

15 What is restitution?

16 What are the provisions against cruel and unusual punishment?

17 What are the "three strikes and you're out" sentencing laws?

18 Explain the organization of the appellate court system.

19 What is the difference between affirming a decision and reversing one?

20 Explain the purpose of a motion for new trial.

21 What guidelines does a court follow in deciding to grant cert?

22 What is reversible error?

23 What is a remand?

24 Explain the purpose of *habeas corpus*.

25 Why does it normally take so long to appeal a criminal case?

QUESTIONS FOR ANALYSIS

1   Are you in favor or against the death penalty? Justify your answer.

2   Are sentences in this country too harsh or too lenient? What do you think?

HYPOTHETICALS

1   After a defendant is found guilty of defrauding local businesses of several thousand dollars, a judge orders that the defendant wear a large sign around his neck with the words, "I am a crook and a deadbeat." He must walk through downtown wearing this sign for five consecutive days, from eight a.m. to five p.m., with a half hour off for lunch. Is this sentence a violation of the U.S. Constitution? Why or why not?

2   Bob has been convicted of battery on Tonya. As part of Bob's sentence, the judge gives Tonya permission to strike him, just once, across the face while under the supervision of sheriff's deputies. Can this sentence be imposed? Should it be imposed?

3   Ted is elected district attorney and as part of his platform, he declares that the age of plea bargains is over. "Every defendant is looking at receiving the maximum sentence if convicted," Ted says. Can he guarantee that outcome? Even if he can, is this a good idea?

The Constitution of the United States of America

We the People of the United States, in Order to form a more perfect Union, establish Justice, insure domestic Tranquility, provide for the common defence, promote the general Welfare, and secure the Blessings of Liberty to ourselves and our Posterity, do ordain and establish this Constitution for the United States of America.

Article I

Section 1

All legislative Powers herein granted shall be vested in a Congress of the United States, which shall consist of a Senate and House of Representatives.

Section 2

1: The House of Representatives shall be composed of Members chosen every second Year by the People of the several States, and the Electors in each State shall have the Qualifications requisite for Electors of the most numerous Branch of the State Legislature.

2: No Person shall be a Representative who shall not have attained to the Age of twenty five Years, and been seven Years a Citizen of the United States, and who shall not, when elected, be an Inhabitant of that State in which he shall be chosen.

3: Representatives and direct Taxes shall be apportioned among the several States which may be included within this Union, according to their respective Numbers, which shall be determined by adding to the whole Number of free Persons, including those bound to Service for a Term of Years, and excluding Indians not taxed, three fifths of all other Persons. The actual Enumeration shall be made within three Years after the first Meeting of the Congress of the United States, and within every subsequent Term of ten Years, in such Manner as they shall by Law direct. The Number of Representatives shall not exceed one for every thirty Thousand, but each State shall have at Least one Representative; and until such enumeration shall be made, the State of New Hampshire shall be entitled to chuse three, Massachusetts eight, Rhode-Island and Providence Plantations one, Connecticut five, New-York six, New Jersey four, Pennsylvania eight, Delaware one, Maryland six, Virginia ten, North Carolina five, South Carolina five, and Georgia three.

4: When vacancies happen in the Representation from any State, the Executive Authority thereof shall issue Writs of Election to fill such Vacancies.

5: The House of Representatives shall chuse their Speaker and other Officers; and shall have the sole Power of Impeachment.

Section 3

1: The Senate of the United States shall be composed of two Senators from each State, chosen by the Legislature thereof for six Years; and each Senator shall have one Vote.

2: Immediately after they shall be assembled in Consequence of the first Election, they shall be divided as equally as may be into three Classes. The Seats of the Senators of the first Class shall be vacated at the Expiration of the second Year, of the second Class at the Expiration of the fourth Year, and of the third Class at the Expiration of the sixth Year, so that one third may be chosen every second Year; and if Vacancies happen by Resignation, or otherwise, during the Recess of the Legislature of any State, the Executive thereof may make temporary Appointments until the next Meeting of the Legislature, which shall then fill such Vacancies.

3: No Person shall be a Senator who shall not have attained to the Age of thirty Years, and been nine Years a Citizen of the United States, and who shall not, when elected, be an Inhabitant of that State for which he shall be chosen.

4: The Vice President of the United States shall be President of the Senate, but shall have no Vote, unless they be equally divided.

5: The Senate shall chuse their other Officers, and also a President pro tempore, in the Absence of the Vice President, or when he shall exercise the Office of President of the United States.

6: The Senate shall have the sole Power to try all Impeachments. When sitting for that Purpose, they shall be on Oath or Affirmation. When the President of the United States is tried, the Chief Justice shall preside: And no Person shall be convicted without the Concurrence of two thirds of the Members present.

7: Judgment in Cases of impeachment shall not extend further than to removal from Office, and disqualification to hold and enjoy any Office of honor, Trust or Profit under the United States: but the Party convicted shall nevertheless be liable and subject to Indictment, Trial, Judgment and Punishment, according to Law.

Section 4

1: The Times, Places and Manner of holding Elections for Senators and Representatives, shall be prescribed in each State by the Legislature thereof; but the Congress may at any time by Law make or alter such Regulations, except as to the Places of chusing Senators.

2: The Congress shall assemble at least once in every Year, and such Meeting shall be on the first Monday in December, unless they shall by Law appoint a different Day.

Section 5

1: Each House shall be the Judge of the Elections, Returns and Qualifications of its own Members, and a Majority of each shall constitute a Quorum to do Business; but a smaller Number may adjourn from day to day, and may be authorized to compel the Attendance of absent Members, in such Manner, and under such Penalties as each House may provide.

2: Each House may determine the Rules of its Proceedings, punish its Members for disorderly Behaviour, and, with the Concurrence of two thirds, expel a Member.

3: Each House shall keep a Journal of its Proceedings, and from time to time publish the same, excepting such Parts as may in their Judgment require Secrecy; and the Yeas and Nays of the Members of either House on any question shall, at the Desire of one fifth of those Present, be entered on the Journal.

4: Neither House, during the Session of Congress, shall, without the Consent of the other, adjourn for more than three days, nor to any other Place than that in which the two Houses shall be sitting.

Section 6

1: The Senators and Representatives shall receive a Compensation for their Services, to be ascertained by Law, and paid out of the Treasury of the United States. They shall in all Cases, except Treason, Felony and Breach of the Peace, be privileged from Arrest during their Attendance at the Session of their respective Houses, and in going to and returning from the same; and for any Speech or Debate in either House, they shall not be questioned in any other Place.

2: No Senator or Representative shall, during the Time for which he was elected, be appointed to any civil Office under the Authority of the United States, which shall have been created, or the Emoluments whereof shall have been encreased during such time; and no Person holding any Office under the United States, shall be a Member of either House during his Continuance in Office.

Section 7

1: All Bills for raising Revenue shall originate in the House of Representatives; but the Senate may propose or concur with Amendments as on other Bills.

2: Every Bill which shall have passed the House of Representatives and the Senate, shall, before it become a Law, be presented to the President of the United States; If he approve he shall sign it, but if not he shall return it, with his Objections to that House in which it shall have originated, who shall enter the Objections at large on their Journal, and proceed to reconsider it. If after such Reconsideration two thirds of that House shall agree to pass the Bill, it shall be sent, together with the Objections, to the other House, by which it shall likewise be reconsidered, and if approved by two thirds of that House, it shall become a Law. But in all such Cases the Votes of both Houses shall be determined by yeas and Nays, and the Names of the Persons voting for and against the Bill shall be entered on the Journal of each House respectively. If any Bill shall not be returned by the President within ten Days (Sundays excepted) after it shall have been presented to him, the Same shall be a Law, in like Manner as if he had signed it, unless the Congress by their Adjournment prevent its Return, in which Case it shall not be a Law.

3: Every Order, Resolution, or Vote to which the Concurrence of the Senate and House of Representatives may be necessary (except on a question of Adjournment) shall be presented to the President of the United States; and before the Same shall take Effect, shall be approved by him, or being disapproved by him, shall be repassed by two thirds of the Senate and House of Representatives, according to the Rules and Limitations prescribed in the Case of a Bill.

Section 8

1: The Congress shall have Power To lay and collect Taxes, Duties, Imposts and Excises, to pay the Debts and provide for the common Defence and general Welfare of the United States; but all Duties, Imposts and Excises shall be uniform throughout the United States;

2: To borrow Money on the credit of the United States;

3: To regulate Commerce with foreign Nations, and among the several States, and with the Indian Tribes;

4: To establish an uniform Rule of Naturalization, and uniform Laws on the subject of Bankruptcies throughout the United States;

5: To coin Money, regulate the Value thereof, and of foreign Coin, and fix the Standard of Weights and Measures;

6: To provide for the Punishment of counterfeiting the Securities and current Coin of the United States;

7: To establish Post Offices and post Roads;

8: To promote the Progress of Science and useful Arts, by securing for limited Times to Authors and Inventors the exclusive Right to their respective Writings and Discoveries;

9: To constitute Tribunals inferior to the supreme Court;

10: To define and punish Piracies and Felonies committed on the high Seas, and Offences against the Law of Nations;

11: To declare War, grant Letters of Marque and Reprisal, and make Rules concerning Captures on Land and Water;

12: To raise and support Armies, but no Appropriation of Money to that Use shall be for a longer Term than two Years;

13: To provide and maintain a Navy;

14: To make Rules for the Government and Regulation of the land and naval Forces;

15: To provide for calling forth the Militia to execute the Laws of the Union, suppress Insurrections and repel Invasions;

16: To provide for organizing, arming, and disciplining, the Militia, and for governing such Part of them as may be employed in the Service of the United States, reserving to the States respectively, the Appointment of the Officers, and the Authority of training the Militia according to the discipline prescribed by Congress;

17: To exercise exclusive Legislation in all Cases whatsoever, over such District (not exceeding ten Miles square) as may, by Cession of particular States, and the Acceptance of Congress, become the Seat of the Government of the United States, and to exercise like Authority over all Places purchased by the Consent of the Legislature of the State in which the Same shall be, for the Erection of Forts, Magazines, Arsenals, dock-Yards, and other needful Buildings; — And

18: To make all Laws which shall be necessary and proper for carrying into Execution the foregoing Powers, and all other Powers vested by this Constitution in the Government of the United States, or in any Department or Officer thereof.

Section 9

1: The Migration or Importation of such Persons as any of the States now existing shall think proper to admit, shall not be prohibited by the Congress prior to the Year one thousand eight hundred and eight, but a Tax or duty may be imposed on such Importation, not exceeding ten dollars for each Person.

2: The Privilege of the Writ of Habeas Corpus shall not be suspended, unless when in Cases of Rebellion or Invasion the public Safety may require it.

3: No Bill of Attainder or ex post facto Law shall be passed.

4: No Capitation, or other direct, Tax shall be laid, unless in Proportion to the Census or Enumeration herein before directed to be taken.

5: No Tax or Duty shall be laid on Articles exported from any State.

6: No Preference shall be given by any Regulation of Commerce or Revenue to the Ports of one State over those of another: nor shall Vessels bound to, or from, one State, be obliged to enter, clear, or pay Duties in another.

7: No Money shall be drawn from the Treasury, but in Consequence of Appropriations made by Law; and a regular Statement and Account of the Receipts and Expenditures of all public Money shall be published from time to time.

8: No Title of Nobility shall be granted by the United States: And no Person holding any Office of Profit or Trust under them, shall, without the Consent of the Congress, accept of any present, Emolument, Office, or Title, of any kind whatever, from any King, Prince, or foreign State.

Section 10

1: No State shall enter into any Treaty, Alliance, or Confederation; grant Letters of Marque and Reprisal; coin Money; emit Bills of Credit; make any Thing but gold and silver Coin a Tender in Payment of Debts; pass any Bill of Attainder, ex post facto Law, or Law impairing the Obligation of Contracts, or grant any Title of Nobility.

2: No State shall, without the Consent of the Congress, lay any Imposts or Duties on Imports or Exports, except what may be absolutely necessary for executing it's inspection Laws: and the net Produce of all Duties and Imposts, laid by any State on Imports or Exports, shall be for the Use of the Treasury of the United States; and all such Laws shall be subject to the Revision and Controul of the Congress.

3: No State shall, without the Consent of Congress, lay any Duty of Tonnage, keep Troops, or Ships of War in time of Peace, enter into any Agreement or Compact with another State, or with a foreign Power, or engage in War, unless actually invaded, or in such imminent Danger as will not admit of delay.

Article II

Section 1

1: The executive Power shall be vested in a President of the United States of America. He shall hold his Office during the Term of four Years, and, together with the Vice President, chosen for the same Term, be elected, as follows

2: Each State shall appoint, in such Manner as the Legislature thereof may direct, a Number of Electors, equal to the whole Number of Senators and Representatives to which the State may be entitled in the Congress: but no Senator or Representative, or Person holding an Office of Trust or Profit under the United States, shall be appointed an Elector.

3: The Electors shall meet in their respective States, and vote by Ballot for two Persons, of whom one at least shall not be an Inhabitant of the same State with themselves. And they shall make a List of all the Persons voted for, and of the Number of Votes for each; which List they shall sign and certify, and transmit sealed to the Seat of the Government of the United States, directed to the President of the Senate. The President of the Senate shall, in the Presence of the Senate and House of Representatives, open all the Certificates, and the Votes shall then be counted. The Person having the greatest Number of Votes shall be the President, if such Number be a Majority of the whole Number of Electors appointed; and if there be more than one who have such Majority, and have an equal Number of Votes, then the House of Representatives shall immediately chuse by Ballot one of them for President; and if no Person have a Majority, then from the five highest on the List the said House shall in like Manner chuse the President. But in chusing the President, the Votes shall be taken by States, the Representation from each State having one Vote; A quorum for this Purpose shall consist of a Member or Members from two thirds of the States, and a Majority of all the States shall be necessary to a Choice. In every Case, after the Choice of the President, the Person having the greatest Number of Votes of the Electors shall be the Vice President. But if there should remain two or more who have equal Votes, the Senate shall chuse from them by Ballot the Vice President.

4: The Congress may determine the Time of chusing the Electors, and the Day on which they shall give their Votes; which Day shall be the same throughout the United States.

5: No Person except a natural born Citizen, or a Citizen of the United States, at the time of the Adoption of this Constitution, shall be eligible to the Office of President; neither shall any Person be eligible to that Office who shall not have attained to the Age of thirty five Years, and been fourteen Years a Resident within the United States.

6: In Case of the Removal of the President from Office, or of his Death, Resignation, or Inability to discharge the Powers and Duties of the said Office, the Same shall devolve on the Vice President, and the Congress may by Law provide for the Case of Removal, Death, Resignation or Inability, both of the President and Vice President, declaring what Officer shall then act as President, and such Officer shall act accordingly, until the Disability be removed, or a President shall be elected.

7: The President shall, at stated Times, receive for his Services, a Compensation, which shall neither be increased nor diminished during the Period for which he shall have been elected, and he shall not receive within that Period any other Emolument from the United States, or any of them.

8: Before he enter on the Execution of his Office, he shall take the following Oath or Affirmation: — "I do solemnly swear (or affirm) that I will faithfully execute the Office of President of the United States, and will to the best of my Ability, preserve, protect and defend the Constitution of the United States."

Section 2

1: The President shall be Commander in Chief of the Army and Navy of the United States, and of the Militia of the several States, when called into the actual Service of the United States; he may require the Opinion, in writing, of the principal Officer in each of the executive Departments, upon any Subject relating to the Duties of their respective Offices, and he shall have Power to grant Reprieves and Pardons for Offences against the United States, except in Cases of Impeachment.

2: He shall have Power, by and with the Advice and Consent of the Senate, to make Treaties, provided two thirds of the Senators present concur; and he shall nominate, and by and with the Advice and Consent of the Senate, shall appoint Ambassadors, other public Ministers and Consuls, Judges of the supreme Court, and all other Officers of the United States, whose Appointments are not herein otherwise provided for, and which shall be established by Law: but the Congress may by Law vest the Appointment of such inferior Officers, as they think proper, in the President alone, in the Courts of Law, or in the Heads of Departments.

3: The President shall have Power to fill up all Vacancies that may happen during the Recess of the Senate, by granting Commissions which shall expire at the End of their next Session.

Section 3

He shall from time to time give to the Congress Information of the State of the Union, and recommend to their Consideration such Measures as he shall judge necessary and expedient; he may, on extraordinary Occasions, convene both Houses, or either of them, and in Case of Disagreement between them, with Respect to the Time of Adjournment, he may adjourn them to such Time as he shall think proper; he shall receive Ambassadors and other public Ministers; he shall take Care that the Laws be faithfully executed, and shall Commission all the Officers of the United States.

Section 4

The President, Vice President and all civil Officers of the United States, shall be removed from Office on Impeachment for, and Conviction of, Treason, Bribery, or other high Crimes and Misdemeanors.

Article III

Section 1

The judicial Power of the United States, shall be vested in one supreme Court, and in such inferior Courts as the Congress may from time to time ordain and establish. The Judges, both of the supreme and inferior Courts, shall hold their Offices during good Behaviour, and shall, at stated Times, receive for their Services, a Compensation, which shall not be diminished during their Continuance in Office.

Section 2

1: The judicial Power shall extend to all Cases, in Law and Equity, arising under this Constitution, the Laws of the United States, and Treaties made, or which shall be made, under their Authority; — to all Cases affecting Ambassadors, other public Ministers and Consuls; — to all Cases of admiralty and maritime Jurisdiction; — to Controversies to which the United States shall be a Party; — to Controversies between two or more States; — between a State and Citizens of another State; — between Citizens of different States, — between Citizens of the same State claiming Lands under Grants of different States, and between a State, or the Citizens thereof, and foreign States, Citizens or Subjects.

2: In all Cases affecting Ambassadors, other public Ministers and Consuls, and those in which a State shall be Party, the supreme Court shall have original Jurisdiction. In all the other Cases before mentioned, the supreme Court shall have appellate Jurisdiction, both as to Law and Fact, with such Exceptions, and under such Regulations as the Congress shall make.

3: The Trial of all Crimes, except in Cases of Impeachment, shall be by Jury; and such Trial shall be held in the State where the said Crimes shall have been committed; but when not committed within any State, the Trial shall be at such Place or Places as the Congress may by Law have directed.

Section 3

1: Treason against the United States, shall consist only in levying War against them, or in adhering to their Enemies, giving them Aid and Comfort. No Person shall be convicted of Treason unless on the Testimony of two Witnesses to the same overt Act, or on Confession in open Court.

2: The Congress shall have Power to declare the Punishment of Treason, but no Attainder of Treason shall work Corruption of Blood, or Forfeiture except during the Life of the Person attainted.

Article IV

Section 1

Full Faith and Credit shall be given in each State to the public Acts, Records, and judicial Proceedings of every other State. And the Congress may by general Laws prescribe the Manner in which such Acts, Records and Proceedings shall be proved, and the Effect thereof.

Section 2

1: The Citizens of each State shall be entitled to all Privileges and Immunities of Citizens in the several States.

2: A Person charged in any State with Treason, Felony, or other Crime, who shall flee from Justice, and be found in another State, shall on Demand of the executive Authority of the State from which he fled, be delivered up, to be removed to the State having Jurisdiction of the Crime.

3: No Person held to Service or Labour in one State, under the Laws thereof, escaping into another, shall, in Consequence of any Law or Regulation therein, be discharged from such Service or Labour, but shall be delivered up on Claim of the Party to whom such Service or Labour may be due.

Section 3

1: New States may be admitted by the Congress into this Union; but no new State shall be formed or erected within the Jurisdiction of any other State; nor any State be formed by the Junction of two or more States, or Parts of States, without the Consent of the Legislatures of the States concerned as well as of the Congress.

2: The Congress shall have Power to dispose of and make all needful Rules and Regulations respecting the Territory or other Property belonging to the United States; and nothing in this Constitution shall be so construed as to Prejudice any Claims of the United States, or of any particular State.

Section 4

The United States shall guarantee to every State in this Union a Republican Form of Government, and shall protect each of them against Invasion; and on Application of the Legislature, or of the Executive (when the Legislature cannot be convened) against domestic Violence.

Article V

The Congress, whenever two thirds of both Houses shall deem it necessary, shall propose Amendments to this Constitution, or, on the Application of the Legislatures of two thirds of the several States, shall call a Convention for proposing Amendments, which, in either Case, shall be valid to all Intents and Purposes, as Part of this Constitution, when ratified by the Legislatures of three fourths of the several States, or by Conventions in three fourths thereof, as the one or the other Mode of Ratification may be proposed by the Congress; Provided that no Amendment which may be made prior to the Year One thousand eight hundred and eight shall in any Manner affect the first and fourth Clauses in the Ninth Section of the first Article; and that no State, without its Consent, shall be deprived of its equal Suffrage in the Senate.

Article VI

1: All Debts contracted and Engagements entered into, before the Adoption of this Constitution, shall be as valid against the United States under this Constitution, as under the Confederation.

2: This Constitution, and the Laws of the United States which shall be made in Pursuance thereof; and all Treaties made, or which shall be made, under the Authority of the United States, shall be the supreme Law of the Land; and the Judges in every State shall be bound thereby, any Thing in the Constitution or Laws of any State to the Contrary notwithstanding.

3: The Senators and Representatives before mentioned, and the Members of the several State Legislatures, and all executive and judicial Officers, both of the United States and of the several States, shall be bound by Oath or Affirmation, to support this Constitution; but no religious Test shall ever be required as a Qualification to any Office or public Trust under the United States.

Article VII

The Ratification of the Conventions of nine States, shall be sufficient for the Establishment of this Constitution between the States so ratifying the Same.

The Word "the," being interlined between the seventh and eight Lines of the first Page, The Word "Thirty" being partly written on an Erazure in the fifteenth Line of the first Page. The Words "is tried" being interlined between the thirty second and thirty third Lines of the first Page and the Word "the" being interlined between the forty third and forty fourth Lines of the second Page.

Attest William Jackson Secretary

done in Convention by the Unanimous Consent of the States present the Seventeenth Day of September in the Year of our Lord one thousand seven hundred and Eighty seven and of the Independence of the United States of America the Twelfth In witness whereof We have hereunto subscribed our Names,

Go. Washington
Presidt. and deputy from Virginia

Delaware
Geo: Read
Gunning Bedford jun
John Dickinson
Richard Bassett
Jaco: Broom

Maryland
James McHenry
Dan of St Thos. Jenifer
Danl Carroll.

Virginia
John Blair
James Madison Jr.

North Carolina
Wm Blount
Richd. Dobbs Spaight.
Hu Williamson

South Carolina
J. Rutledge
Charles Cotesworth Pinckney
Charles Pinckney
Pierce Butler.

Georgia
William Few
Abr Baldwin

New Hampshire
John Langdon
Nicholas Gilman

Massachusetts
Nathaniel Gorham
Rufus King

Connecticut
Wm. Saml. Johnson
Roger Sherman

New York
Alexander Hamilton

New Jersey
Wil. Livingston
David Brearley.
Wm. Paterson.
Jona: Dayton
Pennsylvania
B Franklin
Thomas Mifflin
Robt Morris
Geo. Clymer
Thos. FitzSimons
Jared Ingersoll
James Wilson.
Gouv Morris

Letter of Transmittal

In Convention. Monday September 17th 1787.
Present
The States of
New Hampshire, Massachusetts, Connecticut, Mr. Hamilton from New York, New Jersey, Pennsylvania, Delaware, Maryland, Virginia, North Carolina, South Carolina and Georgia.

Resolved, That the proceeding Constitution be laid before the United States in Congress assembled, and that it is the Opinion of this Convention, that it should afterwards be submitted to a Convention of Delegates, chosen in each State by the People thereof, under the Recommendation of its Legislature, for their Assent and Ratification; and that each Convention assenting to, and ratifying the Same, should give Notice thereof to the United States in Congress assembled. Resolved, That it is the Opinion of this Convention, that as soon as the Conventions of nine States shall have ratified this Constitution, the United States in Congress assembled should fix a Day on which Electors should be appointed by the States which shall have ratified the same, and a Day on which the Electors should assemble to vote for the President, and the Time and Place for commencing Proceedings under this Constitution.

That after such Publication the Electors should be appointed, and the Senators and Representatives elected: That the Electors should meet on the Day fixed for the Election of the President, and should transmit their Votes certified, signed, sealed and directed, as the Constitution requires, to the Secretary of the United States in Congress assembled, that the Senators and Representatives should convene at the Time and Place assigned; that the Senators should appoint a President of the Senate, for the sole Purpose of receiving, opening and counting the Votes for President; and, that after he shall be chosen, the Congress, together with the President, should, without Delay, proceed to execute this Constitution.

By the Unanimous Order of the Convention
Go Washington-Presidt.
W. Jackson Secretary.

Letter of Transmittal to the President of Congress

In Convention. Monday September 17th 1787.

Sir,

We have now the honor to submit to the consideration of the United States in Congress assembled, that Constitution which has appeared to us the most advisable.

The friends of our country have long seen and desired, that the power of making war, peace, and treaties, that of levying money and regulating commerce, and the correspondent executive and judicial authorities should be fully and effectually vested in the general government of the Union: But the impropriety of delegating such extensive trust to one body of men is evident: hence results the necessity of a different organization.

It is obviously impractical in the federal government of these states to secure all rights of independent sovereignty to each, and yet provide for the interest and safety of all. Individuals entering into society must give up a share of liberty to preserve the rest. The magnitude of the sacrifice must depend as well on situation and circumstances, as on the object to be obtained. It is at all times difficult to draw with precision the line between those rights which must be surrendered, and those which may be reserved; and, on the present occasion, this difficulty was encreased by a difference among the several states as to their situation, extent, habits, and particular interests.

In all our deliberations on this subject we kept steadily in our view, that which appears to us the greatest interest of every true American, the consolidation of our Union, in which is involved our prosperity, felicity, safety, perhaps our national existence. This important consideration, seriously and deeply impressed on our minds, led each state in the Convention to be less rigid on points of inferior magnitude than might have been otherwise expected; and thus the Constitution, which we now present, is the result of a spirit of amity, and of that mutual deference and concession which the peculiarity of our political situation rendered indispensable.

That it will meet the full and entire approbation of every state is not perhaps to be expected; but each will doubtless consider that had her interest alone been consulted, the consequences might have been particularly disagreeable or injurious to others; that it is liable to as few exceptions as could reasonably have been expected, we hope and believe; that it may promote the lasting welfare of that country so dear to us all, and secure her freedom and happiness, is our most ardent wish.

With great respect, We have the honor to be, Sir, Your Excellency's most obedient and humble servants,

George Washington, President By Unanimous Order of the Convention.
His Excellency, the President of Congress

Amendments to the Constitution
The Preamble to The Bill of Rights

Congress of the United States

begun and held at the City of New-York, on Wednesday the fourth of March, one thousand seven hundred and eighty nine.

THE Conventions of a number of the States, having at the time of their adopting the Constitution, expressed a desire, in order to prevent misconstruction or abuse of its powers, that further declaratory and restrictive clauses should be added: And as extending the ground of public confidence in the Government, will best ensure the beneficent ends of its institution.

RESOLVED by the Senate and House of Representatives of the United States of America, in Congress assembled, two thirds of both Houses concurring, that the following Articles be proposed to the Legislatures of the several States, as amendments to the Constitution of the United States, all, or any of which Articles, when ratified by three fourths of the said Legislatures, to be valid to all intents and purposes, as part of the said Constitution; viz.

ARTICLES in addition to, and Amendment of the Constitution of the United States of America, proposed by Congress, and ratified by the Legislatures of the several States, pursuant to the fifth Article of the original Constitution.

Article the first. . . . .After the first enumeration required by the first Article of the Constitution, there shall be one Representative for every thirty thousand, until the number shall amount to one hundred, after which, the proportion shall be so regulated by Congress, that there shall be not less than one hundred Representatives, nor less than one Representative for every forty thousand persons, until the number of Representatives shall amount to two hundred, after which the proportion shall be so regulated by Congress, that there shall not be less than two hundred Representatives, nor more than one Representative for every fifty thousand persons.

Article the second. . . . No law, varying the compensation for the services of the Senators and Representatives, shall take effect, until an election of Representatives shall have intervened.

Amendment I

Congress shall make no law respecting an establishment of religion, or prohibiting the free exercise thereof; or abridging the freedom of speech, or of the press; or the right of the people peaceably to assemble, and to petition the Government for a redress of grievances.

Amendment II

A well regulated Militia, being necessary to the security of a free State, the right of the people to keep and bear Arms, shall not be infringed.

Amendment III

No Soldier shall, in time of peace be quartered in any house, without the consent of the Owner, nor in time of war, but in a manner to be prescribed by law.

Amendment IV

The right of the people to be secure in their persons, houses, papers, and effects, against unreasonable searches and seizures, shall not be violated, and no Warrants shall issue, but upon probable cause, supported by Oath or affirmation, and particularly describing the place to be searched, and the persons or things to be seized.

Amendment V

No person shall be held to answer for a capital, or otherwise infamous crime, unless on a presentment or indictment of a Grand Jury, except in cases arising in the land or naval forces, or in the Militia, when in actual service in time of War or public danger; nor shall any person be subject for the same offence to be twice put in jeopardy of life or limb; nor shall be compelled in any criminal case to be a witness against himself, nor be deprived of life, liberty, or property, without due process of law; nor shall private property be taken for public use, without just compensation.

Amendment VI

In all criminal prosecutions, the accused shall enjoy the right to a speedy and public trial, by an impartial jury of the State and district wherein the crime shall have been committed, which district shall have been previously ascertained by law, and to be informed of the nature and cause of the accusation; to be confronted with the witnesses against him; to have compulsory process for obtaining witnesses in his favor, and to have the Assistance of Counsel for his defence.

Amendment VII

In Suits at common law, where the value in controversy shall exceed twenty dollars, the right of trial by jury shall be preserved, and no fact tried by a jury, shall be otherwise re-examined in any Court of the United States, than according to the rules of the common law.

Amendment VIII

Excessive bail shall not be required, nor excessive fines imposed, nor cruel and unusual punishments inflicted.

Amendment IX

The enumeration in the Constitution, of certain rights, shall not be construed to deny or disparage others retained by the people.

Amendment X

The powers not delegated to the United States by the Constitution, nor prohibited by it to the States, are reserved to the States respectively, or to the people.

Attest,
John Beckley, Clerk of the House of Representatives.
Sam. A. Otis Secretary of the Senate.
Frederick Augustus Muhlenberg Speaker of the House of Representatives.
John Adams, Vice-President of the United States, and President of the Senate.

Amendment XI

The Judicial power of the United States shall not be construed to extend to any suit in law or equity, commenced or prosecuted against one of the United States by Citizens of another State, or by Citizens or Subjects of any Foreign State.

Amendment XII

The Electors shall meet in their respective states, and vote by ballot for President and Vice-President, one of whom, at least, shall not be an inhabitant of the same state with themselves; they shall name in their ballots the person voted for as President, and in distinct ballots the person voted for as Vice-President, and they shall make distinct lists of all persons voted for as President, and of all persons voted for as Vice-President, and of the number of votes for each, which lists they shall sign and certify, and transmit sealed to the seat of the government of the United States, directed to the President of the Senate; — The President of the Senate shall, in the presence of the Senate and House of Representatives, open all the certificates and the votes shall then be counted; — The person having the greatest number of votes for President, shall be the President, if such number be a majority of the whole number of Electors appointed; and if no person have such majority, then from the persons having the highest numbers not exceeding three on the list of those voted for as President, the House of Representatives shall choose immediately, by ballot, the President. But in choosing the President, the votes shall be taken by states, the representation from each state having one vote; a quorum for this purpose shall consist of a member or members from two-thirds of the states, and a majority of all the states shall be necessary to a choice. And if the House of Representatives shall not choose a President whenever the right of choice shall devolve upon them, before the fourth day of March next following, then the Vice-President shall act as President, as in the case of the death or other constitutional disability of the President. — The person having the greatest number of votes as Vice-President, shall be the Vice-President, if such number be a majority of the whole number of Electors appointed, and if no person have a majority, then from the two highest numbers on the list, the Senate shall choose the Vice-President; a quorum for the purpose shall consist of two-thirds of the whole number of Senators, and a majority of the whole number shall be necessary to a choice. But no person constitutionally ineligible to the office of President shall be eligible to that of Vice-President of the United States.

Amendment XIII

Neither slavery nor involuntary servitude, except as a punishment for crime whereof the party shall have been duly convicted, shall exist within the United States, or any place subject to their jurisdiction.

Congress shall have power to enforce this article by appropriate legislation.

Amendment XIV

1: All persons born or naturalized in the United States, and subject to the jurisdiction thereof, are citizens of the United States and of the State wherein they reside. No State shall make or enforce any law which shall abridge the privileges or immunities of citizens of the United States; nor shall any State deprive any person of life, liberty, or property, without due process of law; nor deny to any person within its jurisdiction the equal protection of the laws.

2: Representatives shall be apportioned among the several States according to their respective numbers, counting the whole number of persons in each State, excluding Indians not taxed. But when the right to vote at any election for the choice of electors for President and Vice President of the United States, Representatives in Congress, the Executive and Judicial officers of a State, or the members of the Legislature thereof, is denied to any of the male inhabitants of such State, being twenty-one years of age,15 and citizens of the United States, or in any way abridged, except for participation in rebellion, or other crime, the basis of representation therein shall be reduced in the proportion which the number of such male citizens shall bear to the whole number of male citizens twenty-one years of age in such State.

3: No person shall be a Senator or Representative in Congress, or elector of President and Vice President, or hold any office, civil or military, under the United States, or under any State, who, having previously taken an oath, as a member of Congress, or as an officer of the United States, or as a member of any State legislature, or as an executive or judicial officer of any State, to support the Constitution of the United States, shall have engaged in insurrection or rebellion against the same, or given aid or comfort to the enemies thereof. But Congress may by a vote of two-thirds of each House, remove such disability.

4: The validity of the public debt of the United States, authorized by law, including debts incurred for payment of pensions and bounties for services in suppressing insurrection or rebellion, shall not be questioned. But neither the United States nor any State shall assume or pay any debt or obligation incurred in aid of insurrection or rebellion against the United States, or any claim for the loss or emancipation of any slave; but all such debts, obligations and claims shall be held illegal and void.

5: The Congress shall have power to enforce, by appropriate legislation, the provisions of this article.

Amendment XV

The right of citizens of the United States to vote shall not be denied or abridged by the United States or by any State on account of race, color, or previous condition of servitude.

The Congress shall have power to enforce this article by appropriate legislation.

Amendment XVI

The Congress shall have power to lay and collect taxes on incomes, from whatever source derived, without apportionment among the several States, and without regard to any census or enumeration.

Amendment XVII

1: The Senate of the United States shall be composed of two Senators from each State, elected by the people thereof, for six years; and each Senator shall have one vote. The electors in each State shall have the qualifications requisite for electors of the most numerous branch of the State legislatures.

2: When vacancies happen in the representation of any State in the Senate, the executive authority of such State shall issue writs of election to fill such vacancies: Provided, That the legislature of any State may empower the executive thereof to make temporary appointments until the people fill the vacancies by election as the legislature may direct.

3: This amendment shall not be so construed as to affect the election or term of any Senator chosen before it becomes valid as part of the Constitution.

Amendment XVIII

1: After one year from the ratification of this article the manufacture, sale, or transportation of intoxicating liquors within, the importation thereof into, or the exportation thereof from the United States and all territory subject to the jurisdiction thereof for beverage purposes is hereby prohibited.

2: The Congress and the several States shall have concurrent power to enforce this article by appropriate legislation.

3: This article shall be inoperative unless it shall have been ratified as an amendment to the Constitution by the legislatures of the several States, as provided in the Constitution, within seven years from the date of the submission hereof to the States by the Congress.

Amendment XIX

The right of citizens of the United States to vote shall not be denied or abridged by the United States or by any State on account of sex.

Congress shall have power to enforce this article by appropriate legislation.

Amendment XX

1: The terms of the President and Vice President shall end at noon on the 20th day of January, and the terms of Senators and Representatives at noon on the 3d day of

January, of the years in which such terms would have ended if this article had not been ratified; and the terms of their successors shall then begin.

2: The Congress shall assemble at least once in every year, and such meeting shall begin at noon on the 3d day of January, unless they shall by law appoint a different day.

3: If, at the time fixed for the beginning of the term of the President, the President elect shall have died, the Vice President elect shall become President. If a President shall not have been chosen before the time fixed for the beginning of his term, or if the President elect shall have failed to qualify, then the Vice President elect shall act as President until a President shall have qualified; and the Congress may by law provide for the case wherein neither a President elect nor a Vice President elect shall have qualified, declaring who shall then act as President, or the manner in which one who is to act shall be selected, and such person shall act accordingly until a President or Vice President shall have qualified.

4: The Congress may by law provide for the case of the death of any of the persons from whom the House of Representatives may choose a President whenever the right of choice shall have devolved upon them, and for the case of the death of any of the persons from whom the Senate may choose a Vice President whenever the right of choice shall have devolved upon them.

5: Sections 1 and 2 shall take effect on the 15th day of October following the ratification of this article.

6: This article shall be inoperative unless it shall have been ratified as an amendment to the Constitution by the legislatures of three-fourths of the several States within seven years from the date of its submission.

Amendment XXI

1: The eighteenth article of amendment to the Constitution of the United States is hereby repealed.

2: The transportation or importation into any State, Territory, or possession of the United States for delivery or use therein of intoxicating liquors, in violation of the laws thereof, is hereby prohibited.

3: This article shall be inoperative unless it shall have been ratified as an amendment to the Constitution by conventions in the several States, as provided in the Constitution, within seven years from the date of the submission hereof to the States by the Congress.

Amendment XXII

1: No person shall be elected to the office of the President more than twice, and no person who has held the office of President, or acted as President, for more than two years of a term to which some other person was elected President shall be elected to the office of the President more than once. But this article shall not apply to any person holding the office of President when this article was proposed by the Congress, and shall not prevent any person who may be holding the office of President, or acting as President, during the term within which this article becomes operative from holding the office of President or acting as President during the remainder of such term.

2: This article shall be inoperative unless it shall have been ratified as an amendment to the Constitution by the legislatures of three-fourths of the several states within seven years from the date of its submission to the states by the Congress.

Amendment XXIII

1: The District constituting the seat of government of the United States shall appoint in such manner as the Congress may direct: A number of electors of President and Vice President equal to the whole number of Senators and Representatives in Congress to which the District would be entitled if it were a state, but in no event more than the least populous state; they shall be in addition to those appointed by the states, but they shall be considered, for the purposes of the election of President and Vice President, to be electors appointed by a state; and they shall meet in the District and perform such duties as provided by the twelfth article of amendment.

2: The Congress shall have power to enforce this article by appropriate legislation.

Amendment XXIV

1. The right of citizens of the United States to vote in any primary or other election for President or Vice President, for electors for President or Vice President, or for Senator or Representative in Congress, shall not be denied or abridged by the United States or any state by reason of failure to pay any poll tax or other tax.

2. The Congress shall have power to enforce this article by appropriate legislation.

Amendment XXV

1: In case of the removal of the President from office or of his death or resignation, the Vice President shall become President.

2: Whenever there is a vacancy in the office of the Vice President, the President shall nominate a Vice President who shall take office upon confirmation by a majority vote of both Houses of Congress.

3: Whenever the President transmits to the President pro tempore of the Senate and the Speaker of the House of Representatives his written declaration that he is unable to discharge the powers and duties of his office, and until he transmits to them a written declaration to the contrary, such powers and duties shall be discharged by the Vice President as Acting President.

4: Whenever the Vice President and a majority of either the principal officers of the executive departments or of such other body as Congress may by law provide, transmit to the President pro tempore of the Senate and the Speaker of the House of Representatives their written declaration that the President is unable to discharge the powers and duties of his office, the Vice President shall immediately assume the powers and duties of the office as Acting President.

Thereafter, when the President transmits to the President pro tempore of the Senate and the Speaker of the House of Representatives his written declaration that no inability exists, he shall resume the powers and duties of his office unless the Vice President and a majority of either the principal officers of the executive department or of such other body as Congress may by law provide, transmit within four days to the President pro tempore of the Senate and the Speaker of the House of Representatives their written declaration that the President is unable to discharge the powers and duties of his office. Thereupon Congress shall decide the issue, assembling within forty-eight hours for that purpose if not in session. If the Congress, within twenty-one days after receipt of the latter written declaration, or, if Congress is not in session, within twenty-one days after Congress is required to assemble, determines by two-thirds vote of both Houses that the President is unable to discharge the powers and duties of his office, the Vice President shall continue to discharge the same as Acting President; otherwise, the President shall resume the powers and duties of his office.

Amendment XXVI

1: The right of citizens of the United States, who are 18 years of age or older, to vote, shall not be denied or abridged by the United States or any state on account of age.

2: The Congress shall have the power to enforce this article by appropriate legislation.

Amendment XXVII

No law varying the compensation for the services of the Senators and Representatives shall take effect until an election of Representatives shall have intervened.

Glossary

Abandonment When a defendant voluntarily stops the criminal enterprise before it is completed.

Accessory A person who helps commit a crime without being present.

Accessory after the fact A person who finds out that a crime has been committed and helps to conceal the crime or the criminal.

Accessory before the fact A person who, without being present, encourages, orders, or helps another to commit a crime.

Accomplice A person who knowingly and voluntarily helps another person commit or conceal a crime.

Accusation A document that charges a defendant with a misdemeanor in most state courts.

Acquit Finding the defendant in a criminal case not guilty.

Actual possession When a person has a controlled substance in or on his person, with full knowledge of what the substance is.

Actus reus *Latin.* A criminal action.

Admissibility A judicial ruling that evidence is relevant and that it has been properly submitted for review by the jurors.

Admission of evidence The process of tendering evidence to the court and requesting a judge to rule that evidence is admissible and may therefore be shown to the jury.

Affidavit A written statement where a person swears an oath that the facts contained are true.

Affirm A determination by a higher court that declares that a lower court's action was valid and right.

Affirmative defenses Defenses that are something more than a mere denial and that require that the defense present evidence or testimony to prove, either by a preponderance of evidence or by clear and convincing evidence, that the defense is true.

Aggravated assault A felony in most states, the victim is either seriously injured or the defendant uses a deadly weapon in the attack.

Aggravated battery Used interchangeably with the term "aggravated assault."

Aggravated sodomy Non-consensual "crimes against nature" that are carried out with force or threat or that cause serious bodily injury to the victim.

Aggravation of sentence Evidence offered by the state to enhance or lengthen the defendant's sentence.

Alford plea A plea authorized by the U.S. Supreme Court that allows a defendant to enter a guilty plea, but basing the plea on the amount and quantity of evidence against him instead of the defendant's belief in his actual guilt.

Allegata The allegations contained in a charging document

Alternate juror A person selected to sit on the jury, but who will have no right to participate in the deliberations and will not be able to vote to return a verdict.

Answer The defendant's written response to the complaint, usually containing denials of the defendant's responsibility for the plaintiff's injuries.

Anticipatory warrants Warrants issued for contraband or evidence that has not yet arrived at its final destination.

Apparent ability The defendant's obvious capability of carrying through on a threat.

Appeal Asking a higher court to review the actions of a lower court in order to correct mistakes or injustice.

Appellant The party bringing the current appeal from an adverse ruling in a lower court.

Appellee The party who won in the lower court.

Apprehension Dread of an upcoming and an unwanted event.

Arraignment A court hearing where the defendant is informed of the charge against him or her and given the opportunity to enter a plea of guilty or not guilty.

Arrest   Detention and restraint of a suspect by a law enforcement official; a person who is under arrest is not free to leave.

Arson   Intentional (and malicious) burning of a structure.

Asportation (kidnapping)   The movement of the victim, usually against the victim's will or without the victim's consent of the victim or, in the case of theft, of the victim's property.

Asportation (theft)   Movement of an item some distance from its original location.

Assault   The apprehension or fear of a harmful or offensive touching.

Assisted suicide   The crime of actively participating and aiding a person to kill himself or herself.

Attempt   An act that goes beyond preparation, but which is not completed.

Bail   The posting of a monetary amount to guarantee the return of the defendant for subsequent court hearings.

Batson challenge   A challenge to the strikes used by a party during jury selection that claims the party used discriminatory practices in removing members of the panel.

Battered Woman Syndrome   An affirmative defense that asks the jury to excuse a woman's attack on her supposed long-time abuser or asks the judge to mitigate her sentence in reflection of the fact that she was responding to a long period of abuse at the hands of the victim.

Battery   Harmful or offensive touching without consent.

Bench   The place in the courtroom reserved for the judge.

Bench conference   A private conference, held at the judge's bench between the attorneys and the judge.

Bench trial   A trial where the judge decides both questions of law and the final verdict in the case; no jury is present.

Bench warrant   A warrant issued for the arrest of a person who was scheduled to appear in court but failed to do so.

Bestiality   Sexual acts with animals.

Beyond a reasonable doubt   The burden of proof in a criminal case; when one has a reasonable doubt; it is not mere conjecture but a doubt that would cause a prudent, rational person to hesitate before finding a defendant guilty of a crime.

Bifurcated trial   Separate hearings for different issues in the same case; for example, for guilt and sanity or guilt and punishment in a criminal case.

Bill of particulars   A defendant's motion requesting dates, names, locations, and addresses for the charges set out in the indictment.

Binding over   A determination that probable cause exists in a preliminary hearing triggering a transfer of the case to a higher court, usually superior court.

Bond   A promise of specific monetary amount promised to the state and offered as a guarantee for the defendant's return to court at a later date.

Bond forfeiture   A judicial determination that the defendant has violated the conditions of his or her release and that the defendant should be placed into custody pending further hearings.

Bonding company   A private business that posts bonds for individuals who have been charged with crimes and will be forced to pay the balance of the defendant's bond if the defendant flees the jurisdiction or otherwise does not appear for a court date.

Bounty hunter   An employee of a bonding company who works to locate defendants who have absconded and to return these defendants to face their court dates.

***Brady* material**   Information available to the prosecutor that is favorable to the defendant, either because it mitigates his guilt or his sentence. This material must be provided to the defense prior to trial.

Breaking   Any force, even slight, used to gain admittance to a dwelling.

Bribery   Offering money (or something of value) to a public official to influence his or her decisions.

Brief   A written statement prepared by one side in a lawsuit to explain its case to the judge.

Burden of proof   The amount of proof that a party must bring to sustain an action against another party. The burden of proof is different in civil and criminal cases.

Burglary   The intentional breaking and entering of a structure with the intent to commit a theft or a felony.

Burning   Setting a flame to real or personal property.

Calendar or docket   A listing of the cases currently pending before the court, usually by the defendants' names, case file number, and charges brought against them.

Car owner's presumption   A legal presumption that the owner or operator of an automobile has knowledge and is in possession of any items that are recovered from the automobile at the time he or she was driving it.

Case in chief   The body of evidence and testimony offered by a party during its presentation of a jury trial.

Case law   The written decisions by appellate courts explaining the outcome of a case on appeal.

Certiorari   *Latin*. "To make sure"; cert is a court's authority to decide which cases it will hear on appeal and which it will not.

Chain of custody   The chronological list of those in continuous possession of a specific physical object. A person who presents evidence (such as a gun used in a crime) at a trial must account for its possession from time of receipt to time of trial in order for evidence to be admitted by the judge.

Challenge for cause   A formal objection to the qualifications or attitude of a prospective juror.

Charge conference   A meeting held after the close of evidence in a trial and before the closing arguments where the attorneys and the judge discuss what jury instructions will be given to the jurors.

Charging decision   The process that a prosecutor goes through to determine what is the appropriate and just charge to bring against a defendant based on the law and the facts in the case.

Child molestation   Any sexual act with a child.

Child pornography   Any depiction of a child intended to be viewed as a sexual object or for sexual pleasure.

Circumstantial evidence   Facts that suggest a conclusion or indirectly prove a main fact in question, or an object or testimony that suggests a conclusion.

Citizen's arrest   A legal doctrine that holds harmless a citizen who detains a person observed to have committed a crime. When a person makes a citizen's arrest, he or she is immune from civil suit for battery or false imprisonment of the person detained, provided the person detained actually committed a crime.

Clear and convincing evidence   The version presented by the party is highly probable to be true and is a higher standard than preponderance of the evidence.

Clerk   A court official who maintains records of dispositions in both civil and criminal cases.

Closing argument   An attorney's summation of his or her case during which the attorney seeks to convince the jury to return a verdict favorable to his or her side.

Code   A collection of laws.

Coercion   The direct threat of physical violence to make a person commit a crime that he or she would not ordinarily commit.

Common law   1) Either all case law or the case law that is made by judges in the absence of relevant statutes; 2) The legal system that originated in England and is composed of case law and statutes.

Complaint   The document filed by the plaintiff and served on the defendant that sets out the plaintiff's factual allegations that show the defendant is responsible for the plaintiff's injuries.

Complete defense   A defense that would completely exonerate the defendant of the crime charged, assuming the defendant presents sufficient evidence to meet his or her burden of proof (usually preponderance of the evidence).

Concurrent sentencing   Two or more sentences that are served at the same time.

Conditional assault   A form of assault in which the defendant places a condition on the violence.

Conditional plea   A plea entered by the defendant who maintains his or her innocence but states that the evidence against him or her is overwhelming.

Consecutive sentencing   One or more sentences that are served on after the other.

Consent   Voluntary and knowing agreement to a proposed action.

Conspiracy   A crime that may be committed when two or more people agree to do something unlawful.

Constructive breaking   Using fraud, trickery, or deceit to gain access to a dwelling that a person has no right or consent to enter.

Constructive possession When a person has a controlled substance inside or contained in some other object over which the defendant has dominion, custody, or control.

Constructive presence A person who is deemed to be present when the crime occurs even if he or she was not actually in the immediate vicinity when the crime occurred.

Constructive taking When the defendant removes an item from the victim's possession and puts it in a place where the victim cannot access it.

Contempt A judge's power to enforce his or her orders, authority, or dignity by temporarily depriving the offending party of his or her liberty.

Contraband Objects that are illegal to possess, including child pornography, certain types of weapons, and illegal narcotics, among others.

Controlled substance Any drug, including narcotics, that are regulated by the government or classified under state or federal Controlled Substances Acts.

Controlled Substances Acts State and federal laws that regulate, restrict, or forbid the use of certain types of drugs, usually in the form of Schedules that list the drug and the associated penalty.

Conversion An act that transfers the possession of an item from the rightful owner to a person who does not have the owner's consent to possess.

Corpus delicti *Latin.* "The body of the crime," proof that the victim is dead and that the defendant caused the death.

Corroboration Presentation of evidence that supports or adds details to a claim.

Court reporter A trained professional who is responsible for taking down every spoken word in the courtroom during a hearing and reproducing those words as a transcript.

Court-appointed attorney A private, local attorney who is selected by a judge to handle a criminal case; this attorney is paid by the state, usually on an hourly basis.

Cross-examine To question a witness for the opposition about his or possible bias, prejudice, or lack of knowledge about the issues in the case.

Curtilage An area associated with the immediate area of the house, but not necessarily inside the dwelling.

Cyberstalking The crime of using electronic means, including the Internet and social media, to cause the victim emotional distress.

Damages Money that a court orders paid to a person who has suffered damages by the person who caused the injury.

Deadly weapon Any item or device that is likely to cause serious bodily harm to a victim, especially items designed to inflict wounds or death, such as guns or knives.

Defendant 1) A person accused by the state of the commission of a crime; 2) a person who is being sued in a civil action (sometimes referred to as the "respondent").

Defense attorney An attorney who primarily or exclusively represents individuals who have been charged with criminal offenses.

Demonstrative evidence Power points, diagrams, charts, or other aids that are developed by an attorney to persuade the jury to a particular viewpoint.

Diminished capacity Inability of the defendant to understand the actions that he or she took and why his or her actions constituted a crime.

Direct evidence Evidence that proves a fact without the need to resort to any other fact. For example, fingerprints on the murder weapon which prove the defendant held the object.

Direct examination The questions asked of a witness by the attorney who has called him or her to the stand.

Directed verdict A ruling by a judge that there is not sufficient evidence of the defendant's guilt to present to the jury.

Discovery The exchange of information, witness statements, and other evidence between the state and the defense attorney in a criminal case.

DNA Deoxyribonucleic acid, the basic building blocks of cells that direct the overall appearance and structure of an organism.

Documentary evidence A writing that contains facts or data that tend to prove or disprove that a defendant committed a crime.

Double jeopardy A provision of the Fifth Amendment that forbids the retrial of a person who has already been tried for an offense and found not guilty.

Driving under the influence   A charge that can be brought against a driver for operating a motor vehicle with greater than a certain percent of blood/alcohol or operating a vehicle under the influence to the extent that the driver is a threat to others; often abbreviated DUI or DWI (Driving While Intoxicated).

Drug paraphernalia   Any item that can be used to inhale, consume, imbibe, or inject a controlled substance.

Due process   A clause in the Fifth Amendment that guarantees that each and every defendant will receive the same procedural safeguards throughout a criminal case, regardless of the charge.

Duress   Unlawful psychological and mental pressure brought to bear on a person to force him or her to commit a crime that the person would ordinarily not commit.

Dwelling   An occupied structure that is designed for human beings.

Elements   The factual points and statutory requirements of a criminal case that must be proven against the defendant beyond a reasonable doubt.

Embezzlement   The wrongful retention of property, with the intent to permanently deprive the owner of it, after the person has been given temporary consent to possess the property.

Embracery   Another term for jury tampering.

Entering   Proof that any part of the defendant's body entered the victim's dwelling after the defendant satisfied the element of "breaking."

Enticement   Attempting to persuade a child to come to some secluded place with the intent to commit an unlawful sexual act.

Entrapment   A defense that claims government agents induced a defendant to commit a crime when he or she was not pre-disposed to do so.

Evidence   Any type of information that is presented during a trial to prove or disprove a point in contention, including testimony, documents, and physical objects.

Evidence room   A secured area, maintained by law enforcement, where evidence in pending cases is kept and guarded until it is needed at trial.

Ex post facto   *Latin.* An action that is criminalized only after it has been committed.

Exclusionary rule   A court-created doctrine that prevents illegally obtained evidence from being used in a criminal trial.

Exculpatory   Evidence that tends to provide an excuse or a justification for the defendant's actions or that shows that the defendant did not commit the crime charged.

Exigent circumstance   An emergency situation that poses a threat to persons or to evidence.

Expectation of privacy   The Constitutional standard that a court must determine before issuing a search warrant. If an area has a high expectation of privacy, a warrant will be required; if low or non-existent, then no warrant is required.

Expert witness   A person qualified by training, education, or experience to offer an opinion about a scientific or other process; a person with knowledge that is not available to the normal juror.

Fair market value   An estimate of what a willing, knowledgeable buyer, acting without coercion or pressure, would pay for an item.

False imprisonment   The crime of restraining another's movement through force, threat, or intimidation.

Felony   A crime with a sentence of one year or more.

Felony-Murder Doctrine   A statute that exists in most states which allows the state to prosecute a defendant for first-degree murder when he or she causes the death of a person during the commission of a felony.

Fence   A common term for a person who makes a living receiving stolen property from another and then selling it to others.

Flight   When a suspect attempts to elude the police or runs away when confronted by police.

Foundation questions   A series of questions that show that evidence is relevant, admissible, and has not been tampered with or altered in any way.

"Four corners" test   A judicial requirement that a warrant affidavit contain all necessary information in the materials before the warrant was issued.

Fresh pursuit doctrine   A court-created doctrine that allows police officers to arrest suspects without warrants and to cross territorial boundaries while they are still pursuing the suspect.

Fruit of the poisonous tree doctrine   The rule that evidence gathered as a result of evidence gained in an illegal search or questioning cannot be used against the person searched or questioned even if later evidence was gathered lawfully.

Gambling   Paying money for the chance of winning more money or something else of value.

General intent   A showing that the defendant acted knowingly and voluntarily.

Good faith doctrine   A court created doctrine that holds that evidence will not be suppressed under the Exclusionary Rule when officers were acting in good faith and had no reason to know that the warrant was invalid.

Grand jury   A group of citizens who consider felony charges against defendants and make a determination that there is sufficient evidence to warrant further prosecution.

Guilty   The verdict in a criminal case where the jurors have determined that the defendant has committed a crime.

Guilty but mentally ill   A finding that the defendant is guilty of the crime charged, but has some mental problems or mental disease that mitigate his guilt to a small degree.

Habeas corpus   *Latin.* "You have the body"; a judicial order to a prison system ordering that the incarcerated person be brought to court for a hearing; a constitutional mechanism that allows convicts to challenge their sentences.

Homicide   The killing of a human being by another.

Hung jury   A jury that is unable to reach a unanimous verdict.

Identity theft   Unlawful and non-consensual use of another person's identifying information, such as Social Security number, address, and name, to create new credit accounts with no intention of repaying the debts incurred.

Immunity   A grant to an individual that exempts him or her from being prosecuted based on the testimony that the person gives.

Impeachment   To show that a witness is not worthy of belief.

Implied consent   A legal doctrine that provides that when a driver is issued a driver's license under state law, he or she has given consent in advance to any officer who requests a blood or breath test.

In absentia   *Latin.* The defendant is not present.

In camera   *Latin.* "In chambers"; a review of a file by a judge carried out in his or her private office.

Incest   Sexual intercourse between members of a family, who according to state law, are too closely related by blood or adoption to legally marry.

Inchoate   Incomplete, unfinished. An act begun but not finished.

Indictment   A document that charges a defendant with a felony.

Inference   A fact that a person can believe is probably true.

Information   A document that charges a defendant with a misdemeanor in federal court.

Initial appearance   A hearing that takes place within days of the suspect's arrest where the suspect is advised of his or her Constitutional rights, given the opportunity to request a court-appointed attorney and where the court can confirm the defendant's identity.

Insanity   A defense that claims that at the time that the defendant committed the crime, he or she did not know the difference between right and wrong.

Interrogation   The questioning by law enforcement of a suspect concerning the commission of a crime.

Intoxication   When a person is acting under the influence of alcohol or other drugs to the extent that judgment and motor reflexes are impaired.

Join Issue   The parties officially submit the case to a jury for a determination and verdict.

Judge   A member of the judicial branch who is responsible for maintaining order in the courtroom, ruling on motions, making orders and, in many circumstances, sentencing the defendant.

Jurisdiction   The persons about whom and the subject matters about which a court or an official has the right and power to make decisions that are legally binding.

Jury box   An area that is separated from the rest of a courtroom and is reserved exclusively for jurors during a trial.

Jury instructions   A judge's directions to the jury about the law that pertains to the issues in the trial and the jury's function once they retire to the jury room.

Jury tampering   Influencing or attempting to influence a juror's vote in a civil or criminal case.

Jury trial A trial with a judge and jury, not just a judge.

Larceny A general term referring to all types of theft.

Laying the foundation The process, often involving the testimony of several witnesses, to show that evidence is reliable, relevant, and admissible.

Lesser-included offense A crime that has many of the same elements as a more serious crime, but lacks one or two of the elements of that serious crime.

Lewd An act that shows an unlawful indulgence of lust; gross indecency in matters pertaining to sexual relations.

Liable A finding that a party has a duty or obligation to the other party to pay damages or to carry out some other action.

Magistrate A judge who has limited power and authority.

Malice An intentional desire to inflict pain or death on someone that has no legal justification.

Manslaughter The killing of another human being, done without premeditation or malice, often in response to an overwhelming passion or provocation.

Material fact A fact that is central to the negotiations; a fact that is so important to the transaction that, if changed, would alter the outcome.

Mens rea *Latin.* Guilty intent, voluntary action, criminal intent.

Miranda rights The rights that must be read to a person who has been arrested and questioned by the police.

Miranda warnings Rights that are required to be read to persons who have been placed under arrest and whom the police intend to interrogate; required by the U.S. Supreme Court in the case of *Miranda v. Arizona.*

Misdemeanor A criminal offense that is punished by a maximum possible sentence of one year or less in custody.

Mistrial A trial that the judge ends and declares will have no legal effect.

Mitigation of sentence Evidence offered by the defense to lessen or shorten the defendant's sentence.

Motion An oral or written request to a court to take some action.

Motion for change of venue A motion to transfer the location of the trial to another area, often brought when there is extensive pre-trial publicity.

Motion for continuance A request by one party to postpone a trial or other hearing for a future date.

Motion for new trial A motion, filed by the defendant after sentencing, that requests a new trial based on errors or irregularities in the trial; if denied, it begins the appellate process.

Motion in aggravation of sentence A motion filed by the state that seeks to enhance the defendant's sentence based on his or her prior convictions.

Motion *in limine* *Latin.* "At the beginning"; a motion by one party that requests specific judicial rulings at the outset of the trial.

Motion to "reveal the deal" A defense motion seeking any information that a state's witness has negotiated an arrangement with the prosecution to testify in exchange for a lower sentence.

Motion to sever A motion to separate out specific charges or defendants from joint trials.

Motion to suppress A motion that requests a court not allow the jury to hear specific information, such as the defendant's confession or other statements based on improprieties in obtaining the information.

Motive The reasons behind a person's actions.

Murder The unlawful killing of another human being that is done voluntarily, with premeditation or malice.

Mutual combat A defense that claims that the defendant and the victim voluntarily entered into a physical confrontation.

Narcotic A drug that induces sleep, affects the senses, or induces hallucinations.

Necessity The defense that a defendant committed a crime in order to avoid an act of nature or of God.

Necrophilia Sexual acts with human corpses.

No bill A grand jury's determination that there is insufficient probable cause to continue the prosecution against the accused.

Nolle prosequi *Latin.* An order dismissing a criminal charge.

Nolo contendere *Latin.* "I do not contest"; a plea offered in a criminal case where the defendant does not contest his or her guilt and asks for the court's mercy.

Not guilty   The jury's determination that the state has failed to prove that the defendant committed the crime beyond a reasonable doubt.

Not guilty by reason of insanity   A finding that the defendant did not understand the difference between right and wrong when he or she committed the offense and therefore lacks the mental capability to commit a crime.

Notice of appeal   The official docketing and commencement of the appeals process.

Obscene   Sexually oriented lewd and offensive depictions that are in violation of accepted standards of decency.

Open fields doctrine   A court principle that allows police to search without a warrant when the evidence is located in a public setting, such as farmland or beside a road.

Opening statement   A preliminary address to the jury by the prosecutor and defense attorney, outlining the general facts of the case.

Ordinance   A law passed by a local government, such as a town council or city government.

Overbroad   When a search warrant allows police far too much discretion in what they may search; similar to the prohibition against general searches.

Overt act   An action that shows the intent to carry out a behavior; it does not have to be an illegal act, as long as it promotes or makes more likely an illegal activity, such as conspiracy.

Parole   A release from prison, before a sentence is finished, that depends on the person's "keeping clean" and doing what he or she is supposed to do while out.

Peremptory challenge   A strike of a juror for any reason, except based on race or sex.

Perjury   Giving false testimony under oath, about a material fact.

Personal property   Any item that is movable and not considered to be real estate.

Petition for cert   A petition filed by a party on appeal requesting a court to consider its appeal and grant cert.

Photographic lineup   Arranging photographs of persons of similar appearance as the suspect so that the witness can attempt to identify the person who committed the crime.

Physical evidence   Any object that tends to prove that a defendant committed (or did not commit) a crime; physical evidence can consist of murder weapons or other types of evidence like DNA.

Physical lineup   Arranging persons of similar appearance as the suspect so that the witness can attempt to identify the person who committed the crime.

Placing character into evidence   When a criminal defendant testifies and his previous criminal record is allowed into evidence through the cross-examination of the defendant.

Plain view doctrine   A court principle that allows police to search without a warrant when they see evidence of a crime in an unconcealed manner.

Plaintiff   The common name for the party who brings a civil suit against another; also known as a Petitioner.

Plea of former jeopardy   A defendant's motion stating that he or she has already been prosecuted for the underlying offense and any further prosecution is barred by the Fifth Amendment.

Pleadings   1) In a civil case, the pleadings set out the wrong suffered by the parties against one another; 2) in a criminal case, the pleadings are often referred to as indictments (in felony cases) and accusations or information (in misdemeanor cases) where the state sets out an infraction by the defendant which violates the law.

Police   Law enforcement officers who are empowered to investigate criminal cases and to make arrests.

Polling   Requesting the jurors to provide a verbal assurance that the verdict each person reached in the jury room is the still the verdict that they maintain when they return after deliberations.

Pornographic   Any material that depicts sexual behavior and nudity designed to cause sexual excitement.

Possession   When a person has unlawful dominion, custody, or control of a controlled substance.

Preliminary hearing   A court hearing that determines if there is probable cause to believe that the defendant committed the crime with which he or she is charged.

Premeditation   Having sufficient time to think and consider one's actions and proceeding with the crime anyway.

Preponderance of the evidence   A showing by one side in a suit that its version of the facts is more likely to be true than not.

Pre-sentence investigation   An investigation by court-appointed social workers, probation officers, and so on, into a criminal's background to determine the criminal's prospects for rehabilitation.

Presumption   A conclusion about a fact that must be made unless and until refuted by other evidence.

Presumption of innocence   A basic tenet of American law that a defendant enters the criminal process clothed in the assumption that he or she is innocent unless and until the prosecution proves that he or she is guilty beyond a reasonable doubt.

Pretextual stops   The detention or arrest of a person for a minor offense when the officer really suspects that the defendant has committed a more serious crime.

Prima facie   *Latin.* Facts that are considered true as presented until they are disproven by some contrary evidence.

Principal   A person directly involved with committing a crime, as opposed to an accessory.

Privilege   A right to refuse to answer questions and to prevent disclosure of information communicated within a legally recognized confidential relationship.

Pro se   *Latin.* "By oneself"; a person who chooses to represent himself or herself in a legal proceeding.

Probable cause   The Constitutional requirement that law enforcement officers have reasonable belief that a person has committed a crime.

Probata   The proof elicited in a trial.

Probation   Allowing a person convicted of a criminal offense to avoid serving a jail sentence imposed on the person, so long as he or she abides by certain conditions (usually including being supervised by a probation officer).

Property bond   Posting of real estate to guarantee the defendant's return for a subsequent court appearance.

Proportionality   The U.S. Supreme Court has mandated that a sentence must be proportional to the crime to satisfy the Eighth Amendment.

For instance, without some other aggravating circumstance, a life sentence for a petty infraction would be out of proportion and would be a violation of the Eighth Amendment.

Prosecutor   A representative of the local, state, or federal government whose duty is to bring charges against defendants and to prove those charges at trial beyond a reasonable doubt.

Prostitution   The crime of offering a person's body to another for sexual purposes in exchange for money.

Provocation   Words or actions by the victim or another that incite anger or passion that cloud the defendant's judgment and the ability to reason and therefore prevent him from being able to form the necessary intent.

Prurient interest   A work that, taken as a whole, is designed for the purpose of arousing intense, obsessive, or overwhelming sexual intensity.

Public defender attorney   A government attorney who works for an office in the court system whose sole responsibility is to provide legal representation to those individuals who are charged with crimes.

Public indecency   Exposure of a person's sex organs in public.

Quash   Do away with, annul, overthrow, cease.

Rape   When a person forces sex on another without the victim's consent.

Rape Shield Statute   A statute that prevents a rape victim from being cross examined about her sexual history, unless that history involves the defendant; these statutes also protect the name of the rape victim from being released to the media.

Real property   Land and anything permanently attached to land.

Reasonable doubt   The standard of proof that the prosecution must meet in order to prove that a defendant committed a crime.

Rebuttal   To deny or take away the effect of the other party's presentation; a rebuttal attacks claims made by one party with evidence presented by the other.

Recess   A short break in the proceedings in a trial.

Recognizance bond   The person accused simply gives his or her word that he or she will return for a specific court date.

Record   The actual evidence (testimony, physical objects, etc.) as well as the evidence that refused admission by the judge.

Redirect examination   The process of questioning a witness who was originally called on direct examination to clear up any issues raised during cross-examination.

Relevant   Any evidence that makes a fact more or less likely to be true; evidence that tends to prove or disprove a point in contention in the trial.

Remand   Send back. For example, when a higher court requires additional information about a case, it returns it to the trial court.

Resisting arrest   Actively preventing a police officer from arresting a person.

Restitution   Money that a court orders a criminal defendant to pay to the victim of a crime for damage or destruction of the victim's property.

Retainer   A fee charged at the beginning of a case to pay an attorney for all actions carried out.

Reverse   Set aside; when an appellate court decides that the actions of a lower court were incorrect.

Reversible error   A mistake made by a judge in the procedures used at trial, or in making legal ruling during the trial.

Riot   A public disturbance involving three or more persons who create the danger of imminent lawless action.

Roadside sobriety tests   A series of physical evaluations to test a person's responses, balance, and verbal abilities in order to determine if the person is under the influence of alcohol or some other drug.

Robbery   The unlawful taking of property of another through the use of force, threat, or intimidation.

Sale   To exchange a controlled substance for cash or something else of value.

Schedules   A list of assorted items, organized under some guiding principle.

Search warrant   A court order authorizing law enforcement to enter, search, and remove evidence of a crime.

Self-defense   The defense that the defendant injured or killed another, but only as a direct threat to the defendant's well-being.

Self-incrimination   A provision of the Fifth Amendment that prohibits a person from being forced to give evidence against himself.

Sentence   The punishment, which can consist of some combination of prison time and probation, which is imposed on a defendant who has been found guilty at trial who has pled guilty.

Sever   Separate or cut off into constituent parts.

Similar transactions motion   A motion brought by the state showing that the defendant has committed similar offenses and this shows his bent of mind, motive, or course of conduct.

Simple defenses   Defenses that are automatically triggered when a defendant is charged with a crime.

Skimming   Use of an electronic device to surreptitiously acquire credit card information.

Sodomy   A generic term for any "crime against nature" or sexual act that has been branded as degenerate; it includes oral sex, anal sex, homosexual acts, or sex with animals.

Solicitation   Asking for; enticing; strongly requesting; the crime of asking another person to commit a crime.

Specific intent   A requirement that the prosecution prove that the defendant acted with the intent to commit a specific crime.

Speedy trial   A Constitutional guarantee that a person must receive a trial within a reasonable period of time after being arraigned.

Spousal immunity   The legal doctrine that prevents a husband from being charged with the rape of his wife.

Stale   When too much time has passed between the application and issuance of a warrant and the search that it authorizes.

Stalking   Following, contacting, harassing, or annoying another for the purpose of causing emotional distress

Standing   A recognized legal right to bring suit or to challenge a legal decision.

Statute   A law that is voted on by the legislature branch of and enacted by the executive branch.

Statute of limitations   The time period in which a criminal case must be commenced or is barred forever.

Statutory rape   The crime of an adult having sex with an underage boy or girl.

Stop and frisk   The right of a law enforcement officer to pat down a person's outer clothing for weapons, whether the person is under arrest or not.

Strict liability offense A crime where an illegal act occurs and the prosecution is not required to prove the defendant's intent.

Striking a jury The process of questioning and removing panel members until twelve jurors are left; these twelve will serve on the jury.

Style (or caption) The title or heading listing the parties to the case.

Subpoena A court order demanding that a person or item be produced to the court at a specific date and time.

Substantial step Intent and preparation to carry out a crime that is not completed because of some outside act.

Supremacy Clause The provision in Article VI of the U.S. Constitution that the U.S. Constitution, laws, and treaties take precedence over conflicting state constitutions or laws.

Suspect A person of interest to law enforcement and one whom they may believe has committed a criminal action, but is not under arrest.

Tax evasion When a person pays less tax than is legally required.

Tax fraud Creating false documentation or tax schemes that illegally hide income and reduce some or all of the taxes an individual owes to federal or state governments.

Tender Offer to the court.

Term of court The period of time slated for court hearings; it can be as short as a week or as long as a year.

Terry stops A brief detention of a suspect to follow up on specific investigative issues.

Testimonial evidence Evidence given by a witness under oath.

Testimony Oral evidence given by a witness under oath.

Transferred intent A court doctrine that allows the state to apply the defendant's intent to harm one person to another person that the defendant may not have actually been trying to injure.

True bill A grand jury's determination that there is sufficient evidence to continue a felony case against a defendant.

U.S. Supreme Court The name for the highest court of the U.S. federal and state court systems.

Utter To offer as genuine.

Venire The group of local citizens who are summoned for jury duty and from whom a jury will be selected.

Venue The particular geographic area where a court or an official can exercise power; an example of venue would be the county's borders.

Verdict The jury's finding in a trial.

Victim impact statement The right of a victim of a crime to address the court during the defendant's sentencing and to testify about the effect that the defendant's crime has had on the victim.

Voir dire *French.* "To see, to say"; the questioning of a jury panel member to determine if the person is competent to serve on a jury.

Voyeur One who views another, either through a door or window, or by electronic means, to achieve sexual gratification.

Wanton or reckless acts Activities carried out by a defendant who shows a complete indifference to the safety of others.

Warrant An order, issued by a judge, that authorizes a police officer to arrest a suspect or conduct a search.

Wharton's rule Known in some jurisdictions as the "concert of action rule"; a rule that states it is not a conspiracy for two persons to agree to commit a crime if the definition of the crime itself requires the participation of two or more persons.

White-collar crimes A type of theft that is carried out without the direct use of violence and often involves scams, fraud, or the use of technology to defraud victims.

Wiretap Using electronic devices to listen in on a person's telephone calls, whether they are land-based lines or cell calls.

Witness tampering Attempting to influence a witness's testimony during a civil or criminal trial; encouraging a witness to commit perjury.

Work product The principle that a lawyer need not show the other side in a case any facts or things gathered for the case unless the other side can convince the judge that it would be unjust for the thing to remain hidden and there is a special need for it.

Index